Finance (No. 2) Act 2017

CHAPTER 32

CONTENTS

PART 1

DIRECT TAXES

Income tax: employment and pensions

Income tax: investments

Income tax: trading and property businesses

Corporation tax

PART 2

INDIRECT TAXES

PART 3

FULFILMENT BUSINESSES

PART 4

ADMINISTRATION, AVOIDANCE AND ENFORCEMENT

Reporting and record-keeping

Enquiries

Avoidance etc

Information

PART 5

FINAL

Finance (No. 2) Act 2017

2017 CHAPTER 32

An Act to grant certain duties, to alter other duties, and to amend the law relating to the national debt and the public revenue, and to make further provision in connection with finance.   [16th November 2017]

Most Gracious Sovereign

W E, Your Majesty's most dutiful and loyal subjects, the Commons of the United Kingdom in Parliament assembled, towards raising the necessary supplies to defray Your Majesty's public expenses, and making an addition to the public revenue, have freely and voluntarily resolved to give and to grant unto Your Majesty the several duties hereinafter mentioned; and do therefore most humbly beseech Your Majesty that it may be enacted, and be it enacted by the Queen's most Excellent Majesty, by and with the advice and consent of the Lords Spiritual and Temporal, and Commons, in this present Parliament assembled, and by the authority of the same, as follows:—

PART 1

DIRECT TAXES

Income tax: employment and pensions

1   Taxable benefits: time limit for making good

(1)   Part 3 of ITEPA 2003 (employment income: earnings and benefits etc treated as earnings) is amended as follows.

(2)   In section 87 (cash equivalent of benefit of non-cash voucher)—

    (a) in subsection (2)(b), for "to the person incurring it" substitute ", to the person incurring it, on or before 6 July following the relevant tax year", and

    (b) after subsection (2) insert—

        "(2A) If the voucher is a non-cash voucher other than a cheque voucher, the relevant tax year is—

            (a) the tax year in which the cost of provision is incurred, or

            (b) if later, the tax year in which the employee receives the voucher.

        (2B) If the voucher is a cheque voucher, the relevant tax year is the tax year in which the voucher is handed over in exchange for money, goods or services."

(3) In section 88(3) (time at which cheque voucher treated as handed over), at the beginning insert "For the purposes of subsection (2) and sections 87(2B) and 87A(6),".

(4) In section 94(2) (cash equivalent of benefit of credit-token), in paragraph (b), for the words from "employee" to the end substitute "employee—

        (i) to the person incurring it, and

        (ii) on or before 6 July following the tax year which contains the occasion in question."

(5) In section 105(2) (cash equivalent of benefit of living accommodation costing £75,000 or less), in paragraph (b), after "made good" insert ", on or before 6 July following the tax year which contains the taxable period,".

(6) In section 106(3) (cash equivalent of benefit of living accommodation costing over £75,000), in paragraph (a), for the words from "paid" to "exceeds" substitute "paid—

        (i) by the employee,

        (ii) in respect of the accommodation,

        (iii) to the person providing it, and

        (iv) on or before 6 July following the tax year which contains the taxable period,

    exceeds".

(7) In section 144 (deduction for payments for private use of car)—

    (a) in subsection (1)(b), for "in" substitute "on or before 6 July following",

    (b) in subsection (2), after "paid" insert "as mentioned in subsection (1)(b)", and

    (c) in subsection (3), after "paid" insert "as mentioned in subsection (1)(b)".

(8) In section 151(2) (when cash equivalent of benefit of car fuel is nil)—

    (a) in the words before paragraph (a) omit "in the tax year in question",

    (b) in paragraph (a), at the beginning insert "in the tax year in question,", and

    (c) in paragraph (b), at the end insert "on or before 6 July following that tax year".

(9) In section 152(2) (car fuel: proportionate reduction of cash equivalent)—

    (a) in the words before paragraph (a) omit "for any part of the tax year in question",

      (b)   in paragraph (a), at the beginning insert "for any part of the tax year in question,",

      (c)   in paragraph (b), at the beginning insert "for any part of the tax year in question,", and

      (d)   in paragraph (c)—

         (i)   after "employee", in the first place it occurs, insert "—

               (i)   for any part of the tax year in question,", and

         (ii)   for "and the employee does make good that expense" substitute ", and

             (ii)   the employee does make good that expense on or before 6 July following that tax year".

(10)   In section 158 (reduction for payments for private use of van)—

      (a)   in subsection (1)(b), for "in" substitute "on or before 6 July following",

      (b)   in subsection (2), after "paid" insert "as mentioned in subsection (1)(b)", and

      (c)   in subsection (3), after "paid" insert "as mentioned in subsection (1)(b)".

(11)   In section 162(2) (when cash equivalent of benefit of van fuel is nil)—

      (a)   in the words before paragraph (a) omit "in the tax year in question",

      (b)   in paragraph (a), at the beginning insert "in the tax year in question,", and

      (c)   in paragraph (b), at the end insert "on or before 6 July following that tax year".

(12)   In section 163(3) (van fuel: proportionate reduction of cash equivalent)—

      (a)   in the words before paragraph (a) omit "for any part of the tax year in question",

      (b)   in paragraph (a), at the beginning insert "for any part of the tax year in question,",

      (c)   in paragraph (b), at the beginning insert "for any part of the tax year in question,", and

      (d)   in paragraph (c)—

         (i)   after "employee", in the first place it occurs, insert "—

               (i)   for any part of the tax year in question,", and

         (ii)   for "and the employee does make good that expense" substitute ", and

             (ii)   the employee does make good that expense on or before 6 July following that tax year".

(13)   In section 203(2) (cash equivalent of benefit treated as earnings), for "to the persons providing the benefit" substitute ", to the persons providing the benefit, on or before 6 July following the tax year in which it is provided".

(14)   The amendments made by this section have effect for the purpose of calculating income tax charged for the tax year 2017-18 or any subsequent tax year.

2   Taxable benefits: ultra-low emission vehicles

(1)   ITEPA 2003 is amended as follows.

(2)   In section 139 (car with a CO_2 emissions figure: the appropriate percentage), for subsections (1) to (6) substitute—

"(1)   The appropriate percentage for a year for a car with a CO_2 emissions figure of less than 75 is determined in accordance with the following table.

Car	Appropriate percentage
Car with CO_2 emissions figure of 0	2%
Car with CO_2 emissions figure of 1 - 50	
Car with electric range figure of 130 or more	2%
Car with electric range figure of 70 - 129	5%
Car with electric range figure of 40 - 69	8%
Car with electric range figure of 30 - 39	12%
Car with electric range figure of less than 30	14%
Car with CO_2 emissions figure of 51 - 54	15%
Car with CO_2 emissions figure of 55 - 59	16%
Car with CO_2 emissions figure of 60 - 64	17%
Car with CO_2 emissions figure of 65 - 69	18%
Car with CO_2 emissions figure of 70 - 74	19%

(2)   For the purposes of subsection (1) and the table, if a CO_2 emissions figure or an electric range figure is not a whole number, round it down to the nearest whole number.

(3)   The appropriate percentage for a year for a car with a CO_2 emissions figure of 75 or more is whichever is the lesser of—
    (a)   20% plus one percentage point for each 5 grams per kilometre driven by which the CO_2 emissions figure exceeds 75, and
    (b)   37%.

(4)   For the purposes of subsection (3), if a CO_2 emissions figure is not a multiple of 5, round it down to the nearest multiple of 5.

(5)   In this section, an "electric range figure" is the number of miles which is the equivalent of the number of kilometres specified in an EC certificate of conformity, an EC type-approval certificate or a UK approval certificate on the basis of which a car is registered, as being the maximum distance for which the car can be driven in electric mode without recharging the battery."

(3) In section 140 (car without a CO_2 emissions figure: the appropriate percentage) –

    (a) in subsection (2), in the table –

        (i) for "23%" substitute "24%", and

        (ii) for "34%" substitute "35%";

    (b) in subsection (3)(a), for "16%" substitute "2%".

(4) In section 142(2) (car first registered before 1 January 1998: the appropriate percentage), in the table –

    (a) for "23%" substitute "24%", and

    (b) for "34%" substitute "35%".

(5) Omit subsection 170(3).

(6) The amendments made by this section have effect for the tax year 2020-21 and subsequent tax years.

3 Pensions advice

(1) In Chapter 9 of Part 4 of ITEPA 2003, after section 308B insert –

"308C Provision of pensions advice: limited exemption

    (1) No liability to income tax arises in respect of –

        (a) the provision of relevant pensions advice to an employee or former or prospective employee, or

        (b) the payment or reimbursement of costs incurred, by or in respect of an employee or former or prospective employee, in obtaining relevant pensions advice,

    if Condition A or B is met.

    (2) But subsection (1) does not apply in relation to a person in a tax year so far as the value of the exemption in the person's case in that year exceeds £500.

    (3) The "value of the exemption", in relation to a person and a tax year, is the amount exempted by subsection (1) from income tax in the person's case in that year, disregarding subsection (2) for this purpose.

    (4) If in a tax year there is in relation to an individual more than one person who is an employer or former employer, subsections (1) to (3) apply in relation to the individual as employee or former or prospective employee of any one of those persons separately from their application in relation to the individual as employee or former or prospective employee of any other of those persons.

    (5) "Relevant pensions advice", in relation to a person, means information, or advice, in connection with –

        (a) the person's pension arrangements, or

        (b) the use of the person's pension funds.

    (6) Condition A is that the relevant pensions advice, or payment or reimbursement, is provided under a scheme that is open –

        (a) to the employer's employees generally, or

        (b) generally to the employer's employees at a particular location.

   (7)   Condition B is that the relevant pensions advice, or payment or reimbursement, is provided under a scheme that is open generally to the employer's employees, or generally to those of the employer's employees at a particular location, who—

         (a)   have reached the minimum qualifying age, or

         (b)   meet the ill-health condition.

   (8)   The "minimum qualifying age", in relation to an employee, means the employee's relevant pension age less 5 years.

   (9)   "Relevant pension age", in relation to an employee, means—

         (a)   where paragraph 22 or 23 of Schedule 36 to FA 2004 applies in relation to the employee and a registered pension scheme of which the employee is a member, the employee's protected pension age (see paragraph 22(8) and 23(8) of Schedule 36 to FA 2004), or

         (b)   in any other case, the employee's normal minimum pension age, as defined by section 279(1) of FA 2004.

   (10)   The "ill-health condition" is met by an employee if the employer is satisfied, on the basis of evidence provided by a registered medical practitioner, that the employee is (and will continue to be) incapable of carrying on his or her occupation because of physical or mental impairment."

  (2)   In section 228 of ITEPA 2003 (effect of exemptions on liability under provisions outside Part 2 of ITEPA 2003), in subsection (2), after paragraph (da) insert—

      "(db)   section 308C (provision of pensions advice),".

  (3)   Regulation 5 of the Income Tax (Exemption of Minor Benefits) Regulations 2002 (S.I. 2002/205) (exemption in respect of the provision of pensions advice) is revoked.

  (4)   In regulation 2 of the Income Tax (Exemption of Minor Benefits) (Amendment) Regulations 2004 (S.I. 2004/3087) omit the inserted regulation 5.

  (5)   The amendments made by this section have effect for the tax year 2017-18 and subsequent tax years.

4   Legal expenses etc

  (1)   ITEPA 2003 is amended as follows.

  (2)   In section 346 (deduction for employee liabilities)—

         (a)   in the heading, at the end insert "and expenses",

         (b)   after paragraph B (in subsection (1)) insert—

            "BA   Payment of any costs or expenses not falling within paragraph B which are incurred in connection with the employee giving evidence about matters related to the employment in, or for the purposes of—

                (a)   a proceeding or other process (whether or not involving the employee), or

                (b)   an investigation (whether or not likely to lead to any proceeding or other process involving the employee).

BB   Payment of any costs or expenses not falling within paragraph B or BA which are incurred in connection with a proceeding or other process, or an investigation, in which—

      (a)   acts of the employee related to the employment, or

      (b)   any other matters related to the employment,

      are being or are likely to be considered.",

(c)   in paragraph C(b) (in subsection (1)), after "B" insert ", BA or BB",

(d)   in subsection (2) for "or B" substitute "B, BA or BB",

(e)   in subsection (2A), for "paragraph A, B or C" substitute "any of paragraphs A to C", and

(f)   after subsection (3) insert—

     "(4)   In this section and section 349—

      (a)   "acts" includes failures to act and acts are "related to the employment" if the employee was acting—

         (i)   in the employee's capacity as holder of the employment, or

         (ii)   in any other capacity in which the employee was acting in the performance of the duties of the employment,

      (b)   "giving evidence" includes making a formal or informal statement or answering questions,

      (c)   "proceeding or other process" includes any civil, criminal or arbitration proceedings, any disciplinary or regulatory proceedings of any kind and any process operated for resolving disputes or adjudicating on complaints, and

      (d)   references to a proceeding or other process or an investigation include a reference to a proceeding or other process or an investigation that is likely to take place."

(3)   In section 349 (section 346: meaning of "qualifying insurance contract"), in subsection (2)—

     (a)   after paragraph (c) insert—

         "(ca)   the payment of costs or expenses incurred in connection with an employee giving evidence about matters related to the employee's employment in, or for the purposes of—

           (i)   a proceeding or other process (whether or not involving the employee), or

           (ii)   an investigation (whether or not likely to lead to any proceeding or other process involving the employee),

         (cb)   the payment of any costs or expenses incurred in connection with a proceeding or other process, or an investigation, in which—

           (i)   acts of an employee related to the employment, or

           (ii)   any other matters related to the employment of an employee,

         are being or are likely to be considered,", and

     (b)   in subsection (2)(d), after "(c)" insert ", (ca) or (cb)".

(4)   In section 409 (payments and benefits on termination of employment etc: exception for payments and benefits in respect of employee liabilities and indemnity insurance) —

     (a)   in the heading, for "employee liabilities" substitute "certain legal expenses etc", and

     (b)   in subsection (3), at the end insert "or by the employer or former employer on behalf of the individual".

(5)   In section 410 (payments and benefits on termination of employment etc: exception for certain payments and benefits received by personal representatives of deceased individual) —

     (a)   in the heading for "employee liabilities" substitute "certain legal expenses etc", and

     (b)   in subsection (3), at the end insert "or by the former employer on behalf of the individual's personal representatives".

(6)   In section 558 (deductions for liabilities of former employees: meaning of "deductible payment") —

     (a)   after paragraph B (in subsection (1)) insert—

        "BA   Payment of any costs or expenses not falling within paragraph B which are incurred in connection with the former employee giving evidence about matters related to the former employment in, or for the purposes of —

           (a)   a proceeding or other process (whether or not involving the former employee), or

           (b)   an investigation (whether or not likely to lead to any proceeding or other process involving the former employee).

        BB   Payment of any costs or expenses not falling within paragraph B or BA which are incurred in connection with a proceeding or other process, or an investigation, in which —

           (a)   acts of the former employee related to the former employment, or

           (b)   any other matters related to the former employment,

        are being or are likely to be considered.", and

     (b)   in paragraph C(b) (in subsection (1)), after "B" insert ", BA or BB",

     (c)   in subsection (2), for "or B" substitute "B, BA or BB",

     (d)   after subsection (3) insert—

        "(4)   In this section and section 560 —

           (a)   "acts" includes failures to act and acts are "related to the former employment" if the former employee was acting —

              (i)   in the employee's capacity as holder of the former employment, or

              (ii)   in any other capacity in which the former employee was acting in the performance of the duties of that employment,

           (b)   "giving evidence" includes making a formal or informal statement or answering questions,

      (c)   "proceeding or other process" includes any civil, criminal or arbitration proceedings, any disciplinary or regulatory proceedings of any kind and any process operated for resolving disputes or adjudicating on complaints, and

      (d)   references to a proceeding or other process or an investigation include a reference to a proceeding or other process or an investigation that is likely to take place."

  (7) In section 560 (section 558: meaning of "qualifying insurance contract"), in subsection (2) —

    (a) after paragraph (c) insert —

       "(ca) the payment of costs or expenses incurred in connection with a former employee giving evidence about matters related to the former employment in, or for the purposes of —

          (i)   a proceeding or other process (whether or not involving the former employee), or

          (ii) an investigation (whether or not likely to lead to any proceeding or other process involving the former employee).

       (cb) the payment of any costs or expenses incurred in connection with a proceeding or other process, or an investigation, in which —

          (i)   acts of a former employee related to the employment, or

          (ii) any other matters related to the former employment of a former employee,

       are being or are likely to be considered,", and

    (b) in paragraph (d), after "(c)" insert ", (ca) or (cb)".

  (8) The amendments made by this section have effect in relation to the tax year 2017-18 and subsequent tax years.

5   Termination payments etc: amounts chargeable on employment income

  (1) ITEPA 2003 is amended in accordance with subsections (2) to (9).

  (2) In section 7(5) (list of provisions under which amounts are treated as earnings), before the "or" at the end of paragraph (c) insert —

      "(ca) section 402B (termination payments, and other benefits, that cannot benefit from section 403 threshold),".

  (3) Before section 403 (charge on payments and benefits in excess of £30,000 threshold) insert —

"402A Split of payments and other benefits between sections 402B and 403

  (1) In this Chapter "termination award" means a payment or other benefit to which this Chapter applies because of section 401(1)(a).

  (2) Section 402B (termination awards not benefiting from threshold treated as earnings) applies to termination awards to the extent determined under section 402C.

(3) Section 403 (charge on payment or benefit where threshold applies) applies to termination awards so far as they are not ones to which section 402B applies.

(4) Section 403 also applies to payments and other benefits to which this Chapter applies because of section 401(1)(b) or (c) (change in duties or earnings).

402B Termination awards not benefiting from threshold to be treated as earnings

(1) The amount of a termination award to which this section applies is treated as an amount of earnings of the employee, or former employee, from the employment.

(2) See also section 7(3)(b) and (5)(ca) (which cause amounts treated as earnings under this section to be included in general earnings).

(3) Section 403(3) (when benefits are received) does not apply in relation to payments or other benefits to which this section applies.

402C The termination awards to which section 402B applies

(1) This section has effect for the purpose of identifying the extent to which section 402B applies to termination awards in respect of the termination of the employment of the employee.

(2) In this section "relevant termination award" means a termination award that is neither —
   (a) a redundancy payment, nor
   (b) so much of an approved contractual payment as is equal to or less than the amount which would have been due if a redundancy payment had been payable.

(3) If the post-employment notice pay (see section 402D) in respect of the termination is greater than, or equal to, the total amount of the relevant termination awards in respect of the termination, section 402B applies to all of those relevant termination awards.

(4) If the post-employment notice pay in respect of the termination is less than the total amount of the relevant termination awards in respect of the termination but is not nil —
   (a) section 402B applies to a part of those relevant termination awards, and
   (b) the amount of that part is equal to the post-employment notice pay.

(5) Section 309(4) to (6) (meaning of "redundancy payment" and "approved contractual payment" etc) apply for the purposes of subsection (2) as they apply for the purposes of section 309.

402D "Post-employment notice pay"

(1) "The post-employment notice pay" in respect of a termination is (subject to subsection (11)) given by —

$$\left(\frac{BP \times D}{P}\right) - T$$

where —

BP, D and P are given by subsections (3) to (7), and

T is the total of the amounts of any payment or benefit received in connection with the termination which—

    (a)   would fall within section 401(1)(a) but for section 401(3),

    (b)   is taxable as earnings under Chapter 1 of Part 3,

    (c)   is not pay in respect of holiday entitlement for a period before the employment ends, and

    (d)   is not a bonus payable for termination of the employment.

(2)   If the amount given by the formula in subsection (1) is a negative amount, the post-employment notice pay is nil.

(3)   Subject to subsections (5) and (6)—

    BP is the employee's basic pay (see subsection (7)) from the employment in respect of the last pay period of the employee to end before the trigger date,

    P is the number of days in that pay period, and

    D is the number of days in the post-employment notice period.

(4)   See section 402E for the meaning of "trigger date" and "post-employment notice period".

(5)   If there is no pay period of the employee which ends before the trigger date then—

    BP is the employee's basic pay from the employment in respect of the period starting with the first day of the employment and ending with the trigger date,

    P is the number of days in that period, and

    D is the number of days in the post-employment notice period.

(6)   If the last pay period of the employee to end before the trigger date is a month, the minimum notice (see section 402E) is given by contractual terms and is expressed to be a whole number of months, and the post-employment notice period is equal in length to the minimum notice or is otherwise a whole number of months, then—

    BP is the employee's basic pay from the employment in respect of the last pay period of the employee to end before the trigger date,

    P is 1, and

    D is the length of the post-employment notice period expressed in months.

(7)   In this section "basic pay" means—

    (a)   employment income of the employee from the employment but disregarding—

        (i)   any amount received by way of overtime, bonus, commission, gratuity or allowance,

        (ii)   any amount received in connection with the termination of the employment,

        (iii)   any amount treated as earnings under Chapters 2 to 10 of Part 3 (the benefits code) or which would be so treated apart from section 64,

          (iv)   any amount which is treated as earnings under Chapter 12 of Part 3 (amounts treated as earnings),

          (v)   any amount which counts as employment income by virtue of Part 7 (income relating to securities and securities options), and

          (vi)   any employment-related securities that constitute earnings under Chapter 1 of Part 3 (earnings), and

    (b)   any amount which the employee has given up the right to receive but which would have fallen within paragraph (a) had the employee not done so.

(8)   In subsection (7) "employment-related securities" has the same meaning as it has in Chapter 1 of Part 7 (see section 421B).

(9)   The Treasury may by regulations amend this section for the purpose of altering the meaning of "basic pay".

(10)   A statutory instrument containing regulations under subsection (9) may not be made unless a draft of it has been laid before, and approved by a resolution of, the House of Commons.

(11)   Where the purpose, or one of the purposes, of any arrangements is the avoidance of tax by causing the post-employment notice pay calculated under subsection (1) to be less than it would otherwise be, the post-employment notice pay is to be treated as the amount which the post-employment notice pay would have been but for the arrangements.

(12)   In subsection (11) "arrangements" includes any scheme, arrangement or understanding of any kind, whether or not legally enforceable, involving a single transaction or two or more transactions.

402E   Meaning of "trigger date" and "post-employment notice period" in section 402D

(1)   Subsections (2) and (4) to (6) have effect for the purposes of section 402D (and subsection (4) has effect also for the purposes of this section).

(2)   The "trigger date" is—

    (a)   if the termination is not a notice case, the last day of the employment, and

    (b)   if the termination is a notice case, the day the notice is given.

(3)   For the purposes of this section, the termination is a "notice case" if the employer or employee gives notice to the other to terminate the employment, and here it does not matter—

    (a)   whether the notice is more or less than, or the same as, the minimum notice, or

    (b)   if the employment ends before the notice expires.

(4)   The "minimum notice" is the minimum notice required to be given by the employer to terminate the employee's employment by notice in accordance with the law and contractual terms effective—

    (a)   where the termination is not a notice case—

          (i)   immediately before the employment ends, or

          (ii)   where the employment ends by agreement entered into after the start of the employment, immediately before the agreement is entered into, and

> (b) where the termination is a notice case, immediately before the notice is given.

(5) The "post-employment notice period" is the period —

   (a) beginning at the end of the last day of the employment, and

   (b) ending with the earliest lawful termination date.

(But see subsection (8) for provision about limited-term contracts.)

(6) If the earliest lawful termination date is, or precedes, the last day of the employment, the number of days in the post-employment notice period is nil.

(7) "The earliest lawful termination date" is the last day of the period which —

   (a) is equal in length to the minimum notice, and

   (b) begins at the end of the trigger date.

(8) In the case of a contract of employment which is a limited-term contract and which does not include provision for termination by notice by the employer, the post-employment notice period is the period —

   (a) beginning at the end of the last day of the employment, and

   (b) ending with the day of the occurrence of the limiting event.

(9) If, in a case to which subsection (8) applies, on the last day of the employment the day of the occurrence of the limiting event is not ascertained or ascertainable (because, for example, the limiting event is the performance of a task), then subsection (8) has effect as if for paragraph (b) there were substituted —

   "(b) ending with the day on which notice would have expired if the employer had, on the last day of the employment, given to the employee the minimum notice required to terminate the contract under section 86 of the Employment Rights Act 1996 (assuming that that section applies to the employment)."

(10) In this section "limited-term contract" and "limiting event" have the same meaning as in the Employment Rights Act 1996 (see section 235(2A) and (2B))."

(4) In section 403 (charges on payments and benefits which can benefit from threshold) —

   (a) in subsection (1), for "Chapter" substitute "section",

   (b) in subsection (3), after "Chapter" insert "(but see section 402B(3))",

   (c) in subsection (4), for the words from "when" to "exceeds" substitute "when aggregated with —

      (a) other payments or benefits in respect of the employee or former employee that are payments or benefits to which this section applies, and

      (b) other payments or benefits in respect of the employee or former employee that are payments or benefits —

         (i) received in the tax year 2017-18 or an earlier tax year, and

         (ii) to which this Chapter applied in the tax year of receipt,

      it exceeds",

   (d) in subsection (5)(a), for "Chapter" substitute "section",

      (e)   in subsection (6), after "employment income" insert "or, as the case may be, in relation to whom section 402B(1) provides for an amount to be treated as an amount of earnings", and

      (f)   in the heading, at the end insert "where threshold applies".

(5)   In section 404 (how the threshold applies) –

      (a)   in subsection (3)(b) (meaning of "termination or change date"), for "this Chapter" substitute "section 403", and

      (b)   after subsection (5) insert –

         "(6)   In subsection (3)(b), the reference to a payment or other benefit to which section 403 applies includes a reference to a payment or other benefit –

            (a)   received in the tax year 2017-18 or an earlier tax year, and

            (b)   to which this Chapter applied in the tax year of receipt."

(6)   After section 404A insert –

"404B Power to vary threshold

      (1)   The Treasury may by regulations amend the listed provisions by substituting, for the amount for the time being mentioned in those provisions, a different amount.

      (2)   The listed provisions are –
            subsections (1), (4) and (5) of section 403, and
            subsections (1), (4) and (5) of section 404 and its heading.

      (3)   Regulations under this section may include transitional provision.

      (4)   A statutory instrument containing regulations under this section which reduce the mentioned amount may not be made unless a draft of it has been laid before, and approved by a resolution of, the House of Commons."

(7)   In section 406 (exception in cases of death, injury or disability) –

      (a)   the existing text becomes subsection (1), and

      (b)   after that subsection insert –

         "(2)   Although "injury" in subsection (1) includes psychiatric injury, it does not include injured feelings."

(8)   In section 414(2) (proportionate reduction for foreign service in certain cases), for "otherwise count as employment income under this Chapter" substitute "otherwise –

      (a)   be treated as earnings by section 402B(1), or

      (b)   count as employment income as a result of section 403".

(9)   In section 717(4) (regulations etc not subject to negative procedure), before "or section 681F(3)" insert ", section 402D(10) (meaning of basic pay for purpose of calculating charge on termination award), section 404B(4) (reduction of tax-free threshold for employment-termination etc payments)".

(10)   The amendments made by this section have effect for the tax year 2018-19 and subsequent tax years.

6   PAYE settlement agreements

(1)   In Chapter 5 of Part 11 of ITEPA 2003 (PAYE settlement agreements), in sections 703(a) and 704(1)(a), for "an officer of Revenue and Customs" substitute "Her Majesty's Revenue and Customs".

(2)   The amendment made by this section has effect in relation to the tax year 2018-19 and subsequent tax years.

7   Money purchase annual allowance

(1)   Part 4 of FA 2004 is amended as follows.

(2)   In section 227ZA (chargeable amount), in subsection (1)(b), for "£10,000" substitute "£4,000".

(3)   In section 227B (alternative chargeable amount), in subsections (1)(b) and (2), for "£10,000" substitute "£4,000".

(4)   In section 227D (pension input amounts in respect of certain hybrid arrangements), in Steps 4 and 5 of subsection (4), for "£10,000" substitute "£4,000".

(5)   The amendments made by this section have effect for the tax year 2017-18 and subsequent tax years.

Income tax: investments

8   Dividend nil rate for tax year 2018-19 etc

(1)   In section 13A of ITA 2007 (income charged at the dividend nil rate), for "£5000", in each place, substitute "£2000".

(2)   The amendments made by this section have effect for the tax year 2018-19 and subsequent tax years.

9   Life insurance policies: recalculating gains on part surrenders etc

(1)   ITTOIA 2005 is amended as follows.

(2)   After section 507 (method for making periodic calculations in part surrender or assignment cases) insert—

"507A Recalculating gains under section 507

(1)   An interested person may apply to an officer of Revenue and Customs for a review of a calculation under section 507 on the ground that the gain arising from it is wholly disproportionate.

(2)   For the purposes of this section an interested person in relation to a calculation under section 507 is a person who would be liable for all or any part of the amount of tax that would be chargeable under this Chapter if the gain were not recalculated.

(3)   Applications under subsection (1) must be—
       (a)   made in writing, and
       (b)   received by an officer of Revenue and Customs within—

     (i) the four tax years following the tax year in which the gain arose, or

     (ii) such longer period as the officer may agree.

  (4) In considering whether the gain is wholly disproportionate, the officer may take into account (as well as the amount of the gain) any factor which the officer considers appropriate including, so far as the officer considers it appropriate to do so—

    (a) the economic gain on the rights surrendered or assigned,

    (b) the amount of the premiums paid under the policy or contract,

    (c) the amount of tax that would be chargeable under this Chapter if the gain were not recalculated.

  (5) If, following an application under subsection (1), an officer considers that the gain arising from the calculation under section 507 is wholly disproportionate, the officer must recalculate the gain on a just and reasonable basis.

  (6) Following a recalculation under subsection (5), references in this Chapter (but excluding this section) to a calculation under section 507 are to be regarded as references to a recalculation under this section.

  (7) Following a recalculation under subsection (5), an officer of Revenue and Customs must notify the interested person of the result of the recalculation.

  (8) If two or more persons are interested persons in relation to a calculation under section 507—

    (a) an application under subsection (1) may be made only by all the interested persons jointly, and

    (b) subsection (7) applies as if the reference to the interested person were a reference to each of the interested persons.

  (9) Following a recalculation under subsection (5), all necessary adjustments and repayments of income tax are to be made.

  (10) No recalculation is to be made under this section if the gain mentioned in subsection (1) arises as a result of one or more transactions which form part of arrangements, the main purpose, or one of the main purposes, of which is to obtain a tax advantage for any person.

  (11) In this section—

    "arrangements" includes any agreement, understanding, scheme, transaction or series of transactions (whether or not legally enforceable), and

    "tax advantage" has the meaning given by section 1139 of CTA 2010."

 (3) After section 512 (available premium left for relevant transaction in certain part surrender or assignment cases) insert—

"512A Recalculating gains under section 511

  (1) An interested person may apply to an officer of Revenue and Customs for a review of a calculation under section 511 on the ground that the gain arising from it is wholly disproportionate.

(2)   For the purposes of this section an interested person in relation to a calculation under section 511 is a person who would be liable for all or any part of the amount of tax that would be chargeable under this Chapter —

    (a)   if the gain were not recalculated, or

    (b)   if all rights under the policy or contract had been surrendered immediately after the surrender or assignment of rights which gave rise to the calculation.

(3)   Applications under subsection (1) must be —

    (a)   made in writing, and

    (b)   received by an officer of Revenue and Customs within —

        (i)   the four tax years following the tax year in which the gain arose, or

        (ii)   such longer period as the officer may agree.

(4)   In considering whether the gain is wholly disproportionate, the officer may take into account (as well as the amount of the gain) any factor which the officer considers appropriate including, so far as the officer considers it appropriate to do so —

    (a)   the economic gain on the rights surrendered or assigned,

    (b)   the amount of the premiums paid under the policy or contract,

    (c)   the amount of tax that would be chargeable under this Chapter if the gain were not recalculated.

(5)   If, following an application under subsection (1), an officer considers that the gain arising from the calculation under section 511 is wholly disproportionate, the officer must recalculate the gain on a just and reasonable basis.

(6)   Following a recalculation under subsection (5), references in this Chapter (but excluding this section) to a calculation under section 511 are to be regarded as references to a recalculation under this section.

(7)   Following a recalculation under subsection (5), an officer of Revenue and Customs must notify the interested person of the result of the recalculation.

(8)   If two or more persons are interested persons in relation to a calculation under section 511 —

    (a)   an application under subsection (1) may be made only by all the interested persons jointly, and

    (b)   subsection (7) applies as if the reference to the interested person were a reference to each of the interested persons.

(9)   Following a recalculation under subsection (5), all necessary adjustments and repayments of income tax are to be made.

(10)   No recalculation is to be made under this section if the gain mentioned in subsection (1) arises as a result of one or more transactions which form part of arrangements, the main purpose, or one of the main purposes, of which is to obtain a tax advantage for any person.

(11)   In this section —

           "arrangements" includes any agreement, understanding, scheme, transaction or series of transactions (whether or not legally enforceable), and

           "tax advantage" has the meaning given by section 1139 of CTA 2010."

  (4) In section 538 (recovery of tax from trustees), after subsection (6) insert—

     "(7) Subsection (8) applies where—

        (a) an individual has recovered an amount from trustees under this section, and

        (b) subsequently the individual's liability to tax under this Chapter has been reduced (or removed) as a result of a recalculation under section 507A or 512A.

     (8) The individual must repay to the trustees the amount (if any) by which the recovered amount exceeds the individual's revised entitlement.

     (9) In subsection (8) the individual's revised entitlement is the amount to which the individual is entitled under this section calculated by reference to the individual's liability to tax under this Chapter as reduced (or removed) as a result of the recalculation under section 507A or 512A."

  (5) The amendments made by subsection (4) have effect in relation to amounts recovered before, as well as after, the day on which this Act is passed.

10   Personal portfolio bonds

    In section 520 of ITTOIA 2005 (property categories), after subsection (4) insert—

     "(5) The Treasury may by regulations—

        (a) amend the table in subsection (2) by adding, removing or amending a category of property;

        (b) add, remove or amend a definition relating to any category of property in that table; and

        (c) make consequential amendments.

     (6) A statutory instrument containing regulations under this section which have the effect of removing a category of property from the table in subsection (2)—

        (a) must be laid before the House of Commons; and

        (b) ceases to have effect at the end of the period of 28 days beginning with the day on which it was made, unless it is approved during that period by a resolution of the House of Commons.

     (7) In reckoning the period of 28 days, no account is to be taken of any time during which Parliament is dissolved or prorogued, or during which the House of Commons is adjourned for more than four days."

11   EIS and SEIS: the no pre-arranged exits requirement

  (1) ITA 2007 is amended as follows.

(2) In section 177 (EIS: the no pre-arranged exits requirement), for subsection (2) substitute —

   "(2) The arrangements referred to in subsection (1)(a) do not include —
   (a) any arrangements with a view to such an exchange of shares, or shares and securities, as is mentioned in section 247(1), or
   (b) any arrangements with a view to any shares in the issuing company being exchanged for, or converted into, shares in that company of a different class."

(3) In section 257CD (SEIS: the no pre-arranged exits requirement), for subsection (2) substitute —

   "(2) The arrangements referred to in subsection (1)(a) do not include —
   (a) any arrangements with a view to such an exchange of shares, or shares and securities, as is mentioned in section 257HB(1), or
   (b) any arrangements with a view to any shares in the issuing company being exchanged for, or converted into, shares in that company of a different class."

(4) The amendments made by this section have effect in relation to shares issued on or after 5 December 2016.

12 VCTs: follow-on funding

(1) ITA 2007 is amended as follows.

(2) In section 326 (restructuring to which sections 326A and 327 apply) —
   (a) in the heading to section 326, for "section 327 applies" substitute "sections 326A, 327 and 327A apply";
   (b) in subsection (1), for "Sections 326A and 327 apply" substitute "Sections 326A, 327 and 327A apply".

(3) After section 327 insert —

"327A Follow-on funding

   (1) Subsections (2) and (3) apply where —
   (a) this section applies (see section 326(1)),
   (b) the acquisition by the new company of all the old shares, which is provided for by the arrangements mentioned in section 326(1), takes place, and
   (c) the acquisition falls within section 326(2).

   (2) If, after the acquisition, another company makes an investment in the new company, section 280C (the permitted maximum age condition) has effect in relation to that investment as if —
   (a) in subsection (4)(a) the reference to a relevant investment having been made in the relevant company before the end of the initial investing period included a reference to a relevant investment having been made in the old company before the acquisition and before the end of the initial investing period, and
   (b) in subsection (6)(a) the reference to relevant investments made in the relevant company included a reference to relevant investments made in the old company before the acquisition.

    (3)   In relation to any relevant holding issued by the new company after the acquisition, section 294A (the permitted company age requirement) has effect as if—

        (a)   in subsection (3)(a) the reference to a relevant investment having been made in the relevant company before the end of the initial investing period included a reference to a relevant investment having been made in the old company before the acquisition and before the end of the initial investing period, and

        (b)   in subsection (5)(a) the reference to relevant investments made in the relevant company included a reference to relevant investments made in the old company before the acquisition.

    (4)   In subsection (3) "relevant holding" has the same meaning as in Chapter 4."

  (4)   The amendments made by this section have effect—

        (a)   for the purposes of section 280C of ITA 2007, in relation to investments made on or after 6 April 2017;

        (b)   for the purposes of section 294A of ITA 2007, in relation to relevant holdings issued on or after 6 April 2017.

13   VCTs: exchange of non-qualifying shares and securities

  (1)   Section 330 of ITA 2007 (power to facilitate company reorganisations etc involving exchange of shares) is amended as follows.

  (2)   After subsection (1) insert—

    "(1A)   The Treasury may by regulations make provision for the purposes of this Part for cases where—

        (a)   a holding of shares or securities that does not meet the requirements of Chapter 4 is exchanged for other shares or securities not meeting those requirements, and

        (b)   the exchange is made for genuine commercial reasons and does not form part of a scheme or arrangement the main purpose or one of the main purposes of which is the avoidance of tax."

  (3)   In subsection (2), for "subsection (1)" substitute "subsections (1) and (1A)".

  (4)   In subsection (3), for "The regulations" substitute "Regulations under subsection (1)".

  (5)   After subsection (3) insert—

    "(3A)   Regulations under subsection (1A) may, among other things, make provision—

        (a)   for the new shares or securities to be treated in any respect in the same way as the original shares and securities for any period;

        (b)   as to when the new shares or securities are to be regarded as having been acquired;

        (c)   as to the valuation of the original or the new shares or securities."

  (6)   In subsection (4), for "The regulations" substitute "Regulations under this section".

(7)　In subsection (6). in paragraph (c), at the beginning insert "in the case of regulations under subsection (1)".

14　Social investment tax relief

Schedule 1 makes provision about income tax relief for social investments.

15　Business investment relief

(1)　Chapter A1 of Part 14 of ITA 2007 (remittance basis) is amended as follows.

(2)　In section 809VC (qualifying investments), in subsection (1)(a), after "issued to" insert "or acquired by".

(3)　In section 809VD (condition relating to qualifying investments) –

　　(a)　in subsection (1), omit the "or" at the end of paragraph (b) and after that paragraph insert –

　　　　"(ba)　an eligible hybrid company, or";

　　(b)　in subsection (2)(b), for "2" substitute "5";

　　(c)　in subsection (3)(c), for "2" substitute "5";

　　(d)　after subsection (3) insert –

　　　"(3A)　A company is an "eligible hybrid company" if –

　　　　(a)　it is a private limited company,

　　　　(b)　it is not an eligible trading company or an eligible stakeholder company,

　　　　(c)　it carries on one or more commercial trades or is preparing to do so within the next 5 years,

　　　　(d)　it holds one or more investments in eligible trading companies or is preparing to do so within the next 5 years, and

　　　　(e)　carrying on commercial trades and making investments in eligible trading companies are all or substantially all of what it does (or of what it is reasonably expected to do once it begins operating).";

　　(e)　in subsection (4), for "reference in subsection (3)" substitute "references in subsections (3) and (3A)";

　　(f)　in subsection (5)(a), for "2" substitute "5".

(4)　In section 809VE (commercial trades), after subsection (5) insert –

　　"(6)　A company which is a partner in a partnership is not to be regarded as carrying on a trade carried on by the partnership."

(5)　In section 809VH (meaning of "potentially chargeable event") –

　　(a)　in subsection (1)(a), after "eligible stakeholder company" insert "nor an eligible hybrid company";

　　(b)　in subsection (1)(d), for "2-year" substitute "5-year";

　　(c)　in subsection (2), for paragraph (b) substitute –

　　　　"(b)　the value is received from any person in circumstances that are directly or indirectly attributable to the investment, and";

　　(d)　omit subsection (4);

　　(e)　in subsection (5) –

             (i)   for "2-year" substitute "5-year";

             (ii)   in paragraph (a), for "2" substitute "5";

   (f)   in subsection (6), omit the "or" at the end of paragraph (b) and after that paragraph insert—

      "(ba)   it is an eligible hybrid company but is not trading and—

           (i)   it holds no investments in eligible trading companies, or

           (ii)   none of the eligible trading companies in which it holds investments is trading, or";

   (g)   in subsection (10)(b), after "eligible stakeholder company" insert "or an eligible hybrid company".

  (6)   In section 809VJ (grace period), after subsection (2) insert—

   "(2A)   But subsection (2B) applies instead of subsections (1) and (2) where the potentially chargeable event is a breach of the 5-year start-up rule by virtue of section 809VH(5)(b).

   (2B)   The grace period allowed for the steps mentioned in section 809VI(2)(a) and (2)(b) is the period of 2 years beginning with the day on which a relevant person first became aware or ought reasonably to have become aware of the potentially chargeable event referred to in subsection (2A)."

  (7)   In section 809VN (order of disposals etc), in subsections (1)(c) and (5)(a) and (b), after "eligible stakeholder company" insert "or eligible hybrid company".

  (8)   The amendments made by this section have effect where the relevant event as defined in section 809VA of ITA 2007 occurs on or after 6 April 2017.

Income tax: trading and property businesses

16   Calculation of profits of trades and property businesses

Schedule 2 contains provision about the calculation of the profits of a trade, profession or vocation or a property business, in particular the calculation of profits on the cash basis.

17   Trading and property allowances

Schedule 3 contains provision about a trading allowance and a property allowance giving relief from income tax.

Corporation tax

18   Carried-forward losses

  (1)   Schedule 4 makes provision about corporation tax relief for losses and other amounts that are carried forward.

  (2)   The Commissioners for Her Majesty's Revenue and Customs may by regulations made by statutory instrument make provision consequential on any provision made by Schedule 4.

  (3)   Regulations under subsection (2)—

      (a)   may make provision amending or modifying any provision of the Taxes Acts (including any provision inserted by Schedule 4),

      (b)   may make incidental, supplemental, transitional, transitory or saving provision, and

      (c)   may make different provision for different purposes.

(4)   A statutory instrument containing regulations under subsection (2) is subject to annulment in pursuance of a resolution of the House of Commons.

(5)   In this section "the Taxes Acts" has the same meaning as in the Taxes Management Act 1970 (see section 118(1) of that Act).

19 Losses: counteraction of avoidance arrangements

(1)   Any loss-related tax advantage that would (in the absence of this section) arise from relevant tax arrangements is to be counteracted by the making of such adjustments as are just and reasonable.

(2)   Any adjustments required to be made under this section (whether or not by an officer of Revenue and Customs) may be made by way of —

      (a)   an assessment,

      (b)   the modification of an assessment,

      (c)   amendment or disallowance of a claim,

   or otherwise.

(3)   For the purposes of this section arrangements are "relevant tax arrangements" if conditions A and B are met.

(4)   Condition A is that the purpose, or one of the main purposes, of the arrangements is to obtain a loss-related tax advantage.

(5)   Condition B is that it is reasonable to regard the arrangements as circumventing the intended limits of relief under the relevant provisions or otherwise exploiting shortcomings in the relevant provisions.

(6)   In determining whether or not condition B is met all the relevant circumstances are to be taken into account, including whether the arrangements include any steps that—

      (a)   are contrived or abnormal, or

      (b)   lack a genuine commercial purpose.

(7)   In this section "loss-related tax advantage" means a tax advantage as a result of a deduction (or increased deduction) under a provision mentioned in subsection (8).

(8)   The provisions are —

      (a)   sections 457, 459, 461, 462, 463B, 463G and 463H of CTA 2009 (non-trading deficits from loan relationships);

      (b)   section 753 of CTA 2009 (non-trading losses on intangible fixed assets);

      (c)   section 1219 of CTA 2009 (management expenses etc);

      (d)   sections 37, 45, 45A, 45B and 45F of CTA 2010 (deductions in respect of trade losses);

      (e)   section 62(3) of CTA 2010 (losses of a UK property business);

      (f)   Part 5 of CTA 2010 (group relief);

      (g)   Part 5A of CTA 2010 (group relief for carried-forward losses);

    (h)   sections 303B, 303C and 303D of CTA 2010 (non-decommissioning losses of ring-fence trades);

    (i)   sections 124A, 124B and 124C of FA 2012 (carried-forward BLAGAB trade losses).

(9)   In this section—

    "arrangements" includes any agreement, understanding, scheme transaction or series of transactions (whether or not legally enforceable);

    "tax advantage" has the meaning given by section 1139 of CTA 2010.

(10)   This section has effect in relation to a tax advantage that relates (or would apart from this section relate) to an accounting period beginning on or after 1 April 2017 (regardless of when the arrangements in question were made).

(11)   Where a tax advantage would (apart from this subsection) relate to an accounting period beginning before 1 April 2017 and ending on or after that date ("the straddling period")—

    (a)   so much of the straddling period as falls before 1 April 2017, and so much of that period as falls on or after that date, are treated as separate accounting periods, and

    (b)   the extent (if any) to which the tax advantage relates to the second of those accounting periods is to be determined by apportioning amounts—

        (i)   in accordance with section 1172 of CTA 2010 (time basis), or

        (ii)   if that method would produce a result that is unjust or unreasonable, on a just and reasonable basis.

(12)   In the case of a tax advantage as a result of a deduction (or increased deduction) under—

    (a)   section 463H of CTA 2009,

    (b)   section 62(3) of CTA 2010,

    (c)   section 303B, 303C or 303D of CTA 2010, or

    (d)   section 124A or 124C of FA 2012,

subsections (10) and (11) have effect as if the references to 1 April 2017 were to 13 July 2017.

20   Corporate interest restriction

Schedule 5 makes provision about the amounts that may be brought into account for the purposes of corporation tax in respect of interest and other financing costs.

21   Museum and gallery exhibitions

Schedule 6 makes provision about relief in respect of the production of museum and gallery exhibitions.

22   Grassroots sport

(1)   CTA 2010 is amended as follows.

(2)   In section 1(2) (overview of Act)—

    (a)   omit the "and" at the end of paragraph (g), and

(b)   after that paragraph insert—

    "(ga)   relief for expenditure on grassroots sport (see Part 6A), and".

(3)   In section 99(1) (group relief: losses and other amounts which may be surrendered), after paragraph (d) insert—

    "(da)   amounts allowable as qualifying expenditure on grassroots sport (see Part 6A),".

(4)   In section 105(4) (group relief: order in which amounts are treated as surrendered)—

    (a)   after paragraph (a) insert—

        "(aa)   second, expenditure within section 99(1)(da),",

    (b)   in paragraph (b), for "second" substitute "third",

    (c)   in paragraph (c), for "third" substitute "fourth", and

    (d)   in paragraph (d), for "fourth" substitute "fifth".

(5)   After Part 6 insert—

"PART 6A

RELIEF FOR EXPENDITURE ON GRASSROOTS SPORT

217A Relief for expenditure on grassroots sport

(1)   A payment made by a company which is qualifying expenditure on grassroots sport (and which is not refunded) is allowed as a deduction in accordance with this section from the company's total profits in calculating the corporation tax chargeable for the accounting period in which the payment is made.

(2)   The deduction is from the company's total profits for the accounting period after any other relief from corporation tax other than—

    (a)   relief under Part 6,

    (b)   group relief, and

    (c)   group relief for carried-forward losses.

(3)   If the company is a qualifying sport body at the time of the payment, a deduction is allowed for the amount of the payment.

    See section 217C for the meaning of "qualifying sport body".

(4)   If the company is not a qualifying sport body at the time of the payment, a deduction is allowed—

    (a)   if the payment is to a qualifying sport body, for the amount of the payment, and

    (b)   if the payment does not fall within paragraph (a) (a "direct payment"), in accordance with subsections (7) and (8).

(5)   If at any time on or after 1 April 2017 the company receives income for use for charitable purposes which are purposes for facilitating participation in amateur eligible sport, a deduction is allowed only if, and in so far as, the payment exceeds an amount which is equal to the amount of that income which—

    (a)   the company does not have to bring into account for corporation tax purposes, and

    (b)   has not previously been taken into account under this subsection to disallow a deduction under this Part of all or any part of a payment.

See section 217B(3) for the meaning of terms used in this subsection.

(6)   But in any case, the amount of the deduction is limited to the amount that reduces the company's taxable total profits for the accounting period to nil.

(7)   If the total of all the direct payments made by the company in the accounting period is equal to or less than the maximum deduction for direct payments, a deduction is allowed under subsection (4)(b) in respect of that total.

(8)   If the total of all the direct payments made by the company in the accounting period is more than the maximum deduction for direct payments, a deduction is allowed under subsection (4)(b) in respect of so much of that total as does not exceed the maximum deduction for direct payments.

(9)   The maximum deduction for direct payments is £2,500 or, if the accounting period is shorter than 12 months, a proportionately reduced amount.

(10)   The Treasury may by regulations amend subsection (9) by substituting a higher amount for the amount for the time being specified there.

217B Meaning of qualifying expenditure on grassroots sport

(1)   For the purposes of this Part, a payment is qualifying expenditure on grassroots sport if—

    (a)   it is expenditure incurred for charitable purposes which are purposes for facilitating participation in amateur eligible sport, and

    (b)   apart from this Part, no deduction from total profits, or in calculating any component of total profits, would be allowed in respect of the payment.

For the meaning of charitable purposes, see sections 2, 7 and 8 of the Charities Act 2011.

(2)   Where expenditure is incurred for both—

    (a)   charitable purposes which are purposes for facilitating participation in amateur eligible sport, and

    (b)   other purposes,

then, for the purposes of subsection (1), it is to be apportioned between the purposes in paragraph (a) and the purposes in paragraph (b) on a just and reasonable basis.

(3)   For the purposes of section 217A(5) and subsection (1)(a)—

    (a)   paying a person to play or take part in a sport does not facilitate participation in amateur sport, but paying coaches or officials for their services may do so, and

    (b)   "eligible sport" means a sport that for the time being is an eligible sport for the purposes of Chapter 9 of Part 13 (see section 661).

217C Meaning of qualifying sport body

(1) For the purposes of this Part, a "qualifying sport body" is—
    (a) a recognised sport governing body;
    (b) a body which is wholly owned by a recognised sport governing body.

(2) A "recognised sport governing body" is a body which is included from time to time in a list, maintained by the National Sports Councils, of governing bodies of sport recognised by them.

(3) The Treasury may by regulations—
    (a) amend this section for the purpose of altering the meaning of "qualifying sport body";
    (b) designate bodies to be treated as qualifying sport bodies for the purposes of this Part.

(4) Regulations under section (3)(b) may designate a body by reference to its inclusion in a class or description of bodies.

(5) In this section "the National Sports Councils" means—
    (a) the United Kingdom Sports Council,
    (b) the English Sports Council,
    (c) the Scottish Sports Council,
    (d) the Sports Council for Wales, and
    (e) the Sports Council for Northern Ireland.

(6) Regulations under subsection (3)(b) made before 1 April 2018 may include provision having effect in relation to times before the regulations are made (but not times earlier than 1 April 2017).

217D Relationship between this Part and Part 6

If, but for section 217A, an amount—
    (a) would be deductible under Part 6, or
    (b) would be deductible under Part 6 but for Chapter 2A of Part 6,
the amount is not deductible under this Part, and nothing in this Part affects the amount's deductibility (or non-deductibility) under Part 6."

(6) The amendments made by this section have effect for the purpose of allowing deductions for payments made on or after 1 April 2017.

(7) Where a company has an accounting period beginning before 1 April 2017 and ending on or after that date, the accounting period for the purposes of the new section 217A(9) is so much of the accounting period as falls on or after 1 April 2017.

23 Profits from the exploitation of patents: cost-sharing arrangements

(1) Part 8A of CTA 2010 (profits from the exploitation of patents) is amended as follows.

(2) After section 357BLE insert—

"357BLEA Cases where the company is a party to a CSA

(1) Subsection (2) applies if during the relevant period—

  (a) the company is a party to a cost-sharing arrangement (see section 357GC),

  (b) the company incurs expenditure in making payments under the arrangement that are within section 357BLC(2) by reason of section 357GCZC, and

  (c) persons who are not connected with the company make payments under the arrangement to the company in respect of relevant research and development undertaken or contracted out by the company.

(2) So much of the expenditure referred to in paragraph (b) of subsection (1) as is equal to the amount of the payments referred to in paragraph (c) of that subsection is to be disregarded in determining the R&D fraction for the sub-stream.

(3) Subsection (4) applies if during the relevant period —

  (a) the company is a party to a cost-sharing arrangement,

  (b) the company incurs expenditure in making payments under the arrangement that are within subsection (5), and

  (c) the company receives payments under the arrangement that are within subsection (6).

(4) So much of the expenditure referred to in paragraph (b) of subsection (3) as is equal to the amount of the payments referred to in paragraph (c) of that subsection is to be disregarded in determining the R&D fraction for the sub-stream.

(5) A payment is within this subsection if —

  (a) it is within section 357BLD(2) by reason of section 357GCZC, or

  (b) it is within section 357BLE(2) or (3) by reason of section 357GCZD.

(6) A payment is within this subsection if —

  (a) it is made by persons connected with the company in respect of relevant research and development undertaken or contracted out by the company, or

  (b) it is made in respect of an assignment to the company of a relevant qualifying IP right or a grant or transfer to the company of an exclusive licence in respect of such a right."

(3) For section 357GC substitute —

"357GC Meaning of "cost-sharing arrangement" etc

(1) This section applies for the purposes of this Part.

(2) A "cost-sharing arrangement" is an arrangement under which —

  (a) each of the parties to the arrangement is required to contribute to the cost of, or undertake activities for the purpose of, creating or developing an item or process,

  (b) each of those parties —

    (i) is entitled to a share of any income attributable to the item or process, or

    (ii) has one or more rights in respect of the item or process, and

     (c)   the amount of any income received by each of those parties is proportionate to its participation in the arrangement as described in paragraph (a).

(3)   "Invention", in relation to a cost-sharing arrangement, means the item or process that is the subject of the arrangement (or any item or process incorporated within it).

357GCZA Qualifying IP right held by another party to CSA

(1)   This section applies if —
    (a)   a company is a party to a cost-sharing arrangement,
    (b)   another party to the arrangement ("P") holds a qualifying IP right granted in respect of the invention, and
    (c)   the company does not hold an exclusive licence in respect of the right.

(2)   But this section does not apply if the arrangement produces for the company a return within section 357BG(1)(c).

(3)   The company is to be treated for the purposes of this Part as if it held the right.

(4)   The right is to be treated for the purposes of this Part as a new qualifying IP right in relation to the company if —
    (a)   the company or P (or both) became a party to the arrangement on or after 1 April 2017, or
    (b)   the right is a new qualifying IP right in relation to P (or would be if P was a company).

(5)   Subsection (4) does not apply if —
    (a)   the company held an exclusive licence in respect of the right immediately before it became a party to the arrangement, and
    (b)   that licence was granted to the company before the relevant date.

(6)   The right is to be treated for the purposes of this Part as an old qualifying IP right in relation to the company if it is not to be treated as a new qualifying IP right by reason of subsection (4).

(7)   Subsections (7) and (8) of section 357BP (meaning of "relevant date") apply for the purposes of subsection (5) of this section as they apply for the purposes of subsection (6) of that section.

357GCZB Exclusive licence held by another party to CSA

(1)   This section applies if —
    (a)   a company is a party to a cost-sharing arrangement,
    (b)   another party to the arrangement ("P") holds an exclusive licence in respect of a qualifying IP right granted in respect of the invention, and
    (c)   the company does not hold the right or another exclusive licence in respect of it.

(2)   But this section does not apply if the arrangement produces for the company a return within section 357BG(1)(c).

(3) The company is to be treated for the purposes of this Part as if it held an exclusive licence in respect of the right.

(4) The right is to be treated for the purposes of this Part as a new qualifying IP right in relation to the company if—

    (a) the company or P (or both) became a party to the arrangement on or after 1 April 2017, or

    (b) the right is a new qualifying IP right in relation to P (or would be if P was a company).

(5) Subsection (4) does not apply if—

    (a) the company held the right immediately before it became a party to the arrangement, and

    (b) either—

        (i) the right had been granted or issued to the company in response to an application filed before 1 July 2016, or

        (ii) the right had been assigned to the company before the relevant date.

(6) Subsection (4) also does not apply if—

    (a) the company held an exclusive licence in respect of the right immediately before it became a party to the arrangement, and

    (b) that licence was granted to the company before the relevant date.

(7) The right is to be treated for the purposes of this Part as an old qualifying IP right in relation to the company if it is not to be treated as a new qualifying IP right by reason of subsection (4).

(8) Subsections (7) and (8) of section 357BP (meaning of "relevant date") apply for the purposes of subsections (5) and (6) of this section as they apply for the purposes of subsections (5) and (6) of that section.

357GCZC R&D undertaken or contracted out by another party to CSA

(1) Subsection (2) applies if—

    (a) a company is a party to a cost-sharing arrangement, and

    (b) another party to the arrangement ("P") undertakes research and development for the purpose of creating or developing the invention.

(2) The research and development is to be treated for the purposes of sections 357BLC and 357BLD as having been contracted out by the company to P.

(3) Subsection (4) applies if—

    (a) a company is a party to a cost-sharing arrangement,

    (b) another party to the arrangement ("P") contracts out to another person ("A") research and development for the purpose of creating or developing the invention, and

    (c) the company makes a payment under the arrangement in respect of that research and development (whether to P or to A).

(4) For the purposes of sections 357BLC and 357BLD—

(a)   the company is to be treated as having contracted out to P research and development which is the same as that contracted out by P to A, and

(b)   the payment mentioned in subsection (3)(c) is to be treated as if it were a payment made to P in respect of the research and development the company is treated as having contracted out to P.

(5)   In this section "research and development" has the meaning given by section 1138.

357GCZD Acquisition of qualifying IP rights etc by another party to CSA

(1)   Subsection (2) applies if—
    (a)   a company is a party to a cost-sharing arrangement,
    (b)   a person ("A") assigns to another party to the arrangement ("P") a qualifying IP right,
    (c)   the qualifying IP right is a right in respect of the invention, and
    (d)   the company makes under the arrangement a payment in respect of the assignment (whether to A or to P).

(2)   The payment is to be treated for the purposes of section 357BLE as if it were a payment to A in respect of the assignment by A to the company of the right.

(3)   Subsection (4) applies if—
    (a)   a company is a party to a cost-sharing arrangement,
    (b)   a person ("A") grants or transfers to another party to the arrangement ("P") an exclusive licence in respect of qualifying IP right,
    (c)   the qualifying IP right is a right granted in respect of the invention, and
    (d)   the company makes a payment under the arrangement in respect of the grant or transfer (whether to A or to P).

(4)   The payment is to be treated for the purposes of section 357BLE as if it were a payment to A in respect of the grant or transfer by A to the company of the licence.

357GCZE Treatment of expenditure in connection with formation of CSA etc

(1)   Where—
    (a)   a company makes a payment to a person ("P") in consideration of that person entering into a cost-sharing arrangement with the company, and
    (b)   P holds a qualifying IP right granted in respect of the invention or holds an exclusive licence in respect of such a right,

a just and reasonable amount of the payment is to be treated for the purposes of section 357BLE as if it was an amount paid in respect of the assignment to the company of the right or (as the case may be) the transfer to the company of the licence.

(2)   Where—
    (a)   a company makes a payment to a party to a cost-sharing arrangement ("P") in consideration of P agreeing to the

company becoming a party to the arrangement (whether in place of P or in addition to P), and

    (b)   any party to the arrangement holds a qualifying IP right in respect of the invention or holds an exclusive licence in respect of such a right,

a just and reasonable amount of the payment is to be treated for the purposes of section 357BLE as if it was an amount paid in respect of the assignment to the company of the right or (as the case may be) the transfer to the company of the licence.

(3)   Where—

    (a)   a company that is a party to a cost-sharing arrangement makes a payment to another party to the arrangement in consideration of that party agreeing to the company becoming entitled to a greater share of the income attributable to the invention or acquiring additional rights in relation to the invention, and

    (b)   any party to the arrangement holds a qualifying IP right in respect of the invention or holds an exclusive licence in respect of such a right,

a just and reasonable amount of the payment is to be treated for the purposes of section 357BLE as if it was an amount paid in respect of the assignment to the company of the right or (as the case may be) the transfer to the company of the licence.

357GCZF Treatment of income in connection with formation of CSA etc

(1)   Where—

    (a)   a company receives a payment in consideration of its entering into a cost-sharing arrangement, and

    (b)   the company holds a qualifying IP right granted in respect of the invention or holds an exclusive licence in respect of such a right,

a just and reasonable amount of the payment is to be treated as relevant IP income of the company.

(2)   Where—

    (a)   a company that is a party to a cost-sharing arrangement receives a payment from a person in consideration of its agreeing to that person becoming a party to the arrangement (whether in place of the company or in addition to it), and

    (b)   any party to the arrangement holds a qualifying IP right in respect of the invention or holds an exclusive licence in respect of such a right,

a just and reasonable amount of the payment is to be treated as relevant IP income of the company.

(3)   Where—

    (a)   a company that is a party to a cost-sharing arrangement receives a payment from another party to the arrangement in consideration of its agreeing to that party becoming entitled to a greater share of the income attributable to the invention or acquiring additional rights in relation to the invention, and

    (b)   any party to the arrangement holds a qualifying IP right in respect of the invention or holds an exclusive licence in respect of such a right, a just and reasonable amount of the payment is to be treated as relevant IP income of the company."

(4) In section 357BP (meaning of "new qualifying IP right") after subsection (12) insert—

"(13) This section has effect subject to section 357GCZA (qualifying IP right held by another party to a cost-sharing arrangement) and section 357GCZB (exclusive licence held by another party to a cost-sharing arrangement)."

(5) The amendments made by this section have effect in relation to accounting periods beginning on or after 1 April 2017.

24 Hybrid and other mismatches

(1) Part 6A of TIOPA 2010 (hybrid and other mismatches) is amended as follows.

(2) In section 259B(3) (local taxes), for "is not outside the scope of subsection (2) by reason only that" substitute "is outside the scope of subsection (2) if".

(3) In section 259CC(2) (hybrid and other mismatches from financial instruments: meaning of "permitted" taxable period of a payee), for paragraph (b) substitute—

"(b) the period begins at a later time and it is just and reasonable for the amount of ordinary income to arise for the period (rather than an earlier one)."

(4) In section 259DD(2) (hybrid transfer deduction/non-inclusion mismatches: meaning of "permitted" taxable period of a payee), for paragraph (b) substitute—

"(b) the period begins at a later time and it is just and reasonable for the amount of ordinary income to arise for the period (rather than an earlier one)."

(5) In section 259EB (hybrid payer deduction/non-inclusion mismatches and their extent), after subsection (1) insert—

"(1A) But there is no hybrid payer deduction/non-inclusion mismatch so far as the relevant deduction is—
  (a) a debit in respect of amortisation that is brought into account under section 729 or 731 of CTA 2009 (writing down the capitalised cost of an intangible fixed asset), or
  (b) an amount that is deductible in respect of amortisation under a provision of the law of a territory outside the United Kingdom that is equivalent to either of those sections."

(6) In section 259FA (deduction/non-inclusion mismatches relating to transfers by permanent establishments), after subsection (4) insert—

"(4A) For the purposes of this section "the PE deduction" does not include—
  (a) a debit in respect of amortisation that is brought into account under section 729 or 731 of CTA 2009 (writing down the capitalised cost of an intangible fixed asset), or
  (b) an amount that is deductible in respect of amortisation under a provision of the law of a territory outside the United Kingdom that is equivalent to either of those sections."

(7)   In section 259GB (hybrid payee deduction/non-inclusion mismatches and their extent), after subsection (1) insert—

   "(1A)   But there is no hybrid payee deduction/non-inclusion mismatch so far as the relevant deduction is—

   (a)   a debit in respect of amortisation that is brought into account under section 729 or 731 of CTA 2009 (writing down the capitalised cost of an intangible fixed asset), or

   (b)   an amount that is deductible in respect of amortisation under a provision of the law of a territory outside the United Kingdom that is equivalent to either of those sections."

(8)   In section 259HB (multinational payee deduction/non-inclusion mismatches and their extent), after subsection (1) insert—

   "(1A)   But there is no multinational payee deduction/non-inclusion mismatch so far as the relevant deduction is—

   (a)   a debit in respect of amortisation that is brought into account under section 729 or 731 of CTA 2009 (writing down the capitalised cost of an intangible fixed asset), or

   (b)   an amount that is deductible in respect of amortisation under a provision of the law of a territory outside the United Kingdom that is equivalent to either of those sections."

(9)   In section 259KB (imported mismatches: meaning of "excessive PE deduction" etc), after subsection (3) insert—

   "(3A)   For the purposes of this section a "PE deduction" does not include—

   (a)   a debit in respect of amortisation that is brought into account under section 729 or 731 of CTA 2009 (writing down the capitalised cost of an intangible fixed asset), or

   (b)   an amount that is deductible in respect of amortisation under a provision of the law of a territory outside the United Kingdom that is equivalent to either of those sections."

(10)   The amendment made by subsection (2)—

   (a)   has effect, in the case of its application to Chapter 6 of Part 6A of TIOPA 2010, in relation to excessive PE deductions in relation to which the relevant PE period begins on or after 13 July 2017,

   (b)   has effect, in the case of its application to Chapter 9 or 10 of that Part, in relation to accounting periods beginning on or after that date, and

   (c)   has effect, in the case of its application to any other Chapter of that Part, in relation to—

      (i)   payments made on or after date, or

      (ii)   quasi-payments in relation to which the payment period begins on or after that date.

(11)   For the purposes of subsection (10)(a), (b) and (c)(ii), where there is a straddling period—

   (a)   so much of the straddling period as falls before 13 July 2017, and so much of it as falls on or after that date, are to be treated as separate accounting periods or separate taxable periods (as the case may be), and

   (b)   if it is necessary to apportion an amount for the straddling period to the two separate periods, it is to be apportioned—

          (i)   on a time basis according to the respective length of the separate periods, or

          (ii)   if that would produce a result that is unjust or unreasonable, on a just and reasonable basis.

(12)   A "straddling period" means an accounting period or payment period (as the case may be) beginning before 13 July 2017 and ending on or after that date.

(13)   Part 6A of TIOPA 2010 has effect, and is to be deemed always to have had effect, with the amendments set out in subsections (3) to (9).

25   Trading profits taxable at the Northern Ireland rate

Schedule 7 contains —

     (a)   amendments of Part 8B of CTA 2010 (trading profits taxable at the Northern Ireland rate), and

     (b)   amendments consequential on or related to those amendments.

Chargeable gains

26   Elections in relation to assets appropriated to trading stock

(1)   Section 161 of TCGA 1992 (appropriations to and from trading stock) is amended as follows.

(2)   In subsection (3) —

     (a)   for "a person's appropriation of an asset for the purposes of a trade" substitute "a case where a chargeable gain would have accrued to a person on the appropriation of an asset for the purposes of a trade as mentioned in that subsection", and

     (b)   for "the chargeable gain or increased by the amount of the allowable loss referred to in subsection (1), and where that subsection" substitute "that chargeable gain, and where subsection (1)".

(3)   In subsection (3ZB) —

     (a)   in paragraph (a) —

         (i)   omit "or loss", and

         (ii)   omit "or an allowable loss",

     (b)   in paragraph (b) —

         (i)   omit ", or increased by the amount of any loss," and

         (ii)   omit "or allowable loss", and

     (c)   in paragraph (c), at the end insert "and a loss which accrues on that disposal which is not ATED-related is also unaffected by the election".

(4)   The amendments made by this section have effect in relation to appropriations of assets made on or after 8 March 2017.

27   Substantial shareholding exemption

(1)   Schedule 7AC to TCGA 1992 (exemptions for disposals by companies with substantial shareholding) is amended as follows.

(2)   Omit the following (which relate to requirements to be met by investing company) —

      (a)   in paragraph 1(2), "the investing company and";

      (b)   in paragraph 3—

          (i)   in sub-paragraph (2)(b), "(but see sub-paragraph (3) below)";

          (ii)   sub-paragraph (3);

          (iii)   in sub-paragraph (4), "of paragraph 18(1)(b) and";

      (c)   in the heading to Part 3, "investing company and";

      (d)   paragraph 18 and the preceding italic heading;

      (e)   in paragraph 23(3), "a member of a trading group or".

(3)   In paragraph 7 (substantial shareholding requirement), for "two" substitute "six".

(4)   In paragraph 10 (effect of earlier no-gain/no-loss transfer), in sub-paragraph (2)(b), after "but for" insert "subsection (1A) or".

(5)   In paragraph 19 (requirements relating to company invested in)—

      (a)   in sub-paragraph (1)(b), at the beginning insert "in a case where sub-paragraph 1A) applies,";

      (b)   after sub-paragraph (1) insert—

        "(1A) This sub-paragraph applies where—

          (a)   the disposal is a disposal to a person connected with the investing company, or

          (b)   the requirement in paragraph 7 is met by virtue of paragraph 15A.";

      (c)   at the end insert—

        "(4) Section 1122 of CTA 2010 (meaning of "connected" persons) applies for the purposes of sub-paragraph (1A)(a)."

(6)   The amendments made by this section have effect in relation to disposals made on or after 1 April 2017.

28   Substantial shareholding exemption: institutional investors

(1)   Schedule 7AC to TCGA 1992 (exemptions for disposals by companies with substantial shareholding) is amended as follows.

(2)   After paragraph 3 insert—

"Subsidiary exemption: qualifying institutional investors

  3A (1) This paragraph applies in relation to a gain or loss accruing to a company ("the investing company") on a disposal of shares or an interest in shares in another company ("the company invested in").

      (2) This paragraph applies if—

          (a)   the requirement in paragraph 7 is met (substantial shareholder requirement),

          (b)   the requirement in paragraph 19 is not met (requirement relating to company invested in), and

          (c)   the investing company is not a disqualified listed company.

      (3) If, immediately before the disposal, 80% or more of the ordinary share capital of the investing company is owned by qualifying

institutional investors, no chargeable gain or loss accrues on the disposal.

(4) If, immediately before the disposal, at least 25% but less than 80% of the ordinary share capital of the investing company is owned by qualifying institutional investors, the amount of the chargeable gain or loss accruing on the disposal is reduced by the percentage of the ordinary share capital of the investing company which is owned by the qualifying institutional investors.

(5) A company is a "disqualified listed company" for the purposes of this Part of this Schedule if—

  (a) any of the shares forming part of the ordinary share capital of the company are listed on a recognised stock exchange,

  (b) the company is not a qualifying institutional investor, and

  (c) the company is not a qualifying UK REIT

(6) In sub-paragraph (5)(c) "qualifying UK REIT" means a UK REIT within the meaning of Part 12 of CTA 2010 which—

  (a) meets the condition in section 528(4)(b) of that Act (company not a close company by virtue of having an institutional investor as a participant), or

  (b) by virtue of section 443 of that Act (companies controlled by or on behalf of Crown) is not treated as a close company.

3B (1) This paragraph applies for the purposes of paragraph 3A.

(2) A person "owns" ordinary share capital if the person owns it—

  (a) directly,

  (b) indirectly, or

  (c) partly directly and partly indirectly.

(3) Sections 1155 to 1157 of CTA 2010 (meaning of "indirect ownership" and calculation of amounts owned indirectly) apply for the purposes of sub-paragraph (2).

(4) For the purposes of sections 1155 to 1157 of CTA 2010 as applied by sub-paragraph (3)—

  (a) ordinary share capital may not be owned through a disqualified listed company;

  (b) treat references to a body corporate as including an exempt unauthorised unit trust (and references to ordinary share capital, in the case of such a trust, as references to units in the trust).

(5) A person is also to be regarded as owning ordinary share capital in a company in circumstances where a person would, under paragraphs 12 and 13 of this Schedule, be regarded as holding shares in a company.

(6) Where the assets of a partnership include ordinary share capital of a company, each partner is to be regarded as owning a proportion of that share capital equal to the partner's proportionate interest in that ordinary share capital.

      (7) In this Schedule "exempt unauthorised unit trust" has the same meaning as in the Unauthorised Unit Trusts (Tax) Regulations 2013 (SI 2013/2819)."

(3)   After paragraph 8 insert—

    "8A (1) This paragraph applies in a case where at least 25% of the ordinary share capital of the investing company is owned by qualifying institutional investors.

      (2) The investing company also holds a "substantial shareholding" in the company invested in for the purposes of this Schedule if—

          (a) the investing company holds ordinary shares, or interests in ordinary shares, in the company invested in the cost of which on acquisition was at least £20,000,000, and

          (b) by virtue of those shares or interests or any other shares or interests in shares in the company invested in, the investing company—

              (i) is beneficially entitled to not less than a proportionate percentage of the profits available for distribution to equity holders of the company invested in, and

              (ii) would be beneficially entitled on a winding up to not less than a proportionate percentage of the assets of the company invested in available for distribution to equity holders.

      (3) In sub-paragraph (2)—

         "cost" means the amount or value of the consideration, in money or money's worth, given by the investing company or on its behalf wholly and exclusively for the acquisition of the ordinary shares or interests in ordinary shares, together with the incidental costs to it of the acquisition;

         "proportionate percentage" means a percentage equal to the percentage of the ordinary share capital held by the investing company by virtue of the ordinary shares and interests in ordinary shares referred to in sub-paragraph (2)(a).

      (4) For the purposes of sub-paragraph (2)(a) it does not matter whether there was a single acquisition or a series of acquisitions.

      (5) If—

          (a) the percentage ("the actual percentage") of the profits or assets to which the investing company is, or would be, beneficially entitled as mentioned in sub-paragraph (2)(b)(i) or (ii) is less than the proportionate percentage, but

          (b) having regard to the proportion that the actual percentage bears to the proportionate percentage, the difference can reasonably be regarded as insignificant,

      the investing company is treated as meeting the condition in sub-paragraph (2)(b)(i) or (ii) (as the case may be).

      (6) Paragraph 3B (owning ordinary share capital) applies for the purposes of sub-paragraph (1).

      (7) Paragraph 8(2) applies for the purposes of sub-paragraph (2).

(8) In this paragraph "ordinary shares" means shares in the ordinary share capital of the company invested in."

(4) In paragraph 9 (aggregation), in sub-paragraph (1), for "paragraph 7" substitute "paragraphs 7 and 8A(2)".

(5) After paragraph 30 insert—

"Meaning of "qualifying institutional investor"

30A (1) In this Schedule "qualifying institutional investor" means a person falling within any of A to G below.

Pension schemes

A   The trustee or manager of—

    (a) a registered pension scheme, other than an investment-regulated pension scheme, or

    (b) an overseas pension scheme, other than one which would be an investment-regulated pension scheme if it were a registered pension scheme.

"Investment-regulated pension scheme" has the same meaning as in Part 1 of Schedule 29A to the Finance Act 2004.

"Overseas pension scheme" has the same meaning as in Part 4 of that Act.

Life assurance businesses

B   A company carrying on life assurance business, if immediately before the disposal its interest in the investing company is held as part of its long-term business fixed capital.

"Life assurance business" has the meaning given in section 56 of the Finance Act 2012.

Section 137 of that Act applies for the purposes of determining whether an interest forms part of the long-term business fixed capital of a company.

Sovereign wealth funds etc

C   A person who cannot be liable for corporation tax or income tax (as relevant) on the ground of sovereign immunity.

Charities

D   A charity.

Investment trusts

E   An investment trust.

Authorised investment funds

F   An authorised investment fund which meets the genuine diversity of ownership condition throughout the accounting period of the fund in which the disposal is made.

"Authorised investment fund" has the same meaning as in the Authorised Investment Funds (Tax) Regulations 2006 (SI 2006/964).

Regulation 9A of the Authorised Investment Funds (Tax) Regulations 2006 (genuine diversity of ownership) applies for this purpose.

Exempt unauthorised unit trusts

G   The trustees of an exempt unauthorised unit trust, where the trust meets the genuine diversity of ownership condition throughout the accounting period of the trust in which the disposal is made.

Regulation 9A of the Authorised Investment Funds (Tax) Regulations 2006 (genuine diversity of ownership) applies for this purpose (treating references to an authorised investment fund as including an exempt unauthorised unit trust).

(2)   The Treasury may by regulations amend this Schedule so as to add or remove a person as a "qualifying institutional investor" (and may in particular do so by changing the conditions subject to which a person is a qualifying institutional investor)."

(6)   In paragraph 31 (index), at the appropriate places insert—

"Exempt unauthorised unit trust	paragraph 3B(7)"
"Qualifying institutional investor	paragraph 30A".

(7)   The amendments made by this section have effect in relation to disposals made on or after 1 April 2017.

Domicile, overseas property etc

29   Deemed domicile: income tax and capital gains tax

(1)   In Chapter 2A of Part 14 of ITA 2007 (income tax liability: domicile), after section 835B insert—

"835BA Deemed domicile

(1)   This section has effect for the purposes of the provisions of the Income Tax Acts or TCGA 1992 which apply this section.

(2)   An individual not domiciled in the United Kingdom at a time in a tax year ("the relevant tax year") is to be regarded as domiciled in the United Kingdom at that time if—

(a)   condition A is met, or

(b)   condition B is met.

(3)   Condition A is that—

(a)   the individual was born in the United Kingdom,

(b)   the individual's domicile of origin was in the United Kingdom, and

(c)   the individual is UK resident for the relevant tax year.

(4) Condition B is that the individual has been UK resident for at least 15 of the 20 tax years immediately preceding the relevant tax year.

(5) But Condition B is not met if —
   (a) the individual is not UK resident for the relevant tax year, and
   (b) there is no tax year beginning after 5 April 2017 and preceding the relevant tax year in which the individual was UK resident."

(2) Schedule 8 contains —
   (a) provision applying section 835BA of ITA 2007, and
   (b) further provision relating to this section.

30 Deemed domicile: inheritance tax

(1) In section 267 of IHTA 1984 (persons treated as domiciled in the United Kingdom), in subsection (1) —
   (a) in paragraph (a), omit the final "or";
   (b) after that paragraph insert —
      "(aa) he is a formerly domiciled resident for the tax year in which the relevant time falls ("the relevant tax year"), or";
   (c) for paragraph (b) substitute —
      "(b) he was resident in the United Kingdom —
         (i) for at least fifteen of the twenty tax years immediately preceding the relevant tax year, and
         (ii) for at least one of the four tax years ending with the relevant tax year."

(2) In that section, omit subsection (3).

(3) In that section, in subsection (4), for "in any year of assessment" substitute "for any tax year".

(4) In section 48 of that Act (settlements: excluded property) —
   (a) in subsection (3)(b), for "and (3D)" substitute "to (3E)";
   (b) in subsection (3A)(b), for "subsection (3B)" substitute "subsections (3B) and (3E)";
   (c) after subsection (3D) insert —

      "(3E) In a case where the settlor of property comprised in a settlement is not domiciled in the United Kingdom at the time the settlement is made, the property is not excluded property by virtue of subsection (3) or (3A) above at any time in a tax year if the settlor was a formerly domiciled resident for that tax year."

(5) In section 64 of that Act (charge at ten-year anniversary), in subsection (1B), after "was made" insert "and is not a formerly domiciled resident for the tax year in which the ten-year anniversary falls".

(6) In section 65 of that Act (charge at other times), after subsection (7A) insert —

      "(7B) Tax shall not be charged under this section by reason only that property comprised in a settlement becomes excluded property by virtue of section 48(3E) ceasing to apply in relation to it."

(7) In section 82 of that Act (excluded property) —

    (a) for subsection (1) substitute —

        "(1) In a case where, apart from this section, property to which section 80 or 81 applies would be excluded property by virtue of section 48(3)(a) above, that property shall not be taken to be excluded property at any time ("the relevant time") for the purposes of this Chapter (except sections 78 and 79) unless Conditions A and B are satisfied.";

    (b) in subsection (2), for "the condition in subsection (3) below" substitute "Condition A";

    (c) in subsection (3), for "The condition" substitute "Condition A";

    (d) after subsection (3) insert —

        "(4) Condition B referred to in subsection (1) above is —

            (a) in the case of property to which section 80 above applies, that the person who is the settlor in relation to the settlement first mentioned in that section, and

            (b) in the case of property to which subsection (1) or (2) of section 81 above applies, that the person who is the settlor in relation to the first or second of the settlements mentioned in that subsection,

        was not a formerly domiciled resident for the tax year in which the relevant time falls."

(8) In section 272 of that Act (interpretation) —

    (a) for the definition of "foreign-owned" substitute —

        ""foreign-owned", in relation to property at any time, means property —

            (a) in the case of which the person beneficially entitled to it is at that time domiciled outside the United Kingdom, or

            (b) if the property is comprised in a settlement, in the case of which the settlor —

                (i) is not a formerly domiciled resident for the tax year in which that time falls, and

                (ii) was domiciled outside the United Kingdom when the property became comprised in the settlement;";

    (b) at the appropriate place insert —

        ""formerly domiciled resident", in relation to a tax year, means a person —

            (a) who was born in the United Kingdom,

            (b) whose domicile of origin was in the United Kingdom,

            (c) who was resident in the United Kingdom for that tax year, and

            (d) who was resident in the United Kingdom for at least one of the two tax years immediately preceding that tax year;".

(9) The amendments made by this section have effect in relation to times after 5 April 2017, subject to subsections (10) to (12).

(10) The amendment to section 267(1) of IHTA 1984 made by subsection (1)(c) does not have effect in relation to a person if—

    (a) the person is not resident in the United Kingdom for the relevant tax year, and

    (b) there is no tax year beginning after 5 April 2017 and preceding the relevant tax year in which the person was resident in the United Kingdom.

In this subsection "relevant tax year" is to be construed in accordance with section 267(1) of IHTA 1984 as amended by subsection (1).

(11) The amendment to section 267(1) of IHTA 1984 made by subsection (1)(c) also does not have effect in determining—

    (a) whether settled property which became comprised in the settlement on or before that date is excluded property for the purposes of IHTA 1984;

    (b) the settlor's domicile for the purposes of section 65(8) of that Act in relation to settled property which became comprised in the settlement on or before that date;

    (c) whether, for the purpose of section 65(8) of that Act, the condition in section 82(3) of that Act is satisfied in relation to such settled property.

(12) Despite subsection (2), section 267(1) of IHTA 1984, as originally enacted, shall continue to be disregarded in determining—

    (a) whether settled property which became comprised in the settlement on or before 9 December 1974 is excluded property for the purposes of IHTA 1984;

    (b) the settlor's domicile for the purposes of section 65(8) of that Act in relation to settled property which became comprised in the settlement on or before that date;

    (c) whether, for the purpose of section 65(8) of that Act, the condition in section 82(3) of that Act is satisfied in relation to such settled property.

(13) Subsections (14) and (15) apply if an amount of inheritance tax—

    (a) would not be charged but for the amendments made by this section, or

    (b) is, because of those amendments, greater than it would otherwise have been.

(14) Section 233 of IHTA 1984 (interest on unpaid inheritance tax) applies in relation to the amount of inheritance tax as if the reference, in the closing words of subsection (1) of that section, to the end of the period mentioned in paragraph (a), (aa), (b) or (c) of that subsection were a reference to—

    (a) the end of that period, or

    (b) if later, the end of the month immediately following the month in which this Act is passed.

(15) Subsection (1) of section 234 of IHTA 1984 (cases where inheritance tax payable by instalments carries interest only from instalment dates) applies in relation to the amount of inheritance tax as if the reference, in the closing words of that subsection, to the date at which an instalment is payable were a reference to—

    (a) the date at which the instalment is payable, or

    (b) if later, the end of the month immediately following the month in which this Act is passed.

(16) Subsection (17) applies if—

    (a)   a person is liable as mentioned in section 216(1)(c) of IHTA 1984 (trustee liable on 10-year anniversary, and other trust cases) for an amount of inheritance tax charged on an occasion, and

    (b)   but for the amendments made by this section—

        (i)   no inheritance tax would be charged on that occasion, or

       (ii)   a lesser amount of inheritance tax would be charged on that occasion.

(17)   Section 216(6)(ad) of IHTA 1984 (delivery date for accounts required by section 216(1)(c)) applies in relation to the account to be delivered in connection with the occasion as if the reference to the expiration of the period of 6 months from the end of the month in which the occasion occurs were a reference to—

    (a)   the expiration of that period, or

    (b)   if later, the end of the month immediately following the month in which this Act is passed.

31   Settlements and transfer of assets abroad: value of benefits

Schedule 9 makes provision about the value of benefits received in relation to settlements and the transfer of assets abroad.

32   Exemption from attribution of carried interest gains

(1)   TCGA 1992 is amended as follows.

(2)   In section 13(1A) (attribution of gains to members of non-resident companies)—

    (a)   omit the "or" at the end of paragraph (a), and

    (b)   at the end of paragraph (b), insert ", or

        (c)   a chargeable gain treated as accruing under section 103KA(2) or (3) (carried interest gains)."

(3)   In section 86 (attribution of gains to settlors with interest in non-resident or dual resident settlements), after subsection (4ZA) insert—

   "(4ZB)   Where (apart from this subsection) the amount mentioned in subsection (1)(e) would include an amount of chargeable gains treated as accruing under section 103KA(2) or (3) (carried interest gains), the amount of the gains is to be disregarded for the purposes of subsection (1)(e)."

(4)   In section 87 (non-UK resident settlements: attribution of gains to beneficiaries), after subsection (5A) insert—

   "(5B)   Where (apart from this subsection) the amount mentioned in subsection (4)(a) would include an amount of chargeable gains treated as accruing under section 103KA(2) or (3) (carried interest gains), the amount of the gains is to be disregarded for the purposes of determining the section 2(2) amount."

(5)   The amendments made by this section have effect in relation to chargeable gains treated as accruing under section 103KA(2) or (3) of TCGA 1992 at any time before, as well as after, the passing of this Act.

33 Inheritance tax on overseas property representing UK residential property

Schedule 10 makes provision about the extent to which overseas property is excluded property for the purposes of inheritance tax, in cases where the value of the overseas property is attributable to residential property in the United Kingdom.

Disguised remuneration

34 Employment income provided through third parties

(1) In section 554XA of ITEPA 2003 (employment income provided through third parties: exclusion for payments in respect of a tax liability), in subsection (2), omit paragraphs (a) and (b).

(2) The amendment made by subsection (1) has effect in relation to relevant steps taken on or after 21 July 2017.

(3) Schedule 11 makes provision about the application of Part 7A of ITEPA 2003 in relation to loans and quasi-loans that are outstanding on 5 April 2019.

35 Trading income provided through third parties

(1) ITTOIA 2005 is amended as follows.

(2) After section 23 insert—

"Trading income provided through third parties

23A Application of section 23E: conditions

(1) Section 23E (tax treatment of relevant benefits) applies if Conditions A to E are met.

(2) Condition A is that a person ("T") is or has been carrying on a trade (the "relevant trade") alone or in partnership.

(3) Condition B is that—

    (a) there is an arrangement ("the arrangement") in connection with the relevant trade to which T is a party or which otherwise (wholly or partly) covers or relates to T, and

    (b) it is reasonable to suppose that, in essence—

        (i) the arrangement, or

        (ii) the arrangement so far as it covers or relates to T,

    is (wholly or partly) a means of providing, or is otherwise concerned with the provision of, relevant benefits.

(4) Condition C is that—

    (a) a relevant benefit arises to T, or a person who is or has been connected with T, in pursuance of the arrangement, or

    (b) a relevant benefit arises to any other person in pursuance of the arrangement and any of the enjoyment conditions (see section 23F) is met in relation to the relevant benefit.

(5) Condition D is that it is reasonable to suppose that the relevant benefit (directly or indirectly) represents, or has arisen or derives from, or is

otherwise connected with, the whole or part of a qualifying third party payment.

(6) Condition E is that it is reasonable to suppose that a tax advantage would be obtained by T, or a person who is or has been connected with T, as a result of the arrangement.

(7) For the purposes of subsection (3) in particular, all relevant circumstances are to be taken into account in order to get to the essence of the matter.

(8) In this section and sections 23B to 23H, "this group of sections" means this section and those sections.

(9) The provisions of this group of sections apply to professions and vocations as they apply to trades.

(10) See Schedule 12 to F(No.2)A 2017 for provision about the application of this group of sections in relation to loans and quasi-loans that are outstanding on 5 April 2019.

23B Meaning of "relevant benefit"

(1) The following provisions apply for the purposes of this group of sections.

(2) "Relevant benefit" means any payment (including a payment by way of a loan), a transfer of money's worth, or any other benefit.

(3) The assumption of a liability of T by another person is to be treated as the provision of a relevant benefit to T.

(4) The assumption, by a person other than T, of a liability of a person ("C") who is or has been connected with T, is to be treated as the provision of a relevant benefit to C.

(5) "Loan" includes —
   (a) any form of credit;
   (b) a payment that is purported to be made by way of a loan.

23C Meaning of "qualifying third party payment"

(1) The following provisions apply for the purposes of this group of sections.

(2) A payment is a "third party payment" if it is made (by T or another person) to —
   (a) T acting as trustee, or
   (b) any person other than T.

(3) A third party payment is a "qualifying third party payment" if the deduction condition or the trade connection condition is met in relation to the payment.

(4) The "deduction condition" is met in relation to a payment if —
   (a) a deduction for the payment is made in calculating the profits of the relevant trade, or
   (b) where the relevant trade is or has been carried on in partnership, a deduction for the payment is made in calculating

the amount on which T is liable to income tax in respect of the profits of the trade.

(5) The "trade connection condition" is met in relation to a payment if it is reasonable to suppose that in essence –

    (a) the payment is by way of consideration for goods or services provided in the course of the relevant trade, or

    (b) there is some other connection (direct or indirect) between the payment and the provision of goods or services in the course of the relevant trade.

(6) For the purposes of subsection (5) in particular, all relevant circumstances are to be taken into account in order to get to the essence of the matter.

23D   Other definitions

(1) The following provisions apply for the purposes of this group of sections.

(2) "Arrangement" includes any agreement, understanding, scheme, settlement, trust, transaction or series of transactions (whether or not legally enforceable).

(3) A "tax advantage" includes –

    (a) relief or increased relief from tax,

    (b) repayment or increased repayment of tax,

    (c) avoidance or reduction of a charge to tax or an assessment to tax,

    (d) avoidance of a possible assessment to tax,

    (e) deferral of a payment of tax or advancement of a repayment of tax, and

    (f) avoidance of an obligation to deduct or account for tax.

(4) Section 993 of ITA 2007 (meaning of "connected" persons) applies for the purposes of this group of sections as if subsection (4) of that section 993 were omitted.

23E   Tax treatment of relevant benefits

(1) Where this section applies (see section 23A), the relevant benefit amount is to be treated for income tax purposes as profits of the relevant trade for –

    (a) the tax year in which the relevant benefit arises, or

    (b) if T has ceased to carry on the relevant trade in a tax year (the "earlier tax year") before the tax year referred to in paragraph (a), the earlier tax year.

(2) For the purposes of this section, "the relevant benefit amount" means –

    (a) if the relevant benefit is a payment otherwise than by way of a loan, an amount equal to the amount of the payment,

    (b) if the relevant benefit is a payment by way of loan, an amount equal to the principal amount lent, or

    (c) in any other case, an amount equal to the value of the relevant benefit.

(3) For the purposes of subsection (2)(c), the value of a relevant benefit is –

      (a)   its market value at the time it arises, or

      (b)   if higher, the cost of providing it.

  (4)   In subsection (3) "market value" has the same meaning as it has for the purposes of TCGA 1992 by virtue of Part 8 of that Act.

23F   Relevant benefits: persons other than T

  (1)   For the purposes of section 23A(4), the enjoyment conditions are—

      (a)   that the relevant benefit, or part of it, is in fact so dealt with by any person as to be calculated at some time to enure for the benefit of T;

      (b)   that the arising of the relevant benefit operates to increase the value to T of any assets—

          (i)   which T holds, or

          (ii)   which are held for the benefit of T;

      (c)   that T receives, or is entitled to receive, at any time any benefit provided or to be provided out of, or deriving or to be derived from, the relevant benefit (or part of it);

      (d)   where the relevant benefit is the payment of a sum of money (including a payment by way of loan), that T may become entitled to the beneficial enjoyment of the sum or part of the sum if one or more powers are exercised or successively exercised (and for these purposes it does not matter who may exercise the powers or whether they are exercisable with or without the consent of another person);

      (e)   where the relevant benefit is the payment of a sum of money (including a payment by way of loan), that T is able in any manner to control directly or indirectly the application of the sum or part of the sum.

  (2)   Where an enjoyment condition is met in relation to part only of a relevant benefit, that part is to be treated as a separate benefit for the purposes of section 23A(4).

  (3)   In subsection (1) references to T include references to a person who is or has been connected with T.

  (4)   In determining whether any of the enjoyment conditions is met in relation to a relevant benefit, regard must be had to the substantial result and effect of all the relevant circumstances.

23G   Anti-avoidance

  (1)   In determining whether section 23E applies in relation to a relevant benefit, no regard is to be had to any arrangements the main purpose, or one of the main purposes, of which is to secure that section 23E does not apply in relation to the whole, or any part, of—

      (a)   the relevant benefit, or

      (b)   the relevant benefit and one or more other relevant benefits (whether or not all arising to the same person).

  (2)   Where arrangements are disregarded under subsection (1), and a relevant benefit (or part of it)—

      (a)   would, if the arrangements were not disregarded, arise before 6 April 2017, but

     (b)   would, when the arrangements are disregarded, arise on or after that date,

the relevant benefit (or part) is to be regarded for the purposes of this group of sections as arising on the date on which it would arise apart from the arrangements.

23H   Double taxation

(1) This section applies where—

    (a)   income tax is charged on an individual by virtue of the application of section 23E in relation to a relevant benefit amount, and

    (b)   at any time, a tax (whether income tax or another tax) is charged on the individual or another person otherwise than by virtue of the application of section 23E in relation to the relevant benefit concerned.

(2) In order to avoid a double charge to tax, the individual may make a claim for one or more consequential adjustments to be made in respect of the tax charged as mentioned in subsection (1)(b).

(3) On a claim under this section an officer of Revenue and Customs must make such of the consequential adjustments claimed (if any) as are just and reasonable.

(4) The value of any consequential adjustments must not exceed the lesser of—

    (a)   the income tax charged on the individual as mentioned in subsection (1)(a), and

    (b)   the tax charged as mentioned in subsection (1)(b).

(5) Consequential adjustments may be made—

    (a)   in respect of any period,

    (b)   by way of an assessment, the modification of an assessment, the amendment of a claim, or otherwise, and

    (c)   despite any time limit imposed by or under any enactment."

(3) In section 7(2) (income charged: profits of a tax year) at the end insert "(including amounts treated as profits of the tax year under section 23E(1))."

(4) The amendments made by this section have effect in relation to relevant benefits arising on or after 6 April 2017.

(5) Schedule 12 contains provision about the application of new sections 23A to 23H of ITTOIA 2005 in relation to loans and quasi-loans that are outstanding on 5 April 2019.

36   Disguised remuneration schemes: restriction of income tax relief

(1) Section 38 of ITTOIA 2005 (restriction of deductions: employee benefit contributions) is amended in accordance with subsections (2) to (5).

(2) After subsection (1) insert—

"(1A)   No deduction is allowed under this section in respect of employee benefit contributions for a period of account which starts more than 5 years after the end of the period of account in which the contributions are made."

(3)   After subsection (2) insert—

"(2AA)   Subsection (2) is subject to subsections (1A) and (2AB).

(2AB)   Where subsection (3C) applies, no deduction is allowed for an amount in respect of the contributions for the period except so far as the amount is a qualifying amount (see subsection (3D))."

(4)   After subsection (3) insert—

"(3A)   Subsection (3) is subject to subsections (1A) and (3B).

(3B)   Where subsection (3C) applies, an amount disallowed under subsection (2) is allowed as a deduction for a subsequent period only so far as it is a qualifying amount.

(3C)   This subsection applies where the provision of qualifying benefits out of, or by way of, the contributions gives rise both to an employment income tax charge and to an NIC charge.

(3D)   An amount in respect of employee benefit contributions is a "qualifying amount" if the relevant tax charges are paid before the end of the relevant period (and are not repaid).

(3E)   For the purposes of subsection (3D)—
       (a)   the "relevant tax charges", in relation to an amount, are the employment income tax charge and the NIC charge arising in respect of benefits which are provided out of, or by way of, that amount, and
       (b)   the "relevant period" is the period of 12 months immediately following the end of the period of account for which the deduction for the employee benefit contributions would (apart from this section) be allowable.

(3F)   For the purposes of subsections (3C) and (3E),"employment income tax charge" and "NIC charge" have the meaning given by section 40(7)."

(5)   After subsection (3F) (inserted by subsection (4)) insert—

"(3G)   Subsection (3H) applies where—
       (a)   a deduction would, apart from this section, be allowable for an amount (the "remuneration amount") in respect of employees' remuneration, and
       (b)   in consequence of the payment of the employees' remuneration, employee benefit contributions are made, or are to be made, in respect of the remuneration amount.

(3H)   In calculating for income tax purposes the profits of a trade, the deduction referred to in subsection (3G)(a) is to be treated as a deduction in respect of employee benefit contributions made or to be made (and is to be treated as not being a deduction in respect of employees' remuneration)."

(6)   Section 866 of ITTOIA 2005 (employee benefit contributions: non-trades and non-property businesses) is amended in accordance with subsections (7) to (10).

(7) After subsection (2) insert—

"(2A) No deduction is allowed under this section in respect of employee benefit contributions for a period of account which starts more than 5 years after the end of the period of account in which the contributions are made."

(8) After subsection (3) insert—

"(3A) Subsection (3) is subject to subsections (2A) and (3B).

(3B) Where subsection (4C) applies, no deduction is allowed for an amount in respect of the contributions for the period except so far as the amount is a qualifying amount (see subsection (4D))."

(9) After subsection (4) insert—

"(4A) Subsection (4) is subject to subsections (2A) and (4B).

(4B) Where subsection (4C) applies, an amount disallowed under subsection (3) is allowed as a deduction for a subsequent period only so far as it is a qualifying amount.

(4C) This subsection applies where the provision of qualifying benefits out of, or by way of, the contributions gives rise both to an employment income tax charge and to an NIC charge.

(4D) An amount in respect of employee benefit contributions is a "qualifying amount" if the relevant tax charges are paid before the end of the relevant period (and are not repaid).

(4E) For the purposes of subsection (4D)—

   (a) the "relevant tax charges", in relation to an amount, are the employment income tax charge and the NIC charge arising in respect of benefits which are provided out of, or by way of, that amount, and

   (b) the "relevant period" is the period of 12 months immediately following the end of the period of account for which the deduction for the employee benefit contributions would (apart from this section) be allowable.

(4F) For the purposes of subsections (4C) and (4E), "employment income tax charge" and "NIC charge" have the meaning given by section 40(7)."

(10) After subsection (4F) (inserted by subsection (9)) insert—

"(4G) Subsection (4H) applies where—

   (a) a deduction would, apart from this section, be allowable for an amount (the "remuneration amount") in respect of employees' remuneration, and

   (b) in consequence of the payment of the employees' remuneration, employee benefit contributions are made, or are to be made, in respect of the remuneration amount.

(4H) In calculating for income tax purposes a person's profits or other income, the deduction referred to in subsection (4G)(a) is to be treated as a deduction in respect of employee benefit contributions made or to be made (and is to be treated as not being a deduction in respect of employees' remuneration)."

(11) The amendments made by subsections (2) to (4) and (7) to (9) have effect in relation to employee benefit contributions made, or to be made, on or after 6 April 2017.

(12) The amendments made by subsections (5) and (10) have effect in relation to remuneration paid on or after 6 April 2017.

37   Disguised remuneration schemes: restriction of corporation tax relief

(1) Section 1290 of CTA 2009 (restriction of deductions: employee benefit contributions) is amended in accordance with subsections (2) to (5).

(2) After subsection (1) insert—

"(1A)   No deduction is allowed under this section in respect of employee benefit contributions for a period of account which starts more than 5 years after the end of the period of account in which the contributions are made."

(3) After subsection (2) insert—

"(2A)   Subsection (2) is subject to subsections (1A) and (2B).

(2B)   Where subsection (3C) applies, no deduction is allowed for an amount in respect of the contributions for the period except so far as the amount is a qualifying amount (see subsection (3D))."

(4) After subsection (3) insert—

"(3A)   Subsection (3) is subject to subsections (1A) and (3B).

(3B)   Where subsection (3C) applies, an amount disallowed under subsection (2) is allowed as a deduction for a subsequent period only so far as it is a qualifying amount.

(3C)   This subsection applies where the provision of qualifying benefits out of, or by way of, the contributions gives rise both to an employment income tax charge and to an NIC charge.

(3D)   An amount in respect of employee benefit contributions is a "qualifying amount" if the relevant tax charges are paid before the end of the relevant period (and are not repaid).

(3E)   For the purposes of subsection (3D)—
   (a)   the "relevant tax charges", in relation to an amount, are the employment income tax charge and the NIC charge arising in respect of benefits which are provided out of, or by way of, that amount, and
   (b)   the "relevant period" is the period of 12 months immediately following the end of the period of account for which the deduction for the employee benefit contributions would (apart from this section) be allowable.

(3F)   For the purposes of subsections (3C) and (3E), "employment income tax charge" and "NIC charge" have the meaning given by section 1292(7)."

(5) After subsection (3F) (inserted by subsection (4)) insert—

"(3G)   Subsection (3H) applies where—

>   (a) a deduction would, apart from this section, be allowable for an amount (the "remuneration amount") in respect of employees' remuneration, and
>   (b) in consequence of the payment of the employees' remuneration, employee benefit contributions are made, or are to be made, in respect of the remuneration amount.
>
> (3H) In calculating for corporation tax purposes the profits of a company, the deduction referred to in subsection (3G)(a) is to be treated as a deduction in respect of employee benefit contributions made or to be made (and is to be treated as not being a deduction in respect of employees' remuneration)."

(6) The amendments made by subsections (2) to (4) have effect in relation to employee benefit contributions made, or to be made, on or after 1 April 2017.

(7) The amendment made by subsection (5) has effect in relation to remuneration paid on or after 1 April 2017.

Capital allowances

38 First-year allowance for expenditure on electric vehicle charging points

(1) CAA 2001 is amended as follows.

(2) In section 39 (first-year qualifying expenditure) after the entry for section 45E insert—

> "section 45EA   expenditure on plant or machinery for electric vehicle charging point".

(3) After section 45E insert—

"45EA Expenditure on plant or machinery for electric vehicle charging point

> (1) Expenditure is first-year qualifying expenditure if—
>   (a) it is incurred in the relevant period,
>   (b) it is expenditure on plant or machinery for an electric vehicle charging point where the plant or machinery is unused and not second-hand, and
>   (c) it is not excluded by section 46 (general exclusions).
>
> (2) For the purposes of this section expenditure on plant or machinery for an electric vehicle charging point is expenditure on plant or machinery installed solely for the purpose of charging electric vehicles.
>
> (3) The "relevant period" is the period beginning with 23 November 2016 and ending with—
>   (a) in the case of expenditure incurred by a person within the charge to corporation tax, 31 March 2019, and
>   (b) in the case of expenditure incurred by a person within the charge to income tax, 5 April 2019.
>
> (4) The Treasury may by regulations amend subsection (3) so as to extend the relevant period.

    (5) In this section—

        "electric vehicle" means a road vehicle that can be propelled by electrical power (whether or not it can also be propelled by another kind of power);

        "electric vehicle charging point" means a facility for charging an electric vehicle."

    (4) In section 46 (general exclusions), in subsection (1) after the entry for section 45E insert—

        "section 45EA (expenditure on plant or machinery for electric vehicle charging point)".

    (5) In section 52 (amount of first-year allowances)—

      (a) in the table in subsection (3), after the entry for expenditure qualifying under section 45E insert—

"Expenditure qualifying under section 45EA (expenditure on plant or machinery for electric vehicle charging point)	100%"

      (b) after subsection (3) insert—

      "(3A) Subsection (3B) applies where the Treasury make regulations under section 45EA(4) (power to extend relevant period).

        (3B) The regulations may amend the amount specified in column 2 of the Table in subsection (3) for expenditure qualifying under section 45EA, but only in relation to expenditure incurred after the date on which the relevant period would have ended but for the regulations."

Transactions in UK land

39   Disposals concerned with land in United Kingdom

    (1) The FA 2016 amendments have effect (so far as they would not otherwise have effect) in relation to—

      (a) amounts that are recognised in GAAP accounts drawn up for any period of account beginning on or after 8 March 2017, or

      (b) in the case of a straddling period, amounts that would be recognised in GAAP accounts drawn up for a period of account beginning on 8 March 2017 and ending when the straddling period ends.

    (2) In subsection (1)—

        "the FA 2016 amendments" means—

      (a) the amendments made by sections 76, 77 and 80 of FA 2016 (corporation tax treatment of certain profits and gains realised from disposals concerned with land in the United Kingdom), or

      (b) the amendments made by sections 78 and 79 of that Act (corresponding rules for income tax purposes),

        "GAAP accounts" means accounts drawn up in accordance with generally accepted accounting practice,

        "recognised" means recognised as an item of profit or loss, and "straddling period" means a period of account beginning before 8 March 2017 and ending on or after that date.

(3) In section 161 of TCGA 1992 (appropriations to and from stock), in subsection (5)(a), for "CTA 2010" substitute "ITA 2007".

(4) Section 79(10) of FA 2016 (which substitutes paragraph (a) of section 161(5) of TCGA 1992) is to be regarded as always having had effect with the amendment made by subsection (3).

Co-ownership authorised contractual schemes

40 Co-ownership authorised contractual schemes: capital allowances

In Part 2 of CAA 2001 (plant and machinery), in Chapter 20 (supplementary provisions), after the Chapter heading insert—

"Co-ownership authorised contractual schemes

262AA Co-ownership schemes: carrying on qualifying activity

(1) This section applies where the participants in a co-ownership authorised contractual scheme together carry on a qualifying activity.

(2) Each participant in the scheme is for the purposes of this Part to be regarded as carrying on the qualifying activity.

(3) Subsection (2) applies in relation to a participant only to the extent that the profits or gains arising to the participant from the qualifying activity are, or (if there were any) would be, chargeable to tax.

(4) But in determining for the purposes of subsection (1) whether or to what extent the participants in a co-ownership authorised contractual scheme together carry on a qualifying activity, assume that profits or gains arising to all participants from the qualifying activity are, or (if there were any) would be, chargeable to tax.

262AB Co-ownership schemes: election

(1) The operator of a co-ownership authorised contractual scheme may make an election under this section.

(2) The election must specify an accounting period of the scheme as the first accounting period in relation to which the election has effect.

(3) That first accounting period must not—
    (a) be longer than 12 months, or
    (b) begin before 1 April 2017.

(4) The election has effect for that first accounting period and all subsequent accounting periods of the scheme.

(5) The election is irrevocable.

(6) The election is made by notice to an officer of Revenue and Customs.

262AC Co-ownership schemes: calculation of allowance after election

(1) This section applies where an election under section 262AB has effect for an accounting period of a co-ownership authorised contractual scheme ("the relevant period").

(2) The operator of the scheme is to calculate the allowances that would be available to the scheme under this Part in relation to the relevant period on the basis of the assumptions in subsection (3).

(3) The assumptions are—
   (a) the scheme is a person;
   (b) the relevant period is a chargeable period for the purposes of this Act;
   (c) any qualifying activity carried on by the participants in the scheme together is carried on by the scheme;
   (d) property which was subject to the scheme at the beginning of the first accounting period for which the election has effect—
      (i) ceased to be owned by the participants at that time, and
      (ii) was acquired by the scheme at that time;
   (e) the disposal value to be brought into account in relation to the cessation of ownership and the acquisition referred to in paragraph (d) is the tax written-down value;
   (f) any property which became subject to the scheme at a time during an accounting period for which the election has effect was acquired by the scheme at that time;
   (g) property which ceased to be subject to the scheme at any such time ceased to be owned by the scheme at that time;
   (h) the disposal value to be brought into account in relation to the cessation of ownership referred to in paragraph (g) is the tax written-down value;
   (i) the scheme is not entitled to a first-year allowance or an annual investment allowance in respect of any expenditure.

(4) The operator of the co-ownership authorised contractual scheme must allocate to each participant in the scheme a proportion (which may be zero) of the allowances calculated under this section.

(5) The allocation is to be on the basis of what is just and reasonable.

(6) In determining what is just and reasonable—
   (a) regard is to be had in particular to the relative size of each participant's holding of units in the scheme;
   (b) no regard is to be had to—
      (i) whether or to what extent a participant is liable to income tax or corporation tax, or
      (ii) any other circumstances relating to a participant's liability to tax.

(7) If the participants in the scheme together carry on more than one qualifying activity, the calculation and allocation under this section are to be made separately for each activity.

(8) The proportion of an allowance allocated by the operator to a participant under this section for a qualifying activity is the total

amount of the allowance available to the participant under this Part in relation to the relevant period by virtue of carrying on that activity as a participant in the scheme.

(9) In this section "tax written-down value", in relation to any cessation of ownership or acquisition, means such amount as would give rise to neither a balancing allowance nor a balancing charge.

(10) For the purposes of subsection (9) assume that expenditure to which the disposal value relates is in its own pool.

(11) For the purposes of subsections (3)(c) and (9), assume that profits or gains arising to all participants from the qualifying activity are, or (if there were any) would be, chargeable to tax.

262AD Co-ownership schemes: effect of election for participants

(1) This section has effect where an election under section 262AB is made by the operator of a co-ownership authorised contractual scheme.

(2) For the purposes of sections 61(1) and 196(1) (disposal events and values)—
   (a) a participant in the scheme is to be regarded as ceasing to own the participant's interest in the property subject to the scheme at the beginning of the first accounting period of the scheme for which the election has effect, and
   (b) the disposal value to be brought into account in relation to that cessation of ownership is the tax written-down value.

(3) In subsection (2)(b) "tax written-down value" means such amount as would give rise to neither a balancing allowance nor a balancing charge.

(4) For the purposes of subsection (3) assume that—
   (a) expenditure to which the disposal value relates is in its own pool;
   (b) profits or gains arising to all participants from the qualifying activity are, or (if there were any) would be, chargeable to tax.

262AE Co-ownership schemes: effect of election for purchasers

(1) This section has effect where—
   (a) an election under section 262AB is made by the operator of a co-ownership authorised contractual scheme,
   (b) property consisting of a fixture ceased to be subject to the scheme at any time in an accounting period for which the election has effect,
   (c) in a calculation made by the operator of the scheme under section 262AC(2) the assumption in section 262AC(3)(g) was made in relation to that fixture, and
   (d) a person ("the current owner") is treated as the owner of the fixture as a result of incurring capital expenditure on its provision ("the new expenditure").

(2) In determining the current owner's qualifying expenditure—
   (a) if the disposal value statement requirement is not satisfied, the new expenditure is to be treated as nil, and

      (b) in any other case, any amount of the new expenditure which exceeds the assumed disposal value is to be left out of account (or, if such an amount has already been taken into account, is to be treated as an amount that should never have been taken into account).

  (3) The disposal value statement requirement is that—

      (a) the operator of the scheme has, no later than 2 years after the date when the fixture ceased to be property subject to the scheme, made a written statement of the assumed disposal value, and

      (b) the current owner has obtained that statement or a copy of it (directly or indirectly) from the operator of the scheme.

  (4) Sections 185 (fixture on which a plant and machinery allowance has been claimed) and 187A (effect of changes in ownership of fixture) do not apply in relation to the new expenditure.

  (5) In this section "assumed disposal value" means the disposal value that, in making the calculation referred to in subsection (1)(c), was assumed to be brought into account pursuant to section 262AC(3)(h).

262AF Co-ownership schemes: definitions relating to schemes

    In sections 262AA to 262AE and this section—

      "co-ownership authorised contractual scheme" means a co-ownership scheme which is authorised for the purposes of the Financial Services and Markets Act 2000 by an authorisation order in force under section 261D(1) of that Act;

      "co-ownership scheme" has the same meaning as in Part 17 of that Act (see section 235A(2) of that Act);

      "operator" and "units", in relation to a co-ownership authorised contractual scheme, have the meanings given by section 237(2) of that Act;

      "participant", in relation to such a scheme, is to be read in accordance with section 235 of that Act."

41 Co-ownership authorised contractual schemes: information requirements

  (1) The Treasury may by regulations impose requirements on the operator of a co-ownership authorised contractual scheme in relation to—

      (a) the provision of information to participants in the scheme;

      (b) the provision of information to Her Majesty's Revenue and Customs.

  (2) Regulations under subsection (1)(a) may be made only for the purpose of enabling participants in a co-ownership authorised contractual scheme to meet their tax obligations in the United Kingdom with respect to their interests in the scheme.

  (3) Regulations under subsection (1)(b) may in particular require the provision of information about—

      (a) who the participants in the scheme were in any accounting period of the scheme;

      (b) the number and classes of units in the scheme in any such period;

      (c) the amount of income per unit of any class in any such period;

(d)   what information has been provided to participants.

(4)   Regulations under this section may specify –
    (a)   the time when information is to be provided;
    (b)   the form and manner in which information is to be provided.

(5)   Regulations under this section may make provision for the imposition of penalties in respect of contravention of, or non-compliance with, the regulations, including provision –
    (a)   for Her Majesty's Revenue and Customs to exercise a discretion as to the amount of a penalty, and
    (b)   about appeals in relation to the imposition of a penalty.

(6)   Regulations under this section may in particular be framed by reference to an accounting period of a co-ownership authorised contractual scheme beginning on or after 1 April 2017.

(7)   Regulations under this section may contain consequential, supplementary and transitional provision.

(8)   Regulations under this section must be made by statutory instrument.

(9)   A statutory instrument containing regulations under this section is subject to annulment in pursuance of a resolution of the House of Commons.

(10)   In this section –
    "co-ownership authorised contractual scheme" means a co-ownership scheme which is authorised for the purposes of the Financial Services and Markets Act 2000 by an authorisation order in force under section 261D(1) of that Act;
    "co-ownership scheme" has the same meaning as in Part 17 of that Act (see section 235A(2) of that Act);
    "operator" and "units", in relation to a co-ownership authorised contractual scheme, have the meanings given by section 237(2) of that Act;
    "participant", in relation to such a scheme, is to be read in accordance with section 235 of that Act.

42   Co-ownership authorised contractual schemes: offshore funds

(1)   The Treasury may by regulations make provision about how participants in a co-ownership authorised contractual scheme are to be treated for income tax purposes or corporation tax purposes in relation to investments made for the purposes of the scheme in an offshore fund.

(2)   Regulations under subsection (1) may, among other things, make provision –
    (a)   for the operator of a co-ownership authorised contractual scheme to allocate to participants in the scheme amounts relating to investments made for the purposes of the scheme in an offshore fund;
    (b)   for those amounts to be regarded as income of the participants to whom they are allocated;
    (c)   as to when that income is to be brought into account for income tax purposes or corporation tax purposes.

(3)   Regulations under this section may –
    (a)   modify an enactment (whenever passed or made);

(b)   contain consequential, supplementary and transitional provision.

(4)   Regulations under this section must be made by statutory instrument.

(5)   A statutory instrument containing regulations under this section is subject to annulment in pursuance of a resolution of the House of Commons.

(6)   References in this section to investments made for the purposes of a co-ownership authorised contractual scheme in an offshore fund include investments so made through one or more other co-ownership authorised contractual schemes.

(7)   In this section—

"co-ownership authorised contractual scheme" means a co-ownership scheme which is authorised for the purposes of the Financial Services and Markets Act 2000 by an authorisation order in force under section 261D(1) of that Act;

"co-ownership scheme" has the same meaning as in Part 17 of that Act (see section 235A(2) of that Act);

"offshore fund" has the meaning given by section 355 of TIOPA 2010;

"operator", in relation to a co-ownership authorised contractual scheme, has the meaning given by section 237(2) of the Financial Services and Markets Act 2000;

"participant", in relation to such a scheme, is to be read in accordance with section 235 of that Act.

PART 2

INDIRECT TAXES

43   Air passenger duty: rates of duty from 1 April 2018

(1)   In section 30 of FA 1994 (air passenger duty: rates of duty), in subsection (4A) (long haul rates of duty)—

(a)   in paragraph (a), for "£75" substitute "£78";

(b)   in paragraph (b), for "£150" substitute "£156".

(2)   The amendments made by this section have effect in relation to the carriage of passengers beginning on or after 1 April 2018.

44   Petroleum revenue tax: elections for oil fields to become non-taxable

(1)   In Schedule 20B to FA 1993, for paragraphs 2 to 12 substitute—

"Method of election

2   An election must be made in writing.

3   An election must be notified to the Commissioners.

4   An election is deemed to have been made on the date on which notification of the election was sent to the Commissioners.

Effect of election

5   If an election is made, the field ceases to be taxable with effect from the start of the first chargeable period to begin after the election is made.

No unrelievable field losses from field

6   From the start of the first chargeable period to begin after an election is made, no allowable loss that accrues from the oil field is an allowable unrelievable field loss for the purposes of petroleum revenue tax.

Interpretation

7   (1) In this Schedule—
                "Commissioners" means the Commissioners for Her Majesty's Revenue and Customs;
                "participator", in relation to a particular time, means a person who is a participator in the chargeable period which includes that time.

        (2) Expressions used in this Schedule and in Part 1 of the Oil Taxation Act 1975 have the same meaning in this Schedule as in Part 1 of that Act."

(2)   In OTA 1975, in section 6(1A), for "paragraph 5" substitute "paragraph 6".

(3)   In FA 1980, in paragraph 15(9A) of Schedule 17, for "paragraph 5" substitute "paragraph 6".

(4)   The amendment made by this section is to be treated as having come into force on 23 November 2016.

45   Gaming duty: rates

(1)   In section 11(2) of FA 1997 (rates of gaming duty), for the table substitute—

"TABLE

Part of gross gaming yield	Rate
The first £2,423,500	15%
The next £1,670,500	20%
The next £2,925,500	30%
The next £6,175,500	40%
The remainder	50%".

(2)   The amendment made by this section has effect in relation to accounting periods beginning on or after 1 April 2017.

46   Remote gaming duty: freeplay

(1)   Part 3 of FA 2014 (general betting duty, pool betting duty and remote gaming duty) is amended in accordance with subsections (2) to (8).

(2)   In section 159 (remote gaming duty: gaming payments), for subsection (4) substitute—

"(4)   For the purposes of this Chapter—

(a)   where the chargeable person participates in the remote gaming in reliance on an offer which waives all of a gaming payment, the person is to be treated as having made a gaming payment of the amount which would have been required to be paid without the offer ("the full amount"), and

(b)   where the chargeable person participates in the remote gaming in reliance on an offer which waives part of a gaming payment, the person is to be treated as having made an additional gaming payment of the difference between the gaming payment actually made and the full amount.

(5)   Where a person is treated by subsection (4) as having made a gaming payment, the payment is to be treated for the purposes of this Chapter—

(a)   as having been made to the gaming provider at the time when the chargeable person begins to participate in the remote gaming to which it relates, and

(b)   as not having been—

(i)   returned, or

(ii)   assigned to a gaming prize fund.

(6)   The Commissioners may by regulations make further provision about how a gaming payment which a person is treated as having made under subsection (4) is to be treated for the purposes of this Chapter.

(7)   This section has effect subject to section 159A."

(3)   After section 159 insert—

"159A Play using the results of successful freeplay

(1)   Where a chargeable person participates in remote gaming, an amount is not to be taken into account in determining the "gaming payment" (if any) under section 159 so far as the amount is paid out of money in relation to which the first and second conditions are met ("excluded winnings").

(2)   The first condition is that the money has been won by participation in the gaming either—

(a)   in reliance on an offer which waives all or part of a gaming payment, or

(b)   in a case where the gaming payment was paid out of money in relation to which this condition and the second condition were met.

(3)   The second condition is that the chargeable person is not entitled to use the money otherwise than for the purpose of participation in the gaming.

(4) Subsection (5) applies where—

 (a) a chargeable person participates in remote gaming in reliance on an offer which waives all or part of a gaming payment, and

 (b) that offer has been won in the course of the person's participation in the gaming (and the person was not given the choice of receiving a different benefit instead of the offer).

(5) The amount which would, apart from this subsection, be treated by section 159(4)(a) or (b) as a gaming payment (or additional gaming payment) is not to be so treated.

(6) For the purposes of this section, where a payment is made out of moneys which include both excluded winnings and money which is not excluded winnings (the "other funds"), the payment is not taken to be made out of excluded winnings except so far as the amount of the payment exceeds the amount of those other funds.

(7) In this section "money" includes any amount credited and any other money's worth."

(4) In section 160 (remote gaming duty: prizes)—

 (a) in subsection (1), in the opening words, after "account" insert "only",

 (b) omit subsection (2),

 (c) in subsection (3), at the end insert "(but where a gaming payment is returned by being credited to an account this subsection has effect subject to subsection (1))", and

 (d) at the end insert—

  "(9) This section has effect subject to section 160A."

(5) After section 160 insert—

"160A Prizes: freeplay

(1) Where a prize is a freeplay offer (whether or not in the form of a voucher) which does not fall within section 160(4)—

 (a) for the purposes of sections 156 and 157, the expenditure on the prize is nil, and

 (b) subsections (5) to (7) of section 160 do not apply in relation to the prize.

(2) Where a prize is a voucher which gives the recipient a choice of using it in place of money for freeplay or as whole or partial payment for another benefit, section 160(5)(b) has effect as if after "used" there were inserted "if it is used as payment for a benefit other than freeplay".

(3) In this section—

 "freeplay" means participation, in reliance on a freeplay offer, in—

  (a) remote gaming, or

  (b) an activity in respect of which a gambling tax listed in section 161(4) is charged;

 "freeplay offer" means an offer which waives all or part of—

  (a) a gaming payment, or

  (b) a payment in connection with participation in an activity in respect of which a gambling tax listed in section 161(4) is charged."

(6)   In section 188 (gaming), after subsection (2) insert—

    "(3)   But a game is not a "game of chance" for the purposes of this Part if—

       (a)   it can only be played with the participation of two or more persons, and

       (b)   no amounts are paid or required to be paid—

          (i)   in respect of entitlement to participate in the game, or

          (ii)   otherwise for, on account of or in connection with participation in the game."

(7)   In section 190 (index), in the Table, in the entry for "game of chance", for "188(1)(b)" substitute "188(1)(b) and (3)".

(8)   In section 194(4) (regulations under Part 3 to which the procedure in section 194(5) is to apply), before paragraph (a), insert—

    "(za)   regulations under section 159(6);".

(9)   The amendments made by this section have effect with respect to accounting periods beginning on or after 1 August 2017.

47   Tobacco products manufacturing machinery: licensing scheme

(1)   After section 8U of TPDA 1979 insert—

"8V   Tobacco products manufacturing machinery: licensing scheme

    (1)   In this section "tobacco products manufacturing machinery" means machinery that is designed primarily for use for the purpose of (or for purposes including) manufacturing tobacco products.

    (2)   The Commissioners may by regulations—

       (a)   prohibit a person from purchasing, acquiring, owning or being in possession of, or carrying out other specified activities in respect of, an item of tobacco products manufacturing machinery, except in accordance with a licence granted under the regulations;

       (b)   provide that if a person contravenes the prohibition in relation to an item of tobacco products manufacturing machinery, the machinery is liable to forfeiture.

    (3)   The regulations may provide that the prohibition does not apply—

       (a)   in relation to persons, or items of tobacco products manufacturing machinery, of a specified description;

       (b)   in specified circumstances.

    (4)   Regulations under this section may include provision—

       (a)   imposing obligations on licensed persons;

       (b)   for a licensed person who fails to comply with a condition or restriction of a licence, or with an obligation imposed by the regulations, to be liable to a penalty of the amount for the time being specified in section 9(2)(b) of the Finance Act 1994;

       (c)   for exceptions from liability to a penalty under the regulations;

       (d)   for the assessment and recovery of a penalty, including provision for two or more contraventions to be treated as a single contravention for the purposes of assessment;

(e)   for the Commissioners, if they think it right because of special circumstances, to remit, reduce (including reduce to nil) or stay a penalty, or agree a compromise in relation to proceedings for a penalty;

(f)   about reviews by the Commissioners, or by an officer of Revenue and Customs, of decisions in connection with licensing and the imposition of penalties under the regulations and about appeals against those decisions (which may include provision for specified decisions of the Commissioners to be treated as if they were listed in section 13A(2) of, or Schedule 5 to, the Finance Act 1994);

(g)   for the Customs and Excise Management Act 1979 to have effect in relation to licensed persons as it has effect in relation to revenue traders, subject to such modifications as may be specified in the regulations.

(5)   The Commissioners may, by or under regulations under this section, make provision—

(a)   regulating the grant of licences, including provision about the circumstances in which a licence may be granted and the requirements to be met by or in relation to the applicant (which may include a requirement that the applicant is a fit and proper person to hold a licence);

(b)   about the form, manner and content of an application for or in respect of a licence;

(c)   for licences to be subject to specified conditions or restrictions;

(d)   regulating the variation or revocation of a licence, or of any condition or restriction to which a licence is subject;

(e)   about the renewal, surrender or transfer of a licence;

(f)   for communications by or with the Commissioners in connection with a licence to be made electronically;

(g)   as to the arrangements for licensing bodies corporate which are members of the same group (as defined in the regulations);

(h)   for members of a group to be jointly and severally liable for any penalties imposed under the regulations."

(2)   In section 9 of TPDA 1979 (regulations), in subsection (1A), for "or 8U" substitute ", 8U or 8V".

PART 3

FULFILMENT BUSINESSES

48   Carrying on a third country goods fulfilment business

(1)   For the purposes of this Part a person carries on a third country goods fulfilment business if the person, by way of business—

(a)   stores third country goods which are owned by a person who is not established in a Member State, or

(b)   stores third country goods on behalf of a person who is not established in a Member State,

at a time when the conditions in subsection (2) are met in relation to the goods.

(2)   The conditions are that—

    (a)   there has been no supply of the goods in the United Kingdom for the purposes of VATA 1994, and

    (b)   the goods are being offered for sale in the United Kingdom or elsewhere.

(3)   But a person does not carry on a third country goods fulfilment business if the person's activities within subsection (1) are incidental to the carriage of the goods.

(4)   Goods are "third country" goods if they have been imported from a place outside the Member States within the meaning of section 15 of VATA 1994.

(5)   Whether a person is established in a Member State is to be determined in accordance with Article 10 of Council Implementing Regulation (EU) No 282/2011 of 15 March 2011 laying down implementing measures for Directive 2006/112/EC on the common system of value added tax.

49 Requirement for approval

(1)   A person may not carry on a third country goods fulfilment business otherwise than in accordance with an approval given by the Commissioners under this section.

(2)   The Commissioners may approve a person to carry on a third country goods fulfilment business only if they are satisfied that the person is a fit and proper person to carry on the business.

(3)   The Commissioners may approve a person to carry on a third country goods fulfilment business for such periods and subject to such conditions or restrictions as they may think fit or as they may by regulations made by them prescribe.

(4)   The Commissioners may at any time for reasonable cause vary the terms of, or revoke, an approval under this section.

(5)   In this Part "approved person" means a person approved under this section to carry on a third country goods fulfilment business.

50 Register of approved persons

(1)   The Commissioners must maintain a register of approved persons.

(2)   The register is to contain such information relating to approved persons as the Commissioners consider appropriate.

(3)   The Commissioners may make publicly available such information contained in the register as they consider necessary to enable those who deal with a person who carries on a third country goods fulfilment business to determine whether the person in question is an approved person in relation to that activity.

(4)   The information may be made available by such means (including the internet) as the Commissioners consider appropriate.

51 Regulations relating to approval, registration etc.

(1)   The Commissioners may by regulations make provision –

    (a)   regulating the approval and registration of persons under this Part,

(b) regulating the variation or revocation of any such approval or registration, or of any condition or restriction to which such an approval or registration is subject,

(c) about the register maintained under section 50,

(d) regulating the carrying on of a third country goods fulfilment business, and

(e) imposing obligations on approved persons.

(2) The regulations may, in particular, make provision—

(a) requiring applications, and other communications with the Commissioners, to be made electronically;

(b) as to the procedure for the approval and registration of bodies corporate which are members of the same group;

(c) requiring approved persons to keep and make available for inspection such records as may be prescribed by or under the regulations.

52 Disclosure of information by HMRC

(1) The Commissioners may disclose to an approved person information held by Her Majesty's Revenue and Customs in connection with a function of Her Majesty's Revenue and Customs, but only for the purpose mentioned in subsection (2).

(2) The purpose is to assist the approved person in complying with obligations imposed on that person by virtue of section 51.

(3) An approved person to whom information is disclosed under subsection (1)—

(a) may use the information only for the purpose of complying with obligations imposed on that person by virtue of section 51, and

(b) may not further disclose the information except with the consent of the Commissioners.

(4) Section 19 of the Commissioners for Revenue and Customs Act 2005 (offence) applies to a disclosure in contravention of subsection (3)(b) as it applies to a disclosure, in contravention of section 20(9) of that Act, of revenue and customs information relating to a person whose identity is specified in the disclosure or can be deduced from it.

53 Offence

(1) A person who—

(a) carries on a third country goods fulfilment business, and

(b) is not an approved person,

commits an offence.

(2) In proceedings for an offence under subsection (1) it is a defence to show that the person did not know, and had no reasonable grounds to suspect, that the person—

(a) was carrying on a third country goods fulfilment business, or

(b) was not an approved person.

(3) A person is taken to have shown the fact mentioned in subsection (2) if—

(a) sufficient evidence of that fact is adduced to raise an issue with respect to it, and

        (b)   the contrary is not proved beyond reasonable doubt.

  (4)   A person guilty of an offence under this section is liable on summary
        conviction—
        (a)   in England and Wales, to imprisonment for a term not exceeding 12
               months, or a fine, or both;
        (b)   in Scotland, to imprisonment for a term not exceeding 12 months, or a
               fine not exceeding the statutory maximum, or both;
        (c)   in Northern Ireland, to imprisonment for a term not exceeding 6
               months, or a fine not exceeding the statutory maximum, or both.

  (5)   A person guilty of an offence under this section is liable on conviction on
        indictment to—
        (a)   imprisonment for a period not exceeding 7 years,
        (b)   a fine, or
        (c)   both.

  (6)   In relation to an offence committed before the commencement of section 154(1)
        of the Criminal Justice Act 2003 the reference in subsection (4)(a) to 12 months
        is to be read as a reference to 6 months.

54   Forfeiture

  (1)   If a person—
        (a)   carries on a third country goods fulfilment business, and
        (b)   is not an approved person,
        any goods within subsection (2) are liable to forfeiture under CEMA 1979.

  (2)   Goods are within this subsection if—
        (a)   they are stored by the person, and
        (b)   their storage by the person constitutes, or has constituted, the carrying
               on of a third country goods fulfilment business by the person.

55   Penalties

  (1)   Schedule 13 provides for a penalty to be payable by a person who carries on a
        third country goods fulfilment business and is not an approved person.

  (2)   The Commissioners may make regulations ("penalty regulations") imposing a
        penalty for the contravention of—
        (a)   any condition or restriction imposed under this Part;
        (b)   regulations under this Part.

  (3)   The amount of a penalty imposed by the penalty regulations is to be specified
        in the regulations, but must not exceed £3,000.

  (4)   The penalty regulations may make provision for the assessment and recovery
        of a penalty imposed by the regulations.

  (5)   The Commissioners may by regulations make provision for corporate bodies
        which are members of the same group to be jointly and severally liable for any
        penalties imposed under—
        (a)   Schedule 13;
        (b)   penalty regulations.

56   Appeals

(1)   FA 1994 is amended as follows.

(2)   In section 13A(2) (customs and excise reviews and appeals: relevant decisions) after paragraph (gb) insert—

> "(gc)   any decision by HMRC that a person is liable to a penalty, or as to the amount of a person's liability, under—
>
> > (i)   regulations under section 55 of the Finance (No. 2) Act 2017, or
> >
> > (ii)   Schedule 13 to that Act;".

(3)   In Schedule 5 to that Act (decisions subject to review and appeal) after paragraph 9A insert—

> *"The Finance (No. 2) Act 2017*

> 9B   Any decision for the purposes of Part 3 of the Finance (No. 2) Act 2017 (third country goods fulfilment businesses) as to—
>
> > (a)   whether or not, and in which respects, any person is to be, or to continue to be, approved and registered, or
> >
> > (b)   the conditions or restrictions subject to which any person is approved and registered."

57   Regulations

(1)   Regulations under this Part may—

> (a)   make provision which applies generally or only for specified cases or purposes;
>
> (b)   make different provision for different cases or purposes;
>
> (c)   include incidental, consequential, transitional or transitory provision;
>
> (d)   confer a discretion on the Commissioners;
>
> (e)   make provision by reference to a notice to be published by the Commissioners.

(2)   Regulations under this Part are to be made by statutory instrument.

(3)   A statutory instrument containing regulations under this Part is subject to annulment in pursuance of a resolution of the House of Commons.

(4)   This section does not apply to regulations under section 59 (commencement).

58   Interpretation

(1)   In this Part—

> "approved person" has the meaning given by section 49(5);
>
> "the Commissioners" means the Commissioners for Her Majesty's Revenue and Customs.

(2)   For the purposes of this Part two or more bodies corporate are members of a group if—

> (a)   one of them controls each of the others,
>
> (b)   one person (whether a body corporate or an individual) controls all of them, or

     (c)   two or more individuals carrying on a business in partnership control all of them.

(3)   A body corporate is to be taken to control another body corporate if —

     (a)   it is empowered by or under legislation to control that body's activities, or

     (b)   it is that body's holding company within the meaning of section 1159 of, and Schedule 6 to, the Companies Act 2006.

(4)   An individual or individuals are to be taken to control a body corporate if the individual or individuals (were the individual or individuals a company) would be that body's holding company within the meaning of section 1159 of, and Schedule 6 to, the Companies Act 2006.

59   Commencement

(1)   This Part comes into force —

     (a)   so far as it confers powers to make regulations, on the day on which this Act is passed, and

     (b)   for all other purposes, on such day as the Commissioners may by regulations made by statutory instrument appoint.

(2)   Regulations under subsection (1)(b) may appoint different days for different purposes.

PART 4

ADMINISTRATION, AVOIDANCE AND ENFORCEMENT

Reporting and record-keeping

60   Digital reporting and record-keeping for income tax etc

(1)   TMA 1970 is amended as set out in subsections (2) and (3).

(2)   After section 12B insert —

"Digital reporting and record-keeping

12C   Digital reporting and record-keeping

Schedule A1 (digital reporting and record-keeping) has effect."

(3) Before Schedule 1AA insert—

"SCHEDULE A1 Section 12C

DIGITAL REPORTING AND RECORD-KEEPING

PART 1

APPLICATION

Application: persons

1   (1) This Schedule applies to a person within the charge to income tax who, otherwise than in partnership, carries on (or has carried on)—

(a) a trade, profession or vocation the profits of which are chargeable to income tax under Part 2 of ITTOIA 2005,

(b) a property business the profits of which are chargeable to income tax under Part 3 of ITTOIA 2005, or

(c) any other activity which may give rise to profits or other income chargeable to income tax under Part 2 or 3 of ITTOIA 2005.

(2) This is subject to paragraph 2.

2   (1) This Schedule does not apply to—

(a) the trustees of a charitable trust, or

(b) the trustees of an exempt unauthorised unit trust (within the meaning of the Unauthorised Unit Trusts (Tax) Regulations 2013 (S.I. 2013/2819)),

unless the trustees elect for this Schedule to apply to them.

(2) This Schedule does not apply to a person in respect of an excluded activity unless the person elects for this Schedule to apply to the person in respect of the excluded activity.

(3) The following are excluded activities—

(a) the underwriting business of a member of Lloyd's (within the meaning of section 184 of the Finance Act 1993),

(b) holding shares in respect of which a distribution may be made which is chargeable to income tax under Part 3 of ITTOIA 2005 by virtue of section 548(6) of CTA 2010 (distributions to shareholders in real estate investment trusts), and

(c) participating in an open-ended investment company which may make distributions chargeable to income tax under Part 3 of ITTOIA 2005 by virtue of regulation 69Z18 of the Authorised Investment Funds (Tax) Regulations 2006 (S.I. 2006/964) (property income distributions).

(4) The Commissioners may by regulations make provision about elections under this paragraph and the withdrawal of such elections, including provision—

(a) about how an election may be made or withdrawn, and

(b) about the period for which an election or withdrawal has effect.

Application: partnerships

3   (1) This Schedule applies to a partnership if one or more of the partners is within the charge to income tax.

(2) This is subject to paragraph 4.

4   (1) If all the activities of a partnership which may give rise to profits or income are excluded activities, this Schedule does not apply to the partnership unless the partnership elects for this Schedule to apply to it.

(2) The following are excluded activities —
   (a) the underwriting business of a Lloyd's partnership (as defined in section 184(1) of the Finance Act 1993),
   (b) holding shares in respect of which a distribution may be made which is chargeable to income tax under Part 3 of ITTOIA 2005 by virtue of section 548(6) of CTA 2010 (distributions to shareholders in real estate investment trusts), and
   (c) participating in an open-ended investment company which may make distributions chargeable to income tax under Part 3 of ITTOIA 2005 by virtue of regulation 69Z18 of the Authorised Investment Funds (Tax) Regulations 2006 (S.I. 2006/964) (property income distributions).

(3) The Commissioners may by regulations make provision about elections under this paragraph and the withdrawal of such elections, including provision —
   (a) about how an election may be made or withdrawn, and
   (b) about the period for which an election or withdrawal has effect.

Nominated partners

5   (1) Requirements imposed by regulations under this Schedule on a partnership are to be met by a nominated partner.

(2) A "nominated partner" is a partner nominated for the purposes of this Schedule —
   (a) by the partners, or
   (b) by the Commissioners.

(3) A nomination, or a revocation of a nomination, by the partners does not have effect until notice of the revocation or nomination is given to HMRC.

(4) The Commissioners may by regulations make provision about nominations and the revocation of nominations, including provision about the circumstances in which the Commissioners may nominate a partner.

(5) In this Act references to a nominated partner are to a partner nominated for the purposes of this Schedule.

PART 2

DIGITAL REPORTING AND RECORD-KEEPING

Interpretation

6   In this Part of this Schedule "business"—
         (a)   in relation to a person to whom this Schedule applies (see paragraphs 1 and 2), means the activity by virtue of which this Schedule applies to the person (and if more than one, means each of them), and
         (b)   in relation to a partnership to which this Schedule applies (see paragraphs 3 and 4), means any activity of the partnership.

Periodic updates

7   (1)   The Commissioners may by regulations require a person or partnership to whom this Schedule applies to provide to HMRC, by electronic communications, specified information about the business of the person or partnership.

         (2)   The information which may be specified includes any information ("financial information") relevant to calculating profits, losses or income of the business, including information about receipts and expenses.

         (3)   The regulations may require information to be provided at or for specified intervals, times or periods.

         (4)   The regulations may not require financial information about the business to be provided more often than once every 3 months.

End of period statement

8   (1)   The Commissioners may by regulations require a person to whom this Schedule applies to provide to HMRC, by electronic communications, a statement containing specified information about the person's business in relation to each relevant period.

         (2)   "Relevant period" means—
                (a)   in relation to a business the profits or income of which are chargeable to income tax under Chapter 2 of Part 2 of ITTOIA 2005, a basis period (see Chapter 15 of that Part), and
                (b)   otherwise, a tax year.

         (3)   The information which may be specified includes any information relevant to calculating profits, losses or income of the business for the relevant period, including information about receipts and expenses.

         (4)   Regulations under this paragraph may require the statement to include a declaration to the effect that the information included in it is correct and complete.

         (5)   An end of period statement for a tax year must be provided to HMRC at or before—

      (a)   the time at which the person delivers a return under section 8 or 8A for the tax year (see section 8(7)(c) and 8A(7)(c)), or

      (b)   if earlier, the end of 31 January following the tax year.

   (6)   In this Act—

      (a)   references to an end of period statement are to a statement required by regulations under this paragraph;

      (b)   references to an end of period statement for a tax year are to an end of period statement for that tax year or, where the relevant period is a basis period, for the basis period for that tax year.

Facility for complying with notice to file under section 8 or 8A

9   The Commissioners may by regulations make provision for the establishment and use of a facility enabling a person to whom this Schedule applies to file or deliver, by electronic communications—

      (a)   anything which under section 8(1AB) may be required to be filed or delivered by a notice to file under section 8;

      (b)   anything which under section 8A(1AB) may be required to be filed or delivered by a notice to file under section 8A.

Partnership return

10   (1)   The Commissioners may by regulations require a partnership to which this Schedule applies to provide to HMRC, by electronic communications, a return containing specified information about the partnership's business in relation to each tax year.

   (2)   The information which may be specified includes any information which is or may be required to be included in a section 12AA partnership return, including information in respect of any partners within the charge to corporation tax.

   (3)   In particular, the information which may be specified includes the information required to be included in a section 12AA partnership return by section 12AB (partnership statements).

   (4)   Regulations under this paragraph may require the return to include a declaration to the effect that the information included in it is correct and complete.

   (5)   A Schedule A1 partnership return for a tax year must be provided to HMRC on or before 31 January following the tax year.

   (6)   In this Act—

      (a)   references to a Schedule A1 partnership return are to a return required by regulations under this paragraph, and

      (b)   references to a partnership statement, in relation to a Schedule A1 partnership return, are to information required to be included in the return by virtue of sub-paragraph (3).

   (7)   In the Taxes Acts, unless the contrary intention appears, a reference (whether general or specific) to a return under, or a return required under, this Act includes a reference to a Schedule A1 partnership return.

Record-keeping

11 (1) The Commissioners may by regulations require a person or partnership to whom this Schedule applies to—

    (a) keep specified records relating to the business in electronic form, and

    (b) preserve those records in electronic form for a specified period.

(2) The records which may be specified are any records the Commissioners consider relevant to ascertaining information required to be provided by regulations under this Part of this Schedule.

(3) A requirement imposed by regulations under this paragraph is in addition to, and not in place of, any other requirement that the person or partnership keep and preserve records (or keep and preserve records in a particular form).

(4) Paragraph 5(1) (requirements imposed on partnership to be met by nominated partner) does not apply to requirements imposed by regulations under this paragraph.

12 (1) This paragraph applies where requirements imposed by regulations under paragraph 11 for any period are not complied with.

(2) The person, or in the case of a partnership each relevant partner, is liable for a penalty.

(3) "Relevant partner" means any person who was a partner in the partnership at any time during the period in question.

(4) The amount of the penalty must not exceed £3,000.

(5) A person or relevant partner is not liable to a penalty under this paragraph in relation to a period if the person or relevant partner is liable to a penalty under section 12B(5) in relation to that period.

Electronic communications and records: supplementary powers

13 (1) This paragraph applies to regulations under paragraphs 7, 8, 9, 10 and 11.

(2) The regulations may (amongst other things) make provision—

    (a) as to the electronic form to be taken by information provided and records kept or preserved,

    (b) requiring persons to prepare and keep records of information provided by means of electronic communications,

    (c) for the production of the contents of records kept or preserved in accordance with regulations under this Part of this Schedule,

    (d) as to conditions that must be complied with in connection with the use of electronic communications or the keeping or preservation of electronic records,

    (e) for treating information as not having been provided or records as not having been kept or preserved unless conditions are complied with,

    (f)   for determining the time at which and person by whom information is taken to have been delivered, and

    (g)   for authenticating information or records.

(3) The regulations may also make provision (which may include provision for the application of conclusive or other presumptions) about the manner of proving for any purpose—

    (a)   whether any use of electronic communications is to be taken as having resulted in the provision of information,

    (b)   the time at which information was provided,

    (c)   the person by whom information was provided,

    (d)   the contents of any information provided,

    (e)   the contents of any records, and

    (f)   any other matter for which provision may be made by the regulations.

(4) The regulations may allow or require use to be made of intermediaries in connection with—

    (a)   the provision of information by means of electronic communications, and

    (b)   the authentication or security of anything transmitted by any such means.

(5) The regulations may—

    (a)   allow any authorisation or requirement for which the regulations may provide to be given by means of a specific or general direction given by the Commissioners, and

    (b)   provide that the conditions of an authorisation or requirement are to be taken to be satisfied only where the Commissioners are satisfied as to specified matters.

(6) The regulations may provide—

    (a)   that information provided must meet standards of accuracy and completeness set by specific or general directions given by the Commissioners, and

    (b)   that failure to meet those standards may be treated as a failure to provide the information, or as a failure to comply with the requirements of the regulations.

PART 3

EXEMPTIONS

Exemption for the digitally excluded

14   (1) The Commissioners must by regulations make provision—

    (a)   for a person to be exempt from requirements imposed by regulations under paragraphs 7, 8 and 11 if the Commissioners are satisfied that the person is digitally excluded, and

    (b)   for a partnership to be exempt from requirements imposed by regulations under paragraphs 7, 10 and 11 if the Commissioners are satisfied that the partnership is digitally excluded.

(2) A person is digitally excluded if the digital exclusion condition is met in relation to the person.

(3) A partnership is digitally excluded if the digital exclusion condition is met in relation to each partner.

(4) The digital exclusion condition is met in relation to a person or partner if —

    (a) the person or partner is a practising member of a religious society or order whose beliefs are incompatible with using electronic communications or keeping electronic records, or

    (b) for any reason (including age, disability or location) it is not reasonably practicable for the person or partner to use electronic communications or to keep electronic records.

Further exemptions

15 (1) The Commissioners may by regulations make provision for further exemptions.

(2) The exemptions for which provision may be made include exemptions based on income or other financial criteria.

PART 4

SUPPLEMENTARY PROVISION

Appeals

16 (1) An appeal may be brought against any decision made by the Commissioners, or by an officer of Revenue and Customs, under regulations under this Schedule.

(2) Notice of an appeal under this paragraph must be given to HMRC within 30 days after the day on which notice of the decision is given.

(3) The notice of appeal must —

    (a) be in writing, and

    (b) specify the grounds of appeal.

Interpretation

17 Any power in this Schedule to require the provision of information includes power to require the provision of accounts, statements and documents relating to that information.

Regulations

18 (1) Regulations under this Schedule may —

    (a) make provision which applies generally or only for specified cases or purposes;

    (b) make different provision for different cases or purposes;

    (c) include incidental, supplemental, consequential, saving, transitional or transitory provision;

    (d) make provision for matters to be specified by the Commissioners in accordance with the regulations.

  (2) Sub-paragraph (1)(d) does not apply to any interval, time or period specified by virtue of paragraph 7(3) (which may be specified only by the regulations).

  (3) Regulations under this Schedule may make provision for a person or partnership to whom this Schedule applies, but who would not otherwise be subject to a requirement imposed by the regulations, to elect to be subject to that requirement.

  (4) Regulations under this Schedule may provide that, for the purposes of any provision of this Schedule or of the regulations, a change in the accounting date of a business is to be disregarded (and its period of account determined accordingly).

  (5) The power to make regulations under this Schedule is exercisable by statutory instrument.

  (6) A statutory instrument containing regulations under this Schedule is subject to annulment in pursuance of a resolution of the House of Commons."

  (4) Subsections (1) to (3) come into force on such day as the Treasury may by regulations made by statutory instrument appoint.

  (5) Regulations under subsection (4) may appoint different days for different purposes.

61   Digital reporting and record-keeping for income tax etc: further amendments

  (1) Schedule 14 contains provision amending TMA 1970 and other Acts.

  (2) The Commissioners for Her Majesty's Revenue and Customs may by regulations amend or modify any provision of the Taxes Acts in consequence of the provision made by section 60 or Schedule 14.

  (3) Regulations under subsection (2) may make transitional, transitory or saving provision.

  (4) Regulations under subsection (2) must be made by statutory instrument.

  (5) A statutory instrument containing regulations under subsection (2) may not be made unless a draft of the instrument has been laid before, and approved by a resolution of, the House of Commons.

  (6) Subsections (1) to (5) and Schedule 14 come into force on such day as the Treasury may by regulations made by statutory instrument appoint.

  (7) Regulations under subsection (6) may appoint different days for different purposes.

62   Digital reporting and record-keeping for VAT

  (1) Schedule 11 to VATA 1994 (administration, collection and enforcement) is amended as set out in subsections (2) to (4).

  (2) In paragraph 2 (accounting and payment) –

     (a)   in sub-paragraph (1) for "and the making of returns" substitute ", the making of returns and the submission of information";

     (b)   after sub-paragraph (11) insert—

       "(11A) Regulations under this paragraph may include incidental, supplemental, consequential, saving, transitional or transitory provision."

(3)   In paragraph 6 (duty of taxable person to keep records)—

     (a)   omit sub-paragraph (4);

     (b)   at the end insert—

       "(5)   The Commissioners may by regulations make provision about the form in which, and means by which, records are to be kept and preserved.

       (6)   Regulations under sub-paragraph (5) may—

           (a)   make different provision for different cases;

           (b)   provide for any provision of the regulations to be subject to conditions or exceptions specified in writing by the Commissioners;

           (c)   include incidental, supplemental, consequential, saving, transitional or transitory provision.

       (7)   If regulations under sub-paragraph (5) make provision requiring records to be kept or preserved in electronic form they must make provision for a taxable person to be exempt from those requirements for any month ("the current month") if—

           (a)   the value of the person's taxable supplies, in the period of one year ending with the month before the current month, was less than the VAT threshold, and

           (b)   the person was not subject to those requirements in the month before the current month.

       (8)   The regulations may modify the exemption for cases where a business or part of a business carried on by a taxable person is transferred to another person as a going concern.

       (9)   The "VAT threshold" means the amount specified in paragraph 1(1)(a) of Schedule 1 on the first day of the current month.

      (10)   Regulations under sub-paragraph (5) requiring records to be kept or preserved in electronic form may (among other things) make provision—

           (a)   as to the electronic form in which records are to be kept or preserved,

           (b)   for the production of the contents of records kept or preserved in accordance with the regulations,

           (c)   as to conditions that must be complied with in connection with the keeping or preservation of electronic records,

           (d)   for treating records as not having been kept or preserved unless conditions are complied with,

           (e)   for authenticating records,

     (f)   about the manner of proving for any purpose the contents of any records (including provision for the application of conclusive or other presumptions).

  (11) Regulations under sub-paragraph (5) requiring records to be kept or preserved in electronic form may—

     (a)   allow any authorisation or requirement for which the regulations may provide to be given by means of a specific or general direction given by the Commissioners,

     (b)   provide that the conditions of an authorisation or requirement are to be taken to be satisfied only where the Commissioners are satisfied as to specified matters."

  (4) In paragraph 6A (power to direct keeping of records), for sub-paragraph (7) substitute—

     "(7) Regulations under paragraph 6(5) apply for the purposes of this paragraph as they apply for the purposes of paragraph 6."

  (5) In section 83(1) of VATA 1994 (appealable decisions), for paragraph (zc) substitute—

    "(zc) a decision of the Commissioners about the application of any provision of regulations under paragraph 2 or 6 of Schedule 11, or of regulations under section 135 or 136 of the Finance Act 2002 relating to VAT, which—

      (i)   requires returns to be made or information to be submitted by electronic communications, or

     (ii)   requires records to be kept or preserved in electronic form,

    (including in particular a decision as to whether such a requirement applies and a decision to impose a penalty)."

  (6) Subsections (3)(a) and (4) of this section come into force when the first regulations under paragraph 6(5) of Schedule 11 to VATA 1994 come into force.

  (7) Regulations under paragraph 6(5) of Schedule 11 to VATA 1994 may not make provision requiring records to be kept or preserved in electronic form which has effect before 1 April 2019.

Enquiries

63   Partial closure notices

Schedule 15 makes provision for partial closure notices in respect of enquiries under sections 9A, 12ZM and 12AC of TMA 1970 and Schedule 18 to FA 1998.

Avoidance etc

64   Errors in taxpayers' documents

  (1) Schedule 24 to FA 2007 (penalties for errors) is amended as set out in subsections (2) and (3).

(2)   After paragraph 3 insert—

"Errors related to avoidance arrangements

3A   (1)   This paragraph applies where a document of a kind listed in the Table in paragraph 1 is given to HMRC by a person ("P") and the document contains an inaccuracy which—

    (a)   falls within paragraph 1(2), and

    (b)   arises because the document is submitted on the basis that particular avoidance arrangements (within the meaning of paragraph 3B) had an effect which in fact they did not have.

(2)   It is to be presumed that the inaccuracy was careless, within the meaning of paragraph 3, unless—

    (a)   the inaccuracy was deliberate on P's part, or

    (b)   P satisfies HMRC or (on an appeal notified to the tribunal) the tribunal that P took reasonable care to avoid inaccuracy.

(3)   In considering whether P took reasonable care to avoid inaccuracy, HMRC and (on an appeal notified to the tribunal) the tribunal must take no account of any evidence of any reliance by P on advice where the advice is disqualified.

(4)   Advice is "disqualified" if any of the following applies—

    (a)   the advice was given to P by an interested person;

    (b)   the advice was given to P as a result of arrangements made between an interested person and the person who gave the advice;

    (c)   the person who gave the advice did not have appropriate expertise for giving the advice;

    (d)   the advice took no account of P's individual circumstances;

    (e)   the advice was addressed to, or given to, a person other than P;

but this is subject to sub-paragraphs (5) and (7).

(5)   Where (but for this sub-paragraph) advice would be disqualified under any of paragraphs (a) to (c) of sub-paragraph (4), the advice is not disqualified under that paragraph if at the relevant time P—

    (a)   has taken reasonable steps to find out whether the advice falls within that paragraph, and

    (b)   reasonably believes that it does not.

(6)   In sub-paragraph (4) "an interested person" means—

    (a)   a person, other than P, who participated in the avoidance arrangements or any transaction forming part of them, or

    (b)   a person who for any consideration (whether or not in money) facilitated P's entering into the avoidance arrangements.

(7)   Where (but for this sub-paragraph) advice would be disqualified under paragraph (a) of sub-paragraph (4) because it was given by a person within sub-paragraph (6)(b), the advice is not disqualified under that paragraph if—

    (a)   the person giving the advice had appropriate expertise for giving it,

    (b) the advice took account of P's individual circumstances, and

    (c) at the time when the question whether the advice is disqualified arises—

      (i) Condition E in paragraph 3B(5) is met in relation to the avoidance arrangements, but

      (ii) none of Conditions A to D in paragraph 3B(5) is or has at any time been met in relation to them.

 (8) If the document mentioned in sub-paragraph (1) is given to HMRC by P as a personal representative of a deceased person ("D")—

    (a) sub-paragraph (4) is to be read as if—

      (i) the references in paragraphs (a) and (b) to P were to P or D;

      (ii) the reference in paragraph (d) to P were to D, and

      (iii) the reference in paragraph (e) to a person other than P were to a person who is neither P nor D,

    (b) sub-paragraph (6) is to be read as if—

      (i) the reference in paragraph (a) to P were a reference to the person to whom the advice was given, and

      (ii) the reference in paragraph (b) to P were to D (or, where P also participated in the avoidance arrangements, P or D), and

    (c) sub-paragraph (7) is to be read as if the reference in paragraph (b) to P were to D.

 (9) In this paragraph—

    "arrangements" includes any agreement, understanding, scheme, transaction or series of transactions (whether or not legally enforceable);

    "the relevant time" means the time when the document mentioned in sub-paragraph (1) is given to HMRC;

    "the tribunal" has the same meaning as in paragraph 17 (see paragraph 17(5A)).

3B (1) In paragraph 3A "avoidance arrangements" means, subject to sub-paragraph (3), arrangements which fall within sub-paragraph (2).

 (2) Arrangements fall within this sub-paragraph if, having regard to all the circumstances, it would be reasonable to conclude that the obtaining of a tax advantage was the main purpose, or one of the main purposes, of the arrangements.

 (3) Arrangements are not avoidance arrangements for the purposes of paragraph 3A if (although they fall within sub-paragraph (2))—

    (a) they are arrangements which accord with established practice, and

    (b) HMRC had, at the time the arrangements were entered into, indicated its acceptance of that practice.

 (4) If, at any time, any of Conditions A to E is met in relation to particular arrangements—

    (a) for the purposes of this Schedule the arrangements are to be taken to fall within (and always to have fallen within) sub-paragraph (2), and

      (b)   in relation to the arrangements, sub-paragraph (3) (and the reference to it in sub-paragraph (1)) are to be treated as omitted.

This does not prevent arrangements from falling within sub-paragraph (2) other than by reason of one or more of Conditions A to E being met.

(5) Conditions A to E are as follows –

      (a)   Condition A is that the arrangements are DOTAS arrangements within the meaning given by section 219(5) and (6) of FA 2014;

      (b)   Condition B is that the arrangements are disclosable VAT arrangements or disclosable indirect tax arrangements for the purposes of Schedule 18 to FA 2016 (see paragraphs 8A to 9A of that Schedule);

      (c)   Condition C is that both of the following apply –

          (i)   P has been given a notice under a provision mentioned in sub-paragraph (6) stating that a tax advantage arising from the arrangements is to be counteracted, and

         (ii)   that tax advantage has been counteracted under section 209 of FA 2013;

      (d)   Condition D is that a follower notice under section 204 of FA 2014 has been given to P by reference to the arrangements (and not withdrawn) and –

          (i)   the necessary corrective action for the purposes of section 208 of FA 2014 has been taken in respect of the denied advantage, or

         (ii)   the denied advantage has been counteracted otherwise than as mentioned in sub-paragraph (i);

      (e)   Condition E is that a tax advantage asserted by reference to the arrangements has been counteracted (by an assessment, an amendment of a return or claim, or otherwise) on the basis that an avoidance-related rule applies in relation to P's affairs.

(6) The provisions referred to in sub-paragraph (5)(c)(i) are –

      (a)   paragraph 12 of Schedule 43 to FA 2013 (general anti-abuse rule: notice of final decision);

      (b)   paragraph 8 or 9 of Schedule 43A to that Act (pooled or bound arrangements: notice of final decision);

      (c)   paragraph 8 of Schedule 43B to that Act (generic referrals: notice of final decision).

(7) In sub-paragraph (5)(d) the reference to giving a follower notice to P includes giving a partnership follower notice in respect of a partnership return in relation to which P is a relevant partner; and for the purposes of this sub-paragraph –

      (a)   "relevant partner" has the meaning given by paragraph 2(5) of Schedule 31 to FA 2014;

      (b)   a partnership follower notice is given "in respect of" the partnership return mentioned in paragraph 2(2)(a) or (b) of that Schedule.

(8) For the purposes of sub-paragraph (5)(d) it does not matter whether the denied advantage has been dealt with—

    (a) wholly as mentioned in one or other of sub-paragraphs (i) and (ii) of sub-paragraph (5)(d), or

    (b) partly as mentioned in one of those sub-paragraphs and partly as mentioned in the other;

and "the denied advantage" has the same meaning as in Chapter 2 of Part 4 of FA 2014 (see section 208(3) of and paragraph 4(3) of Schedule 31 to that Act).

(9) For the purposes of sub-paragraph (5)(e) a tax advantage has been "asserted by reference to" the arrangements if a return, claim or appeal has been made by P on the basis that the tax advantage results from the arrangements.

(10) In this paragraph—

    "arrangements" has the same meaning as in paragraph 3A;

    "avoidance-related rule" has the same meaning as in Part 4 of Schedule 18 to FA 2016 (see paragraph 25 of that Schedule);

    a "tax advantage" includes—

        (a) relief or increased relief from tax,

        (b) repayment or increased repayment of tax,

        (c) avoidance or reduction of a charge to tax or an assessment to tax,

        (d) avoidance of a possible assessment to tax,

        (e) deferral of a payment of tax or advancement of a repayment of tax,

        (f) avoidance of an obligation to deduct or account for tax, and

        (g) in relation to VAT, anything which is a tax advantage for the purposes of Schedule 18 to FA 2016 under paragraph 5 of that Schedule."

(3) In paragraph 18, after sub-paragraph (5) insert—

    "(6) Paragraph 3A applies where a document is given to HMRC on behalf of P as it applies where a document is given to HMRC by P (and in paragraph 3B(9) the reference to P includes a person acting on behalf of P)."

(4) In FA 2014, omit section 276 (which is superseded by the provision inserted by subsections (2) and (3)).

(5) The amendments made by this section have effect in relation to any document of a kind listed in the Table in paragraph 1 of Schedule 24 to FA 2007 which—

    (a) is given to HMRC on or after the day on which this Act is passed, and

    (b) relates to a tax period that—

        (i) begins on or after 6 April 2017, and

        (ii) ends on or after the day on which this Act is passed.

(6) In subsection (5) "tax period", and the reference to giving a document to HMRC, have the same meaning as in Schedule 24 to FA 2007 (see paragraph 28 of that Schedule).

65   Penalties for enablers of defeated tax avoidance

Schedule 16 makes provision for penalties for persons who enable tax avoidance which is defeated.

66   Disclosure of tax avoidance schemes: VAT and other indirect taxes

(1)   Schedule 17 contains provision about the disclosure of tax avoidance schemes involving VAT or other indirect taxes.

(2)   In consequence of the provision made by Schedule 17, section 58A of, and Schedule 11A to, VATA 1994 (disclosure of VAT avoidance schemes) cease to have effect to require a person to disclose any scheme which—

    (a)   is first entered into by that person on or after 1 January 2018,

    (b)   constitutes notifiable arrangements under Schedule 17,

    (c)   implements proposals which are notifiable proposals under Schedule 17.

(3)   No scheme or proposed scheme may be notified to the Commissioners under paragraph 9 of Schedule 11A to VATA 1994 (voluntary notification of schemes) on or after 1 January 2018.

(4)   This section and Schedule 17 come into force—

    (a)   so far as is necessary for enabling the making of regulations under that Schedule, on the passing of this Act, and

    (b)   for all other purposes, on 1 January 2018.

67   Requirement to correct certain offshore tax non-compliance

Schedule 18 makes provision for and in connection with requiring persons to correct any offshore tax non-compliance subsisting on 6 April 2017.

68   Penalty for transactions connected with VAT fraud etc

(1)   VATA 1994 is amended as follows.

(2)   After section 69B (penalty for breach of record-keeping requirements imposed by directions) insert—

"69C   Transactions connected with VAT fraud

(1)   A person (T) is liable to a penalty where—

    (a)   T has entered into a transaction involving the making of a supply by or to T ("the transaction"), and

    (b)   conditions A to C are satisfied.

(2)   Condition A is that the transaction was connected with the fraudulent evasion of VAT by another person (whether occurring before or after T entered into the transaction).

(3)   Condition B is that T knew or should have known that the transaction was connected with the fraudulent evasion of VAT by another person.

(4)   Condition C is that HMRC have issued a decision ("the denial decision") in relation to the supply which—

    (a)   prevents T from exercising or relying on a VAT right in relation to the supply,

    (b)   is based on the facts which satisfy conditions A and B in relation to the transaction, and

    (c)   applies a relevant principle of EU case law (whether or not in circumstances that are the same as the circumstances in which any relevant case was decided by the European Court of Justice).

  (5)   In this section "VAT right" includes the right to deduct input tax, the right to apply a zero rate to international supplies and any other right connected with VAT in relation to a supply.

  (6)   The relevant principles of EU case law for the purposes of this section are the principles established by the European Court of Justice in the following cases —

    (a)   joined Cases C-439/04 and C-440/04 *Axel Kittel v. Belgian State; Belgium v. Recolta Recycling* (denial of right to deduct input tax), and

    (b)   Case C-273/11 *Mecsek-Gabona Kft v Nemzeti Adó- és Vámhivatal Dél-dunántúli Regionális Adó Főigazgatósága* (denial of right to zero rate),

as developed or extended by that Court (whether before or after the coming into force of this section) in other cases relating to the denial or refusal of a VAT right in order to prevent abuses of the VAT system.

  (7)   The penalty payable under this section is 30% of the potential lost VAT.

  (8)   The potential lost VAT is —

    (a)   the additional VAT which becomes payable by T as a result of the denial decision,

    (b)   the VAT which is not repaid to T as a result of that decision, or

    (c)   in a case where as a result of that decision VAT is not repaid to T and additional VAT becomes payable by T, the aggregate of the VAT that is not repaid and the additional VAT.

  (9)   Where T is liable to a penalty under this section the Commissioners may assess the amount of the penalty and notify it to T accordingly.

  (10)   No assessment of a penalty under this section may be made more than two years after the denial decision is issued.

  (11)   The assessment of a penalty under this section may be made immediately after the denial decision is made (and notice of the assessment may be given to T in the same document as the notice of the decision).

  (12)   Where by reason of actions involved in making a claim to exercise or rely on a VAT right in relation to a supply T —

    (a)   is liable to a penalty for an inaccuracy under paragraph 1 of Schedule 24 to the Finance Act 2007 for which T has been assessed (and the assessment has not been successfully appealed against by T or withdrawn), or

    (b)   is convicted of an offence (whether under this Act or otherwise),

those actions do not give rise to liability to a penalty under this section.

69D Penalties under section 69C: officers' liability

  (1)   Where —

      (a)   a company is liable to a penalty under section 69C, and

      (b)   the actions of the company which give rise to that liability were attributable to an officer of the company ("the officer"),

the officer is liable to pay such portion of the penalty (which may be equal to or less than 100%) as HMRC may specify in a notice given to the officer (a "decision notice").

(2)   Before giving the officer a decision notice HMRC must—

      (a)   inform the officer that they are considering doing so, and

      (b)   afford the officer the opportunity to make representations about whether a decision notice should be given or the portion that should be specified.

(3)   A decision notice—

      (a)   may not be given before the amount of the penalty due from the company has been assessed (but it may be given immediately after that has happened), and

      (b)   may not be given more than two years after the denial decision relevant to that penalty was issued.

(4)   Where the Commissioners have specified a portion of the penalty in a decision notice given to the officer—

      (a)   section 70 applies to the specified portion as to a penalty under section 69C,

      (b)   the officer must pay the specified portion before the end of the period of 30 days beginning with the day on which the notice is given,

      (c)   section 76(9) applies as if the decision notice were an assessment notified under section 76, and

      (d)   a further decision notice may be given in respect of a portion of any additional amount assessed in an additional assessment.

(5)   HMRC may not recover more than 100% of the penalty through issuing decision notices in relation to two or more persons.

(6)   A person is not liable to pay an amount by virtue of this section if the actions of the company concerned are attributable to the person by reference to conduct for which the person has been convicted of an offence.

In this subsection "conduct" includes omissions.

(7)   In this section "company" means a body corporate or unincorporated association but does not include a partnership, a local authority or a local authority association.

(8)   In its application to a body corporate other than a limited liability partnership "officer" means—

      (a)   a director (including a shadow director within the meaning of section 251 of the Companies Act 2006),

      (b)   a manager, or

      (c)   a secretary.

(9)   In in its application to a limited liability partnership "officer" means a member.

(10)   In its application in any other case, "officer" means—

   (a) a director,

   (b) a manager,

   (c) a secretary, or

   (d) any other person managing or purporting to manage any of the company's affairs.

69E Publication of details of persons liable to penalties under section 69C

(1) The Commissioners may publish information about a person if—

   (a) in consequence of an investigation the person has been found liable to one or more penalties under section 69C (the amount of which has been assessed), and

   (b) the potential lost VAT in relation to the penalty (or the aggregate of the potential lost VAT in relation to each of the penalties) exceeds £50,000.

(2) The information that may be published under subsection (1) is—

   (a) the person's name (including any trading name, previous name or pseudonym),

   (b) the person's address (or registered office),

   (c) the nature of any business carried on by the person,

   (d) the amount of the penalty or penalties in question,

   (e) the periods or times to which the actions giving rise to the penalty or penalties relate,

   (f) any other information that the Commissioners consider it appropriate to publish in order to make clear the person's identity.

(3) In a case where—

   (a) the requirements in subsection (1)(a) and (b) are met in relation to a penalty or penalties for which a company is liable,

   (b) information about the company is published by virtue of this section,

   (c) a person ("the officer") has been given a decision notice under section 69D specifying a portion of the penalty (or, if there is more than one penalty, of any of the penalties) payable by the company as a portion which the officer is liable to pay, and

   (d) the amount (or, if the decision notice specifies portions of more than one penalty, the aggregate amount) which the officer is liable to pay under the decision notice exceeds £25, 000,

the Commissioners may publish information about the officer.

(4) The information that may be published under subsection (3) is—

   (a) the officer's name,

   (b) the officer's address,

   (c) the officer's position (or former position) in the company,

   (d) the amount of any penalty imposed on the company of which a portion is payable by the officer under the decision notice and the portion so payable,

   (e) the periods or times to which the actions giving rise to any such penalty relate,

      (f)   any other information that the Commissioners consider it appropriate to publish in order to make clear the officer's identity.

(5)   Information published under this section may be published in any manner that the Commissioners consider appropriate.

(6)   Before publishing any information under this section the Commissioners must—

      (a)   inform the person or officer to which it relates that they are considering doing so (in the case of an officer, on the assumption that they publish information about the company), and

      (b)   afford the person or officer the opportunity to make representations about whether it should be published.

(7)   No information may be published under subsection (1) before the day on which the penalty becomes final or, where more than one penalty is involved, the latest day on which any of the penalties becomes final.

(8)   No information may be published under subsection (1) for the first time after the end of the period of one year beginning with that day.

(9)   No information may be published under subsection (3) before whichever is the later of—

      (a)   the day mentioned in subsection (7), and

      (b)   the day on which the decision notice given to the officer becomes final.

(10)   No information may be published under subsection (3) for the first time after the end of the period of one year beginning with the later of the two days mentioned in subsection (9).

(11)   No information may be published (or continue to be published) under subsection (1) or (3) after the end of the period of three years beginning with the day mentioned in subsection (7).

(12)   For the purposes of this section a penalty or a decision notice becomes final when the time for any appeal or further appeal relating to it expires or, if later, any appeal or final appeal relating to it is finally determined.

(13)   The Treasury may by regulations made by statutory instrument—

      (a)   amend subsection (1) to vary the amount for the time being specified in paragraph (b), or

      (b)   amend subsection (3) to vary the amount for the time being specified in paragraph (d).

(14)   A statutory instrument containing regulations under subsection (13) is subject to annulment in pursuance of a resolution of the House of Commons."

(3)   In section 70 (mitigation of penalties)—

      (a)   in the heading, for "and 67" substitute ", 67, 69A and 69C",

      (b)   in subsection (1) for "or 69A" substitute ", 69A or 69C", and

  (c) after subsection (4) insert—

    "(5) In the application of subsections (3) and (4) in relation to a penalty under section 69C, subsection (4) has effect with the omission of paragraphs (b) and (c)."

(4) In section 76 (assessment of amounts due by way of penalty etc), in subsection (1)(b) for "to 69B" (in both places) substitute "to 69C".

(5) In section 83(1) (appeals), after paragraph (n) insert—

    "(na) any liability to a penalty under section 69C, any assessment of a penalty under that section or the amount of such an assessment;

    (nb) the giving of a decision notice under section 69D or the portion of a penalty assessed under section 69C which is specified in such a notice;".

(6) After paragraph 21 of Schedule 24 to FA 2007 (penalties for errors: double jeopardy) insert—

    "21ZA(1) A person is not liable to a penalty under paragraph 1 in respect of an inaccuracy if—

      (a) the inaccuracy involves a claim by the person to exercise or rely on a VAT right (in relation to a supply) that has been denied or refused by HMRC as mentioned in subsection (4) of section 69C of VATA 1994, and

      (b) the person has been assessed to a penalty under that section (and the assessment has not been successfully appealed against or withdrawn).

    (2) In sub-paragraph (1)(a) "VAT right" has the same meaning as in section 69C of VATA 1994."

(7) Section 69C does not apply in relation to transactions entered into before this section comes into force.

Information

69 Data-gathering from money service businesses

(1) In Part 2 of Schedule 23 to FA 2011 (data-gathering powers: relevant data-holders), after paragraph 13C insert—

  "Money service businesses

  13D (1) A person is a relevant data-holder if the person—

    (a) carries on any of the activities in sub-paragraph (2) by way of business,

    (b) is a relevant person within the meaning of regulation 8(1) of the Money Laundering, Terrorist Financing and Transfer of Funds (Information on the Payer) Regulations 2017 (S.I. 2017/692), and

    (c) is not an excluded credit institution.

  (2) The activities referred to in sub-paragraph (1)(a) are—

    (a) operating a currency exchange office;

      (b)   transmitting money (or any representation of monetary value) by any means;

      (c)   cashing cheques which are made payable to customers.

(3) An excluded credit institution is a credit institution which has permission to carry on the regulated activity of accepting deposits—

      (a)   under Part 4A of the Financial Services and Markets Act 2000 (permission to carry on regulated activities), or

      (b)   resulting from Part 2 of Schedule 3 to that Act (exercise of passport rights by EEA firms).

(4) Sub-paragraph (3) is to be read with section 22 of and Schedule 2 to the Financial Services and Markets Act 2000, and any order under that section (classes of regulated activities).

(5) In this paragraph "credit institution" has the meaning given by Article 4.1(1) of Regulation (EU) No 575/2013 of the European Parliament and of the Council of 26 June 2013 on prudential requirements for credit institutions and investment firms."

(2) This section applies in relation to relevant data with a bearing on any period (whether before, on or after the day on which this Act is passed).

PART 5

FINAL

70 Northern Ireland welfare payments: updating statutory reference

In section 44(2) of FA 2016 (tax treatment of supplementary welfare payments: Northern Ireland) for "the Housing Benefit (Amendment) Regulations (Northern Ireland) 2016 (S.R. (N.I.) 2016 No. 258)" substitute "the Housing Benefit (Amendment No. 2) Regulations (Northern Ireland) 2016 (S.R. (N.I.) 2016 No. 326)".

71 Interpretation

In this Act the following abbreviations are references to the following Acts.

CAA 2001	Capital Allowances Act 2001
CEMA 1979	Customs and Excise Management Act 1979
CTA 2009	Corporation Tax Act 2009
CTA 2010	Corporation Tax Act 2010
CT(NI)A 2015	Corporation Tax (Northern Ireland) Act 2015
FA, followed by a year	Finance Act of that year
F(No.2)A, followed by a year	Finance (No.2) Act of that year
F(No.3)A, followed by a year	Finance (No.3) Act of that year

ICTA	Income and Corporation Taxes Act 1988
ICTA	Income and Corporation Taxes Act 1988
IHTA 1984	Inheritance Tax Act 1984
ITA 2007	Income Tax Act 2007
ITEPA 2003	Income Tax (Earnings and Pensions) Act 2003
ITTOIA 2005	Income Tax (Trading and Other Income) Act 2005
OTA 1975	Oil Taxation Act 1975
TCGA 1992	Taxation of Chargeable Gains Act 1992
TIOPA 2010	Taxation (International and Other Provisions) Act 2010
TMA 1970	Taxes Management Act 1970
TPDA 1979	Tobacco Products Duty Act 1979
VATA 1994	Value Added Tax Act 1994

72   Short title

This Act may be cited as the Finance (No. 2) Act 2017.

SCHEDULES

SCHEDULE 1

Section 14

SOCIAL INVESTMENT TAX RELIEF

PART 1

AMENDMENTS OF PART 5B OF ITA 2007

Introductory

1   ITA 2007 is amended as follows.

Date by which investment must be made to qualify for SI relief

2   In section 257K(1)(a)(iii) (date by which investment must be made to qualify
for SI relief) for "6 April 2019" substitute "6 April 2021".

The existing investments requirement

3   After section 257LD insert —

"257LDA The existing investments requirement

(1)   If at the time immediately before the investment is made the investor
holds any shares in or debentures of —
(a)   the social enterprise, or
(b)   a company which at that time is a qualifying subsidiary of the
social enterprise,
those shares or debentures must be risk finance investments or (in
the case of shares) permitted subscriber shares.

(2)   A share or debenture is a "risk finance investment" for the purposes
of this section if —
(a)   it is a share that was issued to the investor, or a debenture of
which the investor is the holder in return for advancing an
amount, and
(b)   at any time, a compliance statement under section 205, 257ED
or 257PB is provided in respect of it or of shares or
investments including it.

(3)   Subscriber shares are "permitted subscriber shares" for the purposes
of this section if —
(a)   they were issued to the investor and have been continuously
held by the investor since they were issued, or
(b)   they were acquired by the investor at a time when the
company which issued them —

94   *Finance (No. 2) Act 2017 (c. **32**)*
Schedule 1 – Social investment tax relief
Part 1 – Amendments of Part 5B of ITA 2007

       (i)   had issued no shares other than subscriber shares, and

       (ii)   had not begun to carry on or make preparations for carrying on any trade or business.

(4)   In this section "debenture" is to be read in accordance with section 257L(6)."

The no disqualifying arrangements requirement

4   After section 257LE insert—

"257LEA The no disqualifying arrangements requirement

(1)   The investment must not be made, and money raised by the social enterprise from the making of the investment must not be employed,—

    (a)   in consequence or anticipation of disqualifying arrangements, or

    (b)   otherwise in connection with disqualifying arrangements.

(2)   Arrangements are "disqualifying arrangements" if—

    (a)   the main purpose, or one of the main purposes, of the arrangements is to secure both that an activity is or will be carried on by the social enterprise or a 90% social subsidiary of the social enterprise and that—

       (i)   one or more persons (whether or not including any party to the arrangements) may obtain relevant tax relief in respect of a qualifying investment which raises money for the purposes of that activity, or

       (ii)   shares issued by the social enterprise which raise money for the purposes of that activity may comprise part of the qualifying holdings of a VCT,

    (b)   that activity is the relevant qualifying activity, and

    (c)   one or both of conditions A and B are met.

(3)   Condition A is that, as a (direct or indirect) result of the money raised by the investment being employed as required by section 257MM, an amount representing the whole or the majority of the amount raised is, in the course of the arrangements, paid to or for the benefit of a relevant person or relevant persons.

(4)   Condition B is that, in the absence of the arrangements, it would have been reasonable to expect that the whole or greater part of the component activities of the relevant qualifying activity would have been carried on as part of another business by a relevant person or relevant persons.

(5)   For the purposes of this section it is immaterial whether the social enterprise is a party to the arrangements.

(6)   In this section—

       "90% social subsidiary" is to be read in accordance with section 257MV;

Finance (No. 2) Act 2017 (c. 32)
Schedule 1 — Social investment tax relief
Part 1 — Amendments of Part 5B of ITA 2007

95

"component activities" means the carrying on of a qualifying trade or preparing to carry on such a trade, which constitutes the relevant qualifying activity;

a "qualifying investment" means—

(a) shares in the social enterprise, or

(b) a qualifying debt investment in the social enterprise (see section 257L);

"qualifying holdings", in relation to the social enterprise, is to be construed in accordance with section 286 (VCTs: qualifying holdings);

"relevant person" means a person who is a party to the arrangements or a person connected with such a party;

"relevant qualifying activity" means the qualifying trade or activity mentioned in section 257ML(1) for the purposes of which the investment raised money;

"relevant tax relief" has the meaning given by subsection (7).

(7) "Relevant tax relief"—

(a) in relation to a qualifying debt investment, means SI relief in respect of that investment;

(b) in relation to shares, means one or more of the following—

(i) SI relief in respect of the shares;

(ii) EIS relief (within the meaning of Part 5) in respect of the shares;

(iii) SEIS relief (within the meaning of Part 5A) in respect of the shares;

(iv) relief under Chapter 6 of Part 4 (losses on disposal of shares) in respect of the shares;

(v) relief under section 150A or 150E of TCGA 1992 (EIS and SEIS) in respect of the shares;

(vi) relief under Schedule 5B to that Act (EIS: reinvestment) in consequence of which deferral relief is attributable to the shares (see paragraph 19(2) of that Schedule);

(vii) relief under Schedule 5BB to that Act (SEIS: re-investment) in consequence of which SEIS re-investment relief is attributable to the shares (see paragraph 4 of that Schedule)."

5 (1) Section 257SH (power to require information where reason to believe SI relief may not be due because of certain kinds of arrangements, etc) is amended as follows.

(2) In subsection (1) after "257LE," insert "257LEA,".

96

Finance (No. 2) Act 2017 (c. 32)
Schedule 1 — Social investment tax relief
Part 1 — Amendments of Part 5B of ITA 2007

(3) In subsection (4) at the appropriate place insert—

"Section 257LEA	The investor, the social enterprise, any person controlling the social enterprise and any person whom an officer of Revenue and Customs has reason to believe may be a party to the arrangements in question"

Limits on amounts that may be invested

6   (1)   In the italic heading before section 257M, after "enterprise" insert ": general".

(2)   Omit sections 257MA and 257MB (which are superseded by the provision inserted by sub-paragraph (3) below).

(3)   After section 257MN insert—

"Limits on amounts that may be invested

257MNA Maximum amount where investment made in first 7 years

(1)   This section applies where—
    (a)   the investment is made before the end of the period of 7 years beginning with the relevant first commercial sale, or
    (b)   the investment is made after that period but—
        (i)   a relevant investment was made in the social enterprise before the end of that period, and
        (ii)   some or all of the money raised by that relevant investment was employed for the purposes of (or of part of) the qualifying activity for which the money raised by the investment is employed.

(2)   Where this section applies, the total amount of relevant investments made in the social enterprise on or before the date when the investment is made must not exceed £1.5 million.

(3)   The reference in subsection (2) to relevant investments "made in the social enterprise" is to be read with section 257MNB.

(4)   In this section—
    "qualifying activity" means—
        (a)   a qualifying trade within paragraph (a) of section 257ML(1) carried on by the social enterprise or a 90% social subsidiary of the social enterprise, or
        (b)   an activity within paragraph (b) of section 257ML(1) so carried on;
    "the relevant first commercial sale" has the meaning given by section 175A(6), reading—
        (a)   references to the issuing company as references to the social enterprise,
        (b)   references to the issue date as references to the investment date, and

Finance (No. 2) Act 2017 (c. 32)
Schedule 1 — Social investment tax relief
Part 1 — Amendments of Part 5B of ITA 2007

97

      (c)   references to money raised by the issue of the relevant shares as references to money raised by the investment;

"relevant investment" has the meaning given by section 173A(3) (reading references in section 173A(3) to a company as including any social enterprise).

(5)   Section 173A(4) and (5) apply to determine for the purposes of this section when a relevant investment is made.

(6)   Where the social enterprise is an accredited social impact contractor—

      (a)   the reference in subsection (1)(a) to the relevant first commercial sale is to be read as a reference to the date on which the social enterprise first entered into a social impact contract;

      (b)   the reference in subsection (1)(b) to the qualifying activity mentioned there is to be read as a reference to the carrying out of the social impact contract for which the money raised by the investment is employed.

(7)   For provision about maximum amounts where this section does not apply, see section 257MNC.

257MNB Section 257MNA: supplementary

(1)   In section 257MNA(2) the reference to relevant investments "made in the social enterprise" includes—

      (a)   relevant investments made in a company which, at the material date, is or has been a 51% subsidiary of the social enterprise,

      (b)   any other relevant investment made in a company to the extent that the money raised by that relevant investment has been employed for the purposes of a trade carried on by another company ("company X") which, at the material date, is or has been a 51% subsidiary of the social enterprise, and

      (c)   any other relevant investment made in a company if—

          (i)   the money raised by that relevant investment has been employed for the purposes of a trade carried on by that company or another person, and

         (ii)   after that relevant investment was made, but on or before the material date, that trade became a transferred trade (see subsection (5)).

(2)   The investments within paragraph (a) of subsection (1)—

      (a)   include investments made in a company mentioned in that paragraph before it became a 51% subsidiary of the social enterprise, but

      (b)   where a company mentioned in that paragraph is not a 51% subsidiary of the social enterprise at the material date, do not include any investments made in that company after it last ceased to be such a subsidiary.

(3)   For the purposes of subsection (1)(b), where company X is not a 51% subsidiary of the social enterprise at the material date, any money

98   *Finance (No. 2) Act 2017 (c. 32)*
Schedule 1 — Social investment tax relief
Part 1 — Amendments of Part 5B of ITA 2007

employed after company X last ceased to be such a subsidiary is to be ignored.

(4) Where only a proportion of the money raised by a relevant investment is employed for the purposes of a trade which becomes a transferred trade, only the corresponding proportion of that relevant investment is to be treated as falling within subsection (1)(c).

(5) For the purposes of this section, if—

  (a) on or before the material date a trade is transferred—

    (i) to the social enterprise,

    (ii) to a company which, at the material date, is or has been a 51% subsidiary of the social enterprise, or

    (iii) to a partnership of which the social enterprise, or a company within sub-paragraph (ii), is a member, and

  (b) the trade or part of it was at any time before the transfer carried on by another person,

the trade or part mentioned in paragraph (b) becomes a "transferred trade" when it is transferred as mentioned in paragraph (a).

(6) The cases within subsection (5)(a)—

  (a) include the case where the trade is transferred to a company within subsection (5)(a)(ii), or a partnership of which such a company is a member, before the company became a 51% subsidiary of the social enterprise, but

  (b) where a company within subsection (5)(a)(ii) is not a 51% subsidiary of the social enterprise at the material date, do not include the case where the trade is transferred to that company, or a partnership of which that company is a member, after that company last ceased to be such a subsidiary.

(7) In this section—

  "the material date" means the date on which the investment is made;

  "relevant investment" has the meaning given by section 173A(3) (reading references in section 173A(3) to a company as including any social enterprise).

(8) Section 173A(4) and (5) apply to determine for the purposes of this section when a relevant investment is made.

(9) Section 173A(6) and (7) (meaning of "trade" etc) apply also for the purposes of this section.

257MNC Maximum amount for cases outside section 257MNA

(1) This section applies where—

  (a) the investment is made at any time after the period mentioned in section 257MNA(1)(a), and

  (b) it is not the case that the conditions in section 257MNA(1)(b)(i) and (ii) are met.

(2) Where this section applies—

Finance (No. 2) Act 2017 (c. 32)
Schedule 1 — Social investment tax relief
Part 1 — Amendments of Part 5B of ITA 2007

99

    (a)   the total amount of relevant investments made in the social enterprise on or before the date when the investment is made must not exceed £1.5 million, and

    (b)   the amount invested must not be more than the amount mentioned in subsection (3).

(3)   That amount is the amount given by the formula —

$$\left(\frac{\text{€200,000} - \text{M}}{\text{RCG} + \text{RSI}}\right) - \text{T}$$

where —

    T is the total of any relevant investments made in the social enterprise in the aid period,

    M is the total of any de minimis aid, other than relevant investments, that is granted during the aid period —

        (a)   to the social enterprise, or

        (b)   to a qualifying subsidiary of the social enterprise at a time when it is such a subsidiary,

    RCG is the highest rate at which capital gains tax is charged in the aid period, and

    RSI is the highest SI rate in the aid period.

(4)   In subsection (3) "the aid period" means the 3 years —

    (a)   ending with the day on which the investment is made, but

    (b)   in the case of that day, including only the part of the day before the investment is made.

(5)   In this section "de minimis aid" means de minimis aid which fulfils the conditions laid down —

    (a)   in Commission Regulation (EU) No. 1407/2013 (de minimis aid) as amended from time to time, or

    (b)   in any EU instrument from time to time replacing the whole or any part of that Regulation.

(6)   For the purposes of subsection (3), the amount of any de minimis aid is the amount of the grant or, if the aid is not in the form of a grant, the gross grant equivalent amount within the meaning of that Regulation as amended from time to time.

(7)   For the purposes of subsection (3), if —

    (a)   the investment or any relevant investment is made, or

    (b)   any aid is granted,

in sterling or any other currency that is not the euro, its amount is to be converted into euros at an appropriate spot rate of exchange for the date on which the investment is made or the aid is paid.

(8)   In this section "relevant investment" has the meaning given by section 173A(3) (reading references in section 173A(3) to a company as including any social enterprise).

(9)   Section 173A(4) and (5) apply to determine for the purposes of this section when a relevant investment is made.

(10)   Section 257MNB (which expands the meaning of "relevant investments made in the social enterprise") applies for the purposes

100   *Finance (No. 2) Act 2017 (c. **32**)*
Schedule 1 — Social investment tax relief
Part 1 — Amendments of Part 5B of ITA 2007

of each of subsections (2) and (3) above as it applies for the purposes of section 257MNA(2).

257MND Limit on investment in shorter applicable period

(1)   This section applies where condition A or condition B is met.

(2)   Condition A is that—

    (a)   a company becomes a 51% subsidiary of the social enterprise at any time during the shorter applicable period,

    (b)   all or part of the money raised by the investment is employed for the purposes of a qualifying activity which consists wholly or partly of a trade carried on by that company, and

    (c)   that trade (or part of it) was carried on by that company before it became a 51% subsidiary as mentioned in paragraph (a).

(3)   Condition B is that all or part of the money raised by the investment is employed for the purposes of a qualifying activity which consists wholly or partly of a trade which, during the shorter applicable period, becomes a transferred trade (see subsection (9)).

(4)   Where this section applies, at each time in the shorter applicable period ("the relevant time") the total of the relevant investments made in the social enterprise before that time must not exceed £1.5 million.

(5)   In subsection (4) the reference to relevant investments "made in the social enterprise" includes—

    (a)   relevant investments made in a company which at any time before the relevant time has been a 51% subsidiary of the social enterprise,

    (b)   any other relevant investment made in a company to the extent that the money raised by that relevant investment has been employed for the purposes of a trade carried on by another company ("company X") which at any time before the relevant time has been a 51% subsidiary of the social enterprise, and

    (c)   any other relevant investment made in a company if—

        (i)   the money raised by that relevant investment has been employed for the purposes of a trade carried on by that company or another person, and

        (ii)   after that relevant investment was made, but before the relevant time, that trade (or part of it) became a transferred trade.

(6)   The investments within paragraph (a) of subsection (5)—

    (a)   include investments made in a company mentioned in that paragraph before it became a 51% subsidiary of the social enterprise, but

    (b)   where a company mentioned in that paragraph is not a 51% subsidiary of the social enterprise at the relevant time, do not include any investments made in that company after it last ceased to be such a subsidiary.

Finance (No. 2) Act 2017 (c. 32)
Schedule 1 — Social investment tax relief
Part 1 — Amendments of Part 5B of ITA 2007

101

(7) For the purposes of subsection (5)(b), where company X is not a 51% subsidiary of the social enterprise at the relevant time, any money employed after company X last ceased to be such a subsidiary is to be ignored.

(8) Where only a proportion of the money raised by a relevant investment is employed for the purposes of a trade which becomes a transferred trade, only the corresponding proportion of that relevant investment is to be treated as falling within subsection (5)(c).

(9) For the purposes of this section, if—
   (a) before the relevant time, a trade is transferred—
       (i) to the social enterprise,
       (ii) to a company which, at the relevant time, is or has been a 51% subsidiary of the social enterprise, or
       (iii) to a partnership of which the social enterprise, or a company within sub-paragraph (ii), is a member, and
   (b) the trade or part of it was at any time before the transfer carried on by another person,
   the trade or part mentioned in paragraph (b) becomes a "transferred trade" when it is transferred as mentioned in paragraph (a).

(10) The cases within subsection (9)(a)—
   (a) include the case where the trade is transferred to a company within subsection (9)(a)(ii), or a partnership of which such a company is a member, before the company became a 51% subsidiary of the social enterprise, but
   (b) where a company within subsection (9)(a)(ii) is not a 51% subsidiary of the social enterprise at the relevant time, do not include the case where the trade is transferred to that company, or a partnership of which that company is a member, after that company last ceased to be such a subsidiary.

(11) In this section—
   "qualifying activity" has the same meaning as in section 257MNA (see subsection (4) of that section);
   "relevant investment" has the meaning given by section 173A(3) (reading references in section 173A(3) to a company as including any social enterprise).

(12) Section 173A(4) and (5) apply to determine for the purposes of this section when a relevant investment is made.

(13) Section 173A(6) and (7) (meaning of "trade" etc) apply also for the purposes of this section.

257MNE Power to amend limits on amounts that may be invested

(1) The Treasury may by regulations substitute a different figure for the figure for the time being specified in section 257MNA(2), 257MNC(2) or (3) or 257MND(4).

(2) Regulations under this section may make incidental, supplemental, consequential, transitional or saving provision.

102   *Finance (No. 2) Act 2017 (c. 32)*
Schedule 1 — Social investment tax relief
Part 1 — Amendments of Part 5B of ITA 2007

      (3)   Regulations under this section may not be made unless a draft of the instrument containing them has been laid before, and approved by a resolution of, the House of Commons."

  (4) In section 1014 (orders and regulations), in subsection (5)(b) (orders and regulations excluded from subsection (4)) for sub-paragraph (iiia) substitute—

        "(iiia)   section 257MNE (social investment relief: amendment of limits on investments),".

Number of employees limit

7   In section 257MH (the number of employees requirement), in each of subsections (1) and (2) for "500" substitute "250".

Financial health requirement

8   After section 257MI insert—

  "257MIA The financial health requirement

      (1)   The social enterprise must meet the financial health requirement at the beginning of the shorter applicable period.

      (2)   The financial health requirement is that the social enterprise is not in difficulty.

      (3)   The social enterprise is "in difficulty" if it is reasonable to assume that it would be regarded as a firm in difficulty for the purposes of the Community Guidelines on State Aid for Rescuing and Restructuring Firms in Difficulty (2004/C 244/02)."

Purposes for which money raised can be used

9   (1) Section 257MM (requirement to use money raised and to trade for minimum period) is amended as follows.

  (2) After subsection (3) insert—

    "(3A)   Employing money on the repayment of a loan does not amount to employing the money for the funded purpose."

  (3) In subsection (7)(c) after "(3)," insert "(3A),".

Excluded activities

10   (1) Section 257MQ (meaning of "excluded activity") is amended as set out in sub-paragraphs (2) to (4).

  (2) In subsection (1)—
      (a)   in paragraph (b) omit "(but see subsection (2))";
      (b)   after paragraph (b) insert—
          "(ba)   leasing (including letting ships on charter or other assets on hire),
          (bb)   receiving royalties or licence fees,

Finance (No. 2) Act 2017 (c. 32)
Schedule 1 — Social investment tax relief
Part 1 — Amendments of Part 5B of ITA 2007

103

> > (bc) operating or managing nursing homes or residential care homes or managing property used as a nursing home or residential care home (see section 257MQA),
> > (bd) generating electricity, exporting electricity (see subsection (3)) or making electricity generating capacity available,
> > (be) generating heat,
> > (bf) generating any form of energy not within paragraph (bd) or (be),
> > (bg) producing gas or fuel,";
> (c) omit paragraph (f) (subsidised generation or export of electricity).

(3) Omit subsection (2).

(4) After subsection (2) insert —

> "(3) For the purposes of subsection (1)(bd) electricity is exported if it is exported onto a distribution system or transmission system (within the meaning of section 4 of the Electricity Act 1989)."

(5) After section 257MQ insert —

"257MQA Excluded activities: nursing homes and residential care homes

> (1) This section supplements section 257MQ(1)(bc).
>
> (2) "Nursing home" means any establishment which exists wholly or mainly for the provision of nursing care —
> > (a) for persons suffering from sickness, injury or infirmity, or
> > (b) for women who are pregnant or have given birth.
>
> (3) "Residential care home" means any establishment which exists wholly or mainly for the provision of residential accommodation, together with board and personal care, for persons in need of personal care because of —
> > (a) old age,
> > (b) mental or physical disability,
> > (c) past or present dependence on alcohol or drugs,
> > (d) any past illnesses, or
> > (e) past or present mental disorder.
>
> (4) The activities of a person are not to be taken to fall within section 257MQ(1)(bc) unless that person has an estate or interest in, or is in occupation of, the nursing home or residential care home in question."

(6) Omit section 257MS (subsidised generation or export of electricity).

PART 2

CONSEQUENTIAL AMENDMENTS

11 (1) ITA 2007 is amended as follows.

(2) In section 178A (EIS: the no disqualifying arrangements requirement), in subsection (6), in the definition of "relevant tax relief" after paragraph (b)

insert—

"(ba) SI relief under Part 5B in respect of the shares;".

(3) In section 257CF (SEIS: the no disqualifying arrangements requirement), in subsection (6), in the definition of "relevant tax relief" after paragraph (b) insert—

"(ba) SI relief under Part 5B in respect of the shares;".

(4) In section 299A (VCTs: the no disqualifying arrangements requirement), in subsection (6), in the definition of "relevant tax relief" after paragraph (c) insert—

"(ca) SI relief (within the meaning of Part 5B) in respect of the shares;".

12 In Schedule 6 to FA 2015 (investment reliefs: excluded activities) omit paragraph 13 (which is superseded by paragraph 10 of this Schedule).

13 In Part 2 of Schedule 24 to FA 2016 (tax advantages about which information may be obtained from certain persons), after the entry relating to relief granted to investors in a company under the enterprise investment scheme insert—

"Relief granted to investors in a social enterprise	Part 5B of ITA 2007	The social enterprise"

PART 3

COMMENCEMENT

14 (1) The amendments made by paragraphs 3 and 6 to 9 have effect in relation to investments made on or after 6 April 2017.

(2) Nothing in sub-paragraph (1) prevents investments made before 6 April 2017 from constituting "relevant investments" for any purpose of section 257MNA, 257MNB, 257MNC or 257MND of ITA 2007.

(3) Subject to sub-paragraph (4), the amendments made by paragraphs 4 and 5 have effect in relation to investments made on or after 6 April 2017.

(4) Arrangements which include any transaction entered into before 6 April 2017 are not "disqualifying arrangements" for the purposes of section 257LEA of ITA 2007.

15 The amendments made by paragraph 10—
(a) so far as they apply for the purposes of section 257JD of ITA 2007, come into force on 6 April 2017;
(b) so far as they apply for the purposes of sections 257MJ and 257MP of ITA 2007, have effect in relation to investments made on or after 6 April 2017.

16 (1) Subject to sub-paragraph (3), the amendments made by paragraph 11(2) and (3) have effect in relation to shares issued on or after 6 April 2017.

(2) Subject to sub-paragraph (3), the amendment made by paragraph 11(4) has effect for the purpose of determining whether shares or securities issued on

or after 6 April 2017 are to be regarded as comprised in a company's qualifying holdings.

(3) The amendments made by paragraph 11 do not have effect for the purposes of determining any question whether particular arrangements which include any transaction entered into before 6 April 2017 are "disqualifying arrangements" for the purposes of section 178A, 257CF or 299A of ITA 2007.

SCHEDULE 2   Section 16

TRADES AND PROPERTY BUSINESSES: CALCULATION OF PROFITS

PART 1

TRADES ETC: AMENDMENTS OF ITTOIA 2005

1   ITTOIA 2005 is amended as follows.

2   For section 33A (cash basis: capital expenditure) substitute —

"33A Cash basis: capital expenditure

(1) This section applies in relation to the calculation of the profits of a trade on the cash basis.

(2) No deduction is allowed for an item of a capital nature incurred on, or in connection with, the acquisition or disposal of a business or part of a business.

(3) No deduction is allowed for an item of a capital nature incurred on, or in connection with, education or training.

(4) No deduction is allowed for an item of a capital nature incurred on, or in connection with, the provision, alteration or disposal of —
   (a) any asset that is not a depreciating asset (see subsections (6) and (7)),
   (b) any asset not acquired or created for use on a continuing basis in the trade,
   (c) a car (see subsection (14)),
   (d) land,
   (e) a non-qualifying intangible asset (see subsections (8) to (11)), or
   (f) a financial asset (see subsection (12)).

(5) But subsection (4)(d) does not prevent a deduction being made for expenditure that —
   (a) is incurred on the provision of a depreciating asset which, in being provided, is installed or otherwise fixed to land so as to become, in law, part of the land, but
   (b) is not incurred on, or in connection with, the provision of —
      (i) a building,
      (ii) a wall, floor, ceiling, door, gate, shutter or window or stairs,
      (iii) a waste disposal system,

106

Finance (No. 2) Act 2017 (c. 32)
Schedule 2 — Trades and property businesses: calculation of profits
Part 1 — Trades etc: amendments of ITTOIA 2005

        (iv)   a sewerage or drainage system, or

        (v)   a shaft or other structure in which a lift, hoist, escalator or moving walkway may be installed.

(6)   An asset is a "depreciating" asset if, on the date the item of a capital nature is incurred, it is reasonable to expect that before the end of 20 years beginning with that date —

        (a)   the useful life of the asset will end, or

        (b)   the asset will decline in value by 90% or more.

(7)   The useful life of an asset ends when it could no longer be of use to any person for any purpose as an asset of a business.

(8)   "Intangible asset" means anything that is capable of being an intangible asset within the meaning of FRS 105 and, in particular, includes —

        (a)   an internally-generated intangible asset, and

        (b)   intellectual property.

(9)   An intangible asset is "non-qualifying" unless, by virtue of having a fixed maximum duration, it must cease to exist before the end of 20 years beginning with the date on which the item of a capital nature is incurred.

(10)   An intangible asset is "non-qualifying" if it consists of a right, whether conditional or not, to obtain an intangible asset without a fixed maximum duration by virtue of which that asset must, assuming the right is exercised at the last possible time, cease to exist before the end of 20 years beginning with the date on which the item of a capital nature is incurred.

(11)   Where —

        (a)   the trader has an intangible asset, and

        (b)   the trader grants a licence or any other right in respect of that asset to another person,

any intangible asset that consists of a licence or other right granted to the trader in respect of the intangible asset mentioned in paragraph (a) is "non-qualifying".

(12)   A "financial asset" means any right under or in connection with —

        (a)   a financial instrument, or

        (b)   an arrangement that is capable of producing a return that is economically equivalent to a return produced under any financial instrument.

(13)   A reference to acquisition, provision, alteration or disposal includes potential acquisition, provision, alteration or (as the case may be) disposal.

(14)   In this section —

        "arrangement" includes any agreement, understanding, scheme, transaction or series of transactions (whether or not legally enforceable);

        "building" includes any fixed structure;

        "car" has the same meaning as in Part 2 of CAA 2001 (see section 268A of that Act);

Finance (No. 2) Act 2017 (c. 32)
Schedule 2 — Trades and property businesses: calculation of profits
Part 1 — Trades etc: amendments of ITTOIA 2005

107

"financial instrument" has the same meaning as in FRS 105;

"FRS 105" means Financial Reporting Standard 105 (the Financial Reporting Standard applicable to the Micro-entities Regime), issued by the Financial Reporting Council in July 2015;

"intellectual property" means—

    (a) any patent, trade mark, registered design, copyright or design right, plant breeders' rights or rights under section 7 of the Plant Varieties Act 1997,

    (b) any right under the law of a country or territory outside the United Kingdom corresponding or similar to a right within paragraph (a),

    (c) any information or technique not protected by a right within paragraph (a) or (b) but having industrial, commercial or other economic value, or

    (d) any licence or other right in respect of anything within paragraph (a), (b) or (c);

"provision" includes creation, construction or acquisition;

"the trader" means the person carrying on the trade."

3   In section 95A (application of Chapter 6 of Part 2 (trade profits: receipts) to the cash basis)—

    (a) the existing text becomes subsection (1),

    (b) in that subsection, omit the entry relating to section 96A, and

    (c) after that subsection insert—

    "(2) Section 96A makes provision about capital receipts in certain cases where the profits of a trade are calculated on the cash basis or have previously been calculated on the cash basis (and see also section 96B)."

4   (1) Section 96A (cash basis: capital receipts) is amended as follows.

    (2) For the heading substitute "Capital receipts under, or after leaving, cash basis".

    (3) For subsections (1) to (3) substitute—

    "(1) This section applies in relation to a trade carried on by a person in two cases—

        (a) Case 1 (see subsections (2) to (3A)), and

        (b) Case 2 (see subsections (3B) to (3E)).

    (2) Case 1 is a case in which conditions A and B are met.

    (3) Condition A is that the person receives disposal proceeds or a capital refund in relation to an asset at a time when an election under section 25A (cash basis for trades) has effect in relation to the trade.

    For the meaning of "disposal proceeds" and "capital refund" see subsections (3F) and (3G).

    (3A) Condition B is that—

        (a) an amount of capital expenditure (see subsection (3H)) relating to the asset has been brought into account in calculating the profits of the trade on the cash basis, or

108   *Finance (No. 2) Act 2017 (c. 32)*
Schedule 2 — Trades and property businesses: calculation of profits
Part 1 — Trades etc: amendments of ITTOIA 2005

      (b)   an amount of capital expenditure relating to the asset which —

          (i)   has been incurred (or treated as incurred) by the person before the tax year for which the person last entered the cash basis, and

          (ii)   is cash basis deductible in relation to that tax year (see section 96B(4)),

has been brought into account in calculating the profits of the trade for a tax year for which no election under section 25A had effect in relation to the trade.

The reference in this paragraph to expenditure brought into account includes a reference to expenditure brought into account under CAA 2001 (see section 96B(5)).

(3B)   Case 2 is a case in which —

      (a)   condition C is met, and

      (b)   condition D or E is met.

(3C)   Condition C is that disposal proceeds or a capital refund arise to the person in relation to an asset at a time —

      (a)   when no election under section 25A has effect in relation to the trade, and

      (b)   which is after a time when such an election had had effect in relation to the trade.

(3D)   Condition D is that an amount of capital expenditure relating to the asset —

      (a)   has been paid at a time when an election under section 25A had effect in relation to the trade,

      (b)   has been brought into account in calculating the profits of the trade on the cash basis, and

      (c)   on the assumption that an election under section 25A had not had effect at the time the expenditure was paid, would not have been qualifying expenditure.

(3E)   Condition E is that an amount of capital expenditure relating to the asset has been brought into account in calculating the profits of the trade for a tax year —

      (a)   for which no election under section 25A had effect in relation to the trade, and

      (b)   which is before the tax year for which the person last entered the cash basis.

The reference in this subsection to expenditure brought into account does not include a reference to expenditure brought into account under CAA 2001 (see section 96B(5)).

(3F)   "Disposal proceeds" means —

      (a)   any proceeds arising from the disposal of an asset or any part of it,

      (b)   any proceeds arising from the grant of any right in respect of, or any interest in, the asset, or

      (c)   any amount of damages, proceeds of insurance or other compensation received in respect of the asset.

Finance (No. 2) Act 2017 (c. 32)
Schedule 2 — Trades and property businesses: calculation of profits
Part 1 — Trades etc: amendments of ITTOIA 2005

109

See also subsections (4) and (5) for circumstances in which a person is to be regarded as disposing of an asset.

(3G)   "Capital refund" means an amount that is (in substance) a refund of capital expenditure relating to an asset.

(3H)   "Capital expenditure" means expenditure of a capital nature incurred, or treated as incurred, on or in connection with —

    (a)   the provision, alteration or disposal of an asset, or

    (b)   the potential provision, alteration or disposal of an asset.

(3I)   The disposal proceeds or capital refund mentioned in condition A or (as the case may be) condition C are to be brought into account as a receipt in calculating the profits of the trade.

(3J)   In a case where only part of the total capital expenditure incurred, or treated as incurred, by the person in relation to the asset has been brought into account in calculating the profits of the trade (whether or not on the cash basis), the amount brought into account under subsection (3I) is proportionately reduced.

The reference in this subsection to expenditure brought into account includes a reference to expenditure brought into account under CAA 2001 (see section 96B(5)).

(3K)   Subsection (3I) does not apply if the whole of the amount which would otherwise be brought into account under that subsection —

    (a)   has already been brought into account as a receipt in calculating the profits of the trade under this section,

    (b)   is brought into account as a receipt in calculating the profits of the trade under any other provision of this Part (except section 240D(3) (assets not fully paid for)), or

    (c)   is brought into account under any Part of CAA 2001 as a disposal value.

(3L)   If part of the amount which would otherwise be brought into account under subsection (3I) has already been or is brought into account as mentioned in subsection (3K), subsection (3I) applies in relation to the remainder of that amount."

(4) Omit subsection (7).

5   After section 96A insert —

"96B   Section 96A: supplementary provision

(1)   This section has effect for the purposes of section 96A.

(2)   Any question as to whether or to what extent expenditure is brought into account in calculating the profits of a trade is to be determined on such basis as is just and reasonable in all the circumstances.

(3)   A person carrying on a trade "enters the cash basis" for a tax year if —

    (a)   an election under section 25A has effect in relation to the trade for the tax year, and

    (b)   no such election had effect in relation to the trade for the previous tax year.

110

Finance (No. 2) Act 2017 (c. 32)
Schedule 2 — Trades and property businesses: calculation of profits
Part 1 — Trades etc: amendments of ITTOIA 2005

(4) Expenditure is "cash basis deductible" in relation to a tax year if, on the assumption that the expenditure was paid in that tax year, a deduction would be allowed in respect of the expenditure in calculating the profits of the trade on the cash basis for that tax year.

(5) Expenditure is "brought into account under CAA 2001" in calculating the profits of a trade if and to the extent that—

    (a) a capital allowance made under Part 2, 5, 6, 7 or 8 of that Act in respect of the expenditure is treated as an expense in calculating those profits (see, for example, section 247 of that Act), or

    (b) qualifying expenditure (within the meaning of Part 2, 7 or 8 of CAA 2001) is allocated to a pool for the trade and is set-off against different disposal receipts.

(6) An amount of qualifying expenditure is "set-off against different disposal receipts" if—

    (a) the amount would have been unrelieved qualifying expenditure carried forward in the pool for the trade, but

    (b) the amount is not so carried forward because (and only because) one or more disposal values in respect of one or more assets, other than the asset in respect of which the qualifying expenditure was incurred (or treated as incurred), have at any time been brought into account in that pool.

(7) For the purposes of subsection (6), an amount of qualifying expenditure incurred (or treated as incurred) by a person is not to be regarded as not carried forward because the person enters the cash basis.

(8) In this section and in section 96A—

    "disposal value" means—

        (a) in section 96A(3K)(c)—

            (i) a disposal value for the purposes of Part 2, 4A, 5, 6, 7 8 or 10 of CAA 2001 (for example, in relation to Part 2 of that Act, see (in particular) section 61 of that Act), or

            (ii) proceeds from a balancing event for the purposes of Part 3 or 3A of that Act (see sections 316 and 360O of that Act), and

        (b) in subsection (6), a disposal value for the purposes of—

            (i) Part 2 of that Act (see, in particular, section 61 of that Act),

            (ii) Part 7 of that Act (see section 462 of that Act), or

            (iii) Part 8 of that Act (see sections 476 and 477 of that Act);

    "market value amount" means the amount that would be regarded as normal and reasonable—

        (a) in the market conditions then prevailing, and

        (b) between persons dealing with each other at arm's length in the open market;

    "pool" means—

Finance (No. 2) Act 2017 (c. 32)
Schedule 2 — Trades and property businesses: calculation of profits
Part 1 — Trades etc: amendments of ITTOIA 2005

111

    (a) the main pool or a class pool to which qualifying expenditure is allocated under Part 2 of CAA 2001 (see section 54 of that Act),

    (b) a pool to which qualifying expenditure is allocated under Part 7 of that Act (see section 456 of that Act), or

    (c) a pool to which qualifying expenditure is allocated under Part 8 of that Act (see section 470 of that Act);

"provision" includes creation, construction or acquisition;

"qualifying expenditure" means —

    (a) qualifying expenditure within the meaning of Part 2 of CAA 2001 (see section 11(4) of that Act for the general rule),

    (b) qualifying expenditure within the meaning of Part 5 of that Act (see section 395 of that Act),

    (c) qualifying expenditure within the meaning of Part 6 of that Act (see section 439 of that Act),

    (d) qualifying expenditure within the meaning of Part 7 of that Act (see section 454 of that Act), or

    (e) qualifying trade expenditure within the meaning of Part 8 of that Act (see section 468 of that Act);

"unrelieved qualifying expenditure" means unrelieved qualifying expenditure for the purposes of —

    (a) Part 2 of CAA 2001 (see section 59(1) and (2) of that Act),

    (b) Part 7 of that Act (see section 461 of that Act), or

    (c) Part 8 of that Act (see section 475 of that Act)."

6   In section 106D (capital receipts), for "(cash basis: capital receipts)" substitute "(capital receipts under, or after leaving, cash basis)".

7   (1) Section 240C (unrelieved qualifying expenditure) is amended as follows.

    (2) For the heading substitute "Unrelieved qualifying expenditure: Parts 2, 7 and 8 of CAA 2001".

    (3) In subsection (1)(b), after "unrelieved qualifying expenditure" insert "relating to the trade".

    (4) In subsection (3), for "the relevant portion of the expenditure" substitute "any cash basis deductible amount of the expenditure".

    (5) For subsection (4) substitute —

      "(4) A "cash basis deductible amount" of the expenditure means any amount of the expenditure for which a deduction would be allowed in calculating the profits of the trade on the cash basis on the assumption that the expenditure was paid in the current tax year."

    (6) In subsection (5), for "The relevant portion" substitute "Any cash basis deductible amount".

    (7) After subsection (5) insert —

      "(5A) For the purposes of subsection (1)(b), in determining the unrelieved qualifying expenditure the person has to carry forward, disregard sections 59(4), 461A(1) and 475A(1) of CAA 2001 (which provide that

112   *Finance (No. 2) Act 2017 (c. 32)*
Schedule 2 — Trades and property businesses: calculation of profits
Part 1 — Trades etc: amendments of ITTOIA 2005

an amount is not to be carried forward as unrelieved qualifying expenditure when a person enters the cash basis)."

(8) For subsection (6) substitute—

"(6)   In this section "unrelieved qualifying expenditure" means unrelieved qualifying expenditure for the purposes of—

(a)   Part 2 of CAA 2001 (see section 59(1) and (2) of that Act),

(b)   Part 7 of that Act (see section 461 of that Act), or

(c)   Part 8 of that Act (see section 475 of that Act)."

8   After section 240C insert—

"240CA Unrelieved qualifying expenditure: Part 5 of CAA 2001

(1)   This section applies if a person carrying on a mineral extraction trade enters the cash basis for a tax year ("the current tax year").

(2)   But this section does not apply if section 240D applies.

(3)   In calculating the profits of the trade for the current tax year, a deduction is allowed for any amount of expenditure—

(a)   which would, apart from section 419A(1) of CAA 2001, have been unrelieved qualifying expenditure for the current tax year, and

(b)   for which a deduction would be allowed in calculating the profits of the trade on the cash basis on the assumption that the expenditure was paid in the current tax year.

(4)   In this section—

"mineral extraction trade" has the meaning given in section 394 of CAA 2001;

"unrelieved qualifying expenditure" means unrelieved qualifying expenditure for the purposes of Part 5 of CAA 2001 (see section 419 of that Act)."

9   (1) Section 240D (assets not fully paid for) is amended as follows.

(2) In subsection (1)(b), for "obtained" to the end substitute "incurred relevant expenditure, and".

(3) After subsection (1) insert—

"(1A)   "Relevant expenditure" means expenditure—

(a)   for which a deduction would be allowed in calculating the profits of the trade on the cash basis on the assumption that the expenditure was paid in the tax year, and

(b)   in respect of which the person has obtained capital allowances under Part 2, 5, 6, 7 or 8 of CAA 2001."

(4) In subsection (4), for "The amount of any capital allowance obtained in respect of expenditure on the provision of any plant or machinery" substitute "Any question as to whether or to what extent expenditure is relevant expenditure, or as to whether or to what extent any capital allowance obtained is in respect of relevant expenditure,".

(5) In subsection (5), after "given" insert "under Part 2 of CAA 2001".

(6) Omit subsection (6).

Finance (No. 2) Act 2017 (c. 32)
Schedule 2 – Trades and property businesses: calculation of profits
Part 1 – Trades etc: amendments of ITTOIA 2005

113

10   In section 786(6) (meaning of "rent-a-room receipts"), for "(capital receipts)" substitute "(capital receipts under, or after leaving, cash basis)".

11   In section 805(5) (meaning of "qualifying care receipts"), for "(capital receipts)" substitute "(capital receipts under, or after leaving, cash basis)".

PART 2

PROPERTY BUSINESSES: AMENDMENTS OF ITTOIA 2005

12   ITTOIA 2005 is amended as follows.

13   In Chapter 3 of Part 3 (profits of property businesses: basic rules), after section 271 insert—

"Basis of calculation of profits

271A Basis of calculation of profits: GAAP required

(1)   The profits of a property business for a tax year must be calculated in accordance with GAAP if condition A, B, C, D or E is met.

(2)   Condition A is that the business is carried on at any time in the tax year by—

(a)   a company,

(b)   a limited liability partnership,

(c)   a corporate firm, or

(d)   the trustees of a trust.

(3)   For the purposes of subsection (2) a firm is a "corporate firm" if a partner in the firm is not an individual.

(4)   Condition B is that the cash basis receipts for the tax year exceed £150,000.

(5)   In subsection (4) "the cash basis receipts for the tax year" means the total of the amounts that would be brought into account as receipts in calculating the profits of the property business for the tax year on the cash basis (see section 271D).

(6)   If the property business is carried on for only part of the tax year, the sum given in subsection (4) is proportionately reduced.

(7)   Condition C is that—

(a)   the property business is carried on by an individual ("P"),

(b)   a share of joint property income is brought into account in calculating the profits of the business for the tax year,

(c)   a share of that joint property income is brought into account in calculating the profits for the tax year of a property business carried on by another individual ("Q's property business"), and

(d)   the profits of Q's property business for the tax year are calculated in accordance with GAAP.

(8)   In subsection (7) "joint property income" means income to which P and Q are treated for income tax purposes as beneficially entitled in equal shares by virtue of section 836 of ITA 2007.

114

Finance (No. 2) Act 2017 (c. 32)
Schedule 2 — Trades and property businesses: calculation of profits
Part 2 — Property businesses: amendments of ITTOIA 2005

(9) Condition D is that—

    (a) an allowance under Part 3A of CAA 2001 (business premises renovation allowances) is made at any time in calculating the profits of the property business, and

    (b) if the profits of the business were to be calculated in accordance with GAAP for the tax year, there would be a day in the tax year on which the occurrence of a balancing event (within the meaning of that Part) would give rise to a balancing adjustment for the tax year (see section 360M of that Act).

(10) Condition E is that an election under this subsection made by the person who is or has been carrying on the property business has effect in relation to the business for the tax year.

(11) An election under subsection (10) must be made on or before the first anniversary of the normal self-assessment filing date for the tax year for which the election is made.

(12) The Treasury may by regulations—

    (a) amend subsection (2);

    (b) amend subsection (4) so as to substitute another sum for the sum for the time being specified in that subsection.

(13) A statutory instrument containing regulations under subsection (12) may not be made unless a draft of the instrument has been laid before, and approved by a resolution of, the House of Commons.

(14) Subsection (13) does not apply if the regulations omit one or more paragraphs of subsection (2) and make no other provision.

271B Calculation of profits in accordance with GAAP

(1) In this Part, references to calculating the profits of a property business in accordance with GAAP are to calculating the profits in accordance with generally accepted accounting practice, subject to any adjustment required or authorised by law in calculating profits for income tax purposes.

(2) A requirement under this Part to calculate profits in accordance with GAAP does not—

    (a) require a person to comply with the requirements of the Companies Act 2006 or subordinate legislation made under that Act except as to the basis of calculation, or

    (b) impose any requirements as to audit or disclosure.

(3) See section 272 (application of trading income rules: GAAP) which applies only where profits are calculated in accordance with GAAP.

271C Basis of calculation of profits: cash basis required

The profits of a property business for a tax year must be calculated on the cash basis if none of conditions A, B, C, D or E in section 271A is met.

Finance (No. 2) Act 2017 (c. 32)
Schedule 2 — Trades and property businesses: calculation of profits
Part 2 — Property businesses: amendments of ITTOIA 2005

115

271D Calculation of profits on the cash basis

(1) In this Part, references to calculating the profits of a property business on the cash basis are to calculating the profits in accordance with subsections (2) and (3).

(2) In calculating the profits, receipts of the business are brought into account at the time they are received, and expenses of the business are brought into account at the time they are paid.

(3) Subsection (2) is subject to any adjustment required or authorised by law in calculating profits for income tax purposes.

(4) For provision about the application of Chapter 4 (profits of property businesses: lease premiums etc) in relation to profits calculated on the cash basis, see section 276A.

(5) For provision about the application of Chapter 5 (rules about deductions and receipts) in relation to profits calculated on the cash basis, see section 307A.

(6) The following provisions apply only where profits are calculated on the cash basis—

    (a) section 272ZA (application of trading income rules: cash basis), and

    (b) Chapter 7A (cash basis: adjustments for capital allowances)."

14   In the italic heading before section 272, at the end insert ": *application of trading income rules*".

15   After that italic heading insert—

"271E Profits of a property business: application of trading income rules

(1) The profits of a property business are calculated in the same way as the profits of a trade.

(2) But this is subject to—

    (a) section 272, which limits the rule in subsection (1) in relation to a property business whose profits are calculated in accordance with GAAP, and

    (b) section 272ZA, which limits that rule in relation to a property business whose profits are calculated on the cash basis."

16 (1) Section 272 (profits of a property business: application of trading income rules) is amended as follows.

  (2) For the heading substitute "Application of trading income rules: GAAP".

  (3) Omit subsection (1).

  (4) In subsection (2), for the words before the table substitute "In relation to a property business whose profits are calculated in accordance with GAAP, the provisions of Part 2 (trading income) which apply as a result of section 271E(1) are limited to the following—".

  (5) In the table in subsection (2), omit the entry relating to section 25 (generally accepted accounting practice).

116

Finance (No. 2) Act 2017 (c. 32)
Schedule 2 – Trades and property businesses: calculation of profits
Part 2 – Property businesses: amendments of ITTOIA 2005

17   After section 272 insert—

"272ZA Application of trading income rules: cash basis

(1)   In relation to a property business whose profits are calculated on the cash basis, the provisions of Part 2 (trading income) which apply as a result of section 271E(1) are limited to the following—

In Chapter 3 (basic rules) –	
section 26	losses calculated on same basis as profits
section 28A	money's worth
section 29	interest
In Chapter 4 (rules restricting deductions) –	
section 34	expenses not wholly and exclusively for trade and unconnected losses
sections 38 to 42 and 44	employee benefit contributions
sections 45 to 47	business entertainment and gifts
section 52	exclusion of double relief for interest
section 53	social security contributions
section 54	penalties, interest and VAT surcharges
section 55	crime-related payments
section 55A	expenditure on integral features
In Chapter 5 (rules allowing deductions) –	
section 57	pre-trading expenses
sections 58 and 59	incidental costs of obtaining finance
section 69	payments for restrictive undertakings
sections 70 and 71	seconded employees
section 72	payroll deduction schemes: contributions to agents' expenses
sections 73 to 75	counselling and retraining expenses
sections 76 to 80	redundancy payments etc
section 81	personal security expenses
sections 82 to 86	contributions to local enterprise organisations or urban regeneration companies
sections 86A and 86B	contributions to flood and coastal erosion risk management projects

Finance (No. 2) Act 2017 (c. 32)
Schedule 2 — Trades and property businesses: calculation of profits
Part 2 — Property businesses: amendments of ITTOIA 2005

117

sections 87 and 88	scientific research
sections 89 and 90	expenses connected with patents, designs and trade marks
section 91	payments to Export Credits Guarantee Department
In Chapter 6 (receipts) —	
section 96	capital receipts
section 97	debts incurred and later released
section 104	distribution of assets of mutual concerns
section 105(1) and (2)(b) and (c)	industrial development grants
section 106	sums recovered under insurance policies etc
In Chapter 6A (amounts not reflecting commercial transactions) —	
section 106C	amounts not reflecting commercial transactions
section 106D	capital receipts
section 106E	gifts to charities etc
In Chapter 7 (gifts to charities etc) —	
section 109	receipt by donor or connected person of benefit attributable to certain gifts

(2) In those provisions, the expression "this Part" is to be read as a reference to those provisions as applied by subsection (1) and to the other provisions of Part 3.

(3) In section 106D, the reference to subsection (4) or (5) of section 96A is to be read as a reference to subsection (2), (3) or (5) of section 307F (deemed capital receipts under, or after leaving, cash basis)."

18   After section 272ZA insert—

"Calculation of profits: other general rules".

19   In section 272A (restricting deductions for finance costs related to residential property), after subsection (6) insert—

"(7)   See also section 307D (cash basis: modification of deduction for costs of loans)."

20   (1) Section 274 (relationship between rules prohibiting and allowing deductions) is amended as follows.

(2) For subsection (1)(b) substitute—
          "(b)   is subject to—

118

Finance (No. 2) Act 2017 (c. 32)
Schedule 2 – Trades and property businesses: calculation of profits
Part 2 – Property businesses: amendments of ITTOIA 2005

       (i)   section 36 (unpaid remuneration), as applied by section 272,

      (ii)   section 38 (employee benefit contributions), as applied by sections 272 and 272ZA,

    (iii)   section 48 (car hire), as applied by section 272,

    (iv)   section 55 (crime-related payments), as applied by sections 272 and 272ZA,

     (v)   section 272A (finance costs), and

    (vi)   section 307D (cash basis: modification of deduction for costs of loans)."

(3) In subsection (3)—

    (a)   after "section 272" insert ", or sections 38 and 55 as applied by section 272ZA", and

    (b)   for "section 272A" insert "sections 272A and 307D".

(4) In subsection (4), after "section 272" insert "or 272ZA".

21   In section 276(5) (introduction: profits of property businesses: lease premiums etc), after "292" insert "; but see also section 276A".

22   After section 276 insert—

"276A Application of Chapter to property businesses using cash basis

The following provisions of this Chapter do not apply in calculating the profits of a property business on the cash basis—

    (a)   sections 291 to 294 (tenants under taxed leases: deductions), and

    (b)   sections 296 and 298 (ICTA modifications)."

23   In Chapter 5 of Part 3 (profits of property businesses: other rules about receipts and deductions), after the Chapter heading insert—

"Cash basis: application of Chapter

307A Cash basis: application of Chapter

(1) The following provisions of this Chapter apply only where the profits of a property business are calculated on the cash basis—

    (a)   section 307B (cash basis: capital expenditure),

    (b)   section 307C (cash basis: deduction for costs of loans), and

    (c)   section 307D (cash basis: modification of deduction for costs of loans).

(2) Sections 307E and 307F make provision about capital receipts in certain cases where the profits of a property business are calculated on the cash basis or have previously been calculated on the cash basis.

Property businesses using cash basis

307B Cash basis: capital expenditure

(1) This section applies in relation to the calculation of the profits of a property business on the cash basis.

Finance (No. 2) Act 2017 (c. 32)
Schedule 2 — Trades and property businesses: calculation of profits
Part 2 — Property businesses: amendments of ITTOIA 2005

119

(2) No deduction is allowed for an item of a capital nature incurred on, or in connection with, the acquisition or disposal of a business or part of a business.

(3) No deduction is allowed for an item of a capital nature incurred on, or in connection with, education or training.

(4) No deduction is allowed for an item of a capital nature incurred on, or in connection with, the provision, alteration or disposal of land.

(5) But subsection (4) does not prevent a deduction being made for expenditure that—

    (a) is incurred on the provision of a depreciating asset which, in being provided, is installed or otherwise fixed to qualifying land (see subsection (8)) so as to become, in law, part of the land, but

    (b) is not incurred on, or in connection with, the provision of—

        (i) a building,

        (ii) a wall, floor, ceiling, door, gate, shutter or window or stairs,

        (iii) a waste disposal system,

        (iv) a sewerage or drainage system, or

        (v) a shaft or other structure in which a lift, hoist, escalator or moving walkway may be installed.

(6) No deduction is allowed for an item of a capital nature incurred on, or in connection with, the provision, alteration or disposal of an asset for use in ordinary residential property (see subsection (8)).
But see section 311A (replacement domestic items relief).

(7) If an asset is provided partly for use in ordinary residential property and partly for other purposes, such apportionment of the expenditure incurred on, or in connection with, the provision, alteration or disposal of the asset is to be made for the purposes of subsection (6) as is just and reasonable.

(8) In relation to the calculation of profits for a tax year—

    (a) "ordinary residential property" means a dwelling-house or part of a dwelling-house in relation to which an ordinary property business (see subsection (9)) is carried on in the tax year, and

    (b) "qualifying land" means land not falling within paragraph (a).

(9) "Ordinary property business" means—

    (a) so much of a UK property business as does not consist of the commercial letting of furnished holiday accommodation (within the meaning of Chapter 6) in the UK, or

    (b) so much of an overseas property business as does not consist of the commercial letting of furnished holiday accommodation in one or more EEA states.

(10) No deduction is allowed for an item of a capital nature incurred on, or in connection with, the provision, alteration or disposal of—

    (a) any asset that is not a depreciating asset (see subsections (11) and (12)),

120   *Finance (No. 2) Act 2017 (c. 32)*
Schedule 2 — Trades and property businesses: calculation of profits
Part 2 — Property businesses: amendments of ITTOIA 2005

> > (b) any asset not acquired or created for use on a continuing basis in the property business,
> > (c) a car (see subsection (20)),
> > (d) a non-qualifying intangible asset (see subsections (13) to (16)), or
> > (e) a financial asset (see subsection (17)).

> (11) An asset is a "depreciating" asset if, on the date the item of a capital nature is incurred, it is reasonable to expect that before the end of 20 years beginning with that date —
> > (a) the useful life of the asset will end, or
> > (b) the asset will decline in value by 90% or more.

> (12) The useful life of an asset ends when it could no longer be of use to any person for any purpose as an asset of a business.

> (13) "Intangible asset" means anything that is capable of being an intangible asset within the meaning of FRS 105 and, in particular, includes —
> > (a) an internally-generated intangible asset, and
> > (b) intellectual property.

> (14) An intangible asset is "non-qualifying" unless, by virtue of having a fixed maximum duration, it must cease to exist before the end of 20 years beginning with the date on which the item of a capital nature is incurred.

> (15) An intangible asset is "non-qualifying" if it consists of a right, whether conditional or not, to obtain an intangible asset without a fixed maximum duration by virtue of which that asset must, assuming the right is exercised at the last possible time, cease to exist before the end of 20 years beginning with the date on which the item of a capital nature is incurred.

> (16) Where —
> > (a) the person carrying on the property business ("P") has an intangible asset, and
> > (b) P grants a licence or any other right in respect of that asset to another person,
>
> any intangible asset that consists of a licence or other right granted to P in respect of the intangible asset mentioned in paragraph (a) is "non-qualifying".

> (17) A "financial asset" means any right under or in connection with —
> > (a) a financial instrument, or
> > (b) an arrangement that is capable of producing a return that is economically equivalent to a return produced under any financial instrument.

> (18) A reference to acquisition, provision, alteration or disposal includes potential acquisition, provision, alteration or (as the case may be) disposal.

> (19) If there is a letting of accommodation only part of which is furnished holiday accommodation, such apportionments as are just and

Finance (No. 2) Act 2017 (c. 32)
Schedule 2 — Trades and property businesses: calculation of profits
Part 2 — Property businesses: amendments of ITTOIA 2005

121

reasonable in all the circumstances are to be made for the purposes of this section.

(20) In this section—

"arrangement" includes any agreement, understanding, scheme, transaction or series of transactions (whether or not legally enforceable);

"building" includes any fixed structure;

"car" has the same meaning as in Part 2 of CAA 2001 (see section 268A of that Act);

"financial instrument" has the same meaning as in FRS 105;

"FRS 105" means Financial Reporting Standard 105 (the Financial Reporting Standard applicable to the Micro-entities Regime), issued by the Financial Reporting Council in July 2015;

"intellectual property" means—

  (a) any patent, trade mark, registered design, copyright or design right, plant breeders' rights or rights under section 7 of the Plant Varieties Act 1997,

  (b) any right under the law of a country or territory outside the United Kingdom corresponding or similar to a right within paragraph (a),

  (c) any information or technique not protected by a right within paragraph (a) or (b) but having industrial, commercial or other economic value, or

  (d) any licence or other right in respect of anything within paragraph (a), (b) or (c);

"provision" includes creation, construction or acquisition.

307C   Cash basis: deduction for costs of loans

(1) Section 307D applies in calculating the profits of a property business for a tax year if conditions A to D are met.

(2) Condition A is that the profits of the business are calculated on the cash basis for the tax year.

(3) Condition B is that a deduction for costs of a loan is allowed in calculating the profits of the business for the tax year or, ignoring section 272A (restricting deductions for finance costs related to residential property) and section 307D (cash basis: modification of deduction for costs of loans), would be so allowed.

In this section such a loan is referred to as a "relevant loan".

(4) Condition C is that an amount of the principal of one or more relevant loans is outstanding at the end time (and a relevant loan in respect of which such an amount is outstanding at the end time is referred to in this section as an "outstanding relevant loan").

(5) Condition D is that—

$$L > V$$

where—

  L is the total outstanding amount of relevant loans (see subsections (6) and (7)), and

122

Finance (No. 2) Act 2017 (c. 32)
Schedule 2 – Trades and property businesses: calculation of profits
Part 2 – Property businesses: amendments of ITTOIA 2005

V is the sum of the values of all relevant properties (see subsections (8) to (10)).

(6) The "total outstanding amount of relevant loans" —

    (a) if there is only one outstanding relevant loan, is the outstanding business amount of that loan, and

    (b) if there are two or more outstanding relevant loans, is found by calculating the outstanding business amount of each such loan and adding those amounts together.

(7) The "outstanding business amount" of a relevant loan is given by —

$$\frac{X}{Y} \times A$$

where —

    A is the amount of the principal of the loan which is outstanding at the end time,

    X is the amount of the deduction for costs of the loan that would be allowed, apart from sections 272A and 307D, in calculating the profits of the business for the tax year, and

    Y is the amount of the deduction for costs of the loan that would be allowed, apart from the wholly and exclusively rule and sections 272A and 307D, in calculating the profits of the business for the tax year.

(8) A property is a "relevant property" if —

    (a) it is involved in the property business at the end time, or

    (b) although it is not involved in the business at the end time —

        (i) it was last involved in the business at an earlier time in the tax year, and

        (ii) the person carrying on the business holds the property throughout the period beginning with that earlier time and ending with the end time.

(9) The "value" of a relevant property is the total of —

    (a) the market value of the property at the time that it is first involved in the property business, and

    (b) such amount of any expenditure of a capital nature incurred by the person carrying on the business in respect of the property as is not brought into account in calculating the profits of the business for the tax year or any previous tax year.

(10) A property is "involved in the property business" if it is a property whose exploitation forms the whole or part of the business.

(11) The "end time" is —

    (a) the time immediately before the end of the tax year, or

    (b) if in the tax year the person carrying on the business permanently ceases to carry it on, the time immediately before the person permanently ceases to carry on the business.

(12) "Costs", in relation to a loan, means —

    (a) interest on the loan,

Finance (No. 2) Act 2017 (c. 32)
Schedule 2 — Trades and property businesses: calculation of profits
Part 2 — Property businesses: amendments of ITTOIA 2005

123

      (b)   an amount in connection with the loan that, for the person receiving or entitled to the amount, is a return in relation to the loan which is economically equivalent to interest, or

      (c)   incidental costs of obtaining finance by means of the loan.

(13)   Section 58(2) to (4) (meaning of "incidental costs of obtaining finance") apply for the purposes of subsection (12)(c).

(14)   In this section —

    "market value", in relation to a property, means the price which the property might reasonably be expected to fetch —

      (a)   in the market conditions then prevailing, and

      (b)   between persons dealing with each other at arm's length in the open market;

    "property" means an estate, interest or right in or over land;

    "the wholly and exclusively rule" means the rule in section 34 (expenses not wholly and exclusively for trade and unconnected losses), as applied by section 272ZA (application of trading income rules: cash basis).

307D Cash basis: modification of deduction for costs of loans

(1)   Where section 307C provides that this section applies in calculating the profits of a property business for a tax year, the amount which is allowed as a deduction for costs of a loan in calculating the profits for the tax year is the non-adjusted deduction multiplied by the relevant fraction.

This is subject to section 272A (restricting deductions for finance costs related to residential property).

(2)   "The non-adjusted deduction" means the deduction for costs of the loan that would be allowed, apart from section 272A and this section, in calculating the profits of the business for the tax year.

(3)   "The relevant fraction" means —

$$\frac{V}{L}$$

where V and L have the same meaning as in section 307C.

(4)   For the meaning of "costs of a loan" see section 307C.

Property businesses that use, or have used, cash basis

307E Capital receipts under, or after leaving, cash basis

(1)   This section applies in relation to a property business carried on by a person in two cases —

      (a)   Case 1 (see subsections (2) to (4)), and

      (b)   Case 2 (see subsections (5) to (8)).

(2)   Case 1 is a case in which conditions A and B are met.

(3)   Condition A is that the person receives disposal proceeds or a capital refund in relation to an asset in a tax year for which the profits of the property business are calculated on the cash basis (see section 271D).

124   *Finance (No. 2) Act 2017 (c. 32)*
Schedule 2 — Trades and property businesses: calculation of profits
Part 2 — Property businesses: amendments of ITTOIA 2005

For the meaning of "disposal proceeds" and "capital refund" see subsections (9) and (10).

(4) Condition B is that—

    (a) an amount of capital expenditure (see subsection (11)) relating to the asset has been brought into account in calculating the profits of the property business on the cash basis, or

    (b) an amount of relevant capital expenditure (see subsection (17)) relating to the asset has been brought into account in calculating the profits of the property business in accordance with GAAP (see section 271B)—

        (i) by means of a deduction allowed under section 58 or 59 (incidental costs of obtaining finance) (as applied by section 272) or section 311A (replacement domestic items relief), or

        (ii) under CAA 2001 (see subsection (20)).

(5) Case 2 is a case in which—

    (a) condition C is met, and

    (b) condition D or E is met.

(6) Condition C is that disposal proceeds or a capital refund arise to the person in relation to an asset in a tax year—

    (a) for which the profits of the property business are calculated in accordance with GAAP, and

    (b) which is after a tax year for which the profits of the business had been calculated on the cash basis.

(7) Condition D is that an amount of capital expenditure relating to the asset—

    (a) has been paid in a tax year for which the profits of the property business were calculated on the cash basis,

    (b) has been brought into account in calculating the profits of the business on the cash basis, and

    (c) on the assumption that the profits had not been calculated on the cash basis at the time the expenditure was paid, would not have been qualifying expenditure.

(8) Condition E is that—

    (a) an amount of capital expenditure relating to the asset has been brought into account in calculating the profits of the property business for a tax year in accordance with GAAP by means of a deduction allowed under section 58 or 59 (as applied by section 272) or section 311A, and

    (b) that tax year is before the tax year for which the person last entered the cash basis.

(9) "Disposal proceeds" means—

    (a) any proceeds arising from the disposal of an asset or any part of it,

    (b) any proceeds arising from the grant of any right in respect of, or any interest in, the asset, or

Finance (No. 2) Act 2017 (c. 32)
Schedule 2 — Trades and property businesses: calculation of profits
Part 2 — Property businesses: amendments of ITTOIA 2005

125

(c) any amount of damages, proceeds of insurance or other compensation received in respect of the asset.

See also section 307F for circumstances in which a person is to be regarded as disposing of an asset.

(10) "Capital refund" means an amount that is (in substance) a refund of capital expenditure relating to an asset.

(11) "Capital expenditure" means expenditure of a capital nature incurred, or treated as incurred, on or in connection with—

   (a) the provision, alteration or disposal of an asset, or

   (b) the potential provision, alteration or disposal of an asset.

(12) The disposal proceeds or capital refund mentioned in condition A or (as the case may be) condition C are to be brought into account as a receipt in calculating the profits of the property business.

(13) In a case where only part of the total capital expenditure incurred, or treated as incurred, by the person in relation to the asset has been brought into account in calculating the profits of the property business (whether or not on the cash basis), the amount brought into account under subsection (12) is proportionately reduced.

The reference in this subsection to expenditure brought into account includes a reference to expenditure brought into account under CAA 2001 (see subsection (20)).

(14) Subsection (12) does not apply if the whole of the amount which would otherwise be brought into account under that subsection—

   (a) has already been brought into account as a receipt in calculating the profits of the property business under this section,

   (b) is brought into account as a receipt in calculating the profits of the business under any other provision of this Part (except section 334D(4) (assets not fully paid for)), or

   (c) is brought into account under Part 2 or 3A of CAA 2001 as a disposal value.

The reference to any other provision of this Part in paragraph (b) includes a reference to any provision applied by section 272 or 272ZA.

(15) If part of the amount which would otherwise be brought into account under subsection (12) has already been or is brought into account as mentioned in subsection (14), subsection (12) applies in relation to the remainder of that amount.

(16) For the purposes of this section, any question as to whether or to what extent expenditure is brought into account in calculating the profits of a property business is to be determined on such basis as is just and reasonable in all the circumstances.

(17) In subsection (4)(b) "relevant capital expenditure" means capital expenditure which—

   (a) has been incurred (or treated as incurred) by the person before the tax year for which the person last entered the cash basis, and

   (b) is cash basis deductible in relation to that tax year.

126

Finance (No. 2) Act 2017 (c. 32)
Schedule 2 — Trades and property businesses: calculation of profits
Part 2 — Property businesses: amendments of ITTOIA 2005

(18) For the purposes of this section, a person carrying on a property business "enters the cash basis" for a tax year if the profits of the business are calculated—

    (a) on the cash basis for the tax year, and

    (b) in accordance with GAAP for the previous tax year.

(19) Expenditure is "cash basis deductible" in relation to a tax year if, on the assumption that the expenditure was paid in that tax year, a deduction would be allowed in respect of the expenditure in calculating the profits of the property business on the cash basis for that tax year.

(20) For the purposes of this section, expenditure is "brought into account under CAA 2001" in calculating the profits of a property business if and to the extent that—

    (a) a capital allowance made under Part 2 of that Act in respect of the expenditure is treated as an expense in calculating those profits (see sections 248 to 250A of that Act), or

    (b) qualifying expenditure (within the meaning of Part 2 of CAA 2001) is allocated to a pool for a relevant qualifying activity and is set-off against different disposal receipts.

(21) An amount of qualifying expenditure is "set-off against different disposal receipts" if—

    (a) the amount would have been unrelieved qualifying expenditure carried forward in the pool for the relevant qualifying activity, but

    (b) the amount is not so carried forward because (and only because) one or more disposal values in respect of one or more assets, other than the asset in respect of which the qualifying expenditure was incurred (or treated as incurred), have at any time been brought into account in that pool.

(22) For the purposes of subsections (20) and (21), an activity is a "relevant qualifying activity" if—

    (a) it is a qualifying activity mentioned in section 15(1)(b) to (da) of CAA 2001 (property business activities), and

    (b) the property business consists of or includes that qualifying activity.

(23) For the purposes of subsection (21), an amount of qualifying expenditure incurred (or treated as incurred) by a person is not to be regarded as not carried forward because the person enters the cash basis.

(24) In this section—

    "disposal value" means—

        (a) in subsection (14)(c)—

            (i) a disposal value for the purposes of Part 2 of CAA 2001 (see, in particular, section 61 of that Act), or

            (ii) proceeds from a balancing event for the purposes of Part 3A of that Act (see section 360O of that Act), and

Finance (No. 2) Act 2017 (c. 32)
Schedule 2 — Trades and property businesses: calculation of profits
Part 2 — Property businesses: amendments of ITTOIA 2005

127

    (b)   in subsection (21), a disposal value for the purposes of Part 2 of that Act;

"pool" means the main pool or a class pool to which qualifying expenditure is allocated under Part 2 of CAA 2001 (see section 54 of that Act);

"provision" includes creation, construction or acquisition;

"qualifying expenditure" means qualifying expenditure within the meaning of Part 2 of CAA 2001 (see section 11(4) of that Act for the general rule);

"unrelieved qualifying expenditure" means unrelieved qualifying expenditure for the purposes of Part 2 of CAA 2001 (see section 59(1) and (2) of that Act).

307F Deemed capital receipts under, or after leaving, cash basis

(1)   This section makes provision supplementary to section 307E.

(2)   If—

    (a)   at any time a person ceases to use an asset or any part of it for the purposes of a property business (other than in the circumstances mentioned in subsection (5)), but

    (b)   the person does not dispose of the asset (or that part) at that time,

the person is to be regarded for the purposes of section 307E as disposing of the asset (or that part) at that time for an amount equal to the market value amount.

(3)   If at any time there is a material increase in the person's non-business use of an asset or any part of it, the person is to be regarded for the purposes of section 307E as disposing of the asset (or that part) at that time for an amount equal to the relevant proportion of the market value amount.

(4)   For the purposes of subsection (3)—

    (a)   there is an increase in a person's non-business use of an asset (or part of an asset) if—

        (i)   the proportion of the person's use of the asset (or that part) that is for the purposes of the property business decreases, and

        (ii)   the proportion of the person's use of the asset (or that part) that is for other purposes (the "non-business use") increases;

    (b)   "the relevant proportion" is the difference between—

        (i)   the proportion of the person's use of the asset (or part of the asset) that is non-business use, and

        (ii)   the proportion of the person's use of the asset (or that part) that was non-business use before the increase mentioned in subsection (3).

(5)   If—

    (a)   the property business in respect of which capital expenditure relating to an asset has been brought into account as mentioned in section 307E is an overseas property business, and

    (b)   there is a move overseas,

128

Finance (No. 2) Act 2017 (c. 32)
Schedule 2 — Trades and property businesses: calculation of profits
Part 2 — Property businesses: amendments of ITTOIA 2005

the person is to be regarded for the purposes of section 307E as disposing of the asset at the time of the move overseas for an amount equal to the market value amount.

(6) For the purposes of subsection (5) there is a "move overseas" if—

   (a) the person ceases to be UK resident, or

   (b) the tax year is, as respects the person, a split year, and the overseas part of the tax year is the later part.

(7) The move overseas occurs—

   (a) in a case falling within subsection (6)(a), on the last day of the tax year for which the person is UK resident, or

   (b) in a case falling within subsection (6)(b), on the last day of the UK part of the tax year.

(8) In this section—

   "capital expenditure" has the same meaning as in section 307E,

   "market value amount" means the amount that would be regarded as normal and reasonable—

      (a) in the market conditions then prevailing, and

      (b) between persons dealing with each other at arm's length in the open market."

24   In section 311A (replacement domestic items relief), in subsection (15)—

   (a) for the definition of "the capital expenditure rule" substitute—

      ""the capital expenditure rule" means—

         (a) in relation to a property business whose profits are calculated in accordance with GAAP, section 33 (capital expenditure), as applied by section 272, and

         (b) in relation to a property business whose profits are calculated on the cash basis, section 307B (cash basis: capital expenditure);";

   (b) in the definition of "the wholly and exclusively rule"—

      (i) omit "the rule in", and

      (ii) after "section 272" insert "or 272ZA".

25   In section 315 (deduction for expenditure on sea walls), after subsection (6) insert—

   "(7) In calculating the profits of a property business on the cash basis, any reference in this section to the incurring of expenditure is to the paying of expenditure."

26   In section 322 (commercial letting of furnished holiday accommodation), after paragraph (za) in subsections (2) and (2A) insert—

   "(zaa) section 307B (cash basis: capital expenditure),".

27   After section 329 insert—

"329A Application of Chapter where cash basis used

   This Chapter applies if—

      (a) the profits of a property business are calculated—

         (i) on the cash basis for a tax year (see section 271D), and

Finance (No. 2) Act 2017 (c. 32)
Schedule 2 — Trades and property businesses: calculation of profits
Part 2 — Property businesses: amendments of ITTOIA 2005

129

> > (ii) in accordance with GAAP (see section 271B) for the following tax year, or
> (b) the profits of a property business are calculated —
> > (i) in accordance with GAAP for a tax year, and
> > (ii) on the cash basis for the following tax year."

28   In section 331 (income charged) —

> (a) the existing text becomes subsection (1), and
> (b) after that subsection insert —

> > "(2) This is subject to section 334A (spreading on leaving cash basis and related election)."

29   After section 334 insert —

"Spreading of adjustment income on leaving cash basis

334A Spreading on leaving cash basis and related election

> Sections 239A (spreading on leaving cash basis) and 239B (election to accelerate charge under section 239A) apply for the purposes of this Chapter as they apply for the purposes of Chapter 17 of Part 2, but as if —
>
> > (a) for section 239A(1) there were substituted —
> >
> > > "(1) This section applies if the profits of a property business are calculated —
> > > > (a) on the cash basis for a tax year (see section 271D), and
> > > > (b) in accordance with GAAP (see section 271B) for the following tax year.", and
> >
> > (b) any reference to section 239A or 239B were to the section concerned as applied by this section.

CHAPTER 7A

CASH BASIS: ADJUSTMENTS FOR CAPITAL ALLOWANCES

334B "Entering the cash basis"

> For the purposes of this Chapter, a person carrying on a property business enters the cash basis for a tax year if the profits of the business are calculated —
>
> > (a) on the cash basis for the tax year (see section 271D), and
> > (b) in accordance with GAAP (see section 271B) for the previous tax year.

334C Unrelieved qualifying expenditure

> (1) This section applies if —
> > (a) a person carrying on a property business enters the cash basis for a tax year ("the current tax year"), and
> > (b) the person would, apart from section 59(4A) of CAA 2001, have unrelieved qualifying expenditure relating to a relevant property business activity to carry forward from the chargeable period which is the previous tax year.

130 *Finance (No. 2) Act 2017 (c. 32)*
Schedule 2 — Trades and property businesses: calculation of profits
Part 2 — Property businesses: amendments of ITTOIA 2005

(2) But this section does not apply if section 334D applies.

(3) In calculating the profits of the property business for the current tax year, a deduction is allowed for any cash basis deductible amount of the expenditure relating to each relevant property business activity.

(4) A "cash basis deductible amount" of the expenditure means any amount of the expenditure for which a deduction would be allowed in calculating the profits of the property business on the cash basis on the assumption that the expenditure was paid in the current tax year.

(5) Any cash basis deductible amount of the expenditure is to be determined on such basis as is just and reasonable in all the circumstances.

(6) In this section —

"relevant property business activity" means —

(a) in relation to a UK property business, an ordinary UK property business and a UK furnished holiday lettings business (within the meaning of Part 2 of CAA 2001 (see sections 16 and 17 of that Act)), and

(b) in relation to an overseas property business, an ordinary overseas property business and an EEA furnished holiday lettings business (within the meaning of Part 2 of that Act (see sections 17A and 17B of that Act));

"unrelieved qualifying expenditure" means unrelieved qualifying expenditure for the purposes of Part 2 of CAA 2001 (see section 59(1) and (2) of that Act).

334D Assets not fully paid for

(1) This section applies if —

(a) a person carrying on a property business enters the cash basis for a tax year ("the current tax year"),

(b) at any time before the end of the chargeable period which is the previous tax year the person has incurred relevant expenditure, and

(c) not all of the relevant expenditure has actually been paid by the person.

(2) "Relevant expenditure" means expenditure on plant or machinery —

(a) for which a deduction would be allowed in calculating the profits of the property business on the cash basis on the assumption that the expenditure was paid in the current tax year, and

(b) in respect of which the person has obtained capital allowances.

(3) If the amount of the relevant expenditure that the person has actually paid exceeds the amount of capital allowances given in respect of the relevant expenditure, the difference is to be deducted in calculating the profits of the property business for the current tax year.

(4) If the amount of the relevant expenditure that the person has actually paid is less than the amount of capital allowances given in respect of

Finance (No. 2) Act 2017 (c. 32)
Schedule 2 — Trades and property businesses: calculation of profits
Part 2 — Property businesses: amendments of ITTOIA 2005

131

the relevant expenditure, the difference is to be treated as a receipt in calculating the profits of the property business for the current tax year.

(5) Any question as to whether or to what extent expenditure is relevant expenditure, or as to whether or to what extent any capital allowance obtained is in respect of relevant expenditure, is to be determined on such basis as is just and reasonable in all the circumstances.

(6) If the amount of capital allowances given in respect of the relevant expenditure has been reduced under section 205 or 207 of CAA 2001 (reduction where asset provided or used only partly for qualifying activity), the amount of the relevant expenditure that the person has actually paid is to be proportionately reduced for the purposes of this section.

334E Effect of election where predecessor and successor are connected persons

(1) This section applies if —
   (a) a person carrying on a property business enters the cash basis for a tax year,
   (b) the person is the successor for the purposes of section 266 of CAA 2001, and
   (c) as a result of an election under that section, relevant plant or machinery is treated as sold by the predecessor to the successor at any time during the tax year.

(2) The provisions of this Chapter have effect in relation to the successor as if everything done to or by the predecessor had been done to or by the successor.

(3) Any expenditure actually incurred by the successor on acquiring the relevant plant or machinery is to be ignored for the purposes of calculating the profits of the property business for the tax year.

(4) In this section —
   "the predecessor" has the same meaning as in section 266 of CAA 2001, and
   "relevant plant or machinery" has the same meaning as in section 267 of that Act."

30   In section 351 (income charged), after subsection (2) insert —

   "(3) Further to subsection (2), section 254 applies for the purposes of this Chapter as if for subsection (2A) of that section there were substituted —

      "(2A) If the time immediately before the person permanently ceases to carry on the UK property business falls in a cash basis tax year, assume for the purposes of subsection (2) that the profits of the business are calculated on the cash basis."

   (4) For the purposes of sections 254 (as so applied) and 353, a tax year is "a cash basis tax year" in relation to a property business if the profits of the business for the tax year are calculated on the cash basis (see section 271D)."

132

Finance (No. 2) Act 2017 (c. 32)
Schedule 2 — Trades and property businesses: calculation of profits
Part 2 — Property businesses: amendments of ITTOIA 2005

31   In section 353 (basic meaning of "post-cessation receipt"), after subsection (1)
        insert—

        "(1A)   If the time immediately before a person permanently ceases to carry
                on a UK property business falls in a cash basis tax year (see section
                351(4)), a sum is to be treated as a post-cessation receipt only if it
                would have been brought into account in calculating the profits of
                the business on the cash basis had it been received at that time."

32   In section 356 (application to businesses within the charge to corporation
        tax), in subsection (1), for "section 355" substitute "sections 353(1A) and 355,
        and in the modification of section 254 in section 351(3)".

33   In section 786 (meaning of "rent-a-room receipts"), after subsection (6)
        insert—

        "(6A)   Subsections (6B) and (7) apply if—
                (a)   the receipts would otherwise be brought into account in
                      calculating the profits of a UK property business, and
                (b)   the profits are calculated on the cash basis (see section 271D).

        (6B)   Any amounts brought into account under section 307E (capital
                receipts under, or after leaving, cash basis) as a receipt in calculating
                the profits of the property business are to be treated as receipts
                within paragraph (a) of subsection (1) above."

34   In section 860 (adjustment income), in subsection (5), after "Chapter 17 of
        Part 2" insert ", or under section 239B as applied to property businesses by
        section 334A,".

35   In section 866 (employee benefit contributions: non-trades and non-property
        businesses), in subsection (7)(b), for "section 272" substitute "sections 272
        and 272ZA".

36   In section 867 (business entertainment and gifts: non-trades and non-
        property businesses), in subsection (7)(b), for "section 272" substitute
        "sections 272 and 272ZA".

37   In section 868 (social security contributions: non-trades etc), in subsection
        (6)(b), for "section 272" insert "sections 272 and 272ZA".

38   In section 869 (penalties, interest and VAT surcharges: non-trades etc), in
        subsection (6)(b), for "section 272" substitute "sections 272 and 272ZA".

39   In section 870 (crime-related payments: non-trades and non-property
        businesses), in subsection (4)(b), for "section 272" substitute "sections 272
        and 272ZA".

40   In section 872 (losses calculated on same basis as miscellaneous income), in
        subsection (4)(b), for "section 272" substitute "sections 272 and 272ZA".

41   In Part 2 of Schedule 4 (index of defined expressions), at the appropriate
        place insert—

"the cash basis (in Part 3)	section 271D

Finance (No. 2) Act 2017 (c. 32)
Schedule 2 — Trades and property businesses: calculation of profits
Part 2 — Property businesses: amendments of ITTOIA 2005

133

| in accordance with GAAP (in Part 3) | section 271B". |

PART 3

TRADES ETC: AMENDMENTS OF OTHER ACTS

TMA 1970

42   In section 42 of TMA 1970 (procedure for making claims etc), in subsection (7)(e), after "194" insert ", 271A(10)".

TCGA 1992

43   TCGA 1992 is amended as follows.

44   In section 37 (consideration chargeable to tax on income), after subsection (1) insert—

> "(1A) There is to be excluded from the consideration for a disposal of an asset taken into account in the computation of the gain a sum equal to any amount that is taken into account by the person making the disposal as a receipt under section 96A or 307E of ITTOIA 2005 (capital receipts under, or after leaving, cash basis) as a result of the operation of any deemed disposal provision in relation to the asset.
>
> (1B) But subsection (1A) applies only to the extent that the sum has not been excluded from the consideration for an earlier disposal of the asset.
>
> (1C) The following are "deemed disposal provisions"—
>> (a) in relation to trades, professions and vocations, subsections (4) and (5) of section 96A of ITTOIA 2005 (which provide for circumstances in which a person is to be regarded as disposing of an asset for the purposes of that section), and
>> (b) in relation to property businesses, section 307F of ITTOIA 2005 (which provides for circumstances in which a person is to be regarded as disposing of an asset for the purposes of section 307E of that Act)."

45 (1) Section 41 (restriction of losses by reference to capital allowances etc) is amended as follows.

(2) In subsection (4), after paragraph (a) insert—
> "(zaa) any deduction allowable in respect of capital expenditure in calculating profits on the cash basis (see sections 33A and 307B of ITTOIA 2005),".

(3) After subsection (6) insert—
> "(6A) Where—
>> (a) capital allowances have been made or may be made in respect of expenditure, and
>> (b) the capital allowances include a deduction mentioned in subsection (4)(zaa),

134   *Finance (No. 2) Act 2017 (c. 32)*
Schedule 2 — Trades and property businesses: calculation of profits
Part 3 — Trades etc: amendments of other Acts

the capital allowances to be taken into account under this section are to be regarded as equal to the total amount of expenditure which has qualified for capital allowances less any balancing charge to which the person making the disposal is liable under the Capital Allowances Act."

(4) In subsection (7), after "Capital Allowances Act," insert "and subsection (6A) does not apply,".

(5) After subsection (8) insert—

"(9)   In this section—

(a)   in relation to a trade, profession or vocation, references to calculating profits on the cash basis are to calculating the profits of a trade, profession or vocation in relation to which an election under section 25A of ITTOIA 2005 (cash basis for trades) has effect, and

(b)   in relation to a property business, references to calculating profits on the cash basis are to be construed in accordance with section 271D of that Act (calculation of profits of property businesses on the cash basis).

(10)   In this section—

"capital expenditure" means expenditure of a capital nature incurred on, or in connection with, the creation, construction, acquisition, alteration or disposal of an asset, and

"property business" means a UK property business or an overseas property business within the meaning of Part 3 of ITTOIA 2005 (see sections 264 and 265 of that Act)."

46   (1) Section 47A (exemption for disposals by persons using cash basis) is amended as follows.

(2) For the heading substitute "Exemption for certain disposals under, or after leaving, cash basis".

(3) In subsection (1), for "A to D" substitute "A, B and D".

(4) For subsection (2) substitute—

"(2)   Condition A is that the asset is not land."

(5) In subsection (3), for "or vocation" substitute ", vocation or property business".

(6) Omit subsection (4).

(7) For subsection (5) substitute—

"(5)   Condition D is that relevant disposal proceeds—

(a)   are brought into account as a receipt (whether or not on the cash basis) under section 96A(3I) of ITTOIA 2005 in calculating the profits of a trade, profession or vocation (capital receipts under, or after leaving, cash basis: trades, professions and vocations), or

(b)   are brought into account as a receipt (whether or not on the cash basis) under section 307E(12) of that Act in calculating

Finance (No. 2) Act 2017 (c. 32)
Schedule 2 — Trades and property businesses: calculation of profits
Part 3 — Trades etc: amendments of other Acts

135

the profits of a property business (capital receipts under, or after leaving, cash basis: property businesses).

(5A) "Relevant disposal proceeds" means disposal proceeds as mentioned in section 96A(3F) of ITTOIA 2005 or (as the case may be) section 307E(9) of that Act which arise from the disposal mentioned in subsection (1)."

(8) For subsection (6) substitute —

"(6) Subsection (7) applies in the case of the disposal of, or of an interest in, an asset —

    (a) which, in the period of ownership of the person making the disposal —

        (i) has been used partly for the purposes of the trade, profession or vocation and partly for other purposes, or

        (ii) has been used for the purposes of the trade, profession or vocation for part of that period, or

    (b) expenditure on which by the person has qualified in part only for capital allowances."

(9) In subsection (7) —

    (a) in paragraph (a), for "was, or (as the case may be)" to the end substitute "qualified for capital allowances", and

    (b) in paragraph (c), at the end insert ", or to the expenditure qualifying for capital allowances."

(10) After subsection (7) insert —

"(8) In this section "property business" means a UK property business or an overseas property business within the meaning of Part 3 of ITTOIA 2005 (see sections 264 and 265 of that Act)."

47   Section 47B (disposals made by persons after leaving cash basis) is omitted.

CAA 2001

48   CAA 2001 is amended as follows.

49   In section 1 (capital allowances), omit subsections (4) and (5).

50   After section 1 insert —

"1A   Capital allowances and charges: cash basis

(1) This section applies in relation to a chargeable period for which the profits of a trade, profession, vocation or property business ("the relevant activity") carried on by a person are calculated on the cash basis.

(2) The person is not entitled to any allowance or liable to any charge under this Act except as provided by subsections (4) and (7).

(3) No disposal value is to be brought into account except as provided by subsections (5) and (8).

(4) If, apart from subsection (2), the person would be entitled to an allowance in respect of expenditure incurred on the provision of a

136

Finance (No. 2) Act 2017 (c. 32)
Schedule 2 — Trades and property businesses: calculation of profits
Part 3 — Trades etc: amendments of other Acts

car or liable to a charge in connection with such an allowance, the person is so entitled or (as the case may be) so liable.

(5) If, apart from subsection (3), a disposal value would be brought into account in respect of a car, the disposal value is brought into account in respect of the car.

(6) Subsections (7) and (8) apply if—

    (a) a person carrying on a relevant activity incurs qualifying expenditure relating to an asset at a time when the profits of that activity are not calculated on the cash basis,

    (b) after incurring the expenditure, the person enters the cash basis for a tax year, and

    (c) no deduction would be allowed in respect of the expenditure in calculating the profits of the relevant activity on the cash basis for that tax year, on the assumption that the expenditure was paid in that tax year.

(7) If, apart from subsection (2), the person would be liable to a charge in connection with allowances in respect of the qualifying expenditure mentioned in subsection (6), the person is so liable.

(8) If, apart from subsection (3), a disposal value would be brought into account in respect of the asset mentioned in subsection (6), the disposal value is brought into account in respect of the asset.

(9) For the purposes of this section a person carrying on a trade, profession or vocation "enters the cash basis" for a tax year if—

    (a) an election under section 25A of ITTOIA 2005 (cash basis for trades) has effect in relation to the trade, profession or vocation for the tax year, and

    (b) no such election has effect in relation to the trade, profession or vocation for the previous tax year.

(10) For the purposes of this section a person carrying on a property business "enters the cash basis" for a tax year if the profits of the business are calculated—

    (a) on the cash basis for the tax year (see section 271D of ITTOIA 2005), and

    (b) in accordance with GAAP (see section 271B of that Act) for the previous tax year.

(11) In this section—

    (a) references to calculating the profits of a trade, profession or vocation on the cash basis are to calculating the profits of a trade, profession or vocation in relation to which an election under section 25A of ITTOIA 2005 has effect, and

    (b) references to calculating the profits of a property business on the cash basis are to be construed in accordance with section 271D of that Act (calculation of profits of property businesses on the cash basis).

(12) In this section—

    "car" has the same meaning as in Part 2 (see section 268A);

    "disposal value" means—

Finance (No. 2) Act 2017 (c. 32)
Schedule 2 — Trades and property businesses: calculation of profits
Part 3 — Trades etc: amendments of other Acts

137

      (a)   a disposal value for the purposes of Part 2, 4A, 5, 6, 7, 8 or 10, or

      (b)   proceeds from a balancing event for the purposes of Part 3 or 3A;

"qualifying expenditure" means qualifying expenditure within the meaning of any Part of this Act."

51   (1) Section 4 (capital expenditure) is amended as follows.

   (2) In subsection (2) —

      (a)   omit "or" at the end of paragraph (a), and

      (b)   after paragraph (a) insert—

         "(aa)   any cash basis expenditure, other than expenditure incurred on the provision of a car, or".

   (3) After subsection (2) insert—

     "(2ZA)   In subsection (2)(aa) —

        "cash basis expenditure" means any expenditure incurred —

      (a)   in the case of a trade, profession or vocation, at a time when an election under section 25A of ITTOIA 2005 has effect in relation to the trade, profession or vocation, or

      (b)   in the case of a property business, in a tax year for which the profits of the business are calculated on the cash basis (see section 271D of that Act); and

        "car" has the same meaning as in Part 2 (see section 268A)."

52   (1) Section 59 (unrelieved qualifying expenditure) is amended as follows.

   (2) In subsection (4), for "no amount may be carried forward as unrelieved qualifying expenditure" substitute "any cash basis deductible amount may not be carried forward as unrelieved qualifying expenditure in a pool for the trade, profession or vocation".

   (3) After subsection (4) insert—

     "(4A)   If a person carrying on a property business enters the cash basis for a tax year, any cash basis deductible amount may not be carried forward as unrelieved qualifying expenditure in a pool for a relevant qualifying activity from the chargeable period which is the previous tax year."

   (4) Omit subsection (5).

   (5) After subsection (5) insert—

     "(5A)   A "cash basis deductible amount" means any amount of unrelieved qualifying expenditure for which a deduction would be allowed in calculating the profits of the trade, profession, vocation or property business (as the case may be) on the cash basis on the assumption that the expenditure was paid in the tax year for which the person enters the cash basis."

   (6) In subsection (6), for "the amount of unrelieved qualifying expenditure incurred on the provision of a car" substitute "any cash basis deductible amount".

138   *Finance (No. 2) Act 2017 (c. 32)*
Schedule 2 — Trades and property businesses: calculation of profits
Part 3 — Trades etc: amendments of other Acts

(7) For subsection (7) substitute—

> "(7) Subsections (9), (10) and (11) of section 1A (capital allowances and charges: cash basis) apply for the purposes of this section as they apply for the purposes of that section.
>
> (7A) In subsection (4A) "relevant qualifying activity" means—
>> (a) in relation to a UK property business, an ordinary UK property business and a UK furnished holiday lettings business, and
>> (b) in relation to an overseas property business, an ordinary overseas property business and an EEA furnished holiday lettings business."

53 (1) Section 66A (persons leaving cash basis) is amended as follows.

(2) For subsection (1) substitute—

> "(1) This section applies if—
>> (a) a person carrying on a trade, profession, vocation or property business ("the business") leaves the cash basis in a chargeable period,
>> (b) the person has incurred expenditure at a time when the profits of the business are calculated on the cash basis,
>> (c) some or all of the expenditure was brought into account in calculating the profits of the business on the cash basis, and
>> (d) the expenditure would have been qualifying expenditure if the profits of the business had not been calculated on the cash basis at the time the expenditure was incurred."

(3) In subsection (2)(a)—

(a) for "amount of that expenditure for which" substitute "higher of the following",

(b) in sub-paragraphs (i) and (ii), at the beginning insert "the amount of that expenditure for which", and

(c) in both places, for "or vocation" substitute ", vocation or property business".

(4) After subsection (6) insert—

> "(7) For the purposes of this section a person carrying on a property business leaves the cash basis in a chargeable period ("tax year X") if the profits of the business are calculated—
>> (a) in accordance with GAAP (see section 271B of ITTOIA 2005) for tax year X, and
>> (b) on the cash basis (see section 271D of that Act) for the previous tax year.
>
> (8) Subsection (11) of section 1A (capital allowances and charges: cash basis) applies for the purposes of this section as it applies for the purposes of that section."

Finance (No. 2) Act 2017 (c. 32)
Schedule 2 — Trades and property businesses: calculation of profits
Part 3 — Trades etc: amendments of other Acts

139

54   After section 419 insert—

"419A Unrelieved qualifying expenditure: entry to cash basis

(1)   If a person carrying on a mineral extraction trade enters the cash basis for a tax year, for the purpose of determining the person's unrelieved qualifying expenditure for the chargeable period ending with the basis period for the tax year and subsequent chargeable periods (see section 419), only the non-cash basis deductible portion of qualifying expenditure incurred before the chargeable period ending with the basis period for the tax year is to be taken into account.

(2)   The "non-cash basis deductible portion" of qualifying expenditure means the amount of qualifying expenditure for which no deduction would be allowed in calculating the profits of the trade on the cash basis on the assumption that the expenditure was paid in the tax year for which the person enters the cash basis.

(3)   Subsections (9) and (11) of section 1A (capital allowances and charges: cash basis) apply for the purposes of this section as they apply for the purposes of that section."

55   After section 431C insert—

"431D Persons leaving cash basis

(1)   This section applies if—
        (a)   a person carrying on a mineral extraction trade leaves the cash basis in a chargeable period,
        (b)   the person has incurred expenditure at a time when an election under section 25A of ITTOIA 2005 (cash basis for trades) has effect in relation to the trade,
        (c)   some or all of the expenditure was brought into account in calculating the profits of the trade on the cash basis, and
        (d)   the expenditure would have been qualifying expenditure if an election under section 25A of that Act had not had effect at the time the expenditure was incurred.

(2)   In this section—
        (a)   the "relieved portion" of the expenditure is the higher of the following—
                (i)   the amount of that expenditure for which a deduction was allowed in calculating the profits of the trade, or
                (ii)   the amount of that expenditure for which a deduction would have been so allowed if the expenditure had been incurred wholly and exclusively for the purposes of the trade;
        (b)   the "unrelieved portion" of the expenditure is any remaining amount of the expenditure.

(3)   An amount of the expenditure equal to the amount (if any) by which the unrelieved portion of the expenditure exceeds the relieved portion of the expenditure is to be regarded as qualifying expenditure incurred by the person in the chargeable period.

140

Finance (No. 2) Act 2017 (c. 32)
Schedule 2 — Trades and property businesses: calculation of profits
Part 3 — Trades etc: amendments of other Acts

    (4) For the purposes of this section a person carrying on a trade leaves the cash basis in a chargeable period if—

        (a) immediately before the beginning of the chargeable period an election under section 25A of ITTOIA 2005 had effect in relation to the trade, and

        (b) such an election does not have effect in relation to the trade for the chargeable period."

56   After section 461 insert—

"461A Unrelieved qualifying expenditure: entry to cash basis

    (1) If a person carrying on a trade enters the cash basis for a tax year, any cash basis deductible amount may not be carried forward as unrelieved qualifying expenditure in the pool for the trade from the chargeable period ending with the basis period for the previous tax year.

    (2) A "cash basis deductible amount" means any amount of unrelieved qualifying expenditure for which a deduction would be allowed in calculating the profits of the trade on the cash basis on the assumption that the expenditure was paid in the tax year for which the person enters the cash basis.

    (3) Any cash basis deductible amount is to be determined on such basis as is just and reasonable in all the circumstances.

    (4) Subsections (9) and (11) of section 1A (capital allowances and charges: cash basis) apply for the purposes of this section as they apply for the purposes of that section."

57   After section 462 insert—

"462A Persons leaving cash basis

    (1) This section applies if—

        (a) a person carrying on a trade leaves the cash basis in a chargeable period,

        (b) the person has incurred expenditure at a time when an election under section 25A of ITTOIA 2005 (cash basis for trades) has effect in relation to the trade,

        (c) some or all of the expenditure was brought into account in calculating the profits of the trade on the cash basis, and

        (d) the expenditure would have been qualifying expenditure if an election under section 25A of that Act had not had effect at the time the expenditure was incurred.

    (2) In this section the "relieved portion" of the expenditure is the higher of the following—

        (a) the amount of that expenditure for which a deduction was allowed in calculating the profits of the trade, or

        (b) the amount of that expenditure for which a deduction would have been so allowed if the expenditure had been incurred wholly and exclusively for the purposes of the trade.

Finance (No. 2) Act 2017 (c. 32)
Schedule 2 — Trades and property businesses: calculation of profits
Part 3 — Trades etc: amendments of other Acts

141

    (3)   For the purposes of determining the person's available qualifying expenditure in the pool for the trade for the chargeable period (see section 456) —

        (a)   the whole of the expenditure must be allocated to the pool for the trade in that chargeable period, and

        (b)   the available qualifying expenditure in that pool is reduced by the relieved portion of that expenditure.

    (4)   For the purposes of determining any disposal values (see section 462), the expenditure incurred by the person is to be regarded as qualifying expenditure.

    (5)   For the purposes of this section a person carrying on a trade leaves the cash basis in a chargeable period if —

        (a)   immediately before the beginning of the chargeable period an election under section 25A of ITTOIA 2005 had effect in relation to the trade, and

        (b)   such an election does not have effect in relation to the trade for the chargeable period."

58   After section 475 insert —

"475A Unrelieved qualifying expenditure: entry to cash basis

    (1)   If a person carrying on a trade enters the cash basis for a tax year, any cash basis deductible amount may not be carried forward as unrelieved qualifying expenditure in the pool for the trade from the chargeable period ending with the basis period for the previous tax year.

    (2)   A "cash basis deductible amount" means any amount of unrelieved qualifying expenditure for which a deduction would be allowed in calculating the profits of the trade on the cash basis on the assumption that the expenditure was paid in the tax year for which the person enters the cash basis.

    (3)   Any cash basis deductible amount is to be determined on such basis as is just and reasonable in all the circumstances.

    (4)   Subsections (9) and (11) of section 1A (capital allowances and charges: cash basis) apply for the purposes of this section as they apply for the purposes of that section."

59   After section 477 insert —

"477A Persons leaving cash basis

    (1)   This section applies if —

        (a)   a person carrying on a trade leaves the cash basis in a chargeable period,

        (b)   the person has incurred expenditure at a time when an election under section 25A of ITTOIA 2005 (cash basis for trades) has effect in relation to the trade,

        (c)   some or all of the expenditure was brought into account in calculating the profits of the trade on the cash basis, and

142

Finance (No. 2) Act 2017 (c. 32)
Schedule 2 — Trades and property businesses: calculation of profits
Part 3 — Trades etc: amendments of other Acts

        (d)   the expenditure would have been qualifying trade expenditure if an election under section 25A of that Act had not had effect at the time the expenditure was incurred.

    (2)   In this section the "relieved portion" of the expenditure is the amount of that expenditure for which a deduction was allowed in calculating the profits of the trade.

    (3)   For the purposes of determining the person's available qualifying expenditure in the pool for the trade for the chargeable period (see section 470) —

        (a)   the whole of the expenditure must be allocated to the pool for the trade in that chargeable period, and

        (b)   the available qualifying expenditure in that pool is reduced by the relieved portion of that expenditure.

    (4)   For the purposes of determining any disposal receipts (see section 476), the expenditure incurred by the person is to be regarded as qualifying trade expenditure.

    (5)   For the purposes of this section a person carrying on a trade leaves the cash basis in a chargeable period if —

        (a)   immediately before the beginning of the chargeable period an election under section 25A of ITTOIA 2005 had effect in relation to the trade, and

        (b)   such an election does not have effect in relation to the trade for the chargeable period."

ITA 2007

60   ITA 2007 is amended as follows.

61   In Part 4 (loss relief), in section 59 (overview of Part), in subsection (3)(b) —

        (a)   for "section 272" substitute "sections 272 and 272ZA", and

        (b)   for "applies" substitute "apply".

62   (1)   Chapter 4 of Part 4 (losses from property businesses) is amended as follows.

    (2)   In section 120 (deduction of property losses from general income), in subsection (7), at the end insert "and section 127BA (restriction of relief: cash basis)".

    (3)   After section 127B insert —

"127BA Restriction of relief: cash basis

    (1)   This section applies if —

        (a)   in a tax year a person makes a loss in a UK property business or overseas property business (whether carried on alone or in partnership), and

        (b)   the profits of the business are calculated on the cash basis for the tax year (see section 271D of ITTOIA 2005).

    (2)   No property loss relief against general income may be given to the person for the loss."

63   In Chapter 1 of Part 8 (relief for interest payments), in section 384B(1) (restriction on relief for interest payments where cash basis applies), after

Finance (No. 2) Act 2017 (c. 32)
Schedule 2 — Trades and property businesses: calculation of profits
Part 3 — Trades etc: amendments of other Acts

143

"for the tax year" insert "or if the profits of a UK property business or overseas property business carried on by the partnership are calculated on the cash basis for the tax year (see section 271D of ITTOIA 2005)."

PART 4

COMMENCEMENT AND TRANSITIONAL PROVISION

64 (1) The amendments made by this Schedule have effect for the tax year 2017-18 and subsequent tax years.

    (2) If —

        (a) disregarding this sub-paragraph, under section 33A of ITTOIA 2005, as inserted by paragraph 2 of Part 1, a deduction would not be allowed in calculating the profits of a trade, profession or vocation on the cash basis for the tax year 2017-18, but

        (b) if the amendment made by paragraph 2 were not to have effect for that tax year, that deduction would be allowed in calculating the profits of that trade, profession or vocation on that basis for that tax year,

    that deduction is to be allowed in calculating the profits of that trade, profession or vocation on that basis for that tax year.

    (3) Sub-paragraph (2) is to be disregarded in determining any question as to whether or to what extent an amount of expenditure would, on the assumption that it was paid in the tax year 2017-18, be brought into account in calculating the profits of a trade, profession or vocation for the tax year 2017-18 for the purposes of —

        (a) the following provisions of CAA 2001 —

            (i) section 1A (capital allowances and charges: cash basis),

            (ii) section 59 (unrelieved qualifying expenditure),

            (iii) section 419A (unrelieved qualifying expenditure: entry to cash basis),

            (iv) section 461A (unrelieved qualifying expenditure: entry to cash basis), and

            (v) section 475A (unrelieved qualifying expenditure: entry to cash basis); and

        (b) the following provisions of ITTOIA 2005 —

            (i) section 96A (capital receipts under, or after leaving, cash basis),

            (ii) section 240C (unrelieved qualifying expenditure: Parts 2, 7 and 8 of CAA 2001),

            (iii) section 240CA (unrelieved qualifying expenditure: Part 5 of CAA 2001), and

            (iv) section 240D (assets not fully paid for).

    (4) But sub-paragraph (2) is not to be disregarded in determining any question as to whether or to what extent an amount of expenditure is actually brought into account in calculating the profits of a trade, profession or vocation for the tax year 2017-18 for the purposes of the provisions mentioned in paragraphs (a) and (b) of sub-paragraph (3).

SCHEDULE 3   Section 17

TRADING AND PROPERTY ALLOWANCES

PART 1

MAIN PROVISIONS

1   In ITTOIA 2005, after section 783 insert—

"PART 6A

INCOME CHARGED UNDER THIS ACT: TRADING AND PROPERTY ALLOWANCES

CHAPTER 1

TRADING ALLOWANCE

Introduction

783A Relief under this Chapter

(1)   This Chapter gives relief to an individual on—
    (a)   the income of a relevant trade (see section 783AA), and
    (b)   miscellaneous income (see section 783AB).

(2)   If the individual qualifies for full relief (see section 783AE), the individual's relevant income (see section 783AC) is not charged to income tax (see sections 783AF and 783AG).

(3)   If the individual qualifies for partial relief (see section 783AH), the individual's relevant income is calculated by alternative methods (see sections 783AI to 783AK).

(4)   Any provision of this Chapter which gives relief is subject to sections 783AN to 783AQ, which specify circumstances in which relief under this Chapter is not given.

Basic definitions

783AA "Relevant trade" of an individual

(1)   For the purposes of this Chapter, a trade carried on by an individual is a "relevant trade" of the individual for a tax year if—
    (a)   the individual carries on the trade otherwise than in partnership, and
    (b)   the trade is not a rent-a-room trade in relation to the individual for the tax year.

(2)   For the purposes of subsection (1)(b) a trade is a "rent-a-room trade" in relation to an individual for a tax year if—
    (a)   the individual qualifies for rent-a-room relief for the tax year, and
    (b)   the individual has rent-a-room receipts for the tax year which would, apart from Chapter 1 of Part 7 (rent-a-room relief), be brought into account in calculating the profits of the trade.

See section 783AR for definitions relevant to this subsection.

(3)   In this Chapter references to a trade include references to a profession or vocation.

783AB "Miscellaneous income"

(1)   For the purposes of this Chapter, an individual's "miscellaneous income" for a tax year is all the income arising to the individual in the tax year which would be chargeable to income tax under Chapter 8 of Part 5 (income not otherwise charged) for the tax year.

(2)   But if—

    (a)   the individual qualifies for rent-a-room relief for the tax year, and

    (b)   the individual has rent-a-room receipts for the tax year which would, apart from Chapter 1 of Part 7, be chargeable to income tax under Chapter 8 of Part 5,

the rent-a-room receipts are not miscellaneous income.

(3)   The reference in subsection (1) to the amount which would be chargeable to income tax under Chapter 8 of Part 5 is to the amount which would be so chargeable—

    (a)   apart from this Chapter, and

    (b)   if no deduction were made for expenses or any other matter.

783AC The individual's "relevant income"

(1)   For the purposes of this Chapter, an individual's "relevant income" for a tax year is the sum of the following—

    (a)   the receipts for the tax year of the individual's relevant trades for the tax year, and

    (b)   the individual's miscellaneous income for the tax year.

(2)   In subsection (1)(a) the reference to the receipts of a trade for a tax year is to all the amounts which would, apart from this Chapter, be brought into account as a receipt in calculating the profits of the trade for the tax year.

783AD The individual's trading allowance

(1)   For the purposes of this Chapter, an individual's trading allowance for a tax year is £1,000.

(2)   The Treasury may by regulations amend subsection (1) so as to substitute a higher sum for the sum for the time being specified in that subsection.

Full relief

783AE Full relief: introduction

(1)   An individual qualifies for full relief for a tax year if—

    (a)   the individual has relevant income for the tax year,

    (b)   the relevant income does not exceed the individual's trading allowance for the tax year, and

      (c)   no election by the individual under section 783AL has effect for the tax year (election for full relief not to be given).

(2)   An individual also qualifies for full relief for a tax year if—

      (a)   the individual has relevant income for the tax year which consists of or includes receipts of one or more relevant trades,

      (b)   the relevant income exceeds the individual's trading allowance for the tax year,

      (c)   the conditions mentioned in subsection (3) are met,

      (d)   no election by the individual under section 783AL has effect for the tax year, and

      (e)   no election by the individual under section 783AM has effect for the tax year (election for partial relief).

(3)   The conditions are that—

      (a)   no election by the individual under section 25A (cash basis for trades) has effect for the tax year,

      (b)   the individual's relevant income would not exceed the individual's trading allowance for the tax year if it were to be assumed that an election by the individual under section 25A had effect for the tax year,

      (c)   the individual is eligible to make an election under section 25A (see section 31A) for the tax year, and

      (d)   if any trade carried on by the individual in the tax year was carried on in the immediately preceding tax year—

          (i)   an election by the individual under section 25A had effect for that preceding tax year, or

          (ii)   the individual was eligible to make such an election for that preceding tax year.

783AF Full relief: trade profits

(1)   This section applies if—

      (a)   an individual qualifies for full relief for a tax year, and

      (b)   the individual's relevant income for the tax year consists of or includes receipts of one or more relevant trades.

(2)   The profits or losses of each such trade for the tax year are treated as nil.

783AG Full relief: miscellaneous income

(1)   This section applies if—

      (a)   an individual qualifies for full relief for a tax year, and

      (b)   the individual's relevant income for the tax year consists of or includes miscellaneous income.

(2)   The amount of—

      (a)   the miscellaneous income arising in the tax year, less

      (b)   any expenses associated with that income,

is treated as nil.

Partial relief

783AH Partial relief: alternative calculation of profits: introduction

An individual qualifies for partial relief for a tax year if—

    (a)   the individual has relevant income for the tax year,

    (b)   the relevant income exceeds the individual's trading allowance for the tax year, and

    (c)   an election by the individual under section 783AM has effect for the tax year (election for partial relief).

783AI Partial relief: alternative calculation of trade profits

(1)   This section applies if—

    (a)   an individual qualifies for partial relief for a tax year, and

    (b)   the individual's relevant income for the tax year consists of or includes receipts of one or more relevant trades.

(2)   The profits or losses for the tax year of each of the individual's relevant trades are given by taking the following steps—

Step 1

Calculate the total of all the amounts which would, apart from this Chapter, be brought into account as a receipt in calculating the profits of the trade for the tax year.

Step 2

Subtract the deductible amount.

Step 3

Subtract from the amount given by step 2 any deduction for overlap profit allowed in calculating the profits of the trade for the tax year under section 205 (deduction for overlap profit in final tax year) or section 220 (deduction for overlap profit on change of accounting date).

(3)   Subject to section 783AK, the deductible amount is equal to the individual's trading allowance for the tax year.

(4)   "Overlap profit" has the same meaning in this section as it has in Chapter 15 of Part 2 (see sections 204 and 204A).

783AJ Partial relief: alternative calculation of chargeable miscellaneous income

(1)   This section applies if—

    (a)   an individual qualifies for partial relief for a tax year, and

    (b)   the individual's relevant income for the tax year consists of or includes miscellaneous income.

(2)   The amount of miscellaneous income chargeable to income tax for the tax year is—

    (a)   the miscellaneous income for the tax year, less

    (b)   the deductible amount.

(3)   Subject to section 783AK, the deductible amount is equal to the individual's trading allowance for the tax year.

783AK Deductible amount: splitting of trading allowance

(1) This section applies where the individual's relevant income for the tax year includes —

    (a) receipts of a relevant trade, and

    (b) receipts of any other relevant trade or miscellaneous income (or both).

(2) The references in section 783AI and (where it applies) section 783AJ to the deductible amount are to amounts which, in total, equal the individual's trading allowance for the tax year.

(3) The question of how to allocate the individual's trading allowance for the tax year for the purposes of subsection (2) is to be decided by the individual, subject to subsections (4) and (5).

(4) The deductible amount in respect of a relevant trade must not be such that the amount given by step 2 of section 783AI(2) is negative.

(5) The deductible amount in respect of miscellaneous income must not be such as to result in the individual making a loss in the transactions giving rise to the miscellaneous income.

Elections

783AL Election for full relief not to be given

(1) An individual may elect not to be given full relief for a tax year (see sections 783AF and 783AG).

(2) An election must be made on or before the first anniversary of the normal self-assessment filing date for the tax year for which the election is made.

783AM Election for partial relief

(1) An individual may elect for partial relief to be given for a tax year if the individual's relevant income for the tax year exceeds the individual's trading allowance for the tax year (see sections 783AI and 783AJ).

(2) An election must be made on or before the first anniversary of the normal self-assessment filing date for the tax year for which the election is made.

Exclusions from relief

783AN Exclusion from relief: expenses deducted against rent-a-room receipts

(1) No relief under this Chapter is given to an individual for a tax year if —

    (a) the individual qualifies for rent-a-room relief for the tax year,

    (b) the individual has rent-a-room receipts mentioned in subsection (2) for the tax year, and

    (c) condition A or B is met.

(2) The rent-a-room receipts mentioned in subsection (1) are —

     (a)   rent-a-room receipts which would, apart from Chapter 1 of Part 7 (rent-a-room relief), be brought into account in calculating the profits of a trade, or

     (b)   rent-a-room receipts which would, apart from Chapter 1 of Part 7, be chargeable to income tax under Chapter 8 of Part 5 (income not otherwise charged).

(3)   Condition A is that—

     (a)   the individual's total rent-a-room amount for the tax year does not exceed the individual's limit for the tax year (see section 783AR), and

     (b)   an election by the individual under section 799 has effect to disapply full rent-a-room relief for the tax year.

(4)   Condition B is that—

     (a)   the individual's total rent-a-room amount for the tax year exceeds the individual's limit for the tax year, and

     (b)   no election by the individual under section 800 has effect to apply the alternative method of calculating profits for the tax year.

783AO Exclusion from relief: payments by employer

No relief under this Chapter is given to an individual for a tax year if—

     (a)   the individual has relevant income for the tax year, and

     (b)   the income includes a payment made by, or on behalf of, a person at a time when the individual is—

         (i)   an employee of the person, or

         (ii)   the spouse or civil partner of an employee of the person.

783AP Exclusion from relief: payments by firm

No relief under this Chapter is given to an individual for a tax year if—

     (a)   the individual has relevant income for the tax year, and

     (b)   the income includes a payment made by, or on behalf of, a firm at a time when the individual is—

         (i)   a partner in the firm, or

         (ii)   connected with a partner in the firm.

783AQ Exclusion from relief: payments by close company

(1)   No relief under this Chapter is given to an individual for a tax year if—

     (a)   the individual has relevant income for the tax year, and

     (b)   the income includes a payment made by, or on behalf of, a close company at a time when the individual is—

         (i)   a participator in the close company, or

         (ii)   an associate of a participator in the close company.

(2)   In this section "associate" and "participator" have the same meanings as in Part 10 of CTA 2010 (see sections 448 and 454).

Interpretation

783AR Interpretation of this Chapter

In this Chapter —

    (a)   "rent-a-room relief", "rent-a-room receipts" and "total rent-a-room amount" have the same meanings as in Chapter 1 of Part 7 (rent-a-room relief: see sections 784, 786 and 788), and

    (b)   references to "the individual's limit" are to be construed in accordance with section 789 (the individual's limit for the purposes of rent-a-room relief).

CHAPTER 2

PROPERTY ALLOWANCE

Introduction

783B Relief under this Chapter

(1)   This Chapter gives relief to an individual on certain income of a relevant property business (see sections 783BA and 783BB).

(2)   The form of relief depends on whether the individual's relevant property income exceeds the individual's property allowance (see sections 783BC and 783BD).

(3)   If the individual's relevant property income does not exceed the individual's property allowance, the income is not charged to income tax (unless the individual elects otherwise) (see sections 783BE and 783BF).

(4)   If the individual's relevant property income does exceed the individual's property allowance, the individual may elect for an alternative method of calculating the income (see sections 783BG to 783BI).

(5)   Any provision of this Chapter which gives relief is subject to sections 783BL to 783BP, which specify circumstances in which relief under this Chapter is not given.

Basic definitions

783BA "Relevant property business" of an individual

(1)   Subject to subsection (3), for the purposes of this Chapter an individual's property business is a "relevant property business" for a tax year if the business is not a rent-a-room property business in relation to the individual for the tax year.

(2)   For the purposes of subsection (1) a property business is a "rent-a-room property business" in relation to an individual for a tax year if —

    (a)   the individual qualifies for rent-a-room relief for the tax year, and

(b)   all the receipts which would, apart from Chapter 1 of Part 7 (rent-a-room relief), be brought into account in calculating the profits of the business, are rent-a-room receipts.

See section 783BQ for definitions relevant to this subsection.

(3)   If an individual receives—

(a)   property income distributions which are treated as profits of a UK property business by virtue of regulation 69Z18(1) or (2) of the AIF Regulations (property AIF distributions: liability to tax), or

(b)   distributions which are treated as profits of a UK property business by virtue of section 548(6) of CTA 2010 (REIT distributions: liability to tax),

that separate property business (see regulation 69Z18(6) of the AIF Regulations and section 549(5) of CTA 2010) is not a relevant property business of the individual.

(4)   In subsection (3) "the AIF Regulations" means the Authorised Investment Funds (Tax) Regulations 2006 (S.I. 2006/964).

783BB "Relievable receipts" of a property business

(1)   For the purposes of this Chapter, the "relievable receipts" of an individual's relevant property business for a tax year are all the amounts which would, apart from this Chapter, be brought into account as a receipt in calculating the profits of the business for the tax year.

This is subject to subsections (2) and (3).

(2)   If—

(a)   the individual qualifies for rent-a-room relief for the tax year, and

(b)   the individual has rent-a-room receipts for the tax year which would, apart from Chapter 1 of Part 7, be brought into account in calculating the profits of the property business,

the rent-a-room receipts are not relievable receipts of the business.

(3)   Non-relievable balancing charges in respect of the property business for the tax year are not relievable receipts of the business.

(4)   In subsection (3) "non-relievable balancing charges", in respect of a property business for a tax year, means balancing charges falling to be made for the tax year under Part 2 of CAA 2001 which do not relate to a business or transaction which is carried on, or entered into, for the purpose of generating receipts which are relievable receipts of the property business.

783BC The individual's "relevant property income"

For the purposes of this Chapter, an individual's "relevant property income" for a tax year is the relievable receipts for the tax year of the individual's relevant property businesses for the tax year.

783BD The individual's property allowance

(1)   For the purposes of this Chapter, an individual's property allowance for a tax year is £1,000.

(2) The Treasury may by regulations amend subsection (1) so as to substitute a higher sum for the sum for the time being specified in that subsection.

Relief if relevant property income does not exceed property allowance

783BE Full relief: introduction

An individual qualifies for full relief for a tax year if —
  (a) the individual has relevant property income for the tax year,
  (b) the relevant property income does not exceed the individual's property allowance for the tax year, and
  (c) no election by the individual under section 783BJ has effect for the tax year (election for full relief not to be given).

783BF Full relief: property profits

(1) If an individual qualifies for full relief for a tax year, this section applies in relation to the calculation of the profits of the individual's relevant property business for the tax year or, where the individual's relevant property income for the tax year consists of the relievable receipts of two relevant property businesses, the profits of each property business for the tax year.

(2) The following are not brought into account —
  (a) the relievable receipts of the property business for the tax year, and
  (b) any expenses associated with those receipts.

Relief if relevant property income exceeds property allowance

783BG Partial relief: alternative calculation of property profits: introduction

An individual qualifies for partial relief for a tax year if —
  (a) the individual has relevant property income for the tax year,
  (b) the relevant property income exceeds the individual's property allowance for the tax year, and
  (c) an election by the individual under section 783BK has effect for the tax year (election for partial relief).

783BH Partial relief: alternative calculation of property profits

(1) If an individual qualifies for partial relief for a tax year, this section applies in relation to the calculation of the profits of the individual's relevant property business for the tax year or, where the individual's relevant property income for the tax year consists of the relievable receipts of two relevant property businesses, the profits of each property business for the tax year.

(2) The relievable receipts of the property business for the tax year are brought into account.

(3) No relevant expenses are brought into account.

(4) The deductible amount is brought into account.

(5) Subject to section 783BI, the deductible amount is equal to the individual's property allowance for the tax year.

(6) In subsection (3) "relevant expenses" means all the amounts—

    (a) which would, apart from this section, be brought into account as a deduction in calculating the profits of the business for the tax year, and

    (b) which are associated with the relievable receipts.

783BI Deductible amount: splitting of property allowance

(1) This section applies where the individual's relevant property income for the tax year consists of the relievable receipts of two relevant property businesses.

(2) The references in section 783BH to the deductible amount are to amounts which, in total, equal the individual's property allowance for the tax year.

(3) The question of how to allocate the individual's property allowance for the tax year for the purposes of subsection (2) is to be decided by the individual, subject to subsection (4).

(4) The deductible amount in respect of a relevant property business must not be such as to result in a loss of the business.

Elections

783BJ Election for full relief not to be given

(1) An individual may elect not to be given full relief for a tax year (see section 783BF).

(2) An election must be made on or before the first anniversary of the normal self-assessment filing date for the tax year for which the election is made.

783BK Election for partial relief

(1) An individual may elect for partial relief to be given for a tax year if the individual's relevant property income for the tax year exceeds the individual's property allowance for the tax year (see section 783BH).

(2) An election must be made on or before the first anniversary of the normal self-assessment filing date for the tax year for which the election is made.

Exclusions from relief

783BL Exclusion from relief: tax reduction under section 274A

No relief under this Chapter is given to an individual for a tax year if, in calculating the individual's liability to income tax for the tax year, a tax reduction under section 274A (property business: relief for non-deductible costs of a dwelling-related loan) is applied at Step 6 of the calculation in section 23 of ITA 2007.

783BM Exclusion from relief: expenses deducted against rent-a-room receipts

(1)   No relief under this Chapter is given to an individual for a tax year if—

    (a)   the individual qualifies for rent-a-room relief for the tax year,

    (b)   the individual has rent-a-room receipts for the tax year which would, apart from Chapter 1 of Part 7 (rent-a-room relief), be brought into account in calculating the profits of a property business, and

    (c)   condition A or B is met.

(2)   Condition A is that—

    (a)   the individual's total rent-a-room amount for the tax year does not exceed the individual's limit for the tax year (see section 783BQ), and

    (b)   an election by the individual under section 799 has effect to disapply full rent-a-room relief for the tax year.

(3)   Condition B is that—

    (a)   the individual's total rent-a-room amount for the tax year exceeds the individual's limit for the tax year, and

    (b)   no election by the individual under section 800 has effect to apply the alternative method of calculating profits for the tax year.

783BN Exclusion from relief: payments by employer

No relief under this Chapter is given to an individual for a tax year if—

    (a)   the individual has relevant property income for the tax year, and

    (b)   the income includes a payment made by, or on behalf of, a person at a time when the individual is—

        (i)   an employee of the person, or

        (ii)   the spouse or civil partner of an employee of the person.

783BO Exclusion from relief: payments by firm

No relief under this Chapter is given to an individual for a tax year if—

    (a)   the individual has relevant property income for the tax year, and

    (b)   the income includes a payment made by, or on behalf of, a firm at a time when the individual is—

        (i)   a partner in the firm, or

        (ii)   connected with a partner in the firm.

783BP Exclusion from relief: payments by close company

(1)   No relief under this Chapter is given to an individual for a tax year if—

    (a)   the individual has relevant property income for the tax year, and

       (b)   the income includes a payment made by, or on behalf of, a close company at a time when the individual is—

          (i)   a participator in the close company, or

          (ii)   an associate of a participator in the close company.

  (2)   In this section "associate" and "participator" have the same meanings as in Part 10 of CTA 2010 (see sections 448 and 454).

Interpretation

783BQ Interpretation of this Chapter

In this Chapter—

       (a)   "rent-a-room relief", "rent-a-room receipts" and "total rent-a-room amount" have the same meanings as in Chapter 1 of Part 7 (rent-a-room relief: see sections 784, 786 and 788), and

       (b)   references to "the individual's limit" are to be construed in accordance with section 789 (the individual's limit for the purposes of rent-a-room relief)."

PART 2

CONSEQUENTIAL AMENDMENTS

ITTOIA 2005

2   ITTOIA 2005 is amended in accordance with paragraphs 3 to 11.

3   In section 1 (overview of Act), before paragraph (a) of subsection (5) insert—

      "(za)   provision about a trading allowance and property allowance (see Part 6A),".

4   In Chapter 2 of Part 2 (trading income: income taxed as trade profits), after section 22 insert—

"Trading allowance

22A   Trading allowance

  (1)   The rules for calculating the profits of a trade, profession or vocation carried on by an individual are subject to Chapter 1 of Part 6A (trading allowance).

  (2)   That Chapter gives relief on relevant income and, where relief is given, disallows most deductions under this Part (see, in particular, sections 783AC, 783AF and 783AI)."

5   In Chapter 15 of Part 2 (basis periods), after section 204 insert—

"204A Overlap profit and trading allowance under Chapter 1 of Part 6A

  (1)   This section makes provision about the amount of profit treated as arising in an overlap period which falls within the basis period of a trade for two tax years ("tax year A" and "tax year B") where relief is given under Chapter 1 of Part 6A (trading allowance) in respect of the trade for at least one of those tax years.

(2) The profit which arises in the overlap period is treated as nil if—

    (a) the profits or losses of the trade for tax year A or tax year B (or both) are treated as nil under section 783AF (full relief: trade profits), or

    (b) in relation to tax year A or tax year B (or both)—

        (i) section 783AI applies in calculating the profits or losses of the trade (partial relief: alternative calculation of trade profits), and

        (ii) the deductible amount subtracted at step 2 of section 783AI(2) in relation to the trade is greater than or equal to the non-adjusted overlap profit.

(3) Subsection (6) applies if conditions 1 and 2 are met.

(4) Condition 1 is that, in relation to either tax year A or tax year B—

    (a) section 783AI applies in calculating the profits or losses of the trade, and

    (b) the deductible amount subtracted at step 2 of section 783AI(2) in relation to the trade is less than the non-adjusted overlap profit.

(5) Condition 2 is that neither section 783AF nor section 783AI applies in relation to the trade—

    (a) where condition 1 is met in relation to tax year A, for tax year B, or

    (b) where condition 1 is met in relation to tax year B, for tax year A.

(6) The profit which arises in the overlap period is treated as equal to the non-adjusted overlap profit less the deductible amount mentioned in subsection (4)(b).

(7) Subsection (8) applies if, in relation to each of tax year A and tax year B—

    (a) section 783AI applies in calculating the profits or losses of the trade, and

    (b) the deductible amount subtracted at step 2 of section 783AI(2) in relation to the trade is less than the non-adjusted overlap profit.

(8) The profit which arises in the overlap period is treated as equal to the non-adjusted overlap profit less the higher of the following—

    (a) the deductible amount subtracted at step 2 of section 783AI(2) in calculating the profits or losses of the trade for tax year A, and

    (b) the deductible amount subtracted at step 2 of section 783AI(2) in calculating the profits or losses of the trade for tax year B.

(9) In this section "non-adjusted overlap profit" means the amount of profit that would arise in the overlap period apart from—

    (a) Chapter 1 of Part 6A, and

    (b) this section."

6   In section 227A (application of Chapter where cash basis used), after

subsection (2) insert—

"(3)   This section is subject to section 227C (application of Chapter where section 227B applies)."

7   After section 227A insert—

"227B   Cash basis treatment: full relief under Chapter 1 of Part 6A (trading allowance)

(1)   Subsection (2) applies if—
   (a)   an individual carries on a trade in a tax year, and
   (b)   the profits or losses of the trade for the tax year are treated as nil under section 783AF (trade profits: full relief under Chapter 1 of Part 6A) by virtue of the fact that the conditions in section 783AE(2) are met.

(2)   For the purposes of determining if this Chapter applies, an election under section 25A is to be treated as having effect in relation to the trade for the tax year.

227C   Application of Chapter where section 227B applies

(1)   This section applies if, as a result of the operation of section 227B, the basis on which profits of a trade are calculated is treated as changed as mentioned in section 227A(1).

(2)   This Chapter applies as if—
   (a)   in sections 232(1) and 233(1), for "the first period of account for which the new basis is adopted" there were substituted "the first tax year for which the profits or losses of the trade are not treated as nil under section 783AF", and
   (b)   sections 235, 236, 237, 239A and 239B were omitted.

(3)   If there is no tax year after the change of basis for which the profits or losses of the trade are not treated as nil under section 783AF, this Chapter does not apply."

8   After section 307F (inserted by Schedule 2 to this Act) insert—

"Property allowance

307G   Property allowance

(1)   The rules for calculating the profits of an individual's property business are subject to Chapter 2 of Part 6A (property allowance).

(2)   That Chapter gives relief on relevant property income and, where relief is given, disallows all deductions under this Part which relate to that income (see, in particular, sections 783BC, 783BF and 783BH)."

9   In section 688 (income charged under Chapter 8 of Part 5), before paragraph (a) of subsection (2) insert—
   "(za)   Chapter 1 of Part 6A (which gives relief on relevant income which may consist of or include income chargeable under this Chapter: see, in particular, sections 783AB, 783AC, 783AG and 783AJ),".

158   *Finance (No. 2) Act 2017 (c. 32)*
Schedule 3 — Trading and property allowances
Part 2 — Consequential amendments

10 In section 828 (overlap profit), in subsection (3), for "section 204" substitute "sections 204 and 204A".

11 In Part 2 of Schedule 4 (defined expressions)—
    (a)   at the appropriate places insert—

"individual's property allowance (in Chapter 2 of Part 6A)	section 783BD
individual's trading allowance (in Chapter 1 of Part 6A)	section 783AD
miscellaneous income (in Chapter 1 of Part 6A)	section 783AB
relevant income (in Chapter 1 of Part 6A)	section 783AC
relevant property business (in Chapter 2 of Part 6A)	section 783BA
relevant property income (in Chapter 2 of Part 6A)	section 783BC
relevant trade (in Chapter 1 of Part 6A)	section 783AA
relievable receipts (in Chapter 2 of Part 6A)	section 783BB",

    (b)   in the entry for "overlap profit", for "section 204" substitute "sections 204 and 204A".

TIOPA 2010

12 In TIOPA 2010—
    (a)   in section 22(8) (credit for foreign tax on overlap profit if credit for that tax already allowed), in the definition of "overlap profit", for "section 204" substitute "sections 204 and 204A", and
    (b)   in section 24(8) (claw-back of relief under section 22(2)), in the definition of "overlap profit", for "section 204" substitute "sections 204 and 204A".

PART 3

COMMENCEMENT

13 The amendments made by this Schedule have effect for the tax year 2017-18 and subsequent tax years.

Finance (No. 2) Act 2017 (c. 32)
Schedule 4 — Relief for carried-forward losses
Part 1 — Amendment of general rules about carrying forward losses

159

SCHEDULE 4   Section 18

RELIEF FOR CARRIED-FORWARD LOSSES

PART 1

AMENDMENT OF GENERAL RULES ABOUT CARRYING FORWARD LOSSES

Non-trading deficits from loan relationships

1   Part 5 of CTA 2009 (loan relationships) is amended as follows.

2   In the heading of Chapter 16 (non-trading deficits) at the end insert ": pre-1 April 2017 deficits and charities".

3   In section 456 (introduction to Chapter 16) in subsection (1) —
         (a)   after "if" insert "—
                        (a)   ", and
         (b)   at the end insert ", and
                        (b)   either —
                                (i)   that accounting period begins before 1 April 2017, or
                                (ii)   at the end of that accounting period the company is a charity".

4   After section 463 insert —

"CHAPTER 16A

NON-TRADING DEFICITS: POST 1 APRIL 2017 DEFICITS

463A Introduction to Chapter

         (1)   This Chapter applies if —
                (a)   for any accounting period beginning on or after 1 April 2017 a company has a non-trading deficit from its loan relationships under section 301(6), and
                (b)   at the end of that accounting period the company is not a charity.

         (2)   In this Chapter "the deficit" and "the deficit period" mean that deficit and that period respectively.

         (3)   Sections 463B and 463C deal with claims to set off the deficit against profits of the deficit period or earlier periods.

         (4)   Sections 463D to 463F deal with the consequences of such claims.

         (5)   Sections 463G to 463I provide for so much of the deficit as is not —
                (a)   set off against profits under section 463B, or
                (b)   surrendered as group relief under Part 5 of CTA 2010,
                to be carried forward to later accounting periods.

463B Claim to set off deficit against profits of deficit period or earlier periods

         (1)   The company may make a claim for the whole or part of the deficit —

160   *Finance (No. 2) Act 2017 (c. 32)*
Schedule 4 – Relief for carried-forward losses
Part 1 – Amendment of general rules about carrying forward losses

> > (a)   to be set off against any profits of the company (of whatever description) for the deficit period, or
> >
> > (b)   to be carried back to be set off against profits for earlier accounting periods.
>
> (2)   No claim may be made under subsection (1) in respect of so much of the deficit as is surrendered as group relief under Part 5 of CTA 2010.
>
> (3)   For time limits and other provisions applicable to claims under subsection (1), see section 463C.
>
> (4)   For what happens when a claim is made under subsection (1)(a), see section 463D.
>
> (5)   For what happens when a claim is made under subsection (1)(b), and the profits available for relief when such a claim is made, see sections 463E and 463F.

463C Time limits for claims under section 463B(1)

> (1)   A claim under section 463B(1) must be made within—
> > (a)   the period of 2 years after the deficit period ends, or
> > (b)   such further period as an officer of Revenue and Customs allows.
>
> (2)   Different claims may be made in respect of different parts of a non-trading deficit for any deficit period.
>
> (3)   But no claim may be made in respect of any part of a deficit to which another such claim relates.

463D Claim to set off deficit against profits for the deficit period

> (1)   This section applies if a claim is made under section 463B(1)(a) for the whole or part of the deficit to be set off against profits for the deficit period.
>
> (2)   The amount of the deficit to which the claim relates must be set off against the profits of the company for the deficit period which are identified in the claim.
>
> (3)   Those profits are reduced accordingly.
>
> (4)   Relief under this section must be given before relief is given against profits for the deficit period—
> > (a)   under section 37 or 62(1) to (3) of CTA 2010 (deduction of losses from total profits for the same or earlier accounting periods), or
> > (b)   as a result of a claim under section 463B(1)(b) (carry-back) in respect of a deficit for a later period.
>
> (5)   No relief may be given under this section against ring fence profits of the company within the meaning of Part 8 of CTA 2010 (oil activities) or contractor's ring fence profits of the company within the meaning of Part 8ZA of that Act (oil contractors).

Finance (No. 2) Act 2017 (c. 32)
Schedule 4 — Relief for carried-forward losses
Part 1 — Amendment of general rules about carrying forward losses

161

463E Claim to carry back deficit to earlier periods

(1) This section applies if a claim is made under section 463B(1)(b) for the whole or part of the deficit to be carried back to be set off against profits for accounting periods before the deficit period.

(2) The claim has effect only if it relates to an amount no greater than the lesser of —

    (a) so much of the deficit as is not an amount in relation to which a claim is made under section 463B(1)(a), and

    (b) the total amount of the profits available for relief under this section.

(3) Section 463F explains which profits are so available.

(4) The amount to which the claim relates is set off against those profits by treating them as reduced accordingly.

(5) If those profits are profits for more than one accounting period, the relief is applied by setting off the amount to which the claim relates against profits for a later period before setting off any remainder of that amount against profits for an earlier period.

463F Profits available for relief under section 463E

(1) The profits available for relief under section 463E are the amounts which (apart from the relief) would be charged under this Part as profits for accounting periods ending within the permitted period after giving every prior relief.

(2) In this section —

    "the permitted period" means the period of 12 months immediately before the deficit period, and

    "prior relief" means a relief which subsection (5) provides must be given before relief under section 463E.

(3) If an accounting period ending within the permitted period begins before it, only a part of the amount which (apart from the relief) would be chargeable under this Part for the period, after giving every prior relief, is available for relief under section 463E.

(4) That part is so much as is proportionate to the part of the accounting period in the permitted period.

(5) The reliefs which must be given before relief under section 463E are —

    (a) relief as a result of a claim under section 459(1)(a) or section 463B(1)(a) (claim for deficit to be set off against total profits for the deficit period),

    (b) relief in respect of a loss or deficit incurred or treated as incurred in an accounting period before the deficit period,

    (c) relief under Part 6 of CTA 2010 (charitable donations relief in respect of payments made wholly and exclusively for the purposes of a trade),

    (d) relief under section 37 of CTA 2010 (losses deducted from total profits of the same or an earlier accounting period), and

162   *Finance (No. 2) Act 2017 (c. 32)*
Schedule 4 — Relief for carried-forward losses
Part 1 — Amendment of general rules about carrying forward losses

(e) if the company is a company with investment business for the purposes of Part 16 (companies with investment business) —

    (i) any deduction in respect of management expenses under section 1219 (expenses of management of a company's investment business),

    (ii) relief under Part 6 of CTA 2010 in respect of payments made wholly and exclusively for the purposes of its business, and

    (iii) any allowance under Part 2 of CAA 2001 (plant and machinery allowances).

463G Carry forward of unrelieved deficit against total profits

(1) This section applies if conditions A to D are met.

(2) Condition A is that —

    (a) any amount of the deficit ("the unrelieved amount") is not —

        (i) set off against profits on a claim under section 463B(1), or

        (ii) surrendered as group relief under Part 5 of CTA 2010.

(3) Condition B is that it is not the case —

    (a) that the company ceased to be a company with investment business in the deficit period, or

    (b) (if the company was a company with investment business immediately before the beginning of the deficit period) that its investment business became small or negligible in the deficit period.

(4) Condition C is that (if the company is a Solvency 2 insurance company) it is not the case that the whole of the deficit is a shock loss.

(5) Condition D is that (if the company is a general insurance company) the first accounting period after the deficit period is not an excluded accounting period.

(6) The unrelieved amount is carried forward to the first accounting period after the deficit period.

(7) The company may make a claim for the whole or part of the unrelieved amount to be set off against the company's total profits for the first accounting period after the deficit period.

(8) If a claim is made under subsection (7) —

    (a) the unrelieved amount, or the part of it to which the claim relates, must be set off against the company's total profits for the first accounting period after the deficit period, and

    (b) those profits are reduced accordingly.

(9) No claim may be made under subsection (7) in respect of so much of the unrelieved amount as is surrendered under Part 5A of CTA 2010 (group relief for carried-forward losses).

(10) A claim under subsection (7) must be made within —

    (a) the period of two years after the end of the first accounting period after the deficit period, or

Finance (No. 2) Act 2017 (c. 32)
Schedule 4 — Relief for carried-forward losses
Part 1 — Amendment of general rules about carrying forward losses

163

      (b)   such further period as an officer of Revenue and Customs allows.

(11)   No relief may be given under this section against ring fence profits of the company within the meaning of Part 8 of CTA 2010 (oil activities) or contractor's ring fence profits of the company within the meaning of Part 8ZA of that Act (oil contractors).

(12)   If —

      (a)   the company is a Solvency 2 insurance company, and

      (b)   the deficit is partly (but not wholly) a shock loss,

subsections (6) to (9) have effect as if references to the unrelieved amount were to the eligible amount (see subsection (13)).

(13)   In this section "the eligible amount" means so much of the unrelieved amount as is not a shock loss; and for the purpose of determining how much of the unrelieved amount is, or is not, a shock loss, it is to be assumed that in setting off or surrendering amounts as mentioned in subsection (2)(a)(i) and (ii) the company uses shock losses before other amounts.

(14)   In this Chapter—

      "company with investment business" has the same meaning as in Part 16 (see section 1218B);

      "excluded accounting period" has the meaning given by section 269ZG of CTA 2010;

      "general insurance company" is to be interpreted in accordance with section 269ZG of CTA 2010;

      "shock loss" has the meaning given by section 269ZK of CTA 2010;

      "Solvency 2 insurance company" means an insurance company as defined in section 269ZP(2) of CTA 2010.

(15)   In this Chapter references to a company's investment business are to be construed in accordance with section 1219(2).

463H Carry forward of unrelieved deficit against non-trading profits

(1)   Subsections (4) to (8) apply if—

      (a)   section 463G would apply but for the fact that the company's investment business became small or negligible in the accounting period mentioned in subsection (3)(b) of that section,

      (b)   section 463G would apply but for condition D in that section (no carry-forward to an excluded accounting period of a general insurance company), or

      (c)   the company is a Solvency 2 insurance company and any amount of the deficit would be eligible to be carried forward under section 463G(6) were that amount not a shock loss (see section 463G(4), (12) and (13)).

(2)   Subsections (4) to (8) also apply if—

      (a)   subsections (6) to (10) of section 463G would apply but for the fact that the company's investment business became small or negligible in the accounting period mentioned in section 463I(1)(c)(ii), or

164   *Finance (No. 2) Act 2017 (c. 32)*
Schedule 4 — Relief for carried-forward losses
Part 1 — Amendment of general rules about carrying forward losses

      (b)   subsections (6) to (10) of section 463G would apply but for section 463I(1)(d) (no carry-forward under those subsections to an excluded accounting period of a general insurance company).

(3)   In this section the "unrelieved amount"—

      (a)   in a case within paragraph (a) or (b) of subsection (1), is to be interpreted in accordance with section 463G(2);

      (b)   in a case within paragraph (c) of subsection (1), means the amount mentioned in that paragraph;

      (c)   in a case within subsection (2), means so much of the deficit mentioned in section 463I(1)(a) as is not set off as mentioned in section 463I(1)(b)(i) or surrendered as mentioned in section 463I(1)(b)(ii).

(4)   The unrelieved amount is carried forward to the first accounting period ("period 2") after—

      (a)   (in a case within subsection (1)) the deficit period, or

      (b)   (in a case within subsection (2)) the period mentioned in section 463I(1)(a).

(5)   So much of the unrelieved amount as is not the subject of a claim under subsection (7) must be set off against the non-trading profits of the company for period 2.

(6)   Those profits are reduced accordingly.

(7)   The company may make a claim for relief under subsection (5) not to be given in period 2 for the unrelieved amount or so much of it as is specified in the claim.

(8)   A claim under subsection (7) is effective if, and only if, it is made—

      (a)   within the period of two years after the end of period 2, or

      (b)   within such further period as an officer of Revenue and Customs may allow.

(9)   Subsection (10) applies if any amount is carried forward under subsection (4) to an accounting period ("the carry forward period") and—

      (a)   cannot be set off under subsection (5) against non-trading profits of that period, or

      (b)   is the subject of a claim under subsection (7).

(10)   If the company continues to be a company with investment business throughout the carry forward period, subsections (4) to (8) have effect as if—

      (a)   references to the unrelieved amount were to the amount mentioned in subsection (9), and

      (b)   references to—

          (i)   the deficit period, or

          (ii)   the period mentioned in section 463I(1)(a),

      were to the carry forward period.

(11)   In this section "non-trading profits", in relation to a company, means so much of the company's profits as does not consist of trading

Finance (No. 2) Act 2017 (c. 32)
Schedule 4 — Relief for carried-forward losses
Part 1 — Amendment of general rules about carrying forward losses

165

income for the purposes of section 37 of CTA 2010 (deduction of trading losses from total profits of the same or an earlier period).

463I Re-application of section 463G if any deficit remains after previous application

(1) This section applies if—

    (a) any amount of the deficit is carried forward to an accounting period ("the later period") of the company under section 463G(6),

    (b) any of that amount is not—

        (i) set off against the company's total profits for the later period on a claim under section 463G(7), or

        (ii) surrendered as group relief for carried-forward losses under Part 5A of CTA 2010,

    (c) it is not the case—

        (i) that the company ceased to be a company with investment business in the later period, or

        (ii) (if the company was a company with investment business immediately before the beginning of the later period) that its investment business became small or negligible in the later period, and

    (d) it is not the case that the first accounting period after the later period is an excluded accounting period of a general insurance company.

(2) Subsections (6) to (10) of section 463G apply as if—

    (a) references to the unrelieved amount were to so much of the amount of the deficit carried forward to the later period as is not set off or surrendered as mentioned in subsection (1)(b), and

    (b) references to the deficit period were to the later period."

Non-trading losses on intangible fixed assets

5 (1) Section 753 of CTA 2009 (treatment of non-trading loss) is amended as follows.

(2) In subsection (3) (carry forward of non-trading loss)—

    (a) in the words before paragraph (a), after "not" insert ", in any period ("the reference period")";

    (b) in the words after paragraph (b) for "debit of" substitute "loss on intangible fixed assets for".

(3) After subsection (3) insert—

"(4) But subsection (3) does not apply if the company ceased to be a company with investment business in the reference period.

(5) In the application of subsection (3) to an amount of a loss previously carried forward under that subsection, the reference in paragraph (b) to group relief under Part 5 of CTA 2010 is to be read as a reference to group relief for carried-forward losses under Part 5A of that Act.

(6) In this section "company with investment business" has the same meaning as in Part 16 (see section 1218B)."

166   Finance (No. 2) Act 2017 (c. **32**)
Schedule 4 — Relief for carried-forward losses
Part 1 — Amendment of general rules about carrying forward losses

Expenses of management of investment business etc

6   (1) Section 1223 of CTA 2009 (carrying forward expenses of management and other amounts) is amended as follows.

    (2) In subsection (1)(b) —

        (a) for "amounts" substitute "an amount", and

        (b) after "(2)(c)," insert " —

                (i) a claim relating to the whole of the amount has not been made under subsection (3B), or".

    (3) After subsection (3) insert—

      "(3A) But subsection (3) does not apply in relation to so much of the excess as is surrendered as group relief under Part 5 of CTA 2010 or as group relief for carried-forward losses under Part 5A of that Act.

      (3B) A deduction in respect of the excess may be made under section 1219 for the next accounting period only on the making by the company of a claim.

      (3C) A claim may relate to the whole of the excess or to part of it only.

      (3D) A claim must be made —

          (a) within the period of two years after the end of the next accounting period, or

          (b) within such further period as an officer of Revenue and Customs may allow.

      (3E) Subsection (1A) of section 1219 does not apply in relation to a deduction in respect of the excess made for the next accounting period."

Trading losses

7   Chapter 2 of Part 4 of CTA 2010 (trade losses) is amended as follows.

8   In section 36 (introduction to Chapter) for subsection (1) substitute —

    "(1) This Chapter provides relief for a loss made by a company in a trade (see sections 37 to 47)".

9   For the italic heading before section 37 substitute —

        "Relief in loss-making period and carry back relief".

10   (1) Section 45 (carry forward of trade loss against subsequent trade profits) is amended as follows.

    (2) In the heading, after "of" insert "pre-1 April 2017".

    (3) In subsection (1) after "accounting period" insert "beginning before 1 April 2017".

    (4) In subsection (4)(b) for "cannot be" substitute "is not".

Finance (No. 2) Act 2017 (c. 32)
Schedule 4 — Relief for carried-forward losses
Part 1 — Amendment of general rules about carrying forward losses

167

(5) After subsection (4) insert—

"(4A) But the company may make a claim that the profits of the trade of an accounting period specified in the claim are not to be reduced by the unrelieved loss, or are not to be reduced by the unrelieved loss by more than an amount specified in the claim.

(4B) A claim under subsection (4A) may specify an accounting period only if it begins on or after 1 April 2017.

(4C) A claim under subsection (4A) is effective if, and only if, it is made—
  (a) within the period of two years after the end of the accounting period specified in the claim, or
  (b) within such further period as an officer of Revenue and Customs may allow."

(6) In subsection (5) for "section" (in the second place it occurs) substitute ", sections 45B, 45F and".

11   After section 45 insert—

"45A Carry forward of post-1 April 2017 trade loss against total profits

(1) This section applies if—
  (a) in an accounting period ("the loss-making period") beginning on or after 1 April 2017 a company carrying on a trade makes a loss in the trade,
  (b) relief under section 37 or Part 5 (group relief) is not given for an amount of the loss ("the unrelieved amount"),
  (c) the company continues to carry on the trade in the next accounting period ("the later period"), and
  (d) the conditions in subsection (3) are met.

(2) But this section does not apply if the trade is a ring fence trade.

(3) The conditions are that—
  (a) the trade did not become small or negligible in the loss-making period,
  (b) relief under section 37 was not unavailable for the loss by reason of —
    (i) section 37(5), 44, 48 or 52, or
    (ii) section 1209, 1216DA, 1217DA, 1217MA, 1217SA or 1218ZDA of CTA 2009,
  (c) relief under section 37 would not be unavailable by reason of section 44 for a loss (assuming there was one) made in the trade in the later period,
  (d) if the company is a Solvency 2 insurance company the loss is not a shock loss (see subsections (9) and (10)), and
  (e) the later period is not an excluded accounting period of a general insurance company.

(4) The unrelieved amount is carried forward to the later period.

(5) The company may make a claim for relief to be given in the later period for the unrelieved amount or for any part of it specified in the claim.

168   Finance (No. 2) Act 2017 (c. 32)
Schedule 4 — Relief for carried-forward losses
Part 1 — Amendment of general rules about carrying forward losses

(6) If the company makes a claim, the relief is given by deducting the unrelieved amount, or the specified part of it, from the company's total profits of the later period.

(7) A claim under this section must be made—
    (a) within the period of two years after the end of the later period, or
    (b) within such further period as an officer of Revenue and Customs may allow.

(8) Relief under this section is subject to restriction or modification in accordance with provisions of the Corporation Tax Acts.

(9) For the purposes of this section and section 45B, a loss which is partly, but not wholly, a shock loss is to be treated as if—
    (a) the amount that is a shock loss, and
    (b) the amount that is not,
    were separate losses.

(10) In this section—
        "excluded accounting period" has the meaning given by section 269ZG;
        "general insurance company" is to be interpreted in accordance with section 269ZG(6);
        "ring fence trade" has the same meaning as in Part 8 (see section 277);
        "Solvency 2 insurance company" means an insurance company as defined in section 269ZP(2);
        "shock loss" has the meaning given by section 269ZK.

45B   Carry forward of post-1 April 2017 trade loss against trade profits

(1) This section applies if—
    (a) in an accounting period ("the loss-making period") beginning on or after 1 April 2017 a company carrying on a trade makes a loss in the trade,
    (b) relief under section 37 or 42 or Part 5 (group relief) is not given for an amount of the loss ("the unrelieved amount"),
    (c) the company continues to carry on the trade in the next accounting period ("the later period"), and
    (d) case 1, 2 or 3 applies.
    Case 1 is that any of the conditions in section 45A(3) are not met.
    Case 2 is that relief for the unrelieved amount was not available under section 45A by reason of section 1210(5), 1216DB(5) or 1217DB(5) of CTA 2009.
    Case 3 is that the trade is a ring fence trade.

(2) The unrelieved amount is carried forward to the later period.

(3) Relief for the unrelieved amount is given to the company in the later period if the company makes a profit in the trade in the later period.

(4) The relief is given by reducing the profits of the trade of the later period by the unrelieved amount.

Finance (No. 2) Act 2017 (c. 32)
Schedule 4 — Relief for carried-forward losses
Part 1 — Amendment of general rules about carrying forward losses

169

(5)   But the company may make a claim for relief not to be given in the later period for the unrelieved amount or for any part of it specified in the claim.

(6)   A claim under subsection (5) is effective if, and only if, it is made —

    (a)   within the period of two years after the end of the later period, or

    (b)   within such further period as an officer of Revenue and Customs may allow.

(7)   If the trade is a ring fence trade, this section has effect only in relation to so much of the loss mentioned in subsection (1)(a) as is not a non-decommissioning loss.

(8)   Relief under this section is subject to restriction or modification in accordance with provisions of the Corporation Tax Acts.

(9)   In this section —

    "non-decommissioning loss" is to be interpreted in accordance with section 303A;

    "ring fence trade" has the same meaning as in Part 8 (see section 277).

(10)   See also section 45A(9) (splitting for the purposes of that section and this section of losses that are partly, but not wholly, shock losses of insurance companies).

45C   Re-application of section 45A if loss remains after previous application

(1)   This section applies if —

    (a)   an amount of a loss made in a trade is carried forward to an accounting period ("the later period") of a company under section 45A(4),

    (b)   any of that amount is not deducted from the company's total profits of the later period on a claim under section 45A(5) or surrendered by way of group relief for carried forward-losses under Part 5A,

    (c)   the company continues to carry on the trade in the accounting period ("the further period") after the later period, and

    (d)   the conditions in subsection (2) are met.

(2)   The conditions are that —

    (a)   the trade did not become small or negligible in the later period,

    (b)   relief under section 37 would not be unavailable by reason of section 44 for a loss (assuming there was one) made in the trade in the further period, and

    (c)   the further period is not an excluded accounting period of a general insurance company.

(3)   Subsections (4) to (8) of section 45A apply as if —

    (a)   references to the unrelieved amount were to so much of the amount carried forward to the later period as is not deducted or surrendered as mentioned in subsection (1)(b), and

170
Finance (No. 2) Act 2017 (c. 32)
Schedule 4 — Relief for carried-forward losses
Part 1 — Amendment of general rules about carrying forward losses

      (b)   references to the later period were to the further period.

    (4)   In this section "excluded accounting period" and "general insurance company" have the same meaning as in section 45A.

45D   Application of section 45B if loss remains after application of section 45A

    (1)   This section applies if—

        (a)   an amount of a loss made in a trade is carried forward to an accounting period ("the later period") of a company under section 45A(4),

        (b)   any of that amount is not deducted from the company's total profits of the later period on a claim under section 45A(5) or surrendered by way of group relief for carried forward-losses under Part 5A,

        (c)   the company continues to carry on the trade in the accounting period ("the further period") after the later period, and

        (d)   any of the conditions in section 45C(2) is not met.

    (2)   Subsections (2) to (8) of section 45B apply as if—

        (a)   references to the unrelieved amount were to so much of the amount carried forward to the later period as is not deducted or surrendered as mentioned in subsection (1)(b), and

        (b)   references to the later period were to the further period.

45E   Re-application of section 45B if loss remains after previous application

    (1)   This section applies if—

        (a)   an amount of a loss made in a trade is carried forward to an accounting period ("the later period") of a company under section 45B(2),

        (b)   any of that amount is not used under section 45B(4) to reduce profits of the trade for the later period, and

        (c)   the company continues to carry on the trade in the accounting period ("the further period") after the later period.

    (2)   Subsections (2) to (8) of section 45B apply as if—

        (a)   references to the unrelieved amount were to so much of the amount carried forward to the later period as was not used as mentioned in subsection (1)(b), and

        (b)   references to the later period were to the further period.

45F   Terminal losses: relief unrestricted by Part 7ZA and 7A

    (1)   This section applies if—

        (a)   a company makes a loss in a trade in an accounting period (the "loss-making period"),

        (b)   an amount of that loss is carried forward to an accounting period of the company ("the terminal period") under section 45, 45A or 45B,

Finance (No. 2) Act 2017 (c. 32)
Schedule 4 — Relief for carried-forward losses
Part 1 — Amendment of general rules about carrying forward losses

171

      (c)   relief in the terminal period is not given under section 45, 45A or (as the case may be) 45B for that amount or for any part of it, and

      (d)   the company ceases to carry on the trade in the terminal period.

(2)   The company may make a claim for relief to be given for the unrelieved amount under this section.

(3)   If the company makes a claim the relief is given by deducting the unrelieved amount from the relevant profits of the company of —

      (a)   the terminal period, and

      (b)   previous accounting periods so far as they fall (wholly or partly) within the period of 3 years ending with the end of the terminal period.

(4)   But no deduction is to be made under subsection (3) for any accounting period which is —

      (a)   the loss-making period,

      (b)   a period before the loss-making period, or

      (c)   a period beginning before 1 April 2017.

(5)   The amount of a deduction to be made under subsection (3) for any accounting period is the amount of the unrelieved amount so far as it cannot be deducted under that subsection for a subsequent accounting period.

(6)   The company's claim must be made —

      (a)   within the period of two years after the end of the terminal period, or

      (b)   within such further period as an officer of Revenue and Customs may allow.

(7)   In this section —

      "the unrelieved amount" means so much of the amount mentioned in subsection (1)(b) for which relief is not given in the terminal period under section 45, 45A or (as the case may be) 45B, and

      "relevant profits", in relation to the terminal period or any previous accounting period, means —

          (a)   the total profits of the company of the period, in a case where the unrelieved amount was carried forward to the terminal period under section 45A,

          (b)   the profits of the trade of the period, in a case where the unrelieved amount was carried forward to the terminal period under section 45 or 45B.

(8)   Relief under this section is subject to restriction or modification in accordance with provisions of the Corporation Tax Acts.

45G Section 45F: accounting period falling partly within 3 year period

(1)   This section applies if an accounting period falls partly within the period of 3 years mentioned in section 45F(3)(b).

172

Finance (No. 2) Act 2017 (c. 32)
Schedule 4 — Relief for carried-forward losses
Part 1 — Amendment of general rules about carrying forward losses

(2) The amount of the deduction for the unrelieved amount for the accounting period is not to exceed an amount equal to the overlapping proportion of the company's relevant profits of that period.

(3) The overlapping proportion is the same as the proportion that the part of the accounting period falling within the period of 3 years bears to the whole of the accounting period.

(4) In this section "the unrelieved amount" and "relevant profits" have the meaning given by section 45F(7).

45H   Section 45F: transfers of trade to obtain relief

Section 45F does not apply by reason of a company ceasing to carry on a trade if —

    (a) on the company ceasing to carry on the trade, any of the activities of the trade begin to be carried on by a person who is not (or by persons any or all of whom are not) within the charge to corporation tax, and

    (b) the company's ceasing to carry on the trade is part of a scheme or arrangement the main purpose, or one of the main purposes, of which is to secure that that section applies by reason of the cessation."

UK property business losses

12   Chapter 4 of Part 4 of CTA 2010 (property losses) is amended as follows.

13   (1) Section 62 (relief for losses made in UK property business) is amended as follows.

(2) In subsection (4) —

    (a) in the words before paragraph (a), for "Subsection (5) applies" substitute "Subsections (5) to (5C) apply", and

    (b) for paragraph (a) substitute —

        "(a) an amount of the loss is not deducted as mentioned in subsection (3) or surrendered by way of group relief under Part 5,".

(3) In subsection (5), for the words before paragraph (a) substitute "The amount".

(4) After subsection (5) insert —

  "(5A) But relief under subsection (2) for the amount is given to the company in the next accounting period only on the making by the company of a claim.

   (5B) A claim may relate to the whole of the amount or to part of it only.

   (5C) A claim must be made —

    (a) within the period of two years after the end of the next accounting period, or

    (b) within such further period as an officer of Revenue and Customs may allow.

Finance (No. 2) Act 2017 (c. 32)
Schedule 4 – Relief for carried-forward losses
Part 1 – Amendment of general rules about carrying forward losses

173

(5D)   In the application of this section to an amount of a loss previously carried forward under subsection (5), the reference in subsection (4)(a) to group relief under Part 5 is to be read as a reference to group relief for carried-forward losses under Part 5A."

14   (1)   Section 63 (company with investment business ceasing to carry on UK property business) is amended as follows.

(2)   For subsection (2) substitute—

"(2)   Subsections (3) to (7) apply if an amount of loss made in carrying on the UK property business would be carried forward to the next accounting period under section 62(5) but for the company ceasing to carry on the business or to be within the charge to corporation tax in respect of it."

(3)   In subsection (3)(b) for "that" substitute "the next accounting".

(4)   After subsection (3) insert—

"(4)   But a deduction in respect of the amount of loss may be made under section 1219 of CTA 2009 for the next accounting period only on the making by the company of a claim.

(5)   A claim may relate to the whole of the amount of the loss or to part of it only.

(6)   A claim must be made—
   (a)   within the period of two years after the end of the next accounting period, or
   (b)   within such further period as an officer of Revenue and Customs may allow.

(7)   Subsection (1A) of section 1219 of CTA 2009 does not apply in relation to a deduction in respect of the amount of loss made for the next accounting period."

PART 2

RESTRICTION ON DEDUCTIONS IN RESPECT OF CARRIED-FORWARD LOSSES

15   CTA 2010 is amended as follows.

16   After section 269 insert—

"PART 7ZA

RESTRICTIONS ON OBTAINING CERTAIN DEDUCTIONS

Introduction

269ZA Overview of Part

This Part contains provision restricting the amount of certain deductions which a company may make in calculating its taxable total profits for an accounting period.

174

Finance (No. 2) Act 2017 (c. 32)
Schedule 4 – Relief for carried-forward losses
Part 2 – Restriction on deductions in respect of carried-forward losses

Restrictions on obtaining certain deductions

269ZB Restriction on deductions from trading profits

(1) This section has effect for determining the taxable total profits of a company for an accounting period.

(2) The sum of any deductions made by the company for the accounting period which fall within subsection (3) may not exceed the relevant maximum.

But this is subject to subsection (10).

(3) The following deductions fall within this subsection—

    (a) any deductions under section 45(4)(b) or 45B;

    (b) any deduction under section 303B(4) or 303D(5), so far as it is a restricted deduction.

(4) For the purposes of this section a deduction under section 303B(4) or 303D(5) is a "restricted deduction" so far as it would not be available but for section 304(5) (reduction of income derived from related activities).

(5) In this section the "relevant maximum" means the sum of—

    (a) 50% of the company's relevant trading profits for the accounting period, and

    (b) the company's trading profits deductions allowance for the accounting period.

(6) Section 269ZF contains provision for determining a company's relevant trading profits for an accounting period.

(7) A company's "trading profits deductions allowance" for an accounting period—

    (a) is so much of the company's deductions allowance for the period as is specified in the company's tax return as its trading profits deductions allowance for the period, and

    (b) accordingly, is nil if no amount of the company's deductions allowance for the period is so specified.

(8) An amount specified under subsection (7)(a) as a company's trading profits deductions allowance for an accounting period may not exceed the difference between—

    (a) the amount of the company's deductions allowance for the period, and

    (b) the total of any amounts specified for the period under section 269ZC(5)(a) (non-trading profits deductions allowance) and section 124D(4) of FA 2012 (BLAGAB trade profits deductions allowance).

(9) A company's "deductions allowance" for an accounting period is to be determined in accordance with section 269ZR where, at any time in that period—

    (a) the company is a member of a group (see section 269ZZB), and

    (b) one or more other companies within the charge to corporation tax are members of that group.

Finance (No. 2) Act 2017 (c. 32)
Schedule 4 — Relief for carried-forward losses
Part 2 — Restriction on deductions in respect of carried-forward losses

175

Otherwise, a company's "deductions allowance" for an accounting period is to be determined in accordance with section 269ZW.

(10) Subsection (2) does not apply in relation to a company for an accounting period where, in determining the company's relevant trading profits, the amount given by step 1 in section 269ZF(3) is not greater than nil.

269ZC Restriction on deductions from non-trading profits

(1) This section has effect for determining the taxable total profits of a company for an accounting period.

(2) The sum of any deductions made by the company for the accounting period under section 457(3) and 463H(5) of CTA 2009 (carry forward of non-trading deficits from loan relationships against subsequent non-trading profits) may not exceed the relevant maximum.

But this is subject to subsection (8).

(3) In this section the "relevant maximum" means the sum of —
   (a) 50% of the company's relevant non-trading profits for the accounting period, and
   (b) the amount of the company's non-trading profits deductions allowance for the accounting period.

(4) Section 269ZF contains provisions for determining a company's relevant non-trading profits for an accounting period.

(5) A company's "non-trading profits deductions allowance" for an accounting period —
   (a) is so much of the company's deductions allowance for the period as is specified in the company's tax return as its non-trading profits deductions allowance for the period, and
   (b) accordingly, is nil if no amount of the company's deductions allowance for the period is so specified.

(6) An amount specified under subsection (5)(a) as a company's non-trading profits deductions allowance for an accounting period may not exceed the difference between —
   (a) the amount of the company's deductions allowance for the period, and
   (b) the total of any amounts specified for the period under section 269ZB(7)(a) (trading profits deductions allowance) and section 124D(4) of FA 2012 (BLAGAB trade profits deductions allowance).

(7) A company's "deductions allowance" for an accounting period is to be determined in accordance with section 269ZR where, at any time in that period —
   (a) the company is a member of a group (see section 269ZZB), and
   (b) one or more other companies within the charge to corporation tax are members of that group.

Otherwise, a company's "deductions allowance" for an accounting period is to be determined in accordance with section 269ZW.

176   *Finance (No. 2) Act 2017 (c. 32)*
Schedule 4 — Relief for carried-forward losses
Part 2 — Restriction on deductions in respect of carried-forward losses

(8) Subsection (2) does not apply in relation to a company for an accounting period where, in determining the company's relevant non-trading profits for the period, the amount given by step 1 in section 269ZF(3) is not greater than nil.

269ZD Restriction on deductions from total profits

(1) This section has effect for determining the taxable total profits of a company for an accounting period.

(2) The sum of any relevant deductions made by the company for the accounting period may not exceed the difference between—

    (a) the relevant maximum, and

    (b) the sum of—

        (i) any deductions falling within section 269ZB(3) (carry forward of trade loss against subsequent trade profits) made by the company for the accounting period,

        (ii) any deductions made by the company for the accounting period under sections 457(3) and 463H(5) of CTA 2009 (carry forward of non-trading deficits from loan relationships against subsequent non-trading profits), and

        (iii) any deductions made by the company for the accounting period under sections 124(5), 124A(5) and 124C(6) of FA 2012 (carry forward of BLAGAB trade losses against BLAGAB trade profits).

But this is subject to subsection (7) and section 269ZE.

(3) The following deductions made for an accounting period are "relevant deductions" for the purposes of this section—

    (a) a deduction under section 463G of CTA 2009 (carry forward of non-trading deficit against total profits);

    (b) a deduction under section 753 of CTA 2009 (non-trading losses on intangible fixed assets) in respect of a loss treated by subsection (3) of that section (carry forward of losses) as if it were a loss of the accounting period;

    (c) a deduction under section 1219 of CTA 2009 (expenses of management of a company's investment business) in respect of an amount treated by section 1223(3) of that Act (carrying forward of expenses of management and other amounts) as expenses of management deductible for the accounting period;

    (d) a deduction under section 1219 of CTA 2009 (expenses of management of a company's investment business) in respect of a loss treated by section 63(3) (carrying forward of certain losses made by company with investment business which ceases to carry on UK property business) as an expense of management deductible for the accounting period;

    (e) a deduction under section 37 (relief for trade losses against total profits) made in reliance on section 1210(3), 1216DB(3), 1217DB(3), 1217MB(2), 1217SB(2) or 1218ZDB(2) of CTA 2009;

Finance (No. 2) Act 2017 (c. 32)
Schedule 4 — Relief for carried-forward losses
Part 2 — Restriction on deductions in respect of carried-forward losses

177

     (f)   a deduction under section 45A (carry forward of trade loss against total profits);

     (g)   a deduction under section 62(3) (relief for losses made in UK property business) in respect of a loss treated by subsection (5)(b) of that section (carry forward of losses) as a loss made by the company in the accounting period;

     (h)   a deduction under section 303C (excess carried forward non-decommissioning losses of ring fence trade: relief against total profits);

     (i)   a deduction under Part 5 (group relief) made in respect of a loss surrendered under that Part in reliance on section 1210(3), 1216DB(3), 1217DB(3), 1217MB(2), 1217SB(2) or 1218ZDB(2) of CTA 2009;

     (j)   a deduction under Part 5A (group relief for carried-forward losses);

     (k)   a deduction under section 124B of FA 2012 (deduction from total profits of excess carried-forward BLAGAB trade losses),

(but see section 269ZJ (insurance companies: shock losses).

(4)   In this section the "relevant maximum" means the sum of —

     (a)   50% of the company's relevant profits for the accounting period, and

     (b)   the amount of the company's deductions allowance for the accounting period.

(5)   A company's "relevant profits" for an accounting period are the sum of —

     (a)   the company's relevant trading profits for the accounting period (see section 269ZF(1)),

     (b)   the company's relevant non-trading profits for the accounting period (see section 269ZF(2), and

     (c)   the company's relevant BLAGAB trade profits for the accounting period.

In this subsection "relevant BLAGAB trade profits" has the same meaning as in section 124D of FA 2012.

(6)   A company's "deductions allowance" for an accounting period is to be determined in accordance with section 269ZR where, at any time in that period —

     (a)   the company is a member of a group (see section 269ZZB), and

     (b)   one or more other companies within the charge to corporation tax are members of that group.

Otherwise, the company's "deductions allowance" for the accounting period is to be determined in accordance with section 269ZW.

(7)   Subsection (2) does not apply in relation to a company for an accounting period where the sum of —

     (a)   the amount given by paragraph (1) of step 1 in section 269ZF(3), and

     (b)   the company's BLAGAB trade profit for the accounting period,

178   *Finance (No. 2) Act 2017 (c. 32)*
Schedule 4 — Relief for carried-forward losses
Part 2 — Restriction on deductions in respect of carried-forward losses

is not greater than nil.

269ZE Restriction on deductions from total profits: insurance companies

(1) Where the conditions in subsection (2) are met, section 269ZD has effect as if, for subsection (2) of that section there were substituted—

"(2) The sum of any relevant deductions made by the company for the accounting period may not exceed the modified loss cap (as defined in section 269ZE).
But this is subject to subsection (7)."

(2) The conditions are that—

    (a) the company referred to in section 269ZD(1) carries on business to which the charge to corporation tax under section 68 of FA 2012 (charge to tax on I-E profit) applies and has an I-E profit for the accounting period,

    (b) the policyholders' share (if any) of the I-E profit is not the whole of that profit, and

    (c) the adjusted shareholders' I-E profit for the accounting period is less than the BLAGAB-related loss capacity.

(3) The "adjusted shareholders' I-E profit" is equal to—

    (a) the shareholders' share of the I-E profit, less

    (b) any excess capacity.

(4) The "BLAGAB-related loss capacity" is equal to A + B - C where—

A is 50% of the company's relevant BLAGAB trade profits for the accounting period (as defined in section 124D of FA 2012);

B is the company's BLAGAB trade profits deductions allowance for the period (if any) (as defined in section 124D of FA 2012);

C is the total of any deductions made by the company for the accounting period under sections 124(5), 124A(5) and 124C(6) of FA 2012.

(5) To determine the modified loss cap, take the following steps—

Step 1: find the basic loss cap.

Step 2: reduce that amount by the BLAGAB-related loss capacity.

Step 3: add to the result of step 2 the adjusted shareholders' I-E profit.

The result is the modified loss cap.

(6) In this section "the basic loss cap" means the difference referred to in the opening words of section 269ZD(2) (assuming that that section has effect without the modification set out in subsection (1) of this section) (but, if applicable, taking account of section 269ZJ).

(7) In this section "excess capacity" means the amount (if any) by which—

    (a) the section 269ZF step 2 amount, is less than

    (b) what the section 269ZF step 2 amount would be if in paragraph (d) of section 269ZF(4) the reference to any I-E profit were to the policyholders' share of any I-E profit.

Finance (No. 2) Act 2017 (c. 32)
Schedule 4 — Relief for carried-forward losses
Part 2 — Restriction on deductions in respect of carried-forward losses

179

(8)   In subsection (7) the reference to the "section 269ZF step 2 amount" is to the sum given by paragraph (1) of step 2 of section 269ZF(3) in calculating the company's relevant trading profits and relevant non-trading profits for the accounting period: but for this purpose disregard paragraph (4) of step 1 of section 269ZF(3).

(9)   For the purposes of this section the "shareholders' share" of an insurance company's I-E profit for an accounting period is equal to—

    (a)   the amount of the I-E profit, less

    (b)   the policyholders' share (if any) of that profit.

(10)   In this section references to the policyholders' share of I-E profit are to that share as determined in accordance with section 103 of FA 2012.

Relevant profits

269ZF "Relevant trading profits" and "relevant non-trading profits"

(1)   A company's "relevant trading profits" for an accounting period are—

    (a)   the company's qualifying trading profits for the accounting period (see subsection (3)), less

    (b)   the company's trading profits deductions allowance for the accounting period (see section 269ZB(7)).

But if the allowance mentioned in paragraph (b) exceeds the profits mentioned in paragraph (a), the company's "relevant trading profits" for the accounting period are nil.

(2)   A company's "relevant non-trading profits" for an accounting period are—

    (a)   the company's qualifying non-trading profits for the accounting period (see subsection (3)), less

    (b)   the company's non-trading profits deductions allowance for the accounting period (see section 269ZC(5)).

But if the allowance mentioned in paragraph (b) exceeds the profits mentioned in paragraph (a), the company's "relevant non-trading profits" for the accounting period are nil.

(3)   To determine a company's qualifying trading profits and qualifying non-trading profits for an accounting period—

Step 1 - modified total profits

    (1)   Calculate the company's total profits for the accounting period.

    (2)   For the purposes of this subsection assume that the company's total profits for the accounting period are to be calculated with the modifications set out in subsection (4).

    (3)   If the company's total profits for the accounting period (as modified under paragraph (2)) are not greater than nil, the company's qualifying trading profits and relevant non-trading profits for the accounting period are both nil.

    (4)   Otherwise, proceed with steps 2 to 5.

Step 2 - negative amount for apportioning under step 4

180

Finance (No. 2) Act 2017 (c. 32)
Schedule 4 — Relief for carried-forward losses
Part 2 — Restriction on deductions in respect of carried-forward losses

(1) Calculate the sum ("the step 2 amount") of any amounts which (on the assumption set out in paragraph (2) of step 1), could be relieved against the company's total profits of the accounting period.

(2) But in calculating that sum, ignore the amount of any excluded deductions for the accounting period (see subsection (5)).

(3) If the company's total profits for the accounting period (as modified under step 1(2)) do not exceed the amount given by this step, the qualifying trading profits and the qualifying non-trading profits are both nil.

(4) Otherwise, proceed with steps 3 to 5.

Step 3 - trade profits and non-trade profits

Divide the company's total profits for the accounting period (as modified under step 1(2)) into—

(a) profits of a trade of the company (the company's "trade profits"), and

(b) profits that are not profits of a trade of the company (the company's "non-trade profits").

Step 4 - apportioning the step 2 amount

Take the step 2 amount and do one of the following—

(a) reduce the company's trade profits by the whole of that amount,

(b) reduce the company's non-trade profits by the whole of that amount, or

(c) reduce the company's trade profits by part of that amount and reduce the company's non-trade profits by the remaining part of that amount.

Apply this step in a way which ensures that neither the company's trade profits nor the company's non-trade profits are reduced below nil.

Step 5 - amount of qualifying trading or non-trading profits (if not determined under step 1 or 2)

The amounts resulting from step 3, after any reduction under step 4, are—

(a) in the case of the amount in step 3(a), the company's qualifying trading profits, and

(b) in the case of the amount in step 3(b), the company's qualifying non-trading profits.

(4) For the purposes of subsection (3) the company's total profits for an accounting period are to be calculated with the following modifications—

(a) ignore any income so far as it falls within, and is dealt with under, Part 9A of CTA 2009 (company distributions);

(b) ignore any ring fence profits (as defined in section 276);

(c) ignore any contractor's ring fence profits (as defined in section 356LD);

(d) if the company is an insurance company, ignore any I-E profit (see section 141(2) of FA 2012);

(e) make no deductions under sections 45(4)(b) and 45B (carry forward of trade loss against subsequent trade profits) other

Finance (No. 2) Act 2017 (c. 32)
Schedule 4 — Relief for carried-forward losses
Part 2 — Restriction on deductions in respect of carried-forward losses

181

than deductions that would be ignored for the purposes of section 269ZB by reason of—

 (i)   section 1209(3), 1210(5A) or 1211(7A) of CTA 2009 (losses of film trade),

 (ii)   section 1216DA(3), 1216DB(5A) or 1216DC(7A) of that Act (losses of television programme trade),

 (iii)   section 1217DA(3), 1217DB(5A) or 1217DC(7A) of that Act (losses of video game trade),

 (iv)   section 1217MA(3) or 1217MC(9) of that Act (losses of theatrical trade),

 (v)   section 1217SA(3) or 1217SC(9) of that Act (losses of orchestral trade),

 (vi)   section 1218ZDA(3) or 1218ZDC(9) of that Act (losses of museum or gallery exhibition trade),

 (vii)   section 65(4B) or 67A(5A) (losses of UK or EEA furnished holiday lettings business),

 (viii)   section 269ZJ(1) (insurance companies: shock losses),

 (ix)   section 304(7) (certain losses of ring fence trades), or

 (x)   section 356NJ(2) (pre-1 April 2017 loss arising from oil contractor activities);

(f)   make no restricted deductions (as defined in section 269ZB(4)) under section 303B(4) or 303D(5)); and

(g)   make no deductions under section 457(3) or 463H(5) of CTA 2009 (carry forward of non-trading deficits from loan relationships against subsequent non-trading profits), other than deductions that would be ignored for the purposes of section 269ZC by reason of section 269ZJ(2) (insurance companies: shock losses).

(5)   The following are "excluded deductions" for an accounting period ("the current accounting period")—

(a)   a deduction for the current accounting period which is a relevant deduction for the purposes of section 269ZD (see subsection (3) of that section);

(b)   a deduction under section 37 (relief for trade losses against total profits) in relation to a loss made in an accounting period after the current accounting period;

(c)   a deduction under section 45F (terminal losses);

(d)   a deduction under section 260(3) of CAA 2001 (special leasing of plant or machinery: carry back of excess allowances) in relation to capital allowances for an accounting period after the current accounting period; and

(e)   a deduction under section 463E of CTA 2009 (non-trading deficit from loan relationships) in relation to a deficit for a period after the current accounting period.

Exclusion for certain general insurance companies

269ZG General insurance companies: excluded accounting periods

(1)   Nothing in sections 269ZB to 269ZE has effect for determining the taxable total profits of a general insurance company for an excluded accounting period.

182   *Finance (No. 2) Act 2017 (c. 32)*
Schedule 4 — Relief for carried-forward losses
Part 2 — Restriction on deductions in respect of carried-forward losses

(2) An accounting period of a general insurance company is an "excluded accounting period" if conditions A and B are met.

(3) Condition A is that—

    (a) the company is subject to insolvency procedures (see section 269ZH) at the end of the accounting period,

    (b) immediately before it became subject to insolvency procedures the company—

        (i) was unable to pay its debts as they fell due, and

        (ii) met the non-viability condition, and

    (c) the company's liabilities in respect of qualifying latent claims (see section 269ZI) were the main factor contributing to the company's meeting the non-viability condition at that time.

(4) Condition B is that—

    (a) at the end of the accounting period the company meets the non-viability condition, and

    (b) the company's liabilities in respect of qualifying latent claims are the main factor contributing to the company's meeting that condition at that time.

(5) At any time, a general insurance company meets the non-viability condition if there is no realistic prospect that it will subsequently write any new insurance business.

(6) For the purposes of this section a person who carries on the activity of effecting or carrying out contracts of general insurance is a "general insurance company" if—

    (a) the person has permission under Part 4A of the Financial Services and Markets Act 2000 to carry on that activity,

    (b) the person is of the kind mentioned in paragraph 5(d) or (da) of Schedule 3 to the Financial Services and Markets Act 2000 (EEA passport rights) and carries on that activity in the United Kingdom through a permanent establishment there, or

    (c) the person qualifies for authorisation under Schedule 4 to the Financial Services and Markets Act 2000 (Treaty rights) and carries on that activity in the United Kingdom through a permanent establishment there.

(7) The definition in subsection (6) is subject to the following qualifications—

    (a) a friendly society within the meaning of Part 3 of FA 2012 is not a general insurance company, and

    (b) an insurance special purpose vehicle (as defined in section 139 of FA 2012) is not a general insurance company.

(8) In this section—

        "contract of general insurance" means a contract of a type described in Part 1 of Schedule 1 to the Financial Services and Markets Act 2000 (Regulated Activities) Order 2001 (S.I. 2001/544);

        "liability" includes a contingent or prospective liability.

Finance (No. 2) Act 2017 (c. 32)
Schedule 4 — Relief for carried-forward losses
Part 2 — Restriction on deductions in respect of carried-forward losses

183

269ZH "Insolvency procedures"

(1) For the purposes of section 269ZG a company is subject to insolvency procedures if—

    (a) it is in liquidation,

    (b) it is in administration,

    (c) it is in receivership, or

    (d) a relevant scheme has effect in relation to it.

(2) A company is "in liquidation" for the purposes of this section if—

    (a) it is in liquidation within the meaning of section 247 of the Insolvency Act 1986 or Part 3 of the Insolvency (Northern Ireland) Order 1989 (S.I. 1989/2405 (N.I. 19), or

    (b) a corresponding situation under the law of a country or territory outside the United Kingdom exists in relation to the company.

(3) A company is "in administration" for the purposes of this section if—

    (a) it is in administration within the meaning of Schedule B1 to the Insolvency Act 1986 or Schedule B1 to the Insolvency (Northern Ireland) Order 1989, or

    (b) there is in force in relation to it under the law of a country or territory outside the United Kingdom any appointment corresponding to the appointment of an administrator under either of those Schedules.

(4) A company is "in receivership" for the purposes of this section if there is in force in relation to it—

    (a) an order for the appointment of an administrative receiver, a receiver and manager or a receiver under Chapter 1 or 2 of Part 3 of the Insolvency Act 1986 or Part 4 of the Insolvency (Northern Ireland Order) 1989, or

    (b) any corresponding order under the law of a country or territory outside the United Kingdom.

(5) In this section "relevant scheme" means a compromise or arrangement—

    (a) under section 425 of the Companies Act 1985, Article 418 of the Companies (Northern Ireland) Order 1986 (S.I. 1986/1032 (N.I. 6)) or Part 26 of the Companies Act 2006, or

    (b) under any corresponding provision of the law of a country or territory outside the United Kingdom.

269ZI "Qualifying latent claims"

(1) This section applies for the purposes of section 269ZG.

(2) Where a general insurance company has a liability in respect of a claim, the claim is a "qualifying latent claim" if conditions A to C are met.

(3) In this section "claim" means a claim (whether actual or potential) under an insurance policy.

(4) Condition A is that—

184

Finance (No. 2) Act 2017 (c. 32)
Schedule 4 — Relief for carried-forward losses
Part 2 — Restriction on deductions in respect of carried-forward losses

  (a) the claim is of a type that was not reasonably foreseeable at the time when the insurance policy concerned was entered into, and

  (b) it is likely that, had the company foreseen that type of claim, the price or other terms of the policy would have been significantly different.

(5) Condition B is that the latency period associated with that type of claim (see subsection (7)) is more than 10 years.

(6) Condition C is that the insurance policy, or the part of the insurance policy under which the claim is or would be made, is—

  (a) an employer's liability policy, or

  (b) a public or products liability policy.

(7) The "latency period" associated with a type of claim is the mean period for claims of the type between—

  (a) the insured event giving rise to the claim, and

  (b) notification of the claim.

(8) The mean period mentioned in subsection (7) is to be determined as at the end of the accounting period mentioned in section 269ZG(2).

(9) In this section—

  "employer's liability policy" means an insurance policy against the risks of the person insured incurring liabilities to the insured's employees for injury, illness or death arising out of their employment during the course of business;

  "general insurance company" is to be interpreted in accordance with section 269ZG;

  "insurance policy" includes any contract of insurance;

  "liability" includes a contingent or prospective liability;

  "public or products liability policy" means an insurance policy against the risks of the person insured incurring liabilities to third parties for damage to property, injury, illness or death, arising in the course of the insured's business.

269ZJ Exclusion of shock losses from restrictions

(1) If a shock loss is—

  (a) carried forward to an accounting period of an insurance company (see section 269ZP(2)), and

  (b) deducted under section 45B (post-1 April 2017 trade losses carried forward against trade profits),

the deduction is to be treated as not falling within section 269ZB(3).

(2) If a shock loss is—

  (a) carried forward to an accounting period of an insurance company, and

  (b) deducted under section 463H of CTA 2009 (carry forward of unrelieved non-trading deficit from loan relationships against non-trading profits),

the company is to be treated for the purposes of sections 269ZC and 269ZD(2)(b)(ii) as not having made that deduction.

Finance (No. 2) Act 2017 (c. 32)
Schedule 4 — Relief for carried-forward losses
Part 2 — Restriction on deductions in respect of carried-forward losses

185

(3) If an insurance company makes a deduction of (or in respect of) a shock loss, that deduction is not a "relevant deduction" for the purposes of section 269ZD (restriction on deductions from total profits).

(4) See also section 124E of FA 2012 (exclusion from the restriction on deductions from BLAGAB trade profits).

269ZK Meaning of "shock loss": requirement to make a claim

(1) If the conditions in subsection (3) are met, an insurance company may make a claim in respect of —
  (a) a loss or other amount (the "specified loss"), and
  (b) a period of 12 months ("the specified period") which is a solvency shock period (see section 269ZM).

(2) A claim may specify more than one 12 month period under subsection (1)(b) (but periods specified by an insurance company under this section may not overlap with one another).

(3) The conditions are that —
  (a) the accounting period (for corporation tax purposes) in which the specified loss arises ("the loss-making period") begins on or after 1 April 2017,
  (b) the specified loss is, or is capable of being, carried forward to a subsequent accounting period, and
  (c) the loss-making period and the specified period have one or more days in common.

(4) A claim under this section must be made within —
  (a) the period of two years after the end of the loss-making period, or
  (b) such further period as an officer of Revenue and Customs allows.

(5) If —
  (a) a claim is made under this section, and
  (b) the whole of the loss-making period is, or falls within, the specified period,
  the specified loss is a "shock loss".

(6) If —
  (a) a claim is made under this section, and
  (b) the loss-making period falls partly, but not wholly, in the specified period,
  the specified loss is a "shock loss" so far as it is attributable to the specified period.

(7) For the purposes of subsection (6) the specified loss is "attributable to" the specified period in the proportion —

$$\frac{P}{N}$$

186

Finance (No. 2) Act 2017 (c. 32)
Schedule 4 — Relief for carried-forward losses
Part 2 — Restriction on deductions in respect of carried-forward losses

Where P is the number of days of the loss-making period that fall within the specified period and N is the number of days in the loss-making period.

(8) If the method in subsection (7) would produce a result that is unjust or unreasonable, the apportionment of the specified loss for the purposes of subsection (6) is to be made on a just and reasonable basis.

269ZL Further provision about claims under section 269ZK

(1) A claim under section 269ZK is not effective unless —
  (a) the claim —
    (i) states the company's solvency capital requirement at the beginning of the specified period,
    (ii) states the company's shock loss threshold for that period, and sets out the calculation of that amount (as described in steps 2 to 5 of 269ZN(1)), and
    (iii) states the amount of the company's solvency loss for that period (see section 269ZO), and
  (b) the company submits with the claim —
    (i) information ("the submitted information") corresponding to the information specified in the template mentioned in point (i), (j) or (k) (as the case requires) of Article 4 of the technical standards implementing Regulation, and
    (ii) a report provided by the appropriate person which meets the condition in subsection (2).

(2) The condition is that the report includes an opinion confirming that —
  (a) the submitted information is prepared in all material respects in accordance with any relevant requirements which would apply if the submitted information were disclosed as part of the company's report on solvency and financial condition,
  (b) the calculation of the company's shock loss threshold (not including step 1(a) of section 269ZN(1)) complies in all material respects with section 269ZN, and
  (c) the company's solvency loss is calculated in all material respects in accordance with section 269ZO.

(3) In this section "relevant requirements" means —
  (a) requirements under rules made by the Prudential Regulation Authority, and
  (b) requirements under any directly applicable EU regulation made under the Solvency 2 Directive.

(4) In this section "the appropriate person" means —
  (a) the company's chief actuary, or
  (b) (if the company is not a PRA-authorised person) a person with equivalent functions.

(5) Subsections (1)(b)(i), (2)(a) and (3) have effect in relation to a third-country insurance undertaking as if it were an insurance undertaking.

Finance (No. 2) Act 2017 (c. 32)
Schedule 4 — Relief for carried-forward losses
Part 2 — Restriction on deductions in respect of carried-forward losses

187

269ZM Meaning of "solvency shock period"

A period of 12 months is a "solvency shock period" in relation to an insurance company if the company has a solvency loss for that period (see section 269ZO) which exceeds the company's shock loss threshold for that period (see section 269ZN).

269ZN Determination of shock loss threshold

(1) A company's shock loss threshold for a 12 month period is determined as follows.

Step 1

    (a) Calculate the company's solvency capital requirement at the beginning of that period.

    (b) But any adjustment for the loss-absorbing capacity of deferred taxes is to be calculated, and applied, on the assumption that that period is a solvency shock period in relation to the company.

    (c) The resulting amount is the company's "adjusted SCR".

Step 2

Calculate the deductible amount (see subsection (2)) for each relevant ring-fenced fund of the company.

Step 3

Deduct the total of the amounts found under step 2 from the company's adjusted SCR.

Step 4

Multiply the amount found under step 3 by 90%.

Step 5

The result is the company's shock loss threshold for the period.

(2) The deductible amount for a relevant ring-fenced fund is the lesser of A and B, where —

    (a) A is the amount of basic own funds within that fund at the beginning of the period (or zero, if greater);

    (b) B is the notional solvency capital requirement for that fund at the beginning of that period.

(3) But in calculating amount A for the purposes of subsection (2) —

    (a) no account is to be taken of the value of future transfers attributable to shareholders;

    (b) a restricted own-fund item within the fund is to be disregarded if the company's with-profits actuary provides a written opinion confirming that the condition in subsection (4) is met.

(4) The condition is that —

    (a) the item is available as a restricted own-fund item pursuant to conditional support arrangements, and

    (b) if at the time mentioned in subsection (2)(a) or any subsequent time (when the conditional support arrangements are in place) the value of the company's interest in the item were to be (or is in fact) greater than zero, that value would be recognised for the purposes of a balance

188   *Finance (No. 2) Act 2017 (c. 32)*
                                Schedule 4 — Relief for carried-forward losses
                Part 2 — Restriction on deductions in respect of carried-forward losses

sheet drawn up at the time in question by the company in accordance with generally accepted accounting practice.

(5)   In this section "conditional support arrangements" means arrangements under which the relevant restrictions would cease to apply if specified conditions relating to the financial strength of the fund were met.

(6)   In subsection (5) "the relevant restrictions" means the restrictions on transferability as a result of which the item is a restricted own-fund item.

(7)   In this section "adjustment for the loss-absorbing capacity of deferred taxes" means —

     (a)   an adjustment pursuant to Article 103(c) of the Solvency 2 Directive, or

     (b)   any corresponding adjustment made pursuant to Subsection 3 of Section 4 of Chapter 6 of Title 1 of the Solvency 2 Directive (solvency capital requirement full and partial internal models).

(8)   Where the company is a third-country insurance undertaking —

     (a)   steps 1(b) and 2 to 5 of subsection (1), and

     (b)   subsections (2) to (7),

have effect with any modifications that are appropriate as a result of the reference in step 1(a) of subsection (1) to the "solvency capital requirement" having effect in accordance with section 269ZP(1)(b).

269ZO Calculation of solvency loss

(1)   An insurance company's solvency loss (if any) for a 12 month period is determined as follows.

(2)   Calculate, in the manner set out in subsections (5) to (11) —

     (a)   whether the total amount of the company's basic own funds at the beginning of the period ("opening BOF") exceeds the total amount of the company's basic own funds at the end of the period ("closing BOF"), and

     (b)   if so, the amount by which opening BOF exceeds closing BOF.

(3)   The company has a solvency loss for the 12 month period only if an excess of opening BOF over closing BOF is found under subsection (2)(a).

(4)   The amount found under subsection (2)(b) is the amount of the solvency loss.

(5)   The method of calculation under subsection (2) must fairly represent the method by which the company calculates its solvency capital requirement.

But this is subject to subsections (6) to (10).

(6)   Closing BOF is to be calculated on the assumption that the 12 month period mentioned in subsection (1) is a solvency shock period in relation to the company.

(7)   The following adjustments are to be made in calculating the company's basic own funds at the beginning and end of the period —

Finance (No. 2) Act 2017 (c. 32)
Schedule 4 — Relief for carried-forward losses
Part 2 — Restriction on deductions in respect of carried-forward losses

189

1. Find (with respect to each of those times) what that amount would be in the absence of this subsection.

2. Find the surplus in respect of each relevant ring-fenced fund of the company (at the time in question).

3. Deduct the total of the amounts found under paragraph 2 from the amount found under paragraph 1.

The result is to be taken to be the amount of the company's basic own funds at the beginning, or (as the case may be) the end, of the period.

(8) The surplus in respect of a relevant ring-fenced fund (at any time) is equal to—

    (a) the amount of basic own funds attributable to policyholders, or

    (b) zero, if greater.

(9) For any relevant ring-fenced fund, the amount of basic own funds attributable to policyholders (at any time) is equal to—

$$A - B$$

where—

A is the amount of basic own funds within the relevant ring-fenced fund;

B is the total of any items in the fund that fall within subsection (10).

(10) The items are—

    (a) the value of future transfers attributable to shareholders;

    (b) any restricted own-fund item in relation to which the company's with-profits actuary provides a written opinion confirming that the condition in subsection (4) of section 269ZN is met.

(11) In subsection (5) the reference to the "method" of a calculation is to the—

    (a) taking into account, and

    (b) leaving out of account,

of variations in items of basic own funds for the purposes of the calculation.

(12) If the company is a third-country insurance undertaking, subsections (1) to (11) have effect in relation to it as if it were an insurance undertaking.

269ZP Interpretation of sections 269ZJ to 269ZO

(1) In sections 269ZJ to 269ZO "solvency capital requirement"—

    (a) in relation to an insurance undertaking or a reinsurance undertaking, means the solvency capital requirement pursuant to Section 4 of Chapter 6 of Title 1 of the Solvency 2 Directive;

    (b) in relation to a third-country insurance undertaking, means the amount that would be the undertaking's solvency capital

190 Finance (No. 2) Act 2017 (c. 32)
Schedule 4 — Relief for carried-forward losses
Part 2 — Restriction on deductions in respect of carried-forward losses

requirement pursuant to Section 4 of Chapter 6 of Title 1 of
the Solvency 2 Directive if that undertaking were an
insurance undertaking.

(2)   In sections 269ZJ to 269ZO and this section—

"actuarial function", in relation to a PRA-authorised person, has
the meaning given by the PRA Rulebook;

"basic own funds" is to be interpreted in accordance with
Article 88 of the Solvency 2 Directive;

"chief actuary", in relation to a PRA-authorised person, means
a person who has the function of having responsibility for the
actuarial function;

"insurance company" means a company which is an insurance
undertaking, a reinsurance undertaking or a third-country
insurance undertaking;

"insurance undertaking" has the meaning given in Article 13(1)
of the Solvency 2 Directive;

"notional solvency capital requirement", in relation to a ring-
fenced fund, has the same meaning as in Commission
Delegated Regulation (EU) 2015/35 supplementing the
Solvency 2 Directive;

"PRA-authorised person" has the same meaning as in the
Financial Services and Markets Act 2000 (see section 2B(5) of
that Act);

"the PRA Rulebook" means the Rulebook made by the
Prudential Regulation Authority under the Financial Services
and Markets Act 2000 (as that Rulebook has effect from time
to time);

"reinsurance undertaking" has the meaning given in Article
13(4) of the Solvency 2 Directive;

"relevant ring-fenced fund" means a ring-fenced fund that is a
with-profits fund;

"report on solvency and financial condition" means a report on
solvency and financial condition pursuant to Article 51 of the
Solvency 2 Directive;

"restricted own-fund item" is to be interpreted in accordance
with Article 80(2) of Commission Delegated Regulation (EU)
2015/35 supplementing the Solvency 2 Directive;

"ring-fenced fund" has the same meaning as in Commission
Delegated Regulation (EU) 2015/35 supplementing the
Solvency 2 Directive;

"Solvency 2 Directive" means Directive 2009/138/EC of the
European Parliament and the Council of 25 November 2009
on the taking-up and pursuit of the business of Insurance and
Reinsurance (Solvency II);

"technical standards implementing Regulation" means
Commission Implementing Regulation (EU) 2015/2452 of 2
December 2015 laying down implementing technical
standards with regard to the procedures, formats and
templates of the solvency and financial condition report in
accordance with the Solvency 2 Directive;

"third-country insurance undertaking" means an undertaking
that has received authorisation under Article 162 of the

Finance (No. 2) Act 2017 (c. 32)
Schedule 4 — Relief for carried-forward losses
Part 2 — Restriction on deductions in respect of carried-forward losses

191

Solvency 2 Directive from the Prudential Regulation Authority or the Financial Conduct Authority;

"value of future transfers attributable to shareholders" has the same meaning as in Article 80 of Commission Delegated Regulation (EU) 2015/35 supplementing the Solvency 2 Directive;

"with-profits fund" has the meaning given by the Glossary forming part of the PRA Rulebook;

"with-profits actuary" has the meaning given by the Glossary forming part of the Handbook made by the Financial Conduct Authority under the Financial Services and Markets Act 2000 (as that Handbook has effect from time to time).

269ZQ Power to amend

(1) The Treasury may by regulations make such amendments of the provisions mentioned in subsection (2) as they consider appropriate in consequence of —

    (a) any change made to, or replacement of, the PRA Rulebook or the FCA Handbook;

    (b) any regulatory requirement, or change to a regulatory requirement, imposed by EU legislation, or by or under any Act (whenever adopted, enacted or made).

(2) The provisions are —

    (a) sections 269ZJ to 269ZP,

    (b) sections 124A to 124E of FA 2012.

(3) Regulations under this section may include transitional provision.

(4) In this section —

"the PRA Rulebook" means the Rulebook made by the Prudential Regulation Authority under the Financial Services and Markets Act 2000 (as that Rulebook has effect from time to time);

"the FCA Handbook means the Handbook made by the Financial Conduct Authority under the Financial Services and Markets Act 2000 (as that Handbook has effect from time to time).

Deductions allowance

269ZR Deductions allowance for company in a group

(1) This section makes provision as to the deductions allowance of a company for an accounting period where, at any time in the period —

    (a) the company is a member of a group, and

    (b) one or more other companies within the charge to corporation tax are members of that group.

(2) The company's deductions allowance for the accounting period is the sum of —

    (a) any amounts of group deductions allowance allocated to the company for the period in accordance with sections 269ZS to 269ZV, and

192

Finance (No. 2) Act 2017 (c. 32)
Schedule 4 — Relief for carried-forward losses
Part 2 — Restriction on deductions in respect of carried-forward losses

  (b) the appropriate amount of non-group deductions allowance of the company for the period,

up to a limit of £5,000,000.

(3) The "appropriate amount of non-group deductions allowance" of the company, for the accounting period, is—

$$\frac{DNG}{DAC} \times £5{,}000{,}000$$

where—

  "DNG" is the number of days in the period on which the company is not a member of a group that has another member that is a company within the charge to corporation tax, and

  "DAC" is the total number of days in the period.

(4) If the accounting period is less than 12 months—

  (a) the appropriate amount of non-group deductions allowance, and

  (b) the limit in subsection (2),

are proportionally reduced.

269ZS Group deductions allowance and the nominated company

(1) This section applies where—

  (a) two or more members of a group are companies within the charge to corporation tax, and

  (b) all the companies within the charge to corporation tax that are members of the group together nominate ("the group allowance nomination") one of their number ("the nominated company") for the purposes of this Part.

(2) The "group deductions allowance" for the group is £5,000,000 for each accounting period of the nominated company throughout which the group allowance nomination has effect.

(3) If the group allowance nomination takes effect, or ceases to have effect, part of the way through an accounting period of the nominated company, the "group deductions allowance" for the group for that period is—

$$\frac{DN}{DAC} \times £5{,}000{,}000$$

where—

  "DN" is the number of days in the accounting period on which a group allowance nomination that nominates the nominated company in relation to the group has effect, and

  "DAC" is the total number of days in the accounting period.

(4) If an accounting period of the nominated company is less than 12 months, the group deductions allowance for that period is proportionally reduced.

(5) A group allowance nomination must state the date on which it is to take effect (which may be earlier than the date the nomination is made).

Finance (No. 2) Act 2017 (c. 32)
Schedule 4 — Relief for carried-forward losses
Part 2 — Restriction on deductions in respect of carried-forward losses

193

(6) A group allowance nomination is of no effect unless it is signed by the appropriate person on behalf of each company that is, when the nomination is made, a member of the group and within the charge to corporation tax.

(7) A group allowance nomination ceases to have effect—

    (a) immediately before the date on which a new group allowance nomination in respect of the group takes effect,

    (b) upon the appropriate person in relation to a company within the charge to corporation tax that is a member of the group notifying an officer of Revenue and Customs, in writing, that the group allowance nomination is revoked, or

    (c) upon the nominated company ceasing to be a company within the charge to corporation tax or ceasing to be a member of the group.

(8) The Commissioners for Her Majesty's Revenue and Customs may by regulations make further provision about a group allowance nomination or any notification under this section including, in particular, provision—

    (a) about the form and manner in which a nomination or notification may be made,

    (b) about how a nomination may be revoked and the form and manner of such revocation,

    (c) requiring a person to notify HMRC of the making or revocation of a nomination,

    (d) requiring a person to give information to HMRC in connection with the making or revocation of a nomination or the giving of a notification,

    (e) imposing time limits in relation to making or revoking a nomination or giving a notification, and

    (f) providing that a nomination or its revocation, or a notification, is of no effect, or ceases to have effect, if time limits or other requirements under the regulations are not met.

(9) In this Part "the appropriate person", in relation to a company, means—

    (a) the proper officer of the company, or

    (b) such other person as may for the time being have the express, implied or apparent authority of the company to act on its behalf for the purposes of this Part.

(10) Subsections (3) and (4) of section 108 of TMA 1970 (responsibility of company officers: meaning of "proper officer") apply for the purposes of subsection (9) as they apply for the purposes of that section.

269ZT Group allowance allocation statement: submission

(1) A company must submit a group allowance allocation statement to HMRC for each of its accounting periods in which it is the nominated company in relation to a group.

This is subject to subsections (2) and (3).

194

Finance (No. 2) Act 2017 (c. 32)
Schedule 4 — Relief for carried-forward losses
Part 2 — Restriction on deductions in respect of carried-forward losses

(2) If a company ceases to be the nominated company in relation to a group before it submits a group allowance allocation statement to HMRC for an accounting period —

    (a) that company may not submit the statement, and

    (b) the company that is for the time being the nominated company in relation to the group must do so.

(3) But if a new group allowance nomination in respect of the group takes effect on a date before it is made, that does not affect the validity of the submission of any group allowance allocation statement submitted before the date the new nomination is made.

(4) A group allowance allocation statement under this section must be received by HMRC before the first anniversary of the filing date for the company tax return for the accounting period to which the statement relates.

(5) A group allowance allocation statement under this section may be submitted at a later time if an officer of Revenue and Customs allows it.

(6) A group allowance allocation statement under this section must comply with the requirements of section 269ZV.

269ZU Group allowance allocation statement: submission of revised statement

(1) This section applies if a group allowance allocation statement has been submitted under section 269ZT, or this section, in respect of an accounting period of a company that is, or was, a nominated company ("the nominee's accounting period").

(2) A revised group allowance allocation statement in respect of the nominee's accounting period may be submitted to HMRC by the company that is for the time being the nominated company in relation to the group.

(3) But if a new group allowance nomination in respect of the group takes effect on a date before it is made, that does not affect the validity of the submission of any revised group allowance allocation statement submitted before the date the new nomination is made.

(4) A revised group allowance allocation statement may be submitted on or before whichever is the latest of the following dates —

    (a) the first anniversary of the filing date for the company tax return for the nominee's accounting period,

    (b) if notice of enquiry (within the meaning of Schedule 18 to FA 1998) is given into a relevant company tax return, 30 days after the enquiry is completed,

    (c) if, after such an enquiry, an officer of Revenue and Customs amends the return under paragraph 34(2) of that Schedule, 30 days after the notice of amendment is issued,

    (d) if an appeal is brought against such an amendment, 30 days after the date on which the appeal is finally determined.

(5) A revised group allowance allocation statement may be submitted at a later time if an officer of Revenue and Customs allows it.

Finance (No. 2) Act 2017 (c. 32)
Schedule 4 — Relief for carried-forward losses
Part 2 — Restriction on deductions in respect of carried-forward losses

195

(6) In this section "relevant company tax return" means a company tax return of a company for an accounting period for which an amount of group deductions allowance was, or could have been, allocated by a previous group allowance allocation statement in respect of the nominee's accounting period.

(7) The references in subsection (4) to an enquiry into a relevant company tax return do not include an enquiry resulting from an amendment of such a return where—

(a) the scope of the enquiry is limited as mentioned in paragraph 25(2) of Schedule 18 to FA 1998 (enquiry into amendments when time limit for enquiry into return as originally submitted is passed), and

(b) the amendment relates only to the allocation of group deductions allowance for the nominee's accounting period.

(8) A group allowance allocation statement under this section must comply with the requirements of section 269ZV.

269ZV Group allowance allocation statement: requirements and effects

(1) This section applies in relation to a group allowance allocation statement submitted under section 269ZT or 269ZU.

(2) The statement must be signed by the appropriate person in relation to the company giving the statement.

(3) The statement must—

(a) identify the group to which it relates,

(b) specify the accounting period, of the company that is or was the nominated company, to which the statement relates ("the nominee's accounting period"),

(c) specify the days in the nominee's accounting period on which that company was the nominated company in relation to the group or state that that company was the nominated company throughout the period,

(d) state the group deductions allowance the group has for the nominee's accounting period,

(e) list one or more of the companies that were members of the group and within the charge to corporation tax in the nominee's accounting period ("listed companies"),

(f) allocate amounts of the group deductions allowance to the listed companies, and

(g) for each amount of group deductions allowance allocated to a listed company, specify the accounting period of the listed company for which it is allocated.

(4) An amount of group deductions allowance allocated to a listed company must be allocated to that company for an accounting period that falls wholly or partly in the nominee's accounting period.

(5) The maximum amount of group deductions allowance that may be allocated, by the group allowance allocation statement, to a listed company for an accounting period of that company is—

$$\frac{\text{DAP}}{\text{DNAP}} \times \text{GSA}$$

196   *Finance (No. 2) Act 2017 (c. 32)*
Schedule 4 — Relief for carried-forward losses
Part 2 — Restriction on deductions in respect of carried-forward losses

where —

"DAP" is the number of days in the accounting period of the listed company that are —

(a) days in the nominee's accounting period, and

(b) days on which the company was a member of the group,

"DNAP" is the number of days in the nominee's accounting period, and

"GSA" is the group deductions allowance of the group for the nominee's accounting period.

(6) The sum of the amounts allocated to listed companies by the group allowance allocation statement may not exceed the group deductions allowance for the nominee's accounting period.

(7) If a group allowance allocation statement is submitted that does not comply with subsection (5) or (6), the company that is, for the time being, the nominated company in relation to the group must submit a revised group allowance allocation statement that does comply with those subsections within 30 days of the date on which the group allowance allocation statement that did not comply was submitted or within such further period as an officer of Revenue and Customs allows.

(8) If a group allowance allocation statement —

(a) complies with those subsections when it is submitted, but

(b) subsequently ceases to comply with either of them,

the company that is, for the time being, the nominated company in relation to the group must submit a revised group allowance allocation statement that does comply with those subsections within 30 days of the date on which the group allowance allocation statement ceased to comply with one of those subsections or within such further period as an officer of Revenue and Customs allows.

(9) If a company fails to comply with subsection (7) or (8), an officer of Revenue and Customs may by written notice to the company amend the group allowance allocation statement as the officer thinks fit for the purpose of making it comply with subsections (5) and (6).

(10) An officer of Revenue and Customs who issues a notice under subsection (9) to a company must, at the same time, send a copy of the notice to each of the listed companies.

(11) The time limits otherwise applicable to the amendment of a company tax return do not apply to any such amendment to the extent that it is made in consequence of a group allowance allocation statement being submitted in accordance with section 269ZT or 269ZU.

(12) The Commissioners for Her Majesty's Revenue and Customs may by regulations make further provision about a group allowance allocation statement including, in particular, provision —

(a) about the form of a statement and the manner in which it is to be submitted,

(b) requiring a person to give information to HMRC in connection with a statement,

Finance (No. 2) Act 2017 (c. 32)   197
Schedule 4 – Relief for carried-forward losses
Part 2 – Restriction on deductions in respect of carried-forward losses

    (c)   as to the circumstances in which a statement that is not received by the time specified in section 269ZU(4) is to be treated as if it were so received, and

    (d)   as to the circumstances in which a statement that does not comply with the requirements of this section is to be treated as if it did comply.

269ZW Deductions allowance for company not in a group

(1)   This section makes provision as to the deductions allowance of a company for an accounting period where section 269ZR (deductions allowance for company in a group) does not apply.

(2)   The company's deductions allowance for the accounting period is £5,000,000.

(3)   If the accounting period is less than 12 months, the company's deductions allowance for the period is proportionally reduced.

269ZX Increase of deductions allowance where provision for onerous lease reversed

(1)   This section applies if—

    (a)   a relevant reversal credit (see section 269ZY) is brought into account in calculating a company's specified profits for an accounting period, and

    (b)   the amount of the company's specified profits for the accounting period is greater than nil.

(2)   For the purposes of this section a company's "specified profits" for an accounting period are the sum of—

    (a)   the company's total profits for the accounting period, calculated with the modifications set out in section 269ZF(4), and

    (b)   any I-E profit of the company for the accounting period.

(3)   The company's deductions allowance for the accounting period (as determined in accordance with section 269ZR or 269ZW) is to be treated (for all purposes) as increased by—

    (a)   the amount of the relevant reversal credit, or

    (b)   if lower, the amount of the specified profits.

269ZY Meaning of "relevant reversal credit"

(1)   For the purposes of section 269ZX a "relevant reversal credit" is a credit, or other income, brought into account in respect of the relevant reversal (see subsections (3) and (5)) of a relevant onerous lease provision.

(2)   A provision in the accounts of a company ("C") is a "relevant onerous lease provision" if—

    (a)   the provision relates to a lease of land under which C is the tenant (and "L" is the landlord),

    (b)   the provision is required, for accountancy purposes, as a provision for an onerous lease, and

    (c)   the lease was entered into at arm's length.

198   *Finance (No. 2) Act 2017 (c. 32)*
Schedule 4 — Relief for carried-forward losses
Part 2 — Restriction on deductions in respect of carried-forward losses

(3) The reversal (in whole or in part) of a relevant onerous lease provision is a "relevant reversal" if—

    (a) the reversal is required for accountancy purposes as a result of an arrangement ("C's arrangement") made at arm's length under which C's obligations under the lease are varied or cancelled,

    (b) subsection (4) does not apply, and

    (c) at least one of conditions X, Y and Z in subsection (7) is met.

(4) This subsection applies if—

    (a) C and L are connected at the time when C's arrangement is made, or

    (b) the landlord who granted the lease (whether that was L or another person) and the tenant to whom it was granted (whether that was C or another person) were connected at the time when the lease was granted.

(5) The reversal (in whole or in part) of a relevant onerous lease provision is a "relevant reversal" if—

    (a) the lease has been granted out of a lease ("the superior lease"),

    (b) L and C are members of the same group of companies,

    (c) the reversal would be a relevant reversal by virtue of subsection (3) if the condition in subsection (3)(b) (lack of connection between C and L) were met,

    (d) the terms of C's arrangement substantially reflect those of an arrangement ("L's arrangement") made at arm's length under which L's obligations under the superior lease are varied or cancelled, and

    (e) subsection (6) does not apply.

(6) This subsection applies if—

    (a) at the time when L's arrangement is made, the landlord under the superior lease ("S") is connected with L or C, or

    (b) the landlord who granted the superior lease (whether that is S or another person) and the tenant to whom it was granted (whether that was L or another person) were connected at the time when that lease was granted.

(7) The conditions mentioned in subsection (3)(c) are as follows.
Condition X is that—

    (a) it is reasonable to suppose that immediately before C's arrangement was made there was a material risk that at some time within the next 12 months C would be unable to pay its debts as they fell due, and

    (b) the sole or main purpose of C's arrangement was to avert that risk (whether directly or indirectly).

Debts due to a person connected with C are to be regarded as not being debts for the purposes of paragraph (a).
Condition Y is that C is in insolvent administration.
Condition Z is that C's arrangement is, or is part of, a statutory insolvency arrangement.

(8) In this section "statutory insolvency arrangement" means—

Finance (No. 2) Act 2017 (c. 32)
Schedule 4 — Relief for carried-forward losses
Part 2 — Restriction on deductions in respect of carried-forward losses

199

  (a) a voluntary arrangement that has taken effect under, or as a result of, the Insolvency Act 1986 or the Insolvency (Northern Ireland) Order 1989 (S.I. 1989/ 2405 (N.I. 19)),

  (b) a compromise or arrangement that has taken effect under Part 26 of the Companies Act 2006, or

  (c) an arrangement or compromise of a kind corresponding to any of those mentioned in paragraph (a) or (b) that has taken effect under, or as a result of, the law of a country or territory outside the United Kingdom,

(and for the purposes of this section an arrangement which is, or is part of, a statutory insolvency arrangement is taken to be "made" when the statutory insolvency arrangement takes effect).

 (9) For the purposes of this section a company in administration is in insolvent administration if—

  (a) it entered administration under Schedule B1 to the Insolvency Act 1986, or Schedule B1 to the Insolvency (Northern Ireland) Order 1989, at a time when its assets were insufficient for the payment of its debts and other liabilities and the expenses of the administration, or

  (a) under the law of a country or territory outside the United Kingdom circumstances corresponding to those mentioned in paragraph (a) exist.

 (10) In the application of subsection (5) to Scotland, the reference to the lease having been granted out of the superior lease is to the lease being a sublease of land subject to the superior lease.

 (11) Section 152 (groups of companies) applies for the purposes of this section as it applies for the purposes of Part 5.

 (12) For the purposes of this section any question whether a person is connected with another is to be determined in accordance with section 1122.

269ZZ Company tax return to specify amount of deductions allowance

 (1) A company's tax return for an accounting period must specify—

  (a) the amount of the company's deductions allowance for the period, and

  (b) if section 269ZX (increase of deductions allowance where provision for onerous lease reversed) applies, what that amount would be without the increase provided for by subsection (3) of that section.

 (2) But subsection (1) applies only if the company makes for the accounting period a deduction to which section 269ZB(2), 269ZC(2) or 269ZD(2) or section 124D(1) of FA 2012 applies.

269ZZA Excessive specifications of deductions allowance

 (1) This section applies if a company's tax return for an accounting period specifies an excessive amount as—

  (a) the company's deductions allowance for the period,

  (b) the company's trading profits deductions allowance for the period,

200   *Finance (No. 2) Act 2017 (c. 32)*
Schedule 4 — Relief for carried-forward losses
Part 2 — Restriction on deductions in respect of carried-forward losses

     (c)   the company's non-trading profits deductions allowance for the period,

     (d)   the company's contractor's ring fence profits deductions allowance for the period, or

     (e)   the company's BLAGAB trade profits deductions allowance for the period.

(2)   The company must, so far as it may do so, amend the company tax return so that the amount specified is not excessive.

(3)   If an officer of Revenue and Customs considers that an undue amount of relief has been given as a consequence of the amount specified being excessive, the officer may make an assessment to tax in the amount which in the officer's opinion ought to be charged.

(4)   If—

     (a)   the amount specified became excessive in consequence of an alteration being made to the amount of group deductions allowance allocated to the company for the accounting period concerned, and

     (b)   the company has failed, or is unable, to amend its company tax return in accordance with subsection (2),

an assessment under subsection (3) is not out of time if it is made within 12 months of the date on which the alteration took place.

(5)   The power in subsection (3) is without prejudice to the power to make a discovery assessment under paragraph 41(1) of Schedule 18 to FA 1998.

269ZZB Meaning of "group"

(1)   In this Part "group" means two or more companies which together meet the following condition.

(2)   The condition is that one of the companies is—

     (a)   the ultimate parent of each of the other companies, and

     (b)   is not the ultimate parent of any other company.

(3)   A company ("A") is the "ultimate parent" of another company ("B") if—

     (a)   A is the parent of B, and

     (b)   no company is the parent of both A and B.

(4)   A company ("A") is the "parent" of another company ("B") if—

     (a)   B is a 75% subsidiary of A,

     (b)   A is beneficially entitled to at least 75% of any profits available for distribution to equity holders of B, or

     (c)   A would be beneficially entitled to at least 75% of any assets of B available for distribution to its equity holders on a winding up.

(5)   The following apply for the purposes of subsection (4)—

     (a)   Chapter 6 of Part 5 (equity holders and profits or assets available for distribution) other than sections 169 to 182, and

     (b)   Chapter 3 of Part 24 (subsidiaries).

This is subject to subsections (6) and (7).

Finance (No. 2) Act 2017 (c. 32)
Schedule 4 — Relief for carried-forward losses
Part 2 — Restriction on deductions in respect of carried-forward losses

201

(6) In applying Chapter 3 of Part 24 for the purposes of subsection (4)—

    (a) share capital of a registered society is to be treated as if it were ordinary share capital, and

    (b) a company ("the shareholder") that directly owns shares in another company is to be treated as not owning those shares if a profit on their sale would be a trading receipt of the shareholder.

(7) In applying Chapter 6 of Part 5 (other than sections 169 to 182) and Chapter 3 of Part 24 for the purposes of subsection (4), they are to be read with all modifications necessary to ensure that—

    (a) they apply to a company which does not have share capital, and to holders of corresponding ordinary holdings in such a company, in a way which corresponds to the way they apply to companies with ordinary share capital and holders of ordinary shares in such companies,

    (b) they apply to a company which is an unincorporated association in a way which corresponds to the way they apply to companies which are bodies corporate,

    (c) they apply in relation to ownership through an entity (other than a company), or any trust or other arrangement, in a way which corresponds to the way they apply to ownership through a company, and

    (d) for the purposes of achieving paragraphs (a) to (c), profits or assets are attributed to holders of corresponding ordinary holdings in unincorporated associations, entities, trusts or other arrangements in a manner which corresponds to the way profits or assets are attributed to holders of ordinary shares in a company which is a body corporate.

(8) In this section "corresponding ordinary holding" in an unincorporated association, entity, trust or other arrangement means a holding or interest which provides the holder with economic rights corresponding to those provided by a holding of ordinary shares in a body corporate".

17 (1) Section 269C (overview of Chapter 3 of Part 7A: restriction on banking company obtaining certain deductions) is amended as follows.

(2) After subsection (1) insert—

"(1A) This Chapter applies in relation to a banking company in addition to Part 7ZA (which contains provision restricting the amount of certain deductions which any kind of company may make in calculating its taxable total profits for an accounting period)."

(3) In subsection (2) for "269CD" substitute "269CC"

18 (1) Section 269CA (restriction on deductions for pre-1 April 2015 trading losses) is amended as follows.

(2) In subsection (2), in the second sentence—

    (a) for "269CD" substitute "269ZF", and

    (b) omit "step 5 in".

(3) In subsection (3), for the words from "where" to the end substitute "in relation to a banking company for an accounting period where, in

202

Finance (No. 2) Act 2017 (c. 32)
Schedule 4 — Relief for carried-forward losses
Part 2 — Restriction on deductions in respect of carried-forward losses

determining the company's relevant trading profits for the period, the amount given by step 1 in section 269ZF(3) is not greater than nil".

19 (1) Section 269CB (restriction on deductions for pre-1 April 2015 non-trading deficits from loan relationships) is amended as follows.

(2) In subsection (2), in the second sentence—
(a) for "269CD" substitute "269ZF", and
(b) for "step 6 in subsection (1)" substitute "subsection (2)".

(3) In subsection (3), for the words from "where" to the end substitute "in relation to a banking company for an accounting period where, in determining the company's relevant non-trading profits for the period, the amount given by step 1 in section 269ZF(3) is not greater than nil"

20 (1) Section 269CC (restriction on deductions for pre-1 April 2015 management expenses etc) is amended as follows.

(2) In subsection (3) for the words from "does not apply" to the end substitute "is subject to subsection (8)".

(3) In subsection (7)—
(a) in the second sentence of step 1, for "269CD" substitute "269ZD(5)",
(b) in step 2 for the words from "which are" to the end substitute "under—
(a) section 45 (carry forward of pre-1 April 2017 trade loss against subsequent trade profits),
(b) section 45B (carry forward of post-1 April 2017 trade loss against subsequent trade profits), or
(c) section 457 of CTA 2009 (carry forward of pre-1 April 2017 non-trading deficits from loan relationships)."

(4) After subsection (7) insert—

"(8) Subsection (2) does not apply in relation to a banking company for an accounting period where, in determining the company's relevant profits for the period, the amount given by step 1 in section 269ZF(3) is not greater than nil."

21 Section 269CD (relevant profits) is omitted.

22 (1) Section 269CN (definitions for the purposes of Part 7A) is amended as follows.

(2) In the definition of "relevant non-trading profits" for the words from "means" to the end substitute "has the meaning given by section 269ZF(2)".

(3) In the definition of "relevant profits" for the words from "means" to the end substitute "has the meaning given by section 269ZD(5)".

(4) In the definition of "relevant trading profits" for the words from "means" to the end substitute "has the meaning given by section 269ZF(1)".

Finance (No. 2) Act 2017 (c. 32)
Schedule 4 – Relief for carried-forward losses
Part 3 – Group relief for carried-forward losses

203

PART 3

GROUP RELIEF FOR CARRIED-FORWARD LOSSES

23   After section 188 of CTA 2010 insert—

"PART 5A

GROUP RELIEF FOR CARRIED-FORWARD LOSSES

CHAPTER 1

INTRODUCTION

188AA Introduction to Part

(1)   This Part—

    (a)   allows a company to surrender losses and other amounts that have been carried forward to an accounting period of the company (see Chapter 2), and

    (b)   enables, in certain cases involving groups or consortiums of companies, other companies to claim corporation tax relief for the losses and other amounts that are surrendered (see Chapter 3).

(2)   Chapters 4 and 5 contain limitations on the amount of corporation tax relief which may be given on a claim under Chapter 3.

(3)   See Chapter 5 for definitions that apply for the purposes of this Part and miscellaneous provisions.

(4)   The corporation tax relief mentioned in this section is called "group relief for carried-forward losses."

CHAPTER 2

SURRENDER OF COMPANY'S CARRIED-FORWARD LOSSES ETC

188BA Overview of Chapter

(1)   This Chapter allows a company to surrender losses and other amounts that have been carried forward to an accounting period of the company.

(2)   Section 188BB sets out the basic provisions about the surrendering of losses and other amounts.

(3)   Sections 188BC to 188BJ place restrictions on the surrendering of losses and other amounts.

188BB Surrender of carried-forward losses and other amounts

(1)   Subsection (2) applies if—

    (a)   a loss or other amount is carried forward to an accounting period of a company under any of the following provisions—

204   *Finance (No. 2) Act 2017 (c. 32)*
Schedule 4 — Relief for carried-forward losses
Part 3 — Group relief for carried-forward losses

        (i)   section 463G(6) of CTA 2009 (carry forward of post-1 April 2017 non-trading deficit from loan relationships);

        (ii)   section 753(3) of that Act (carry forward of non-trading loss on intangible fixed assets);

        (iii) section 1223 of that Act (carry forward of expenses of management of investment business);

        (iv) section 45A(4) of this Act (carry forward of post-1 April 2017 trade loss);

        (v)   sections 62(5)(a) and 63(3)(a) of this Act (carry forward of loss made in UK property business); or

    (b)   section 303C of this Act (excess carried forward non-decommissioning losses of ring fence trade: relief against total profits) applies in relation to an amount.

(2)   The company may surrender the loss or other amount under this Chapter so far as the loss or other amount is eligible for corporation tax relief (apart from this Part).

(3)   Subsection (4) applies if any of a BLAGAB trade loss made by an insurance company for an accounting period is carried forward to an accounting period of the company ("the later period") under section 124A(2) or 124C(3) of FA 2012.

(4)   The company may surrender the remaining carried forward amount under this Chapter so far as that amount is eligible for corporation tax relief (apart from this Part).

(5)   In subsection (4) "the remaining carried forward amount" means so much of the amount carried forward (as mentioned in subsection (3)) as cannot be deducted under section 124A(5) or 124C(6) of FA 2012 from the company's BLAGAB trade profit (if any) of the later period.

(6)   Under paragraph 70(1) of Schedule 18 to FA 1998, the company surrenders losses or other amounts, so far as eligible for surrender under this Chapter, by consenting to one or more claims for group relief for carried-forward losses in relation to the amounts (see requirement 1 in section 188CB(3) and requirement 1 in section 188CC(3)).

(7)   In this Part, in relation to losses or other amounts within subsection (1) or (4) that a company has carried forward to an accounting period—

        "the surrenderable amounts" means those losses and other amounts so far as eligible for surrender under this Chapter,

        "surrendering company" means the company that has the losses or other amounts,

        "the surrender period" means the accounting period to which the losses and other amounts have been carried forward.

(8)   See sections 188BC to 188BJ for provisions restricting what the surrendering company may surrender under this section.

188BC Restriction on surrendering pre-1 April 2017 losses etc

(1)   The surrendering company may not surrender under this Chapter—

Finance (No. 2) Act 2017 (c. 32)
Schedule 4 — Relief for carried-forward losses
Part 3 — Group relief for carried-forward losses

205

      (a)   a loss carried forward to the surrender period under section 753(3) of CTA 2009 in so far as the loss is made up of an amount previously carried forward under that section from an accounting period beginning before 1 April 2017,

      (b)   expenses carried forward to the surrender period under section 1223 of CTA 2009 if the expenses were first deductible under section 1219 of that Act for an accounting period beginning before that date, or

      (c)   a loss carried forward to the surrender period under section 62(5)(a) or 63(3)(a) of this Act if the loss was made in an accounting period beginning before that date.

(2)   The surrendering company may not surrender under this Chapter a qualifying charitable donation carried forward to the surrender period under section 1223 of CTA 2009.

188BD Restriction where investment business has become small or negligible

(1)   The surrendering company may not surrender under this Chapter —

      (a)   a loss carried forward to the surrender period under section 753(3) of CTA 2009 if an investment business carried on by the surrendering company became small or negligible before the beginning of that period,

      (b)   expenses carried forward to the surrender period under section 1223 of CTA 2009 if the surrendering company's investment business became small or negligible before the beginning of that period, or

      (c)   a loss carried forward to the surrender period under section 62(5)(a) or 63(3)(a) if the surrendering company's investment business became small or negligible before the beginning of that period.

(2)   In this section —

      (a)   "company with investment business" has the same meaning as in Part 16 of CTA 2009 (see section 1218B of that Act);

      (b)   references to a company's investment business are to be construed in accordance with section 1219(2) of CTA 2009.

188BE Restriction where surrendering company could use losses etc itself

The surrendering company may not surrender any losses or other amounts under this Chapter if —

      (a)   section 269ZD(2) applies in determining the taxable total profits of the surrendering company for the surrender period, and

      (b)   the sum of the relevant deductions (within the meaning of section 269ZD(3)) made for the surrender period is less than the maximum permitted by section 269ZD(2).

188BF Restriction where surrendering company has no income-generating assets

The surrendering company may not surrender any losses or other amounts under this Chapter if at the end of the surrender period the surrendering company has no assets capable of producing income.

206   *Finance (No. 2) Act 2017 (c. 32)*
Schedule 4 — Relief for carried-forward losses
Part 3 — Group relief for carried-forward losses

188BG Restrictions for certain insurance companies

(1) If the surrendering company is a general insurance company and the surrender period is an excluded accounting period, the company may not surrender under this Chapter—

    (a) a loss carried forward to the surrender period under section 753(3) of CTA 2009;

    (b) expenses carried forward to the surrender period under section 1223 of CTA 2009;

    (c) a loss carried forward to the surrender period under section 62(5)(a) or 63(3)(a).

(2) In subsection (1) "excluded accounting period" and "general insurance company" are to be interpreted in accordance with section 269ZG.

(3) If the surrendering company is a Solvency 2 insurance company it may not surrender under this Chapter—

    (a) a loss carried forward to the surrender period under section 753(3) of CTA 2009,

    (b) expenses carried forward to the surrender period under section 1223 of CTA 2009, or

    (c) a loss carried forward to the surrender period under section 62(5)(a) or 63(3)(a),

so far as the loss is, or (as the case may be) the expenses are, a shock loss.

188BH Restriction on surrender of losses etc made when UK resident

(1) This section applies in relation to a loss or other amount carried forward to the surrender period if the surrendering company was UK resident during the loss-making period.

(2) The surrendering company may not surrender the loss or other amount under this Chapter so far as the loss or other amount—

    (a) is attributable to a permanent establishment through which the company carried on a trade outside the United Kingdom during the loss-making period (see subsection (3)), and

    (b) is, or represents, an amount within subsection (5).

(3) A loss or other amount is attributable to a permanent establishment of the surrendering company if (ignoring this section) the amount could be included in the company's surrenderable amounts for the surrender period if those amounts were determined—

    (a) by reference to that establishment alone, and

    (b) by applying, in relation to that establishment, principles corresponding in all material respects to those mentioned in subsection (4).

(4) The principles are those that would be applied for corporation tax purposes in determining an equivalent loss or other amount in the case of a permanent establishment through which a non-UK resident company carried on a trade in the United Kingdom.

(5) An amount is within this subsection if, for the purposes of non-UK tax chargeable under the law of the territory in which the permanent

Finance (No. 2) Act 2017 (c. 32)
Schedule 4 — Relief for carried-forward losses
Part 3 — Group relief for carried-forward losses

207

establishment was situated, the amount is or at any time has been (in any period) deductible from or otherwise allowable against non-UK profits of a person other than the surrendering company.

(6) Subsection (7) applies for the purposes of subsection (5) if, in order to determine if an amount is or at any time has been deductible or otherwise allowable for the purposes of non-UK tax chargeable under the law of a territory, it is necessary under that law to know if the amount (or a corresponding amount) is or has been deductible or otherwise allowable for tax purposes in the United Kingdom.

(7) The amount is to be treated as deductible or otherwise allowable for the purposes of the non-UK tax chargeable under the law of the territory concerned if (and only if) the surrendering company is treated as resident in that territory for the purposes of the non-UK tax.

(8) In this section and section 188BI—

"the loss-making period", in relation to a loss or other amount, means the accounting period in which the loss was made or the amount arose,

"non-UK tax" has the meaning it has in Part 5 (see section 187), and

"non-UK profits" has the meaning given by section 108.

188BI Restriction on surrender of losses made when non-UK resident

(1) This section applies in relation to a loss or other amount carried forward to the surrender period if during the loss-making period the surrendering company was a non-UK resident company—

(a) carrying on a trade of dealing in or developing UK land, or

(b) carrying on a trade in the United Kingdom through a permanent establishment.

(2) If the surrendering company was established in the EEA during the loss-making period, it may surrender the loss or other amount under this Chapter only so far as conditions A and B are met.

Subsection (8) imposes restrictions on a surrender under this subsection.

(3) In any other case, the surrendering company may surrender the loss or other amount under this Chapter only so far as conditions A, B and C are met in relation to the loss or amount.

(4) Condition A is that the loss or other amount is attributable to activities of the surrendering company in respect of which it is within the charge to corporation tax for the loss-making period.

(5) Condition B is that the loss or other amount is not attributable to activities of the surrendering company that are double taxation exempt for the loss-making period (within the meaning given by section 186).

(6) Condition C is that—

(a) the loss or other amount does not correspond to, and is not represented in, an amount with subsection (7), and

208   *Finance (No. 2) Act 2017 (c. 32)*
Schedule 4 — Relief for carried-forward losses
Part 3 — Group relief for carried-forward losses

     (b)   no amount brought into account in calculating the loss or other amount corresponds to, or is represented in, an amount within subsection (7).

(7)   An amount is within this subsection if, for the purposes of non-UK tax chargeable under the law of a territory, the amount is or at any time has been (in any period) deductible from or otherwise allowable against non-UK profits of any person.

(8)   A loss or other amount may not be surrendered by virtue of subsection (2) if and to the extent that it, or any amount brought into account in calculating it, corresponds to, or is represented in, amounts within subsection (9).

(9)   An amount is within this subsection if, for the purposes of non-UK tax chargeable under the law of a territory, the amount has (in any period) been deducted from or otherwise allowed against non-UK profits of any person.

(10)   But an amount is not to be taken to be within subsection (7) or (9) by reason only that it is —

     (a)   an amount of profits brought into account for the purpose of being excluded from non-UK profits of the person, or

     (b)   an amount brought into account in calculating an amount of profits brought into account as mentioned in paragraph (a).

(11)   Subsection (12) applies for the purposes of subsection (7) if, in order to determine if an amount is or at any time has been deductible or otherwise allowable for the purposes of non-UK tax chargeable under the law of a territory, it is necessary under that law to know if the amount (or a corresponding amount) is or at any time has been deductible or otherwise allowable for tax purposes in the United Kingdom.

(12)   The amount is to be treated as deductible or otherwise allowable for the purposes of the non-UK tax chargeable under the law of the territory concerned.

(13)   For the purposes of this section a company is established in the EEA if —

     (a)   it is constituted under the law of the United Kingdom or an EEA territory, and

     (b)   it has its registered office, central administration or principal place of business within the European Economic Area.

(14)   In subsection (13) "EEA territory", in relation to any time, means a territory outside the United Kingdom that is within the European Economic Area at that time.

188BJ Restriction on surrender losses etc made when dual resident

The surrendering company may not surrender a loss or other amount under this Chapter if the company was not eligible to surrender the loss or other amount under Chapter 2 of Part 5 by reason of section 109 (restriction on losses etc surrenderable by dual resident).

Finance (No. 2) Act 2017 (c. 32)
Schedule 4 — Relief for carried-forward losses
Part 3 — Group relief for carried-forward losses

209

CHAPTER 3

CLAIMS FOR GROUP RELIEF FOR CARRIED-FORWARD LOSSES

Introduction

188CA Overview of Chapter

This Chapter sets out how a company may claim group relief for carried-forward losses and how the relief is given.

Claiming group relief for carried-forward losses

188CB Claims in relation to all the surrenderable amounts

(1) This section applies in relation to the surrendering company's surrenderable amounts for the surrender period under Chapter 2.

(2) If the requirements in subsection (3) are met, a company ("the claimant company") may make a claim for group relief for carried-forward losses for an accounting period ("the claim period") in relation to the surrenderable amounts.

(3) The requirements are as follows —
Requirement 1
The surrendering company consents to the claim.
Requirement 2
There is a period ("the overlapping period") that is common to the claim period and the surrender period.
Requirement 3
At a time during the overlapping period —
    (a) the group condition is met (see section 188CE)
    (b) consortium condition 1 is met (see section 188CF), or
    (c) consortium condition 2 is met (see section 188CG).

(4) A claim under this section may relate to the whole of the surrenderable amounts or to part of them only.

(5) This section is subject to section 188CD (claim not allowed by company with unused carried-forward losses of its own).

188CC Claims in relation to the surrenderable amounts that are attributable to a specified accounting period

(1) This section applies in relation to the surrendering company's surrenderable amounts for the surrender period under Chapter 2.

(2) If the requirements in subsection (3) are met, a company ("the claimant company") may make a claim for group relief for carried-forward losses for an accounting period ("the claim period") in relation to the surrenderable amounts that are attributable to an accounting period of the surrendering company specified in the claim ("the specified loss-making period").

(3) The requirements are as follows —
Requirement 1

210   *Finance (No. 2) Act 2017 (c. 32)*
Schedule 4 — Relief for carried-forward losses
Part 3 — Group relief for carried-forward losses

The surrendering company consents to the claim.

Requirement 2

There is a period ("the overlapping period") that is common to the claim period and the surrender period.

Requirement 3

Consortium condition 3 (see section 188CH) or consortium condition 4 (see section 188CI) is met throughout a period which —

    (a)   begins before or during the specified loss-making period, and

    (b)   ends during or after the overlapping period.

(4)   A claim under this section may relate to the whole of the surrenderable amounts attributable to the specified loss-making period or to part of them only.

(5)   This section is subject to section 188CD (claim not allowed by company with unused carried-forward losses of its own)

188CD Claim not allowed by company with unused carried-forward losses of its own

A company may not make a claim for group relief for carried-forward losses for an accounting period if —

    (a)   any amount carried forward to that period under any provision mentioned in section 188BB(1), or any amount which is carried forward to that period and falls within section 124B(1)(b) of FA 2012, is not deducted in full from the total profits of the company for that period at Step 2 of section 4(2),

    (b)   the company makes a claim under section 458(1) of CTA 2009 for any amount of a deficit to be excepted from being set off against profits of that period,

    (c)   the company makes a claim under section 45(4A) that the profits of a trade of that period are not to be reduced or are not to be reduced by more than a specified amount, or

    (d)   the company makes a claim under section 45B(5) for relief not to be given in that period for an amount of a loss or for a specified part of an amount of a loss.

188CE The group condition

(1)   The group condition is met if the surrendering company and the claimant company —

    (a)   are members of the same group of companies, and

    (b)   are both UK related.

(2)   For the meaning of "UK related" in subsection (1)(b) and in sections 188CF to 188CI, see section 188CJ.

188CF Consortium condition 1

(1)   Consortium condition 1 is met if —

    (a)   the claimant company is a trading company or a holding company,

    (b)   the claimant company is owned by a consortium,

    (c)   the surrendering company is a member of the consortium, and

Finance (No. 2) Act 2017 (c. 32)
Schedule 4 — Relief for carried-forward losses
Part 3 — Group relief for carried-forward losses

211

(d)   both companies are UK related.

(2)   But consortium condition 1 is not met if a profit on a sale within subsection (3) by the surrendering company would be a trading receipt of the surrendering company.

(3)   A sale is within this subsection if it is a sale of —
 (a)   the share capital the surrendering company owns in the claimant company, or
 (b)   if the claimant company is owned by the consortium as a result of section 153(3) (consortiums involving holding companies), the share capital the surrendering company owns in the holding company in question.

188CG Consortium condition 2

(1)   Consortium condition 2 is met if —
 (a)   the claimant company is a trading company or a holding company,
 (b)   the claimant company is owned by a consortium,
 (c)   the surrendering company is not a member of the consortium,
 (d)   the surrendering company is a member of the same group of companies as a third company ("the link company"),
 (e)   the link company is a member of the consortium,
 (f)   the surrendering company and the claimant company are both UK related.

(2)   But consortium condition 2 is not met if a profit on a sale within subsection (3) by the link company would be a trading receipt of that company.

(3)   A sale is within this subsection if it is a sale of —
 (a)   the share capital the link company owns in the claimant company, or
 (b)   if the claimant company is owned by the consortium as a result of section 153(3) (consortiums involving holding companies), the share capital the link company owns in the holding company in question.

188CH Consortium condition 3

(1)   Consortium condition 3 is met if —
 (a)   the surrendering company is a trading company or a holding company,
 (b)   the surrendering company is owned by a consortium,
 (c)   the claimant company is a member of the consortium, and
 (d)   both companies are UK related.

(2)   But consortium condition 3 is not met if a profit on a sale within subsection (3) by the claimant company would be a trading receipt of the claimant company.

(3)   A sale is within this subsection if it is a sale of —
 (a)   the share capital the claimant company owns in the surrendering company, or

212   *Finance (No. 2) Act 2017 (c. 32)*
Schedule 4 — Relief for carried-forward losses
Part 3 — Group relief for carried-forward losses

       (b)   if the surrendering company is owned by the consortium as a result of section 153(3) (consortiums involving holding companies), the share capital the claimant company owns in the holding company in question.

188CI Consortium condition 4

(1)   Consortium condition 4 is met if—

       (a)   the surrendering company is a trading company or a holding company,

       (b)   the surrendering company is owned by a consortium,

       (c)   the claimant company is not a member of the consortium,

       (d)   the claimant company is a member of the same group of companies as a third company ("the link company"),

       (e)   the link company is a member of the consortium, and

       (f)   the claimant company and the surrendering company are both UK related.

(2)   But consortium condition 4 is not met if a profit on a sale within subsection (3) by the link company would be a trading receipt of that company.

(3)   A sale is within this subsection if it is a sale of—

       (a)   the share capital the link company owns in the surrendering company, or

       (b)   if the surrendering company is owned by the consortium as a result of section 153(3) (consortiums involving holding companies), the share capital the link company owns in the holding company in question.

188CJ Meaning of "UK related" company

For the purpose of sections 188CE to 188CI a company is UK related if—

       (a)   it is a UK resident company, or

       (b)   it is a non-UK resident company carrying on a trade in the United Kingdom through a permanent establishment.

Giving group relief for carried-forward losses

188CK Deductions from total profits

(1)   If a claimant company makes a claim under section 188CB or 188CC, the group relief for carried-forward losses is given by the making of a deduction from the claimant company's total profits of the claim period.

(2)   In the case of a claim under section 188CB, the amount of the deduction under subsection (1) is—

       (a)   an amount equal to the surrendering company's surrenderable amounts for the surrender period, or

       (b)   if the claim is in relation to only part of those amounts, an amount equal to that part.

(3)   Subsection (2) is subject to—

       (a)   subsections (6) to (9),

Finance (No. 2) Act 2017 (c. 32)
Schedule 4 — Relief for carried-forward losses
Part 3 — Group relief for carried-forward losses

213

      (b)   the limitations set out in Chapter 4, and

      (c)   section 269ZD (restriction on deductions from total profits).

(4)   In the case of a claim under section 188CC, the amount of the deduction under subsection (1) is—

      (a)   an amount equal to the surrendering company's surrenderable amounts for the surrender period that are attributable to the specified loss-making period, or

      (b)   if the claim is in relation to only part of those amounts, an amount equal to that part.

(5)   Subsection (4) is subject to—

      (a)   subsections (6) to (9),

      (b)   the limitations set out in Chapter 5, and

      (c)   section 269ZD (restriction on deductions from total profits).

(6)   A deduction under subsection (1) is to be made—

      (a)   before deductions for relief within subsection (7), but

      (b)   after all other deductions to be made at Step 2 in section 4(2) (apart from deductions for group relief for carried-forward losses on other claims).

(7)   The deductions within this subsection are deductions for relief—

      (a)   under section 37 in relation to a loss made in an accounting period after the claim period,

      (b)   under section 260(3) of CAA 2001 in relation to capital allowances for an accounting period after the claim period, and

      (c)   under section 389 or 463B of CTA 2009 in relation to a deficit of a deficit period after the claim period.

(8)   For the purposes of subsection (6)(b) it is to be assumed that the claimant company has claimed all relief available to it for the claim period under section 37 of this Act or section 260(3) of CAA 2001.

(9)   Corporation tax relief is not to be given more than once for the same amount, whether—

      (a)   by giving group relief for carried-forward losses and by giving some other relief (for any accounting period) to the surrendering company, or

      (b)   by giving group relief for carried-forward losses more than once.

CHAPTER 4

LIMITATIONS ON RELIEF: CLAIMS UNDER SECTION 188CB

Introduction

188DA Overview

This Chapter sets out limitations on the amount of relief which may be given on a claim under section 188CB.

214

Finance (No. 2) Act 2017 (c. 32)
Schedule 4 — Relief for carried-forward losses
Part 3 — Group relief for carried-forward losses

General limitation on amount of relief

188DB Limitation on amount of relief applying to all claims under section 188CB

(1) The amount of group relief for carried-forward losses to be given on a claim under section 188CB ("the current claim") is limited to whichever is the lesser of —

    (a) the amount mentioned in subsection (2), and

    (b) the amount mentioned in subsection (3).

(2) The amount referred to in subsection (1)(a) is the unused part of the surrenderable amounts (see section 188DC).

(3) The amount referred to in subsection (1)(b) is the difference between —

    (a) the claimant company's relevant maximum for the overlapping period (see section 188DD), and

    (b) the amount of previously claimed group relief for carried-forward losses for the overlapping period (see section 188DE).

188DC Unused part of the surrenderable amounts

(1) The unused part of the surrenderable amounts is the amount equal to —

    (a) the surrenderable amount for the overlapping period (see subsection (2)), less

    (b) the amount of prior surrenders for that period (see subsections (3) to (5)).

(2) To determine the surrenderable amount for the overlapping period —

    (a) take the proportion of the surrender period included in the overlapping period, and

    (b) apply that proportion to the surrenderable amounts for the surrender period.

The surrenderable amount for the overlapping period is the amount given as a result of paragraph (b).

(3) To determine the amount of prior surrenders for the overlapping period —

    (a) identify any prior claims for the purposes of this section (see subsection (4)), and

    (b) take the steps set out in subsection (5) in relation to each such claim.

The amount of prior surrenders for the overlapping period is the total of the previously used amounts given at step 3 in subsection (5) for all the prior claims.

(4) A claim is a prior claim for the purposes of this section if —

    (a) it is either —

        (i) a claim under section 188CB by any company which relates to the same amounts as the current claim, or

Finance (No. 2) Act 2017 (c. 32)
Schedule 4 — Relief for carried-forward losses
Part 3 — Group relief for carried-forward losses

215

(ii) a claim under section 188CC by any company which relates to amounts included in the amounts to which the current claim relates,

(b) it is made before the current claim, and

(c) it has not been withdrawn.

(5) These are the steps referred to in subsection (3)(b) to be taken in relation to each prior claim.

Step 1

Identify the overlapping period for the prior claim.

Step 2

Identify any period that is common to the overlapping period for the current claim and the overlapping period for the prior claim.

If there is a common period, go to step 3.

If there is no common period, there is no previously used amount in relation to the prior claim (and ignore step 3).

Step 3

Determine the previously used amount of group relief for carried-forward losses in relation to the prior claim (see subsection (6)).

(6) To determine the previously used amount of group relief for carried-forward losses in relation to a prior claim —

(a) take the proportion of the overlapping period for the prior claim that is included in the common period identified at step 2 in relation to that claim, and

(b) apply that proportion to the amount of group relief for carried-forward losses given on the prior claim.

The previously used amount of group relief for carried-forward losses in relation to the prior claim is the amount given as a result of paragraph (b).

(7) For the meaning of the "overlapping period" see section 188DG.

188DD Claimant company's relevant maximum for overlapping period

(1) The claimant company's relevant maximum for the overlapping period is determined as follows —

Step 1

Calculate the claimant company's relevant maximum for the claim period in accordance with section 269ZD(4).

Step 2

Deduct from that amount the sum of —

(a) any deductions made by the company for the claim period
(i) under section 45(4)(b) or 45B(4), or
(ii) under section 303B or 303D by virtue of section 304(5),

(b) any deductions made by the company for the claim period under section 457(3) or 463H(5) of CTA 2009,

(c) any deductions made by the company for the claim period under section 124(5), 124A(5) or 124C(6) of FA 2012, and

(d) any deductions made by the company for the claim period which are deductions within any of paragraphs (a) to (i) and (k) of section 269ZD(3).

Step 3

216

Finance (No. 2) Act 2017 (c. 32)
Schedule 4 — Relief for carried-forward losses
Part 3 — Group relief for carried-forward losses

Take the proportion of the claim period included in the overlapping period and apply that proportion to the amount arrived at under step 2.

(2) In step 2 of subsection (1) —

    (a) in paragraph (a)(i), the references to deductions under section 45(4)(b) or 45B(4) do not include deductions that would be ignored for the purposes of section 269ZB by reason of —

        (i) section 1209(3), 1210(5A) or 1211(7A) of CTA 2009 (losses of film trade),

        (ii) section 1216DA(3), 1216DB(5A) or 1216DC(7A) of that Act (losses of television programme trade),

        (iii) section 1217DA(3), 1217DB(5A) or 1217DC(7A) of that Act (losses of video game trade),

        (iv) section 1217MA(3) or 1217MC(9) of that Act (losses of theatrical trade),

        (v) section 1217SA(3) or 1217SC(9) of that Act (losses of orchestral trade),

        (vi) section 1218ZDA(3) or 1218ZDC(9) of that Act (losses of museum or gallery exhibition trade),

        (vii) section 65(4B) or 67A(5A) (losses of UK or EEA furnished holiday lettings business),

        (viii) section 269ZJ(1) (insurance companies: shock losses),

        (ix) section 304(7) (certain losses of ring fence trades), or

        (x) section 356NJ(2) (pre-1 April 2017 loss arising from oil contractor activities);

    (b) in paragraph (b) the reference to a deduction under section 463H(5) does not include the deduction of a shock loss.

(3) If the amount of the claimant company's relevant profits for the claim period (calculated in accordance with section 269ZD(5)) is less than the amount of the claimant company's deductions allowance for the claim period (determined in accordance with section 269ZD(6)), subsection (1) has effect as if step 1 was modified as follows —

Step 1

Calculate the claimant company's relevant profits for the claim period in accordance with section 269ZD(5).

(4) If section 269ZD has effect in relation to the claimant company for the claim period with the modifications set out in section 269ZE(1) (special loss cap for insurance companies in certain cases), subsection (1) has effect as if steps 1 and 2 were modified as follows —

Step 1

Determine, in accordance with section 269ZE(5), the modified loss cap for the claimant company and the claim period.

Step 2

Reduce that amount by the total of any deductions made by the claimant company for the claim period which are deductions within any of paragraphs (a) to (i) and (k) of section 269ZD(3).

(5) Subsection (2) is to be ignored if subsection (3) applies.

Finance (No. 2) Act 2017 (c. 32)
Schedule 4 — Relief for carried-forward losses
Part 3 — Group relief for carried-forward losses

217

188DE Previously claimed group relief for carried-forward losses

(1) To determine the amount of previously claimed group relief for carried-forward losses for the overlapping period —

    (a) identify any prior claims for the purposes of this section (see subsection (2)), and

    (b) take the steps set out in subsection (3) in relation to each such claim.

The amount of previously claimed group relief for carried-forward losses for the overlapping period is the total of the previously claimed amounts given at step 3 in subsection (3) for all the prior claims.

(2) A claim is a prior claim for the purposes of this section if —

    (a) it is a claim under section 188CB or 188CC by the claimant company for group relief for carried-forward losses which would be given by way of a deduction from the company's total profits of the claim period,

    (b) it is made before the current claim, and

    (c) it has not been withdrawn.

(3) These are the steps referred to in subsection (1)(b) to be taken in relation to each prior claim.

Step 1

Identify the overlapping period for the prior claim.

Step 2

Identify any period that is common to the overlapping period for the current claim and the overlapping period for the prior claim.

If there is a common period, go to step 3.

If there is no common period, there is no previously claimed amount in relation to the prior claim (and ignore step 3).

Step 3

Determine the previously claimed amount of group relief for carried forward losses in relation to the prior claim (see subsection (4)).

(4) To determine the previously claimed amount of group relief for carried-forward losses in relation to a prior claim —

    (a) take the proportion of the overlapping period for the prior claim that is included in the common period identified at step 2 in relation to that claim, and

    (b) apply that proportion to the amount of group relief for carried-forward losses given on the prior claim.

The previously claimed amount of group relief for carried-forward losses in relation to the prior claim is the amount given as a result of paragraph (b).

188DF Sections 188DC to 188DE: supplementary

(1) If two or more claims for group relief for carried-forward losses are made at the same time, for the purpose of section 188DC and 188DE treat the claims as made —

    (a) in such order as the company making them may elect or the companies making them may jointly elect, or

218   *Finance (No. 2) Act 2017 (c. 32)*
Schedule 4 — Relief for carried-forward losses
Part 3 — Group relief for carried-forward losses

    (b)   if no such election is made, in such order as an officer of Revenue and Customs may direct.

(2)   For the purpose of step 3 in each of section 188DC(5) and 188DE(3) the amount of group relief for carried-forward losses given on a prior claim is determined on the basis that relief is given on the claim before it is given on any later claim.

(3)   If the use of any proportion mentioned in subsection (4), would, in the circumstances of a particular case, produce a result that is unjust or unreasonable, the proportion is to be modified so far as necessary to produce a result that is just and reasonable.

(4)   The proportions are those found in—
    (a)   section 188DC(2),
    (b)   section 188DC(6),
    (c)   step 3 in section 188DD(1), and
    (d)   section 188DE(4).

188DG Sections 188DC and 188DE: meaning of "the overlapping period"

(1)   In sections 188DC and 188DE "the overlapping period", in relation to a claim for group relief for carried-forward losses, means the period that is common to the claim period and the surrender period (see Requirement 2 in section 188CB(3) and Requirement 2 in section 188CC(3)).

(2)   But if during any part of the overlapping period the relief condition is not met, that part is treated as not forming part of the overlapping period but instead as forming—
    (a)   a part of the surrender period that is not included in the overlapping period, and
    (b)   a part of the claim period that is not included in the overlapping period.

(3)   The relief condition is the condition on which the claim for group relief for carried forward losses is based, that is—
        the group condition,
        consortium condition 1,
        consortium condition 2,
        consortium condition 3, or
        consortium condition 4.

Further limitations on amount of relief if claim based on consortium conditions 1 or 2

188DH Condition 1: ownership proportion

(1)   This section applies if—
    (a)   the claimant company makes a claim under section 188CB for group relief for carried-forward losses, and
    (b)   the claim is based on consortium condition 1.

(2)   The relief to be given on the claim is limited to the ownership proportion of the claimant company's relevant maximum for the

Finance (No. 2) Act 2017 (c. 32)
Schedule 4 — Relief for carried-forward losses
Part 3 — Group relief for carried-forward losses

219

overlapping period (see section 188DD to determine the claimant company's relevant maximum for the overlapping period).

(3) The ownership proportion is the same as the lowest of the following proportions prevailing during the overlapping period —

    (a) the proportion of the ordinary share capital of the claimant company that is beneficially owned by the surrendering company,

    (b) the proportion of any profits available for distribution to equity holders of the claimant company to which the surrendering company is beneficially entitled,

    (c) the proportion of any assets of the claimant company available for distribution to such equity holders on a winding up to which the surrendering company would be beneficially entitled, and

    (d) the proportion of the voting power in the claimant company that is directly possessed by the surrendering company.

(4) If any of the proportions in subsection (3) changes during the overlapping period, use the average of that proportion during that period.

(5) If the claimant company is owned by the consortium company as a result of section 153(3) (consortium company involving holding companies), references in subsection (3) to the claimant company are to be read as references to the holding company in question.

(6) In this section "the overlapping period" is to be read in accordance with section 188DG.

(7) Chapter 6 of Part 5 (equity holders and profits or assets available for distribution) applies for the purposes of subsection (3)(b) and (c).

188DI Condition 2: ownership proportion

(1) This section applies if —

    (a) the claimant company makes a claim under section 188CB for group relief for carried-forward losses, and

    (b) the claim is based on consortium condition 2.

(2) The limitation on relief in section 188DH applies in relation to the claim, but for this purpose references in section 188DH(3) to the surrendering company are to be read as reference to the link company.

188DJ Condition 2: companies in link company's group

(1) Where —

    (a) the claimant company makes a claim under section 188CB, and

    (b) the claim is based on consortium condition 2,

the amount of relief to be given on the claim is limited by subsections (2) and (3).

(2) There is a limit on the amount of group relief for carried-forward losses that can be given, in total, to the claimant company for the claim period on consortium claims made in relation to losses and

220   *Finance (No. 2) Act 2017 (c. **32**)*
Schedule 4 — Relief for carried-forward losses
Part 3 — Group relief for carried-forward losses

         other amounts surrendered by the link company and group companies.

(3)   That limit is the same as the limit that, as a result of section 188DH(2), would apply for the purposes of a consortium claim made by the claimant company for the claim period in relation to losses or other amounts surrendered by the link company, assuming that the link company was UK related.

(4)   In determining the limit that would apply as a result of section 188DH(2) it is to be assumed that the accounting period of the link company is the same as the accounting period of the claimant company.

(5)   In this section—

        "consortium claim" means a claim for group relief for carried-forward losses under section 188CB,

        "group company" means a company that is a member of the same group of companies as the link company (other than the link company itself), and

        "UK related", in relation to a company, has the meaning given by section 188CJ.

188DK Conditions 1 and 2: claimant company not controlled by surrendering company etc

(1)   This section applies if—

    (a)   the claimant company makes a claim under section 188CB for group relief for carried-forward losses,

    (b)   the claim is based on consortium condition 1, and

    (c)   during any part of the overlapping period, arrangements within subsection (3) are in place which enable a person to prevent the surrendering company, either alone or together with one or more other companies that are members of the consortium, from controlling the claimant company.

(2)   This section also applies if—

    (a)   the claimant company makes a claim under section 188CB for group relief for carried-forward losses,

    (b)   the claim is based on consortium condition 2, and

    (c)   during any part of the overlapping period, arrangements within subsection (3) are in place which enable a person to prevent the link company, either alone or together with one or more other companies that are members of the consortium, from controlling the claimant company.

(3)   Arrangements are within this subsection if—

    (a)   the company, either alone or together with one or more other companies that are members of the consortium, would control the claimant company, but for the existence of the arrangements, and

    (b)   the arrangements form part of a scheme the main purpose, or one of the main purposes, of which is to enable the claimant company to obtain a tax advantage under this Chapter.

Finance (No. 2) Act 2017 (c. 32)
Schedule 4 – Relief for carried-forward losses
Part 3 – Group relief for carried-forward losses

221

(4) The relief to be given on the claim is to be determined as if the claimant company's relevant maximum for the overlapping period was 50% of what it would be but for this section (see section 188DD to determine the claimant company's relevant maximum for the overlapping period).

(5) In this section "the overlapping period" is to be read in accordance with section 188DG

(6) Section 1139 ("tax advantage") applies for the purposes of this section.

188DL Conditions 1 and 2: claimant company in group of companies

(1) This section applies if—
  (a) the claimant company makes a claim under section 188CB based on consortium condition 1 or 2, and
  (b) the claimant company is a member of a group of companies.

(2) In determining the claimant company's relevant maximum for the overlapping period under section 188DD, the amount calculated at step 1 of that section is to be treated as reduced (but not below nil) by the group's potential relief.

(3) The group's potential relief is the sum of—
  (a) the maximum amount of group relief for carried-forward losses that could be claimed by the claimant company for the claim period on claims under section 188CB based on the group condition, and
  (b) the maximum amount of group relief under Part 5 that could be claimed by the claimant company for the claim period on claims under section 130 based on the group condition.

(4) Before determining the maximum amount of potential group relief for carried-forward losses or potential group relief under subsection (3) take account of any claim made before the claim mentioned in subsection (1) that—
  (a) is a claim for group relief or group relief for carried-forward losses based on the group condition made by another member of the same group of companies as the claimant company, and
  (b) is in relation to losses or other amounts surrendered.

CHAPTER 5

LIMITATIONS ON RELIEF: CLAIMS UNDER SECTION 188CC

Introduction

188EA Overview of Chapter

This Chapter sets out limitations on the amount of relief which may be given on a claim under section 188CC.

222

Finance (No. 2) Act 2017 (c. 32)
Schedule 4 — Relief for carried-forward losses
Part 3 — Group relief for carried-forward losses

General limitation on amount of relief

188EB Limitation on amount of relief applying to all claims under section 188CC

(1) The amount of group relief for carried-forward losses to be given on a claim under section 188CC ("the current claim") is limited to whichever is the lesser of—

    (a) the amount mentioned in subsection (2),

    (b) the amount mentioned in subsection (3), and

    (c) the amount mentioned in subsection (4).

(2) The amount referred to in subsection (1)(a) is the unused part of the surrenderable amounts that are attributable to the specified loss-making period (see section 188EC).

(3) The amount referred to in subsection (1)(b) is the difference between—

    (a) the claimant company's relevant maximum for the overlapping period (see section 188ED), and

    (b) the amount of previously claimed group relief for carried-forward losses for the overlapping period (see section 188EE).

(4) The amount referred to in subsection (1)(c) is the potential Part 5 group relief amount (see section 188EF).

188EC Unused part of surrenderable amounts attributable to specified loss-making period

(1) The unused part of the surrenderable amounts that are attributable to the specified loss-making period is the amount equal to—

    (a) the surrenderable amount for the overlapping period (see subsection (2)), less

    (b) the amount of prior surrenders for that period (see subsections (3) to (5)).

(2) To determine the surrenderable amount for the overlapping period—

    (a) take the proportion of the surrender period included in the overlapping period, and

    (b) apply that proportion to the surrenderable amounts for the surrender period that are attributable to the specified loss-making period.

The surrenderable amount for the overlapping period is the amount given as a result of paragraph (b).

(3) To determine the amount of prior surrenders for the overlapping period—

    (a) identify any prior claims for the purposes of this section (see subsection (4)), and

    (b) take the steps set out in subsection (5) in relation to each such claim.

The amount of prior surrenders for the overlapping period is the total of the previously used amounts given at step 3 in subsection (5) for all the prior claims.

Finance (No. 2) Act 2017 (c. 32)
Schedule 4 — Relief for carried-forward losses
Part 3 — Group relief for carried-forward losses

223

(4) A claim is a prior claim for the purposes of this section if —

    (a) it is either —

        (i) a claim under section 188CB by any company which relates to the amounts to which the current claim relates (as well as any other amounts), or

        (ii) a claim under section 188CC by any company which relates to the same amounts to which the current claim relates,

    (b) it is made before the current claim, and

    (c) it has not been withdrawn.

(5) These are the steps referred to in subsection (3)(b) to be taken in relation to each prior claim.

Step 1

Identify the overlapping period for the prior claim.

Step 2

Identify any period that is common to the overlapping period for the current claim and the overlapping period for the prior claim.

If there is a common period, go to step 3.

If there is no common period, there is no previously used amount in relation to the prior claim (and ignore step 3).

Step 3

Determine the previously used amount of group relief for carried-forward losses in relation to the prior claim (see subsections (6) to (8)).

(6) To determine the previously used amount of group relief for carried-forward losses in relation to a prior claim made under section 188CB —

Step 1

Take the proportion of the overlapping period for the prior claim that is included in the common period identified at step 2 in subsection (5) in relation to that claim.

Step 2

Apply that proportion to the amount of group relief for carried-forward losses given on the claim.

Step 3

Multiply the amount arrived at under step 2 by the fraction set out in subsection (7).

(7) The fraction is —

$$\frac{A}{B}$$

where —

    A is the sum of the surrenderable amounts that are attributable to the specified loss-making period, and

    B is the sum of all the surrenderable amounts.

(8) To determine the previously used amount of group relief for carried-forward losses in relation to a prior claim made under section 188CC —

224

Finance (No. 2) Act 2017 (c. 32)
Schedule 4 — Relief for carried-forward losses
Part 3 — Group relief for carried-forward losses

    (a)   take the proportion of the overlapping period for the prior claim that is included in the common period identified at step 2 in subsection (5) in relation to that claim, and

    (b)   apply that proportion to the amount of group relief for carried-forward losses given on the prior claim.

The previously used amount of group relief for carried-forward losses in relation to the prior claim is the amount given as a result of paragraph (b).

188ED Claimant company's relevant maximum for the overlapping period

(1)   The claimant company's relevant maximum for the overlapping period is determined as follows—

Step 1

Calculate the claimant company's relevant maximum for the claim period in accordance with section 269ZD(4).

Step 2

Deduct from that amount the sum of—

    (a)   any deductions made by the company for the claim period
        (i)   under section 45(4)(b) or 45B(4), or
       (ii)   under section 303B or 303D by virtue of section 304(5),

    (b)   any deduction made by the company for the claim period under section 457(3) or 463H(5) of CTA 2009,

    (c)   any deductions made by the company for the claim period under section 124(5), 124A(5) or 124C(6) of FA 2012, and

    (d)   any deductions made by the company for the claim period which are deductions within any of paragraphs (a) to (i) and (k) of section 269ZD(3).

Step 3

Take the proportion of the claim period included in the overlapping period and apply that proportion to the amount arrived at under step 2.

(2)   In step 2 of subsection (1)—

    (a)   in paragraph (a)(i), the references to deductions under section 45(4)(b) or 45B(4) do not include deductions that would be ignored for the purposes of section 269ZB by reason of—

        (i)   section 1209(3), 1210(5A) or 1211(7A) of CTA 2009 (losses of film trade),

       (ii)   section 1216DA(3), 1216DB(5A) or 1216DC(7A) of that Act (losses of television programme trade),

      (iii)   section 1217DA(3), 1217DB(5A) or 1217DC(7A) of that Act (losses of video game trade),

      (iv)   section 1217MA(3) or 1217MC(9) of that Act (losses of theatrical trade),

       (v)   section 1217SA(3) or 1217SC(9) of that Act (losses of orchestral trade),

      (vi)   section 1218ZDA(3) or 1218ZDC(9) of that Act (losses of museum or gallery exhibition trade),

      (vii)   section 65(4B) or 67A(5A) (losses of UK or EEA furnished holiday lettings business),

Finance (No. 2) Act 2017 (c. 32)
Schedule 4 — Relief for carried-forward losses
Part 3 — Group relief for carried-forward losses

225

        (viii)   section 269ZJ(1) (insurance companies: shock losses),

        (ix)   section 304(7) (certain losses of ring fence trades), or

        (x)   section 356NJ(2) (pre-1 April 2017 loss arising from oil contractor activities);

    (b)   in paragraph (b) the reference to a deduction under section 463H(5) does not include the deduction of a shock loss.

(3) If the amount of the claimant company's relevant profits for the claim period (calculated in accordance with section 269ZD(5)) is less than the amount of the claimant company's deductions allowance for the claim period (determined in accordance with section 269ZD(6)), subsection (1) has effect as if step 1 was modified as follows —

Step 1

Calculate the claimant company's relevant profits for the claim period in accordance with section 269ZD(5).

(4) If section 269ZD has effect in relation to the claimant company for the claim period with the modifications set out in section 269ZE(1) (special loss cap for insurance companies in certain cases), subsection (1) has effect as if steps 1 and 2 were modified as follows —

Step 1

Determine, in accordance with section 269ZE(5), the modified loss cap for the claimant company and the claim period.

Step 2

Reduce that amount by the total of any deductions made by the claimant company for the claim period which are deductions within any of paragraphs (a) to (i) and (k) of section 269ZD(3).

(5) Subsection (2) is to be ignored if subsection (4) applies.

188EE Previously claimed group relief for carried-forward losses

(1) To determine the amount of previously claimed group relief for carried-forward losses for the overlapping period —

    (a)   identify any prior claims for the purposes of this section (see subsection (2)), and

    (b)   take the steps set out in subsection (3) in relation to each such claim.

The amount of previously claimed group relief for carried-forward losses for the overlapping period is the total of the previously claimed amounts given at step 3 in subsection (3) for all the prior claims.

(2) A claim is a prior claim for the purposes of this section if —

    (a)   it is a claim under section 188CB or 188CC by the claimant company for group relief for carried-forward losses which would be given by way of a deduction from the company's total profits of the claim period,

    (b)   it is made before the current claim, and

    (c)   it has not been withdrawn.

(3) These are the steps referred to in subsection (1)(b) to be taken in relation to each prior claim.

Step 1

226

Finance (No. 2) Act 2017 (c. 32)
Schedule 4 — Relief for carried-forward losses
Part 3 — Group relief for carried-forward losses

Identify the overlapping period for the prior claim.

Step 2

Identify any period that is common to the overlapping period for the current claim and the overlapping period for the prior claim.

If there is a common period, go to Step 3.

If there is no common period, there is no previously claimed amount in relation to the prior claim (and ignore step 3).

Step 3

Determine the previously claimed amount of group relief for carried forward losses in relation to the prior claim (see subsection (4)).

(4) To determine the previously claimed amount of group relief for carried-forward losses in relation to a prior claim —

    (a) take the proportion of the overlapping period for the prior claim that is included in the common period identified at step 2 in subsection (3) in relation to that claim, and

    (b) apply that proportion to the amount of group relief for carried-forward losses given on the prior claim.

The previously claimed amount of group relief for carried-forward losses in relation to the prior claim is the amount given as a result of paragraph (b).

188EF The potential Part 5 group relief amount

(1) The potential Part 5 group relief amount is determined as follows —

Step 1

Calculate the maximum amount of group relief that could have been given to the claimant company under Part 5 in relation to losses or other amounts within section 99(1) which the surrendering company had for the specified loss-making period.

In applying this step, ignore any lack of profits of the claimant company from which deductions could have been made as mentioned in section 137(1).

Step 2

Deduct from the amount arrived at under step 1 the amount of any group relief actually given to the claimant company under Part 5 in relation to losses or other amounts within section 99(1) which the surrendering company had for the specified loss-making period.

Step 3

Multiply the amount arrived at following step 2 by the fraction in subsection (2).

Step 4

Deduct from the amount arrived at following step 3 any group relief for carried-forward losses previously given to the claimant company on claims under section 188CC which are related to the current claim.

(2) The fraction referred to in step 3 is —

$$\frac{A}{B}$$

where —

    A is the sum of the losses or other amounts within section 99(1)(a), (c), (e), (f) and (g) which the surrendering company had for the specified loss-making period, and

Finance (No. 2) Act 2017 (c. 32)
Schedule 4 — Relief for carried-forward losses
Part 3 — Group relief for carried-forward losses

227

B is the sum of the losses or other amounts within section 99(1) (a) to (g) which the surrendering company had for the specified loss-making period.

(3) References in subsection (2) to losses or other amounts are references to losses or other amounts only in so far as they were eligible for surrender under Chapter 2 of Part 5.

(4) A claim under section 188CC is related to the current claim if the surrendering company and the specified loss-making period are the same in relation to both claims.

188EG Sections 188EC to 188EE: supplementary

(1) If two or more claims for group relief for carried-forward losses are made at the same time, for the purpose of section 188EC and 188EE treat the claims as made—

    (a) in such order as the company making them may elect or the companies making them may jointly elect, or

    (b) if no such election is made, in such order as an officer of Revenue and Customs may direct.

(2) For the purpose of step 3 in each of sections 188EC(5) and 188EE(3) the amount of group relief for carried-forward losses given on a prior claim is determined on the basis that relief is given on the claim before it is given on any later claim.

(3) If the use of any proportion mentioned in subsection (4), would, in the circumstances of a particular case, produce a result that is unjust or unreasonable, the proportion is to be modified so far as necessary to produce a result that is just and reasonable.

(4) The proportions are those found in—

    (a) section 188EC(2)(a),

    (b) step 1 in section 188EC(6),

    (c) section 188EC(8)(a),

    (d) step 3 in section 188ED(1), and

    (e) section 188EE(4)(a).

188EH Sections 188EC and 188EE: meaning of "the overlapping period"

(1) In sections 188EC and 188EE "the overlapping period", in relation to a claim for group relief for carried-forward losses, means the period that is common to the claim period and the surrender period (see Requirement 2 in section 188CB(3) and Requirement 2 in section 188CC(3)).

(2) But if during any part of the overlapping period the relief condition is not met, that part is treated as not forming part of the overlapping period but instead as forming—

    (a) a part of the surrender period that is not included in the overlapping period, and

    (b) a part of the claim period that is not included in the overlapping period.

(3) The relief condition is the condition on which the claim for group relief for carried forward losses is based, that is—

228   *Finance (No. 2) Act 2017 (c. 32)*
Schedule 4 — Relief for carried-forward losses
Part 3 — Group relief for carried-forward losses

the group condition,

consortium condition 1,

consortium condition 2,

consortium condition 3, or

consortium condition 4.

Further limitations on amount of relief that apply in particular cases

188EI Condition 4: companies in link company's group

(1)   Where—

    (a)   the claimant company makes a claim under section 188CC, and

    (b)   the claim is based on consortium condition 4

the amount of relief to be given on the claim is limited by subsections (2) and (3).

(2)   There is a limit on the amount of group relief for carried-forward losses that can be given, in total, on relevant consortium claims made by the link company and group companies.

(3)   That limit is the maximum amount of group relief for carried-forward losses that could be given to the link company on relevant consortium claims—

    (a)   assuming that no relevant consortium claims were made by group companies based on consortium condition 4,

    (b)   assuming that the link company was UK related, and

    (c)   ignoring any lack of profits of the link company from which deductions could be made as mentioned in section 188CK(1).

(4)   In this section—

"consortium claim" means a claim made under section 188CC for group relief for carried-forward losses,

"group company" means a company that is a member of the same group of companies as the link company (other than the link company),

"relevant consortium claim" means a consortium claim in relation to which the surrendering company, the surrender period and the specified loss-making period are the same as is the case for the claim mentioned in subsection (1), and

"UK related", in relation to a company, has the meaning given by section 188CJ.

188EJ Condition 3 or 4: surrendering company not controlled by claimant company etc

(1)   This section applies if—

    (a)   the claimant company makes a claim under section 188CC for group relief for carried-forward losses,

    (b)   the claim is based on consortium condition 3, and

    (c)   during any part of the overlapping period, arrangements within subsection (3) are in place which enable a person to prevent the claimant company, either alone or together with

Finance (No. 2) Act 2017 (c. 32)
Schedule 4 — Relief for carried-forward losses
Part 3 — Group relief for carried-forward losses

229

one or more other companies that are members of the consortium, from controlling the surrendering company.

(2) This section also applies if —

   (a) the claimant company makes a claim under section 188CC for group relief for carried-forward losses,

   (b) the claim is based on consortium condition 4, and

   (c) during any part of the overlapping period, arrangements within subsection (3) are in place which enable a person to prevent the link company, either alone or together with one or more other companies that are members of the consortium, from controlling the surrendering company.

(3) Arrangements are within this subsection if —

   (a) the company, either alone or together with one or more other companies that are members of the consortium, would control the surrendering company, but for the existence of the arrangements, and

   (b) the arrangements form part of a scheme the main purpose, or one of the main purposes, of which is to enable the claimant company to obtain a tax advantage under this Chapter.

(4) The relief to be given on the claim is to be determined as if the surrenderable amount for the overlapping period were 50% of what it would be but for this section (see section 188EC(2) to determine the surrenderable amount for the overlapping period).

(5) In this section "the overlapping period" is to be read in accordance with section 188EH.

(6) Section 1139 ("tax advantage") applies for the purposes of this section.

188EK Condition 3 or 4: surrendering company in group of companies

(1) This section applies if —

   (a) the claimant company makes a claim under section 188CC for group relief for carried-forward losses, and

   (b) the surrendering company is a member of a group of companies.

(2) The surrendering company's surrenderable amounts for the surrender period that are attributable to the specified loss-making period are to be treated as reduced (but not below nil) by the relevant amount.

(3) To determine the relevant amount —

   Step 1

   Calculate the group's potential relief.

   Step 2

   Multiply the amount arrived at under step 1 by the fraction set out in subsection (6).

(4) The group's potential relief is the maximum amount of group relief for carried-forward losses that could be given if every claim that could be made based on the group condition in respect of the surrenderable amounts for the surrender period was in fact made

230   *Finance (No. 2) Act 2017 (c. 32)*
Schedule 4 — Relief for carried-forward losses
Part 3 — Group relief for carried-forward losses

(and for this purpose it is to be assumed that the maximum possible claim is made in each case).

(5) Before determining the maximum amount of potential group relief for carried-forward losses under subsection (4), take account of any claim made before the current claim that—

    (a) is a claim for group relief for carried-forward losses based on the group condition, and

    (b) is in relation to losses or other amounts surrendered by a member of the same group of companies as the surrendering company (other than the surrendering company itself).

(6) The fraction mentioned in step 2 in subsection (3) is—

$$\frac{A}{B}$$

where—

    A is the sum of the surrendering company's surrenderable amounts for the surrender period that are attributable to the specified loss-making period, and

    B is the sum of all the surrendering company's surrenderable amounts for the surrender period.

CHAPTER 6

MISCELLANEOUS PROVISIONS AND INTERPRETATION OF PART

Miscellaneous

188FA Payments for group relief for carried-forward losses

(1) This section applies if—

    (a) the surrendering company and the claimant company have an agreement between them in relation to losses and other amounts of the surrendering company ("the agreed loss amounts"),

    (b) group relief for carried-forward losses is given to the claimant company in relation to the agreed loss amounts, and

    (c) as a result of the agreement the claimant company makes a payment to the surrendering company that does not exceed the total amount of the agreed loss amounts.

(2) The payment—

    (a) is not to be taken into account in determining the profits or losses of either company for corporation tax purposes, and

    (b) for corporation tax purposes is not to be regarded as a distribution.

Interpretation

188FB Subsidiaries, groups and consortiums

Chapter 5 of Part 5 (which explains certain key concepts for the purposes of Part 5, including (in particular) how to determine if a company is a member of a group of companies or is a member of, or

Finance (No. 2) Act 2017 (c. **32**)
Schedule 4 — Relief for carried-forward losses
Part 3 — Group relief for carried-forward losses

231

is owned by a consortium) applies for the purposes of this Part as it applies for the purposes of Part 5.

188FC "Trading company" and "holding company"

(1) In this Part "trading company" means a company the business of which consists wholly or mainly in the carrying on of a trade.

(2) In this Part "holding company" means a company the business of which consists wholly or mainly in the holding of shares or securities that—

    (a) are its 90% subsidiaries, and

    (b) are trading companies.

188FD Other definitions

(1) In this Part—

"the claimant company" has the meaning given by section 188CB(2) or 188CC(2),

"the claim period" has the meaning given by section 188CB(2) or 188CC(2),

"company" means any body corporate,

"group relief for carried-forward losses" has the meaning given by section 188AA(4),

"profits" means income and chargeable gains, except in so far as the context otherwise requires,

"shock loss" has the meaning given by section 269ZK,

"Solvency 2 insurance company" means an insurance company as defined in section 269ZP(2),

"the specified loss-making period", in relation to a claim for group relief for carried forward losses made under section 188CC, has the meaning given by subsection (2) of that section,

"the surrenderable amounts" has the meaning given by section 188BB(7),

"surrendering company" has the meaning given by 188BB(7), and

"the surrender period" has the meaning given by section 188BB(7).

(2) In this Part, except in so far as the context otherwise requires—

    (a) references to a trade include an office, and

    (b) reference to carrying on a trade include holding an office."

PART 4

INSURANCE COMPANIES: CARRYING FORWARD BLAGAB TRADE LOSSES

24   Chapter 9 of Part 2 of FA 2012 (relief for BLAGAB trade losses) is amended as follows.

25 (1) Section 124 (carry forward of BLAGAB trade losses against subsequent profits) is amended as follows.

    (2) In the heading, after "of" insert "pre-1 April 2017".

232   *Finance (No. 2) Act 2017 (c. 32)*
Schedule 4 — Relief for carried-forward losses
Part 4 — Insurance companies: carrying forward BLAGAB trade losses

(3) In subsection (1), after "accounting period" insert "beginning before 1 April 2017".

(4) In subsection (5), at the end insert "(but see also section 124D)".

26   After section 124 insert—

"124A Carry forward of post-1 April 2017 BLAGAB trade losses against subsequent profits

(1) This section applies if—

    (a) an insurance company carrying on basic life assurance and general annuity business makes a BLAGAB trade loss for an accounting period beginning on or after 1 April 2017 ("the loss-making period"),

    (b) relief under—

        section 37 of CTA 2010 (as applied by section 123), or

        Part 5 of CTA 2010 (group relief) (as applied by section 125),

    is not given for an amount of the loss ("the unrelieved amount"), and

    (c) the company continues to carry on basic life assurance and general annuity business in the next accounting period ("the later period").

(2) The unrelieved amount is carried forward to the later period.

(3) Relief for the unrelieved amount is given to the company in the later period if the company has a BLAGAB trade profit for the later period.

(4) The relief is given as set out in subsection (5).

(5) For the purposes of—

    (a) section 93 (minimum profits charge), and

    (b) section 104 (policyholders' rate of tax),

    the BLAGAB trade profit of the later period is reduced by the unrelieved amount (but see also section 124D).

(6) Relief under this section is subject to restriction or modification in accordance with section 137(7) of CTA 2010 and other applicable provisions of the Corporation Tax Acts.

124B Excess carried forward post-1 April 2017 losses: relief against total profits

(1) This section applies if—

    (a) an amount of an insurance company's BLAGAB trade loss for an accounting period is carried forward to an accounting period of the company ("the later period") under section 124A(2) or 124C(3), and

    (b) any of that amount ("the unrelieved amount") is not deducted under section 124A(5) or 124C(6) (as the case may be) from the company's BLAGAB trade profit (if any) of the later period.

Finance (No. 2) Act 2017 (c. 32)
Schedule 4 – Relief for carried-forward losses
Part 4 – Insurance companies: carrying forward BLAGAB trade losses

233

(2)   The company may make a claim for relief to be given for the unrelieved amount under this section.

(3)   If the company makes a claim, the relief is given by deducting the unrelieved amount, or any part of it specified in the claim, from the company's total profits of the later period.

(4)   But (if the company is a Solvency 2 insurance company) –

   (a)   the company may not make a claim under this section if the unrelieved amount is wholly a shock loss, and

   (b)   the company may not make a claim specifying a part of the unrelieved amount if that part is (to any extent) a shock loss.

(5)   For the purposes of subsection (4) assume that in any use by the company of the BLAGAB trade loss for relief under –

   (a)   section 37 of CTA 2010 (as applied by section 123),

   (b)   Part 5 of CTA 2010 (as applied by section 125), or

   (c)   section 124A(5) or 124C(6),

   any part of it that is a shock loss is used before any part of it that is not a shock loss.

(6)   A claim under this section must be made –

   (a)   within the period of two years after the end of the later period, or

   (b)   within such further period as an officer of Revenue and Customs may allow.

(7)   Relief under this section is subject to restriction or modification in accordance with section 137(7) of CTA 2010 and other applicable provisions of the Corporation Tax Acts.

(8)   In this section –

   "Solvency 2 insurance company" means an insurance undertaking, a reinsurance undertaking or a third-country insurance undertaking;

   "insurance undertaking" has the meaning given in Article 13(1) of the Solvency 2 Directive;

   "reinsurance undertaking" has the meaning given in Article 13(4) of the Solvency 2 Directive;

   "Solvency 2 Directive" means Directive 2009/138/EC of the European Parliament and the Council of 25 November 2009 on the taking-up and pursuit of the business of Insurance and Reinsurance (Solvency II);

   "shock loss" has the meaning given by section 269ZK of CTA 2010;

   "third-country insurance undertaking" means an undertaking that has received authorisation under Article 162 of the Solvency 2 Directive from the Prudential Regulation Authority or the Financial Conduct Authority.

124C   Further carry forward against subsequent profits of post-1 April 2017 loss not fully used

(1)   This section applies if –

234

Finance (No. 2) Act 2017 (c. 32)
Schedule 4 — Relief for carried-forward losses
Part 4 — Insurance companies: carrying forward BLAGAB trade losses

    (a)   an amount of an insurance company's BLAGAB trade loss for an accounting period is carried forward to an accounting period ("the later period") of the company under section 124A(2) or subsection (3) of this section,

    (b)   any of that amount is unrelieved in the later period, and

    (c)   the company continues to carry on basic life assurance and general annuity business in the accounting period ("the further period") after the later period.

(2)   An amount carried forward as mentioned in subsection (1)(a) is "unrelieved in the later period" so far as it is not—

    (a)   deducted under section 124A(5) or subsection (6) of this section from the company's BLAGAB trade profit (if any) of the later period,

    (b)   deducted from the company's total profits of the later period on a claim under 124B, or

    (c)   surrendered by way of group relief for carried-forward losses under Part 5A of CTA 2010.

(3)   So much of the amount mentioned in subsection (1)(a) as is unrelieved in the later period is carried forward to the further period.

(4)   Relief for the amount carried forward under subsection (3) ("the remaining carried forward amount") is given to the company in the further period if the company has a BLAGAB trade profit for that period.

(5)   The relief is given as set out in subsection (6).

(6)   For the purposes of—

    (a)   section 93 (minimum profits charge), and

    (b)   section 104 (policyholders' rate of tax),

the BLAGAB trade profit of the further period is reduced by the remaining carried forward amount (but see also section 124D).

(7)   Relief under this section is subject to restriction or modification in accordance with section 137(7) of CTA 2010 and other applicable provisions of the Corporation Tax Acts.

124D Restriction on deductions from BLAGAB trade profits

(1)   The sum of any deductions made by a company for an accounting period under sections 124(5), 124A(5) and 124C(6) may not exceed the relevant maximum.

But this is subject to subsection (6).

(2)   In this section the "relevant maximum" means the sum of—

    (a)   50% of the company's relevant BLAGAB trade profits for the accounting period, and

    (b)   the company's BLAGAB trade profits deductions allowance for the accounting period.

(3)   A company's "relevant BLAGAB trade profits" for an accounting period are—

    (a)   the company's BLAGAB trade profit for the accounting period, less

Finance (No. 2) Act 2017 (c. 32)
Schedule 4 — Relief for carried-forward losses
Part 4 — Insurance companies: carrying forward BLAGAB trade losses

235

(b) the company's BLAGAB trade profits deductions allowance for the accounting period.

But if the allowance mentioned in paragraph (b) exceeds the profit mentioned in paragraph (a), the company's "relevant BLAGAB trade profits" for the accounting period are nil.

(4) A company's "BLAGAB trade profits deductions allowance" for an accounting period —

(a) is so much of the company's deductions allowance for the period as is specified in the company's tax return as its BLAGAB trade profits deductions allowance for the period, and

(b) accordingly, is nil if no amount of the company's deductions allowance for the period is so specified.

(5) An amount specified under subsection (4)(a) as a company's BLAGAB trade profits deductions allowance for an accounting period may not exceed the difference between —

(a) the amount of the company's deductions allowance for the period, and

(b) the total of any amounts specified for the period under sections 269ZB(7)(a) of CTA 2010 (trading profits deduction allowance) and 269ZC(5)(a) of CTA 2010 (non-trading profits deduction allowance).

(6) Subsection (1) does not apply to a company for an accounting period if the company's BLAGAB trade profit for the accounting period is not greater than nil.

(7) Section 269ZB(9) of CTA 2010 gives the meaning of "deductions allowance" in relation to a company and an accounting period.

124E Section 124D: shock losses excluded from the restriction

(1) Subsection (2) applies where the company making a deduction under section 124A(5) or 124C(6) is a Solvency 2 insurance company.

(2) The deduction is to be ignored for the purposes of section 124D(1) and section 269ZD(2)(b)(iii) of CTA 2010 so far as it is a deduction of a shock loss.

(3) Where, by virtue of subsection (2), any deductions made by a Solvency 2 insurance company for an accounting period would be ignored for the purposes of section 124D(1), the references in section 124D(3)(a) and (6) to the company's BLAGAB trade profit have effect as references to that profit as reduced by those deductions.

(4) In this section "Solvency 2 insurance company" and "shock loss" have the same meaning as in section 124B."

236   *Finance (No. 2) Act 2017 (c. 32)*
Schedule 4 — Relief for carried-forward losses
Part 5 — Carrying forward trade losses in certain creative industries

PART 5

CARRYING FORWARD TRADE LOSSES IN CERTAIN CREATIVE INDUSTRIES

Losses of film trade

27   Chapter 4 of Part 15 of CTA 2009 (losses of separate film trade) is amended as follows.

28   (1) Section 1209 (restriction on use of losses while film in production) is amended as follows.

     (2) In subsection (2)—

         (a) after "45" insert "or 45B", and

         (b) for "set against" substitute "deducted from".

     (3) After subsection (2) insert—

        "(3) If the loss is carried forward under section 45 or 45B of CTA 2010 and deducted from profits of the separate film trade in a subsequent period, the deduction is to be ignored for the purposes of section 269ZB of CTA 2010 (restriction on deductions from trading profits)."

29   (1) Section 1210 (use of losses in later periods) is amended as follows.

     (2) In subsection (2) after "45" insert "or 45B".

     (3) In subsection (3) for "loss relief" substitute "section 37 and Part 5 of CTA 2010".

     (4) In subsection (4) for "Subsection (5) applies" substitute "Subsections (5) and (5A) apply".

     (5) In subsection (5) after paragraph (a) insert—

        "(ab) carried forward under section 45A of that Act to be deducted from the total profits of a later period,"

     (6) After subsection (5) insert—

        "(5A) A deduction under section 45 or 45B of CTA 2010 which is made in respect of so much of the loss as is attributable to film tax relief is to be ignored for the purposes of section 269ZB of that Act (restriction on deductions from trading profits)."

30   (1) Section 1211 (terminal losses) is amended as follows.

     (2) In subsection (1)(c)—

         (a) after "45" insert ", 45A or 45B", and

         (b) omit "trade X in".

     (3) In subsection (3) for the words after "treated" to the end substitute "—

         (a) in a case where the loss could have been carried forward under section 45 of CTA 2010 had trade X not ceased, as if it were a loss carried forward under that section to be set against the profits of trade Y of the first accounting period beginning after the cessation and so on, and

         (b) in a case where the loss could have been carried forward under section 45A or 45B of CTA 2010 had trade X not ceased, as if it were a loss made in trade Y which has been carried

Finance (No. 2) Act 2017 (c. 32)
Schedule 4 – Relief for carried-forward losses
Part 5 – Carrying forward trade losses in certain creative industries

237

forward under section 45B of that Act to the first accounting period beginning after the cessation."

(4) In subsection (6) for the words after "treated" to the end substitute "–

    (a) in a case where the amount could have been carried forward under section 45 of CTA 2010 had trade X not ceased, as if it were a loss carried forward under that section to be set against the profits of trade Z of the first accounting period beginning after the cessation and so on, and

    (b) in a case where the amount could have been carried forward under section 45A or 45B of CTA 2010 had trade X not ceased, as if it were a loss made in trade Z which has been carried forward under section 45B of that Act to the first accounting period beginning after the cessation."

(5) After subsection (7) insert–

    "(7A) A deduction under section 45 or 45B of CTA 2010 which is made in reliance on this section is to be ignored for the purposes of section 269ZB of that Act (restriction on deductions from trading profits)."

Losses of television programme trade

31   Chapter 4 of Part 15A of CTA 2009 (losses of separate television programme trade) is amended as follows.

32   (1) Section 1216DA (restriction on use of losses while programme in production) is amended as follows.

    (2) In subsection (2)–

        (a) after "45" insert "or 45B", and

        (b) for "set against" substitute "deducted from".

    (3) After subsection (2) insert–

        "(3) If the loss is carried forward under section 45 or 45B of CTA 2010 and deducted from profits of the separate programme trade in a subsequent period, the deduction is to be ignored for the purposes of section 269ZB of CTA 2010 (restriction on deductions from trading profits)."

33   (1) Section 1216DB (use of losses in later periods) is amended as follows.

    (2) In subsection (2) after "45" insert "or 45B".

    (3) In subsection (3) for "loss relief" substitute "section 37 and Part 5 of CTA 2010".

    (4) In subsection (4) for "Subsection (5) applies" substitute "Subsections (5) and (5A) apply".

    (5) In subsection (5) after paragraph (a) insert–

        "(ab) carried forward under section 45A of that Act to be deducted from the total profits of a later period,"

    (6) After subsection (5) insert–

        "(5A) A deduction under section 45 or 45B of CTA 2010 which is made in respect of so much of the loss as is attributable to television tax relief

238   *Finance (No. 2) Act 2017 (c. 32)*
Schedule 4 — Relief for carried-forward losses
Part 5 — Carrying forward trade losses in certain creative industries

is to be ignored for the purposes of section 269ZB of that Act (restriction on deductions from trading profits)."

34   (1)   Section 1216DC (terminal losses) is amended as follows.

      (2)   In subsection (1)(c) —

          (a)   after "45" insert ", 45A or 45B", and

          (b)   omit "trade X in".

      (3)   In subsection (3) for the words after "treated" to the end substitute "—

          (a)   in a case where the loss could have been carried forward under section 45 of CTA 2010 had trade X not ceased, as if it were a loss carried forward under that section to be set against the profits of trade Y of the first accounting period beginning after the cessation and so on, and

          (b)   in a case where the loss could have been carried forward under section 45A or 45B of CTA 2010 had trade X not ceased, as if it were a loss made in trade Y which has been carried forward under section 45B of that Act to the first accounting period beginning after the cessation."

      (4)   In subsection (6) for the words after "treated" to the end substitute "—

          (a)   in a case where the amount could have been carried forward under section 45 of CTA 2010 had trade X not ceased, as if it were a loss carried forward under that section to be set against the profits of trade Z of the first accounting period beginning after the cessation and so on, and

          (b)   in a case where the amount could have been carried forward under section 45A or 45B of CTA 2010 had trade X not ceased, as if it were a loss made in trade Z which has been carried forward under section 45B of that Act to the first accounting period beginning after the cessation."

      (5)   After subsection (7) insert—

        "(7A)   A deduction under section 45 or 45B of CTA 2010 which is made in reliance on this section is to be ignored for the purposes of section 269ZB of that Act (restriction on deductions from trading profits)."

Losses of video game trade

35   Chapter 4 of Part 15B of CTA 2009 (losses of separate video game trade) is amended as follows.

36   (1)   Section 1217DA (restriction on use of losses while video game in development) is amended as follows.

      (2)   In subsection (2) —

          (a)   after "45" insert "or 45B", and

          (b)   for "set against" substitute "deducted from".

      (3)   After subsection (2) insert—

        "(3)   If the loss is carried forward under section 45 or 45B of CTA 2010 and deducted from profits of the separate video game trade in a subsequent period, the deduction is to be ignored for the purposes of

Finance (No. 2) Act 2017 (c. 32)
Schedule 4 — Relief for carried-forward losses
Part 5 — Carrying forward trade losses in certain creative industries

239

        section 269ZB of CTA 2010 (restriction on deductions from trading profits)."

37   (1) Section 1217DB (use of losses in later periods) is amended as follows.

    (2) In subsection (2) after "45" insert "or 45B".

    (3) In subsection (3) for "loss relief" substitute "section 37 and Part 5 of CTA 2010".

    (4) In subsection (4) for "Subsection (5) applies" substitute "Subsections (5) and (5A) apply".

    (5) In subsection (5) after paragraph (a) insert—

        "(ab) carried forward under section 45A of that Act to be deducted from the total profits of a later period,"

    (6) After subsection (5) insert—

        "(5A) A deduction under section 45 or 45B of CTA 2010 which is made in respect of so much of the loss as is attributable to video games tax relief is to be ignored for the purposes of section 269ZB of that Act (restriction on deductions from trading profits)."

38   (1) Section 1217DC (terminal losses) is amended as follows.

    (2) In subsection (1)(c)—

        (a) after "45" insert ", 45A or 45B", and

        (b) omit "trade X in".

    (3) In subsection (3) for the words after "treated" to the end substitute "—

        (a) in a case where the loss could have been carried forward under section 45 of CTA 2010 had trade X not ceased, as if it were a loss carried forward under that section to be set against the profits of trade Y of the first accounting period beginning after the cessation and so on, and

        (b) in a case where the loss could have been carried forward under section 45A or 45B of CTA 2010 had trade X not ceased, as if it were a loss made in trade Y which has been carried forward under section 45B of that Act to the first accounting period beginning after the cessation."

    (4) In subsection (6) for the words after "treated" to the end substitute "—

        (a) in a case where the amount could have been carried forward under section 45 of CTA 2010 had trade X not ceased, as if it were a loss carried forward under that section to be set against the profits of trade Z of the first accounting period beginning after the cessation and so on, and

        (b) in a case where the amount could have been carried forward under section 45A or 45B of CTA 2010 had trade X not ceased, as if it were a loss made in trade Z which has been carried forward under section 45B of that Act to the first accounting period beginning after the cessation."

240

Finance (No. 2) Act 2017 (c. 32)
Schedule 4 — Relief for carried-forward losses
Part 5 — Carrying forward trade losses in certain creative industries

(5) After subsection (7) insert—

"(7A) A deduction under section 45 or 45B of CTA 2010 which is made in reliance on this section is to be ignored for the purposes of section 269ZB of that Act (restriction on deductions from trading profits)."

Losses of theatrical trade

39   Part 15C of CTA 2009 (theatrical productions) is amended as follows.

40   (1) Section 1217MA (restriction on use of losses before completion period) is amended as follows.

        (2) In subsection (1) for "Subsection (2)" substitute "This section".

        (3) In subsection (2)—
            (a)   after "45" insert "or 45B", and
            (b)   for "set against" substitute "deducted from".

        (4) After subsection (2) insert—

            "(3) If the loss is carried forward under section 45 or 45B of CTA 2010 and deducted from profits of the separate theatrical trade in a subsequent period, the deduction is to be ignored for the purposes of section 269ZB of CTA 2010 (restriction on deductions from trading profits)."

41   (1) Section 1217MB (use of losses in the completion period) is amended as follows.

        (2) In subsection (1) after "45" insert "or 45B".

        (3) In subsection (2) for "loss relief" substitute "section 37 and Part 5 of CTA 2010".

42   (1) Section 1217MC (terminal losses) is amended as follows.

        (2) In subsection (1)(b) after "45" insert "or 45B".

        (3) In subsection (3) for the words after "treated" to the end substitute "—
            (a)   in a case where the loss could have been carried forward under section 45 of CTA 2010 had trade 1 not ceased, as if it were a loss carried forward under that section to be set against the profits of trade 2 of the first accounting period beginning after the cessation and so on, and
            (b)   in a case where the loss could have been carried forward under section 45B of CTA 2010 had trade 1 not ceased, as if it were a loss made in trade 2 which has been carried forward under that section to the first accounting period beginning after the cessation."

        (4) In subsection (6) for the words after "treated" to the end substitute "—
            (a)   in a case where the amount could have been carried forward under section 45 of CTA 2010 had trade 1 not ceased, as if it were a loss carried forward by company B under that section to be set against the profits of company B's trade of the first accounting period beginning after the cessation and so on, and

Finance (No. 2) Act 2017 (c. 32)
Schedule 4 — Relief for carried-forward losses
Part 5 — Carrying forward trade losses in certain creative industries

241

(b) in a case where the amount could have been carried forward under section 45B of CTA 2010 had trade 1 not ceased, as if it were a loss made in company B's trade which has been carried forward under that section to the first accounting period beginning after the cessation."

(5) After subsection (8) insert—

"(9) A deduction under section 45 or 45B of CTA 2010 which is made in reliance on this section is to be ignored for the purposes of section 269ZB of that Act (restriction on deductions from trading profits)."

Losses of orchestral trade

43 Chapter 4 of Part 15D of CTA 2009 (losses of separate orchestral trade) is amended as follows.

44 (1) Section 1217SA (restriction on use of losses before completion period) is amended as follows.

(2) In subsection (1) for "Subsection (2)" substitute "This section".

(3) In subsection (2)—
    (a) after "45" insert "or 45B", and
    (b) for "set against" substitute "deducted from".

(4) After subsection (2) insert—

"(3) If the loss is carried forward under section 45 or 45B of CTA 2010 and deducted from profits of the separate orchestral trade in a subsequent period, the deduction is to be ignored for the purposes of section 269ZB of CTA 2010 (restriction on deductions from trading profits)."

45 (1) Section 1217SB (use of losses in the completion period) is amended as follows.

(2) In subsection (1) after "45" insert "or 45B".

(3) In subsection (2) for "loss relief" substitute "section 37 and Part 5 of CTA 2010".

46 (1) Section 1217SC (terminal losses) is amended as follows.

(2) In subsection (1)(b) after "45" insert "or 45B".

(3) In subsection (3) for the words after "treated" to the end substitute "—
    (a) in a case where the loss could have been carried forward under section 45 of CTA 2010 had trade 1 not ceased, as if it were a loss carried forward under that section to be set against the profits of trade 2 of the first accounting period beginning after the cessation and so on, and
    (b) in a case where the loss could have been carried forward under section 45B of CTA 2010 had trade 1 not ceased, as if it were a loss made in trade 2 which has been carried forward under that section to the first accounting period beginning after the cessation."

242   *Finance (No. 2) Act 2017 (c. 32)*
Schedule 4 — Relief for carried-forward losses
Part 5 — Carrying forward trade losses in certain creative industries

(4) In subsection (6) for the words after "treated" to the end substitute "—

    (a) in a case where the amount could have been carried forward under section 45 of CTA 2010 had trade 1 not ceased, as if it were a loss carried forward by company B under that section to be set against the profits of company B's trade of the first accounting period beginning after the cessation and so on, and

    (b) in a case where the amount could have been carried forward under section 45B of CTA 2010 had trade 1 not ceased, as if it were a loss made in company B's trade which has been carried forward under that section to the first accounting period beginning after the cessation."

(5) After subsection (8) insert—

    "(9) A deduction under section 45 or 45B of CTA 2010 which is made in reliance on this section is to be ignored for the purposes of section 269ZB of that Act (restriction on deductions from trading profits)."

PART 6

OIL ACTIVITIES

47   Part 8 of CTA 2010 (oil activities) is amended as follows.

48   After section 303 insert—

"303A Introduction to sections 303B to 303D: post-1 April 2017 non-decommissioning losses of ring fence trades

    (1) This section has effect for the purposes of sections 303B to 303D.

    (2) A loss made by a company in a ring fence trade is a "non-decommissioning loss" so far as it is not attributable to expenditure which is relevant expenditure in relation to a decommissioning relief agreement.

    (3) Where a company makes a loss for an accounting period in a ring fence trade, the amount (if any) of that loss that is "attributable to" expenditure which is relevant expenditure in relation to a decommissioning relief agreement is equal to—

        (a) the total amount of such expenditure brought into account in calculating that loss, or

        (b) if lower, the amount of the loss.

    (4) Expenditure is "relevant expenditure" in relation to a decommissioning relief agreement if it is decommissioning expenditure (as defined in section 81 of FA 2013) to which the provision of the agreement described in section 80(2)(b) of that Act relates.

    In this subsection the reference to section 81 of FA 2013 is to that section as it has effect when the agreement in question is made.

    (5) In this section "decommissioning relief agreement" has the meaning given by section 80 of FA 2013.

303B Carry forward of losses against subsequent profits

(1) This section applies if—

    (a) in an accounting period beginning on or after 1 April 2017 ("the loss-making period") a company makes a non-decommissioning loss in a ring fence trade,

    (b) relief under—

        section 37 or 42, or

        Part 5 (group relief),

    is not given for an amount of the loss ("the unrelieved amount"), and

    (c) the company continues to carry on the ring fence trade in the next accounting period ("the later period").

(2) The unrelieved amount is carried forward to the later period.

(3) Relief for the unrelieved amount is given to the company in the later period if the company makes a profit in the trade for the later period.

(4) The relief is given by reducing the profits of the trade in the later period by the unrelieved amount.

(5) Relief under this section is subject to restriction or modification in accordance with the provisions of the Corporation Tax Acts.

303C Excess carried forward losses: relief against total profits

(1) This section applies if—

    (a) an amount of a non-decommissioning loss made in a ring fence trade is carried forward to an accounting period of a company ("the later period") under section 303B(2) or 303D(3), and

    (b) any of that amount ("the unrelieved amount") is not deducted under section 303B(4) or 303D(5) (as the case may be) from the company's profits of the trade (if any) of the later period.

(2) The company may make a claim for relief to be given for the unrelieved amount under this section (but see subsection (4)).

(3) If the company makes a claim, the relief is given by deducting the unrelieved amount, or any part of it specified in the claim, from the company's total profits of the later period.

(4) The company may not make a claim if—

    (a) the ring fence trade became small or negligible in the loss-making period or any intervening period,

    (b) relief under section 37 was unavailable for the non-decommissioning loss by reason of section 37(5) or 44, or

    (c) relief under section 37 would be unavailable by reason of section 44 for a loss (assuming there was one) made in the ring fence trade in the later period or any intervening period.

(5) In subsection (4)—

    "intervening period" means an accounting period of the company which begins after the loss-making period and before the later period, and

244   *Finance (No. 2) Act 2017 (c. 32)*
Schedule 4 — Relief for carried-forward losses
Part 6 — Oil activities

"the loss-making period" means the accounting period of the company in which the non-decommissioning loss was made.

(6) A claim under this section must be made—

    (a) within the period of two years after the end of the later period, or

    (b) within such further period as an officer of Revenue and Customs may allow.

(7) Relief under this section is subject to restriction or modification in accordance with the provisions of the Corporation Tax Acts.

303D Further carry forward against subsequent profits of loss not fully used

(1) This section applies if—

    (a) an amount of a loss made in a ring fence trade is carried forward to an accounting period ("the later period") of a company under section 303B(2) or subsection (3) of this section,

    (b) any of that amount is unrelieved in the later period, and

    (c) the company continues to carry on the ring fence trade in the accounting period ("the further period") after the later period.

(2) An amount carried forward as mentioned in subsection (1)(a) is "unrelieved in the later period" so far as it is not—

    (a) deducted under section 303B(4) or subsection (5) of this section from the company's profit (if any) of the later period,

    (b) deducted from the company's total profits of the later period on a claim under section 303C, or

    (c) surrendered by way of group relief for carried-forward losses under Part 5A of CTA 2010.

(3) So much of the amount mentioned in subsection (1)(a) as is unrelieved in the later period is carried forward to the further period.

(4) Relief for the amount carried forward under subsection (3) ("the remaining carried forward amount") is given to the company in the further period if the company has a profit in the trade for that period.

(5) The relief is given by reducing the profits of the trade of the further period by the remaining carried forward amount.

(6) Relief under this section is subject to restriction or modification in accordance with the provisions of the Corporation Tax Acts."

49 (1) Section 304 (losses) is amended as follows.

(2) After subsection (1) insert—

  "(1A) Relief in respect of a loss incurred by a company may not be given against that company's ring fence profits under any provision listed in subsection (1B).

  (1B) The provisions are—

    (a) section 753 of CTA 2009 (non-trading losses on intangible fixed assets);

    (b) section 45A (carry forward of trade loss against total profits);

    (c)   section 62(3) (relief for losses made in UK property business)."

(3) In subsection (5), after "45" insert "45B, 303B(4) or 303D(5)".

(4) After subsection (6) insert—

    "(7)   A deduction in respect of a loss made in a ring fence trade is to be ignored for the purposes of section 269ZB (restriction on deductions from trading profits) if the deduction is under—

        (a)   section 45 (carry forward of pre-1 April 2017 trade loss against subsequent profits), or

        (b)   section 45B (carry forward of post-1 April 2017 trade loss against total profits)."

50   (1) Section 305 (group relief) is amended as follows.

(2) In the heading, at the end insert "and group relief for carried-forward losses".

(3) After subsection (1) insert—

    "(1A)   On a claim under Chapter 3 of Part 5A, group relief for carried-forward losses may not be allowed against the claimant company's ring fence profits."

(4) For subsection (4) substitute—

    "(4)   In this section—

        "claimant company" is to be read in accordance with Part 5 (see section 188) or Part 5A (see sections 188CB(2) and 188CC(2)), as the case requires;

        "surrendering company" is to be read in accordance with Part 5 (see section 188)."

51   In section 307 (overview of Chapter 5 of Part 8: ring fence expenditure supplement) in subsection (6) for paragraph (c) substitute—

    "(c)   relief given under sections 45, 45B, 303B, 303C and 303D for ring fence losses carried forward from earlier periods,".

52   (1) Section 321 (supplement in respect of a post-commencement period) is amended as follows.

(2) In subsection (2) (treatment of supplement as loss etc)—

    (a)   in the words before paragraph (a) after "period" insert "beginning before 1 April 2017", and

    (b)   in paragraph (b) after "forward of" insert "pre-1 April 2017".

(3) After subsection (2) insert—

    "(2A)   Any post-commencement supplement allowed on a claim in respect of a post-commencement period beginning on or after 1 April 2017 is to be treated for the purposes of the Corporation Tax Acts (other than the post-commencement supplement provisions or Part 4 of Schedule 19B to ICTA) as if it were a loss—

        (a)   which is incurred in carrying on the ring fence trade in that period, and

      (b)   which falls in whole to be used under section 45B (carry forward of post-1 April 2017 trade loss against subsequent trade profits) to reduce trading income from the ring fence trade in succeeding accounting periods."

53   (1)   Section 323 (meaning of "ring fence losses") is amended as follows.

    (2)   In subsection (1)—

      (a)   for paragraph (b) substitute—

         "(b)   some or all of the loss falls to be carried forward to the following accounting period under section 45, 45B or 303B (carry forward of trade losses against subsequent profits)", and

      (b)   in the words after paragraph (b) for "used" substitute "carried forward".

    (3)   In subsection (2) for "used" substitute "carried forward".

54   For section 327 substitute—

"327   Reductions in respect of relief for carried-forward ring fence losses

    (1)   Reductions are to be made in accordance with this section in a post-commencement period if the relevant amount for the period (see subsection (4)) is not nil.

    (2)   If the company has a non-qualifying pool, the amount in the non-qualifying pool is to be reduced (but not below nil) by setting against it a sum equal to the relevant amount for the post-commencement period.

    (3)   If—

      (a)   any of that sum remains after being so set against the amount in the non-qualifying pool, or

      (b)   the company does not have a non-qualifying pool,

      the amount in the ring fence pool is to be reduced (but not below nil) by setting against it so much of that sum as so remains or (as the case may be) a sum equal to the relevant amount for the post-commencement period.

    (4)   For the purposes of this section, the relevant amount for a post-commencement period is the sum of—

      (a)   the amount of any relief given in respect of ring fence losses in the post-commencement period under sections 45, 45B, 303B, 303C and 303D, and

      (b)   the amount of any relief prevented from being given in respect of ring fence losses in the post-commencement period by claims made under sections 45(4A) and 45B(5)."

55   In section 328A (adjustment of pool to remove pre-2013 losses after the initial 6 periods) in subsection (11)—

      (a)   in paragraph (a) for the words from the beginning to "a loss" substitute "no account is to be taken of a loss in determining under section 327(4) the relevant amount for a post-commencement period", and

      (b)   in paragraph (b) for the words from "ring fence losses" to the end substitute "any such profits are reduced by the use under section 45,

45B, 303B, 303C and 303D of ring fence losses that are not represented by the reduction".

PART 7

OIL CONTRACTORS

56   Part 8ZA of CTA 2010 (oil contractors) is amended as follows.

57   (1) Section 356NE (losses) is amended as follows.

(2) The existing text becomes subsection (1) of that section.

(3) In subsection (1) —
   (a) after "the contractor" insert "(or an amount of such a loss)";
   (b) after "profits)" insert "or section 45A (carry forward of post-1 April 2017 trade loss against total profits)";
   (c) after "the loss" insert "(or amount)".

(4) After subsection (1) insert —

"(2) Relief in respect of a loss incurred by the contractor may not be given against the contractor's ring fence profits under any provision listed in subsection (3).

(3) The provisions are —
   (a) section 753 of CTA 2009 (non-trading losses on intangible fixed assets);
   (b) section 62(3) (relief for losses made in UK property business);
   (c) section 303C(3) (excess carried forward non-decommissioning losses of ring fence trade: relief against total profits)."

58   (1) Section 356NF (group relief) is amended as follows.

(2) In the heading, at the end insert "and group relief for carried-forward losses".

(3) After subsection (3) insert —

"(3A) On a claim under Chapter 3 of Part 5A, group relief for carried-forward losses may not be allowed against the claimant company's contractor's ring fence profits, except so far as the claim relates to losses incurred by the surrendering company that arose from oil contractor activities."

(4) For subsection (4) substitute —

"(4) In this section —
         "claimant company" is to be read in accordance with Part 5 (see section 188) or Part 5A (see sections 188CB(2) and 188CC(2)), as the case requires;
         "surrendering company" is to be read in accordance with Part 5 (see section 188) or Part 5A (see section 188BB(7)), as the case requires."

59   After section 356NG insert—

"Restriction on obtaining certain deductions

356NH Restriction on deductions from contractor's ring fence profits

    (1)   For the purpose of determining the contractor's taxable total profits for an accounting period, the sum of any relevant deductions from total profits made by the contractor for the accounting period may not exceed the relevant Part 8ZA maximum.

    (2)   In this section "relevant deduction from total profits" means—

        (a)   any deduction of a loss (or an amount of a loss) under section 45(4)(b) (carry forward of pre-1 April 2017 loss against subsequent profits), so far as the loss arises from oil contractor activities,

        (b)   any deduction of a loss (or an amount of a loss) under section 45A (carry forward of post-1 April 2017 trade loss against total profits), so far as the amount is set against the contractor's ring fence profits, and

        (c)   any deduction of a loss or other amount under Part 5A (group relief for carried-forward losses), so far as the amount in question is set against the contractor's ring fence profits.

    (3)   In this section "the relevant Part 8ZA maximum" means the sum of—

        (a)   50% of the contractor's ring fence profits for the accounting period, and

        (b)   the amount of the contractor's ring fence profits deductions allowance for the period.

356NI Deductions allowances where company has contractor's ring fence profits

    (1)   This section applies if a company ("C") has contractor's ring fence profits for an accounting period.

    (2)   Subsections (3) to (6) set out how to determine, for the accounting period—

        (a)   C's deductions allowance for the purposes of Part 7ZA (restrictions on obtaining certain deductions), and

        (b)   C's contractor's ring fence profits deductions allowance.

    (3)   Determine in accordance with Part 7ZA what C's deductions allowance for the period would be in the absence of this section (and call this "amount A").

    (4)   Determine C's contractor's ring fence profits deductions allowance for the period in accordance with subsection (5).

    (5)   C's "contractor's ring fence profits deductions allowance" for an accounting period—

        (a)   is so much of amount A as is specified in C's company tax return as its contractor's ring fence profits deductions allowance for the period, and

        (b)   accordingly, is nil if no amount is so specified.

(6) Subsection (7) applies if a relevant reversal credit is brought into account in calculating C's contractor's ring fence profits for the accounting period.

In this subsection the reference to bringing into account a relevant reversal credit is to be interpreted in accordance with section 269ZY.

(7) C's contractor's ring fence profits deductions allowance for the accounting period (as determined in accordance with subsection (5)) is to be treated for all purposes as increased by—

(a) the amount of the relevant reversal credit, or

(b) if lower, the amount of the contractor's ring fence profits for the accounting period.

(8) C's deductions allowance for the period for the purposes of Part 7ZA is to be taken to be an amount equal to amount A less the amount of C's ring fence profits deductions allowance for the period.

356NJ Modification of provisions restricting the use of losses

(1) The following deductions are to be treated as not being relevant deductions for the purposes of section 269ZD (restrictions on deductions from total profits)—

(a) the deduction of a loss (or an amount of a loss) under section 45A (carry forward of post- 1 April 2017 trade loss against total profits), so far as the amount is set against the company's contractor's ring fence profits for the accounting period;

(b) the deduction under Part 5A (group relief for carried-forward losses) of a loss or other amount, so far as the amount is set against the company's contractor's ring fence profits for the accounting period.

(2) A deduction under section 45(4)(b) (carry forward of pre-1 April 2017 trade loss against subsequent profits) of a loss arising from oil contractor activities is to be ignored for the purposes of section 269ZB of CTA 2010 (restriction on deductions from trading profits)."

PART 8

TRANSFERRED TRADES

61   Chapter 1 of Part 22 of CTA 2010 (transfers of trade without a change of ownership) is amended as follows.

62   In section 940A (overview of Chapter) in subsection (4) for "944" substitute "943A".

63   Before section 944 (but after the italic heading preceding that section) insert—

"943A Disapplication of section 39

If this Chapter applies to a transfer of a trade, section 39 (terminal losses: extension of periods for which relief may be given) does not apply in relation to a claim under section 37 by the predecessor for relief for a loss made in the transferred trade."

64 (1) Section 944 (modified application of Chapter 2 of Part 4) is amended as follows.

(2) In the heading for "Chapter 2 of Part 4" substitute "section 45".

(3) Omit subsections (1) and (2).

(4) In subsection (3)—

  (a) for "Relief" substitute "If this Chapter applies to a transfer of a trade, relief", and

  (b) after "carry forward of" insert "pre-1 April 2017".

(5) In subsection (4) after paragraph (a) insert—

  "(ab) any claim made by the predecessor under section 45F in reliance on subsection (2) of section 944C,".

65　　After section 944 insert—

"944A Modified application of section 45A

  (1) Subsection (2) applies if—

    (a) this Chapter applies to a transfer of a trade,

    (b) the transferred trade is not a ring fence trade,

    (c) the predecessor made a loss in the transferred trade in the accounting period in which it ceased to carry it on,

    (d) that accounting period began on or after 1 April 2017,

    (e) relief for an amount of that loss is not given under section 37 or Part 5,

    (f) relief under section 37 was not unavailable for that loss by reason of a provision mentioned in section 45A(3)(b)(i) or (ii), and

    (g) relief under section 37 would not be unavailable by reason of section 44 for a loss (assuming there was one) made by the successor in the transferred trade in the accounting period in which the successor begins to carry on the transferred trade ("the successor's start-up accounting period").

  (2) Subsections (4) to (8) of section 45A (carry-forward of post-1 April 2017 trade loss against total profits) apply as if—

    (a) references to the unrelieved amount were to the amount referred to in subsection (1)(e),

    (b) references to the later period were to the successor's start-up accounting period, and

    (c) references to the company were to the successor.

  (3) Subsection (4) applies if—

    (a) this Chapter applies to a transfer of a trade,

    (b) an amount of a loss made in the transferred trade was carried forward under section 45A(4) to the accounting period of the predecessor in which the predecessor ceased to carry on the trade,

    (c) any of that amount was not deducted from the predecessor's total profits on a claim under section 45A(5) or surrendered by the predecessor by way of group relief for carried-forward losses under Part 5A, and

(d) relief under section 37 would not be unavailable by reason of section 44 for a loss (assuming there was one) made by the successor in the transferred trade in the accounting period in which the successor begins to carry on the transferred trade ("the successor's start-up accounting period").

(4) Subsections (4) to (8) of section 45A apply as if —

    (a) references to the unrelieved amount were to so much of the amount referred to in subsection (3)(b) as was not deducted or surrendered as mentioned in subsection (3)(c),

    (b) references to the later period were to the successor's start-up accounting period, and

    (c) references to the company were to the successor.

(5) In this section "ring fence trade" has the same meaning as in Part 8 (see section 277).

944B Modified application of section 45B

(1) Subsection (2) applies if —

    (a) this Chapter applies to a transfer of a trade,

    (b) the predecessor made a loss in the transferred trade in the accounting period in which it ceased to carry it on,

    (c) that accounting period began on or after 1 April 2017,

    (d) relief under section 37 or 42 or Part 5 is not given for an amount of the loss, and

    (e) it is the case that —

        (i) relief under section 37 was unavailable for the loss by reason of any provision mentioned in section 45A(3)(b)(i) or (ii),

        (ii) relief under section 37 would be unavailable by reason of section 44 for a loss (assuming there was one) made by the successor in the transferred trade in the accounting period in which the successor begins to carry on the transferred trade ("the successor's start-up accounting period"), or

        (iii) the transferred trade is a ring fence trade.

(2) Subsections (2) to (8) of section 45B (carry forward of post-1 April 2017 trade loss against trade profits) apply as if —

    (a) references to the unrelieved amount were to the amount mentioned in subsection (1)(d),

    (b) references to the later period were to the successor's start-up accounting period,

    (c) references to the company were to the successor, and

    (d) references to the trade were to the transferred trade.

(3) Subsection (4) applies if —

    (a) this Chapter applies to a transfer of a trade,

    (b) an amount of a loss made in the transferred trade was carried forward under section 45B(2) to the accounting period in which the predecessor ceased to carry on the trade, and

   (c)   any of that amount is not used under section 45B(4) to reduce profits of the transferred trade of the accounting period in which the predecessor ceases to carry on the trade.

(4)   Subsections (2) to (8) of section 45B apply as if—

   (a)   references to the unrelieved amount were to so much of the amount referred to in subsection (3)(b) as is not used as mentioned in subsection (3)(c),

   (b)   references to the later period were to the accounting period of the successor in which the successor begins to carry on the transferred trade,

   (c)   references to the company were to the successor, and

   (d)   references to the trade were to the transferred trade.

944C Modified application of section 45F

(1)   If this Chapter applies to a transfer of a trade, the predecessor may not make a claim under section 45F for relief to be given for an amount of a loss made in the transferred trade.

(2)   But subsection (1) does not apply if—

   (a)   the trade is transferred before 13 July 2017, and

   (b)   the amount of the loss is carried forward to the accounting period in which the predecessor ceases to carry on the trade under section 45 (carry forward of pre-1 April 2017 trade losses).

(3)   Subsection (4) applies if—

   (a)   this Chapter applies to a transfer of a trade,

   (b)   an amount of a loss made by the predecessor in the transferred trade is carried forward under section 45, 45A or 45B to the accounting period of the successor in which the successor ceases to carry on the transferred trade, and

   (c)   relief in that accounting period is not given to the successor under section 45, 45A or (as the case may be) 45B for that amount or for any part of it.

(4)   Section 45F has effect as if the loss was made by the successor in the transferred trade in the accounting period in which it began carrying on the transferred trade.

944D Modified application of section 303B

(1)   Subsection (2) applies if—

   (a)   this Chapter applies to a transfer of a trade,

   (b)   the transferred trade is a ring-fence trade,

   (c)   the predecessor made a non-decommissioning loss in the transferred trade in the accounting period in which it ceased to carry it on,

   (d)   that accounting period began on or after 1 April 2017, and

   (e)   relief under section 37 or 42 or Part 5 is not given for an amount of the loss.

(2)   Subsections (2) to (5) of section 303B (carry forward of non-decommissioning losses against subsequent profits) have effect as if—

(a) references to the unrelieved amount were to the amount mentioned in subsection (1)(e),

(b) references to the later period were to the accounting period of the successor in which the successor begins to carry on the transferred trade,

(c) references to the company were to the successor, and

(d) references to the trade were to the transferred trade.

(3) Section 303A (meaning of non-decommissioning loss) applies for the purposes of this section.

(4) In this section "ring fence trade" has the same meaning as in Part 8 (see section 277).

944E Modified application of section 303D

(1) Subsection (2) applies if—

(a) this Chapter applies to a transfer of a trade,

(b) the trade is a ring-fence trade,

(c) an amount of a loss made in the trade was carried forward under section 303B(2) or 303D(3) to the accounting period in which the predecessor ceased to carry on the trade ("the cessation period"), and

(d) any of that amount was not—

   (i) deducted under section 303B(4) or 303D(5) from the predecessor's profit (if any) of the cessation period,

   (ii) deducted from the predecessor's total profits of the cessation period on a claim under section 303C(2), or

   (iii) surrendered by the predecessor by way of group relief for carried-forward losses under Part 5A.

(2) Subsections (3) to (6) of section 303D have effect as if—

(a) the reference to so much of the amount mentioned in section 303D(1)(a) as is unrelieved in the later period were to so much of the amount mentioned in subsection (1)(c) of this section as was not deducted or surrendered as mentioned in subsection (1)(d),

(b) references to the further period were to the accounting period of the successor in which the successor begins to carry on the transferred trade,

(c) references to the company were to the successor, and

(d) references to the trade were to the transferred trade.

(3) In this section "ring fence trade" has the same meaning as in Part 8 (see section 277)."

66   In section 945 (cases in which predecessor retains more liabilities than assets) in subsection (4), for "section 944(3)" (in both places where those words occur) substitute "sections 944 to 944E".

67 (1) Section 951 (part of trade treated as separate trade) is amended as follows.

(2) After subsection (6) insert—

"(7) Subsection (8) applies if—

> (a) a company ("the transferor") ceases to carry on a trade ("trade Z"),
>
> (b) another company ("the transferee") begins to carry on the activities of trade Z as part of its trade ("part Z") and
>
> (c) by reason of this Chapter an amount of a loss made in trade Z is carried forward under section 45A(4), 45B(2), 303B(2) or 303D(3) to an accounting period of the transferee.
>
> (8) The provisions of sections 45A to 45F and 303B to 303D have effect, in so far as they apply (or re-apply) in relation to the amount carried forward (or any part of it), as if the transferee carries or carried on part Z as a separate trade."

68   In section 952 (apportionment if part of trade treated as separate trade) in subsection (1) for "or (4)" substitute ", (4) or (8)"."

PART 9

TAX AVOIDANCE

Restriction on refreshing losses

69   (1) Section 730F of CTA 2010 (meaning of "relevant carried-forward loss") is amended as follows.

(2) In subsection (1)—

   (a) after paragraph (a) insert—

   > "(aa) a carried-forward UK property business loss (see subsection (2A),";

   (b) after paragraph (b) insert—

   > "(ba) a carried-forward non-trading loss on intangible fixed assets (see subsection (3A),".

(3) In subsection (2)—

   (a) after "45" insert ", 45A or 45B";

   (b) omit "against subsequent trade profits".

(4) In subsection (3), after "457" insert ", 463G or 463H".

(5) After subsection (2) insert—

   > "(2A) "Carried-forward UK property business loss", in relation to a company and an accounting period, means a loss in a UK property business carried on by the company which is carried forward from a previous accounting period under section 62(5)."

(6) After subsection (3) insert—

   > "(3A) "Carried-forward non-trading loss on intangible fixed assets", in relation to a company and an accounting period, means a non-trading loss on intangible fixed assets which is carried forward from a previous accounting period under section 753 of CTA 2009 (treatment of non-trading losses)."

(7) At the end insert—

> "(5) In this section "non-trading loss on intangible fixed assets" is to be read in accordance with Part 8 of CTA 2009."

Change in company ownership

70   Part 14 of CTA 2010 (change in company ownership) is amended as follows.

71   In section 672 (overview of Part) after subsection (1) insert—

> "(1A) Chapter 2A restricts relief in some further cases involving a change in the company's activities.
>
> (1B) Chapter 2B restricts relief for trading losses in some cases involving the transfer of an asset.
>
> (1C) Chapters 2C and 2D restrict group relief for carried-forward losses in some cases.
>
> (1D) Chapter 2E restricts relief for trading losses in some cases involving the transfer of a trade."

72 (1) Section 673 (introduction to Chapter 2: disallowance of trading losses) is amended as follows.

(2) In subsection (2), for "of 3 years in which the change in ownership" substitute "beginning no more than 3 years before the change in ownership occurs which is a period of 5 years in which that change".

(3) In subsection (4), in the words after paragraph (b), for "3" substitute "5".

(4) The amendments made by this paragraph do not have effect unless both the change in ownership referred to in section 673(1) and the major change in the nature or conduct of a trade referred to in section 673(2) occur on or after 1 April 2017.

73 (1) Section 674 (disallowance of trading losses) is amended as follows.

(2) In subsection (2), after "45" insert ", 45B, 303B or 303D".

(3) After subsection (2) insert—

> "(2A) No relief may be given under section 45A or 303C for a loss made by the company in an accounting period beginning before the change in ownership by carrying forward the loss and deducting it from a company's total profits of an accounting period ending after the change in ownership."

74   After section 674 insert—

> **"674A Section 674: exception for certain losses of ring fence trade**
>
> (1) Section 674 does not prevent relief being given for a loss if—
>   (a) the loss is made in a ring fence trade,
>   (b) the loss is not a non-decommissioning loss,
>   (c) it is condition A in section 673 that is met, and
>   (d) the major change by reference to which that condition is met did not occur within a period of 3 years in which the change in ownership occurred.

(2) In this section—

"non-decommissioning loss" is to be interpreted in accordance with section 303A;

"ring fence trade" has the same meaning as in Part 8 (see section 277)."

75 After Chapter 2 insert—

"CHAPTER 2A

POST-1 APRIL 2017 LOSSES: FURTHER CASES INVOLVING A CHANGE IN THE COMPANY'S ACTIVITIES

676AA Introduction to Chapter

(1) This Chapter applies if conditions 1 and 2 are met.

(2) Condition 1 is that on or after 1 April 2017 there is a change in the ownership of a company ("the transferred company").

(3) Condition 2 is that a major change in the business of the transferred company or a co-transferred company occurs within the required period but not before 1 April 2017.

(4) The required period is—

(a) for the purposes of section 676AF, any period beginning no more than 3 years before the change in ownership occurs which is a period of 5 years in which that change occurs,

(b) for the purposes of sections 676AG to 676AK, the period of 8 years beginning 3 years before the change in ownership.

(5) In this Chapter—

"the change in ownership" means the change in ownership mentioned in subsection (2);

"the transferred company" has the meaning given by subsection (2);

"trade" includes an office.

676AB Priority of provisions of Chapters 2 and 3 over this Chapter

(1) If and so far as —

(a) a relevant provision of this Chapter, and

(b) a relevant provision of Chapter 2 or 3,

would each (if the other provision were ignored) apply in relation to the same loss or other amount, the relevant provision of this Chapter does not apply in relation to that amount.

(2) In this section "relevant provision"—

(a) in relation to this Chapter means any of the provisions of sections 676AF to 676AK;

(b) in relation to Chapters 2 and 3 means any of the provisions of sections 674 and 679 to 683.

676AC "Major change in the business" of a company

(1) In this Chapter references to a "major change in the business" of a company include—

      (a)   a major change in the nature or conduct of any trade or business carried on by the company,

      (b)   a major change in the scale of any trade or business carried on by the company, and

      (c)   beginning or ceasing to carry on a particular trade or business.

(2)   In subsection (1) the reference to a major change in the "nature or conduct" of a trade or business includes —

      (a)   a major change in the type of property dealt in, or services or facilities provided in, the trade or business concerned,

      (b)   a major change in customers, outlets or markets of the trade or business concerned,

      (c)   a major change in the nature of the investments held by the company for the purposes of an investment business.

(3)   The definitions in subsections (1) and (2) apply even if the change is the result of a gradual process which began before the period of 5 years mentioned in section 676AA(4)(a) or (as the case may be) the period of 8 years mentioned in section 676AA(4)(b).

(4)   Where the condition in subsection (5) is met in the case of any two companies, the transfer of a trade or business, or any property, from one of them to the other is to be disregarded in determining for the purposes of section 676AA(3) whether or not there is a major change in the business of either of those companies.

(5)   The condition is that the companies are related to one another both —

      (a)   immediately before the change in ownership, and

      (b)   at the time of the transfer mentioned in subsection (4).

676AD Notional split of accounting period in which change in ownership occurs

(1)   This section applies for the purposes of this Chapter.

(2)   The accounting period in which the change in ownership occurs ("the actual accounting period") is treated as two separate accounting periods ("notional accounting periods"), the first ending with the change and the second consisting of the remainder of the period.

(3)   Section 685 (apportionment of amounts) applies for the purposes of this Chapter as it applies for the purposes of Chapter 3.

(4)   The amounts for the actual accounting period in column 1 of the table in section 685(2) are apportioned to the two notional accounting periods in accordance with section 685.

(5)   In this Chapter, and in sections 685 and 686 as they apply by virtue of subsection (3), "the actual accounting period" and "notional accounting periods" have the same meaning as in this section.

676AE "Affected profits"

(1)   This section has effect for the purposes of this Chapter.

(2) Profits of an accounting period ending after the change in ownership are "affected profits" if and so far as—

    (a) they arise before the 5th anniversary of the end of the accounting period of the transferred company in which the change in ownership occurs, and

    (b) they can fairly and reasonably be attributed to activities, or other sources of income, as a result of which, or partly as a result of which, the major change referred to in section 676AA(3) has occurred.

(3) If an accounting period of the company begins before, and ends after, the anniversary mentioned in subsection (2), then for the purposes of that subsection—

    (a) the accounting period is treated as two separate accounting periods, the first ending with that date and the second consisting of the remainder of the period, and

    (b) the profits or losses of the accounting period are apportioned to the two periods.

(4) Any apportionment under subsection (3)(b) is to be made on a time basis according to the respective lengths of the two deemed accounting periods.

(5) But if that method of apportionment would work unjustly or unreasonably in any case, such other method is to be used as is just and reasonable.

676AF Restriction on use of carried-forward post-1 April 2017 trade losses

A loss made by the transferred company in an accounting period beginning before the change in ownership may not be deducted from affected profits of an accounting period ending after the change in ownership under any of the following provisions—

    (a) section 45A(5) (carry-forward of post-1 April 2017 trade losses),

    (b) section 45F(3) (carried-forward losses: terminal relief),

    (c) section 303C(3) (excess carried-forward non-decommissioning losses of ring fence trade), and

    (d) section 124B(3) of FA 2012 (excess carried-forward BLAGAB trade losses).

676AG Restriction on debits to be brought into account

(1) This section has effect for the purpose of restricting the debits to be brought into account for the purposes of Part 5 of CTA 2009 (loan relationships) in respect of the transferred company's loan relationships.

(2) The debits to be brought into account for the purposes of Part 5 of CTA 2009 for—

    (a) the accounting period beginning immediately after the change in ownership, or

    (b) any subsequent accounting period,

do not include relevant non-trading debits so far as amount A exceeds amount B.

(3) Amount A is the sum of —

    (a) the amount of those relevant non-trading debits, and

    (b) the amount of any relevant non-trading debits which have been brought into account for the purposes of that Part for any previous accounting period ending after the change in ownership.

(4) Amount B is the amount of the taxable total profits of the accounting period ending with the change in ownership.

(5) For the meaning of "relevant non-trading debit", see section 730.

676AH Restriction on the carry forward of post-1 April 2017 non-trading deficit from loan relationships

(1) This section has effect for the purpose of restricting the carry forward under Chapter 16A of Part 5 of CTA 2009 (non-trading deficits: post 1 April 2017 deficits) of a pre-acquisition non-trading deficit from the transferred company's loan relationships.

(2) For the purposes of this section an amount is a "pre-acquisition" non-trading deficit from a company's loan relationships if it is a non-trading deficit from the company's loan relationships for an accounting period beginning before the change in ownership.

(3) Subsection (4) applies if, in the case of a pre-acquisition non-trading deficit from the transferred company's loan relationships, the non-trading deficit in column 1 of row 4 of the table in section 685(2) is apportioned in accordance with section 685(2) to the first notional accounting period.

(4) None of that deficit may, by virtue of section 463G (carry forward of unrelieved deficit), be set off against affected profits of —

    (a) the accounting period beginning immediately after the change in ownership, or

    (b) any subsequent accounting period.

676AI Restriction on relief for post-1 April 2017 non-trading loss on intangible fixed assets

(1) This section has effect for the purpose of restricting relief under section 753 of CTA 2009 (treatment of non-trading losses) in respect of a relevant non-trading loss on intangible fixed assets.

(2) An amount is a "relevant non-trading loss on intangible fixed assets" if and so far as —

    (a) it is by virtue of section 751 of CTA 2009 a non-trading loss on intangible fixed assets for a relevant pre-acquisition accounting period, or

    (b) it is made up of an amount falling within paragraph (a) which has been carried forward under section 753(3) of CTA 2009.

(3) "Relevant pre-acquisition accounting period" means an accounting period beginning —

    (a) before the change in ownership, and

    (b) on or after 1 April 2017.

(4) In the case of a relevant non-trading loss on intangible fixed assets, relief under section 753 of CTA 2009 against the total profits of the actual accounting period is available only in relation to each of the notional accounting periods considered separately.

(5) A relevant non-trading loss on intangible fixed assets may not be deducted as a result of section 753(3) of CTA 2009 (losses carried forward) from affected profits of an accounting period ending after the change in ownership.

676AJ Restriction on deduction of post-1 April 2017 expenses of management

(1) This section has effect for the purpose of restricting deductions for post-1 April 2017 relevant expenses of management of the transferred company.

(2) Any amounts which—
    (a) are, or are treated as, expenses of management referable to the actual accounting period, and
    (b) are apportioned to either of the two notional accounting periods in accordance with section 685,
are treated for the purposes of Chapter 2 of Part 16 of CTA 2009 (companies with investment business) as expenses of management referable to that notional accounting period.

(3) Any allowances which are apportioned to either of the notional accounting periods in accordance with section 685 are treated for the purposes of section 253 of CAA 2001 and section 1233 of CTA 2009 (companies with investment business: excess capital allowances) as falling to be made in that notional accounting period.

(4) In calculating the taxable total profits of an accounting period of the transferred company ending after the change in ownership—
    (a) relevant expenses of management, and
    (b) relevant allowances,
may not be deducted from affected profits of the accounting period.

(5) In this section "relevant expenses of management" means expenses of management which are first deductible under section 1219 of CTA 2009 for an accounting period beginning—
    (a) on or after 1 April 2017, and
    (b) before the change in ownership.

(6) In this section "relevant allowances" means allowances falling to be made for an accounting period beginning—
    (a) on or after 1 April 2017, and
    (b) before the change in ownership.

676AK Restriction on use of post-1 April 2017 UK property business losses

(1) This section has effect for the purpose of restricting relief under sections 62 and 63 for a relevant UK property business loss made by the transferred company.

(2) In this section "relevant UK property business loss" means a loss made in a UK property business in an accounting period beginning—

    (a)   on or after 1 April 2017, and

    (b)   before the change in ownership.

(3) In relation to a relevant UK property business loss, relief under section 62(3) is available only in relation to each of the notional accounting periods considered separately.

(4) A relevant UK property business loss may not be deducted as a result of section 62(5) or 63(3) from affected profits of an accounting period ending after the change in ownership.

676AL "Co-transferred company" and "related company"

(1) In this Chapter "co-transferred company" means any company which is related to the transferred company both immediately before and immediately after the change in ownership.

(2) For the purposes of this Chapter any two companies ("T") and ("C") are "related" to one another at any time when—

    (a)   the group condition is met in relation to T and C, or

    (b)   any of consortium conditions 1 to 4 is met in relation to T and C,

(whether on the assumption that T is the claimant company and C is the surrendering company or vice versa).

(3) In this Chapter—

    "consortium condition 1" is to be interpreted in accordance with section 188CF,

    "consortium condition 2" is to be interpreted in accordance with section 188CG,

    "consortium condition 3" is to be interpreted in accordance with section 188CH,

    "consortium condition 4" is to be interpreted in accordance with section 188CI,

    "the group condition" is to be interpreted in accordance with section 188CE."

76   After Chapter 2A insert—

"CHAPTER 2B

ASSET TRANSFERRED WITHIN GROUP: RESTRICTION OF RELIEF FOR POST-1 APRIL TRADE LOSSES

676BA Introduction to Chapter

(1) This section applies if there is a change in the ownership of a company ("the company") on or after 1 April 2017 and—

    (a)   conditions 1 and 2 are met, or

    (b)   condition 3 is met.

(2) Condition 1 is that after the change in ownership the company acquires an asset from another company in circumstances such that—

    (a) section 171 of TCGA 1992 (no gain/no loss transfer within group), or

    (b) section 775 of CTA 2009 (tax-neutral transfer within group),

applies to the acquisition.

(3) Condition 2 is that—

    (a) in a case within subsection (2)(a), a chargeable gain accrues to the company on a disposal of the asset within the period of 5 years beginning with the change in ownership, or

    (b) in a case within subsection (2)(b), there is a non-trading chargeable realisation gain on the realisation of the asset within that period.

(4) Condition 3 is that a chargeable gain on a disposal of an asset within the period of 5 years beginning immediately after the change in ownership (or an amount of such a gain) is treated as accruing to the company by virtue of an election under section 171A of TCGA 1992 (notional transfers within a group).

(Accordingly, references in this Chapter to the accrual of a relevant gain are to be read in the light of section 171B(2) and (3) of TCGA 1992.)

(5) For the purposes of subsection (3), an asset (P) acquired by the company as mentioned in subsection (2) is treated as the same as an asset (Q) owned at a later time by the company if the value of Q is derived in whole or in part from P.

(6) In particular, P is treated as the same as Q for those purposes if—

    (a) Q is a freehold,

    (b) P was a leasehold, and

    (c) the lessee has acquired the reversion.

(7) In this Chapter—

    "the change in ownership" means the change in ownership mentioned in subsection (1),

    "the company" has the same meaning as in this section,

    "non-trading chargeable realisation gain" means a chargeable realisation gain (within the meaning of Part 8 of CTA 2009 (intangible fixed assets)) which is a non-trading credit for the purposes of that Part (see section 746 of that Act),

    "realisation" has the meaning given by section 734 of CTA 2009, and

    "the relevant gain" means the gain (or amount of a gain) within subsection (3)(a) or (b) or (4).

676BB Notional split of accounting period in which change in ownership occurs

(1) This section applies for the purposes of this Chapter.

(2) The accounting period in which the change in ownership occurs ("the actual accounting period") is treated as two separate

accounting periods ("notional accounting periods"), the first ending with the change and the second consisting of the remainder of the period.

(3) Section 702 (apportionment of amounts) applies for the purposes of this Chapter as it applies for the purposes of Chapter 4.

(4) The amounts for the actual accounting period in column 1 of the table in section 702(2) are apportioned to the two notional accounting periods in accordance with section 702.

(5) In this Chapter, and in sections 702 and 703 as they apply by virtue of subsection (3), "the actual accounting period" and "notional accounting periods" have the same meaning as in this section.

676BC Disallowance of relief for trade losses

(1) This section has effect for the purposes of restricting relief under sections 45A, 45F and 303C of this Act and section 124B of FA 2012 for a loss made by the company in a trade before the change in ownership.

(2) But this section applies only if, in accordance with the relevant provisions and section 702, an amount is included in respect of chargeable gains or, as the case may be, non-trading chargeable realisation gains in the total profits of the accounting period in which the relevant gain accrues or arises.

(3) Relief under section 45A or 303C of this Act or section 124B of FA 2012 is available only in relation to each of the notional accounting periods considered separately.

(4) A loss made in an accounting period beginning before the change in ownership—

(a) may not be deducted as a result of section 45A or 303C of this Act or section 124B of FA 2012 from so much of the total profits of an accounting period ending after the change in ownership as represents the relevant gain;

(b) may not be deducted by virtue of paragraph (a) of the definition of "relevant profits" in section 45F(7) from so much of the total profits of an accounting period ending after the change in ownership as represents the relevant gain.

676BD Meaning of "the relevant provisions"

In this Chapter "the relevant provisions" means—

(a) section 8(1) of, and Schedule 7A to, TCGA 1992 (amounts included in respect of chargeable gains in total profits), or

(b) Chapter 6 of Part 8 of CTA 2009 (intangible fixed assets: how credits and debits are given effect).

676BE Meaning of "amount of profits which represents a relevant gain"

(1) In this Chapter, the amount of any profits which represents a relevant gain is found by comparing—

(a) the amount ("Y") of the relevant gain, with

      (b)   the amount ("Z") which is included in respect of chargeable gains or, as the case may be, non-trading chargeable realisation gains for the accounting period concerned.

(2)   If Y does not exceed Z, the amount of the profits which represents the relevant gain equals Y.

(3)   If Y exceeds Z, the amount of those profits equals Z."

77   After Chapter 2B insert—

"Chapter 2C

Disallowance of group relief for carried-forward losses: general provision

676CA Introduction to Chapter

(1)   This Chapter applies if on or after 1 April 2017 there is a change in the ownership of a company ("the transferred company").

(2)   In this Chapter—

      "the change in ownership" means the change in ownership mentioned in subsection (1);

      "the transferred company" has the meaning given by subsection (1).

676CB Restriction on surrender of carried-forward losses

(1)   Subsection (3) applies if a company ("the claimant company") would, (apart from this section), be eligible under Part 5A to make a relevant claim for group relief for carried-forward losses.

(2)   For the purposes of this section a claim for group relief for carried-forward losses is a "relevant claim" if it is—

      (a)   for an accounting period ending after the change in ownership, and

      (b)   in respect of an amount surrendered by the transferred company or a co-transferred company which is a relevant pre-acquisition loss.

(3)   The general rule is that the relief is not available.

(4)   The general rule is subject to the exceptions in sections 676CD and 676CE.

(5)   For the purposes of this section—

      (a)   the accounting period of the company mentioned in subsection (2)(b) in which the change in ownership occurs is treated as two separate accounting periods, the first ending with the change and the second consisting of the remainder of the period, and

      (b)   the profits or losses of the accounting period are apportioned to the two periods.

(6)   Any apportionment under subsection (5)(b) is to be made on a time basis according to the respective lengths of the two periods.

(7) But if that method of apportionment would work unjustly or unreasonably in any case, such other method is to be used as is just and reasonable.

676CC Cases where consortium condition 1 or 2 was previously met

(1) Subsection (4) applies in relation to a claim for group relief for carried-forward losses by the transferred company if conditions A and B are met.

(2) Condition A is that the claim is —
    (a) for an accounting period ending after the change in ownership, and
    (b) in respect of a relevant pre-acquisition loss.

(3) Condition B is that consortium condition 1 was met in relation to —
    (a) the transferred company (as the company owned by a consortium as mentioned in section 188CF(1)(b)), and
    (b) the surrendering company (as the company mentioned in section 188CF(1)(c)),
immediately before the change in ownership ("time T").

(4) The relief given under section 188CK in respect of the transferred company's total profits of the claim period may not exceed the relief that would be available on the assumption that the claim is based on consortium condition 1 and the ownership proportion for the purposes of that condition is equal to the lowest of the following proportions —
    (a) the proportion of the ordinary share capital of the transferred company that was beneficially owned by the surrendering company at time T,
    (b) the proportion of any profits available for distribution to equity holders of the transferred company to which the surrendering company was beneficially entitled at that time,
    (c) the proportion of any assets of the transferred company available for distribution to such equity holders on a winding up to which the surrendering company would be beneficially entitled (as determined at that time), and
    (d) the proportion of the voting power in the transferred company that was directly possessed by the surrendering company at that time.

(5) Subsection (8) applies in relation to a claim for group relief for carried-forward losses by the transferred company if conditions A and B are met.

(6) Condition A is that the claim is —
    (a) for an accounting period ending after the change in ownership, and
    (b) in respect of a a relevant pre-acquisition loss.

(7) Condition B is that consortium condition 2 was met in relation to —
    (a) the transferred company (as the company owned by a consortium as mentioned in section 188CG(1)(b)), and
    (b) the surrendering company (as the company mentioned in section 188CG(1)(c)),

266   *Finance (No. 2) Act 2017 (c. 32)*
Schedule 4 — Relief for carried-forward losses
Part 9 — Tax avoidance

immediately before the change in ownership ("time T").

(8) The relief given under section 188CK in respect of the transferred company's total profits of the claim period may not exceed the relief that would be available on the assumption that the claim is based on consortium condition 2 and the ownership proportion for the purposes of that condition is equal to the lowest of the following proportions—

 (a) the proportion of the ordinary share capital of the transferred company that was beneficially owned by the link company at time T,

 (b) the proportion of any profits available for distribution to equity holders of the transferred company to which the link company was beneficially entitled at that time,

 (c) the proportion of any assets of the transferred company available for distribution to such equity holders on a winding up to which the link company would be beneficially entitled (as determined at that time), and

 (d) the proportion of the voting power in the transferred company that was directly possessed by the link company at that time.

(9) For the purposes of this section—

 (a) the accounting period of the surrendering company mentioned in subsection (3)(b) or (7)(b) (as the case may be) in which the change in ownership occurs is treated as two separate accounting periods, the first ending with the change and the second consisting of the remainder of the period, and

 (b) the profits or losses of the accounting period are apportioned to the two periods.

(10) Any apportionment under subsection (9)(b) is to be made on a time basis according to the respective lengths of the two periods.

(11) In this section—

  "the link company" means the company which is the link company (see section 188CG(1)(d)) for the purposes of the meeting of consortium condition 2 as mentioned in subsection (7),

  "the claim period" and "the surrendering company" has the same meaning as in Part 5A (see section 188FD(1)).

(12) Chapter 6 of Part 5 (equity holders and profits or assets available for distribution) applies for the purposes of subsections (4)(b) and (c) and (8)(b) and (c).

676CD Cases where consortium condition 3 or 4 was previously met

(1) If the requirement in subsection (3) is met, section 676CB(3) does not prevent a company from making under section 188CC a claim for group relief for carried-forward losses falling within subsection (2).

(2) A claim falls within this subsection if it is—

 (a) for an accounting period ("the claim period") ending after the change in ownership, and

     (b)   in relation to an amount surrendered by the transferred company which is a relevant pre-acquisition loss and is attributable to an accounting period of that company specified in the claim ("the specified loss-making period").

(3)   The requirement is that consortium condition 3 or consortium condition 4 is met throughout a period which—

     (a)   begins before or during the specified loss-making period, and

     (b)   ends with or after the time when the change in ownership occurs.

(4)   For the purposes of a claim by virtue of this section, section 188CC(3) has effect as if requirement 3 were omitted.

676CE Exceptions to restrictions

(1)   Nothing in section 676CB(3) or 676CC affects the giving of group relief for carried-forward losses by the making of a deduction under section 188CK(1) from total profits of the claimant company which arise after the 5th anniversary of the end of the accounting period of the transferred company in which the change in ownership occurs.

(2)   Nothing in section 676CB(3) or 676CC affects the availability of relief under Part 5A if immediately before the change in ownership the group condition was met in relation to the transferred company and the claimant company.

But see also section 676CF.

(3)   If an accounting period of the claimant company begins before, and ends after, the anniversary mentioned in subsection (1), then for the purposes of that subsection—

     (a)   the accounting period is treated as two separate accounting periods, the first ending with that date and the second consisting of the remainder of the period, and

     (b)   the profits or losses of the accounting period are apportioned to the two periods.

(4)   Any apportionment under subsection (3)(b) is to be made on a time basis according to the respective lengths of the two periods.

(5)   But if that method of apportionment would work unjustly or unreasonably in any case, such other method is to be used as is just and reasonable.

(6)   In this section "the claimant company" has the same meaning as in Part 5A (see section 188FD(1)).

676CF Cases where Chapter 2, 2A or 3 also applies

(1)   This section applies if—

     (a)   Chapter 2 applies in relation to the change in ownership by virtue of condition A in section 673 being met,

     (b)   Chapter 2A applies in relation to the change in ownership, or

     (c)   Chapter 3 applies in relation to the change in ownership by virtue of condition B in section 677 being met.

(2)   This section also applies if—

(a) the condition in subsection (1)(a) would be met if in subsection (4A) of section 719 (meaning of "change in the ownership of a company") the reference to Chapter 2C included a reference to Chapter 2, or

(b) the condition in subsection (1)(c) would be met if in subsection (4A) of section 719 the reference to Chapter 2C included a reference to Chapter 3.

(3) Where the company in relation to which the major change mentioned in section 673(4), 676AA(3) or 677(3) has occurred would (apart from this section) be eligible under Part 5A to claim in respect of a relevant pre-acquisition loss group relief for carried-forward losses for an accounting period ending after the change in ownership, no deduction in respect of that loss may be made from affected profits under section 188CK.

See section 676CG for the meaning of "affected profits".

(4) For the purposes of this section—

(a) the accounting period in which the change in ownership occurs is treated as two separate accounting periods, the first ending with the change and the second consisting of the remainder of the period, and

(b) the profits or losses of the accounting period are apportioned to the two periods.

(5) Any apportionment under subsection (4)(b) is to be made on a time basis according to the respective lengths of the two deemed accounting periods.

(6) But if that method of apportionment would work unjustly or unreasonably in any case, such other method is to be used as is just and reasonable.

676CG "Affected profits"

(1) This section has effect for the purposes of section 676CF.

(2) Profits of an accounting period ending after the change in ownership are "affected profits" if and so far as—

(a) they arise before the 5th anniversary of the end of the accounting period of the transferred company in which the change in ownership occurs, and

(b) they can fairly and reasonably be attributed to activities, or other sources of income, as a result of which, or partly as a result of which, the major change mentioned in section 673(4), 676AA(3) or 677(3) (as the case may be) has occurred.

(3) If an accounting period of the company in relation to which the major change mentioned in section 673(4), 676AA(3) or 677(3) has occurred begins before, and ends after, the anniversary mentioned in subsection (2), then for the purposes of that subsection—

(a) the accounting period is treated as two separate accounting periods, the first ending with that date and the second consisting of the remainder of the period, and

(b) the profits or losses of the accounting period are apportioned to the two periods.

(4) Any apportionment under subsection (3)(b) is to be made on a time basis according to the respective lengths of the two deemed accounting periods.

(5) But if that method of apportionment would work unjustly or unreasonably in any case, such other method is to be used as is just and reasonable.

676CH "Relevant pre-acquisition loss"

(1) In this Chapter "relevant pre-acquisition loss" means —

    (a) a non-trading deficit from loan relationships for an accounting period beginning before the change in ownership carried forward to the surrender period under section 463G(6) of CTA 2009,

    (b) a loss on intangible fixed assets so far as it is made up of amounts carried forward to the surrender period under section 753(3) of CTA 2009 from one or more accounting periods beginning before the change in ownership,

    (c) expenses carried forward to the surrender period under section 1223 of CTA 2009 (carry forward of expenses of management of investment business) which were first deductible in an accounting period beginning before the change in ownership,

    (d) a loss made in an accounting period beginning before the change in ownership and carried forward to the surrender period under section 45A(3) (post- 1 April 2017 trade loss),

    (e) a loss made in an accounting period beginning before the change in ownership and carried forward to the surrender period under section 62(5)(b) or 63(3)(a) (loss made in UK property business),

    (f) a loss made in an accounting period beginning before the change in ownership and carried forward to the surrender period under section 303B(2) or 303D(3) (post-1 April non-decommissioning losses of ring fence trade),

    (g) a BLAGAB trade loss made in an accounting period beginning before the change in ownership and carried forward to the surrender period under section 124A(2) or 124C(3) of FA 2012.

(2) In this section "the surrender period" is to be interpreted in accordance with section 188BB(7).

676CI Interpretation of Chapter

(1) In this Chapter "co-transferred company" means any company which is related to the transferred company both immediately before and immediately after the change in ownership.

(2) For the purposes of this Chapter any two companies ("T") and ("C") are "related" to one another at any time when —

    (a) the group condition is met in relation to T and C, or

    (b) any of consortium conditions 1 to 4 is met in relation to T and C,

(whether on the assumption that T is the claimant company and C is the surrendering company or vice versa).

270   *Finance (No. 2) Act 2017 (c. 32)*
Schedule 4 — Relief for carried-forward losses
Part 9 — Tax avoidance

    (3)   In this Chapter—

        "consortium condition 1" is to be interpreted in accordance with section 188CF,

        "consortium condition 2" is to be interpreted in accordance with section 188CG,

        "consortium condition 3" is to be interpreted in accordance with section 188CH,

        "consortium condition 4" is to be interpreted in accordance with section 188CI,

        "the group condition" is to be interpreted in accordance with section 188CE."

78   After Chapter 2C insert—

"CHAPTER 2D

ASSET TRANSFERRED WITHIN GROUP: RESTRICTION OF GROUP RELIEF FOR CARRIED-FORWARD LOSSES

676DA Introduction to Chapter

    (1)   This section applies if—

        (a)   there is a change in the ownership of a company ("the company") on or after 1 April 2017, and

        (b)   the following are met—

               conditions 1 and 2, or

               condition 3.

    (2)   Condition 1 is that after the change in ownership the company acquires an asset from another company in circumstances such that—

        (a)   section 171 of TCGA 1992 (no gain/no loss transfer within a group), or

        (b)   section 775 of CTA 2009 (tax-neutral transfer within a group),

    applies to the acquisition.

    (3)   Condition 2 is that—

        (a)   in a case within subsection (2)(a), a chargeable gain accrues to the company on a disposal of the asset within the period of 5 years beginning with the change in ownership, or

        (b)   in a case within subsection (2)(b), there is a non-trading chargeable realisation gain on the realisation of the asset within that period.

    (4)   Condition 3 is that a chargeable gain on a disposal of an asset within the period of 5 years beginning immediately after the change in ownership (or an amount of such a gain) is treated as accruing to the company by virtue of an election under section 171A of TCGA 1992 (notional transfers within a group).

        (Accordingly, references in this Chapter to the accrual of a relevant gain are to be read in the light of section 171B(2) and (3) of TCGA 1992.)

    (5)   For the purposes of subsection (3), an asset (P) acquired by the company as mentioned in subsection (2) is treated as the same as an

asset (Q) owned at a later time by the company if the value of Q is derived in whole or in part from P.

(6) In particular, P is treated as the same as Q for those purposes if—
  (a) Q is a freehold,
  (b) P was a leasehold, and
  (c) the lessee has acquired the reversion.

(7) In this Chapter

"the change in ownership" means the change in ownership mentioned in subsection (1),

"the company" has the same meaning as in this section,

"non-trading chargeable realisation gain" means a chargeable realisation gain (within the meaning of Part 8 of CTA 2009 (intangible fixed assets)) which is a non-trading credit for the purposes of that Part (see section 746 of that Act),

"realisation" has the meaning given by section 734 of CTA 2009, and

"the relevant gain" means the gain (or amount of a gain) within subsection (3)(a) or (b) or (4).

676DB Notional split of accounting period in which change in ownership occurs

(1) This section applies for the purposes of this Chapter.

(2) The accounting period in which the change in ownership occurs ("the actual accounting period") is treated as two separate accounting periods ("notional accounting periods"), the first ending with the change and the second consisting of the remainder of the period.

(3) Section 702 (apportionment of amounts) applies for the purposes of this Chapter as it applies for the purposes of Chapter 4.

(4) The amounts for the actual accounting period in column 1 of the table in section 702(2) are apportioned to the two notional accounting periods in accordance with section 702.

(5) In this Chapter, and in sections 702 and 703 as they apply by virtue of subsection (3), "the actual accounting period" and "notional accounting periods" have the same meaning as in this section.

676DC Disallowance of group relief for carried-forward losses

(1) This section has effect for the purposes of restricting relief under Chapter 3 of Part 5A (group relief for carried-forward losses).

(2) But this section applies only if, in accordance with the relevant provisions and section 702, an amount is included in respect of chargeable gains or, as the case may be, non-trading chargeable realisation gains in the total profits of the accounting period in which the relevant gain accrues or arises.

(3) In calculating the company's taxable total profits of the accounting period in which the relevant gain accrues or arises, a relevant pre-acquisition loss may not be deducted, as a result of section 188CK (group relief for carried-forward losses: deductions from total

profits) from so much of the total profits of the accounting period as represents the relevant gain.

(4) "Relevant pre-acquisition loss" means —

    (a) a non-trading deficit from loan relationships for an accounting period beginning before the change in ownership carried forward to the surrender period under section 463G(6) of CTA 2009,

    (b) a loss on intangible fixed assets so far as it is made up of amounts carried forward to the surrender period under section 753(3) of CTA 2009 from one or more accounting periods beginning before the change in ownership,

    (c) expenses carried forward to the surrender period under section 1223 of CTA 2009 (carrying forward expenses of management and other amounts) which were first deductible in an accounting period beginning before the change in ownership,

    (d) a loss made in an accounting period beginning before the change in ownership and carried forward to the surrender period under section 45A(3) (post- 1 April 2017 trade loss);

    (e) a loss made in an accounting period beginning before the change in ownership and carried forward to the surrender period under section 62(5)(b) or 63(3)(a) (loss made in UK property business),

    (f) a loss made in an accounting period beginning before the change in ownership and carried forward to the surrender period under section 303B(2) or 303D(3) (post-1 April non-decommissioning losses of ring fence trade),

    (g) a BLAGAB trade loss made in an accounting period beginning before the change in ownership and carried forward to the surrender period under section 124A(2) or 124C(3) of FA 2012.

(5) In this section "the surrender period" is to be interpreted in accordance with section 188BB(7).

676DD Meaning of "the relevant provisions"

In this Chapter "the relevant provisions" means —

    (a) section 8(1) of, and Schedule 7A to, TCGA 1992 (amounts included in respect of chargeable gains in total profits), or

    (b) Chapter 6 of Part 8 of CTA 2009 (intangible fixed assets: how credits and debits are given effect).

676DE Meaning of "amount of profits which represents a relevant gain"

(1) In this Chapter, the amount of any profits which represents a relevant gain is found by comparing —

    (a) the amount ("Y") of the relevant gain, with

    (b) the amount ("Z") which is included in respect of chargeable gains or, as the case may be, non-trading chargeable realisation gains for the accounting period concerned.

(2) If Y does not exceed Z, the amount of the profits which represents the relevant gain equals Y.

(3)   If Y exceeds Z, the amount of those profits equals Z."

79   After Chapter 2D insert—

"CHAPTER 2E

POST-1 APRIL 2017 TRADE LOSSES: CASES INVOLVING THE TRANSFER OF A TRADE

676EA Introduction to Chapter

(1)   This Chapter applies if on or after 1 April 2017 there is a change in the ownership of a company ("the transferred company").

(2)   In this Chapter—
         "the change in ownership" means the change in ownership mentioned in subsection (1);
         "the transferred company" has the meaning given by subsection (1).

676EB Restriction on use of trade losses carried-forward on transfer of trade

(1)   Subsection (2) applies if—
         (a)   the transferred company transfers a trade to another company ("the successor company") within the period of 8 years beginning 3 years before the change in ownership,
         (b)   the transfer is a transfer to which Chapter 1 of Part 22 applies, and
         (c)   the transferred company and the successor company are not related to one another both immediately before the change in ownership and at the time of the transfer.

(2)   A loss made by the transferred company in the transferred trade in an accounting period beginning before the change in ownership may not be deducted under section 45A or 303C from the relevant profits of an accounting period of the successor company ending after the change in ownership.

(3)   Profits of an accounting period of the successor company ending after the change in ownership are "relevant profits" if and so far as—
         (a)   they arise before the 5th anniversary of the end of the accounting period of the transferred company in which the change in ownership occurs, and
         (b)   they cannot fairly and reasonably be attributed to the carrying on by the successor company of the transferred trade.

(4)   If an accounting period of the transferred company begins before, and ends after the change in ownership, then for the purposes of subsection (2)—
         (a)   the accounting period is treated as two separate accounting period, the first ending with the change and the second consisting on the remainder of the period, and
         (b)   a loss made in the trade in the accounting period is apportioned to the two periods.

(5) If an accounting period of the successor company begins before, and ends after, the anniversary mentioned in subsection (3), then for the purposes of that subsection —

    (a) the accounting period is treated as two separate accounting periods, the first ending with that date and the second consisting of the remainder of the period, and

    (b) the profits of the accounting period are apportioned to the two periods.

(6) Any apportionment under subsection (4)(b) or (5)(b) is to be made on a time basis according to the respective lengths of the two deemed accounting periods.

(7) But if that method of apportionment would work unjustly or unreasonably in any case, such other method is to be used as is just and reasonable.

676EC Restriction on surrender of trade losses carried forward on transfer of trade

(1) This section applies if —

    (a) the transferred company or a co-transferred company transfers a trade to another company ("the successor company") within the period of 8 years beginning 3 years before the change in ownership,

    (b) the transfer is a transfer to which Chapter 1 of Part 22 applies, and

    (c) another company ("the claimant company") would, apart from this section, be eligible under Part 5A to make a relevant claim for group relief for carried-forward losses.

(2) For the purposes of this section a claim for group relief for carried forward-losses is a relevant claim if it is —

    (a) for an accounting period ending after the change in ownership, and

    (b) in respect of an amount surrendered by the successor company which is an amount of a loss —

        (i) made in the trade by the transferred company or the co-transferred company in an accounting period beginning before the change in ownership, and

        (ii) carried forward to the surrender period of the successor company under section 45A(3), 303B(2) or 303D(3).

(3) The general rule is that the relief is not available.

(4) Subsection (3) does not affect the giving of group relief for carried-forward losses by the making of a deduction under section 188CK(1) from the total profits of the claimant company which arise after the 5th anniversary of the end of the accounting period of the transferred company in which the change in ownership occurs.

(5) Subsection (3) does not affect the availability of relief under Part 5A if immediately before the change in ownership the group condition was met in relation to the claimant company and the transferred company.

(6) If an accounting period of the transferred company or co-transferred company begins before, and ends after the change in ownership, then for the purposes of subsection (2)(b) —

  (a) the accounting period is treated as two separate accounting period, the first ending with the change and the second consisting on the remainder of the period, and

  (b) a loss made in the trade in the accounting period is apportioned to the two periods.

(7) If an accounting period of the claimant company begins before, and ends after, the anniversary mentioned in subsection (4), then for the purposes of that subsection —

  (a) the accounting period is treated as two separate accounting period, the first ending with that date and the second consisting of the remainder of the period, and

  (b) the profits of the accounting period are apportioned to the two periods.

(8) Any apportionment under subsection (6)(b) or (7)(b) is to be made on a time basis according to the respective lengths of the two deemed accounting periods.

(9) But if that method of apportionment would work unjustly or unreasonably in any case, such other method is to be used as is just and reasonable.

676ED Indirect transfers of a trade

(1) Subsections (2) and (3) apply if a trade transferred by the transferred company or a co-transferred company is transferred on a subsequent occasion to another company.

(2) The transferred company or (as the case may be) the co-transferred company is to be treated for the purposes of this Chapter —

  (a) as having transferred the trade to that other company, and

  (b) as having done so at the time it was actually transferred to that other company.

(3) The deemed transfer is to be treated for the purposes of this Chapter as a transfer to which Chapter 1 of Part 22 applies if the actual transfer to the other company was a transfer to which that Chapter applies.

(4) Subsections (5) and (6) apply if —

  (a) a trade ("the original trade") is transferred by the transferred company or a co-transferred company,

  (b) the activities of the original trade are included in the activities of another trade ("the composite trade"), and

  (c) the composite trade is transferred to another company.

(5) The transferred company or (as the case may be) the co-transferred company is to be treated for the purposes of this Chapter —

  (a) as having transferred the original trade to that other company, and

  (b) as having done so at the time the composite trade was actually transferred to that other company.

276   *Finance (No. 2) Act 2017 (c. 32)*
Schedule 4 – Relief for carried-forward losses
Part 9 – Tax avoidance

    (6)   The deemed transfer is to be treated for the purposes of this Chapter as a transfer to which Chapter 1 of Part 22 applies if the transfer of the composite trade to the other company was a transfer to which that Chapter applies.

676EE Interpretation of Chapter

    (1)   Section 940B (meaning of "transfer of trade" and related expressions) applies for the purposes of this Chapter as it applies for the purposes of Chapter 1 of Part 22.

    (2)   In this Chapter "co-transferred company" means any company which is related to the transferred company both immediately before and immediately after the change in ownership.

    (3)   For the purposes of this Chapter any two companies ("T") and ("C") are "related" to one another at any time when —

        (a)   the group condition is met in relation to T and C, or

        (b)   any of consortium conditions 1 to 4 is met in relation to T and C,

    (whether on the assumption that T is the claimant company and C is the surrendering company or vice versa).

    (4)   In this Chapter —

        "consortium condition 1" is to be interpreted in accordance with section 188CF,

        "consortium condition 2" is to be interpreted in accordance with section 188CG,

        "consortium condition 3" is to be interpreted in accordance with section 188CH,

        "consortium condition 4" is to be interpreted in accordance with section 188CI,

        "the group condition" is to be interpreted in accordance with section 188CE.""

80   (1)   Section 677 (introduction to Chapter 3) is amended as follows.

    (2)   In subsection (3), for "6" substitute "8".

    (3)   In subsection (5), for "6" substitute "8".

    (4)   The amendments made by this paragraph do not have effect unless both the change in ownership referred in section 677(1) and the major change in the nature or conduct of a business referred to in section 677(3) occur on or after 1 April 2017.

81   (1)   Section 681 (restriction on relief for non-trading loss on intangible fixed assets) is amended as follows.

    (2)   In subsection (3)(b), for "debit of" substitute "loss on intangible fixed assets for".

82   (1)   Section 685 (apportionment of amounts) is amended as follows.

    (2)   In subsection (2), in column 1 of row 4 in the table, for the words from "of CTA 2009" to the end substitute ", 463G(6) or 463H(4) of CTA 2009."

(3) In subsection (2), in column 1 of row 6 of the table, for "debit of" substitute "loss on intangible fixed assets for".

(4) Where the change in ownership referred to in section 677(1) occurs before 13 July 2017 this paragraph has effect as if sub-paragraph (2) provided as follows—

"(2) In subsection (2), in column 1 of row 4 in the table, for the words from "of CTA 2009" to the end substitute "or 463G(6) of CTA 2009.""

83 (1) In section 690 (meaning of "significant increase in the amount of a company's capital: amount B), in subsection (3) for "3" substitute "5".

(2) The amendment made by this paragraph does not have effect unless the change in ownership referred in section 677(1) occurs on or after 1 April 2017.

84 (1) Section 692 (introduction to Chapter 4) is amended as follows.

(2) In subsection (1), for paragraph (b) substitute—
    "(b)   the following are met—
        condition 1, and
        conditions 2 and 3 or condition 4.

(3) In subsection (4)(a), for "3" substitute "5".

(4) After subsection (4) insert—

    "(4A)   Condition 4 is that a chargeable gain on a disposal of an asset within the period of 5 years beginning immediately after the change in ownership (or an amount of such a gain) is treated as accruing to the company by virtue of an election under section 171A of TCGA 1992 (election to reallocate gain or loss to another member of the group).
    (Accordingly, references in this Chapter to the accrual of a relevant gain are to be read in the light of section 171B(2) and (3) of TCGA 1992.)"

(5) In subsection (7), in the definition of "the relevant gain", for "within subsection (4)(a) or (b)" substitute "(or amount of a gain) within subsection (4)(a) or (b) or (4A)".

(6) The amendments made by this paragraph do not have effect unless the change in ownership referred to in section 692(1) occurs on or after 1 April 2017.

85 In section 696 (restriction of debits to be brought into account), in subsection (4)(b), after "461" insert "or 463B(1)(a)".

86 (1) Section 702 (apportionment of amounts) is amended as follows.

(2) In subsection (2), in column 1 of row 5 of the table, for the words from "of CTA 2009" to the end substitute ", 463G(6) or 463H(4) of CTA 2009."

(3) In subsection (2), in column 1 of row 7 of the table, for "debit of" substitute "loss on intangible fixed assets for".

(4) Where the change in ownership referred to in section 692(1) occurs before 13 July 2017 this paragraph has effect as if sub-paragraph (2) provided as

follows —

"(2)　In subsection (2), in column 1 of row 5 in the table, for the words from "of CTA 2009" to the end substitute "or 463G(6) of CTA 2009.""

87　(1)　Section 704 (company carrying on UK property business) is amended as follows.

(2)　In subsection (2), for "3" substitute "5".

(3)　In subsection (10), in the words after paragraph (b), for "3" substitute "5".

(4)　The amendments made this paragraph do not have effect unless both the change in ownership referred in section 704(1) and the major change in the nature or conduct of a trade or business referred to in section 704(2) occur on or after 1 April 2017.

88　(1)　Section 705 (company carrying on overseas property business) is amended as follows.

(2)　In subsection (2), for "3" substitute "5".

(3)　In subsection (9), in the words after paragraph (b), for "3" substitute "5".

(4)　The amendments made by this paragraph do not have effect unless both the change in ownership referred in section 705(1) and the major change in the nature or conduct of a trade or business referred to in section 705(2) occur on or after 1 April 2017.

89　In section 719 (meaning of "change of ownership of a company"), after subsection (4) insert —

"(4A)　For the purposes of Chapters 2A to 2D there is also a change in the ownership of a company ("C") if, as a result of the acquisition by a person of a holding of the ordinary share capital of the company, the group condition (as defined in section 188CE) is met in relation to C and another company ("A") (which was not a member of the same group of companies as C before the acquisition).

In this subsection the reference to membership of a group of companies is to be interpreted in accordance with section 188FB."

90　In section 721 (when things other than ordinary share capital may be taken into account), in subsection (4), in the words before paragraph (a), after "2," insert "2A, 2B, 2C, 2D,".

91　In section 727 (extended time limit for assessment) for "3" substitute "5".

Deduction buying

92　(1)　Section 730C of CTA 2010 is amended as follows.

(2)　In subsection (2) —
　　(a)　omit "or" at the end of paragraph (a),
　　(b)　after paragraph (b) insert ", or
　　　　　　(c)　Chapter 3 of Part 5A (group relief for carried-forward losses).""

(3) In subsection (3), for "A deductible amount that meets conditions A and B" substitute "In the case of a relevant claim within subsection (2)(a) or (b), a deductible amount that meets conditions A and B (a "restricted deductible amount")".

(4) After subsection (3) insert—

"(3A) A relevant claim within subsection (2)(c) may not be made in respect of a loss or other amount which has been carried forward under any provision mentioned in paragraphs (a) to (e) of section 188BB(1), so far as that amount is made up of an amount which was (in a previous accounting period) a restricted deductible amount."

(5) In subsection (4)—

(a) for "subsection (3) does" substitute "subsections (3) and (3A) do", and

(b) for "the claim" substitute "or as a result of, the claim concerned".

(6) After subsection (7) insert—

"(7A) For the purposes of determining how much of an amount carried forward as mentioned in subsection (3A) is made up of an amount which was (in a previous accounting period) a restricted deductible amount, assume that in previous accounting periods amounts have been brought into account as deductions (see section 730B(2)) in the order that results in the greatest amount being excluded by subsection (3A)."

(7) The amendments made by this paragraph do not have effect if the relevant day (as defined in section 730B(1) of CTA 2010) is before 1 April 2017.

PART 10

NORTHERN IRELAND TRADING LOSSES ETC

93   Part 8B of CTA 2010 (trading profits taxable at the Northern Ireland rate) is amended as follows.

94   In the italic heading before section 357JB for "section 37" substitute "Chapter 2 of Part 4".

95   For sections 357JB to 357JE substitute—

"357JB Availability of relief

(1) The references in section 37 and sections 45A to 45F (relief for trade losses) to a loss are, where a company carrying on a trade in an accounting period has Northern Ireland losses of the trade or mainstream losses of the trade, references to those Northern Ireland losses or mainstream losses.

(2) If a company has a Northern Ireland loss and a mainstream loss in the same accounting period, sections 37 and 45A to 45F have effect in relation to each of those losses separately.

(3) If by reason of this section a company is entitled under section 37(2), 45A(5), 45B(5) or 45F(2) to make a claim in relation to a Northern Ireland loss (or an amount of such a loss) and a claim in relation to a

280

Finance (No. 2) Act 2017 (c. 32)
Schedule 4 — Relief for carried-forward losses
Part 10 — Northern Ireland trading losses etc

mainstream loss (or an amount of such a loss), the company may make—

    (a)   one of those claims only, or

    (b)   both of those claims in either order.

(4)   Where—

    (a)   relief is given under section 37, 45A, 45B or 45F for a Northern Ireland loss (or an amount of such a loss), and

    (b)   the profits against which the relief is given includes some profits of the trade that are Northern Ireland profits and some that are not,

the relief is given first, so far as possible, against the Northern Ireland profits.

(5)   Where—

    (a)   relief is given under section 37, 45, 45A, 45B or 45F for a loss (or an amount of a loss) that is not a Northern Ireland loss, and

    (b)   the profits against which the relief is given include some profits of the trade that are Northern Ireland profits and some that are not,

the relief is given first, so far as possible, against the profits that are not Northern Ireland profits.

357JC Restriction on deductions

(1)   Subsection (2) applies where—

    (a)   relief is given under section 37 for a Northern Ireland loss ("the loss"),

    (b)   the profits against which the relief is given include profits that are not Northern Ireland profits, and

    (c)   at any time during the accounting period for which the relief is given ("the profit period") the Northern Ireland rate is lower than the main rate.

(2)   The reference in section 37(4) to "the amount of the loss" is to the restricted deduction for the loss, as determined under section 357JJ (restricted deduction where Northern Ireland rate lower than main rate).

(3)   Subsection (4) applies where—

    (a)   relief is given under section 45A, 45B or 45F for an amount of a Northern Ireland loss ("the loss"),

    (b)   the profits against which the relief is given include profits that are not Northern Ireland profits, and

    (c)   at any time during the accounting period for which the relief is given ("the profit period"), the Northern Ireland rate is lower than the main rate.

(4)   The reference in section 45A(6), 45B(4) or (as the case may be) 45F(5) to "the unrelieved amount" is to so much of that amount as is equal to the restricted deduction for the loss, as determined under section 357JJ."

Finance (No. 2) Act 2017 (c. 32)
Schedule 4 — Relief for carried-forward losses
Part 10 — Northern Ireland trading losses etc

281

96   After section 357JH insert—

"*Loss relief in relation to Northern Ireland profits and losses: Part 5A*

357JHA Availability of relief

(1)   The reference in section 188BB(1)(a) (group relief for carried-forward losses: surrendering of carried-forward losses and other amounts) to a loss carried forward to an accounting period of a company under section 45A(4) is, where a company has Northern Ireland losses or mainstream losses carried forward to an accounting period under that section, a reference to those Northern Ireland losses or mainstream losses.

(2)   Where—
   (a)   a company makes a claim for group relief for carried-forward losses under Part 5A in relation to a surrenderable amount that is a Northern Ireland loss, and
   (b)   the profits against which the relief is claimed include some profits that are Northern Ireland profits and some that are not,
   the relief in relation to that surrenderable amount is given first, so far as possible, against the Northern Ireland profits.

(3)   Where—
   (a)   a company makes a claim for group relief for carried-forward losses under Part 5A in relation to a surrenderable amount that is not a Northern Ireland loss, and
   (b)   the profits against which the relief is claimed include some profits that are Northern Ireland profits and some that are not,
   the relief in relation to that surrenderable amount is given first, so far as possible, against the profits that are not Northern Ireland profits.

357JHB Restriction on deductions

(1)   Subsection (2) applies where—
   (a)   a company makes a claim for group relief for carried-forward losses under Part 5A in relation to a surrenderable amount that is a Northern Ireland loss ("the loss"),
   (b)   the profits against which the relief is claimed include profits that are not Northern Ireland profits, and
   (c)   at any time during the accounting period for which the relief is claimed ("the profit period"), the Northern Ireland rate is lower than the main rate.

(2)   In section 188CK(2) and (4) (amount of deduction)—
   (a)   the reference in paragraph (a) to "an amount equal to" the surrendering company's surrenderable amounts is, so far as those surrenderable amounts comprise the loss, to the restricted deduction for the loss, as determined under section 357JJ (restricted deduction where Northern Ireland rate lower than main rate);
   (b)   the reference in paragraph (b) to "an amount equal to" part of the surrendering company's surrenderable amounts is, so far

282

Finance (No. 2) Act 2017 (c. 32)
Schedule 4 – Relief for carried-forward losses
Part 10 – Northern Ireland trading losses etc

as that part comprises the loss, to the restricted deduction for the loss, as determined under section 357JJ.

357JHC Modifications of Chapter 4 of Part 5A

(1) Chapter 4 of Part 5A (limitations on group relief for carried-forward losses: claims under section 188CB) has effect, in relation to a claim under section 188CB in relation to surrenderable amounts that include a Northern Ireland loss, subject to the following provisions of this section.

(2) In section 188DB(1) (limitation on amount of group relief for carried-forward losses applying to all claims under section 188CB) –

    (a) paragraphs (a) and (b) are treated as imposing separate limits;

    (b) the limit in paragraph (a) on the amount of group relief for carried-forward losses to be given on a claim under section 188CB has effect as a limit on the amount of losses and other surrenderable amounts in relation to which relief is to be given on the claim;

    (c) the limit in paragraph (b) on the amount of group relief for carried-forward losses to be given on a claim under section 188CB has effect as a limit on the amount of the deduction to be made as a result of the claim.

(3) In section 188DC(6)(b) (unused part of the surrenderable amounts), and in section 188DF(2) so far as it applies in relation to section 188DC, references to the amount of group relief for carried-forward losses given on a claim are to the amount of losses and other surrenderable amounts in relation to which relief is given on the claim.

(4) In section 188DE(4)(b) (previously claimed group relief for carried-forward losses), and in section 188DF(2) so far as it applies in relation to section 188DE, references to the amount of group relief for carried-forward losses given on a claim are to the amount of the deduction made as a result of the claim.

(5) In section 188DH (limitation on group relief for carried-forward losses where claim under section 188CB is based on consortium condition 1), the limit in subsection (2) on the amount of group relief for carried-forward losses to be given on a claim has effect as a limit on the amount of the deduction to be made as a result of the claim.

(6) In section 188DL (limitation on group relief for carried-forward losses where claim under section 188CB is made by member of a group of companies) –

    (a) the reference in subsection (3)(a) to the maximum amount of group relief for carried-forward losses that could be claimed by the claimant company has effect as a reference to the maximum amount of the deduction that could be made as a result of claims by the claimant company, and

    (b) the reference in subsection (3)(b) to the maximum amount of group relief under Part 5 that could be claimed by the claimant company has effect as a reference to the maximum amount of the deduction that could be made as a result of claims by the claimant company.

Finance (No. 2) Act 2017 (c. 32)
Schedule 4 — Relief for carried-forward losses
Part 10 — Northern Ireland trading losses etc

283

357JHD Modifications of Chapter 5 of Part 5A

(1) Chapter 5 of Part 5A (limitations on group relief for carried-forward losses: claims under section 188CC) has effect, in relation to a claim under section 188CC in relation to surrenderable amounts that include a Northern Ireland loss, subject to the following provisions of this section.

(2) In section 188EB(1) (limitation on amount of group relief for carried-forward losses applying to all claims under section 188CC)—

  (a) paragraphs (a), (b) and (c) are treated as imposing separate limits;

  (b) the limit in paragraph (a) on the amount of group relief for carried-forward losses to be given on a claim under section 188CC has effect as a limit on the amount of losses and other surrenderable amounts in relation to which relief is to be given on the claim;

  (c) the limits in paragraphs (b) and (c) on the amount of group relief for carried-forward losses to be given on a claim under section 188CC have effect as limits on the amount of the deduction to be made as a result of the claim.

(3) In section 188EC(6) and (8)(b) (unused part of the surrenderable amounts attributable to the specified-loss making period), and in section 188EG(2) so far as it applies in relation to section 188EC, references to the amount of group relief for carried-forward losses given on a claim are to the amount of losses and other surrenderable amounts in relation to which relief is given on the claim.

(4) In section 188EE(4)(b) (previously claimed group relief for carried-forward losses), and in section 188EG(2) so far as it applies in relation to section 188EE, references to the amount of group relief for carried-forward losses given on a claim are to the amount of the deduction made as a result of the claim.

(5) In section 188EI (condition 4: companies in link company's group), the limit in subsections (2) and (3) on the amount of group relief for carried-forward losses to be given on a claim has effect as a limit on the amount of the deduction to be made as a result on the claim.

(6) In section 188EK (condition 3 or 4: surrendering company in group of companies), the reference in subsection (4) to the maximum amount of group relief for carried-forward losses that could be given has effect as a reference to the maximum amount of losses and other surrenderable amounts in relation to which relief could be given."

97 In section 357JJ (restricted deduction: Northern Ireland rate lower than main rate)—

  (a) in subsection (1) for "357JC(2), 357JE(2) or 357JG(2)" substitute "357JC(2) or (4), 357JG(2) or 357JHB(2)", and

  (b) in subsection (6) for "section 357JC(1), 357JE(1) or 357JG(1)" substitute "357JC(1) or (3), 357JG(1) or 357JHB(1)".

98 In section 357RF (losses of film trade: restriction on use of losses while film is in production) in subsection (2) for "subsection (2)" substitute "subsections (2) and (3)".

284 Finance (No. 2) Act 2017 (c. 32)
Schedule 4 — Relief for carried-forward losses
Part 10 — Northern Ireland trading losses etc

99   In section 357RG (losses of film trade: use of losses in later periods) in subsection (3) after "subsections (5)" insert ", (5A)".

100   In section 357SF (losses of television programme trade: restriction on use of losses while programme in production) in subsection (2) for "subsection (2)" substitute "subsections (2) and (3)".

101   In section 357SG (losses of television programme trade: use of losses in later periods) in subsection (3) after "subsections (5)" insert ", (5A)".

102   In section 357TF (losses of video game trade: restriction on use of losses while video game in development) in subsection (2) for "subsection (2)" substitute "subsections (2) and (3)".

103   In section 357TG (losses of video game trade: use of losses in later periods) in subsection (3) after "subsections (5)" insert ", (5A)".

104   In section 357UF (losses of theatrical trade: restriction on use of losses before completion period) in subsection (2) for "subsection (2)" substitute "subsections (2) and (3)".

105   In section 357UO (losses of orchestral trade: restriction on use of losses before completion period) in subsection (2) for "subsection (2)" substitute "subsections (2) and (3)".

PART 11

MINOR AND CONSEQUENTIAL AMENDMENTS

ICTA

106   (1)   Section 826 of ICTA (interest on tax overpaid) is amended as follows.

      (2)   After subsection (7A) insert—

      "(7AA)   In any case where—
                (a)   a company ceases to carry on a trade in an accounting period ("the terminal period"),
                (b)   as a result of a claim under section 45F of CTA 2010, the whole or any part of a loss made in the trade is relieved for the purposes of corporation tax against profits (of whatever description) of an earlier accounting period ("the earlier period") which does not fall wholly within the period of 12 months immediately preceding the terminal period, and
                (c)   a repayment falls to be made of corporation tax paid for the earlier period or of income tax in respect of a payment received by the company in that accounting period,
                then, in determining the amount of interest (if any) payable under this section on the repayment referred to in paragraph (c) above, no account shall be taken of so much of the amount of that repayment as falls to be made as a result of the claim under section 45F, except so far as concerns interest for any time after the date on which any corporation tax for the terminal period became (or, as the case may be, would have become) due and payable, as mentioned in subsection (7D) below."

Finance (No. 2) Act 2017 (c. 32)
Schedule 4 — Relief for carried-forward losses
Part 11 — Minor and consequential amendments

285

(3) In subsection (7D) (meaning of references to the date on which corporation tax became payable) after "(7A)," insert "(7AA),".

(4) In subsection (7E) (power conferred by section 59E of TMA 1970 not to include power to change the meaning of references to the date on which corporation tax became payable) after "(7A)," insert "(7AA)".

FA 1998

107   Schedule 18 to FA 1998 (company tax returns, assessments and related matters) is amended in accordance with paragraphs 108 to 122.

108   In paragraph 61(1)(c) (consequential claims etc arising out of certain Revenue amendments or assessments), in the words in brackets, after "relief" insert "or group relief for carried-forward losses".

109   In the heading of Part 8 (claims for group relief) at the end insert "and group relief for carried-forward losses".

110   For paragraph 66 (introduction to Part 8) substitute —

"66 (1) This Part of this Schedule applies to —
    (a) claims for group relief under Part 5 of the Corporation Tax Act 2010, and
    (b) claims for group relief for carried-forward losses under Part 5A of that Act.

    (2) In this Part of this Schedule (except where otherwise indicated) —
    (a) references to "relief" are to either of those forms of relief, and
    (b) references to "a claim" are to a claim for either of those forms of relief."

111   In paragraph 67 (claim to be included in company tax return) omit "for group relief".

112 (1) Paragraph 68 (content of claims) is amended as follows.

    (2) In sub-paragraph (1), in the words before paragraph (a), omit "for group relief".

    (3) After sub-paragraph (4) insert —

    "(5) A claim for group relief for carried-forward losses made under section 188CB of the Corporation Tax Act 2010 must also state whether or not there is a company mentioned in sub-paragraph (6) that was not resident in the United Kingdom in either or both of the following periods —
    (a) the accounting period of the surrendering company to which the claim relates,
    (b) the corresponding accounting period of the claimant company.

    (6) Those companies are the claimant company, the surrendering company and any other company by reference to which —
    (a) the claimant company and the surrendering company are members of the same group,

286

Finance (No. 2) Act 2017 (c. 32)
Schedule 4 — Relief for carried-forward losses
Part 11 — Minor and consequential amendments

> > (b) consortium condition 1 in section 188CF or consortium condition 2 in section 188CG of the Corporation Tax Act 2010 is satisfied in the case of the claimant company and the surrendering company.

> (7) A claim for group relief for carried forward-losses made under section 188CC of the Corporation Tax Act 2010 must also state whether or not there is a company mentioned in sub-paragraph (8) that was not resident in the United Kingdom in any or all of the following periods—
> > (a) the specified loss-making period of the surrendering company,
> > (b) the accounting period of the surrendering company to which the surrender relates,
> > (c) the accounting period of the claimant company that corresponds with the period mentioned in paragraph (b).

> (8) Those companies are the claimant company, the surrendering company and any other company by reference to which consortium condition 3 in section 188CH or consortium condition 4 in section 188CI is satisfied in the case of the claimant company and the surrendering company."

113 (1) Paragraph 69 (claims for more or less than the amount available for surrender) is amended as follows.

> (2) In subsection (1) omit "for group relief".

> (3) In subsection (3), in the first step, after "Part 5" insert "or (as the case may be) Part 5A".

114 (1) Paragraph 70 (consent to surrender) is amended as follows.

> (2) For sub-paragraph (1) substitute—

> > "(1) In accordance with Requirement 1 in section 130(2), 135(2), 188CB(3) or (as the case may be) 188CC(3) of the Corporation Tax Act 2010, a claim requires the consent of the surrendering company."

> (3) In sub-paragraph (4) omit "for group relief".

> (4) In sub-paragraph (6)—
> > (a) after "means" insert "—
> > > (a) ",
> > (b) at the end insert— ",
> > > (b) a claim for group relief for carried-forward losses under section 188CB of that Act based on consortium condition 1 or 2 (see Requirement 3 in that section), and
> > > (c) a claim for group relief for carried-forward losses under section 188CC of that Act based on consortium condition 3 or 4 (see Requirement 3 in that section).

Finance (No. 2) Act 2017 (c. 32)
Schedule 4 — Relief for carried-forward losses
Part 11 — Minor and consequential amendments

287

115   In Paragraph 71 (notice of consent) after sub-paragraph (1) insert—

> "(1A) Notice of consent given in respect of a claim for carried-forward losses made under section 188CC of the Corporation Tax Act 2010 must also state which accounting period of the surrendering company is the specified loss-making period.
> Otherwise the notice is ineffective.

116   After paragraph 71 insert—

> *"Notice of consent: additional requirements where claim is for group relief for carried-forward losses*
>
> 71A (1) Where notice of consent by the surrendering company is given in respect of a claim for carried-forward losses, the notice must comply with the additional requirements in this paragraph.
> Otherwise the notice is ineffective.
>
> (2) The notice must identify the particular losses and other amounts carried forward to the surrender period that are to be treated as surrendered in satisfaction of the claim.
>
> (3) The notice must identify a loss or other amount by specifying—
>> (a)   the provision of the Corporation Tax Act 2009 or the Corporation Tax Act 2010 under which it was carried forward to the surrender period, and
>> (b)   in a case where the surrendering company is owned by a consortium, the accounting period of the surrendering company to which the loss or other amount is attributable.
>
> (4) Section 153 of the Corporation Tax Act 2010 (companies owned by consortiums) applies for the purposes of this paragraph."

117 (1) Paragraph 72 (notice of consent requiring amendment of return) is amended as follows.

   (2) For sub-paragraph (1) substitute—

> "(1) Where notice of consent by the surrendering company relates to a loss or other amount in respect of which corporation tax relief has been given to the company for any accounting period, the company must at the same time amend its company tax return for that accounting period so as to reflect the notice of consent."

   (3) Omit sub-paragraph (2).

   (4) In sub-paragraph (3) omit "or (2)".

   (5) In sub-paragraph (4) omit "or (2)".

118 (1) Paragraph 73 (withdrawal or amendment of claim) is amended as follows.

   (2) In sub-paragraph (1) omit "for group relief".

   (3) In sub-paragraph (2) omit "for group relief".

119 (1) Paragraph 74 (time limit for claims) is amended as follows.

   (2) In sub-paragraph (1), in the words before paragraph (a), omit "for group relief".

288   *Finance (No. 2) Act 2017 (c. 32)*
Schedule 4 — Relief for carried-forward losses
Part 11 — Minor and consequential amendments

(3) In sub-paragraph (2) omit "for group relief".

(4) In sub-paragraph (3) omit "for group relief".

(5) In sub-paragraph (4) omit "for group relief" in both places those words occur.

120 (1) Paragraph 75A (assessment on other claimant companies) is amended as follows.

(2) In sub-paragraph (2) omit "group".

(3) In sub-paragraph (6) omit "for group relief".

121 (1) Paragraph 76 (assessment to recover excessive relief) is amended as follows.

(2) In the italic heading omit "group".

(3) In sub-paragraph (1) omit "group".

122 (1) Paragraph 77 (joint amended returns) is amended as follows.

(2) In sub-paragraph (1) —
    (a) in paragraph (a) omit "for group relief", and
    (b) in paragraph (b) omit "group" in the second and third places that word occurs.

(3) In sub-paragraph (3), in paragraph (a), omit "for group relief".

CAA 2001

123   CAA 2001 is amended as follows.

124 (1) Section 212Q (restrictions on capital allowance buying when there are postponed allowances) is amended as follows.

(2) In subsection (4) after "37," insert "45A,".

(3) In subsection (6) —
    (a) after "may not be set off" insert "by a company ("the claimant company")",
    (b) after "CTA 2010" insert "or group relief for carried forward losses in accordance with Part 5A of CTA 2010", and
    (c) omit "by a company ("the claimant company")".

125   In section 138 (deferment of balancing charge arising when there is a disposal event in respect of a ship: limit on amount of deferral) in subsection (2)(b) after "45" insert ", 45A or 45B".

126   In Schedule A1 (first-year tax credits) in paragraph 20 (list of provisions to which restriction on carrying forward losses applies) in paragraph (a) for "section 45" substitute "sections 45, 45A and 45B".

Energy Act 2004

127   In section 27 of the Energy Act 2004 (tax exemption for NDA activities) in subsection (1)(b) for the words from "relieved" to the end substitute " —
        (i) relieved under section 37, 45, 45A, 45B or 45F of the Corporation Tax Act 2010 (relief for trading losses),

Finance (No. 2) Act 2017 (c. 32)
Schedule 4 — Relief for carried-forward losses
Part 11 — Minor and consequential amendments

289

       (ii)   surrendered under Part 5 of that Act (group relief), or

      (iii)   surrendered under Part 5A of that Act (group relief for carried-forward losses)."

CTA 2009

128   CTA 2009 is amended as follows.

129   In section 39(3) (losses of mines, quarries and other concerns) —

    (a)   omit "and", and

    (b)   after "(group relief)" insert "and Part 5A of that Act (group relief for carried forward losses)".

130 (1) Section 364 (group relief claims involving impaired or released consortium debts) is amended as follows.

  (2) In subsection (4) at the end insert ", and

      "group relief" means —

    (a)   group relief under Part 5 of CTA 2010 (see section 97(2) of that Act), and

    (b)   group relief for carried-forward losses under Part 5A of CTA 2010 (see section 188AA(4) of that Act)."

  (3) In subsection (5) for "or 144" substitute ", 144 or 188DH".

131   In section 371 (group relief claims involving impaired or released consortium debts: interpretation) for the definition of "group relief" substitute —

      "group relief" has the meaning given by section 364(4),".

132   In section 387 (treatment of deficit on basic life assurance and general annuity business: introduction) in subsection (1) for "Chapter 16" substitute "Chapters 16 and 16A".

133 (1) Section 1048 (treatment of deemed trading loss under section 1045) is amended as follows.

  (2) In subsection (1) at the end insert "("the deemed loss-making period")".

  (3) In subsection (3) —

    (a)   before paragraph (a) insert —

        "(za)   the deemed loss-making period begins before 1 April 2017",

    (b)   in paragraph (a) for "the accounting period" substitute "the deemed loss-making period".

  (4) After subsection (4) insert —

    "(4A)   Subsection (4B) applies if —

      (a)   the deemed loss-making period begins on or after 1 April 2017,

      (b)   the company —

        (i)   begins to carry on a trade in the deemed loss-making period which it continues to carry on in the following accounting period, or

290 *Finance (No. 2) Act 2017 (c. 32)*
Schedule 4 — Relief for carried-forward losses
Part 11 — Minor and consequential amendments

    (ii) begins to carry on a trade in an accounting period after the deemed-loss making period, and

  (c) the trade is derived from the research and development in relation to which the relief mentioned in subsection (1) was obtained.

 (4B) In that case, so far as—

  (a) the company has not obtained relief in respect of the trading loss under any other provision, and

  (b) the loss has not been surrendered under Part 5 of CTA 2010 (group relief) (surrender of relief to group or consortium members),

 the trading loss is to be treated as if it were a loss of that trade brought forward under the relevant provision (see subsection (4C)) to the relevant period (see subsection (4D).

 (4C) In subsection (4B) "the relevant provision" is—

  (a) section 45A(4) of CTA 2010 if—

    (i) the trade is not a ring fence trade within the meaning of Part 8 of CTA 2010 (see section 277 of that Act), and

    (ii) relief under section 37 of CTA 2010 would not be unavailable by reason of section 44 of that Act for a loss (assuming there was one) made in the trade in the relevant period (see subsection (4D), and

  (b) section 45B(2) of CTA 2010 if either of the conditions in paragraph (a) is not met.

 (4D) In subsection (4B) and (4C) "the relevant period" means—

  (a) in a case where the company began the trade in the deemed loss-making period and continued to carry on the trade in the following accounting period, that following accounting period, and

  (b) in a case where the company began the trade in an accounting period after the deemed loss-making period, the accounting period in which the company began the trade."

 (5) In subsection (5) for "Subsection (4) is" substitute "Subsections (4) and (4B) are".

134 In section 1056 (amount of trading loss which is "unrelieved")—

  (a) in subsection (2)(c) after "Part 5" insert "or Part 5A", and

  (b) in subsection (3)(a) after "45" insert ", 45A or 45B".

135 In section 1062(2) (restriction on losses carried forward where R&D tax credit claimed)—

  (a) for "section 45" substitute "sections 45, 45A and 45B", and

  (b) omit "trading" in the second place that word occurs.

136 In section 1116 (meaning of "the actual reduction in tax liability") in subsection (4) after "Part 5" insert "or Part 5A".

137 In section 1153 (amount of loss which is "unrelieved")—

  (a) in subsection (1)(c) after "Part 5" insert "or Part 5A", and

  (b) in subsection (2)(a) after "45" insert ", 45A, 45B".

Finance (No. 2) Act 2017 (c. 32)
Schedule 4 – Relief for carried-forward losses
Part 11 – Minor and consequential amendments

291

138   In section 1158(2) (restriction on losses carried forward where land remediation tax credit claimed) –

      (a)   for "section 45" substitute "sections 45, 45A and 45B", and

      (b)   omit "trading" in the second place that word occurs.

139   In section 1201 (film tax credit claimable if company has surrenderable loss) in subsection (2B)(b) after "45" insert "or 45B".

140   In section 1216CH (television tax credit claimable if company has surrenderable loss) in subsection (4)(b) after "45" insert "or 45B".

141   In section 1217CH (video game tax credit claimable if company has surrenderable loss) in subsection (4)(b) after "45" insert "or 45B".

142   In section 1217KA (theatre tax credits: amount of surrenderable loss) in subsection (3)(b) after "45" insert "or 45B".

143   In section 1217RH (orchestra tax credits: amount of surrenderable loss) in subsection (3)(b) after "45" insert "or 45B".

144   In section 1223 (carry forward expenses of management and other amounts), in subsection (1)(b), after sub-paragraph (i) (as inserted by paragraph 6(2)(b)) insert –

           "(ii)   section 269ZD of CTA 2010 (restrictions on deductions from total profits) has effect for the accounting period, or

           (iii)   ".

CTA 2010

145   CTA 2010 is amended as follows.

146 (1) Section 1 (overview of Act) is amended as follows.

    (2) In subsection (2) (list of reliefs provided by Parts 4 to 7) after paragraph (f) insert –

        "(fa)   group relief for carried-forward losses (see Part 5A),"

    (3) After subsection (2) insert –

    "(2A) Part 7ZA contains provision restricting the amount of certain deductions which may be made in calculating the profits of a company on which corporation tax is chargeable."

147 (1) Section 17 (interpretation of Chapter 4 of Part 2) is amended as follows.

    (2) In subsection (2) (meaning of "carried-back amount") –

      (a)   after paragraph (a) insert –

          "(aa)   an amount carried back under section 45F (relief for terminal trade losses),", and

      (b)   in paragraph (c) after "459(1)(b)" insert "or 463B(1)(b)".

    (3) In subsection (3) (meaning of "carried-forward amount") –

      (a)   in paragraph (a) after "forward of" insert "pre-1 April 2017",

      (b)   after paragraph (a) insert –

          "(aa)   an amount carried forward under section 45A (carry forward of post 1-April 2017 trade loss against total profits),

292   *Finance (No. 2) Act 2017 (c. 32)*
Schedule 4 — Relief for carried-forward losses
Part 11 — Minor and consequential amendments

          (ab)   an amount carried forward under section 45B (carry forward of post-1 April 2017 trade loss against subsequent trade profits),", and

    (c)   in paragraph (i) after "457(3)" insert ", 463G(6) or 463H(4)".

148 (1) Section 46 (use of trade-related interest and dividends if insufficient trade profits) is amended as follows.

    (2) For subsection (1) substitute —

       "(1) This section applies if in an accounting period a company carrying on a trade makes a loss in the trade and either —

          (a)   relief for the loss could be given in a later accounting period under section 45(4)(b) or 45B(4) but for the fact that there are no profits of the trade of the later accounting period, or

          (b)   the amount of relief for the loss that could be given in a later accounting period under section 45(4)(b) or 45B(4) is limited by reason of the amount of profits of the trade of the later accounting period."

    (3) In subsection (2) at the beginning insert "For the purposes of section 45 and 45B,".

149   In section 47 (registered societies), in subsection (1), for "section 45" substitute "sections 45 and 45B".

150   In section 53 (leasing contracts and company reconstructions), in subsection (1)(e), for "or 45" substitute ", 45, 45A or 45B".

151   In section 54 (non-UK resident company: receipts of interest, dividends or royalties), in subsection (2), for "or 45" substitute ", 45, 45A or 45B".

152 (1) Section 56 (restriction on reliefs for limited partners) is amended as follows.

    (2) In subsection (2) —

        (a)   in paragraph (a) after "37" insert "or 45A",

        (b)   omit "or" at the end of paragraph (a), and

        (c)   after paragraph (b) insert ", or

            (c)   under Part 5A (group relief for carried-forward losses)".

    (3) In subsection (4) —

        (a)   after "37" insert "or 45A", and

        (b)   after "5" insert "or 5A".

153 (1) Section 59 (restriction on relief for members of LLPs) is amended as follows.

    (2) In subsection (2) —

        (a)   in paragraph (a) after "37" insert "or 45A",

        (b)   omit "or" at the end of paragraph (a), and

        (c)   after paragraph (b) insert ", or

            (c)   under Part 5A (group relief for carried-forward losses)".

    (3) In subsection (4) —

        (a)   after "37" insert "or 45A", and

        (b)   after "5" insert "or 5A".

Finance (No. 2) Act 2017 (c. 32)
Schedule 4 – Relief for carried-forward losses
Part 11 – Minor and consequential amendments

293

154 (1) Section 61 (unrelieved losses of member of LLP brought forward) is amended as follows.

   (2) In subsection (1), in the words before paragraph (a), for "This section" substitute "Subsection (2)".

   (3) After subsection (2) insert—

> "(2A) Subsection (2B) applies if—
>> (a) a company ("the member company") carries on a trade as a member of an LLP at a time during an accounting period ("the current period"), and
>> (b) as a result of section 59, relief under section 45A or Part 5A (group relief for carried forward losses) has not been given for an amount of loss made in the trade by the member company as a member of the LLP in a previous accounting period.
>
> (2B) For the purposes of determining the relief under section 45A or Part 5A to be given to any company, the amount of loss is treated as having been made by the member company in the current period so far as it is not excluded by subsection (3) or (4)."

   (4) In subsection (3)—
> (a) after "37" insert "or 45A", and
> (b) after "Part 5" insert "or Part 5A".

155 (1) Chapter 4 of Part 4 (property losses) is amended as follows.

   (2) In section 65 (UK furnished holiday lettings business treated as trade) for subsection (4A) substitute—

> "(4A) Chapter 2 applies as if the following were omitted—
>> (a) sections 37 to 44,
>> (b) the words "beginning before 1 April 2017" in section 45(1),
>> (c) sections 45A to 45H, and
>> (d) sections 48 to 54.
>
> (4B) Any deduction made under section 45(4)(b) from the profits of the trade treated as carried on under this section is to be ignored for the purposes of section 269ZB (restriction on deductions from trading profits)."

   (3) In section 67A (EEA furnished holiday lettings business treated as trade) for subsection (5) substitute—

> "(5) Chapter 2 applies as if the following were omitted—
>> (a) sections 37 to 44,
>> (b) the words "beginning before 1 April 2017" in section 45(1),
>> (c) sections 45A to 45H, and
>> (d) sections 48 to 54.
>
> (5A) Any deduction made under section 45(4)(b) from the profits of the trade treated as carried on under this section is to be ignored for the purposes of section 269ZB (restriction on deductions from trading profits)."

294   *Finance (No. 2) Act 2017 (c. 32)*
Schedule 4 — Relief for carried-forward losses
Part 11 — Minor and consequential amendments

156 (1) Section 95 (write-off of government investment: meaning of "carry forward losses") is amended as follows.

(2) In subsection (1), in Type 1, after "45," insert "45A, 45B,".

(3) In subsection (2) after "(group relief)" insert "or Part 5A (group relief for carried forward losses)".

157   In section 99 (surrendering of losses and other amounts) in subsection (1)(c) after "16" insert "or 16A".

158   In section 104 (meaning of "non-trading loss on intangible fixed assets" for purposes of section 99(1)(g)), for subsection (2) substitute —

   "(2)   But it does not include a loss treated as a non-trading loss on intangible fixed assets for the surrender period as a result of section 753(3) of CTA 2009."

159   In section 137 (giving of group relief: deduction from total profits) in subsection (5) (list of deductions to be made after group relief is given) —
   (a)   omit "and" at the end of paragraph (b),
   (b)   in paragraph (c) for "or 459" substitute ", 459 or 463B", and
   (c)   after paragraph (c) insert ", and
            (d)   under section 188CK (giving of group relief for carried-forward losses: deductions from total profits)".

160   In section 189(2) (relief for qualifying charitable donations) at the end insert "and group relief for carried-forward losses".

161   In section 269DA (surcharge on banking companies) in subsection (2) (calculation of "surcharge profits") —
   (a)   in the formula, after "NBGR+" insert "NBGRCF+", and
   (b)   after the definition of "NBGR" insert —
            "NBGRCF" is the amount (if any) of non-banking group relief for carried-forward losses that is given in determining those taxable total profits (see section 269DBA);".

162   After section 269DB insert —

"269DBA Meaning of "non-banking group relief for carried-forward losses"

   (1)   In section 269DA(2) "non-banking group relief for carried-forward losses" means group relief for carried-forward losses that relates to losses or other amounts that the surrendering company has for a surrender period in relation to which it is not a banking company.

   (2)   In this section "surrendering company" and "surrender period" have the same meaning as in Part 5A (see section 188FD)."

163 (1) Section 269DC (surcharge on banking companies: meaning of "non-banking or pre-2016 loss relief) is amended as follows.

(2) In subsection (3)(b) —
   (a)   after "45" insert ", 45A or 45B", and
   (b)   omit "trade" in the second place that word occurs.

(3) In subsection (4)(b) —

Finance (No. 2) Act 2017 (c. 32)
Schedule 4 — Relief for carried-forward losses
Part 11 — Minor and consequential amendments

295

(a)   after "457" insert ", 463G or 463H", and

(b)   omit "non-trading".

(4)   Omit subsection (5).

164   In section 385 (sales of lessors: no carry back of loss against the income) in subsection (2) after "periods)" insert "or section 45F (relief for terminal trade losses)".

165   In section 398D (sales of lessors: restrictions on use of losses etc) after subsection (2) insert—

"(2A)   Group relief for carried-forward losses is not to be given under Part 5A against so much of the total profits of A as are attributable to the carrying on of the relevant activity."

166   In section 427 (sales of lessors: no carry back of loss against the income) in subsection (2) after "periods)" insert "or section 45F (relief for terminal trade losses)".

167   (1)   Chapter 5 of Part 9 (sales of lessors: anti-avoidance provisions) is amended as follows.

(2)   In section 432 (introduction to section 433) —

(a)   in subsection (1), in the words before paragraph (a), for "Section 433 applies" substitute "Sections 433 and 433A apply", and

(b)   in subsection (2) after "that section" insert "and section 433A".

(3)   In section 433 (restrictions on relief for expenses treated as incurred under Chapter 3 or 4) —

(a)   in subsection (3) —

(i)   in paragraph (a) after "of" insert "pre-1 April 2017",

(ii)   after that paragraph insert—

"(ab)   section 45B (carry forward of post-1 April 2017 trade loss against subsequent trade profits),

(b)   in subsection (5) after "profits)" insert "or section 45A (carry forward of trade loss against total profits)", and

(c)   in subsection (6) —

(i)   after "set off" insert "—

(a)   ", and

(ii)   at the end insert ", or

"(b)   by way of group relief for carried-forward losses in accordance with Chapter 2 of Part 5A (surrender of company's carried forward losses)".

(4)   After section 433 insert—

"433A Restrictions not applying to the restricted loss amount

(1)   Any deduction made under section 45 or 45B in respect of the restricted loss amount is to be ignored for the purposes of the restriction in section 269ZB (restriction on sum of deductions from trading profits).

296   *Finance (No. 2) Act 2017 (c. 32)*
Schedule 4 — Relief for carried-forward losses
Part 11 — Minor and consequential amendments

(2)   Any deduction made under section 62 or 63 in respect of the restricted loss amount is to be ignored for the purposes of the restriction in section 269ZD (restriction on sum of deductions from total profits)."

168   In section 599 (real estate investment trusts: calculation of profits) after subsection (8) insert—

"(9)   No account is to be taken of Part 7ZA of this Act (restrictions on obtaining certain deductions in respect of carried-forward losses)."

169   In section 601 (availability of group reliefs to a group UK REIT) in subsection (2)—
   (a)   omit "and" at the end of paragraph (f), and
   (b)   after paragraph (g) insert ", and
            "(h)   Part 5A of this Act (group relief for carried-forward losses)".

170   In section 705E (shell companies: restriction on relief for non-trading loss on intangible fixed assets), in subsection (3)(b), for "debit of" substitute "loss on intangible fixed assets for".

171   In section 705F(2) (shell companies: apportionment of amounts), in column 1 of the table—
   (a)   in row 4, after "457(1)" insert ", 463G or 463H",
   (b)   in row 4, omit "basic rule for deficits:",
   (c)   in row 5, omit from ", but excluding" to the end, and
   (d)   in row 6, omit from "and treated" to the end.

172   In section 730C (disallowance of deductible amounts: relevant claims) in subsection (2) (meaning of "relevant claim")—
   (a)   omit "or" at the end of paragraph (a),
   (b)   after paragraph (a) insert—
            "(aa)   section 45A (carry forward of post-1 April 2017 trade loss against total profits)," and
   (c)   after paragraph (b) insert ", or
            (c)   Chapter 3 of Part 5A (group relief for carried-forward losses)".

173 (1)   Section 888 (restrictions on leasing partnership losses) is amended as follows.

   (2)   In subsection (3) after "37" insert "or 45A".

   (3)   In subsection (4)—
      (a)   after "set off" insert "—
            (a)   ", and
      (b)   at the end insert ", or
            (b)   by way of group relief for carried-forward losses in accordance with Chapter 2 of Part 5A (surrender of company's carried-forward losses etc)".

   (4)   In subsection (6) in the definition of "relevant loss relief provision"—
      (a)   in paragraph (a) after "of" insert "pre-1 April 2017", and

Finance (No. 2) Act 2017 (c. 32)
Schedule 4 – Relief for carried-forward losses
Part 11 – Minor and consequential amendments

297

   (b) after that paragraph insert—

     "(ab) section 45B (carry forward of post-1 April 2017 trade loss against subsequent trade profits),".

174 (1) Schedule 4 (index of defined expressions) is amended as follows.

  (2) At the appropriate places insert—

"the claimant company (in Part 5A)	section 188FD"
"the claim period (in Part 5A)	section 188FD"
"company (in Part 5A)	section 188FD"
"group relief for carried-forward losses"	section 188AA(4)"
"holding company (in Part 5A)	section 188FC(2)"
"member of a consortium (in Part 5A)	section 153(2) (applied by section 188FB)"
"member of the same group of companies (in Part 5A)	section 152 (applied by section 188FB)"
"owned by a consortium (in Part 5A)	section 153(1) and (3) (applied by section 188FB)"
"profits (in Part 5A)	section 188FD"
"the specified loss-making period" (in Part 5A)	section 188FD"
"75% subsidiary (in Part 5A)	section 151 (applied by section 188FB)"
"the surrenderable amounts (in Part 5A)	section 188FD"
"the surrendering company (in Part 5A)	section 188FD
"the surrender period (in Part 5A)	section 188FD"
"trade (in Part 5A)	section 188FD"
"trading company (in Part 5A)	section 188FC(1)"

  (3) In the entry for "75% subsidiary (except in Part 5)" after "Part 5" insert "and Part 5A".

TIOPA 2010

175 TIOPA 2010 is amended as follows.

298

Finance (No. 2) Act 2017 (c. 32)
Schedule 4 — Relief for carried-forward losses
Part 11 — Minor and consequential amendments

176   In section 54 (double taxation relief by way of credit: non-trading debits on loan relationships) in subsection (7) —

    (a)   in paragraph (b) of the definition of "carry-back claim", after "459(1)(b)" insert "or 463B(1)(b)",

    (b)   in paragraph (b) of the definition of "carry-forward provision", after "457(1)" insert ", 463G(5) or 463H(4)", and

    (c)   in paragraph (b) of the definition of "current-year provision or claim", after "459(1)(a)" insert "or 463B(1)(a)".

177   In section 55 (double taxation relief by way of credit: current year's non-trading deficits on loan relationships) —

    (a)   in subsection (4)(b), after "459(1)(a)" insert "or 463B(1)(a)", and

    (b)   in subsection (5), for "or 459(1)(a)" substitute ", 459(1)(a) or 463B(1)(a)".

178   In section 156(1) (meaning of "losses" in Part 4) —

    (a)   in paragraph (e) after "Chapter 16" insert "or Chapter 16A",

    (b)   omit "or" at the end of paragraph (f), and

    (c)   after paragraph (g) insert ", or

        (h)   Part 5A of CTA 2010 (group relief for carried-forward losses)."

179   In section 371IF (determining the profits of a CFC's qualifying loan relationship), in paragraph (b) of step 5, after "16" insert "or Chapter 16A".

180   After section 371SK insert—

"371SKA Restrictions on certain deductions: deductions allowances

    (1)   This section applies for the purposes of —

        (a)   applying Part 7ZA of CTA 2010 (restrictions on obtaining certain deductions), and

        (b)   applying any provision of Part 7ZA of CTA 2010 for the purposes of Part 7A of that Act (restrictions on obtaining certain deductions: banking companies).

    (2)   Assume that each of the following is nil —

        (a)   the CFC's deductions allowance for the relevant accounting period,

        (b)   the CFC's trading profits deductions allowance for the relevant accounting period, and

        (c)   the CFC's non-trading profits deductions allowance for the relevant accounting period.

    (3)   But if section 269ZX of CTA 2010 (increase of deductions allowance where provision for onerous lease reversed) applies in relation to the relevant accounting period, the reference in subsection (2) to "nil" is to be read as a reference to an amount equal to the increase provided for by subsection (3) of that section."

181   In subsection (2)(a) of section 371SL (group relief etc) —

    (a)   after "(group relief)" insert "or Part 5A of that Act (group relief for carried-forward losses)", and

    (b)   after "by way of group relief" insert "or group relief for carried-forward losses".

Finance (No. 2) Act 2017 (c. 32)
Schedule 4 — Relief for carried-forward losses
Part 11 — Minor and consequential amendments

299

F (No. 3) A 2010

182 (1) In paragraph 10 of Schedule 9 to F(No.3)A 2010 (interest), the new Part A1 to be inserted into Schedule 54 to FA 2009 is amended as follows.

(2) In paragraph A1 (interest on tax repaid as a result of carrying back a non-trading deficit on company's loan relationships) —

(a) in sub-paragraph (1)(c) for "or 459(1)(b)" substitute ", 459(1)(b) or 463B(1)(b)", and

(b) in sub-paragraph (2) for "or 459(1)(b)" substitute ", 459(1)(b) or 463B(1)(b)".

(3) After paragraph A2 insert —

"A2A(1) This paragraph applies where —

(a) a company has profits arising in an accounting period ("the earlier period"),

(b) the company ceases to carry on a trade in a later accounting period ("the later period"),

(c) on a claim under section 45F of CTA 2010 (terminal losses), the whole or any part of a loss incurred in the trade has been set off for the purposes of corporation tax against the profits of the earlier period,

(d) the earlier period does not fall wholly within the period of 12 months immediately preceding the later period, and

(e) a repayment falls to be made of corporation tax paid for the earlier period or of income tax in respect of a payment received by the company in that period.

(2) So much of the repayment mentioned in sub-paragraph (1)(e) as falls to be made as a result of the claim under section 45F does not carry repayment interest.

(3) But sub-paragraph (2) does not apply (and, accordingly, the amount mentioned in that sub-paragraph carries repayment interest) after the expiry of 9 months from the end of the later period."

(4) In paragraph A3 (interest on tax repaid as a result of a claim under section 77 of TIOPA 2010) in sub-paragraph (4) after "A4" insert "or A5".

(5) After paragraph A4 insert —

"A5 (1) This paragraph applies where —

(a) a company has profits arising in an accounting period ("the middle period"),

(b) the company ceases to carry on a trade in a later accounting period ("the later period"),

(c) on a claim under section 45F of CTA 2010 (terminal losses), the whole or any part of a loss incurred in the trade has been set off for the purposes of corporation tax against the profits of the middle period,

(d) the middle period does not fall wholly within the period of 12 months immediately preceding the later period,

(e) as a result of the claim under section 45F, an excess or increased excess arises in the middle period as described in

300   *Finance (No. 2) Act 2017 (c. 32)*
Schedule 4 − Relief for carried-forward losses
Part 11 − Minor and consequential amendments

section 72 of TIOPA 2010 (amounts of unrelieved foreign tax),

(f)   on a claim under section 77 of that Act, credit for the whole or any part of the excess is allowed against corporation tax in respect of an accounting period before the middle period ("the earlier period") and,

(g)   a repayment falls to be made of corporation tax paid for the earlier period or of income tax in respect of a payment received by the company in that period.

(2)   So much of the repayment mentioned in sub-paragraph (1)(g) as falls to be made as a result of the claim under section 77 does not carry repayment interest.

(3)   But sub-paragraph (2) does not apply (and, accordingly, the amount mentioned in that sub-paragraph carries repayment interest) after the expiry of 9 months from the end of the later period."

FA 2012

183   FA 2012 is amended as follows.

184   In section 78 (meaning of expressions used in section 76), in subsection (5), for the words from "means" to the end substitute "means any of the following−

(a)   a BLAGAB trade loss of the company for the accounting period in question, so far as relief is given for the loss under−

(i)   section 37 of CTA 2010 (relief for trade losses against total income), as applied by section 123, or

(ii)   Chapter 4 of Part 5 of that Act (group relief), as applied by section 125;

(b)   an amount deducted under section 124B (relief for excess carried forward post-1 April BLAGAB trade losses) from the company's total profits of the accounting period in question;

(c)   an amount of a BLAGAB trade loss of the company relieved under Chapter 3 of Part 5A of CTA 2010 (group relief for carried-forward losses) if the surrender period (see section 188BB(7)) to which the claim relates is the accounting period in question."

185   In section 93 (minimum profits test), in subsection (2), in the words after paragraph (b), for "and 124" substitute ", 124, 124A and 124C".

186   In section 104 (meaning of "the adjusted amount")−

(a)   in subsection (3), after "124" insert ", 124A or 124C";

(b)   in subsection (4), for "that section" substitute "any of those sections";

(c)   in subsection (5)(a), for "or no relief is available under that section," substitute ", 124A or 124C or no relief is available under those sections,".

187   In section 125 (group relief), at the end insert−

"(4)   For provision about the application of Part 5A of CTA 2010 (group relief for carried-forward losses) in relation to BLAGAB trade losses see subsections (3) to (5) of section 188BB of that Act."

Finance (No. 2) Act 2017 (c. 32)
Schedule 4 — Relief for carried-forward losses
Part 11 — Minor and consequential amendments

301

188 (1) Section 126 (restrictions in respect of non-trading deficit) is amended as follows.

(2) After subsection (1) insert—

> "(1A) A loss falls within subsection (1B) so far as it—
>
>   (a) would (apart from that subsection) be available for relief under section 124B (excess carried forward post-1 April 2017 losses: relief against total profits), and
>
>   (b) arose in an accounting period for which the insurance company has a relevant non-trading deficit.
>
> (1B) A loss (or amount of a loss) falling within this subsection is available for relief under section 124B only so far as it exceeds the amount of that relevant non-trading deficit.
>
> (1C) A loss falls within subsection (1D) so far as it—
>
>   (a) is an amount which a company ("the surrendering company") may surrender by virtue of section 188BB(4) (surrender of carried-forward BLAGAB trade losses), and
>
>   (b) arose in an accounting period for which the surrendering company has a relevant non-trading deficit.
>
> (1D) A loss (or amount of a loss) falling within this subsection is available for relief under Chapter 3 of Part 5A of CTA 2010 (claims for group relief) only so far as it exceeds the amount of that relevant non-trading deficit.
>
> (1E) For the purposes of subsections (1A) and (1C) it is to be assumed (where relevant) that in previous accounting periods losses which arose earlier have been utilised before losses which arose later."

(3) In subsection (2)—

    (a) for "The reference" substitute "In this section references";

    (b) for "is a reference" substitute "are".

189   In section 127 (no relief against policyholders' share of I-E profit), in subsection (3)—

    (a) before paragraph (a) insert—

> "(za) relief under section 124B (relief of excess carried-forward BLAGAB trade losses against total profits),";

    (b) after paragraph (c) insert—

> "(ca) relief under Chapter 3 of Part 5A of CTA 2010 (group relief for carried-forward losses),".

PART 12

COMMENCEMENT ETC

Parts 1 to 9 and 11

190 (1) The amendments made by Parts 1 to 9 and 11 of this Schedule have effect in relation to accounting periods beginning on or after 1 April 2017.

(2) For the purposes of those amendments, where a company has an accounting period beginning before 1 April 2017 and ending on or after that date ("the straddling period") —

    (a) so much of the straddling period as falls before 1 April 2017, and so much of that period as falls on or after that date, are treated as separate accounting periods, and

    (b) where it is necessary to apportion an amount for the straddling period to the two separate accounting periods, it is to be apportioned —

        (i) in accordance with section 1172 of CTA 2010 (time basis), or

        (ii) if that method would produce a result that is unjust or unreasonable, on a just and reasonable basis.

(3) But sub-paragraph (2)(b) is to be ignored if paragraph 191 or 192 applies.

191 (1) This paragraph applies if —

    (a) an accounting period of a company ("the straddling period") is treated as two separate accounting periods under paragraph 190(2)(a),

    (b) it is necessary to apportion an amount ("the amount concerned") for the straddling period to the two separate accounting periods, and

    (c) the amount concerned is either —

        (i) an amount chargeable to corporation tax which would have been less but for Part 10 of TIOPA 2010 (corporate interest restriction), or

        (ii) an amount in respect of which corporation tax relief is available which would have been greater but for Part 10 of TIOPA 2010.

(2) The amount concerned is to be apportioned as follows —

Step 1

Determine what the amount concerned would have been but for Part 10 of TIOPA 2010 ("the notional amount").

Step 2

Determine what amount of the notional amount would have been apportioned to the first separate accounting period had paragraph 190(2)(b) applied ("the notional apportioned amount").

If the notional apportioned amount is less than the amount concerned, proceed with steps 3 and 4.

If the notional apportioned amount is equal to or greater than the amount concerned, the whole of the amount concerned is to be apportioned to the first separate accounting period.

Step 3

Take so much of the amount concerned as is equal to the notional apportioned amount and apportion it to the first accounting period.

Step 4

Take the remainder of the amount concerned and apportion it to the second separate accounting period.

192 (1) This paragraph applies if —

    (a) an accounting period of a company ("the straddling period") is treated as two separate accounting periods under paragraph 190(2)(a),

(b) it is necessary to apportion an amount ("the amount concerned") for the straddling period to the two separate accounting period,

(c) the amount concerned is an amount chargeable to corporation tax, and

(d) the amount concerned would not have arisen but for Part 10 of TIOPA 2010 (whether or not an amount in respect of which corporation tax relief would have been available would have arisen instead).

(2) The whole of the amount concerned is apportioned to the second separate accounting period.

Part 10

193   Section 5(4) to (6) of CT(NI)A 2015 (commencement) has effect as if references to Part 8B of CTA 2010 were to that Part as amended by Part 10 of this Schedule.

Transitional provision

194 (1) An amount of a non-trading deficit from a company's loan relationships which is carried forward under section 463H of CTA 2009 is to be disregarded for the purposes of section 730F of CTA 2010 (as amended by paragraph 69(4)), unless it is a post-13 July 2017 amount.

(2) An amount of a non-trading deficit from a company's loan relationships which is deducted under section 463H(5) of CTA 2009 is to be disregarded for the purposes sections 188DD and 188ED of CTA 2010, unless it is a post-13 July 2017 amount.

(3) For the purposes of this paragraph an amount of a non-trading deficit from a company's loan relationships ("the deficit amount") is a post-13 July 2017 amount —

(a) if the deficit period begins on or after 13 July 2017 or,

(b) (where the deficit period is one that begins before, and ends on or after 13 July 2017 (a "straddling deficit period")), so far as the deficit is apportioned under sub-paragraphs (4) and (5) to the part of the deficit period that begins with 13 July 2017.

(4) For the purposes of sub-paragraph (3)(b) —

(a) a straddling deficit period is to be treated as consisting of two parts, namely the part that precedes, and the part that begins with, 13 July 2017,

(b) the deficit amount is to be apportioned to those parts (see sub-paragraph (5)).

(5) The apportionment is to be made —

(a) in accordance with section 1172 of CTA 2010 (time basis), or

(b) if that method would produce a result that is unjust or unreasonable, on a just and reasonable basis.

(6) In this paragraph "deficit period" is to be interpreted in accordance with section 463A(2) of CTA 2009.

SCHEDULE 5 Section 20

CORPORATE INTEREST RESTRICTION

PART 1

NEW PART 10 OF TIOPA 2010

1   In TIOPA 2010, after Part 9A insert—

"PART 10

CORPORATE INTEREST RESTRICTION

CHAPTER 1

INTRODUCTION

372 Overview

(1)   This Part contains provision that—
   (a)   disallows certain amounts that a company would (apart from this Part) be entitled to bring into account for the purposes of corporation tax in respect of interest and other financing costs, and
   (b)   allows certain amounts disallowed under this Part in previous accounting periods to be brought into account in later accounting periods.

(2)   In this Chapter—
   (a)   section 373 defines some key concepts including, in particular, "the total disallowed amount" in relation to a period of account of a worldwide group, and
   (b)   section 374 provides for Schedule 7A to have effect.

(3)   Chapter 2 provides for—
   (a)   the disallowance in certain circumstances of tax-interest expense amounts of companies that are members of a worldwide group, and
   (b)   the carrying forward of disallowed tax-interest expense amounts, and for bringing those amounts into account in certain circumstances in relation to a later period of account of the worldwide group.

(4)   Chapter 3—
   (a)   defines "a tax-interest expense amount" and "a tax-interest income amount" of a company for a period of account of a worldwide group, which are amounts that are (or apart from this Part would be) brought into account for the purposes of corporation tax,
   (b)   defines "the net tax-interest expense" of a company for a period of account of a worldwide group, which is any excess of the company's tax-interest expense amounts for the period over its tax-interest income amounts for the period,

    (c)   defines "the net tax-interest income" of a company for a period of account of a worldwide group, which is any excess of the company's tax-interest income amounts for the period over its tax-interest expense amounts for the period, and

    (d)   defines "aggregate net tax-interest expense" and "aggregate net tax-interest income" of a worldwide group for a period of account of the worldwide group, which are made up of each member of the group's net tax-interest expense or net tax-interest income for the period.

(5)   Chapter 4 contains provision about the calculation of "the interest capacity" of a worldwide group for a period of account of the group, which is the aggregate of the interest allowance for the period and any unused interest allowance of the group from the previous 5 years (or, if that aggregate is less than the de minimis amount, the de minimis amount).

(6)   Chapter 5 makes provision about the calculation of "the interest allowance" of a worldwide group for a period of account of the group.

The interest allowance for a period of account is calculated using the fixed ratio method unless the group elects for the group ratio method to be used for the period.

(7)   Chapter 6 defines concepts used in Chapter 5 including —

        the "tax-EBITDA" of a company for a period of account of a worldwide group (which is an amount derived from amounts brought into account for the purposes of corporation tax);

        the "aggregate tax-EBITDA" of a worldwide group for a period of account of the group (which is an amount derived from the tax-EBITDA of members of the group).

(8)   Chapter 7 defines additional concepts used in Chapter 5 including —

        "the net group-interest expense", "the adjusted net group-interest expense" and "the qualifying net group-interest expense" of a worldwide group for a period of account of the group (which are amounts derived from the financial statements of the worldwide group);

        the "group-EBITDA" of the worldwide group for a period of account of the group (which is an amount derived from the financial statements of the worldwide group).

(9)   Chapter 8 contains provision altering the way in which this Part has effect in relation to the provision of public infrastructure assets or the carrying on of certain other related activities.

(10)   Chapter 9 contains special provision altering the operation of certain provisions of this Part in relation to —

    (a)   particular types of company (for example, banking companies, companies carrying on oil-related activities, REITs or insurance companies), or

    (b)   particular types of transaction or accounting (for example, long funding operating leases or fair value accounting).

(11)   Chapter 10 contains rules connected with tax avoidance.

(12) Chapter 11 contains the remaining interpretative and supplementary provision, including definitions of —

"related party";

"a worldwide group";

"ultimate parent";

"period of account" of a worldwide group.

373 Meaning of "subject to interest restrictions", "the total disallowed amount" etc

(1) A worldwide group is "subject to interest restrictions" in a period of account of the group if —

    (a) the aggregate net tax-interest expense of the group for the period (see section 390), exceeds

    (b) the interest capacity of the group for the period (see section 392).

(2) "The total disallowed amount" of a worldwide group in a period of account of the group is —

    (a) if the group is subject to interest restrictions in the period, the amount of the excess mentioned in subsection (1);

    (b) otherwise, nil.

(3) "The interest reactivation cap" of a worldwide group in a period of account of the group is (subject to subsection (4)) —

    (a) the interest allowance of the group for the period (see section 396), less

    (b) the aggregate net tax-interest expense of the group for the period.

(4) If the amount determined under subsection (3) is a negative amount, the interest reactivation cap of the worldwide group in the period is nil.

(5) A worldwide group is "subject to interest reactivations" in a period of account of the group if —

    (a) the interest reactivation cap of the group in the period is not nil, and

    (b) at least one member of the group is within the charge to corporation tax at any time during the period, and has an amount available for reactivation in the return period that is not nil (see paragraph 26 of Schedule 7A).

(6) This section has effect for the purposes of this Part.

374 Interest restriction returns

(1) Schedule 7A makes provision about —

    (a) the preparation and submission of interest restriction returns by reporting companies of worldwide groups, and

    (b) other related matters such as enquiries and information powers.

(2) Part 1 of that Schedule includes provision —

    (a) for the appointment of a reporting company of a worldwide group for a period of account, but

(b) for companies ("non-consenting companies") to elect to be unaffected by allocations of interest restrictions made by the company.

(3) Part 2 of that Schedule includes provision—

    (a) for various elections to be made in an interest restriction return that are relevant to the operation of this Part (for example, the group ratio election),

    (b) entitling the reporting company of a worldwide group to allocate interest restrictions among its members but with a rule that allocates a pro-rata share to a non-consenting company, and

    (c) entitling the reporting company of a worldwide group to allocate interest reactivations among its members.

(4) The remaining Parts of that Schedule contain provision about—

    (a) the keeping and preservation of records (see Part 3),

    (b) enquiries into interest restriction returns (see Part 4),

    (c) determinations made by officers of Revenue and Customs in the event of the breach of filing or other obligations (see Part 5),

    (d) information powers exercisable by members of the group (see Part 6),

    (e) information powers exercisable by officers of Revenue and Customs (see Part 7), and

    (f) the amendment of company tax returns to reflect the effect of this Part of this Act and supplementary matters (see Parts 8 and 9).

CHAPTER 2

DISALLOWANCE AND REACTIVATION OF TAX-INTEREST EXPENSE AMOUNTS

375 Disallowance of deductions: full interest restriction return submitted

(1) This section applies where—

    (a) an interest restriction return is submitted for a period of account of a worldwide group ("the relevant period of account"),

    (b) the return complies with the requirements of paragraph 20(3) of Schedule 7A (requirements for full interest restriction return), and

    (c) the return includes a statement that the group is subject to interest restrictions in the return period.

(2) A company that is listed on the statement under paragraph 22 of Schedule 7A (statement of allocated interest restrictions) must, in any accounting period for which the statement specifies an allocated disallowance, leave out of account tax-interest expense amounts that, in total, equal that allocated disallowance.

(3) A non-consenting company in relation to the return may—

> > (a) elect that subsection (2) is not to apply in relation to such relevant accounting period of the company as is specified in the election, or
> >
> > (b) revoke an election previously made.

> (4) If —
> > (a) an election under this section has effect in relation to an accounting period of a company, and
> >
> > (b) paragraph 24 of Schedule 7A allocates to that period a pro-rata share of the total disallowed amount that is not nil,
>
> the company must leave out of account in that period tax-interest expense amounts that, in total, equal that pro-rata share.

> (5) See section 377 for provision as to which tax-interest expense amounts are to be left out of account as a result of this section.

376 Disallowance of deductions: no return, or non-compliant return, submitted

> (1) This section applies where —
> > (a) a worldwide group is subject to interest restrictions in a period of account of the group ("the relevant period of account"),
> >
> > (b) the relevant date has passed, and
> >
> > (c) condition A, B or C is met.

> (2) In this section "the relevant date" means —
> > (a) where the appointment of a reporting company has effect in relation to the relevant period of account, the filing date in relation to the period (see paragraph 7(5) of Schedule 7A);
> >
> > (b) otherwise, the last day of the period of 12 months beginning with the end of the relevant period of account.

> (3) Condition A is that no appointment of a reporting company has effect in relation to the relevant period of account.

> (4) Condition B is that —
> > (a) the appointment of a reporting company has effect in relation to the relevant period of account, and
> >
> > (b) no interest restriction return has been submitted for the period.

> (5) Condition C is that —
> > (a) the appointment of a reporting company has effect in relation to the relevant period of account,
> >
> > (b) an interest restriction return has been submitted for the period, and
> >
> > (c) the return does not comply with the requirements of paragraph 20(3) of Schedule 7A (for example by including inaccurate figures).

> (6) A relevant company must, in any accounting period to which paragraph 24 of Schedule 7A allocates a pro-rata share of the total disallowed amount that is not nil, leave out of account tax-interest expense amounts that, in total, equal that pro-rata share.

(7) See section 377 for provision as to which tax-interest expense amounts are to be left out of account as a result of this section.

(8) In this section "relevant company" means a company that was a member of the worldwide group at any time during the relevant period of account.

377 Disallowance of deductions: identification of the tax-interest amounts to be left out of account

(1) This section applies where—

   (a) a company is required to leave tax-interest expense amounts out of account in an accounting period under section 375 or 376, and

   (b) the total of the tax-interest expense amounts that, apart from that provision, would be brought into account in the accounting period exceeds the total of the tax-interest expense amounts that are required by that provision to be left out of account in that period.

(2) Tax-interest expense amounts must (subject to the following provisions of this section) be left out of account in the following order.

First, leave out of account tax-interest expense amounts that meet condition A in section 382 and would (if brought into account) be brought into account under Part 5 of CTA 2009 (non-trading debits in respect of loan relationships).

Second, leave out of account tax-interest expense amounts that meet condition B in section 382 and would (if brought into account) be brought into account under Part 5 of CTA 2009 as a result of section 574 of that Act (non-trading debits in respect of derivative contracts).

Third, leave out of account tax-interest expense amounts that meet condition A in section 382 and would (if brought into account) be brought into account under Part 3 of CTA 2009 as a result of section 297 of that Act (debits in respect of loan relationships treated as expenses of trade).

Fourth, leave out of account tax-interest expense amounts that meet condition B in section 382 and would (if brought into account) be brought into account under Part 3 of CTA 2009 as a result of section 573 of that Act (debits in respect of derivative contracts treated as expenses of trade).

Fifth, leave out of account tax-interest expense amounts that meet condition C in section 382 and do not also meet condition A or B in that section (finance leases, debt factoring and service concession arrangements).

(3) The company may—

   (a) elect that subsection (2) is not to apply to the accounting period, or

   (b) revoke an election previously made.

(4) An election under this section must specify the particular tax-interest expense amounts that are to be left out of account.

310   *Finance (No. 2) Act 2017 (c. 32)*
Schedule 5 – Corporate interest restriction
Part 1 – New Part 10 of TIOPA 2010

378   Disallowed tax-interest expense amounts carried forward

(1)   For the purposes of this Part a tax-interest expense amount of a company is "disallowed" in an accounting period if the company is required to leave it out of account in that accounting period under section 375 or 376.

(2)   A tax-interest expense amount of a company that is disallowed in an accounting period is (subject to the remaining provisions of this section) carried forward to subsequent accounting periods.

(3)   Where—

    (a)   a tax-interest expense amount of a company would (apart from this Part) be brought into account in calculating the profits or losses of a trade carried on by the company in an accounting period,

    (b)   the tax-interest expense amount is disallowed in that accounting period, and

    (c)   in a subsequent accounting period ("the later accounting period") the company ceases to carry on the trade, or the scale of the activities in the trade becomes small or negligible,

the tax-interest expense amount is not carried forward to the later accounting period or accounting periods after the later accounting period.

(4)   Where—

    (a)   a tax-interest expense amount of a company would (apart from this Part) be brought into account in calculating the profits or losses of a trade carried on by the company in an accounting period,

    (b)   the tax-interest expense amount is disallowed in that accounting period, and

    (c)   in a subsequent accounting period ("the later accounting period") the trade is uncommercial and non-statutory,

the tax-interest expense amount is not carried forward to the later accounting period or accounting periods after the later accounting period.

(5)   For the purposes of subsection (4), a trade is "uncommercial and non-statutory" in an accounting period if, were the company to have made a loss in the trade in the period, relief for the loss under section 37 of CTA 2010 (relief for trade losses against total profits) would have been unavailable by virtue of section 44 of that Act (trade must be commercial or carried on for statutory functions).

(6)   Where—

    (a)   a tax-interest expense amount of a company would (apart from this Part) be brought into account in calculating the profits or losses of an investment business carried on by the company in an accounting period,

    (b)   the tax-interest expense amount is disallowed in that accounting period, and

    (c)   in a subsequent accounting period ("the later accounting period") the company ceases to carry on the investment business, or the scale of the activities in the investment business becomes small or negligible,

the tax-interest expense amount is not carried forward to the later accounting period or accounting periods after the later accounting period.

(7) Where a tax-interest expense amount—

   (a) is disallowed in an accounting period,

   (b) is carried forward to a subsequent accounting period ("the later accounting period"), and

   (c) is brought into account in the later accounting period in accordance with section 379,

it is not carried forward to accounting periods after the later accounting period.

379 Reactivation of interest

(1) This section applies where—

   (a) an interest restriction return is submitted for a period of account of a worldwide group ("the relevant period of account"),

   (b) the return complies with the requirements of paragraph 20(3) of Schedule 7A (requirements for full interest restriction return), and

   (c) the return contains a statement that the group is subject to interest reactivations in the return period.

(2) A company that is listed on the statement under paragraph 25 of Schedule 7A (statement of allocated interest reactivations) must, in the specified accounting period, bring into account tax-interest expense amounts that—

   (a) are brought forward to the specified accounting period from an earlier accounting period, and

   (b) in total, equal the allocated reactivation for the return period.

(3) A tax-interest expense amount is brought into account in the specified accounting period under subsection (2) by being treated as a tax-interest expense amount of the specified accounting period (so that, for example, a tax-interest expense amount that is a relevant loan relationship debit falling within section 383(2)(a)(ii) is brought into account in the specified period as a non-trading debit under Part 5 of CTA 2009).

(4) See section 380 for provision as to which tax-interest expense amounts are to be brought into account under subsection (2).

(5) In this section "the specified accounting period" means—

   (a) the earliest relevant accounting period of the company, or

   (b) where the company became a member of the relevant worldwide group during the relevant period of account, the earliest relevant accounting period of the company in which it was a member of the group.

380 Reactivation of deductions: identification of the tax-interest amounts to be brought into account

(1) This section applies where—

    (a) a company is required to bring tax-interest expense amounts into account in an accounting period under section 379, and

    (b) the total of the tax-interest expense amounts that are brought forward to the accounting period from earlier accounting periods exceeds the total of the tax-interest expense amounts that are required by that provision to be brought into account in that accounting period.

(2) Tax-interest expense amounts must (subject to the following provisions of this section) be brought into account in the following order.

First, bring into account tax-interest expense amounts that meet condition A in section 382 and are brought into account under Part 5 of CTA 2009 (non-trading debits in respect of loan relationships).

Second, bring into account tax-interest expense amounts that meet condition B in section 382 and are brought into account under Part 5 of CTA 2009 as a result of section 574 of that Act (non-trading debits in respect of derivative contracts).

Third, bring into account tax-interest expense amounts that meet condition A in section 382 and are brought into account under Part 3 of CTA 2009 as a result of section 297 of that Act (debits in respect of loan relationships treated as expenses of trade).

Fourth, bring into account tax-interest expense amounts that meet condition B in section 382 and are brought into account under Part 3 of CTA 2009 as a result of section 573 of that Act (debits in respect of derivative contracts treated as expenses of trade).

Fifth, bring into account tax-interest expense amounts that meet condition C in section 382 and do not also meet condition A or B in that section (finance leases, debt factoring and service concession arrangements).

(3) The company may—

    (a) elect that subsection (2) is not to apply to the accounting period, or

    (b) revoke an election previously made.

(4) An election under this section must specify the particular tax-interest expense amounts that are to be brought into account.

381 Set-off of disallowances and reactivations in the same accounting period

(1) This section applies where, as a result of the operation of this Part in relation to different periods of account (whether of the same or a different worldwide group), a company would, apart from this section—

    (a) be required to leave out of account one or more tax-interest expense amounts in an accounting period under section 375 or 376, and

      (b)   be required to bring one or more tax-interest expense amounts into account in that accounting period under section 379.

  (2)   In this section—

      (a)   "the gross disallowed amount" means the amount, or total of the amounts, mentioned in subsection (1)(a);

      (b)   "the gross reactivated amount" means the amount, or total of the amounts, mentioned in subsection (1)(b).

  (3)   Where the gross disallowed amount is equal to the gross reactivated amount, no tax-interest expense amounts are to be left out of account in the accounting period under this Part or brought into account in the accounting period under this Part.

  (4)   Where the gross disallowed amount is more than the gross reactivated amount—

      (a)   the requirement in section 375 or 376 is to leave out of account tax-interest expense amounts that, in total, equal the gross disallowed amount less the gross reactivated amount, and

      (b)   no amount is to be brought into account in the accounting period under section 379.

  (5)   Where the gross reactivated amount is more than the gross disallowed amount—

      (a)   no amount to be left out of account in the accounting period under section 375 or 376, and

      (b)   the requirement in section 379 is to bring into account the gross reactivated amount less the gross disallowed amount.

CHAPTER 3

TAX-INTEREST AMOUNTS

Tax-interest expense and income amounts: basic rules

382   The tax-interest expense amounts of a company

  (1)   References in this Part to a "tax-interest expense amount" of a company for a period of account of a worldwide group are to any amount that—

      (a)   is (or apart from this Part would be) brought into account for the purposes of corporation tax in a relevant accounting period of the company, and

      (b)   meets condition A, B or C.

  (2)   Condition A is that the amount is a relevant loan relationship debit (see section 383).

  (3)   Condition B is that the amount is a relevant derivative contract debit (see section 384).

  (4)   Condition C is that the amount is in respect of the financing cost implicit in amounts payable under a relevant arrangement or transaction.

(5) In subsection (4) "relevant arrangement or transaction" means —

    (a) a finance lease,

    (b) debt factoring, or any similar transaction, or

    (c) a service concession arrangement if and to the extent that the arrangement is accounted for as a financial liability.

(6) Subsection (8) applies if an accounting period in which a tax-interest expense amount is (or apart from this Part would be) brought into account for the purposes of corporation tax contains one or more disregarded periods.

(7) A "disregarded period" is any period falling within the accounting period —

    (a) which does not fall within the period of account of the worldwide group, or

    (b) throughout which the company is not a member of the group.

(8) Where this subsection applies, the tax-interest expense amount mentioned in subsection (6) is reduced by such amount as is referable, on a just and reasonable basis, to the disregarded period or periods mentioned in that subsection.

(9) An amount may be reduced to nil under subsection (8).

(10) If —

    (a) an amount would have met condition A, B or C but for the application of a rule preventing its deduction,

    (b) some or all of it is deductible at a subsequent time as a result of the application of another rule, and

    (c) none of conditions A to C are met at that time,

so much of the amount as is subsequently deductible is treated, at that time, as meeting whichever of condition A, B or C would have been met but for the application of the rule mentioned in paragraph (a).

(11) An example of a case to which subsection (10) applies is a case where —

    (a) an amount is prevented from being deducted as a result of any provision made by Part 6A (hybrid and other mismatches), and

    (b) another provision of that Part subsequently applies so as to permit some or all of it to be deducted from total profits.

383 Relevant loan relationship debits

(1) This section applies for the purposes of section 382.

(2) An amount is a "relevant loan relationship debit" if —

    (a) it is a debit that is (or apart from this Part would be) brought into account for the purposes of corporation tax in respect of a loan relationship under —

        (i) Part 3 of CTA 2009 as a result of section 297 of that Act (loan relationships for purposes of trade), or

        (ii) Part 5 of that Act (other loan relationships), and

    (b) is not an excluded debit.

(3) A debit is "excluded" for the purposes of subsection (2)(b) if—

    (a) it is in respect of an exchange loss (within the meaning of Parts 5 and 6 of CTA 2009), or

    (b) it is in respect of an impairment loss.

384 Relevant derivative contract debits

(1) This section applies for the purposes of section 382.

(2) An amount is a "relevant derivative contract debit" if—

    (a) it is a debit that is (or apart from this Part would be) brought into account for the purposes of corporation tax in respect of a derivative contract under—

        (i) Part 3 of CTA 2009 as a result of section 573 of that Act (derivative contracts for purposes of trade), or

        (ii) Part 5 of that Act as a result of section 574 of that Act (other derivative contracts),

    (b) it is not an excluded debit, and

    (c) the condition in subsection (4) is met.

(3) A debit is "excluded" for the purposes of subsection (2)(b) if—

    (a) it is in respect of an exchange loss (within the meaning of Part 7 of CTA 2009),

    (b) it is in respect of an impairment loss, or

    (c) it is in respect of a derivative contract which hedges risks arising in the ordinary course of a trade where the contract was entered into wholly for reasons unrelated to the capital structure of the worldwide group (or any member of the worldwide group).

(4) The condition referred to in subsection (2)(c) is that the underlying subject matter of the derivative contract consists only of one or more of the following—

    (a) interest rates;

    (b) any index determined by reference to income or retail prices;

    (c) currency;

    (d) an asset or liability representing a loan relationship;

    (e) any other underlying subject matter which is—

        (i) subordinate in relation to any of the matters mentioned in paragraphs (a) to (d), or

        (ii) of small value in comparison with the value of the underlying subject matter as a whole.

(5) For the purposes of this section, whether part of the underlying subject matter of the derivative contract is subordinate or of small value is to be determined by reference to the time when the company enters into or acquires the contract.

(6) In this section "underlying subject matter" has the same meaning as in Part 7 of CTA 2009.

385   The tax-interest income amounts of a company

(1)   References in this Part to a "tax-interest income amount" of a company for a period of account of a worldwide group are to any amount that—

    (a)   is (or apart from this Part would be) brought into account for the purposes of corporation tax in a relevant accounting period of the company, and

    (b)   meets condition A, B, C or D.

(2)   Condition A is that the amount is a relevant loan relationship credit (see section 386).

(3)   Condition B is that the amount is a relevant derivative contract credit (see section 387).

(4)   Condition C is that the amount is in respect of the financing income implicit in amounts receivable under a relevant arrangement or transaction.

(5)   In subsection (4) "relevant arrangement or transaction" means—

    (a)   a finance lease,

    (b)   debt factoring, or any similar transaction, or

    (c)   a service concession arrangement if and to the extent that the arrangement is accounted for as a financial asset.

(6)   Condition D is that the amount is in respect of income that—

    (a)   is receivable from another company, and

    (b)   is in consideration of the provision of a guarantee of any borrowing of that other company.

(7)   Subsection (9) applies if an accounting period in which a tax-interest income amount is (or apart from this Part would be) brought into account for the purposes of corporation tax contains one or more disregarded periods.

(8)   A "disregarded period" is any period falling within the accounting period—

    (a)   which does not fall within the period of account of the worldwide group, or

    (b)   throughout which the company is not a member of the group.

(9)   Where this subsection applies, the tax-interest income amount mentioned in subsection (7) is reduced by such amount as is referable, on a just and reasonable basis, to the disregarded period or periods mentioned in that subsection.

(10)   An amount may be reduced to nil under subsection (9).

386   Relevant loan relationship credits

(1)   This section applies for the purposes of section 385.

(2)   An amount is a "relevant loan relationship credit" if—

    (a)   it is a credit that is (or apart from this Part would be) brought into account for the purposes of corporation tax in respect of a loan relationship under—

      (i)   Part 3 of CTA 2009 as a result of section 297 of that Act (loan relationships for purposes of trade), or

      (ii)   Part 5 of that Act (other loan relationships), and

  (b)   it is not an excluded credit.

(3)   A credit is "excluded" for the purposes of subsection (2)(b) if —

  (a)   it is in respect of an exchange gain (within the meaning of Parts 5 and 6 of CTA 2009), or

  (b)   it is in respect of the reversal of an impairment loss.

387 Relevant derivative contract credits

(1)   This section applies for the purposes of section 385.

(2)   An amount is a "relevant derivative contract credit" if —

  (a)   it is a credit that is (or apart from this Part would be) brought into account for the purposes of corporation tax in respect of a derivative contract under —

      (i)   Part 3 of CTA 2009 as a result of section 573 of that Act (derivative contracts for purposes of trade), or

      (ii)   Part 5 of that Act as a result of section 574 of that Act (other derivative contracts),

  (b)   is not an excluded credit, and

  (c)   the condition in subsection (4) is met.

(3)   A credit is "excluded" for the purposes of subsection (2)(b) if —

  (a)   it is in respect of an exchange gain (within the meaning of Part 7 of CTA 2009),

  (b)   it is in respect of the reversal of an impairment loss, or

  (c)   it is in respect of a derivative contract which hedges risks arising in the ordinary course of a trade where the contract was entered into wholly for reasons unrelated to the capital structure of the worldwide group (or any member of the worldwide group).

(4)   The condition referred to in subsection (2)(c) is that the underlying subject matter of the derivative contract consists only of one or more of the following —

  (a)   interest rates;

  (b)   any index determined by reference to income or retail prices;

  (c)   currency;

  (d)   an asset or liability representing a loan relationship;

  (e)   any other underlying subject matter which is —

      (i)   subordinate in relation to any of the matters mentioned in paragraphs (a) to (d), or

      (ii)   of small value in comparison with the value of the underlying subject matter as a whole.

(5)   For the purposes of this section, whether part of the underlying subject matter of the derivative contract is subordinate or of small value is to be determined by reference to the time when the company enters into or acquires the contract.

(6)   In this section "underlying subject matter" has the same meaning as in Part 7 of CTA 2009.

Double taxation relief

388   Double taxation relief

    (1)   This section applies where—

        (a)   apart from this section, an amount ("the relevant amount") would be a tax-interest income amount brought into account for the purposes of corporation tax in a relevant accounting period ("the relevant accounting period") of a company, and

        (b)   the amount of corporation tax chargeable in respect of the relevant amount is reduced under section 18(2) (entitlement to credit for foreign tax reduces UK tax by amount of the credit).

    (2)   The relevant amount is not a tax-interest income amount to the extent that it consists of notional untaxed income.

    (3)   For this purpose, the amount of the relevant amount that consists of "notional untaxed income" is—

$$\frac{A}{B}$$

where—

    A is the amount of the reduction mentioned in subsection (1)(b);

    B is the rate of corporation tax payable by the company, before any credit under Part 2 (double taxation relief), on the company's profits for the relevant accounting period.

Net tax-interest expense

389   The "net tax-interest expense" or "net tax-interest income" of a company

    (1)   A company has "net tax-interest expense" for a period of account of a worldwide group if the total of its tax-interest expense amounts for the period exceeds the total of its tax-interest income amounts for the period.

    (2)   The amount of the net tax-interest expense of the company for the period is the amount of the excess.

    (3)   A company has "net tax-interest income" for a period of account of a worldwide group if the total of its tax-interest income amounts for the period exceeds the total of its tax-interest expense amounts for the period.

    (4)   The amount of the net tax-interest income of the company for the period is the amount of the excess.

    (5)   The net tax-interest expense or net tax-interest income of a company for a period of account of a worldwide group is "referable" to an accounting period of the company to the extent that it comprises tax-interest expense amounts or tax-interest income amounts that are (or apart from this Part would be) brought into account in the accounting period.

    (6)   This section applies for the purposes of this Part.

390 The worldwide group's aggregate net tax-interest expense and income

(1) The "aggregate net tax-interest expense" of a worldwide group for a period of account of the group is (subject to subsection (2)) —

(a) the total of the net tax-interest expense for the period of each relevant company that has such an amount, less

(b) the total of the net tax-interest income for the period of each relevant company that has such an amount.

(2) Where the amount determined under subsection (1) is negative, the "aggregate net tax-interest expense" of the group for the period is nil.

(3) The "aggregate net tax-interest income" of a worldwide group for a period of account of the group is (subject to subsection (4)) —

(a) the total of the net tax-interest income for the period of each relevant company that has such an amount, less

(b) the total of the net tax-interest expense for the period of each relevant company that has such an amount.

(4) Where the amount determined under subsection (3) is negative, the "aggregate net tax-interest income" of the group for the period is nil.

(5) In this section "relevant company" means a company that was a member of the group at any time during the period of account of the group.

(6) This section applies for the purposes of this Part.

Interpretation

391 Meaning of "impairment loss"

(1) In this Part "impairment loss" means a loss in respect of the impairment of a financial asset.

(2) A reference to a debit in respect of an impairment loss does not include a debit that is (or apart from this Part would be) brought into account in an accounting period in respect of an asset for which fair value accounting is used.

CHAPTER 4

INTEREST CAPACITY

392 The interest capacity of a worldwide group for a period of account

(1) For the purposes of this Part "the interest capacity" of a worldwide group for a period of account of the group ("the current period") is (subject to subsection (2)) —

$$A + B$$

where —

A is the interest allowance of the group for the current period (see Chapter 5);

B is the aggregate of the interest allowances of the group for periods before the current period so far as they are available in the current period (see section 393).

(2) Where the amount determined under subsection (1) is less than the de minimis amount for the current period, the interest capacity of the worldwide group for the period is the de minimis amount.

(3) For this purpose "the de minimis amount" for a period of account is—

    (a) £2 million, or

    (b) where the period is more than or less than a year, the amount mentioned in paragraph (a) proportionately increased or reduced.

393 Amount of interest allowance for a period that is "available" in a later period

(1) This section applies for the purposes of this Chapter.

(2) The amount of the interest allowance of a worldwide group for a period of account ("the originating period") that is "available" in a later period of account of the group ("the receiving period") is (subject to subsection (5)) the lower of amounts A and B.

(3) Amount A is—

    (a) the amount of the interest allowance for the originating period, less

    (b) the total of the amount or amounts (if any) of that interest allowance that were used in the originating period, or in any subsequent period of account of the group before the receiving period (see section 394).

(4) Amount B is the amount (if any) of the interest allowance for the originating period that is unexpired in the receiving period (see section 395).

(5) The amount of the interest allowance for the originating period that is "available" in the receiving period is nil if—

    (a) an abbreviated return election is made in relation to the originating period, the receiving period or any intervening period of account of the group, or

    (b) an interest restriction return is not submitted for any such period.

394 When interest allowance is "used"

(1) This section applies for the purposes of this Chapter.

(2) The amount of the interest allowance of a worldwide group for a period of account of the group ("the originating period") that is "used" in the originating period is the lower of—

    (a) the interest allowance for the originating period, and

    (b) the sum of—

        (i) the aggregate net tax-interest expense of the group for the originating period;

        (ii)   the total amount of tax-interest expense amounts required to be brought into account in the originating period under section 379 (reactivation of interest) by members of the group.

(3)   The amount of the interest allowance for the originating period that is "used" in a later period of account of the group ("the receiving period") is the lower of —

        (a)   the interest allowance so far as it is available in the receiving period (see section 393), and

        (b)   the relevant part of the aggregate net tax-interest expense of the group for the receiving period (see subsection (4)).

(4)   In subsection (3)(b) "the relevant part of the aggregate net tax-interest expense of the group for the receiving period" is (subject to subsection (5)) —

$$A - B - C$$

where —

    A is the aggregate net tax-interest expense of the group for the receiving period;

    B is the interest allowance of the group for the receiving period;

    C is the amount of the interest allowance of the group for any period before the originating period that is used in the receiving period.

(5)   Where the amount determined under subsection (4) is negative, "the relevant part of the aggregate net tax-interest expense of the group for the receiving period" is nil.

395   Amount of interest allowance for a period of account that is "unexpired" in later period

(1)   This section contains provision for determining for the purposes of this Chapter the extent to which an interest allowance of a worldwide group for a period of account ("the originating period") is "unexpired" in a later period of account of the group ("the receiving period").

(2)   If the receiving period —

        (a)   begins 5 years or less after the originating period begins, and

        (b)   ends 5 years or less after the originating period ends,

    all of the interest allowance for the originating period is unexpired in the receiving period.

(3)   If the receiving period begins 5 years or more after the originating period ends, none of the interest allowance for the originating period is unexpired in the receiving period.

(4)   Subsection (5) applies if the receiving period —

        (a)   begins more than 5 years after the originating period begins, and

        (b)   ends 5 years or less after the originating period ends.

(5) The amount of the interest allowance for the originating period that is unexpired in the receiving period is—

$$(A - B) \times \frac{X}{Y}$$

where—

A is the interest allowance for the originating period;

B is—

    (a) the aggregate net tax-interest expense of the group for the originating period, or

    (b) if lower, the interest allowance for the originating period;

X is the number of days in the period—

    (a) beginning with the day on which the receiving period begins, and

    (b) ending with the day 5 years after the day on which the originating period ends;

Y is the number of days in the originating period.

(6) Subsection (7) applies if the receiving period—

    (a) begins 5 years or less after the originating period begins, and

    (b) ends more than 5 years after the originating period ends.

(7) The amount of the interest allowance for the originating period that is unexpired in the receiving period is—

$$(C - D) \times \frac{X}{Z}$$

where—

C is the aggregate net tax-interest expense of the group for the receiving period;

D is—

    (a) the interest allowance of the group for the receiving period, or

    (b) if lower, the aggregate net tax-interest expense of the group for the receiving period;

X has the same meaning as in subsection (5);

Z is the number of days in the receiving period.

(8) Subsection (9) applies if—

    (a) the receiving period—

        (i) begins more than 5 years after the originating period begins, and

        (ii) ends more than 5 years after the originating period ends, and

    (b) subsection (3) does not apply.

(9) The amount of the interest allowance for the originating period that is unexpired in the receiving period is the lower of the amounts determined under subsections (5) and (7).

CHAPTER 5

INTEREST ALLOWANCE

Interest allowance

396 The interest allowance of a worldwide group for a period of account

(1) For the purposes of this Part "the interest allowance" of a worldwide group for a period of account of the group is—

$$A + B$$

where—

   A is the basic interest allowance of the group for the period;

   B is the amount (if any) of the aggregate net tax-interest income of the group for the period (see section 390(3) and (4)).

(2) In subsection (1) "the basic interest allowance" means—

   (a) where no group ratio election is in force in relation to the period, the basic interest allowance calculated using the fixed ratio method (see section 397);

   (b) where such an election is in force in relation to the period, the basic interest allowance calculated using the group ratio method (see section 398).

397 Basic interest allowance calculated using fixed ratio method

(1) For the purposes of section 396, the basic interest allowance of a worldwide group for a period of account of the group, calculated using the fixed ratio method, is the lower of the following amounts—

   (a) 30% of the aggregate tax-EBITDA of the group for the period;

   (b) the fixed ratio debt cap of the group for the period.

(2) See—

   section 400 for the meaning of "fixed ratio debt cap";

   section 405 for the meaning of "aggregate tax-EBITDA".

398 Basic interest allowance calculated using group ratio method

(1) For the purposes of section 396, the basic interest allowance of a worldwide group for a period of account of the group, calculated using the group ratio method, is the lower of the following amounts—

   (a) the group ratio percentage of the aggregate tax-EBITDA of the group for the period;

   (b) the group ratio debt cap of the group for the period.

(2) See—

   section 399 for the meaning of "group ratio percentage";

   section 400 for the meaning of "group ratio debt cap";

   section 405 for the meaning of "aggregate tax-EBITDA".

324   *Finance (No. 2) Act 2017 (c. 32)*
Schedule 5 — Corporate interest restriction
Part 1 — New Part 10 of TIOPA 2010

399   The group ratio percentage

(1)   For the purposes of this Part "the group ratio percentage" of a worldwide group for a period of account of the group is (subject to subsection (2)) the following proportion expressed as a percentage —

$$\frac{A}{B}$$

where —

     A is the qualifying net group-interest expense of the group for the period;

     B is the group-EBITDA of the group for the period.

(2)   "The group ratio percentage" is 100% where —

     (a)   the percentage determined under subsection (1) is negative or higher than 100%, or

     (b)   B in that subsection is zero.

(3)   See —

     section 414 for the meaning of "qualifying net group-interest expense";

     section 416 for the meaning of "group-EBITDA".

400   The debt cap

(1)   For the purposes of section 397 (and this section), "the fixed ratio debt cap" of a worldwide group for a period of account of the group is the sum of the following amounts —

     (a)   the adjusted net group-interest expense of the group for the period;

     (b)   the excess debt cap of the group that was generated in the immediately preceding period of account of the group (if any) (see subsections (3) to (7)).

(2)   For the purposes of section 398 (and this section), "the group ratio debt cap" of a worldwide group for a period of account of the group is the sum of the following amounts —

     (a)   the qualifying net group-interest expense of the group for the period;

     (b)   the excess debt cap of the group that was generated in the immediately preceding period of account of the group (if any) (see subsections (3) to (7)).

(3)   Where no group ratio election is in force in relation to a period of account of a worldwide group ("the generating period"), "the excess debt cap" of the group that is generated in the period is (subject to subsections (5) and (6)) —

$$A - B$$

where —

     A is the fixed ratio debt cap of the group for the generating period;

     B is 30% of the aggregate tax-EBITDA of the group for the generating period.

(4)   Where a group ratio election is in force in relation to a period of account of a worldwide group ("the generating period"), "the excess debt cap" of the group that is generated in the period is (subject to subsections (5) and (6)) —

$$A - B$$

where —

> A is the group ratio debt cap of the group for the generating period;
>
> B is the group ratio percentage of the aggregate tax-EBITDA of the group for the generating period.

(5)   Where the amount determined under subsection (3) or (4) is negative, "the excess debt cap" of the group that is generated in the period is nil.

(6)   Where the amount determined under subsection (3) or (4) is greater than the carry-forward limit, "the excess debt cap" of the group that is generated in the period is the carry-forward limit.

(7)   For this purpose the "carry-forward limit" is the sum of the following amounts —

   (a)   the excess debt cap generated in the period of account of the group immediately preceding the generating period (if any);

   (b)   the total disallowed amount of the group in the generating period.

(8)   See —

> section 373 for the meaning of "the total disallowed amount";
>
> section 405 for the meaning of "aggregate tax-EBITDA";
>
> section 413 for the meaning of "adjusted net group-interest expense";
>
> section 414 for the meaning of "qualifying net group-interest expense".

Effect of group ratio (blended) election

401   Effect of group ratio (blended) election on group ratio percentage

(1)   Where a group ratio (blended) election (see paragraph 14 of Schedule 7A) has effect in relation to a period of account of a worldwide group ("the relevant period of account"), this Chapter applies subject to this section.

(2)   Section 399 (meaning of "group ratio percentage") does not apply for the purpose of determining the group ratio percentage of the group for the relevant period of account.

(3)   Instead, the group ratio percentage of the group for the relevant period of account is determined by taking the following steps —

Step 1

For each investor in the group, multiply the investor's applicable percentage by the investor's share in the group.

Step 2

Add together the amounts found under Step 1.

326   *Finance (No. 2) Act 2017 (c. 32)*
Schedule 5 – Corporate interest restriction
Part 1 – New Part 10 of TIOPA 2010

(4) For the purposes of this section, an investor's "applicable percentage" is the highest of the following percentages—

    (a) 30%;

    (b) the percentage determined under section 399;

    (c) in the case of a related party investor that, throughout the relevant period of account, is a member of a worldwide group ("the investor's worldwide group") other than that mentioned in subsection (1), the group ratio percentage of the investor's worldwide group for the relevant period of account.

(5) Subsection (6) applies where financial statements of the investor's worldwide group are drawn up in respect of one or more periods ("the investor's periods of account") that are comprised in or overlap with (but are not coterminous with) the relevant period of account.

(6) The group ratio percentage of the investor's worldwide group for the relevant period of account is to be determined for the purposes of subsection (4)(c) by taking the following steps—

Step 1

Find the group ratio percentage of the investor's worldwide group for each of the investor's periods of account.

Step 2

Find the proportion of the relevant period of account that coincides with each of the investor's periods of account.

Step 3

For each of the investor's periods of account, multiply the group ratio percentage found under Step 1 by the proportion found under Step 2.

Step 4

Add together the amounts found under Step 3.

402   Effect of group ratio (blended) election on group ratio debt cap

(1) Where a group ratio (blended) election (see paragraph 14 of Schedule 7A) has effect in relation to a period of account of a worldwide group ("the relevant period of account"), this Chapter applies subject to this section.

(2) In section 400 (the debt cap), subsection (2)(a) is treated as if—

    (a) it did not refer to the qualifying net group-interest expense of the group for the period, and

    (b) instead it referred to the blended net group-interest expense of the group for the period, as determined in accordance with this section.

(3) The blended net group-interest expense of the group for the relevant period of account is determined by taking the following steps—

Step 1

For each investor in the group whose applicable percentage for the purposes of section 401 is the percentage mentioned in subsection (4)(a) of that section, multiply the adjusted net group-interest expense of the group for the period by the investor's share in the group.

Step 2

For each investor in the group whose applicable percentage for the purposes of section 401 is the percentage mentioned in subsection (4)(b) of that section, multiply the qualifying net group-interest expense of the group for the period by the investor's share in the group.

Step 3

For each investor in the group whose applicable percentage for the purposes of section 401 is the percentage mentioned in subsection (4)(c) of that section, find the applicable net group-interest expense of the investor's worldwide group for the period (see subsections (4) to (8) of this section).

Step 4

Add together the amounts found under Steps 1, 2 and 3.

(4) For the purposes of this section, the "applicable net group-interest expense" of the investor's worldwide group for a period of account is so much of the qualifying net group-interest expense of the investor's worldwide group for the period as relates to loans to, or other financial arrangements with, members of the investor's worldwide group that are used to fund (directly or indirectly) loans to, or other financial arrangements with, members of the worldwide group mentioned in subsection (1).

(5) Subsection (6) applies where periods of account of the investor's worldwide group ("the investor's periods of account") are comprised in or overlap with (but are not coterminous with) the relevant period of account.

(6) The applicable net group-interest expense of the investor's worldwide group for the relevant period of account is the aggregate of so much of the applicable net group-interest expense of the investor's worldwide group for each of the investor's periods of account as is referable, on a just and reasonable basis, to the relevant period of account.

(7) Subsection (8) applies where—
    (a) a loan is made to, or another financial arrangement is entered into with, a member of the investor's worldwide group, and
    (b) the loan or other financial arrangement is—
        (i) in part used to fund (directly or indirectly) loans to, or other financial arrangements with, members of the worldwide group mentioned in subsection (1), and
        (ii) in part used for other purposes.

(8) In determining the applicable net group-interest expense of the investor's worldwide group for any period, the amount of the qualifying net group-interest expense of the investor's worldwide group for the period that is brought into account, in respect of the loan or other financial arrangement mentioned in subsection (7)(a), is confined to such amount as is referable, on a just and reasonable basis, to the use mentioned in subsection (7)(b)(i).

(9) In this section—

"financial arrangements" does not include the holding of shares;

"the investor's worldwide group" has the same meaning as in section 401.

403 Calculations under sections 401 and 402: investor worldwide groups

(1) This section applies—

    (a) in determining, under section 401, the group ratio percentage of the investor's worldwide group for a period of account;

    (b) in determining, under section 402, the qualifying net group-interest expense of the investor's worldwide group for a period of account.

(2) Where the group ratio (blended) election specifies that a particular election under Schedule 7A ("the investor's election") is to be treated as having effect, or as not having effect, in relation to periods of account of the investor's worldwide group, the investor's election is to be so treated in determining the amounts mentioned in subsection (1).

(3) Where the group ratio (blended) election does not specify that a particular election under Schedule 7A ("the investor's election") is to be treated as having effect, or as not having effect, in relation to periods of account of the investor's worldwide group, the investor's election is to be treated as having effect in determining the amounts mentioned in subsection (1) only if it was in fact made in relation to the period of account in question by a reporting company of the investor's worldwide group.

(4) In this section "the investor's worldwide group" has the same meaning as in section 401.

404 Meaning of "investor", "related party investor" and investor's "share"

(1) An entity is an "investor" in a worldwide group if it has an interest in the ultimate parent of the group that entitles it to a proportion of the profits or losses of the group.

(2) An investor in a worldwide group is a "related party investor" of the group in relation to a period of account of the group if, throughout the period, it is a related party of the ultimate parent of the group.

(3) The "share" of an investor in a worldwide group, in relation to a period of account of the group, is the proportion (expressed as a percentage) of the profits or losses of the group that arise in the period to which the investor is entitled by virtue of the investor's interest in the group's ultimate parent.

(4) This section has effect for the purposes of this Part.

CHAPTER 6

TAX-EBITDA

405 The aggregate tax-EBITDA of a worldwide group

For the purposes of this Part "the aggregate tax-EBITDA" of a worldwide group for a period of account of the group is—

    (a)   the total of the tax-EBITDAs for the period of each company that was a member of the group at any time during the period, or

    (b)   where the amount specified in paragraph (a) is negative, nil.

406 The tax-EBITDA of a company

(1)   For the purposes of this Part the "tax-EBITDA" of a company for a period of account of the worldwide group is—

    (a)   where the company has only one relevant accounting period, the company's adjusted corporation tax earnings for that accounting period;

    (b)   where the company has more than one relevant accounting period, the total of the company's adjusted corporation tax earnings for each of those accounting periods.

(2)   The company's "adjusted corporation tax earnings" for an accounting period is the total (which may be negative) of the amounts that meet condition A or B.

(3)   Condition A is that the amount—

    (a)   is brought into account by the company in determining its taxable total profits of the period (within the meaning given by section 4(2) of CTA 2010), and

    (b)   is not an excluded amount for the purposes of this condition (see section 407).

(4)   Condition B is that the amount—

    (a)   is not brought into account as mentioned in subsection (3)(a), but would have been so brought into account if the company had made profits, or more profits, of any description in the period, and

    (b)   is not an excluded amount for the purposes of this condition (see section 407).

(5)   Subsection (7) applies if an amount—

    (a)   is brought into account as mentioned in subsection (3)(a), or

    (b)   is not brought into account as mentioned in subsection (4)(a),

in an accounting period which contains one or more disregarded periods.

(6)   A "disregarded period" is any period falling within the accounting period—

    (a)   which does not fall within the period of account of the worldwide group, or

    (b)   throughout which the company is not a member of the group.

330   *Finance (No. 2) Act 2017 (c. 32)*
Schedule 5 – Corporate interest restriction
Part 1 – New Part 10 of TIOPA 2010

(7) Where this subsection applies, the amount mentioned in subsection (5) is reduced, for the purposes of subsection (2), by such amount (if any) as is referable, on a just and reasonable basis, to the disregarded period or periods mentioned in subsection (5).

(8) An amount may be reduced to nil under subsection (7).

407 Amounts not brought into account in determining a company's tax-EBITDA

(1) An amount is an excluded amount for the purposes of conditions A and B in section 406 if it is any of the following—

    (a) a tax-interest expense amount or a tax-interest income amount;

    (b) an allowance or charge under CAA 2001;

    (c) an excluded relevant intangibles debit or an excluded relevant intangibles credit (see section 408);

    (d) a loss that—

        (i) is made by the company in an accounting period other than that mentioned in section 406(2), and

        (ii) is not an allowable loss for the purposes of TCGA 1992;

    (e) a deficit from the company's loan relationships for an accounting period other than that mentioned in section 406(2);

    (f) expenses of management of the company that are referable to an accounting period other than that mentioned in section 406(2);

    (g) a deduction under section 137 of CTA 2010 (group relief) or section 188CK of that Act (group relief for carried-forward losses) if and to the extent that it constitutes a loss of the worldwide group;

    (h) a qualifying tax relief.

(2) For the purposes of subsection (1)(g) the deduction constitutes a "loss of the worldwide group" if and to the extent that it comprises surrenderable amounts that are referable to times at which the surrendering company was a member of the worldwide group.

(3) An amount is a qualifying tax relief for the purposes of subsection (1)(h) if it is any of the following—

    (a) an R&D expenditure credit within the meaning of section 104A of CTA 2009;

    (b) a deduction under section 1044, 1063, 1068 or 1087 of CTA 2009 (additional relief for expenditure on research and development);

    (c) an amount which is treated as a trading loss as a result of section 1092 of CTA 2009 (SMEs: deemed trading loss for pre-trading expenditure);

    (d) a deduction under section 1147 or 1149 of CTA 2009 (relief for expenditure on contaminated or derelict land);

    (e) a deduction under section 1199 of CTA 2009 (film tax relief);

    (f) a deduction under section 1216CF of CTA 2009 (television tax relief);

(g) a deduction under section 1217CF of CTA 2009 (video games tax relief);

(h) a deduction under section 1217H of CTA 2009 (relief in relation to theatrical productions);

(i) a deduction under section 1217RD of CTA 2009 (orchestra tax relief);

(j) a deduction under section 1218ZCE of CTA 2009 (museums and galleries exhibition tax relief);

(k) a qualifying charitable donation (whether made in the accounting period mentioned in section 406(2) or an earlier one);

(l) a deduction under section 357A of CTA 2010 (profits from patents etc chargeable at lower rate of corporation tax).

(4) An amount is an excluded amount for the purposes of condition B in section 406 if it is an allowable loss for the purposes of TCGA 1992.

408 Excluded relevant intangibles debits and excluded relevant intangibles credits

(1) For the purposes of section 407 (and this section)—

(a) a debit is a "relevant intangibles debit" if it is brought into account under a provision of Part 8 of CTA 2009 (intangible fixed assets) that is listed in column 1 of the following table;

(b) a relevant intangibles debit is "excluded" to the extent indicated in the corresponding entry in column 2 of the table.

Provision	Excluded debits
section 729	excluded in full
section 731	excluded in full
section 732	excluded if and to the extent that its amount is determined by reference to an excluded intangibles credit
section 735	excluded in full
section 736	excluded in full
section 872	excluded in full
section 874	excluded in full

(2) For the purposes of section 407 (and this section)—

(a) a credit is a "relevant intangibles credit" if it is brought into account under a provision of Part 8 of CTA 2009 (intangible fixed assets) that is listed in column 1 of the following table;

(b) a relevant intangibles credit is "excluded" to the extent indicated in the corresponding entry in column 2 of the table.

332   *Finance (No. 2) Act 2017 (c. 32)*
Schedule 5 — Corporate interest restriction
Part 1 — New Part 10 of TIOPA 2010

Provision	Excluded credits
section 723	excluded if and to the extent that its amount is determined by reference to excluded intangible debits and excluded intangible credits
section 725	excluded if and to the extent that its amount is determined by reference to an excluded intangibles debit
section 735	excluded if and to the extent that the cost of the asset in question exceeds its tax written-down value
section 872	excluded in full
section 874	excluded in full

    (3)   In the table in subsection (2) —

        (a)   "tax written-down value" has the same meaning as in Part 8 of CTA 2009 (see Chapter 5 of that Part);

        (b)   "the cost of the asset" has the same meaning as in section 736 of that Act.

409   Double taxation relief

    (1)   This section applies where —

        (a)   apart from this section, an amount of income ("the relevant amount") would meet condition A or B in section 406 in relation to a relevant accounting period of a company, and

        (b)   the amount of corporation tax chargeable in respect of the relevant amount is reduced under section 18(2) (entitlement to credit for foreign tax reduces UK tax by amount of the credit).

    (2)   The relevant amount is treated, for the purposes of section 406(2) (meaning of "adjusted corporation tax earnings") as not meeting the condition mentioned in subsection (1)(a) to the extent that it consists of notional untaxed income.

    (3)   For this purpose, the amount of the relevant amount that consists of "notional untaxed income" is —

$$\frac{A}{B}$$

where —

    A is the amount of the reduction mentioned in subsection (1)(b);

    B is the rate of corporation tax payable by the company, before any credit under Part 2 (double taxation relief), on the company's profits for the relevant accounting period.

CHAPTER 7

GROUP-INTEREST AND GROUP-EBITDA

Group-interest

410 Net group-interest expense

(1) For the purposes of this Part the "net group-interest expense" of a worldwide group for a period of account of the group ("the relevant period of account") is—

$$A - B$$

where—

A is the sum of the relevant expense amounts that are recognised in the financial statements of the group for the period as items of profit or loss;

B is the sum of the relevant income amounts that are recognised in the financial statements of the group for the period as items of profit or loss.

(2) Subsection (3) applies where—

(a) a relevant expense amount ("the capitalised expense") is brought into account in financial statements of the group (whether for the relevant period of account or any earlier period) in determining the carrying value of an asset,

(b) the asset is not a relevant asset, and

(c) in the financial statements of the group for the relevant period of account, any of the carrying value is written down.

(3) A in subsection (1) is treated as including so much of the amount written down as is attributable to the capitalised expense.

(4) Subsection (5) applies where—

(a) a relevant income amount ("the capitalised income") is brought into account in financial statements of the group (whether for the relevant period of account or any earlier period) in determining the carrying value of an asset,

(b) the asset is not a relevant asset, and

(c) in the financial statements of the group for the relevant period of account, any of the carrying value is written down.

(5) B in subsection (1) is treated as including the amount of the reduction in the amount written down that is attributable to the capitalised income.

(6) See—

section 411 for the definitions of "relevant expense amount" and "relevant income amount";

section 417(5) and (6) for the definition of "relevant asset";

section 420 for provision affecting amounts recognised in financial statements in respect of certain profits or losses arising from derivative contracts.

411 **"Relevant expense amount" and "relevant income amount"**

(1) In this Chapter "relevant expense amount" means (subject to subsection (3)) an amount in respect of any of the following—

    (a) interest payable under a loan relationship;

    (b) expenses ancillary to a loan relationship;

    (c) losses arising from a loan relationship or a related transaction, other than—

        (i) exchange losses, and

        (ii) impairment losses;

    (d) dividends payable in respect of preference shares accounted for as a financial liability;

    (e) losses arising from a relevant derivative contract or a related transaction, other than—

        (i) exchanges losses,

        (ii) impairment losses, and

        (iii) losses where the contract hedges risks arising in the ordinary course of a trade and the contract was entered into wholly for reasons unrelated to the capital structure of the worldwide group (or any member of the worldwide group);

    (f) expenses ancillary to a relevant derivative contract or related transaction;

    (g) financing charges implicit in payments made under a finance lease;

    (h) financing charges relating to debt factoring;

    (i) financing charges implicit in payments made under a service concession arrangement if and to the extent that the arrangement is accounted for as a financial liability;

    (j) interest payable in respect of a relevant non-lending relationship;

    (k) alternative finance return payable under alternative finance arrangements;

    (l) manufactured interest payable;

    (m) financing charges in respect of the advance under a debtor repo or debtor quasi-repo;

    (n) financing charges so far as they are made up of amounts which—

        (i) are treated as interest payable under a loan relationship under a relevant provision of Chapter 2 of Part 16 of CTA 2010 (finance arrangements), or

        (ii) would be so treated if the company in question were within the charge to corporation tax.

(2) In this Chapter "relevant income amount" means (subject to subsection (3)) an amount in respect of any of the following—

    (a) interest receivable under a loan relationship;

    (b) profits arising from a loan relationship or a related transaction, other than—

        (i) exchange gains, and

        (ii) the reversal of impairment losses;

    (c)   dividends receivable in respect of preference shares accounted for as a financial asset;

    (d)   gains arising from a relevant derivative contract or a related transaction, other than—

        (i)   exchange gains,

        (ii)   the reversal of impairment losses, and

        (iii)   gains where the contract hedges risks arising in the ordinary course of a trade and the contract was entered into wholly for reasons unrelated to the capital structure of the worldwide group (or any member of the worldwide group);

    (e)   financing income implicit in amounts received under a finance lease;

    (f)   financing income relating to debt factoring;

    (g)   financing income implicit in amounts received under a service concession arrangement if and to the extent that the arrangement is accounted for as a financial asset;

    (h)   interest receivable in respect of a relevant non-lending relationship;

    (i)   alternative finance return receivable under alternative finance arrangements;

    (j)   manufactured interest receivable;

    (k)   financing income in respect of the advance under a creditor repo or creditor quasi-repo;

    (l)   financing income so far as it is made up of amounts which—

        (i)   are treated as interest receivable under a loan relationship under a relevant provision of Chapter 2 of Part 16 of CTA 2010 (finance arrangements), or

        (ii)   would be so treated if the company in question were within the charge to corporation tax.

(3)   In this Chapter—

    (a)   "relevant expense amount" does not include an amount payable under a pension scheme;

    (b)   "relevant income amount" does not include an amount receivable under a pension scheme.

(4)   In subsection (3) "pension scheme" has the meaning given by section 150(1) of FA 2004.

412   Section 411: interpretation

(1)   For the purposes of section 411(1)(b), expenses are "ancillary" to a loan relationship if and only if they are incurred directly—

    (a)   in bringing, or attempting to bring, the relationship into existence,

    (b)   in making payments under the loan relationship, or

    (c)   in taking steps to ensure the receipt of payments under the loan relationship.

(2)   For the purposes of section 411(1)(e) and (2)(d) a derivative contract is "relevant" if its underlying subject matter consists only of one or more of the following—

    (a)   interest rates;

    (b)   any index determined by reference to income or retail prices;

    (c)   currency;

    (d)   an asset or liability representing a loan relationship;

    (e)   any other underlying subject matter which is—

        (i)   subordinate in relation to any of the matters mentioned in paragraphs (a) to (d), or

        (ii) of small value in comparison with the value of the underlying subject matter as a whole.

(3)   Whether part of the underlying subject matter of a derivative contract is subordinate or of small value is to be determined for the purposes of subsection (2)(e) by reference to the time when the company enters into or acquires the contract.

(4)   For the purposes of section 411(1)(f) expenses are "ancillary" to a relevant derivative contract or related transaction if and only if they are incurred directly—

    (a)   in bringing, or attempting to bring, the derivative contract into existence,

    (b)   in entering into or giving effect to, or attempting to enter into or give effect to, the related transaction,

    (c)   in making payments under the derivative contract or as a result of the related transaction, or

    (d)   in taking steps to secure the receipt of payments under the derivative contract or in accordance with the related transaction.

(5)   For the purposes of section 411(1)(n) and (2)(l), the following provisions of Chapter 2 of Part 16 of CTA 2010 are "relevant"—

    (a)   section 761(3) (type 1 finance arrangements: borrower a company);

    (b)   section 762(3) (type 1 finance arrangements: borrower a partnership);

    (c)   section 766(3) (type 2 finance arrangements);

    (d)   section 769(3) (type 3 finance arrangements).

(6)   In section 411—

    (a)   in subsections (1)(c) and (2)(b), "related transaction", "exchange loss" and "exchange gain" have the same meaning as in Parts 5 and 6 of CTA 2009 (see sections 304 and 475 of that Act);

    (b)   in subsections (1)(e) and (2)(d), "related transaction", "exchange loss" and "exchange gain" have the same meaning as in Part 7 of that Act (see sections 596 and 705 of that Act).

(7)   In section 411 and this section—

    "alternative finance arrangements" has the same meaning as in Parts 5 and 6 of CTA 2009 (see section 501(2) of that Act);

    "alternative finance return" has the same meaning as in Part 6 of CTA 2009 (see sections 511 to 513 of that Act);

    "creditor quasi-repo" has the same meaning as in Chapter 10 of Part 6 of CTA 2009 (see section 544 of that Act);

"creditor repo" has the same meaning as in Chapter 10 of Part 6 of CTA 2009 (see section 543 of that Act);

"debtor quasi-repo" has the same meaning as in Chapter 10 of Part 6 of CTA 2009 (see section 549 of that Act);

"debtor repo" has the same meaning as in Chapter 10 of Part 6 of CTA 2009 (see section 548 of that Act);

"manufactured interest" has the same meaning as in Chapter 9 of Part 6 of CTA 2009 (see section 539(5) of that Act);

"relevant non-lending relationship" has the same meaning as in Chapter 2 of Part 6 of CTA 2009 (see sections 479 and 480 of that Act);

"underlying subject matter" has the same meaning as in Part 7 of CTA 2009 (see section 583 of that Act).

413 Adjusted net group-interest expense

(1) For the purposes of this Part the "adjusted net group-interest expense" of a worldwide group for a period of account of the group is (subject to subsection (2)) –

$$A + B - C$$

where –

A is the net group-interest expense of the group for the period (see section 410);

B is the sum of any upward adjustments (see subsection (3));

C is the sum of any downward adjustments (see subsection (4)).

(2) Where the amount determined under subsection (1) is negative, the "adjusted net group-interest expense" of the group for the period is nil.

(3) In this section "upward adjustment" means any of the following amounts –

  (a) a relevant expense amount that is brought into account in the financial statements of the group for the period in determining the carrying value of an asset or liability;

  (b) an amount that is included in the net group-interest expense of the group for the period by virtue of section 410(5) (capitalised income written off);

  (c) a relevant expense amount that –

    (i) in the financial statements of the group for the period is recognised in equity or shareholders' funds, and is not recognised as an item of profit or loss or as an item of other comprehensive income, and

    (ii) is brought into account for the purposes of corporation tax by a member of the group under a relevant enactment, or would be so brought into account if the member were within the charge to corporation tax;

  (d) a relevant income amount that is recognised in the financial statements of the group for the period, as an item of profit or loss, so far as it –

   (i) is prevented from being brought into account for the purposes of corporation tax by a member of the group by section 322(2) or 323A of CTA 2009 (cases where credits not required to be brought into account), or

   (ii) would be so prevented if the member were within the charge to corporation tax.

(4) In this section "downward adjustment" means any of the following amounts—

  (a) a relevant income amount that is brought into account in the financial statements of the group for the period in determining the carrying value of an asset or liability;

  (b) an amount that is included in the net group-interest expense of the group for the period by virtue of section 410(3) (capitalised expense written off);

  (c) a relevant income amount that—

   (i) in the financial statements of the group for the period is recognised in equity or shareholders' funds, and is not recognised as an item of profit or loss or as an item of other comprehensive income, and

   (ii) is brought into account for the purposes of corporation tax by a member of the group under a relevant enactment, or would be so brought into account if the member were within the charge to corporation tax;

  (d) a relevant expense amount that is recognised in the financial statements of the group for the period, as an item of profit or loss, so far as it—

   (i) is prevented from being brought into account for the purposes of corporation tax by a member of the group by section 323A of CTA 2009 (cases where credits not required to be brought into account), or

   (ii) would so prevented if the member were within the charge to corporation tax;

  (e) a relevant expense amount that is recognised in the financial statements of the group for the period, as an item of profit or loss, so far as—

   (i) the amount represents a dividend payable in respect of preference shares, and

   (ii) those shares are recognised as a liability in the financial statements of the group for the period.

(5) The references in subsections (3)(a) and (4)(a) to amounts brought into account in determining the carrying value of an asset or liability do not include amounts so brought into account as the result of writing off any part of an amount which was itself so brought into account.

(6) In subsections (3)(c)(ii) and (4)(c)(ii), "relevant enactment" means—

  (a) section 321 or 605 of CTA 2009 (credits and debits recognised in equity), or

  (b) regulation 3A of the Taxation of Regulatory Capital Securities Regulations 2013 (S.I. 2013/3209) (amounts recognised in equity).

414 Qualifying net group-interest expense

(1) For the purposes of this Part the "qualifying net group-interest expense" of a worldwide group for a period of account of the group is (subject to subsection (2)) —

$$A - B$$

where
> A is the adjusted net group-interest expense of the group for the period (see section 413);
> B is the sum of any downward adjustments (see subsection (3)).

(2) Where the amount determined under subsection (1) is negative, "the qualifying net group-interest expense" of the group for the period is nil.

(3) In this section "downward adjustment" means a relevant expense amount that meets the condition in subsection (4), so far as it relates to —

> (a) a transaction with, or a financial liability owed to, a person who, at any time during the period, is a related party of a member of the group,
> (b) results-dependent securities, or
> (c) equity notes.

(4) The condition mentioned in subsection (3) is that the amount —

> (a) is recognised in the financial statements of the group for the period, as an item of profit and loss, and is not (and is not comprised in) a downward adjustment for the purposes of section 413 (adjusted net group-interest expense), or
> (b) is (or is comprised in) an upward adjustment for the purposes of that section.

(5) In a case where —

> (a) the person mentioned in subsection (3)(a) is not a related party of a member of the group during any part of the period of account, or
> (b) during any part of the period of account, the financial liability mentioned in subsection (3)(a) is owed to a person who is not a related party of a member of the group,

the amount of the downward adjustment under subsection (3)(a) is to be reduced by such amount (if any) as is attributable, on a just and reasonable basis, to that part.

415 Section 414: interpretation

(1) For the purposes of section 414 a person is treated as not being a related party of a member of the group at any time ("the relevant time") if at the relevant time —

> (a) the person would (apart from this subsection) be a related party of the member by virtue only of section 466(2) (parties to loan relationship treated as related parties by virtue of financial assistance provided by a related party), and

340   *Finance (No. 2) Act 2017 (c. 32)*
Schedule 5 − Corporate interest restriction
Part 1 − New Part 10 of TIOPA 2010

            (b)   any of the following conditions is met in relation to the guarantee, indemnity or other financial assistance in question.

     (2)   The conditions are—

            (a)   that the financial assistance is provided before 1 April 2017;

            (b)   that the financial assistance is provided by a member of the group;

            (c)   that the financial assistance relates only to an undertaking in relation to—

                  (i)   shares in the ultimate parent of the group, or

                  (ii)   loans to a member of the group;

            (d)   that the financial assistance is a non-financial guarantee.

     (3)   Financial assistance is "a non-financial guarantee" if—

            (a)   it guarantees the performance by any person of contractual obligations to provide goods or services to a member of the group,

            (b)   it is given by the person providing the goods or services or by a related party of that person, and

            (c)   the maximum amount for which the guarantor is liable does not exceed the consideration given under the contract for the provision of the goods or services.

     (4)   The reference in section 414(3)(b) to "results-dependent securities" is (subject to subsection (8)) to securities issued by an entity where the consideration given by the entity for the use of the principal secured depends (to any extent) on—

            (a)   the results of the entity's business, or

            (b)   the results of the business of any other entity that was a member of the group at any time during the period of account of the group.

In this subsection references to a business include part of a business.

     (5)   For the purposes of subsection (4) the consideration given by the entity for the use of the principal secured does not fall within paragraph (a) or (b) of that subsection merely because the terms of the security provide—

            (a)   for the consideration to be reduced if the results mentioned in that paragraph improve, or

            (b)   for the consideration to be increased if the results mentioned in that paragraph deteriorate.

     (6)   An amount does not fall within section 414(3)(b) so far as it is relevant alternative finance return (within the meaning given by section 1019(2) of CTA 2010).

     (7)   The reference in section 414(3)(c) to "equity notes" is (subject to subsection (8)) to equity notes within the meaning given by section 1016 of CTA 2010.

     (8)   A regulatory capital security (within the meaning of Taxation of Regulatory Capital Securities Regulations 2013 (S.I. 2013/3209)) is not—

      (a)   a results-dependent security for the purposes of section 414(3)(b), or

      (b)   an equity note for the purposes of section 414(3)(c).

Group-EBITDA

416   Group-EBITDA

(1)   For the purposes of this Part "the group-EBITDA" of a worldwide group for a period of account of the group ("the relevant period of account") is —

$$PBT + I + DA$$

where —

    PBT is the group's profit before tax (which may be a negative amount) (see subsection (2));

    I is the net group-interest expense of the group for the period (which may be a negative amount) (see section 410);

    DA is the group's depreciation and amortisation adjustment (which may be a negative amount) (see subsection (3)).

(2)   For the purposes of this Chapter a worldwide group's "profit before tax" is —

      (a)   the sum of the amounts that are recognised in the financial statements of the group for the period, as items of profit or loss, in respect of income of any description other than tax income, less

      (b)   the sum of the amounts that are recognised in the financial statements of the group for the period, as items of profit or loss, in respect of expenses of any description other than tax expense.

In this subsection "tax income" and "tax expense" have the meaning they have for accounting purposes.

(3)   In this section the group's "depreciation and amortisation adjustment" means the sum of the following amounts (any of which may be negative) —

      (a)   the capital (expenditure) adjustment (see section 417);

      (b)   the capital (fair value movement) adjustment (see section 418);

      (c)   the capital (disposals) adjustment (see section 419).

(4)   The following expressions have the same meaning in sections 417 to 419 as they have in this section —

    "the relevant period of account";

    "the group's profit before tax".

(5)   For provision affecting amounts recognised in financial statements in respect of certain profits or losses arising from derivative contracts, see section 420.

417 The capital (expenditure) adjustment

(1) For the purposes of section 416, "the capital (expenditure) adjustment" is—

$$A - B - C$$

where—

A is the sum of the amounts (if any) in respect of relevant capital expenditure which are brought into account in determining the group's profit before tax;

B is the sum of the amounts (if any) in respect of relevant capital expenditure reversals which are brought into account in determining the group's profit before tax;

C is the sum of the amounts (if any) in respect of relevant capital income which are brought into account in determining the group's profit before tax.

(2) In this section "relevant capital expenditure" means—

(a) expenditure of a capital nature that relates to relevant assets (including any relevant expense amounts previously included in the carrying value of relevant assets) that is recognised in the relevant period of account by way of depreciation or amortisation, or as the result of an impairment review,

(b) expenditure of a capital nature that relates to relevant assets that is incurred and recognised in the relevant period of account, and

(c) amounts recognised in the relevant period of account by way of provision in respect of future expenditure of a capital nature that relates to relevant assets.

(3) In this section "relevant capital expenditure reversals" means the reversal in the relevant period of account of any relevant capital expenditure recognised in an earlier period of account.

(4) In this section "relevant capital income" means income of a capital nature that relates to relevant assets.

(5) In this Chapter "relevant asset" means an asset that is—

(a) plant, property and equipment,

(b) an investment property,

(c) an intangible asset,

(d) goodwill,

(e) shares in a company, or

(f) an interest in an entity which entitles the holder to a share of the profits of the entity.

(6) In subsection (5)—

(a) "plant, property and equipment" has the meaning it has for accounting purposes;

(b) "investment property" has the meaning it has for accounting purposes;

      (c)   "intangible asset" has the meaning it has for accounting purposes (and includes an internally-generated intangible asset);

      (d)   "goodwill" has the meaning it has for accounting purposes (and includes internally-generated goodwill);

      (e)   "entity" includes anything which is treated as an entity in the financial statements of the group (regardless of whether it has a legal personality as a body corporate).

Section 712(2) and (3) of CTA 2009 ("intangible asset" includes intellectual property) applies for the purposes of paragraph (c).

(7)   An amount does not fall within A in subsection (1) if it is brought into account in determining a profit or loss on the disposal of a relevant asset.

418   The capital (fair value movement) adjustment

(1)   In section 416, "the capital (fair value movement) adjustment" means the sum of any relevant fair value movements.

(2)   For the purposes of subsection (1) there is a "relevant fair value movement" where−

      (a)   the carrying value of a relevant asset is measured, for the purposes of the financial statements of the group, using fair value accounting, and

      (b)   an amount representing a change in the carrying value of the asset is brought into account in determining the group's profit before tax.

(3)   The amount of the relevant fair value movement is the amount of the change mentioned in subsection (2)(b) and−

      (a)   is a positive amount where the change is a loss;

      (b)   is a negative amount where the change is a profit.

(4)   References in this section to a change in the carrying value of a relevant asset do not include a change where the amount brought into account in respect of the change as mentioned in subsection (2)(b) is of a revenue nature.

419   The capital (disposals) adjustment

(1)   For the purposes of section 416, "the capital (disposals) adjustment" is−

$$A - B + C$$

where−

    A is the sum of the amounts (if any) that are brought into account in determining the group's profit before tax and that represent losses on disposals of relevant assets;

    B is the sum of the amounts (if any) that are brought into account in determining the group's profit before tax and that represent profits on disposals of relevant assets;

    C is the sum of any recalculated profit amounts (see subsections (2) to (8)).

(2) For the purposes of the definition of C in subsection (1) there is a "recalculated profit amount" where the following two conditions are met.

(3) The first condition is that an amount is brought into account in determining the group's profit before tax in respect of a profit or loss on the disposal of a relevant asset.

(4) The second condition is that—
   (a) the relevant proceeds, exceeds
   (b) the relevant cost.

(5) The amount of the recalculated profit amount is the amount of the excess mentioned in subsection (4).

(6) In this section "the relevant proceeds" means the amount of income of a capital nature that is brought into account in determining the profit or loss mentioned in subsection (3).

(7) In this section "the relevant cost" means (subject to subsection (8)) the amount of expenditure of a capital nature that is brought into account in determining the profit or loss mentioned in subsection (3).

(8) For the purposes of subsection (7), any adjustment made to the amount brought into account as mentioned in that subsection is to be disregarded where the adjustment is in respect of amounts that—
   (a) are otherwise recognised, in the financial statements of the group for the relevant period of account, as items of profit or loss, or
   (b) were so recognised in the financial statements of the group for an earlier period.

(9) References in this section to a relevant asset include part of a relevant asset.

(10) References in this section to the disposal of a relevant asset do not include a disposal where the profit or loss (if any) on the disposal is of a revenue nature.

(11) The condition in subsection (3) is met even if no amount is brought into account as mentioned in that subsection if that is because no gain or loss accrued on the disposal; and subsections (6) to (8) apply accordingly.

Treatment of derivative contracts in financial statements of worldwide group

420 Derivative contracts subject to fair value accounting

(1) This section makes provision about the amounts recognised in a worldwide group's financial statements for a period of account ("the relevant period of account") in respect of derivative contracts.

(2) Subsection (3) applies where one or more excluded derivative contract amounts are recognised in the group's financial statements for the relevant period of account as items of profit or loss.

(3) The financial statements are treated for the purposes of this Part (apart from this section) as if the excluded derivative contract

amounts were not recognised in the group's financial statements for the relevant period of account.

(4) In subsections (2) and (3) "excluded derivative contract amount" means an amount which would, on the relevant assumptions, be excluded from section 597(1) of CTA 2009 (amounts recognised in determining a company's profit or loss) as a result of a relevant provision of the Disregard Regulations.

(5) Subsection (6) applies where, on the relevant assumptions, one or more amounts ("replacement derivative contract amounts") would be brought into account by members of the group for the purposes of corporation tax in relevant accounting periods as a result of regulation 9 or 10 of the Disregard Regulations.

(6) The financial statements are treated for the purposes of this Part (apart from this section) as if the replacement derivative contract amounts were recognised in the group's financial statements for the relevant period of account.

(7) Subsection (9) applies if an accounting period in which a replacement derivative contract amount would, on the relevant assumptions, be brought into account for the purposes of corporation tax contains one or more disregarded periods.

(8) A "disregarded period" is any period falling within the accounting period—
   (a) which does not fall within the relevant period of account, or
   (b) throughout which the company is not a member of the group.

(9) Where this subsection applies, the replacement derivative contract amount mentioned in subsection (7) is reduced by such amount as is referable, on a just and reasonable basis, to the disregarded period or periods mentioned in that subsection.

(10) An amount may be reduced to nil under subsection (9).

421 Derivative contracts subject to fair value accounting: interpretation

(1) In section 420 "the relevant assumptions" means the following assumptions—
   (a) that all members of the group are within the charge to corporation tax;
   (b) that elections under regulation 6A of the Disregard Regulations have effect in relation to each derivative contract of each member of the group;
   (c) that paragraph (5) of regulation 7 of the Disregard Regulations is of no effect;
   (d) that where—
      (i) a member of the group ("member A") holds a derivative contract,
      (ii) the group has a hedging relationship between that derivative contract (on the one hand), and an asset, liability, receipt or expense (on the other), and
      (iii) the asset, liability, receipt or expense is held, or is expected to be received or incurred, by a member of the group other than member A,

the asset, liability, receipt or expense is held, or is expected to be received or incurred, by member A;

    (e)   that the financial statements of members of the group deal with derivative contracts and hedged items in the same way as they are dealt with in the group's financial statements.

(2)   For the purposes of subsection (1)(d) the group has a "hedging relationship" between a derivative contract (on the one hand) and an asset, liability, receipt or expense (on the other) if, were those things held, received or incurred by a single company, the company would have a hedging relationship between them.

(3)   Regulation 2(5) of the Disregard Regulations (hedging relationships of a company) applies for the purposes of this section.

(4)   For the purposes of section 420 and this section —

    (a)   "the Disregard Regulations" means the Loan Relationship and Derivative Contracts (Disregard and Bringing into Account of Profits and Losses) Regulations 2004 (S.I. 2004/3256);

    (b)   the following are "relevant provisions" of the Disregard Regulations —

        (i)   regulation 7 (fair value profits or losses arising from derivative contracts which are currency contracts);

        (ii)   regulation 8 (profits or losses arising from derivative contracts which are commodity contracts or debt contracts);

        (iii)   regulation 9 (profits or losses arising from derivative contracts which are interest rate contracts).

Effect of group-EBITDA (chargeable gains) election

422   Group-EBITDA (chargeable gains) election

(1)   Where a group-EBITDA (chargeable gains) election has effect in relation to a period of account of a worldwide group ("the relevant period of account"), this Chapter applies in relation to the period subject to this section.

(2)   Section 419 (the capital (disposals) adjustment) has effect as if —

    (a)   the definition of C in subsection (1) of that section did not apply, and

    (b)   instead, C were defined for the purposes of that section as —

        (i)   the sum of any relevant gains, less

        (ii)   the sum of any relevant losses,

    or, where that is a negative amount, nil.

(3)   For the purposes of this section, there is a "relevant gain" or "relevant loss" where condition A or B is met.

(4)   Condition A is that a member of the group disposes of a relevant asset during the relevant period of account.

(5)   Condition B is that —

    (a)   a member of the group ceases to be a member of the group during the relevant period of account, and

    (b)   the member held a relevant asset immediately before ceasing to be a member of the group.

(6)   Where condition A is met, the amount of the relevant gain or relevant loss is the amount of the chargeable gain or allowable loss that would, on the assumptions in subsection (8), accrue to the member on the disposal.

(7)   Where condition B is met, the amount of the relevant gain or relevant loss is the amount of the chargeable gain or allowable loss that would, on the assumptions in subsection (8), accrue to the member if the member —

    (a)   disposed of the relevant asset immediately before ceasing to be a member of the group, and

    (b)   received such consideration for that disposal as it is just and reasonable to attribute to it, having regard to the consideration received by the group for its interests in the member.

(8)   The assumptions mentioned in subsections (6) and (7) are that—

    (a)   all members of the group are within the charge to corporation tax;

    (b)   Schedule 7AC to TCGA 1992 (exemptions for disposals by companies with substantial shareholdings) is of no effect;

    (c)   Part 2 (double taxation relief) is of no effect.

(9)   Where—

    (a)   the sum of any relevant losses, exceeds

    (b)   the sum of any relevant gains,

the amount of the excess is treated as a relevant loss in relation to the period of account of the group immediately after the relevant period of account.

(10)   In this section "relevant asset" does not include shares in (or other interests giving an entitlement to share in the profits of) a member of the group.

Effect of interest allowance (alternative calculation) election

423   Capitalised interest brought into account for tax purposes in accordance with GAAP

(1)   Where an interest allowance (alternative calculation) election (see paragraph 16 of Schedule 7A) has effect in relation to a period of account of a worldwide group ("the relevant period of account"), this Chapter applies in relation to the period subject to this section.

(2)   Section 413 (adjusted net group-interest expense of a worldwide group) has effect as if —

    (a)   subsections (3)(a) and (4)(a) (which relate to capitalised interest) did not apply in relation to a GAAP-taxable asset or liability, and

    (b)   subsections (3)(b) and (4)(b) (which relate to capitalised interest written off) did not apply in relation to a GAAP-taxable asset or liability.

(3)   But subsection (2)(b) of this section is of no effect where the adjusted net group-interest expense of the group for a period of account before the relevant period of account included any amount by virtue of section 413(3)(a) or (4)(a) in respect of the GAAP-taxable asset or liability.

(4)   For the purposes of this section an asset or liability is "GAAP-taxable" if any profit or loss for corporation tax purposes in relation to the asset or liability falls to be calculated in accordance with generally accepted accounting practice.

(5)   For the purposes of this section, all members of the group are treated as within the charge to corporation tax.

424   Employers' pension contributions

(1)   Where an interest allowance (alternative calculation) election has effect in relation to a period of account of a worldwide group, this Chapter applies in relation to the period subject to this section.

(2)   The definition of "the group's profit before tax" in subsection (2) of section 416 has effect as if references to amounts that are recognised in the financial statements of the group for the period, as items of profit or loss, did not include amounts so recognised in respect of employer pension contributions.

(3)   The group's profit before tax, as defined in that section, is reduced by the total of the relief to which members of the group are entitled, by virtue of sections 196 to 200 of FA 2004, in respect of relevant employer pension contributions paid during the period.

(4)   In this section—
   (a)   "employer pension contributions" means contributions paid by an employer under a registered pension scheme in respect of an individual;
   (b)   employer pension contributions are "relevant" if they are paid at a time at which the employer is a member of the group.

425   Employee share acquisitions

(1)   Where an interest allowance (alternative calculation) election has effect in relation to a period of account of a worldwide group, this Chapter applies in relation to the period subject to this section.

(2)   The definition of "the group's profit before tax" in subsection (2) of section 416 has effect as if references to amounts that are recognised in the financial statements of the group for the period, as items of profit or loss, did not include amounts so recognised in respect of employee share acquisition arrangements.

(3)   The group's profit before tax, as defined in that section, is reduced by such amount as, on a just and reasonable basis, reflects the effect on the group in the period of—
   (a)   deductions allowed to members of the group under Part 11 of CTA 2009 (relief for particular employee share acquisition schemes) and amounts treated as received by members of the group under that Part, and

      (b)   relief given to members of the group under Part 12 of that Act (other relief for employee share acquisitions).

(4)   In this section "employee share acquisition arrangements" means arrangements the corporation tax treatment of which is determined under Part 11 or 12 of CTA 2009.

(5)   For the purposes of this section, all members of the group are treated as within the charge to corporation tax.

426 Changes in accounting policy

(1)   Where an interest allowance (alternative calculation) election has effect in relation to a period of account of a worldwide group ("the relevant period of account"), this Chapter applies in relation to the period subject to this section.

(2)   The financial statements of the group for the relevant period of account are to be treated as subject to such adjustments as would be made to them under the change of accounting policy provisions if the group were a company that—

    (a)   was within the charge to corporation tax,

    (b)   held the assets and owed the liabilities recognised in the financial statements, to the extent that they are so recognised, and

    (c)   carried on the trades and other activities giving rise to amounts recognised in the financial statements as items of profit and loss.

(3)   In this section "the change of accounting policy provisions" means—

    (a)   Chapter 14 of Part 3 of CTA 2009 (trading profits);

    (b)   sections 315 to 319 of that Act (loan relationships);

    (c)   sections 613 to 615 of that Act (derivative contracts);

    (d)   Chapter 15 of Part 8 of that Act (intangible fixed assets);

    (e)   the Loan Relationships and Derivative Contracts (Change of Accounting Practice) Regulations 2004 (S.I. 2004/3271).

(4)   For the purposes of subsection (2)—

    (a)   the change of accounting policy provisions are to be read subject to the necessary modifications, and

    (b)   it is to be assumed that any election under the change of accounting policy provisions (as applied) has been made.

Effect of interest allowance (non-consolidated investment) election

427 Group interest and group-EBITDA

(1)   Where an interest allowance (non-consolidated investment) election (see paragraph 17 of Schedule 7A) has effect in relation to a period of account of a worldwide group, this Chapter applies in relation to the period subject to this section.

(2)   In this section and section 428 (which contains further interpretative provision)—

    (a)   "the principal worldwide group" means the worldwide group mentioned in subsection (1);

     (b)   "the relevant period of account" means the period of account mentioned in subsection (1).

(3) The financial statements of the principal worldwide group for the relevant period of account are treated as if—

     (a)   no relevant income amounts were recognised in them, as items of profit or loss, so far as they relate to financial liabilities owed to any member of the principal worldwide group by any member of an associated worldwide group, and

     (b)   no amounts were recognised in them, as items of profits or loss, in respect of any profit or loss attributable to an interest held by any member of the principal worldwide group in any member of an associated worldwide group

(4) The adjusted net group-interest expense of the principal worldwide group for the relevant period of account is treated as increased by the appropriate proportion of the adjusted net group-interest expense for the period of each associated worldwide group.

(5) The qualifying net group-interest expense of the principal worldwide group for the relevant period of account is treated as increased by the appropriate proportion of the qualifying net group-interest expense for the period of each associated worldwide group.

(6) The group-EBITDA of the principal worldwide group for the relevant period of account is treated as increased by the appropriate proportion of the group-EBITDA of each associated worldwide group for the period.

(7) In this section "the appropriate proportion", in relation to an associated worldwide group means the proportion of the profits or losses of the associated worldwide group arising in the relevant period of account to which the principal worldwide group is entitled.

428 Section 427: associated worldwide groups

(1) This section has effect for the purposes of section 427 and this section.

(2) "Associated worldwide group" means the worldwide group of which a specified non-consolidated associate is the ultimate parent.

(3) Where (apart from this subsection) a specified non-consolidated associate does not fall within section 473(1)(a) (conditions for being the ultimate parent of a worldwide group), it is treated as if it did fall within that provision.

(4) Where (apart from this subsection) financial statements of an associated worldwide group are not drawn up in respect of the relevant period of account, IAS financial statements of the associated worldwide group are treated as having been drawn up in respect of that period.

(5) The associated worldwide group's financial statements for the relevant period of account are treated as if no relevant expense amounts were recognised in them, as items of profit or loss, so far as they relate to financial liabilities owed to any member of the

principal worldwide group by any member of the associated worldwide group.

(6) The reference in section 427(6) to profits or losses of the associated worldwide group to which the principal worldwide group is entitled does not include any profits or losses that relate to times when the non-consolidated associate is a member of the principal worldwide group.

(7) Subsection (8) has effect in the application of this Part (for the purposes mentioned in subsection (1)) in relation to the financial statements of an associated worldwide group for the relevant period of account.

(8) The associated worldwide group is treated —
  (a) as having made an interest allowance (alternative calculation) election if and only if such an election has effect in relation to the relevant period of account of the principal worldwide group, and
  (b) as not having made any other election under this Part.

(9) In this section "specified" means specified in the interest allowance (non-consolidated investment) election.

429 Meaning of "non-consolidated associate"

(1) An entity is a "non-consolidated associate" of a worldwide group, in relation to a period of account of the group ("the relevant period of account") if condition A, B or C is met.

(2) Condition A is that the entity is accounted for in the financial statements of the group for the relevant period of account —
  (a) as a joint venture or an associate, and
  (b) using the gross equity method or the equity method.

(3) Condition B is that —
  (a) the entity is a partnership, and
  (b) an interest allowance (consolidated partnership) election has effect in relation to the relevant period of account.

(4) Condition C is the entity is a non-consolidated subsidiary of the ultimate parent at any time during the relevant period of account.

(5) In this section the following expressions have the meaning they have for accounting purposes —
  "associate";
  "equity method";
  "gross equity method";
  "joint venture".

(6) In this section "entity" includes anything which is treated as an entity in the financial statements of the worldwide group (regardless of whether it has a legal personality as a body corporate).

(7) This section has effect for the purposes of this Part.

Effect of interest allowance (consolidated partnerships) election

430 Interest allowance (consolidated partnerships) election

(1) Where an interest allowance (consolidated partnerships) election (see paragraph 18 of Schedule 7A) has effect in relation to a period of account of a worldwide group, this Chapter applies in relation to the period subject to this section.

(2) The financial statements of the group for the period are treated as if—

    (a) no amounts were recognised in them, as items of profit or loss, in respect of any income or expenses of a specified consolidated partnership, and

    (b) instead, each specified consolidated partnership were accounted for using the equity method.

(3) In subsection (2)(b) "the equity method" has the meaning it has for accounting purposes.

(4) In this Part "consolidated partnership", in relation to a period of account of a worldwide group, means a partnership in relation to which conditions A and B are met.

(5) Condition A is that, in the financial statements of the worldwide group for the period, the results of the partnership are consolidated with those of the ultimate parent as the results of a single economic entity.

(6) Condition B is that at no time during the period does the partnership have a subsidiary that is a company.

(7) In this section—

    (a) "specified" means specified in the interest allowance (consolidated partnerships) election or elections;

    (b) "subsidiary" has the meaning given by international accounting standards.

Interpretation

431 Interpretation of Chapter

In this Chapter the following expressions have the meaning they have for accounting purposes—

"item of profit or loss";

"item of other comprehensive income".

CHAPTER 8

PUBLIC INFRASTRUCTURE

Overview

432 Overview of Chapter

(1) This Chapter —

      (a)   alters the way in which this Part has effect in relation to companies (referred to as "qualifying infrastructure companies") that are fully taxed in the United Kingdom, and

      (b)   operates by reference to the provision of public infrastructure assets or the carrying on of certain other related activities.

(2)   In addition to the requirement for the company to be fully taxed in the United Kingdom, the qualifying requirements are—

      (a)   a requirement designed to ensure that the company's income and assets are referable to activities in relation to public infrastructure assets, and

      (b)   a requirement for the company to make an election (which may be revoked, subject to a 5-year rule in relation to the revocation and the ability to make a fresh election).

(3)   Two different types of asset meet the definition of a "public infrastructure asset", namely—

      (a)   tangible assets forming part of the infrastructure of the United Kingdom (or the UK sector of the continental shelf) that meet a public benefit test, and

      (b)   buildings (or parts of buildings) that are part of a UK property business and are let (or sub-let) on a short-term basis to unrelated parties.

(4)   In either case an asset counts as a public infrastructure asset only if—

      (a)   it has had, has or is likely to have an expected economic life of at least 10 years, and

      (b)   it is shown in a balance sheet of a member of the group that is fully taxed in the United Kingdom.

(5)   The detail of the above tests is set out in sections 433 to 437.

(6)   The substantive rules provide that an amount does not count as a tax-interest expense amount if—

      (a)   the creditor in relation to the amount is an unrelated party or another qualifying infrastructure company or the amount is in respect of a loan relationship entered into on or before 12 May 2016 (see sections 438 and 439), and

      (b)   the recourse of the creditor in relation to the amount is limited to the income or assets of, or shares in or debt issued by, a qualifying infrastructure company (ignoring certain financial assistance and certain non-financial guarantees).

(7)   In addition—

      (a)   provision is made for adjusting the operation of this Part to take into account the effect of the above rules (for example, the tax-EBITDA of a qualifying infrastructure company is treated as nil (see section 441)),

      (b)   provision is made modifying the operation of this Chapter in the case of joint venture companies or partnerships or other transparent entities (see sections 444 to 447), and

      (c)   provision is made in relation to the decommissioning of a public infrastructure asset (see section 448).

Key concepts

433   Meaning of "qualifying infrastructure company"

(1)   For the purposes of this Chapter a company is a "qualifying infrastructure company" throughout an accounting period if—

    (a)   it meets the public infrastructure income test for the accounting period (see subsections (2) to (4)),

    (b)   it meets the public infrastructure assets test for the accounting period (see subsections (5) to (10)),

    (c)   it is fully taxed in the United Kingdom in the accounting period (see subsection (11)), and

    (d)   it has made an election for the purposes of this section that has effect for the accounting period (see section 434).

(2)   A company meets the public infrastructure income test for an accounting period if all, or all but an insignificant proportion, of its income for the accounting period derives from—

    (a)   qualifying infrastructure activities carried on by the company (see sections 436 and 437),

    (b)   shares in a qualifying infrastructure company, or

    (c)   loan relationships or other financing arrangements to which the only other party is a qualifying infrastructure company.

(3)   A company also meets the public infrastructure income test for an accounting period if it has no income for the period.

(4)   In determining whether the public infrastructure income test for an accounting period is met, income which does not derive from any of the matters mentioned in subsection (2)(a) to (c) is ignored if, having regard to all the circumstances, it is reasonable to regard the amount of the income as insignificant.

(5)   A company meets the public infrastructure assets test for an accounting period if all, or all but an insignificant proportion, of the total value of the company's assets recognised in an appropriate balance sheet on each day in that period derives from—

    (a)   tangible assets that are related to qualifying infrastructure activities,

    (b)   service concession arrangements in respect of assets that are related to qualifying infrastructure activities,

    (c)   financial assets to which the company is a party for the purpose of the carrying on of qualifying infrastructure activities by the company or another associated qualifying infrastructure company,

    (d)   shares in a qualifying infrastructure company, or

    (e)   loan relationships or other financing arrangements to which the only other party is a qualifying infrastructure company.

(6)   If a company has no assets recognised in an appropriate balance sheet on any day in an accounting period, the company is to be taken as meeting the public infrastructure assets test in respect of that day.

(7)   In determining whether the public infrastructure assets test for an accounting period is met in respect of any day, the value of an asset which does not derive from any of the matters mentioned in

subsection (5)(a) to (e) is ignored if, having regard to all the circumstances, it is reasonable to regard the value of the asset as insignificant.

(8) For the purposes of subsection (5)(a) and (b) assets are "related to qualifying infrastructure activities" in the case of a company if the assets are—

(a) public infrastructure assets (see section 436(2) and (5)) in relation to the company that are provided by the company, or

(b) other assets used in the course of a qualifying infrastructure activity carried on by the company or by an associated qualifying infrastructure company.

(9) For the purposes of this section the reference to the value of an asset recognised in an appropriate balance sheet of a company on a day is to the value which is, or would be, recognised in a balance sheet of the company drawn up on that day.

(10) A company is not to be taken as failing to meet the public infrastructure assets test for an accounting period if, ignoring this subsection, that test would have been failed on a particular day or days merely as a result of particular circumstances—

(a) which existed, and

(b) which were always intended to exist,

for a temporary period of an insignificant duration.

(11) A company is fully taxed in the United Kingdom in an accounting period if—

(a) every activity that the company carries on at any time in the accounting period is within the charge to corporation tax,

(b) the company has not made an election under section 18A of CTA 2009 (exemption for profits or losses of foreign permanent establishments) that has effect for the accounting period, and

(c) the company has not made a claim for relief under Chapter 2 of Part 2 (double taxation relief) for the accounting period.

434 Elections under section 433

(1) An election under section 433—

(a) must be made before the beginning of the accounting period in relation to which it is to have effect, and

(b) has effect in relation to that accounting period and all subsequent accounting periods (subject to subsections (2) to (4)).

(2) An election under section 433 may be revoked.

(3) A revocation of an election under section 433—

(a) must be made before the beginning of the accounting period from which the revocation is to have effect, but

(b) cannot have effect in relation to any accounting period that begins before the end of the period of 5 years beginning with the first day of the first accounting period in relation to which the election had effect.

(4) Once revoked, a fresh election may be made under section 433 but cannot have effect in relation to any accounting period that begins before the end of the period of 5 years beginning with the first day of the accounting period from which the revocation had effect.

(5) If—

    (a) a qualifying infrastructure company transfers to another company a business, or a part of a business, that consists of the carrying on of qualifying infrastructure activities, and

    (b) the transferee has not made an election under section 433 that has effect for the accounting period in which the transfer takes place,

the transferee is to be treated as if it had made the election under that section that the transferor had made.

(6) If a company has made an election under section 433 that has effect in relation to an accounting period, the company—

    (a) may not make an election under section 18A of CTA 2009 that has effect for the accounting period, and

    (b) may not make a claim for relief under Chapter 2 of Part 2 for the accounting period.

435 Group elections modifying the operation of sections 433 and 434

(1) Two or more companies which are members of the same worldwide group may jointly make an election under this section modifying the operation of sections 433 and 434 in relation to them for the times during which they remain members of that group.

(2) An election under this section—

    (a) has effect from a date specified in the election;

    (b) may be revoked jointly by the members of the group in relation to which the election has effect from a date specified in the revocation;

    (c) ceases to have effect in relation to a company which gives a notice to an officer of Revenue and Customs, and to the companies in relation to which the election has effect, notifying them of its withdrawal from the election from a date specified in the notice.

(3) A date specified in an election, revocation or notice may not be before the date on which it is made or given.

(4) An election under this section which has effect at particular times ("relevant times") in relation to particular companies ("elected companies") modifies the operation of sections 433 and 434 as follows.

(5) If an elected company ("C") has made an election under section 433 which has effect for an accounting period that includes relevant times, that section has effect as if, in determining whether anything is insignificant for the purposes of section 433(2), (4), (5) or (7), C also had the income and assets that the other elected companies had at those times.

(6) If—

     (a)   an elected company ("C") has made an election under section 433 which has effect for an accounting period including relevant times, and

     (b)   C fails to meet one or more of the tests in subsection (1)(a) to (c) of that section in relation to that accounting period otherwise than as a result of this subsection,

all the other elected companies are also treated as failing to meeting those tests for so much of their accounting periods as consists of the relevant times in the accounting period of C.

(7)   If, in a case where subsection (6) applies, the deemed failed period does not coincide with an accounting period of another elected company ("E"), the accounting period of E is treated for the purposes of this Part as if it consisted of separate accounting periods beginning and ending at such times as secure that none of the separate accounting periods fall partly within the deemed failed period.

(8)   For this purpose "the deemed failed period" means the period consisting of the relevant times in the accounting period of C mentioned in subsection (6).

(9)   All such apportionments as are necessary for the purposes of, or in consequence of, subsections (5) to (7) are to be made on a just and reasonable basis.

(10)   If—

     (a)   elected companies have made elections under section 433 which have effect for accounting periods including relevant times, and

     (b)   more than half of those elected companies have each made an election under that section that has had effect for a period of at least 5 years,

section 434(3)(b) does not apply in relation to any of the elected companies.

436 Meaning of "qualifying infrastructure activity"

(1)   For the purposes of this Chapter a company carries on a "qualifying infrastructure activity" if the company—

     (a)   provides an asset that is a public infrastructure asset in relation to it (see subsections (2) and (5)), or

     (b)   carries on any other activity that is ancillary to, or facilitates, the provision of an asset that is a public infrastructure asset in relation to it.

(2)   For the purposes of this Chapter an asset is a "public infrastructure asset" in relation to a company at any time if—

     (a)   the asset is, or is to be, a tangible asset forming part of the infrastructure of the United Kingdom or the UK sector of the continental shelf,

     (b)   the asset meets the public benefit test (see subsections (3) and (4)),

     (c)   the asset has had, has or is likely to have an expected economic life of at least 10 years, and

     (d)   the asset meets the group balance sheet test (see subsection (10)) in relation to the company.

(3) An asset meets the "public benefit test" if —

    (a) the asset is, or is to be, procured by a relevant public body, or

    (b) the asset is, or is to be, used in the course of a regulated activity.

(4) An asset is used in the course of a "regulated activity" if its use —

    (a) is regulated by an infrastructure authority (see section 437(2)), or

    (b) could be regulated by an infrastructure authority if the authority exercised any of its powers.

(5) For the purposes of this Chapter a building, or part of a building, is also a "public infrastructure asset" in relation to a company at any time if —

    (a) the company, or another member of the worldwide group of which it is a member at that time, carries on a UK property business consisting of or including the building or part,

    (b) the building or part is, or is to be, let on a short-term basis to persons who, at that time, are not related parties of the company or member,

    (c) the building or part has had, has or is likely to have an expected economic life of at least 10 years, and

    (d) the building or part meets the group balance sheet test in relation to the company.

(6) A building, or part of a building, is "let" to a person if the person is entitled to the use of the building or part under a lease or other arrangement.

(7) A building, or part of a building, is let on a "short-term basis" if the lease or other arrangement in question —

    (a) has an effective duration which is 50 years or less, and

    (b) is not an arrangement to which any provision of Chapter 2 of Part 16 of CTA 2010 applies (finance arrangements).

(8) Whether or not a lease or other arrangement has an effective duration which is 50 years or less is determined in accordance with Chapter 4 of Part 4 of CTA 2009 (reading any reference to a lease as a reference to a lease or other arrangement within subsection (6)).

(9) For the purposes of this section references to a building or part of a building being let include the building or part being sub-let, and, accordingly, references to a lease include a sub-lease.

(10) An asset meets the "group balance sheet test" in relation to a company at any time if —

    (a) an entry in respect of the asset is, or would be, recognised (whether as a tangible asset or otherwise) in a balance sheet of the company, or an associated company, that is drawn up at that time, and

    (b) the company or associated company is within the charge to corporation tax at that time in respect of all of its sources of income and no election or claim mentioned in section 433(11)(b) or (c) has effect for a period including that time.

(11) For the purposes of this Chapter references to provision, in relation to a public infrastructure asset, include its acquisition, design, construction, conversion, improvement, operation or repair.

437 Section 436: supplementary

(1) In section 436 "infrastructure" includes—

    (a) water, electricity, gas, telecommunications or sewerage facilities,

    (b) oil pipelines, oil terminals or oil refineries,

    (c) railway facilities (including rolling stock), roads or other transport facilities,

    (d) health or educational facilities,

    (e) facilities or housing accommodation provided for use by members of any of the armed forces or of any police force,

    (f) court or prison facilities,

    (g) waste processing facilities, and

    (h) buildings (or parts of buildings) occupied by any relevant public body.

(2) Each of the following is an "infrastructure authority" for the purposes of section 436(4)—

    (a) the Civil Aviation Authority so far as exercising functions in relation to the provision of airports (within the meaning of the Airports Act 1986),

    (b) each of the following so far as exercising functions in relation to waste processing—

        (i) the Environment Agency,

        (ii) the Scottish Environmental Protection Agency,

        (iii) the Northern Ireland Environment Agency, or

        (iv) Natural Resources Wales,

    (c) the Gas and Electricity Markets Authority,

    (d) each of the following so far as exercising functions in relation to the management of ports or harbours—

        (i) a harbour authority within the meaning of the Harbours Act 1964, or

        (ii) a harbour authority within the meaning of the Harbours Act (Northern Ireland) 1970,

    (e) the Northern Ireland Authority for Utility Regulation,

    (f) the Office of Communications so far as exercising functions in relation to the provision of electronic communication services (within the meaning of the Communications Act 2003) or the management of the radio spectrum,

    (g) the Office of Nuclear Regulation,

    (h) the Office of Rail and Road,

    (i) the Oil and Gas Authority,

    (j) the Water Services Regulation Authority or the Water Industry Commission for Scotland, or

    (k) any other public authority which has functions of a regulatory nature exercisable in relation to the use of tangible assets forming part of the infrastructure of the United Kingdom or the UK sector of the continental shelf.

(3) The Commissioners may by regulations amend the definition of "infrastructure authority".

Exemption and related provision

438 Exemption for interest payable to third parties etc

(1) Amounts that arise to a qualifying infrastructure company in a relevant accounting period are not to be regarded for the purposes of this Part as tax-interest expense amounts of the company so far as they qualify as exempt amounts in that period (see subsections (2) and (3)).

(2) An amount qualifies as an exempt amount so far as it is attributable, on a just and reasonable apportionment, to the times in the relevant accounting period when—

    (a) each creditor in relation to the amount is within subsection (3) or the amount is in respect of a qualifying old loan relationship (see section 439), and

    (b) the recourse of each creditor in relation to the amount is limited to relevant infrastructure matters (see subsections (4) to (6)).

(3) A creditor is within this subsection if—

    (a) the creditor is not a related party of the company, or

    (b) the creditor is a company which is a qualifying infrastructure company,

but section 466(2) does not apply for the purposes of paragraph (a).

(4) The recourse of a creditor is limited to relevant infrastructure matters if, in the event that the company fails to perform its obligations in question, the recourse of the creditor is limited to—

    (a) income of a qualifying infrastructure company,

    (b) assets of a qualifying infrastructure company, or

    (c) shares in or debt issued by a qualifying infrastructure company,

whether the income, assets, shares or debt relate to the company concerned or another qualifying infrastructure company.

(5) For the purposes of subsection (4) a guarantee, indemnity or other financial assistance in favour of the creditor is ignored if—

    (a) it is provided before 1 April 2017, or

    (b) it is provided at any later time by a person who, at that time, is not a related party of the company or is a relevant public body.

(6) For the purposes of subsection (4) a non-financial guarantee in favour of the creditor is ignored if—

    (a) it guarantees the performance by any person of contractual obligations to provide goods or services to a qualifying infrastructure company,

    (b) it is given by the person providing the goods or services or by a person who is a related party of that person, and

    (c)   the maximum amount for which the guarantor is liable does not exceed the consideration given under the contract for the provision of the goods or services.

(7)   In this section "creditor" means—

    (a)   if the amount meets condition A in section 382, the person who is party to the loan relationship as creditor,

    (b)   if the amount meets condition B in that section, the person other than the company who is party to the derivative contract, and

    (c)   if the amount meets condition C in that section, the person other than the company who is party to the relevant arrangement or transaction.

439   Exemption in respect of certain pre-13 May 2016 loan relationships

(1)   A loan relationship is a "qualifying old loan relationship" of a qualifying infrastructure company if—

    (a)   the company entered into the loan relationship on or before 12 May 2016, and

    (b)   as at that date, at least 80% of the total value of the company's future qualifying infrastructure receipts for the qualifying period was highly predictable by reference to qualifying public contracts,

but see subsection (8) for cases where a loan relationship is not a qualifying old loan relationship of the company.

(2)   For the purposes of this section "the qualifying period" means—

    (a)   in a case where the loan relationship would cease to subsist at any time before 12 May 2026 (if any amendments of the loan relationship made on or after 12 May 2016 are ignored), the period beginning with 12 May 2016 and ending with that time, and

    (b)   in any other case, the period of 10 years beginning with 12 May 2016.

(3)   For the purposes of this section "qualifying infrastructure receipts", in relation to a company ("C"), means—

    (a)   receipts arising from qualifying infrastructure activities carried on by C, and

    (b)   such proportion of the receipts arising from qualifying infrastructure activities carried on by another company as, on a just and reasonable basis, is attributable to C's interests in the other company (whether direct or indirect) arising as a result of shares or loans.

(4)   For the purposes of this section receipts are highly predictable by reference to qualifying public contracts so far as their value can be predicted with a high degree of certainty because—

    (a)   the amounts of the receipts are fixed by a qualifying public contract, and

    (b)   the factors affecting the volume of receipts are fixed by a qualifying public contract or are otherwise capable of being predicted with a high degree of certainty.

(5) For this purpose any provision of a qualifying public contract (however expressed) that adjusts the amount of a receipt for changes in the general level of prices or earnings is to be ignored.

(6) For the purposes of this section a contract is a "qualifying public contract" if—

    (a) it was entered into at any time on or before 12 May 2016 and, as at that time, it was expected to have effect for at least 10 years, and

    (b) it was entered into either with a relevant public body or following bids made in an auction conducted by a relevant public body.

(7) If a qualifying old loan relationship is amended after 12 May 2016 so as to increase the amount lent or extend the period for which the relationship is to subsist—

    (a) section 438 is to have effect as if none of those amendments were made (and, accordingly, the exemption under that section has no effect in relation to the increase in the amount or the period of the extension), and

    (b) such apportionments of amounts in respect of the relationship are to be made as are just and reasonable.

(8) A loan relationship to which a qualifying infrastructure company is a party at any time is not a qualifying old loan relationship of the company at that or any subsequent time if, on the relevant assumptions, the condition in subsection (1)(b) would not have been met.

(9) The relevant assumptions are that—

    (a) the assets held by the company at that time were the only assets that the company held on 12 May 2016,

    (b) the assets held at that time by any other company in which it has interests (whether direct or indirect) arising as a result of shares or loans were the only assets that the other company held on 12 May 2016, and

    (c) a qualifying infrastructure receipt could not be regarded as highly predictable if, on 12 May 2016, the public infrastructure asset in question did not exist or was not in the course of being constructed or converted.

(10) For the purposes of this section the value of a receipt on 12 May 2016 is taken to be its present value on that date, discounted using a rate that can reasonably be regarded as one that, in accordance with normal commercial criteria, is appropriate for the purpose.

(11) In this section "receipts" means receipts of a revenue nature.

440　Loans etc made by qualifying infrastructure companies to be ignored

(1) This section applies where—

    (a) a company is a qualifying infrastructure company throughout an accounting period, and

    (b) the company would (but for this section) have had tax-interest income amounts in the accounting period.

(2) For the purposes of this Part, the company is treated as if it did not have any tax-interest income amounts in the accounting period.

441 Tax-EBITDA of qualifying infrastructure company to be nil

(1) This section applies where a company is a qualifying infrastructure company throughout an accounting period.

(2) For the purposes of this Part, the tax-EBITDA of the company for the accounting period is nil.

442 Amounts of qualifying infrastructure company left out of account for other purposes

(1) This section applies where a company is a qualifying infrastructure company throughout a relevant accounting period.

(2) In calculating—
    (a) the adjusted net group-interest expense of the worldwide group for the period of account concerned, or
    (b) the qualifying net group-interest expense of the worldwide group for the period of account concerned,

    amounts that are exempt amounts of the company under section 438, or are treated as mentioned in section 440, are to be left out of account.

(3) For the purposes of this Part the group EBITDA of the worldwide group for the period of account concerned is to be calculated as if the group did not include the company in respect of the relevant accounting period.

443 Interest capacity for group with qualifying infrastructure company etc

(1) If a worldwide group for a period of account includes a qualifying infrastructure company at any time, the general rule is that the interest capacity of the group for the period is calculated as if section 392 did not contain the de minimis provisions.

(2) But this is subject to an exception that depends on the following comparison.

(3) The following amounts must be compared with each other—
    (a) the total disallowed amount of the group in the period calculated as if this Chapter (including subsection (1) of this section but ignoring the remainder of it) were contained in this Part ("the Chapter 8 amount"), and
    (b) the total disallowed amount of the group in the period calculated as if this Chapter were not contained in this Part and as if section 392 contained only the de minimis provisions ("the ordinary amount").

(4) If the Chapter 8 amount exceeds the ordinary amount, the interest capacity of the worldwide group for the period is taken to be the de minimis amount (as defined by 392(3)).

(5) If the interest capacity of the worldwide group for the period is given by subsection (4), nothing else in this Chapter has effect in relation to the worldwide group for the period.

(6) For the purposes of this section the reference to section 392 not containing the de minimis provisions is a reference to that section not containing subsections (2) and (3) of that section.

(7) For the purposes of this section the reference to section 392 containing only the de minimis provisions is a reference to that section having effect as if for subsections (1) and (2) of that section there were substituted —

"(1) For the purposes of this Part the "interest capacity" of a worldwide group for a period of account of the group is the de minimis amount."

Supplementary

444 Joint venture companies

(1) This section makes modifications of this Part in relation to an accounting period of a qualifying infrastructure company ("the joint venture company") where —

   (a) one or more qualifying infrastructure companies ("the qualifying investor or investors") have shares in the joint venture company,

   (b) other persons ("the other investors") who are not qualifying infrastructure companies have all the other shares in the joint venture company,

   (c) each of the investors (that is to say, the qualifying investor or investors and the other investors) has lent money to the joint venture company,

   (d) the amounts each of the investors has lent stand in the same, or substantially the same, proportion as the shares in the joint venture company that each of them has,

   (e) at all times in the accounting period the investors have the same rights in relation to the shares in or assets of the joint venture company and the same rights in relation to the money debt or debts in question, and

   (f) the joint venture company makes an election for the purposes of this section that has effect for the accounting period (but see section 445 for further provision about elections).

(2) Section 401 has effect as if the qualifying investor or investors were not investors in the group for times in the accounting period falling in the relevant period of account.

(3) Section 427 has effect as if, in determining the appropriate proportion in relation to an associated worldwide group, it is assumed that the qualifying investor or investors were not investors in the group for times in the accounting period falling in the relevant period of account.

(4) In consequence of subsection (2) or (3), the shares of the qualifying investor or investors in the group are treated as distributed for times in the accounting period falling in the relevant period of account among the other investors in proportion to the actual shares of the other investors in the group.

(5) For the purposes of section 438 there is a reduction in any amount that would otherwise qualify as an exempt amount in the accounting period where—

    (a) the exemption operates by reference to creditors being within subsection (3) of that section, and

    (b) the creditor in relation to the amount is not an investor.

(6) The amount qualifying as an exempt amount is to be reduced so that only the qualifying proportion of it qualifies.

(7) For the purposes of this section—

    "the qualifying proportion" means the proportion of the shares that the qualifying investor or investors have in the joint venture company in the accounting period, and

    "the non-qualifying proportion" means the proportion of the shares that the other investors have in the joint venture company in the accounting period.

(8) The treatment mentioned in section 440(2) is to extend only to the qualifying proportion of the tax-interest income amounts in the accounting period.

(9) Section 441(2) has effect as if the tax-EBITDA of the company for the accounting period were the amount determined as follows.

Step 1

Find the tax-EBIDTA of the company for the accounting period if section 441 were ignored.

Step 2

The tax-EBITDA of the company for the accounting period is equal to the non-qualifying proportion of that amount.

(10) Section 442(3) has effect as if for the words "the group did not include the company" there were substituted "amounts of the company were limited to the non-qualifying proportion of those amounts".

445 Joint venture groups

(1) This section applies if the joint venture company is the ultimate parent of a multi-company worldwide group at any time in the accounting period.

(2) An election made by the joint venture company under section 444 in relation to the accounting period is of no effect unless all the other members of the group—

    (a) are qualifying infrastructure companies for the accounting period,

    (b) are wholly-owned subsidiaries of the joint venture company throughout the accounting period, and

    (c) have the same accounting periods as the joint venture company.

(3) In determining whether the conditions in section 444(1)(c) to (e) are met in relation to the accounting period of the joint venture company, any loans made to any of the other members of the group are treated as if they were made to the joint venture company.

(4) If the joint venture company makes an election under section 444 for the accounting period, the modifications made by subsections (5) to (10) of that section are also to apply in relation to each of the other members of the group.

446 Joint ventures: supplementary

(1) If—
  (a) the joint venture company makes an election under section 444 in relation to an accounting period,
  (b) that company, or any member of the worldwide group of which it is a member, is the creditor for the purposes of section 438 in any case, and
  (c) the company mentioned in that section in that case is a not a member of that group at any time in the accounting period,

section 438 has effect in that case as if subsection (3)(b) were of no effect in relation to that time.

(2) Section 434(1) to (5) apply to an election under section 444 as they apply to an election under section 433.

(3) For the purposes of section 444 the investors are not to be regarded as having the same rights in relation to the shares in or assets of the joint venture company, or in relation to the money debt or debts in question, at any time if—
  (a) provision is in force at that time in respect of any of the relevant matters that differs in relation to different persons or has, or is capable of having, a different effect in relation to different persons (whether at that or any subsequent time),
  (b) arrangements are in place at that time the effect of which is that, at that or any subsequent time, the rights of some persons in relation to any of the relevant matters differ, or will or may differ, from the rights of others in relation to the matters in question, or
  (c) any other circumstances exist at that time as a result of which the rights of some persons in relation to any of the relevant matters cannot reasonably be regarded as being, in substance, the same rights as others in relation to the matters in question at that or any subsequent time.

(4) In this section—
  (a) "the relevant matters" means the shares in or assets of the joint venture company or the money debt or debts in question,
  (b) "rights" includes powers,
  (c) "different persons" includes persons of a different class or description, and
  (d) "arrangements" include any agreement, understanding, scheme, transaction or series of transactions (whether or not legally enforceable).

447 Partnerships and other transparent entities

(1) Subsections (2) to (4) apply where a company is a member of a partnership.

(2) For the purposes of section 433 the cases in which assets recognised in a balance sheet of the company are regarded as deriving their value from the matters mentioned in subsection (5)(a) to (e) of that section include any case where—

    (a) the company's interest in the partnership is recognised in the balance sheet of the company, and

    (b) that partnership interest derives its value from those matters.

(3) For the purposes of section 436 the cases in which an entry in respect of an asset is (or would be) recognised in a balance sheet of the company include any case where—

    (a) the asset is (or would be) recognised in a balance sheet of the partnership, and

    (b) the company has a significant interest in the partnership.

(4) For the purposes of section 438(4)—

    (a) the obligations mentioned there include any case where the obligations are those of the partnership, and

    (b) references to a qualifying infrastructure company in that case include the partnership.

(5) Subsections (2) to (4) apply (with any necessary modifications) in relation to transparent entities that are not partnerships as they apply in relation to partnerships.

(6) For this purpose an entity is "transparent" if it is not chargeable to corporation tax or income tax as a person (ignoring any exemptions).

448 Decommissioning

(1) This Chapter applies in relation to an activity consisting of the decommissioning of a public infrastructure asset as it applies in relation to its provision.

(2) In determining whether a company is a qualifying infrastructure company the following assets of the company are ignored (and the income arising from them is, accordingly, also ignored)—

    (a) any shares in a decommissioning fund, and

    (b) any loan relationships or other financing arrangements to which a decommissioning fund is party.

(3) A decommissioning fund is to be regarded as a qualifying infrastructure company.

(4) For the purposes of this section "a decommissioning fund" means a fund which—

    (a) holds particular investments for the sole purpose of funding activities for, or in connection with, the decommissioning or other provision of public infrastructure assets, and

    (b) is prevented from using the proceeds of the investments, or the income arising from them, for any purpose other than the purpose mentioned in paragraph (a) or returning surplus funds.

(5) In this section "decommissioning" includes demolishing and putting out of use.

368   *Finance (No. 2) Act 2017 (c. 32)*
Schedule 5 — Corporate interest restriction
Part 1 — New Part 10 of TIOPA 2010

449 Minor definitions for purposes of this Chapter

(1) For the purposes of this Chapter—

"balance sheet" means a balance sheet that is drawn up in accordance with generally accepted accounting practice,

"financial asset" has the same meaning as it has for accounting purposes,

"loan relationships or other financing arrangements" means—

(a) loan relationships,

(b) derivative contracts in relation to which the condition in section 387(4) is met (underlying subject matter to be interest rates etc),

(c) finance leases, or

(d) debt factoring or similar transactions, and

"the UK sector of the continental shelf" means the areas designated by Order in Council under section 1(7) of the Continental Shelf Act 1964.

(2) For the purposes of this Chapter references to a company which is "associated" with another company at any time are references to companies that are members of the same worldwide group at that time.

CHAPTER 9

CASES INVOLVING PARTICULAR TYPES OF COMPANY OR BUSINESS

Banking companies

450 Banking companies

(1) This section applies in relation to a banking company carrying on a trade so far as the activities of the trade consist of or include dealing in financial instruments.

(2) For the purposes of section 382 an amount is treated as meeting condition A, B or C if it is a debit arising directly from dealing in financial instruments other than one in respect of an impairment loss.

(3) An amount—

(a) which is treated as meeting condition A, B or C for the purposes of section 382 as a result of subsection (2) of this section, and

(b) which, but for that subsection, would not be a tax-interest expense amount,

is to be left out of account, or brought into account, as a result of section 377(2) or 380(2) after the second but before the third kind of tax-interest expense amounts mentioned there.

(4) For the purposes of section 385 an amount is treated as meeting condition A, B, C or D if it is a credit arising directly from dealing in financial instruments other than one in respect of the reversal of an impairment loss.

(5) In determining a relevant expense amount under section 411 in the case of the company, that section has effect as if it also included a reference to losses arising directly from dealing in financial instruments other than impairment losses.

(6) In determining a relevant income amount under section 411 in the case of the company, that section has effect as if it also included gains arising directly from dealing in financial instruments other than the reversal of impairment losses.

(7) In this section—

"banking company" has the same meaning as in Part 7A of CTA 2010 (see sections 269B to 269BD), and

"financial instruments" includes—

(a) loan relationships,

(b) derivative contracts, and

(c) shares or other securities.

Oil and gas

451 Oil and gas

(1) For the purposes of this Part any amount which is, or is taken into account in calculating—

(a) the ring fence income of a company within the meaning of section 275 of CTA 2010, or

(b) a company's aggregate gain or loss under section 197(3) of TCGA 1992,

is to be ignored.

(2) For the purpose of applying subsection (1) in relation to the financial statements of a worldwide group of which the company is a member such adjustments are to be made to those statements as are just and reasonable.

REITs

452 Real Estate Investment Trusts

(1) This section applies if a company (a "property rental business company")—

(a) is a company which has profits for an accounting period which are not charged to corporation tax as a result of section 534(1) or (2) of CTA 2010, or

(b) is a company to which gains accrue in an accounting period that are not chargeable gains as a result of section 535(1) or (5) of CTA 2010.

(2) In this section "the residual business company" means the company which—

(a) so far as it carries on residual business, is treated, as a result of section 541 of CTA 2010, as a separate company distinct from the property rental business company, but

(b) ignoring that section, is in fact the same company as the property rental business company.

(3) In applying the provisions of this Part—

    (a) the property rental business company and the residual business company are at all times to be regarded as separate members of the same worldwide group (despite the provisions of section 541(3) of CTA 2010), but

    (b) in the case of the application of section 433 (qualifying infrastructure company), the property rental business company and the residual business company are to be regarded as being one company (and any election (or its revocation) is, therefore, regarded as made by each company).

(4) This Part has effect as if—

    (a) section 534(1) and (2) of CTA 2010, and

    (b) section 535(1) and (5) of CTA 2010,

do not apply in relation to the property rental business company for the accounting period.

(5) The allocated disallowance for the property rental business company (if any) for the accounting period must be limited to such amount as secures that section 530(3)(b) or (5) of CTA 2010 (distribution of profits not required if would result in unlawful distribution) do not apply.

(6) This subsection—

    (a) sets out steps to be taken in order to facilitate the operation of Chapter 2 (disallowance and reactivation of tax-interest expense amounts), and

    (b) has effect in relation to an accounting period of the residual business company whether or not it has net tax-interest expense referable to that period.

If the residual business company does not have net tax-interest expense referable to that period, it is treated for the purposes of steps 1 to 4 in the rest of this subsection as if it had instead a nil amount of tax-interest expense referable to that period.

Step 1

Determine the maximum amount that could be the allocated disallowance for the property rental business company for the accounting period if subsection (5) were ignored and the maximum amount that could be the allocated disallowance for the residual business company for the accounting period (ignoring step 5).

The sum of those maximum amounts is referred to in this subsection as "the total REIT expenses".

Step 2

Determine the amount (if any) that is the allocated disallowance for the property rental business for the accounting period, applying subsection (5) and all other rules in this Part.

This amount is referred to in this subsection as "the actual disallowed amount".

Step 3

Deduct from the total REIT expenses the actual disallowed amount.

Step 4

Determine whether so much of the total REIT expenses as remains after step 3 exceeds the net tax-interest expense of the residual business company referable to the accounting period (ignoring step 5).

Step 5

If the application of step 4 produces an excess, the residual business company is required to bring into account in the accounting period matching tax-interest expense and income amounts in accordance with the following provisions of this section.

(7) The residual business company —

    (a) must bring a tax-interest expense amount equal to the excess into account in the accounting period, and

    (b) must bring a tax-interest income amount equal to the excess into account in the accounting period,

but nothing in this subsection affects any calculation required under any other provision of this Part in relation to the accounting period of the residual business company.

(8) The bringing into account of a tax-interest expense amount under subsection (7) is subject to the operation of the other provisions of this Part (which may result in some or all of the amount not being brought into account).

(9) The tax-interest expense amount under subsection (7) must be matched in amount and nature to an amount comprised in the total REIT expenses.

Section 377(2) to (4) (which, subject to an election made by the company, set out the order in which amounts are left out of account) apply for the purposes of this subsection.

(10) The tax-interest expense or income amounts under subsection (7) are treated as being of the same nature as each other.

(11) An interest restriction return —

    (a) must, in relation to any company carrying on residual business or property rental business, specify that fact, and

    (b) must contain information about how the return has taken into account the effect of this section.

(12) Expressions which are used in this section and in Part 12 of CTA 2010 have the same meaning in this section as they have in that Part.

Insurance companies etc

453   Insurance entities

(1) This section applies where —

    (a) an insurance entity is a member of a worldwide group,

    (b) the entity has a subsidiary ("S") which it holds as a portfolio investment, and

    (c) apart from this section, S would be a member of the group.

(2) For the purposes of this Part —

    (a) the group does not include S (or its subsidiaries), and

372   *Finance (No. 2) Act 2017 (c. 32)*
Schedule 5 — Corporate interest restriction
Part 1 — New Part 10 of TIOPA 2010

    (b)   accordingly, none of those entities is regarded as a consolidated subsidiary of any member of the group.

(3)   For the purposes of this section an insurance entity holds an interest in an entity as "a portfolio investment" if —

    (a)   the insurance entity holds the interest as an investment, and

    (b)   the insurance entity judges the value that the interest has to it wholly or mainly by reference to the market value of the interest.

(4)   In this section —

    "insurance entity" means —

        (a)   an insurance company,

        (b)   a friendly society within the meaning of Part 3 of FA 2012 (see section 172), or

        (c)   a body corporate which carries on underwriting business as a member of Lloyd's, and

    "subsidiary" has the meaning given by international accounting standards.

454   Members of Lloyd's

In the case of a body corporate carrying on underwriting business as a member of Lloyd's —

    (a)   any reference in this Part to an amount being brought into account under Part 3 of CTA 2009 as a result of section 297 or 573 of that Act is to be read as a reference to its being brought into account under that Part as a result of section 219 of FA 1994, and

    (b)   any reference in this Part to a derivative contract is to be read as if subsection (3) of section 226 of FA 1994 (which provides that relevant contracts forming part of a premium trust fund are not derivative contracts) were omitted.

Shipping companies

455   Shipping companies subject to tonnage tax

(1)   This section applies in relation to an accounting period of a tonnage tax company.

(2)   The company's tonnage tax profits for the accounting period are treated as nil for the purpose of calculating the company's adjusted corporation tax earnings for the accounting period under section 406(2).

(3)   In this section "tonnage tax company" and "tonnage tax profits" have the same meaning as in Schedule 22 to FA 2000 (see paragraphs 2 to 5).

Fair value accounting

456 Creditor relationships of companies determined on basis of fair value accounting

(1) A company may elect for all of its creditor relationships which are dealt with on the basis of fair value accounting ("fair-value creditor relationships") to be subject to the provision made by this section for all of its accounting periods.

(2) For the purpose of calculating under this Part—
    (a) tax-interest expense amounts of the company, and
    (b) tax-interest income amounts of the company,
    the relevant loan relationship debits and relevant loan relationship credits in respect of the company's fair-value creditor relationships are instead to be determined for the accounting periods on an amortised cost basis of accounting.

(3) If—
    (a) a company has a hedging relationship between a relevant contract ("the hedging instrument") and the asset representing a loan relationship subject to the election, and
    (b) the loan relationship is dealt with in the company's accounts on the basis of fair value accounting,
    it is to be assumed in applying the amortised cost basis of accounting that the hedging instrument has where possible been designated for accounting purposes as a fair value hedge of the loan relationship.

(4) An election under this section—
    (a) must be made before the end of 12 months from the end of the relevant accounting period,
    (b) has effect for that accounting period and all subsequent accounting periods, and
    (c) is irrevocable.

(5) For this purpose "relevant accounting period" means—
    (a) the first accounting period in which the company has a fair-value creditor relationship, or
    (b) if that accounting period has ended before 1 April 2017, the first accounting period in relation to which any provision of this Part applies.

(6) In this section "amortised cost basis of accounting", in relation to an accounting period, has the same meaning as in Part 5 of CTA 2009 (see section 313), but, in the case of creditor relationships relating to insurance activities, as if that basis of accounting required recognition only of—
    (a) interest accrued for the period in respect of the creditor relationships, or
    (b) if the creditor relationships arise as a result of section 490 of CTA 2009 (OEICs, unit trusts and offshore funds), amounts that can reasonably be regarded as equating to interest accrued for the period in respect of those relationships.

(7) In subsection (6) "creditor relationships relating to insurance activities" means creditor relationships which—

374   *Finance (No. 2) Act 2017 (c. 32)*
Schedule 5 — Corporate interest restriction
Part 1 — New Part 10 of TIOPA 2010

    (a)   are held by an insurance company, a friendly society within the meaning of Part 3 of FA 2012 (see section 172) or a body corporate which carries on underwriting business as a member of Lloyd's, or

    (b)   are held in connection with the regulation of underwriting business carried on by members of Lloyd's.

(8)   The Commissioners may by regulations amend the definition of "amortised cost basis of accounting" in this section.

(9)   Other expressions which are used in this section and in Part 5 of CTA 2009 have the same meaning in this section as they have in that Part.

457   Elections under section 456: deemed debits and credits

(1)   This section applies if—

    (a)   as a result of an election under section 456, the tax-interest expense amounts of a company include notional debits for an accounting period,

    (b)   the worldwide group of which the company is a member is subject to interest restrictions for a period of account, and

    (c)   the total disallowed amount for the period of account consists of or includes the notional debits.

(2)   In order to facilitate the operation of Chapter 2 (disallowance and reactivation of tax-interest expense amounts)—

    (a)   the company must bring a debit equal to the amount of the notional debits into account in the accounting period, and

    (b)   the company must bring a credit equal to the amount of the notional debits into account in the accounting period,

but nothing in this subsection affects any calculation required under any other provision of this Part in relation to the accounting period of the company.

(3)   The bringing into account of a debit under subsection (2)(a) is subject to the operation of the other provisions of this Part (which may result in some or all of the debit not being brought into account).

(4)   The debits and credits under subsection (2) are of the same nature as the notional debits that give rise to them.

(5)   For the purposes of this section a debit is a "notional debit" if the debit is created as a result of the determination required by the election or so far as the amount of the debit is increased as a result of that determination.

Exemption for tax-interest expense or income amounts

458   Co-operative and community benefit societies etc

(1)   This section applies where—

    (a)   apart from this section, an amount would be a tax-interest expense amount or tax-interest income amount of a company as a result of meeting condition A in section 382 or 385 (loan relationships), and

    (b)   the amount meets that condition only because of section 499 of CTA 2009 (certain sums payable by co-operative and community benefit societies or UK agricultural or fishing co-operatives treated as interest under loan relationship).

(2)   The amount is treated as not being a tax-interest expense amount or tax-interest income amount of the company.

459   Charities

(1)   This section applies where—

    (a)   apart from this section, an amount would be a tax-interest expense amount of a company as a result of meeting condition A in section 382 (loan relationship debits),

    (b)   the creditor is a charity,

    (c)   the company is a wholly-owned subsidiary of the charity, and

    (d)   the charitable gift condition is met at all times during the accounting period in which the amount is (or apart from this Part would be) brought into account.

(2)   The amount is treated as not being a tax-interest expense amount of the company.

(3)   For the purposes of this section the "charitable gift condition" is met at any time at which, were the company to make a donation to the charity at that time, it would be a qualifying charitable donation (see section 190 of CTA 2010).

(4)   In this section—

    "charity" has the same meaning as in Chapter 2 of Part 6 of CTA 2010 (see section 202 of that Act as read with Schedule 6 to FA 2010), and

    "the creditor" means the person who is party to the loan relationship in question as creditor.

Leases

460   Long funding operating leases and finance leases

(1)   In calculating a company's adjusted corporation tax earnings for an accounting period under section 406(2), each of the following amounts is to be ignored—

    (a)   the amount of a deduction under section 363 of CTA 2010 (lessor under long funding operating lease);

    (b)   the amount by which a deduction is reduced under section 379 of CTA 2010 (lessee under long funding operating lease);

    (c)   the capital component of the company's rental earnings under a finance lease which is not a long funding finance lease;

    (d)   the amount of depreciation in respect of any asset leased to the company under a finance lease which is not a long funding finance lease.

(2)   The definition of "relevant capital expenditure" in section 417(2) includes the amount of depreciation in respect of any relevant asset

leased under a finance lease for some or all of the relevant period of account to a company that is a member of the worldwide group in question.

(3) For the purposes of this section the capital component of a company's rental earnings under a finance lease is so much of those earnings as do not constitute tax-interest income amounts of the company.

(4) For the purposes of this section the amount of depreciation in respect of any asset leased to a company under a finance lease is the amount which, in accordance with generally accepted accounting practice, falls (or would fall) to be shown as depreciation in respect of the asset in the applicable accounts.

(5) In this section "the applicable accounts" are—

    (a) in a case within subsection (1)(d), the company's accounts for any period, and

    (b) in a case within subsection (2), the financial statements of the worldwide group for the relevant period of account in question.

(6) In this section "long funding finance lease" means a finance lease which is a long funding lease (within the meaning of section 70G of CAA 2001).

CHAPTER 10

ANTI-AVOIDANCE

461 Counteracting effect of avoidance arrangements

(1) Any tax advantage that would (in the absence of this section) arise from relevant avoidance arrangements is to be counteracted by the making of such adjustments as are just and reasonable.

(2) Any adjustments required to be made under this section (whether or not by an officer of Revenue and Customs) may be made by way of an assessment, the modification of an assessment, amendment or disallowance of a claim or otherwise.

(3) For the purposes of this section arrangements are "relevant avoidance arrangements" if conditions A and B are met.

(4) Condition A is that the main purpose, or one of the main purposes, of the arrangements is to enable a company to obtain a tax advantage.

(5) Condition B is that the tax advantage is attributable (or partly attributable) to any company—

    (a) not leaving tax-interest expense amounts out of account that it otherwise would have left out of account,

    (b) leaving tax-interest expense amounts out of account that are lower than they otherwise would have been,

    (c) leaving tax-interest expense amounts out of account in an accounting period other than that in which it otherwise would have left them out of account,

    (d)   bringing tax-interest expense amounts into account that it otherwise would not have brought into account,

    (e)   bringing tax-interest expense amounts into account that are higher than they otherwise would have been, or

    (f)   bringing tax-interest expense amounts into account in an accounting period other than that in which it otherwise would have brought them into account.

(6)   In subsection (5)—

    (a)   references to leaving amounts out of account are to leaving them out of account under this Part;

    (b)   references to bringing amounts into account are to bringing them into account under this Part.

(7)   In this section—

    "arrangements" includes any agreement, understanding, scheme, transaction or series of transactions (whether or not legally enforceable), and

    "tax advantage" includes—

    (a)   relief or increased relief from tax,

    (b)   repayment or increased repayment of tax,

    (c)   avoidance or reduction of a charge to tax or an assessment to tax,

    (d)   avoidance of a possible assessment to tax,

    (e)   deferral of a payment of tax or advancement of a repayment of tax, and

    (f)   avoidance of an obligation to deduct or account for tax.

(8)   For the purposes of the definition of "tax advantage" any reference to tax includes—

    (a)   any amount chargeable as if it were corporation tax or treated as if it were corporation tax, and

    (b)   diverted profits tax.

CHAPTER 11

INTERPRETATION ETC

Related parties

462   Expressions relating to "related parties": introduction

(1)   Section 463 sets out the circumstances in which a person is a related party of another person for the purposes of this Part.

(2)   That section—

    (a)   applies generally in relation to any amount, and

    (b)   is supplemented by sections 464 and 465 (which contain provisions that have effect for the purposes of that section).

(3)   Sections 466 and 467 make provision for treating persons as if they were related parties of each other but only in relation to certain matters.

(4) Sections 468 to 472 –

    (a) make provision for treating persons as if they were not related parties of each other but only in relation to certain matters, and

    (b) take priority over sections 466 and 467.

463 Whether a person is generally a "related party" of another

(1) For the purposes of this Part a person ("A") is a "related party" of another person ("B") –

    (a) throughout any period for which A and B are consolidated for accounting purposes,

    (b) on any day on which the participation condition is met in relation to them, or

    (c) on any day on which the 25% investment condition is met in relation to them.

(2) A and B are consolidated for accounting purposes for a period if –

    (a) their financial results for a period are required to be comprised in group accounts,

    (b) their financial results for the period would be required to be comprised in group accounts but for the application of an exemption, or

    (c) their financial results for a period are in fact comprised in group accounts.

(3) In subsection (2) "group accounts" means accounts prepared under –

    (a) section 399 of the Companies Act 2006, or

    (b) any corresponding provision of the law of a territory outside the United Kingdom.

(4) The participation condition is met in relation to A and B ("the relevant parties") on a day if, within the period of 6 months beginning or ending with that day –

    (a) one of the relevant parties directly or indirectly participates in the management, control or capital of the other, or

    (b) the same person or persons directly or indirectly participate in the management, control or capital of each of the relevant parties.

(5) For the interpretation of subsection (4), see sections 157(1), 158(4), 159(1) and 160(1) (which have the effect that references in that subsection to direct or indirect participation are to be read in accordance with provisions of Chapter 2 of Part 4).

(6) If one of the relevant parties is a securitisation company within the meaning of Chapter 4 of Part 13 of CTA 2010, the relevant parties are not to be regarded as related parties of each other as a result of subsection (4) merely by reference to the fact that –

    (a) the securitisation company is held by a trustee of a settlement, and

    (b) the other relevant party is a settlor in relation to that settlement.

(7) The 25% investment condition is met in relation to A and B if—

    (a) one of them has a 25% investment in the other, or

    (b) a third person has a 25% investment in each of them.

(8) Sections 464 and 465 apply for the purpose of determining whether a person has a "25% investment" in another person.

464 Meaning of "25% investment"

(1) A person ("P") has a 25% investment in another person ("C") if—

    (a) P possesses or is entitled to acquire 25% or more of the voting power in C,

    (b) in the event of a disposal of the whole of the equity in C, P would receive 25% or more of the proceeds,

    (c) in the event that the income in respect of the equity in C were distributed among the equity holders in C, P would receive 25% or more of the amount so distributed, or

    (d) in the event of a winding-up of C or in any other circumstances, P would receive 25% or more of C's assets which would then be available for distribution among the equity holders in C in respect of the equity in C.

(2) In this section references to the equity in C are to—

    (a) the shares in C other than restricted preference shares, or

    (b) loans to C other than normal commercial loans.

(3) For this purpose "shares in C" includes—

    (a) stock, and

    (b) any other interests of members in C.

(4) For the purposes of this section a person is an equity holder in C if the person possesses any of the equity in C.

(5) For the purposes of this section—

    "normal commercial loan" means a loan which is a normal commercial loan for the purposes of section 158(1)(b) or 159(4)(b) of CTA 2010, and

    "restricted preference shares" means shares which are restricted preference shares for the purposes of section 160 of CTA 2010.

(6) In applying for the purposes of this section the definitions of "normal commercial loan" and "restricted preference shares" in a case where—

    (a) C is not a company, or

    (b) C is a company which does not have share capital,

sections 160(2) to (7) and 161 to 164 of CTA 2010 (and any other relevant provisions of that Act) have effect with the necessary modifications.

(7) In this section references to a person receiving any proceeds, amount or assets include—

    (a) the direct or indirect receipt of the proceeds, amount or assets, and

380   *Finance (No. 2) Act 2017 (c. 32)*
Schedule 5 – Corporate interest restriction
Part 1 – New Part 10 of TIOPA 2010

    (b)   the direct or indirect application of the proceeds, amount or assets for the person's benefit,

and it does not matter whether the receipt or application is at the time of the disposal, distribution, winding-up or other circumstances or at a later time.

(8)   If—

    (a)   there is a direct receipt or direct application of any proceeds, amount or assets by or for the benefit of a person ("A"), and

    (b)   another person ("B") directly or indirectly owns a percentage of the equity in A,

there is, for the purposes of subsection (7), an indirect receipt or indirect application of that percentage of the proceeds, amount or assets by or for the benefit of B.

(9)   For this purpose the percentage of the equity in A directly or indirectly owned by B is to be determined by applying the rules in sections 1155 to 1157 of CTA 2010 with such modifications (if any) as may be necessary.

(10)   Subsection (7) is not to result in a person being regarded as having a 25% investment in another person merely as a result of their being parties to a normal commercial loan.

(11)   Any reference in this section, in the case of a person who is a member of a partnership, to the proceeds, amount or assets of the person includes the person's share of the proceeds, amount or assets of the partnership (apportioning those things between the partners on a just and reasonable basis).

465   Attribution of rights and interests

(1)   In determining for the purposes of section 464 the investment that a person ("P") has in another person, P is to be taken to have all of the rights and interests of—

    (a)   any person connected with P,

    (b)   any person who is a member of a partnership, or is connected with a person who is member of a partnership, of which P is a member, or

    (c)   any person who is a member of a partnership, or is connected with a person who is a member of a partnership, of which a person connected with P is a member.

(2)   For the purposes of subsection (1)—

    (a)   section 1122 of CTA 2010 ("connected" persons) applies but as if subsections (7) and (8) of that section were omitted, but

    (b)   a person is not to be regarded as connected with another person merely as a result of their being parties to a loan that is a normal commercial loan for the purposes of section 464.

(3)   In determining for the purposes of section 464 the investment that a person ("P") has in another person ("U"), P is to be taken to have all of the rights and interests of a third person ("T") with whom P acts together in relation to U.

(4)   For this purpose P "acts together" with T in relation to U if (and only if)—

    (a) for the purpose of influencing the conduct of U's affairs –

        (i) P is able to secure that T acts in accordance with P's wishes (or vice versa), or

        (ii) T can reasonably be expected to act, or typically acts, in accordance with P's wishes (or vice versa),

    (b) P and T are party to an arrangement that it is reasonable to conclude is designed to affect the value of any equity in U possessed by T, or

    (c) the same person manages some or all of any equity in U possessed by P and T.

In paragraphs (b) and (c) references to equity in U are to be read in accordance with section 464.

(5) But P does not "act together" with T in relation to U under subsection (4)(c) if –

    (a) the managing person does so as the operator of different collective investment schemes, and

    (b) the management of the schemes is not coordinated for the purpose of influencing the conduct of U's affairs.

(6) For this purpose "collective investment scheme" and "operator" have the same meaning as in Part 17 of the Financial Services and Markets Act 2000 (see sections 235 and 237).

(7) In determining for the purposes of section 464 the investment that a person ("P") has in another person ("U"), P is to be taken to have all of the rights and interests of one or more third persons with whom P has entered into a qualifying arrangement in relation to U.

(8) For this purpose P has entered into a qualifying arrangement with one or more third persons in relation to U if they are parties to an arrangement concerning U as a result of which, by reference to shares held, or to be held, by any one or more of them in U, they can reasonably be expected to act together –

    (a) so as to exert greater influence in relation to U than any one of them would be able to exert if acting alone, or

    (b) otherwise so as to be able to achieve an outcome in relation to U that, if attempted by any one of them acting alone, would be significantly more difficult to achieve.

(9) For this purpose the reference to shares in U includes shares in U that may be held as a result of the exercise of any right or power and includes rights or interests in U that are of a similar character to shares.

(10) In this section "arrangement" includes any agreement, understanding, scheme, transaction or series of transactions (whether or not legally enforceable).

466 Certain loan relationships etc to be treated as made between related parties

(1) This section –

    (a) makes provision for treating a person ("D") who is not a related party of another person ("C") as if they were related parties of each other but only in respect of particular liabilities or transactions, and

(b)   is expressed to apply in relation to loan relationships but also applies (with any necessary modifications) in relation to any other financial liability owed to, or any transaction with, C.

(2)   If at any time—

(a)   D is party to a loan relationship as debtor and C is party to the relationship as creditor, and

(b)   another person ("G") who is a related party of D provides a guarantee, indemnity or other financial assistance in respect of the liability of D that represents the loan relationship,

D and C are treated for the purposes of this Part as if, in relation to the loan relationship concerned (and anything done under or for the purposes of it), they were related parties of each other at that time.

(3)   Subsection (2) is subject to—

(a)   section 415 (qualifying net group-interest expense), and

(b)   section 438(3) (infrastructure: interest payable to third parties etc).

(4)   If at any time—

(a)   D is party to a loan relationship as debtor and C is party to the relationship as creditor, and

(b)   another person ("G") who is a related party of D indirectly stands in the position of a creditor as respects the debt in question by reference to a series of loan relationships or other arrangements,

D and C are treated for the purposes of this Part as if, in relation to the loan relationship concerned (and anything done under or for the purposes of it), they were related parties of each other at that time.

(5)   For the purposes of this section "arrangements" include any agreement, understanding, scheme, transaction or series of transactions (whether or not legally enforceable).

467   Holdings of debt and equity in same proportions

(1)   This section applies at any time where—

(a)   persons have lent money to another person ("U"),

(b)   the lenders also have shares or voting power in U,

(c)   the amounts each of the lenders has lent stand in the same, or substantially the same, proportion as the shares or voting power in U that each of them has, and

(d)   for the purposes of section 464 the lenders (taken together) have a 25% investment in U.

(2)   The lenders are treated for the purposes of this Part as if, in relation to the loans (and anything done under or for the purposes of them), they were related parties of U at that time (so far as that would not otherwise be the case).

(3)   If—

(a)   some or all of the rights under the loan are transferred, and

(b) the transferred rights are held by, or for the benefit of, another person ("the transferee") at any time,

the transferee is treated for the purposes of this Part as if, in relation to the loan (and anything done under or for the purposes of it), the transferee were a related party of U at that time (so far as that would not otherwise be the case).

(4) This applies whether or not the transferee has any shares or voting power in U.

(5) For the purposes of this section references to shares in U include shares in U that may be held as a result of the exercise of any right or power and include rights or interests in U that are of a similar character to shares.

(6) This section applies (with any necessary modifications) in relation to any other financial liability owed to, or any transaction with, U as it applies to loans made to U.

468 Debts with same rights where unrelated parties hold more than 50%

(1) This section applies if —

    (a) a person ("D") is party to a loan relationship as debtor in a period of account of a worldwide group of which it is a member,

    (b) a person ("C") who is party to the loan relationship as creditor is a related party of D at any time in that period,

    (c) there are persons ("the relevant creditors") other than C who are parties to the loan relationship, or are parties to other loan relationships entered into at the same time, as creditors but who are not related parties of D at any time in that period,

    (d) at all times in that period the rights of the relevant creditors are rights in relation to at least 50% of the total amount of the money debt or debts in question, and

    (e) at all times in that period C and the relevant creditors have the same rights in relation to the money debt or debts in question.

(2) D and C are treated for the purposes of this Part as if, in relation to the loan relationship concerned (and anything done under or for the purposes of it), they were not related parties of each other at any time in that period.

(3) Persons are not to be regarded as having the same rights in relation to a money debt or debts at any time if —

    (a) the terms or conditions on which any of the money is lent and which are in force at that time make different provision in relation to different persons or have, or are capable of having, a different effect in relation to different persons (whether at that or any subsequent time),

    (b) arrangements are in place at that time the effect of which is that, at that or any subsequent time, the rights of some persons in relation to any of the debts differ, or will or may differ, from the rights of others in relation to any of the debts, or

384   *Finance (No. 2) Act 2017 (c. 32)*
Schedule 5 — Corporate interest restriction
Part 1 — New Part 10 of TIOPA 2010

      (c)   any other circumstances exist at that time as a result of which the rights of some persons in relation to any of the debts cannot reasonably be regarded as being, in substance, the same rights as others in relation any of the debts at that or any subsequent time.

(4)   For the purposes of this section—

"arrangements" include any agreement, understanding, scheme, transaction or series of transactions (whether or not legally enforceable),

"different persons" includes persons of a different class or description, and

"rights" includes powers.

469   Debt restructuring

(1)   This section—

      (a)   makes provision for treating a person ("D") who is a related party of another person ("C") as if they were not related parties of each other but only in respect of particular liabilities or transactions, and

      (b)   is expressed to apply in relation to loan relationships but also applies (with any necessary modifications) in relation to any other financial liability owed to, or any transaction with, C.

(2)   If—

      (a)   D is party to a loan relationship as debtor and C is party to the loan relationship as creditor,

      (b)   D subsequently becomes a related party of C in consequence of a relevant release of debt, and

      (c)   before D became a related party of C in consequence of the release none of the parties to the loan relationship had been related parties of each other,

D and C are treated for the purposes of this Part as if, in relation to the loan relationship (and anything done under or for the purposes of it), they were not related parties of each other at times on or after the release.

(3)   There is a "relevant release of debt" at any time for the purposes of this section if—

      (a)   a liability to pay an amount under a person's debtor relationship is released under the arrangements,

      (b)   that person is D or a person who is a related party of D at that time, and

      (c)   immediately before the release, it is reasonable to conclude that, without the release and any arrangements of which the release forms part, there would be a material risk that, at some time within the next 12 months, D or the related party would be unable to pay its debts.

(4)   For the purposes of this section "debtor relationship" has the meaning given by section 302(6) of CTA 2009 (reading the references in that subsection to a company as references to a person).

470 Ordinary independent financing arrangements by banks and others

(1) This section applies where—

    (a) at any time, a person ("C") is party to a loan relationship as creditor and the party to the loan relationship as debtor ("D") is a related party of C as a result of any circumstances, and

    (b) the loan relationship is not one to which C is a party at that time directly or indirectly in consequence of, or otherwise in connection with, the existence of any of those circumstances.

(2) C and D are treated for the purposes of this Part as if, in relation to the loan relationship (and anything done under or for the purposes of it), they were not related parties of each other at that time.

471 Loans made by relevant public bodies

(1) This section applies at any time where—

    (a) a relevant public body ("B") lends money to a person ("P"),

    (b) B is a related party of P, and

    (c) the realising of a profit is merely incidental to the making of the loan.

(2) B and P are treated for the purposes of this Part as if, in relation to the loan (and anything done under or for the purposes of it), they were not related parties of each other at that time.

472 Finance leases granted before 20 March 2017

(1) This section applies at any time where an asset is leased by a person ("A") to another ("B") under a lease which is granted before 20 March 2017 and which, in the case of B, is a finance lease.

(2) A and B are treated for the purposes of this Part as if, in relation to the lease (and anything done under or for the purposes of it), they were not related parties of each other at that time.

Determining the worldwide group

473 Meaning of "a worldwide group", "ultimate parent" etc

(1) In this Part "a worldwide group" means—

    (a) any entity which—

        (i) is a relevant entity (see section 474), and

        (ii) meets the first or second non-consolidation condition (see subsections (2) and (3)), and

    (b) each consolidated subsidiary (if any) of the entity mentioned in paragraph (a).

(2) The first non-consolidation condition is that the entity—

    (a) is a member of an IAS group, and

    (b) is not a consolidated subsidiary of an entity that—

        (i) is a relevant entity, and

        (ii) itself meets the first non-consolidation condition.

(3) The second non-consolidation condition is that the entity is not a member of an IAS group.

(4) In this Part—

   (a) references to "a member" of a worldwide group are to an entity mentioned in subsection (1)(a) or (b);

   (b) references to "the ultimate parent" of a worldwide group are to the entity mentioned in subsection (1)(a);

   (c) references to "a single-company worldwide group" are to a worldwide group whose only member is its ultimate parent;

   (d) references to "a multi-company worldwide group" are to a worldwide group with two or more members.

(5) In this section "IAS group" means a group within the meaning given by international accounting standards.

474 Interpretation of section 473: "relevant entity"

(1) In section 473 "relevant entity" means—

   (a) a company, or

   (b) an entity the shares or other interests in which are listed on a recognised stock exchange and are sufficiently widely held.

(2) Shares or other interests in an entity are "sufficiently widely held" if no participator in the entity holds more than 10% by value of all the shares or other interests in the entity.

Section 454 of CTA 2010 (meaning of participator) applies for the purposes of this subsection.

(3) The following are not relevant entities—

   (a) the Crown,

   (b) a Minister of the Crown,

   (c) a government department,

   (d) a Northern Ireland department, or

   (e) a foreign sovereign power.

475 Meaning of "non-consolidated subsidiary" and "consolidated subsidiary"

(1) An entity ("X") is a "non-consolidated subsidiary" of another entity ("Y") at any time ("the relevant time") if—

   (a) X is a subsidiary of Y at the relevant time, and

   (b) if Y were required at the relevant time to measure its investment in X, it would be required to do so using fair value accounting.

(2) An entity ("X") is a "consolidated subsidiary" of another entity ("Y") at any time if, at that time, X is a subsidiary, but not a non-consolidated subsidiary, of Y.

(3) In this section "subsidiary" has the meaning given by international accounting standards.

(4) For the purposes of this section, assume that all entities are subject to international accounting standards.

(5) This section has effect for the purposes of this Part.

476 Continuity of identity of a worldwide group through time

(1) This section applies for the purpose of determining whether a group of entities that constitutes a worldwide group at any time ("Time 2") is the same worldwide group as a group of entities that constitutes a worldwide group at an earlier time ("Time 1").

(2) The group at Time 2 is the same worldwide group as the group at Time 1 if and only if the entity that is the ultimate parent of the group at Time 2—

    (a) was the ultimate parent of the group at Time 1, and

    (b) was the ultimate parent of a worldwide group at all times between Time 1 and Time 2.

477 Treatment of stapled entities

(1) This section applies where two or more entities—

    (a) would, apart from this section, each be the ultimate parent of a worldwide group, and

    (b) are stapled to each other.

(2) This Part has effect as if—

    (a) the entities were consolidated subsidiaries of another entity (the "deemed parent"), and

    (b) the deemed parent fell within section 473(1)(a) (conditions for being the ultimate parent of a worldwide group).

(3) For the purpose of this section an entity ("entity A") is "stapled" to another entity ("entity B") if, in consequence of the nature of the rights attaching to the shares or other interests in entity A (including any terms or conditions attaching to the right to transfer the interests), it is necessary or advantageous for a person who has, disposes of or acquires shares or other interests in entity A also to have, dispose of or acquire shares or other interests in entity B.

478 Treatment of business combinations

(1) This section applies where two entities—

    (a) would, apart from this section, each be the ultimate parent of a worldwide group, and

    (b) are treated under international accounting standards as a single economic entity by reason of being a business combination achieved by contract.

(2) This Part has effect as if—

    (a) the two entities were consolidated subsidiaries of another entity (the "deemed parent"), and

    (b) the deemed parent fell within section 473(1)(a) (conditions for being the ultimate parent of a worldwide group).

(3) In this section "business combination" has the meaning given by international accounting standards.

Financial statements and periods of account

479 "Financial statements" of a worldwide group

(1) References in this Part to "financial statements" of a worldwide group for a period are (subject to subsection (2)) to consolidated financial statements of the worldwide group's ultimate parent and its subsidiaries in respect of the period.

(2) Where the worldwide group is at all times during the period a single-company worldwide group, the references are to financial statements of the ultimate parent in respect of the period.

(3) The basic rule is that the references mentioned in subsections (1) and (2) are to financial statements that are drawn up by or on behalf of the ultimate parent.

(4) But see —

    (a) section 481 for provision under which, in specified circumstances, financial statements of a worldwide group are treated as having been drawn up in accordance with different accounting standards from those in accordance with which they are drawn up by or on behalf of the ultimate parent;

    (b) section 482 for provision under which, in specified circumstances, financial statements of a worldwide group are treated as consolidating different subsidiaries from those consolidated in financial statements drawn up by or on behalf of the ultimate parent;

    (c) section 483 for provision under which, in specified circumstances, financial statements of a worldwide group are treated as having been drawn up where the ultimate parent has drawn up consolidated financial statements covering more than one worldwide group;

    (d) sections 484 to 486 for provision under which, where financial statements of a worldwide group are not drawn up by or on behalf of the ultimate parent, financial statements of the group are treated as having been drawn up.

(5) See also section 487 (under which financial statements drawn up by or on behalf of an entity, but for too long a period or too late, are ignored for the purposes of this Part).

480 "Period of account" of worldwide group

References in this Part to a "period of account" of a worldwide group are to —

    (a) a period in respect of which financial statements of the group are drawn up by or on behalf of the ultimate parent, or

    (b) a period in respect of which financial statements of the group are treated as drawn up for the purposes of this section (whether under any of sections 481 to 485 or under any other enactment).

481 Actual financial statements not drawn up on acceptable principles

(1) This section applies where financial statements of a worldwide group for a period drawn up by or on behalf of the ultimate parent are not drawn up on acceptable principles.

(2) For the purposes of this Part (apart from this section)—

   (a) the financial statements mentioned in subsection (1) are to be ignored, and

   (b) IAS financial statements of the worldwide group are treated as having been drawn up in respect of the period.

(3) For the purposes of this Chapter financial statements are "drawn up on acceptable principles" only if condition A, B, C or D is met.

(4) Condition A is that the financial statements are IAS financial statements.

(5) Condition B is that the amounts recognised in the financial statements are not materially different from those that would be recognised in IAS financial statements of the worldwide group, if such statements were drawn up.

(6) Condition C is that the financial statements are drawn up in accordance with UK generally accepted accounting practice.

(7) Condition D is that the financial statements are drawn up in accordance with generally accepted accounting principles and practice of one of the following territories—

   (a) Canada;

   (b) China;

   (c) India;

   (d) Japan;

   (e) South Korea;

   (f) the United States of America.

(8) The Commissioners may by regulations amend this section so as to alter the circumstances in which financial statements are "drawn up on acceptable principles" for the purposes of this Chapter.

482 Actual financial statements drawn up on acceptable principles but consolidating wrong subsidiaries

(1) This section applies where financial statements of a worldwide group for a period drawn up by or on behalf of the ultimate parent are drawn up on acceptable principles but—

   (a) do not consolidate one or more entities that are IAS subsidiaries, or

   (b) consolidate one or more entities that are not IAS subsidiaries.

(2) In this section "IAS subsidiary", in relation to a period, means an entity which would be required to be consolidated with those of the ultimate parent in IAS financial statements of the group for the period.

(3) For the purposes of this Part (apart from this section)—

> (a) the financial statements mentioned in subsection (1) are to be ignored, and
>
> (b) consolidated financial statements of the ultimate parent and its IAS subsidiaries are treated as having been drawn up in respect of the period.

(4) The financial statements treated by subsection (3)(b) as drawn up are treated as drawn up in accordance with the same accounting principles and practice as the financial statements mentioned in subsection (1).

(5) In this section a reference to financial statements consolidating the results of an entity is to consolidating its results with those of the ultimate parent as the results of a single economic entity.

483 Actual financial statements covering more than one worldwide group

(1) This section applies where —
> (a) consolidated financial statements of an entity and its subsidiaries are drawn up by or on behalf of the entity in respect of a period ("the actual period of account"), and
>
> (b) the entity was the ultimate parent of a worldwide group for a part (but not all) of that period.

(2) For the purposes of this Part (apart from this section) —
> (a) the financial statements mentioned in subsection (1)(a) are to be ignored, and
>
> (b) consolidated financial statements of the entity and its IAS subsidiaries are treated as having been drawn up in respect of the part of the actual period of account mentioned in subsection (1)(b).

(3) The financial statements treated by subsection (2)(b) as drawn up are treated as drawn up —
> (a) where the financial statements mentioned in subsection (1)(a) are drawn up on acceptable principles, in accordance with the same accounting principles and practice as those financial statements;
>
> (b) otherwise, in accordance with international accounting standards.

(4) In this section "IAS subsidiary" has the same meaning as in section 482.

484 No actual financial statements: ultimate parent draws up financial statements

(1) Subsection (2) applies where —
> (a) financial statements of the ultimate parent of a worldwide group are drawn up by or on behalf of the ultimate parent in respect of a period ("the relevant period"),
>
> (b) consolidated financial statements of the ultimate parent and its subsidiaries are not drawn up by or on behalf of the ultimate parent in respect of the relevant period or any part of it, and

      (c)   the group was, at any time during the relevant period, a multi-company worldwide group.

   (2)   For the purposes of this Part (apart from this section) IAS financial statements of the worldwide group are treated as drawn up in respect of the relevant period.

   (3)   The ultimate parent may elect that subsection (2) is not to apply in relation to financial statements of the ultimate parent.

   (4)   An election under subsection (3) —

      (a)   has effect in relation to financial statements in respect of periods ending on or after such date as is specified in the election, and

      (b)   is irrevocable.

   (5)   The date specified in the election may not be before the day on which the election is made.

485   No actual financial statements: other cases

   (1)   In this section "accounts-free period" means (subject to subsection (2)) any period —

      (a)   which begins on or after 1 April 2017,

      (b)   throughout which a worldwide group exists, and

      (c)   in respect of no part of which are financial statements of the group —

         (i)   drawn up by or on behalf of the ultimate parent, or

         (ii)   treated as drawn up for the purposes of this section (whether under section 481, 482, 483 or 484 or any other enactment).

   (2)   A period is not an "accounts-free period" if it forms part of an accounts-free period.

   (3)   If an accounts-free period in relation to a worldwide group is 12 months or less, IAS financial statements of the worldwide group are treated for the purposes of this Part (apart from this section) as having been drawn up for the accounts-free period.

   (4)   If an accounts-free period in relation to a worldwide group is more than 12 months, IAS financial statements of the worldwide group are treated for the purposes of this Part (apart from this section) as having been drawn up for each of the following periods —

      (a)   the first period of 12 months falling within the accounts-free period;

      (b)   any subsequent period of 12 months falling within the accounts-free period;

      (c)   any period of less than 12 months which —

         (i)   begins immediately after the end of a period mentioned in paragraph (a) or (b), and

         (ii)   ends at the end of the accounts-free period.

486   Election altering period of account deemed under section 485

   (1)   This section applies where, disregarding this section, IAS financial statements of a worldwide group would be treated under section

485(4)(a) or (b) as drawn up for a period ("the default period of account") during an accounts-free period.

(2) The ultimate parent of the group may make an election under this section in relation to the default period of account.

(3) Where an election under this section is made, section 485 has effect as if subsection (4)(a) or (b) of that section—

   (a) did not treat IAS financial statements of the group as having been drawn up for the default period of account;

   (b) instead, treated IAS financial statements of the group as having been drawn up for the period—

      (i) beginning with the day on which the default period of account begins ("the start day"), and

      (ii) ending with such day after the start day as is specified in the election ("the end day").

(4) The end day must—

   (a) fall within the accounts-free period, and

   (b) not be later than the final day of the period of 18 months beginning with the start day.

(5) An election under this section—

   (a) must be made before the end day, and

   (b) is irrevocable.

(6) The fact that the ultimate parent of a worldwide group makes an election under this section in relation to a default period of account ("the earlier elected period") does not prevent it from making an election in relation to a later default period of account ("the later elected period").

(7) But where it does so, the end day in relation to the later elected period must be 3 years or more after the end day in relation to the earlier elected period.

(8) Where this section modifies section 485(4)(a) or (b) so that it treats IAS financial statements of the group as having been drawn up for the period mentioned in subsection (3)(b) of this section ("the elected period"), section 485(4)(b) and (c) apply in relation to any part of the accounts-free period following the end of the elected period.

(9) In this section "accounts-free period" has the same meaning as in section 485.

487 Actual financial statements ignored if for too long a period or too late

Financial statements drawn up by or on behalf of any entity are to be ignored for the purposes of this Part (apart from this section) if—

   (a) the period in respect of which they are drawn up is more than 18 months, or

   (b) they are drawn up after the end of the period of 30 months beginning with the beginning of the period in respect of which they are drawn up.

488 Meaning of "IAS financial statements"

(1) References in this Part to "IAS financial statements" of a worldwide group for a period are (subject to subsection (2)) to consolidated financial statements of the worldwide group's ultimate parent and its subsidiaries, drawn up in respect of the period in accordance with international accounting standards.

(2) If the worldwide group is at all times during the period a single-company worldwide group, the references are instead to financial statements of the ultimate parent, drawn up in respect of the period in accordance with international accounting standards.

489 References to amounts recognised in financial statements

(1) References in this Part to an amount "recognised" in financial statements —

   (a) include an amount comprised in an amount so recognised;

   (b) are, where the amount is expressed in a currency other than sterling, to that amount translated into its sterling equivalent.

(2) The exchange rate by reference to which an amount is to be translated under subsection (1)(b) is the average rate of exchange for the period of account, calculated from daily spot rates.

(3) References in this Part to an amount recognised in financial statements "for a period" as an item of profit or loss include references to an amount that —

   (a) was previously recognised as an item of other comprehensive income, and

   (b) is transferred to become an item of profit or loss in determining the profit or loss for the period.

Other definitions

490 Meaning of "relevant accounting period"

For the purposes of this Part a "relevant accounting period" of a company, in relation to a period of account of a worldwide group, means any accounting period that falls wholly or partly within the period of account of the worldwide group.

491 Meaning of "relevant public body"

(1) In this Part "relevant public body" means —

   (a) the Crown,

   (b) a Minister of the Crown,

   (c) a government department,

   (d) a Northern Ireland department,

   (e) a foreign sovereign power,

   (f) a designated educational establishment (within the meaning given by section 106 of CTA 2009),

   (g) a health service body (within the meaning given by section 986 of CTA 2010),

   (h) a local authority or local authority association,

394   *Finance (No. 2) Act 2017 (c. 32)*
Schedule 5 — Corporate interest restriction
Part 1 — New Part 10 of TIOPA 2010

    (i)   any other body that acts under any enactment for public purposes and not for its own profit, or

    (j)   any wholly-owned subsidiary of any body falling within any of the above paragraphs of this subsection.

(2)   In this section "enactment" includes—

    (a)   an enactment contained in subordinate legislation within the meaning of the Interpretation Act 1978,

    (b)   an enactment contained in, or in an instrument made under, an Act of the Scottish Parliament,

    (c)   an enactment contained in, or in an instrument made under, a Measure or Act of the National Assembly for Wales, and

    (d)   an enactment contained in, or in an instrument made under, Northern Ireland legislation.

(3)   The Commissioners may by regulations amend this section so as to alter the meaning of "relevant public body".

(4)   The provision that may be made by the regulations does not include provision altering the meaning of "relevant public body" so that it includes a person who has no functions of a public nature.

492   Meaning of "UK group company"

In this Part "UK group company", in relation to any time during a period of account of a worldwide group, means a company—

    (a)   which is within the charge to corporation tax at that time, and

    (b)   which is a member of the group at that time.

493   Embedded derivatives

Sections 415 and 585 of CTA 2009 (loan relationships with embedded derivatives) apply for the purposes of this Part of this Act.

494   Other interpretation

(1)   In this Part—

    "the Commissioners" means the Commissioners for Her Majesty's Revenue and Customs;

    "fair value accounting" means a basis of accounting under which—

        (a)   assets and liabilities are measured in the company's balance sheet at their fair value, and

        (b)   changes in the fair value of assets and liabilities are recognised as items of profit or loss;

    "fair value" has the meaning it has for accounting purposes;

    "finance lease", in relation to a company or a worldwide group, means a lease that, in accordance with generally accepted accounting practice, falls (or would fall) to be treated as a finance lease or loan in the accounts of the company or the financial statements of the group;

    "interest restriction return" means a return submitted under any provision of Schedule 7A;

    "reporting company" means a company which is for the time being appointed under any provision of Schedule 7A;

> "the return period", in relation to an interest restriction return of a worldwide group, means the period of account of the group to which the return relates;
>
> "service concession arrangement" has the meaning given by international accounting standards;
>
> "wholly-owned subsidiary" has the meaning given by section 1159(2) of the Companies Act 2006.

(2) For the purposes of this Part a person who is not a company is regarded as being a party to a loan relationship if the person would be so regarded for the purposes of Part 5 of CTA 2009 if the person were a company.

Regulations

495 Financial statements: different treatment by group or members

(1) The Commissioners may make regulations for the purpose of altering any calculation under Chapter 7 where—

    (a) the financial statements of a worldwide group for a period include or omit an amount in respect of any matter, and

    (b) any member of the group deals with that matter for tax or accounting purposes in a different way.

(2) The regulations—

    (a) may make provision subject to an election or other specified circumstances, and

    (b) may make provision having effect in relation to any period beginning before the regulations are made if the period begins at some time in the calendar year in which the regulations are made.

496 Parties to capital market arrangements

(1) The Commissioners may make regulations entitling—

    (a) a UK group company which has a liability to corporation tax as a result of this Part and which is a party to a capital market arrangement, and

    (b) another UK group company,

to make a joint election transferring the liability to the other UK group company.

(2) The regulations may include provision—

    (a) specifying other conditions that must be met for an election to be made,

    (b) requiring an election to be made on or before a particular time (for example, before the accounting period for which the liability arises),

    (c) authorising or requiring an officer of Revenue and Customs (on the exercise of a discretion or otherwise) to accept or reject an election,

    (d) authorising or requiring an officer of Revenue and Customs (on the exercise of a discretion or otherwise) to revoke an election previously in force and dealing with the effect of the revocation, and

(e) dealing with the effect of the transfer of the corporation tax liability on any other liabilities that relate to the transferred corporation tax liability.

(3) In this section "capital market arrangement" has the same meaning as in section 72B(1) of the Insolvency Act 1986 (see paragraph 1 of Schedule 2A to that Act).

497 Change in accounting standards

(1) The Treasury may by regulations amend this Part to take account of a change in the way in which amounts are, or may be, presented or disclosed in financial statements where the change results from the issue, revocation, amendment or recognition of, or withdrawal of recognition from, an accounting standard by an accounting body.

(2) For this purpose—
   "accounting standard" includes any statement of practice, guidance or other similar document, and
   "accounting body" means—
   (a) the International Accounting Standards Board (or successor body), or
   (b) the Accounting Standards Board (or successor body).

(3) The regulations—
   (a) may make provision subject to an election or other specified circumstances, and
   (b) may make provision having effect in relation to any period beginning before the regulations are made if the change mentioned in subsection (1) is relevant to that period.

(4) A statutory instrument containing regulations which are capable of increasing the liability of a company to corporation tax may not be made unless a draft of the instrument is laid before, and approved by a resolution of, the House of Commons.

498 Regulations

Regulations under this Part may—
   (a) make different provision for different cases or circumstances,
   (b) include supplementary, incidental and consequential provision, or
   (c) make transitional provision and savings."

Finance (No. 2) Act 2017 (c. 32)
Schedule 5 — Corporate interest restriction
Part 2 — New Schedule 7A to TIOPA 2010

397

PART 2

NEW SCHEDULE 7A TO TIOPA 2010

2   In TIOPA 2010, after Schedule 7 insert—

"SCHEDULE 7A   Section 374

INTEREST RESTRICTION RETURNS

PART 1

THE REPORTING COMPANY

Appointment by a worldwide group of a reporting company

1   (1) A member of a worldwide group may, by notice to an officer of
         Revenue and Customs, appoint an eligible company to be the
         group's reporting company.

     (2) The notice must specify the first period of account of the group
         ("the specified period of account") in relation to which the
         appointment is to have effect.

     (3) An appointment under this paragraph has effect in relation to—
         (a)   the specified period of account, and
         (b)   subsequent periods of account of the group.

     (4) The notice is of no effect unless—
         (a)   it is given during the period of six months beginning with
               the end of the specified period of account,
         (b)   it is authorised by at least 50% of eligible companies, and
         (c)   it is accompanied by a statement containing the required
               information.

     (5) For this purpose "the required information" means—
         (a)   a list of the eligible companies that have authorised the
               notice, and
         (b)   a statement that the listed companies constitute at least
               50% of eligible companies.

     (6) The notice may be accompanied by a statement that such of the
         companies listed under sub-paragraph (5)(a) as are specified in the
         statement do not wish to be consenting companies in relation to
         returns submitted by the reporting company.
         For provision as to the effect of a statement under this sub-
         paragraph, see paragraph 11.

     (7) For the purposes of this paragraph a company is "eligible" if and
         only if the company —
         (a)   was a UK group company at a time during the specified
               period of account, and
         (b)   was not dormant throughout that period.

398

Finance (No. 2) Act 2017 (c. 32)
Schedule 5 — Corporate interest restriction
Part 2 — New Schedule 7A to TIOPA 2010

Revocation by worldwide group of appointment under paragraph 1

2   (1) A member of a worldwide group may, by notice to an officer of Revenue and Customs, revoke an appointment previously made under paragraph 1.

(2) The notice must specify the first period of account of the group ("the specified period of account") in relation to which the appointment is to be revoked.

(3) An appointment that is revoked under this paragraph ceases to have effect in relation to —
     (a) the specified period of account, and
     (b) subsequent periods of account of the group.

(4) The notice is of no effect unless —
     (a) it is given during the period of six months beginning with the end of the specified period of account,
     (b) it is authorised by at least 50% of eligible companies, and
     (c) it is accompanied by a statement containing the required information.

(5) For this purpose "the required information" means —
     (a) a list of the eligible companies that have authorised the notice, and
     (b) a statement that the listed companies constitute at least 50% of eligible companies.

(6) The revocation of an appointment does not prevent the making of a further appointment under paragraph 1 (whether at the same time as the revocation, or later).

(7) For the purposes of this paragraph a company is "eligible" if and only if the company —
     (a) was a UK group company at a time during the specified period of account, and
     (b) was not dormant throughout that period.

Regulations supplementing paragraphs 1 and 2

3   The Commissioners may by regulations make further provision about an appointment under paragraph 1 or the revocation of such an appointment under paragraph 2, including in particular provision —
     (a) about the form and manner in which an appointment or revocation may be made;
     (b) requiring a person to give information to an officer of Revenue and Customs in connection with the making of an appointment or revocation;
     (c) prohibiting a company from being appointed unless it meets conditions specified in the regulations;
     (d) about the time from which an appointment or revocation has effect;

Finance (No. 2) Act 2017 (c. 32)
Schedule 5 — Corporate interest restriction
Part 2 — New Schedule 7A to TIOPA 2010

399

      (e)   providing that an appointment or revocation is of no effect, or (in the case of an appointment) ceases to have effect, if a requirement under the regulations is not met.

Appointment of reporting company by Revenue and Customs

4   (1)   This paragraph applies where —

      (a)   no appointment of a reporting company under paragraph 1 has effect in relation to a period of account of a worldwide group ("the relevant period of account"), and

      (b)   as a result of sub-paragraph (4)(a) of that paragraph, an appointment of a reporting company under that paragraph that has effect in relation to the relevant period of account is no longer possible.

    (2)   An officer of Revenue and Customs may, by notice to an eligible company, appoint it to be the group's reporting company.

    (3)   The notice must specify the relevant period of account (whether by specifying the dates on which it begins and ends or, if the officer does not have that information, by reference to a date or dates).

    (4)   The appointment has effect in relation to the relevant period of account.

    (5)   The appointment may be made —

      (a)   at any time before the end of the period of 36 months beginning with the end of the relevant period of account, or

      (b)   at any time after the end of that period if, at that time, an amount stated in the company tax return of a UK group company for a relevant accounting period can be altered.

    (6)   Paragraph 88(3) to (5) of Schedule 18 to FA 1998 (meaning of "can no longer be altered") applies for the purposes of this paragraph.

    (7)   For the purposes of this paragraph a company is "eligible" if and only if the company —

      (a)   was a UK group company at a time during the relevant period of account, and

      (b)   was not dormant throughout that period.

Appointment by officer of Revenue and Customs of replacement reporting company

5   (1)   This paragraph applies where —

      (a)   an appointment of a reporting company under paragraph 1 or 4 or this paragraph has effect in relation to a period of account of a worldwide group ("the relevant period of account"), and

      (b)   condition A or B is met.

    (2)   Condition A is that an officer of Revenue and Customs considers that the reporting company mentioned in sub-paragraph (1)(a) has not complied with, or will not comply with, a requirement under or by virtue of this Schedule.

400

Finance (No. 2) Act 2017 (c. 32)
Schedule 5 — Corporate interest restriction
Part 2 — New Schedule 7A to TIOPA 2010

(3) Condition B is that the reporting company mentioned in sub-paragraph (1)(a) has agreed that an officer of Revenue of Customs may exercise the power in this paragraph.

(4) An officer of Revenue and Customs may, by notice —

    (a) revoke the appointment of the reporting company mentioned in sub-paragraph (1)(a), and

    (b) appoint in its place an eligible company to be the reporting company of the group.

(5) The notice must —

    (a) be given to each of the companies mentioned in sub-paragraph (4), and

    (b) specify the relevant period of account (whether by specifying the dates on which it begins and ends or, if the officer does not have that information, by reference to a date or dates).

(6) Where the power in sub-paragraph (4) is exercised —

    (a) the appointment that is revoked ceases to have effect in relation to —

        (i) the relevant period of account, and

        (ii) subsequent periods of account of the group;

    (b) the appointment of the replacement has effect in relation to the relevant period of account.

(7) For the purposes of this paragraph a company is "eligible" if and only if the company —

    (a) was a UK group company at a time during the relevant period of account, and

    (b) was not dormant throughout that period.

Obligation of reporting company to notify group members of its status

6   (1) This paragraph applies where the appointment of a reporting company has effect in relation to a period of account of a worldwide group ("the relevant period of account").

    (2) The reporting company must, as soon as reasonably practicable after the relevant time, notify each relevant company that it is the group's reporting company in relation to the relevant period of account.

    (3) In sub-paragraph (2) "the relevant time" means —

        (a) if the relevant period of account is the first period of account in relation to which the appointment has effect, the time of the appointment;

        (b) otherwise, the end of the period of 6 months beginning with the end of the relevant period of account.

    (4) Sub-paragraph (2) does not require the reporting company to notify a relevant company if the reporting company notified that company under that sub-paragraph in relation to an earlier period of account.

(5) The duty to comply with sub-paragraph (2) is enforceable by the company required to be notified under that sub-paragraph.

(6) For the purposes of this paragraph a company is "relevant" if and only if the company meets condition A or B.

(7) Condition A is that the company —
    (a) was a UK group company at a time during the relevant period of account, and
    (b) was not dormant throughout that period.

(8) Condition B is that the company is the ultimate parent of the worldwide group.

Obligation of reporting company to submit interest restriction return

7   (1) This paragraph applies where the appointment of a reporting company has effect in relation to a period of account of a worldwide group.

(2) If the reporting company was appointed under paragraph 1 or 4, it must submit a return for the period of account to an officer of Revenue and Customs.

(3) If the reporting company was appointed under paragraph 5, it must submit a return for the period of account to an officer of Revenue and Customs unless a return for the period has already been submitted under sub-paragraph (2) or this sub-paragraph.

(4) A return submitted under this paragraph must be received by an officer of Revenue and Customs before the filing date in relation to the period of account.

(5) In this Part of this Act "the filing date", in relation to a period of account of a worldwide group, means —
    (a) the end of the period of 12 months beginning with the end of the period of account, or
    (b) if later, the end of the period of 3 months beginning with the day on which the appointment of a reporting company that has effect in relation to the period was made.

(6) A return submitted under this paragraph is of no effect unless it is received by an officer of Revenue and Customs before —
    (a) the end of the period of 36 months beginning with the end of the period of account, or
    (b) if later, the end of the period of 3 months beginning with the day on which the reporting company was appointed.
This is subject to paragraph 57.

Revised interest restriction return

8   (1) This paragraph applies where —
    (a) the appointment of a reporting company has effect in relation to a period of account of a worldwide group, and

402   *Finance (No. 2) Act 2017 (c. 32)*
Schedule 5 — Corporate interest restriction
Part 2 — New Schedule 7A to TIOPA 2010

    (b)   a return ("the previous interest restriction return") was submitted under paragraph 7, or this paragraph, for the period of account.

(2)   The reporting company may submit a revised interest restriction return for the period of account to an officer of Revenue and Customs.

(3)   A revised interest restriction return submitted under sub-paragraph (2) is of no effect unless it is received by an officer of Revenue and Customs before—

    (a)   the end of the period of 36 months beginning with the end of the period of account, or

    (b)   if later, the end of the period of 3 months beginning with the day on which the reporting company was appointed.

This is subject to paragraphs 9 and 57.

(4)   Where—

    (a)   a member of the group amends, or is treated as amending, its company tax return, and

    (b)   as a result of the amendment any of the figures contained in the previous interest restriction return have become incorrect,

the reporting company must submit a revised interest restriction return to an officer of Revenue and Customs.

(5)   A revised interest restriction return submitted under sub-paragraph (4) must be received by an officer of Revenue and Customs before the end of the period of 3 months beginning with—

    (a)   the day on which the amended company tax return was received by an officer of Revenue and Customs, or

    (b)   (as the case may be) the day as from which the company tax return was treated as amended.

(6)   A return submitted under this paragraph—

    (a)   must indicate the respects in which it differs from the previous return, and

    (b)   supersedes the previous return.

Extended period for submission of full return in place of abbreviated return

9   (1)   This paragraph applies where—

    (a)   a reporting company has submitted an abbreviated interest restriction return for a period of account of a worldwide group in accordance with this Schedule, and

    (b)   the worldwide group is not subject to interest restrictions in the return period.

(2)   Despite the passing of the time limit in paragraph 8(3), a full interest restriction return for the period of account submitted under paragraph 8 has effect if it is received before the end of the period of 60 months beginning with the end of the period of account.

Finance (No. 2) Act 2017 (c. 32)
Schedule 5 — Corporate interest restriction
Part 2 — New Schedule 7A to TIOPA 2010

403

Meaning of "consenting company" and "non-consenting company"

10 (1) This paragraph makes provision for the purposes of this Part of this Act about whether a company is a "consenting company" in relation to an interest restriction return submitted by a reporting company.

(2) The company is a "consenting company" in relation to the return if, before the return is submitted —

    (a) it has notified the appropriate persons that it wishes to be a consenting company in relation to interest restriction returns submitted by the reporting company, and

    (b) it has not notified the appropriate persons that it no longer wishes to be a consenting company in relation to such returns.

(3) In sub-paragraph (2) "the appropriate persons" means —

    (a) an officer of Revenue and Customs, and

    (b) the reporting company in relation to the period of account.

(4) The company is a "non-consenting company", in relation to the return, if it is not a consenting company in relation to the return.

Company authorising reporting company appointment treated as consenting company

11 (1) This paragraph applies where a company —

    (a) is listed in a statement under sub-paragraph (4)(c) of paragraph 1 (list of companies authorising appointment of reporting company), and

    (b) is not included in a statement under sub-paragraph (6) of that paragraph (companies authorising appointment of reporting company but not wishing to be consenting companies).

(2) The company is treated as having given, at the time of the appointment, a notice under paragraph 10(2)(a) in relation to interest restriction returns submitted by the reporting company.

(3) Sub-paragraph (2) does not prevent the company, at any time after the appointment, from giving a notice under paragraph 10(2)(b) in relation to interest restriction returns submitted by the reporting company.

PART 2

CONTENTS OF INTEREST RESTRICTION RETURN

Elections

12 (1) An election to which this paragraph applies must be made in an interest restriction return for the period of account (or, as the case may be, the first period of account) to which the election relates.

(2) If an election to which this paragraph applies is capable of being revoked, the revocation must be made in an interest restriction

return for the period of account (or, as the case may be, the first period of account) to which the revocation relates.

    (3) This paragraph applies to the following elections —

       (a)   a group ratio election (see paragraph 13);

       (b)   a group ratio (blended) election (see paragraph 14);

       (c)   a group-EBITDA (chargeable gains) election (see paragraph 15);

       (d)   an interest allowance (alternative calculation) election (see paragraph 16);

       (e)   an interest allowance (non-consolidated investment) election (see paragraph 17);

       (f)   an interest allowance (consolidated partnerships) election (see paragraph 18);

       (g)   an abbreviated return election (see paragraph 19).

Group ratio election

13   (1) This paragraph applies where the appointment of a reporting company has effect in relation to a period of account of a worldwide group.

    (2) The reporting company may —

       (a)   elect that the interest allowance of the group is to be calculated using the group ratio method, or

       (b)   revoke an election previously made.

    (3) An election or revocation under this paragraph has effect in relation to the period of account.

    (4) An election under this paragraph is referred to in this Part of this Act as a "group ratio election".

    (5) For provision as to the effect of a group ratio election, see section 396.

Group ratio (blended) election

14   (1) This paragraph applies where —

       (a)   the appointment of a reporting company has effect in relation to a period of account of a worldwide group,

       (b)   the reporting company makes a group ratio election in respect of the period of account, and

       (c)   a related party investor in relation to the period of account is, throughout the period of account, a member of a worldwide group (an "investor worldwide group") other than that mentioned in paragraph (a).

    (2) The reporting company may —

       (a)   elect that Chapter 5 of Part 10 (interest allowance) is to apply subject to the blended group ratio provisions, or

       (b)   revoke an election previously made.

    (3) An election under this paragraph may —

       (a)   specify one or more investor worldwide groups,

Finance (No. 2) Act 2017 (c. 32)
Schedule 5 — Corporate interest restriction
Part 2 — New Schedule 7A to TIOPA 2010

405

    (b)   specify, in relation to any such group, one or more elections under this Schedule that are capable of being made in relation to a period of account by a reporting company of a worldwide group, and

    (c)   specify that the election is to be treated, for the purposes of the blended group ratio provisions, as having effect, or as not having effect, in relation to periods of account of the investor's worldwide group.

(4) Sub-paragraph (5) applies where—

    (a)   an election under this paragraph is made in relation to a period of account,

    (b)   an election under this paragraph was made in relation to any earlier period of account of the group,

    (c)   the election mentioned in paragraph (b) specified, under sub-paragraph (3)(c), that an election ("the investor's election") was to be treated as having effect in relation to periods of account of the investor's worldwide group, and

    (d)   the investor's election was an election which, if made by a reporting company of a worldwide group, would have been irrevocable.

(5) The election mentioned in sub-paragraph (4)(a) must specify, under sub-paragraph (3)(c), that the investor's election is to be treated as having effect in relation to periods of account of the investor's worldwide group.

(6) An election or revocation under this paragraph has effect in relation to the period of account.

(7) An election under this paragraph is referred to in this Part of this Act as a "group ratio (blended) election".

(8) In this paragraph "the blended group ratio provisions" means the provisions of sections 401 to 403.

Group-EBITDA (chargeable gains) election

15 (1) This paragraph applies where the appointment of a reporting company has effect in relation to a period of account of a worldwide group.

(2) The reporting company may elect that Chapter 7 of Part 10 (group-interest and group-EBITDA) is to apply subject to the chargeable gains provisions.

(3) An election under this paragraph—

    (a)   has effect in relation to the period of account and subsequent periods of account of the worldwide group, and

    (b)   is irrevocable.

(4) An election under this paragraph is referred to in this Part of this Act as a "group-EBITDA (chargeable gains) election".

(5) In this paragraph "the chargeable gains provisions" means the provisions of section 422.

406

Finance (No. 2) Act 2017 (c. 32)
Schedule 5 — Corporate interest restriction
Part 2 — New Schedule 7A to TIOPA 2010

Interest allowance (alternative calculation) election

16   (1) This paragraph applies where the appointment of a reporting company has effect in relation to a period of account of a worldwide group.

(2) The reporting company may elect that Chapter 7 of Part 10 (group-interest and group-EBITDA) is to apply subject to the alternative calculation provisions.

(3) An election under this paragraph—
   (a)   has effect in relation to the period of account and subsequent periods of account of the worldwide group, and
   (b)   is irrevocable.

(4) An election under this paragraph is referred to in this Part of this Act as an "interest allowance (alternative calculation) election".

(5) In this paragraph "the alternative calculation provisions" means sections 423 to 426.

Interest allowance (non-consolidated investment) election

17   (1) This paragraph applies where the appointment of a reporting company has effect in relation to a period of account of a worldwide group.

(2) The reporting company may—
   (a)   elect that Chapter 7 of Part 10 (group-interest and group-EBITDA) is to apply subject to the non-consolidated investment provisions, or
   (b)   revoke an election previously made.

(3) An election under this paragraph must specify, for the purposes of the non-consolidated investment provisions, one or more non-consolidated associates of the worldwide group.

(4) An election or revocation under this paragraph has effect in relation to the period of account.

(5) An election under this paragraph is referred to in this Part of this Act as an "interest allowance (non-consolidated investment) election".

(6) In this paragraph "the non-consolidated investment provisions" means sections 427 and 428.

Interest allowance (consolidated partnerships) election

18   (1) This paragraph applies where the appointment of a reporting company has effect in relation to a period of account of a worldwide group.

(2) The reporting company may elect that Chapter 7 of Part 10 (group-interest and group-EBITDA) is to apply subject to the consolidated partnership provisions.

Finance (No. 2) Act 2017 (c. 32)
Schedule 5 — Corporate interest restriction
Part 2 — New Schedule 7A to TIOPA 2010

407

(3) An election under this paragraph must specify, for the purposes of the consolidated partnership provisions, one or more consolidated partnerships of the worldwide group.

(4) Where an election under this paragraph has been made in relation to a worldwide group, a further election may be made specifying, for the purposes of the consolidated partnership provisions, one or more additional consolidated partnerships of the worldwide group.

(5) An election under this paragraph —
    (a) has effect in relation to the period of account and subsequent periods of account of the worldwide group, and
    (b) is irrevocable.

(6) An election under this paragraph is referred to in this Part of this Act as an "interest allowance (consolidated partnerships) election".

(7) In this paragraph "the consolidated partnership provisions" means the provisions of section 430.

Abbreviated return election

19 (1) This paragraph applies where the appointment of a reporting company has effect in relation to a period of account of a worldwide group.

(2) The reporting company may —
    (a) elect to submit an abbreviated interest restriction return, or
    (b) revoke an election previously made.

(3) An election or revocation under this paragraph has effect in relation to the period of account.

(4) An election under this paragraph is referred to in this Part of this Act as an "abbreviated return election".

(5) For provision as to the effect of an abbreviated return election, see —

    paragraph 20 of this Schedule (which limits the required contents of the interest restriction return);
    section 393 (which deprives the group of the use of the interest allowance for the return period, or any earlier period, in future periods of account).

Required contents of interest restriction return: full returns and abbreviated returns

20 (1) This paragraph makes provision about the contents of an interest restriction return submitted by the reporting company of a worldwide group.

(2) Sub-paragraph (3) applies if —
    (a) the worldwide group is subject to interest restrictions in the return period, or

408   *Finance (No. 2) Act 2017 (c. 32)*
Schedule 5 — Corporate interest restriction
Part 2 — New Schedule 7A to TIOPA 2010

     (b)   the worldwide group is not subject to interest restrictions in the return period, and no abbreviated return election has effect in relation to the period.

(3) The interest restriction return must—

     (a)   state the name and (where it has one) the Unique Taxpayer Reference of the ultimate parent of the worldwide group;

     (b)   specify the return period;

     (c)   state the names and Unique Taxpayer References (where they have them) of the companies that were UK group companies at any time during the return period, specifying in relation to each whether it is a consenting or a non-consenting company in relation to the return;

     (d)   contain a statement of calculations (see paragraph 21);

     (e)   if the group is subject to interest restrictions in the return period—

          (i)   contain a statement of that fact,

          (ii)   specify the total disallowed amount, and

          (iii)   contain a statement of allocated interest restrictions (see paragraph 22);

     (f)   if the group is subject to interest reactivations in the return period—

          (i)   contain a statement of that fact,

          (ii)   specify the interest reactivation cap,

          (iii)   contain a statement of allocated interest reactivations (see paragraph 25);

     (g)   contain a declaration by the person making the return that the return is, to the best of that person's knowledge, correct and complete.

(4) Sub-paragraph (5) applies if—

     (a)   the worldwide group is not subject to interest restrictions in the return period, and

     (b)   an abbreviated return election has effect in relation to the period.

(5) The interest restriction return must—

     (a)   state that the group is not subject to interest restrictions in the return period, and

     (b)   comply with paragraphs (a) to (c) and (g) of sub-paragraph (3).

(6) If the ultimate parent of the worldwide group is a deemed parent by virtue of section 477 (stapled entities) or 478 (business combinations), the requirement in sub-paragraph (3)(a) is to state the name and (where it has one) Unique Taxpayer Reference of each of the entities mentioned in that paragraph.

(7) In this Part of this Act—

     (a)   a return prepared in accordance with sub-paragraph (3) is referred to as "a full interest restriction return";

     (b)   a return prepared in accordance with sub-paragraph (5) is referred to as "an abbreviated interest restriction return".

Finance (No. 2) Act 2017 (c. 32)
Schedule 5 — Corporate interest restriction
Part 2 — New Schedule 7A to TIOPA 2010

409

Statement of calculations

21 The statement of calculations required by paragraph 20(3)(d) to be included in a full interest restriction return must include the following information—

 (a) for each company that was a UK group company at any time during the return period—

  (i) the company's net tax-interest expense, or net tax-interest income, for the return period (see section 389);

  (ii) the company's tax-EBITDA for the return period (see section 406);

 (b) the aggregate net tax-interest expense, and aggregate net tax-interest income, of the group for the return period (see section 390);

 (c) the interest capacity of the group for the return period (see section 392);

 (d) the aggregate of interest allowances of the group for periods before the return period so far as they are available in the return period (see section 393);

 (e) the interest allowance of the group for the return period (see section 396);

 (f) the aggregate tax-EBITDA of the group for the return period (see section 405);

 (g) where the interest allowance is calculated using the fixed ratio method and that allowance is given by section 397(1)(b), the adjusted net group-interest expense of the group for the return period (see section 413);

 (h) where the interest allowance is calculated using the group ratio method—

  (i) the group ratio percentage (see section 399 or 401);

  (ii) the qualifying net group-interest expense of the group for the return period (see section 414);

  (iii) the group-EBITDA of the group for the return period (see section 416).

Statement of allocated interest restrictions

22 (1) The statement of allocated interest restrictions required by paragraph 20(3)(e) to be included in a full interest restriction return must—

 (a) list one or more companies that—

  (i) were UK group companies at any time during the return period, and

  (ii) had net tax-interest expense for the period,

 (b) in relation to each company listed under paragraph (a), specify an amount, and

 (c) show the total of the amounts specified under paragraph (b).

410   *Finance (No. 2) Act 2017 (c. 32)*
Schedule 5 — Corporate interest restriction
Part 2 — New Schedule 7A to TIOPA 2010

(2) The amount specified under sub-paragraph (1)(b) in relation to a company is referred to in this Part of this Act as the "allocated disallowance" of the company for the return period.

(3) The allocated disallowance of a company for the return period—

    (a) must not exceed the net tax-interest expense of the company for the return period,

    (b) where the company is a non-consenting company in relation to the return, must not exceed the company's pro-rata share of the total disallowed amount (see paragraph 23), and

    (c) must not be a negative amount.

(4) The sum of the allocated disallowances for the return period of the companies listed in the statement must equal the total disallowed amount.

(5) The statement must also specify an amount in relation to each relevant accounting period of each company listed in the statement.

(6) The amount specified under sub-paragraph (5) in relation to an accounting period of a company is referred to in this Part of this Act as the "allocated disallowance" of the company for the accounting period.

(7) In the case of a company that has only one relevant accounting period, the allocated disallowance of the company for that accounting period must be equal to the allocated disallowance of the company for the return period.

(8) In the case of a company that has more than one relevant accounting period, the allocated disallowance of the company for any of those accounting periods—

    (a) must not exceed so much of the net tax-interest expense of the company for the return period as is referable to the accounting period,

    (b) where the company is a non-consenting company in relation to the return, must not exceed the accounting period's pro-rata share of the total disallowed amount (see paragraph 24), and

    (c) must not be a negative amount.

(9) The sum of the allocated disallowances of the company for its relevant accounting periods must be equal to the allocated disallowance of the company for the return period.

A company's pro-rata share of the total disallowed amount

23   (1) This paragraph—

    (a) applies in relation to a worldwide group that is subject to interest restrictions in a period of account of the group, and

    (b) allocates the total disallowed amount of the group in the period to companies that are UK group companies at any time during the period.

(2) The amount allocated to a company under this paragraph is referred to in this Part of this Act as the company's "pro-rata share" of the total disallowed amount.

(3) Sub-paragraph (4) applies in relation to a company that has net tax-interest expense for the period of account.

(4) The amount of the total disallowed amount that is allocated to the company is—

$$A \times \frac{B}{C}$$

where—
   A is the total disallowed amount;
   B is the net tax-interest expense of the company for the period of account;
   C is the sum of the net tax-interest expense for the period of account of each company that has net tax-interest expense for the period.

(5) Where this paragraph does not allocate any of the total disallowed amount to a company, the company's "pro-rata share" of the total disallowed amount is nil.

Accounting period's pro-rata share of the total disallowed amount

24 (1) This paragraph—
   (a) applies in relation to a worldwide group that is subject to interest restrictions in a period of account of the group ("the relevant period of account"), and
   (b) allocates the total disallowed amount of the group in the period of account to relevant accounting periods of companies that are UK group companies at any time during that period.

(2) The amount allocated to an accounting period under this paragraph is referred to in this Part of this Act as the accounting period's "pro-rata share" of the total disallowed amount.

(3) Sub-paragraph (4) applies where—
   (a) a company's pro-rata share of the total disallowed amount is not nil, and
   (b) the company has only one relevant accounting period.

(4) The amount of the total disallowed amount that is allocated to the accounting period is the company's pro-rata share of the total disallowed amount.

(5) Sub-paragraph (6) applies where—
   (a) a company's pro-rata share of the total disallowed amount is not nil, and
   (b) the company has more than one relevant accounting period.

412   *Finance (No. 2) Act 2017 (c. 32)*
Schedule 5 — Corporate interest restriction
Part 2 — New Schedule 7A to TIOPA 2010

(6) The amount of the total disallowed amount that is allocated to a relevant accounting period of the company is—

$$A \times \frac{B}{C}$$

where—

  A is the company's pro-rata share of the total disallowed amount;

  B is the net tax-interest expense of the company for the accounting period;

  C is the sum of the net tax-interest expenses of the company for each relevant accounting period.

(7) Where this paragraph does not allocate any of the total disallowed amount to an accounting period of a company, the accounting period's "pro-rata share" of the total disallowed amount is nil.

(8) For the purposes of this paragraph, the "net tax-interest expense" of a company for a relevant accounting period is—

 (a) so much of the net tax-interest expense of the company for the relevant period of account as is referable to the accounting period, or

 (b) if the amount determined under paragraph (a) is negative, nil.

Statement of allocated interest reactivations

25 (1) The statement of allocated interest reactivations required by paragraph 20(3)(f) to be included in a full interest restriction return must—

 (a) list one or more companies that are UK group companies at any time during the return period,

 (b) in relation to each company listed under paragraph (a), specify an amount, and

 (c) show the total of the amounts specified under paragraph (b).

(2) The amount specified under sub-paragraph (1)(b) in relation to a company is referred to in this Part of this Act as the "allocated reactivation" of the company for the return period.

(3) The allocated reactivation of a company for the return period—

 (a) must not exceed the amount available for reactivation of the company in the return period (see paragraph 26), and

 (b) must not be a negative amount.

(4) The sum of the allocated reactivations for the return period of the companies listed in the statement must equal—

 (a) the sum of the amounts available for reactivation of each company in the return period, or

 (b) if lower, the interest reactivation cap of the worldwide group in the return period.

"Amount available for reactivation" of company in period of account of group

26   (1)   This paragraph applies for the purposes of this Part of this Act.

       (2)   The "amount available for reactivation" of a company in a period of account of a worldwide group ("the relevant worldwide group") is—

          (a)   the amount determined under sub-paragraph (3), or

          (b)   if lower, the company's interest reactivation cap (see sub-paragraph (5)).

       (3)   The amount referred to in sub-paragraph (2)(a) is—

$$A + B - C + D - E$$

where—

A is the total of the disallowed tax-interest expense amounts (if any) that are brought forward to the specified accounting period from earlier accounting periods;

B is the total of the tax-interest expense amounts (if any) that the company is required to leave out of account in the specified accounting period as a result of the operation of this Part of this Act in relation to a period of account of the worldwide group before the period of account;

C is the total of the disallowed tax-interest expense amounts (if any) that the company is required to bring into account in the specified accounting period as a result of the operation of this Part of this Act in relation to a period of account of the worldwide group before the period of account;

D is the total of the tax-interest expense amounts (if any) that the company is required to leave out of account in the specified accounting period as a result of the operation of this Part of this Act in relation to a period of account of a worldwide group of which the company was a member before it became a member of the relevant worldwide group;

E is the total of the disallowed tax-interest expense amounts (if any) that the company is required to bring into account in the specified accounting period as a result of the operation of this Part of this Act in relation to a period of account of a worldwide group of which the company was a member before it became a member of the relevant worldwide group.

       (4)   In sub-paragraph (3) "the specified accounting period" means—

          (a)   the earliest relevant accounting period of the company, or

          (b)   where the company became a member of the relevant worldwide group during the period of account, the earliest relevant accounting period of the company in which it was a member of the group.

414

Finance (No. 2) Act 2017 (c. 32)
Schedule 5 — Corporate interest restriction
Part 2 — New Schedule 7A to TIOPA 2010

(5) For the purposes of sub-paragraph (2)(b) "the interest reactivation cap" of the company is—

$$A \times B$$

where—

A is the interest reactivation cap of the worldwide group in the period of account;

B is the proportion of the period of account in which the company is a UK group company.

Estimated information in statements

27 (1) This paragraph applies in relation to a statement under—
   (a) paragraph 21 (statement of calculations),
   (b) paragraph 22 (statement of allocated interest restrictions), or
   (c) paragraph 25 (statement of allocated interest reactivations).

(2) Where any information is included in the statement that is (or is derived from) estimated information, the statement—
   (a) must state that fact, and
   (b) must identify the information in question.

(3) Where—
   (a) estimated information (or information deriving from estimated information) is included in an interest restriction return for a period of account in reliance on this paragraph, and
   (b) a period of 36 months beginning with the end of that period of account has passed without the information becoming final,
   the reporting company must give a notice to an officer of Revenue and Customs within the period of 30 days beginning with the end of that 36-month period.

(4) The notice—
   (a) must identify the information in question that is not final, and
   (b) must indicate when the reporting company expects the information to become final.

(5) If a company fails to comply with the duty under sub-paragraph (3), it is liable to a penalty of £500.

(6) An officer of Revenue and Customs may, in a particular case, treat a revised interest restriction submitted after the end of the applicable period under paragraph 8(3)(a) or (b) as having effect if—
   (a) the revisions to the return are limited to those necessary to take account of information that has become final,
   (b) the officer considers that it was not possible to make those revisions before the end of that period, and

Finance (No. 2) Act 2017 (c. 32)
Schedule 5 — Corporate interest restriction
Part 2 — New Schedule 7A to TIOPA 2010

415

(c) the reporting company has complied with the duty under sub-paragraph (3).

Correction of return by officer of Revenue and Customs

28 (1) An officer of Revenue and Customs may amend an interest restriction return submitted by a company so as to correct—

(a) obvious errors or omissions in the return (whether errors of principle, arithmetical mistakes or otherwise), and

(b) anything else in the return that the officer has reason to believe is incorrect in the light of information available to the officer.

(2) A correction under this paragraph is made by notice to the company.

(3) A correction under this paragraph must not be made more than 9 months after the day on which the return was submitted.

(4) A correction under this paragraph is of no effect if the company—

(a) revises the return so as to reject the correction, or

(b) after the end of the period mentioned in paragraph 8(3)(a) or (b) but within 3 months from the date of the issue of the notice of correction, gives notice rejecting the correction.

(5) Notice under sub-paragraph (4)(b) must be given to the officer of Revenue and Customs by whom notice of the correction was given.

Penalty for failure to deliver return

29 (1) A company is liable to a penalty if the company—

(a) is required to submit an interest restriction return under paragraph 7 for a period of account of a worldwide group, and

(b) fails to do so by the filing date in relation to the period (see sub-paragraph (5) of that paragraph).

(2) The penalty is—

(a) £500 if the return is delivered within 3 months after the filing date, and

(b) £1,000 in any other case.

(3) If a company becomes liable to a penalty under this paragraph, an officer of Revenue and Customs must—

(a) assess the penalty, and

(b) notify the company.

(4) The assessment must be made within the period of 12 months beginning with the filing date mentioned in sub-paragraph (1)(b).

(5) A company may, by notice, appeal against a decision of an officer of Revenue and Customs that a penalty is payable under this paragraph.

(6) Notice of appeal under this paragraph must be given—

416

Finance (No. 2) Act 2017 (c. 32)
Schedule 5 — Corporate interest restriction
Part 2 — New Schedule 7A to TIOPA 2010

> (a) within 30 days after the penalty was notified to the company,
>
> (b) to the officer of Revenue and Customs who notified the company.

(7) A penalty under this paragraph must be paid before the end of the period of 30 days beginning with—

> (a) the day on which the company was notified of the penalty, or
>
> (b) if notice of appeal against the penalty is given, the day on which the appeal is finally determined or withdrawn.

Penalty for incorrect or uncorrected return

30 (1) A company is liable to a penalty if—

> (a) the company (or a person acting on its behalf) submits an interest restriction return to an officer of Revenue and Customs for a period of account of a worldwide group,
>
> (b) there is an inaccuracy in the return which meets condition A or B, and
>
> (c) the inaccuracy is due to a failure by the company (or a person acting on its behalf) to take reasonable care (a "careless inaccuracy") or the company makes the inaccuracy deliberately (a "deliberate inaccuracy").

(2) An inaccuracy meets condition A if it consists of understating the total disallowed amount in the period of account of the group (including a case where no amount is specified in the return).

(3) An inaccuracy meets condition B if it consists of overstating the interest reactivation cap in the period of account of the group.

(4) A penalty payable under this paragraph is equal to the appropriate part of the notional tax.

(5) For the purposes of this Part of this Schedule—

> "the appropriate part" means—
>
> > (a) in the case of a careless inaccuracy, 30%,
> >
> > (b) in the case of a deliberate inaccuracy that is not concealed, 70%, and
> >
> > (c) in the case of a deliberate inaccuracy that is concealed, 100%, and
>
> "the notional tax" means the result produced by applying the average rate of the main corporation tax rate applicable in each of the days of the period of account to the total of the amount of the understatement referred to in condition A and the amount of the overstatement referred to in condition B.

(6) A company is not liable to a penalty under this paragraph in respect of anything done or omitted to be done by the company's agent if the company took reasonable care to avoid the inaccuracy.

Finance (No. 2) Act 2017 (c. 32)
Schedule 5 — Corporate interest restriction
Part 2 — New Schedule 7A to TIOPA 2010

417

Meaning of "deliberate inaccuracy that is concealed" and discovering inaccuracy after return submitted

31 (1) For the purposes of this Part of this Schedule a deliberate inaccuracy made by a company is concealed if the company makes arrangements to conceal it (for example, by submitting false evidence in support of an inaccurate figure).

(2) An inaccuracy in an interest restriction return which was not a careless or deliberate inaccuracy made by a company (or a person acting on its behalf) when the return was submitted is taken to be a careless inaccuracy made by the company for the purposes of this Part of this Schedule if the company (or a person acting on its behalf) —

    (a) discovers the inaccuracy at some later time, and

    (b) does not take reasonable steps to inform an officer of Revenue and Customs.

Inaccuracy in return attributable to another company

32 (1) A company ("C") is liable to a penalty if —

    (a) another company submits an interest restriction return for a period of account of a worldwide group,

    (b) there is an inaccuracy in the return which meets condition A or B in paragraph 30, and

    (c) the inaccuracy was attributable to C deliberately supplying false information to the other company, or to C deliberately withholding information from the other company, with the intention of the return containing the inaccuracy.

(2) A penalty is payable under this paragraph in respect of an inaccuracy whether or not the other company is liable to a penalty under paragraph 30 in respect of the same inaccuracy.

(3) A penalty payable under this paragraph is equal to the notional tax.

Reductions in amount of penalty for disclosure or special circumstances

33 (1) If a company liable to a penalty under paragraph 30 or 32 in respect of an inaccuracy discloses the inaccuracy —

    (a) the penalty must be reduced to one that reflects the quality of the disclosure (including its timing, nature and extent), but

    (b) the penalty may not be reduced below the applicable minimum.

(2) In the case of a penalty under paragraph 30, the applicable minimum is —

    (a) in the case of a careless inaccuracy, 0% of the notional tax if the disclosure is unprompted and 15% otherwise,

    (b) in the case of a deliberate inaccuracy that is not concealed, 30% of the notional tax if the disclosure is unprompted and 45% otherwise, and

418   *Finance (No. 2) Act 2017 (c. 32)*
Schedule 5 — Corporate interest restriction
Part 2 — New Schedule 7A to TIOPA 2010

    (c)   in the case of a deliberate inaccuracy that is concealed, 40% of the notional tax if the disclosure is unprompted and 60% otherwise.

(3) In the case of a penalty under paragraph 32, the applicable minimum is 40% of the notional tax if the disclosure is unprompted and 60% otherwise.

(4) For the purposes of this paragraph—

    (a)   a person makes a disclosure of an inaccuracy by telling an officer of Revenue and Customs about it, giving an officer of Revenue and Customs reasonable help in quantifying it and allowing an officer of Revenue and Customs access to records to ensure that it is fully corrected, and

    (b)   a person makes an "unprompted" disclosure at any time if the person has no reason at that time to believe that an officer of Revenue and Customs have discovered, or are about to discover, the inaccuracy.

(5) If they think it right because of special circumstances, an officer of Revenue and Customs may—

    (a)   reduce a penalty under paragraph 30 or 32, or

    (b)   stay the penalty or agree a compromise in relation to proceedings for the penalty.

(6) The reference to special circumstances does not include an ability to pay but, subject to that, is taken to include, or exclude, such other circumstances as are prescribed by regulations made by the Commissioners.

(7) The power to prescribe circumstances includes power to prescribe circumstances by reference to the notional tax and the extent to which the notional tax exceeds, or is likely to exceed, any actual loss of tax to the Crown.

Assessment, payment and enforcement of penalty

34   (1) If a person becomes liable to a penalty under paragraph 30 or 32, an officer of Revenue and Customs must—

    (a)   assess the penalty, and

    (b)   notify the person.

(2) The assessment must be made within the period of 12 months beginning with the day on which the inaccuracy is corrected.

(3) The penalty must be paid before the end of the period of 30 days beginning with—

    (a)   the day on which the person was notified of the penalty, or

    (b)   if notice of appeal against the penalty is given, the day on which the appeal is finally determined or withdrawn.

(4) An assessment may be enforced—

    (a)   as if it were an assessment to corporation tax (which, among other things, secures the application of Chapters 6 and 7 of Part 22 of CTA 2010 (corporation tax payable by non-UK resident companies: recovery from others)), and

Finance (No. 2) Act 2017 (c. 32)
Schedule 5 — Corporate interest restriction
Part 2 — New Schedule 7A to TIOPA 2010

419

       (b)   as if that assessment were also an assessment to corporation tax of any company which was a UK group company of the group at any time in the period of account in relation to which the interest restriction return contained an inaccuracy.

Right to appeal against penalty or its amount

35   A person may, by notice, appeal against—

       (a)   a decision of an officer of Revenue and Customs that a penalty under paragraph 30 or 32 is payable, or

       (b)   a decision of an officer of Revenue and Customs as to the amount of a penalty under paragraph 30 or 32.

Procedure on appeal

36   (1)   Notice of an appeal under paragraph 35 must be given—

       (a)   within 30 days after the penalty was notified to the person,

       (b)   to an officer of Revenue and Customs.

    (2)   On an appeal notified to the tribunal against a decision that a penalty is payable, the tribunal may confirm or cancel the decision.

    (3)   On an appeal notified to the tribunal against the amount of a penalty, the tribunal may—

       (a)   confirm the decision, or

       (b)   substitute for the decision another decision that an officer of Revenue and Customs had power to make.

    (4)   If the tribunal substitutes its decision for a decision of an officer of Revenue and Customs, the tribunal may rely on paragraph 33(5)—

       (a)   to the same extent as an officer of Revenue and Customs (which may mean applying the same percentage reduction as the officer to a different starting point), or

       (b)   to a different extent, but only if the tribunal thinks that the decision in respect of the application of paragraph 33(5) was flawed.

    (5)   For this purpose "flawed" means flawed when considered in the light of the principles applicable in proceedings for judicial review.

    (6)   Subject to this Part of this Schedule, the provisions of Part 5 of TMA 1970 relating to appeals have effect in relation to appeals under this Part of this Schedule as they have effect in relation to appeals against an assessment to corporation tax.

Payments between companies in respect of penalties

37   (1)   This paragraph applies if—

       (a)   a company ("P") liable to a penalty under this Part of this Schedule has an agreement in relation to the penalty with one or more other companies within the charge to corporation tax, and

420   *Finance (No. 2) Act 2017 (c. 32)*
Schedule 5 — Corporate interest restriction
Part 2 — New Schedule 7A to TIOPA 2010

(b) as a result of the agreement, P receives a payment or payments in respect of the penalty that do not, in total, exceed the amount of the penalty.

(2) The payment—

 (a) is not to be taken into account in calculating the profits for corporation tax purposes of either P or the company making the payment, and

 (b) is not to be regarded as a distribution for corporation tax purposes.

PART 3

DUTY TO KEEP AND PRESERVE RECORDS

Duty to keep and preserve records

38 (1) A company which is a reporting company in relation to a period of account of a worldwide group must—

 (a) keep such records as may be needed to enable it to submit a correct and complete interest restriction return for the period, and

 (b) preserve those records in accordance with this paragraph.

(2) The records must be preserved until the end of the relevant day.

(3) In this paragraph "the relevant day" means—

 (a) the sixth anniversary of the end of the period of account, or

 (b) such earlier date as may be specified in writing by an officer of Revenue and Customs (and different days may be specified for different cases).

(4) If the company is required to submit an interest restriction return for the period before the end of the relevant day, the records must be preserved until any later date on which—

 (a) any enquiry into the return is complete, or

 (b) if there is no enquiry, an officer of Revenue and Customs no longer has the power to enquire into the return (but, for this purpose, paragraph 42 is to be ignored).

(5) If the company is required to submit an interest restriction return for the period after the end of the relevant day and has in its possession at that time any records that may be needed to enable it to submit a correct and complete return, it is under a duty to preserve those records until the date on which—

 (a) any enquiry into the return is complete, or

 (b) if there is no enquiry, an officer of Revenue and Customs no longer has the power to enquire into the return (but, for this purpose, paragraph 42 is to be ignored).

(6) The duty under this paragraph to preserve records may be discharged—

 (a) by preserving them in any form and by any means, or

 (b) by preserving the information contained in them in any form and by any means,

Finance (No. 2) Act 2017 (c. 32)
Schedule 5 – Corporate interest restriction
Part 2 – New Schedule 7A to TIOPA 2010

421

subject to any conditions or exceptions specified in writing by an officer of Revenue and Customs.

(7) The Commissioners may by regulations –

    (a) provide that the records required to be kept and preserved under this paragraph include, or do not include, records specified in the regulations, and

    (b) provide that those records include supporting documents so specified.

(8) The regulations may make provision by reference to things specified in a notice published by the Commissioners in accordance with the regulations (and not withdrawn by a subsequent notice).

Penalty for failure to keep and preserve records

39 (1) A company which fails to comply with paragraph 38 is liable to a penalty not exceeding £3,000.

(2) If a company becomes liable to a penalty under this paragraph, an officer of Revenue and Customs must –

    (a) assess the penalty, and

    (b) notify the company.

(3) The assessment must be made within the period of 12 months beginning with the day on which an officer of Revenue and Customs first becomes aware that the company has failed to comply with paragraph 38.

(4) A company may, by notice, appeal against a decision of an officer of Revenue and Customs that a penalty is payable under this paragraph.

(5) Notice of appeal under this paragraph must be given –

    (a) within 30 days after the penalty was notified to the company,

    (b) to the officer of Revenue and Customs who notified the company.

(6) A penalty under this paragraph must be paid before the end of the period of 30 days beginning with –

    (a) the day on which the company was notified of the penalty, or

    (b) if notice of appeal against the penalty is given, the day on which the appeal is finally determined or withdrawn.

PART 4

ENQUIRY INTO INTEREST RESTRICTION RETURN

Notice of enquiry

40 (1) An officer of Revenue and Customs may enquire into an interest restriction return submitted by a reporting company if the officer

422

Finance (No. 2) Act 2017 (c. 32)
Schedule 5 – Corporate interest restriction
Part 2 – New Schedule 7A to TIOPA 2010

gives notice to the company of the officer's intention to do so ("notice of enquiry").

(2) The general rule is that an interest restriction return which has been the subject of one notice of enquiry may not be the subject of another.

(3) If a return ("the previous return") is superseded by an interest restriction return submitted under paragraph 8 ("the revised return"), notice of enquiry may be given in relation to the revised return even though notice of enquiry has been given in relation to the previous return.

(4) But see paragraph 43(5) for a limitation in certain circumstances on the scope of an enquiry into an interest restriction return submitted under paragraph 8.

(5) The power to give notice of enquiry into an interest restriction return for a period of account of a worldwide group does not restrict the power to give notice of enquiry into a company tax return of a company that is a member of the group at any time in that period.

(6) Accordingly, an amendment of the company's company tax return may be required as a result of an enquiry into the interest restriction return even though a closure notice has been given in respect of an enquiry into that company tax return.

(7) But see paragraph 43(2) for a limitation on the scope of an enquiry into an interest restriction return so far as affecting amounts in a company tax return.

Normal time limits for opening enquiry

41 (1) This paragraph applies where an interest restriction return is submitted by a reporting company for a period of account.

(2) Notice of enquiry may be given at any time before whichever is the latest of—

   (a) the end of the period of 39 months beginning with the end of the period of account;

   (b) the end of the period of 6 months beginning with the day on which the reporting company was appointed; and

   (c) the end of 31 January, 30 April, 31 July or 31 October next following the first anniversary of the day on which an officer of Revenue and Customs receives the revised return.

(3) If—

   (a) estimated information (or information deriving from estimated information) is included in an interest restriction return for a period of account in reliance on paragraph 27, and

   (b) a period of 36 months beginning with the end of that period of account has passed without the information becoming final,

Finance (No. 2) Act 2017 (c. 32)
Schedule 5 — Corporate interest restriction
Part 2 — New Schedule 7A to TIOPA 2010

423

notice of enquiry may be given at any time up to and including the end of the period of 12 months beginning with the end of that 36-month period.

(4) This paragraph is subject to paragraph 42 (which allows notices of enquiry to be given after the time allowed by this paragraph or an enquiry previously closed to be re-opened).

Extended time limits for opening enquiries: discovery of errors

42 (1) Notice of enquiry may be given later than the time allowed under paragraph 41, or a closed enquiry may be re-opened, if—

   (a) an officer of Revenue and Customs discovers that an interest restriction return submitted to an officer of Revenue and Customs does not, or might not, comply with the requirements of paragraph 20(3) in any respect,

   (b) there would be, or might be, an increase in tax payable by any company for any accounting period if the return had complied with those requirements in that respect,

   (c) the discovery is made after the time allowed under paragraph 41 or after an enquiry into the return has been closed, and

   (d) the officer could not, at the relevant time and by reference to the relevant information, have been reasonably expected to be aware of the respects in which the return might not comply with those requirements.

(2) For this purpose "the relevant time" means—

   (a) in a case where no notice of enquiry has been given within the time allowed under paragraph 41, when an officer of Revenue and Customs ceased to be entitled to give a notice, or

   (b) in a case where an enquiry has been closed, when the officer gave the closure notice.

(3) For this purpose "the relevant information" means information which—

   (a) is contained in the interest restriction return in question or either of the two returns for the immediately preceding periods of account of the group,

   (b) is contained in any documents, financial statements or other accounts or information produced or provided to an officer of Revenue or Customs for the purposes of an enquiry into the interest restriction return in question or either of the two returns for the immediately preceding periods of account of the group,

   (c) is information the existence of which, and the relevance of which as regards the situation mentioned in sub-paragraph (1)(b), could reasonably be expected to be inferred by an officer of Revenue and Customs from information falling with paragraph (a) or (b) of this sub-paragraph, or

   (d) is information the existence of which, and the relevance of which as regards the situation mentioned in sub-

424

Finance (No. 2) Act 2017 (c. 32)
Schedule 5 — Corporate interest restriction
Part 2 — New Schedule 7A to TIOPA 2010

paragraph (1)(b), are notified in writing to an officer of Revenue and Customs by the reporting company for the period of account or a person acting on its behalf.

(4) Notice of enquiry into an interest restriction return for a period of account may not be given, or a closed enquiry may not be re-opened, as a result of this paragraph more than the applicable number of years after the end of the period of account.

(5) The "applicable number of years" is—

    (a) 20 years in a case involving deliberate non-compliance by the reporting company for the period of account or by a qualifying person,

    (b) 6 years in a case involving careless non-compliance by the reporting company for the period of account or by a qualifying person, and

    (c) 4 years in any other case.

(6) For this purpose "qualifying person" means—

    (a) a person acting on behalf of the reporting company for the period of account, or

    (b) a person who was a partner of the reporting company for the period of account at the relevant time.

(7) For the purposes of this paragraph an enquiry is "closed" when a closure notice is given in relation to the enquiry.

Scope of enquiry

43 (1) An enquiry into an interest restriction return extends to anything contained, or required to be contained, in the return (including any election included in the return).

(2) But the enquiry does not extend to an enquiry into an amount—

    (a) which is contained, or required to be contained, in a company tax return of a UK group company, and

    (b) which is taken into account in any calculation required for the purposes of the interest restriction return.

(3) Sub-paragraph (2) does not affect—

    (a) any question as to whether or not, as a result of this Part of this Act, the amount falls to be left out of account, or to be brought into account, in any accounting period of the company, or

    (b) the way in which, by reference to that amount and other matters, any provision of this Part of this Act has effect to determine whether or not the amount, or any other amount, is to be left out of, or brought into account, in any accounting period (whether of that company or another company).

(4) Nor does sub-paragraph (2) limit the operation of any provision of Part 4 of Schedule 18 to FA 1998 (determinations and assessments made by officers of Revenue and Customs).

(5) If—

Finance (No. 2) Act 2017 (c. 32)
Schedule 5 — Corporate interest restriction
Part 2 — New Schedule 7A to TIOPA 2010

425

    (a)   at any time an enquiry into an interest restriction return ("the previous return") has been closed, and

    (b)   the previous return is subsequently superseded by an interest restriction return submitted under paragraph 8 ("the revised return"),

the enquiry into the revised return extends only to matters arising as a result of information that was not included in the previous return.

(6)   For this purpose an enquiry is "closed" when a closure notice is given in relation to the enquiry.

Enquiry into return for wrong period or wrong group

44   (1)   If it appears to an officer of Revenue and Customs that the period of account for which an interest restriction return has been submitted is or may be the wrong period, the power to enquire into the return includes power to enquire into the period for which the return ought to have been made.

(2)   If sub-paragraph (1) applies, paragraph 41 (normal time limits for opening enquiry) has effect as if the return were one that had been submitted for the correct period of account.

(3)   If it appears to an officer of Revenue and Customs that the worldwide group ("the relevant group") in relation to which an interest restriction return has been submitted —

    (a)   consists of, or may consist of, two or more worldwide groups,

    (b)   includes, or may include, entities that are members of a different worldwide group or groups, or

    (c)   does not include, or may not include, entities that should be members of the relevant group,

the power to enquire into the return includes power to enquire into the returns for the periods of account of the worldwide groups which ought to have been made.

Amendment of self-assessment during enquiry to prevent loss of tax

45   (1)   If after notice of enquiry has been given into an interest restriction return but before the enquiry is completed, an officer of Revenue and Customs forms the opinion that —

    (a)   the amount stated in the self-assessment of a company as the amount of tax payable is insufficient,

    (b)   the deficiency is attributable to matters in relation to which the enquiry extends, and

    (c)   unless the assessment is immediately amended there is likely to be a loss of tax to the Crown,

the officer may by notice to the company amend its self-assessment to make good the deficiency.

(2)   In sub-paragraph (1) the reference to a company is to a company that was a member of the group at any time in the period of account for which the interest restriction return was submitted.

426

Finance (No. 2) Act 2017 (c. 32)
Schedule 5 — Corporate interest restriction
Part 2 — New Schedule 7A to TIOPA 2010

(3) An appeal may be brought, by notice, against an amendment of a company's self-assessment by an officer of Revenue and Customs under this paragraph.

(4) Notice of appeal must be given —

    (a) within 30 days after the amendment was notified to the company,

    (b) to the officer of Revenue and Customs by whom the notice of amendment was given.

(5) None of the steps mentioned in section 49A(2)(a) to (c) of TMA 1970 (reviews of the matter or notification of appeal to tribunal) may be taken in relation to the appeal before the completion of the enquiry.

(6) In this paragraph "self-assessment" has the meaning given by paragraph 7 of Schedule 18 to FA 1998.

Revision of interest restriction return during enquiry

46 (1) This paragraph applies if a reporting company submits a revised interest restriction return at a time when an enquiry is in progress into the previous return.

(2) The submission of the revised return does not restrict the scope of the enquiry but the revisions may be taken into account (together with any matter arising) in the enquiry.

(3) So far as the revised return affects the tax payable by a company, it does not take effect until the enquiry is completed (and, accordingly, paragraph 70 has effect subject to this sub-paragraph).

(4) But sub-paragraph (3) does not affect any claim by the company under section 59DA of TMA 1970 (claim for repayment in advance of liability being established).

(5) The submission of a revised return whose effect is deferred under sub-paragraph (3) takes effect as follows —

    (a) if the conclusions in the closure notice state either —

        (i) that the revisions were not taken into account in the enquiry, or

        (ii) that no revision of the revised return is required arising from the enquiry,

    the revision takes effect on the completion of the enquiry, and

    (b) in any other case, the revisions take effect as part of the steps required to be taken in order to give effect to the conclusions stated in the closure notice.

(6) For the purposes of this paragraph the period during which an enquiry into an interest restriction return is in progress is the whole of the period —

    (a) beginning with the day on which an officer of Revenue and Customs gives notice of enquiry into the return, and

    (b) ending with the day on which the enquiry is completed.

Completion of enquiry

47 (1) An enquiry into an interest restriction return submitted by a reporting company is completed when an officer of Revenue and Customs by notice (a "closure notice") —

    (a) informs the company that the officer has completed the enquiry, and

    (b) states the officer's conclusions.

(2) The closure notice takes effect when it is given.

(3) If an officer of Revenue and Customs concludes that the return should have been made for one or more different periods of account of the group, the closure notice must designate the period of account (or periods of account) for which the return should have been made.

(4) If an officer of Revenue and Customs concludes that an interest restriction return in relation to a worldwide group should have been submitted —

    (a) in relation to one or more different worldwide groups, or

    (b) in relation to a different membership,

the closure notice must designate each period of account of a worldwide group for which an interest restriction return should have been made or for which an interest restriction return should have been submitted in relation to a different membership.

(5) If the officer concludes that the group in relation to which the return was submitted has a different membership, the designation under sub-paragraph (4) must also include details of the members of the group that the officer considers are UK group companies.

(6) If the officer concludes that the return should have been submitted in relation to one or more different worldwide groups, the designation under sub-paragraph (4) must also include —

    (a) sufficient details to identify the different worldwide group or groups, and

    (b) details of the members of the group that the officer considers are UK group companies.

(7) A designation by a closure notice of a period of account under this paragraph must specify the dates on which the period of account begins and ends.

(8) In this paragraph references to UK group companies, in relation to a period of account, do not include UK group companies that are dormant throughout the period.

Direction to complete enquiry

48 (1) An application may be made at any time to the tribunal for a direction that an officer of Revenue and Customs gives a closure notice in respect of an enquiry into an interest restriction return within a specified period.

428

Finance (No. 2) Act 2017 (c. 32)
Schedule 5 — Corporate interest restriction
Part 2 — New Schedule 7A to TIOPA 2010

(2) The application is to be made by the reporting company for the period of account of the group for which the return was submitted.

(3) The application is subject to the relevant provisions of Part 5 of TMA 1970 (see, in particular, section 48(2)(b) of that Act).

(4) The tribunal must give a direction unless satisfied that an officer of Revenue and Customs has reasonable grounds for not giving a closure notice within a specified period.

Conclusions of enquiry

49 (1) This paragraph applies where a closure notice is given under paragraph 47 to a company by an officer.

(2) The closure notice must—
 (a) state that, in the officer's opinion, no steps are required to be taken by the company as a result of the enquiry, or
 (b) state the steps that the company is required to take in order to give effect to the conclusions stated in the notice.

(3) The closure notice may (but need not) specify the allocated disallowance for particular companies specified in the notice.

(4) If—
 (a) the return was made for the wrong period, and
 (b) a period of account designated under paragraph 47(3) begins or ends at any time in that period,
the closure notice must require the company to take steps to make the return one appropriate to that designated period of account.

(5) If there is more than one designated period of account within sub-paragraph (4), the closure notice must require the company to submit an interest restriction return for each of those designated periods of account.

(6) If—
 (a) a period of account of a worldwide group ("the relevant group") is designated under paragraph 47(4),
 (b) the company is a member of the relevant group for that period of account, and
 (c) condition A or B is met,
the closure notice must require the company to submit an interest restriction return for the designated period of account of the relevant group.

(7) Condition A is met if the UK group companies comprised in the relevant group were regarded as members of the worldwide group in relation to which the return was made.

(8) Condition B is met if—
 (a) the relevant group includes UK group companies that were not regarded as members of the group in relation to which the return was made, and

Finance (No. 2) Act 2017 (c. 32)
Schedule 5 — Corporate interest restriction
Part 2 — New Schedule 7A to TIOPA 2010

429

(b) the ultimate parent of the relevant group is not the ultimate parent of a worldwide group in relation to which a reporting company has been appointed for a period of account that includes a time falling within the designated period of account of the relevant group.

(9) If sub-paragraph (6) applies in relation to two or more designated periods of account of a worldwide group (whether those periods are of the same or different groups), the closure notice must require the company to submit separate interest restriction returns for each of the designated periods of account.

(10) If, as a result of this paragraph, a closure notice requires a company to submit an interest restriction return for a period of account of a worldwide group, the company is treated for the purposes of this Part of this Act as if it had been appointed as the reporting company of the group in relation to the period.

(11) For this purpose it does not matter whether the return that was subject to the enquiry was submitted in relation to a different worldwide group.

(12) Sub-paragraph (10) is ignored in determining the period within which the return must be submitted (as to which, see instead paragraph 50(2)).

Interest restriction returns to be submitted to an officer of Revenue and Customs

50 (1) If, as a result of a closure notice given under paragraph 47 (closure notice in respect of a return subject to enquiry), a company is required to submit one or more interest restriction returns, the return or returns must—

(a) be submitted to an officer of Revenue and Customs,

(b) give effect to the conclusions stated in the notice, and

(c) contain such consequential provision as the company considers appropriate.

(2) A return submitted in compliance with the closure notice is of no effect unless it is received by an officer of Revenue and Customs before the end of the period of 3 months beginning with the day on which the closure notice is given to the company.

(3) A return submitted in compliance with the closure notice—

(a) must indicate the respects in which it differs from the return that was the subject of the enquiry, and

(b) supersedes that return.

(4) For provision dealing with cases where no return is submitted before the end of the period mentioned in sub-paragraph (2), see paragraph 58.

Return in relation to a worldwide group: other entities part of another group

51 (1) This paragraph applies if—

430

Finance (No. 2) Act 2017 (c. 32)
Schedule 5 — Corporate interest restriction
Part 2 — New Schedule 7A to TIOPA 2010

    (a)   an enquiry has been made into an interest restriction return ("the original return") for a period of account of a worldwide group ("the original group"),

    (b)   a closure notice has been given in respect of the enquiry that designates a period of account of a worldwide group under paragraph 47(4) ("the new group"),

    (c)   the new group consists of both UK group companies that were not regarded as members of the original group and other UK group companies, and

    (d)   the ultimate parent of the new group is the ultimate parent of a worldwide group ("the existing group") in relation to which a reporting company has been appointed for a period of account that includes a time falling within the designated period of account of the new group.

(2) An officer of Revenue and Customs must give a notice to that company appointing it as the reporting company in relation to each designated period of account of the new group.

(3) The notice of appointment must be given within the period of 30 days beginning with the day on which the closure notice was given.

(4) If—

    (a)   an interest restriction return has been submitted for a period of account of the existing group, and

    (b)   that period of account begins or ends at any time in a designated period of account of the new group,

the return is to be treated as withdrawn.

(5) Accordingly—

    (a)   any notice of enquiry or closure notice in relation to the return is also to be treated as withdrawn,

    (b)   any appeal in respect of any matter stated in a closure notice in relation to the return is treated as withdrawn, and

    (c)   any determination of any such appeal is treated as being of no effect.

(6) If—

    (a)   an interest restriction return for a period of account is treated as withdrawn as a result of sub-paragraph (4), and

    (b)   the period of account begins at any time before a designated period of account of the new group,

the notice under sub-paragraph (2) is also to be treated as if it constituted, on the day on which it is given, the appointment of the company in relation to a period of account of the existing group beginning with that time and ending immediately before the beginning of the designated period of account.

(7) If—

    (a)   enquiries are open at any time in relation to more than one interest restriction return, and

    (b)   this paragraph is capable of applying by reference to a closure notice to be given in respect of any one of those

Finance (No. 2) Act 2017 (c. 32)
Schedule 5 – Corporate interest restriction
Part 2 – New Schedule 7A to TIOPA 2010

431

enquiries (so that a worldwide group could be either the original group or the existing group),

an officer of Revenue and Customs must select the company that, in the officer's opinion, ought to be the reporting company in relation to the new group.

(8) For this purpose an enquiry is "open" in relation to an interest restriction return if no closure notice has been given in relation to the enquiry.

Appeal against closure notice or notice under paragraph 51

52 (1) If a closure notice –
    (a)   is given to a company under paragraph 47, and
    (b)   contains a statement under paragraph 49(2)(b),
the company may appeal against the statement.

(2) If a notice is given to a company under paragraph 51, the company may appeal against the notice.

(3) Notice of appeal under this paragraph must be given –
    (a)   within 30 days after the notice was given to the company,
    (b)   to the officer of Revenue and Customs by whom the notice in question was given.

New groups without existing reporting company

53 (1) This paragraph applies if –
    (a)   a closure notice is given to a company under paragraph 47,
    (b)   a period of account of a worldwide group ("the new group") is designated under paragraph 47(4) in the closure notice,
    (c)   the company is not a member of the new group at any time in that period of account, and
    (d)   paragraph 51 does not apply.

(2) An officer of Revenue and Customs may appoint a company to be the reporting company of the new group in relation to that period.

(3) The appointment –
    (a)   must be of a company that was a UK group company at any time during that period and was not dormant throughout that period, and
    (b)   must be made before the end of the period of 3 months beginning with the day on which the closure notice is given to the company.

Matters required to be done on a "just and reasonable" basis

54 (1) This paragraph applies if –
    (a)   anything is required to be done under any provision of this Part of this Act on a "just and reasonable" basis,

432

Finance (No. 2) Act 2017 (c. 32)
Schedule 5 — Corporate interest restriction
Part 2 — New Schedule 7A to TIOPA 2010

      (b)   in preparing an interest restriction return the reporting company adopts a particular basis for dealing with that thing, and

      (c)   notice of enquiry is given into the return.

(2) An officer of Revenue and Customs may determine that, in preparing the return, a different just and reasonable basis should have been adopted for dealing with that thing.

(3) A closure notice given in respect of the return must require the reporting company to whom the notice is given to revise the return to give effect to that determination.

(4) The officer's determination may be questioned on an appeal under paragraph 52 on the ground that the basis to be adopted is not just and reasonable (but not on any other ground).

References to a reporting company where replaced

55   (1) This paragraph applies where—

      (a)   the appointment of a reporting company has effect in relation to a period of account of a worldwide group, and

      (b)   another reporting company is appointed in place of that company and the appointment has effect in relation to that period of account.

(2) Any reference in this Part of this Schedule (however expressed) to the reporting company in relation to that period of account at any time is to the company which is the reporting company at that time in relation to that period of account.

PART 5

DETERMINATIONS BY OFFICERS OF REVENUE AND CUSTOMS

Power of Revenue and Customs to make determinations where no return filed etc

56   (1) This paragraph applies where—

      (a)   an officer of Revenue and Customs considers that a worldwide group was subject to interest restrictions in a period of account of the group ("the relevant period of account"),

      (b)   the determination date has passed, and

      (c)   condition A, B or C is met.

(2) In this paragraph "the determination date", in relation to a period of account of a worldwide group, means—

      (a)   where the appointment of a reporting company has effect in relation to the period of account, the filing date in relation to the period (see paragraph 7(5));

      (b)   otherwise, the end of the period of 12 months beginning with the end of the period of account.

(3) Condition A is that no appointment of a reporting company has effect in relation to the relevant period of account.

(4) Condition B is that—

    (a) the appointment of a reporting company has effect in relation to the relevant period of account, and

    (b) no interest restriction return has been submitted for the period.

(5) Condition C is that—

    (a) the appointment of a reporting company has effect in relation to the relevant period of account,

    (b) an interest restriction return has been submitted for the period, and

    (c) the return does not comply with the requirements of paragraph 20(3) (for example by including inaccurate figures).

(6) An officer of Revenue and Customs may determine, to the best of the officer's information and belief—

    (a) a company's pro-rata share of the total disallowed amount of the group for the relevant period of account, and

    (b) in relation to each relevant accounting period of the company, the accounting period's pro-rata share of the total disallowed amount.

(7) If, as a result of the determination, an accounting period's pro-rata share of the total disallowed amount is not nil, the company must leave out of account tax-interest expense amounts in that period that, in total, equal that pro-rata share.

(8) A notice of determination under this paragraph must be given to the company, and to the reporting company, stating the date on which the determination is made.

(9) No determination under this paragraph may be made after the end of the period of 3 years beginning with the determination date.

Time limit: interest restriction return following determination under paragraph 56

57 (1) Sub-paragraph (2) applies where—

    (a) a notice of determination under paragraph 56 is given to a company, and

    (b) at the time the notice is given, no interest restriction return for the relevant period of account has been submitted under paragraph 7.

(2) Despite the passing of the time limit in paragraph 7(6), an interest restriction return for the relevant period of account submitted under paragraph 7 has effect if it is received before the end of the period of 12 months beginning with the date on which the notice is given.

(3) Sub-paragraph (4) applies where—

    (a) a notice of determination under paragraph 56 is given to a company, and

434

Finance (No. 2) Act 2017 (c. 32)
Schedule 5 – Corporate interest restriction
Part 2 – New Schedule 7A to TIOPA 2010

  (b) at the time the notice is given, an interest restriction return for the relevant period of account has been submitted under paragraph 7.

(4) Despite the passing of the time limit in paragraph 8(3), an interest restriction return for the relevant period of account submitted under paragraph 8 has effect if it is received before the end of the period of 12 months beginning with the date on which the notice is given.

(5) In this paragraph "the relevant period of account" means the period of account to which the determination in question relates.

Power of Revenue and Customs to make determinations following enquiry

58 (1) This paragraph applies where—

  (a) as a result of a closure notice given under paragraph 47 (closure notice in respect of a return subject to enquiry), a company is required to submit an interest restriction return ("the return") in relation to a worldwide group,

  (b) the worldwide group is subject to interest restrictions in the return period, and

  (c) condition A or B is met.

(2) Condition A is that the time limit in paragraph 50(2) for submission of the return has passed without the return being received by an officer of Revenue and Customs.

(3) Condition B is that—

  (a) the return has been received by an officer of Revenue and Customs before the time limit in paragraph 50(2), and

  (b) the officer considers that the return does not comply with the requirements of the closure notice.

(4) An officer of Revenue and Customs may determine, to the best of the officer's information and belief—

  (a) a company's pro-rata share of the total disallowed amount of the group for the period of account in question, and

  (b) in relation to each relevant accounting period of the company, the accounting period's pro-rata share of the total disallowed amount.

(5) If, as a result of the determination, an accounting period's pro-rata share of the total disallowed amount is not nil, the company must leave out of account tax-interest expense amounts in that period that, in total, equal that pro-rata share.

(6) A notice of determination under this paragraph must be given to the company, and to the reporting company, stating the date on which the determination is made.

(7) No determination under this paragraph may be made after the end of the period of 3 months beginning with the end of the period mentioned in paragraph 50(2).

Appeal against determination under paragraph 58

59 (1) If a notice of determination under paragraph 58 is given to a company, the company may appeal against the notice.

(2) The only ground on which an appeal under this paragraph may be brought is that the determination is inconsistent with the requirements of the closure notice to which it relates.

(3) Notice of appeal under this paragraph must be given –

    (a) within 30 days after the notice of determination was given to the company,

    (b) to the officer of Revenue and Customs by whom the notice of determination was given.

PART 6

INFORMATION POWERS EXERCISABLE BY MEMBERS OF GROUP

Provision of information to and by the reporting company

60 (1) The reporting company in relation to a period of account of a worldwide group may, by notice, require a company that was a UK group company at any time during the period to provide it with information that it needs for the purpose of exercising functions under or by virtue of this Part of this Act.

(2) A notice under sub-paragraph (1) must specify the information to be provided.

(3) The duty to comply with a notice under sub-paragraph (1) is enforceable by the reporting company.

(4) As soon as reasonably practicable after submitting an interest restriction return to an officer of Revenue and Customs under any provision of this Schedule, the reporting company must send a copy of it to each company that was a UK group company at any time during the period of account.

(5) If a reporting company receives a closure notice under paragraph 47, the reporting company must, as soon as reasonably practicable, send a copy of the notice to every company that was a UK group company at any time during the period of account that was subject to the enquiry.

(6) The duty to comply with sub-paragraph (4) or (5) is enforceable by any person to whom the duty is owed.

Provision of information between members of group where no reporting company appointed

61 (1) This paragraph applies where condition A or B is met in relation to a period of account of a worldwide group.

(2) Condition A is that –

    (a) no appointment of a reporting company has effect in relation to the period of account, and

436   *Finance (No. 2) Act 2017 (c. 32)*
Schedule 5 – Corporate interest restriction
Part 2 – New Schedule 7A to TIOPA 2010

    (b)   as a result of sub-paragraph (4)(a) of paragraph 1, an appointment of a reporting company under that paragraph that has effect in relation to the relevant period of account is no longer possible.

  (3) Condition B is that—

    (a)   an appointment of a reporting company has effect in relation to the period of account,

    (b)   a full interest restriction return has not been submitted in accordance with this Part for the period, and

    (c)   the filing date in relation to the period has passed (see paragraph 7(5)).

  (4) A company that was a UK group company at any time during the period of account may, by notice, require any other such company to provide it with information that it needs for the purpose of determining whether, or the extent to which, it is required to leave tax-interest expense amounts out of account, or bring them into account, under this Part of this Act.

  (5) A notice under sub-paragraph (4) must specify the information to be provided.

  (6) The duty to comply with a notice under sub-paragraph (4) is enforceable by the company that gives the notice.

PART 7

INFORMATION POWERS EXERCISABLE BY OFFICERS OF REVENUE AND CUSTOMS

Power to obtain information and documents from members of worldwide group

62   (1) An officer of Revenue and Customs may, by notice, require a group member—

    (a)   to provide information, or

    (b)   to produce a document,

if the information or document is reasonably required by the officer for the purpose of checking an interest restriction return for, or exercising any of the powers under this Part of this Act in relation to, a period of account of a worldwide group.

  (2) For the purposes of this Part of this Schedule a person is a "group member" if, in the opinion of an officer of Revenue and Customs, the person is or might be a member of the worldwide group at any time in the period of account.

  (3) A group member may (subject to the operation of any provision of Part 4 of Schedule 36 to FA 2008 as applied by paragraph 66(1) of this Schedule) be required to provide information, or produce a document, that relates to one or more other group companies.

  (4) A notice under this paragraph may be given to a person even if the person is not within the charge to corporation tax or income tax.

  (5) A notice under this paragraph may specify or describe the information or documents to be provided or produced.

Finance (No. 2) Act 2017 (c. 32)
Schedule 5 – Corporate interest restriction
Part 2 – New Schedule 7A to TIOPA 2010

437

Power to obtain information and documents from third parties

63   (1)   An officer of Revenue and Customs may, by notice, require a third party –

      (a)   to provide information, or

      (b)   to produce a document,

if the information or document is reasonably required by the officer for the purpose of checking an interest restriction return for, or exercising any of the powers under this Part of this Act in relation to, a period of account of a worldwide group.

  (2)   A person is a "third party" if the person is not a group member at any time in the period of account.

  (3)   A notice may not be given under this paragraph unless –

      (a)   a company which is a UK group company of the group at any time in the period of account agrees to the giving of the notice, or

      (b)   on an application made by an officer of Revenue and Customs, the tribunal approves the giving of the notice.

  (4)   The tribunal may not approve the giving of a notice to a third party unless –

      (a)   the tribunal is satisfied that, in the circumstances, the officer giving the notice is justified in doing so, and

      (b)   either the requirements of sub-paragraph (5) are met or the tribunal is satisfied that it is appropriate to dispense with meeting those requirements because to meet them might prejudice the assessment or collection of tax.

  (5)   The requirements in this sub-paragraph are met if –

      (a)   the third party has been told that the information or documents referred to in the notice are required,

      (b)   the third party has been given a reasonable opportunity to make representations to an officer of Revenue and Customs,

      (c)   the tribunal has been given a summary of any representations made by the third party, and

      (d)   a company which is a UK group company of the group at any time in the period of account has been given a summary of the reasons why the information and documents are required.

  (6)   Sub-paragraph (5)(d) does not apply if an officer of Revenue and Customs has insufficient information to identify a company mentioned in that paragraph.

  (7)   No notice of the application for the approval of the tribunal needs to be given to the third party by an officer of Revenue and Customs.

  (8)   A notice under this paragraph to the third party must give details of the worldwide group unless –

      (a)   the notice is approved by the tribunal, and

438

Finance (No. 2) Act 2017 (c. 32)
Schedule 5 – Corporate interest restriction
Part 2 – New Schedule 7A to TIOPA 2010

     (b)   the tribunal is satisfied that no details should be given because to do so might seriously prejudice the assessment or collection of tax.

(9) An officer of Revenue and Customs must give a copy of a notice under this paragraph to a company which is a UK group company of the group at any time in the period of account unless—

     (a)   the tribunal has approved the notice and is satisfied that no copy should be given because to do so might prejudice the assessment or collection of tax, or

     (b)   an officer of Revenue and Customs has insufficient information to identify such a company.

(10) A decision of the tribunal under this paragraph is final (despite the provisions of sections 11 and 13 of the Tribunals, Courts and Enforcement Act 2007).

(11) A notice under this paragraph—

     (a)   may specify or describe the information or documents to be provided or produced, and

     (b)   if given with the approval of the tribunal, must state that fact.

Notices following submitted interest restriction returns

64   (1) The general rule is that, if an interest restriction return for a period of account of a worldwide group has been received by an officer of Revenue and Customs, a notice under paragraph 62 or 63 may not be given in relation to the period of the account of the group.

    (2) But the general rule does not apply if—

     (a)   a notice of enquiry has been given in respect of the return, and

     (b)   the enquiry has not been completed.

Appeals

65   (1) A group member may appeal against a notice under paragraph 62.

    (2) A person to whom a notice is given under paragraph 63 in a case where the tribunal has not approved the giving of the notice may appeal against the notice on the ground that it would be unduly onerous to comply with it.

    (3) No appeal may be made under this paragraph in relation to a requirement to provide any information, or produce any documents, that forms part of the statutory records of any company which is a UK group company of the group at any time in the period of account.

    (4) "Statutory records" has the same meaning given by paragraph 62 of Schedule 36 to FA 2008.

    (5) In this Part of this Schedule references to an appeal against a notice include an appeal against a requirement of the notice.

Finance (No. 2) Act 2017 (c. 32)
Schedule 5 — Corporate interest restriction
Part 2 — New Schedule 7A to TIOPA 2010

439

Application of provisions of Schedule 36 to FA 2008

66 (1) The following provisions of Schedule 36 to FA 2008 (information and inspection powers) apply in relation to notices under paragraph 62 or 63 —

    (a) paragraph 7 (complying with notices),

    (b) paragraph 8 (producing copies of documents),

    (c) paragraph 15 (power to copy documents),

    (d) paragraph 16 (power to remove documents),

    (e) paragraph 18 (documents not in person's possession or power),

    (f) paragraph 19 (types of information),

    (g) paragraph 20 (old documents),

    (h) paragraph 23 (privileged communications),

    (i) paragraphs 24 to 27 (auditors and tax advisers),

    (j) every paragraph contained in Part 7 (penalties),

    (k) every paragraph contained in Part 8 (offence), and

    (l) paragraph 56 (application of provisions of TMA 1970).

(2) Paragraph 32 of Schedule 36 to FA 2008 (procedure on appeals) applies in relation to an appeal under this Part of this Schedule against a notice under this Part of this Schedule.

References to checking an interest restriction return etc

67 (1) For the purposes of this Part of this Schedule references to checking an interest restriction return include —

    (a) determining whether or not an interest restriction return should be submitted for a period of account of a worldwide group,

    (b) determining whether or not a worldwide group is, or may be, subject to interest restrictions in a period of account, (and, if so, determining the total disallowed amount of the group),

    (c) determining the membership of a worldwide group (or determining the members that are UK group companies), and

    (d) determining any other question that is relevant to the operation of this Part of this Schedule in relation to an interest restriction return or anything required to be included in it.

(2) For the purposes of this Part of this Schedule references to a worldwide group include one that an officer of Revenue and Customs suspects may exist.

PART 8

COMPANY TAX RETURNS

Elections under section 375, 377 or 380

68   The following elections (or their revocation) must be made by a company in its company tax return (whether as originally made or by amendment) for the accounting period to which the election (or revocation) relates –

    (a)   an election under section 375 (a non-consenting company leaving pro-rata share of total disallowed amount out of account),

    (b)   an election under section 377 (a company specifying tax-interest expense amounts to be left out of account), and

    (c)   an election under section 380 (a company specifying tax-interest expense amounts to be brought into account).

Amendments to take account of operation of this Part of this Act (including elections)

69   (1)   A company may amend its company tax return for an accounting period so as to make (or revoke) an election under section 375 at any time before –

    (a)   the filing date in relation to the period of account of the worldwide group to which the interest restriction return in question relates (see paragraph 7(5)), or

    (b)   if later, the end of the period of 3 months beginning with the day on which the interest restriction return in question is received by an officer of Revenue and Customs.

(2)   A company that amends its company tax return for an accounting period as mentioned in sub-paragraph (1) must, before the time limit specified in that sub-paragraph, also amend the return to take account of the election (or revocation).

(3)   If –

    (a)   a company is required by section 376 to leave an amount out of account in an accounting period, and

    (b)   the company has already delivered a company tax return for the period,

the company must amend its company tax return to take account of the requirement.

(4)   The amendment must be made before the end of the period of 3 months beginning with the day after the relevant date (within the meaning of section 376).

(5)   A company may amend its company tax return for an accounting period so as to make (or revoke) an election under section 377 or 380 at any time before –

    (a)   the end of the period of 36 months beginning with the day after the end of the accounting period, or

    (b)   if later, the end of the period of 3 months beginning with the day on which a relevant interest restriction return was received by an officer of Revenue and Customs.

Finance (No. 2) Act 2017 (c. 32)
Schedule 5 — Corporate interest restriction
Part 2 — New Schedule 7A to TIOPA 2010

441

(6) A company that amends its company tax return for an accounting period as mentioned in sub-paragraph (5) must, before the time limit specified in that sub-paragraph, also amend the return to take account of the election (or revocation).

(7) In sub-paragraph (5) "a relevant interest restriction return" means an interest restriction return for a period of account in relation to which the accounting period is a relevant accounting period.

(8) The time limit for amending a company tax return given by paragraph 15(4) of Schedule 18 to FA 1998 is subject to the time limits given by this paragraph.

Cases where company treated as amending return

70 (1) If—
    (a) a company has delivered a company tax return for an accounting period, but
    (b) as a result of the submission of an interest restriction return, information contained in the company tax return is incorrect (for example, there is a change in the amount of profits on which corporation tax is chargeable),

the company is treated as having amended its company tax return for the accounting period so as to correct the information.

(2) If—
    (a) a notice of determination under paragraph 56 or 58 is given to a company in relation to an accounting period, and
    (b) the company has already delivered a company tax return for the period,

the company is treated as having amended its company tax return to take account of the determination.

Regulations for purposes of paragraph 70 etc

71 (1) The Commissioners may by regulations—
    (a) make provision generally for the purposes of paragraph 70, and
    (b) make provision for other cases where a company is to be treated as having amended its company tax return.

(2) The provision that may be made by the regulations includes provision—
    (a) permitting or requiring the company to deliver an amended company tax return for the accounting period;
    (b) specifying amendments that may or must be made in the return;
    (c) specifying a time limit for the delivery of the return that is later than that determined under paragraph 15(4) of Schedule 18 to FA 1998 (amendment of return by company).

Consequential claims to company tax returns

72 (1) This paragraph applies if—

442

Finance (No. 2) Act 2017 (c. 32)
Schedule 5 — Corporate interest restriction
Part 2 — New Schedule 7A to TIOPA 2010

(a) a company amends, or is treated as amending, its company tax return for an accounting period in consequence of a closure notice given in respect of an interest restriction return under paragraph 47 or a notice of determination given to the company under paragraph 56 or 58, and

(b) the amendment has the effect of increasing the amount of corporation tax payable by the company for the accounting period.

(2) Any qualifying claim may be made or given within the period of one year beginning with the day on which the company receives a copy of the closure notice under paragraph 60(5) or the notice of determination.

(3) Any qualifying claim previously made which is not irrevocable —

(a) may be revoked or varied within that one-year period, and

(b) if it is revoked or varied, must be done so in the same manner as it was made and by or with the consent of the same person or persons who made or consented to it (or, if a person has died, by or with the consent of the person's personal representatives).

(4) For the purposes of this paragraph a claim is a "qualifying" claim if its making, revocation or variation has the effect of reducing the liability of the company to corporation tax for the accounting period (whether or not it also reduces the liability to tax of the company for other periods).

(5) But a claim is not a "qualifying" claim if —

(a) the making, revocation or variation of the claim would alter the liability to tax of any person other than the company, or

(b) the making, revocation or variation of the claim is such that, if it were to be made, revoked or varied, the total of the reductions in liability to tax of the company would exceed the additional liability to corporation tax resulting from the amendment.

(6) If a qualifying claim is made, revoked or varied as a result of this paragraph, all such adjustments must be made as are required to take account of the effect of taking that action on the liability of the company to tax for any period.

(7) The adjustments may be made by way of discharge or repayment of tax or the making of amendments, assessments or otherwise.

(8) The provisions of TMA 1970 relating to appeals against decisions on claims apply with any necessary modifications to a decision on the revocation or variation of a claim as a result of this paragraph.

(9) In this paragraph (except in sub-paragraph (8)) "claim" includes an election, an application and a notice, and references to making a claim are to be read accordingly.

(10) In this paragraph "tax" (except in the expression "corporation tax") includes income tax and capital gains tax.

Finance (No. 2) Act 2017 (c. 32)
Schedule 5 — Corporate interest restriction
Part 2 — New Schedule 7A to TIOPA 2010

443

Meaning of "company tax return"

73   In this Schedule "company tax return" has the meaning given by paragraph 3 of Schedule 18 to FA 1998.

PART 9

SUPPLEMENTARY

Double jeopardy

74   A person is not liable to a penalty under any provision of this Schedule in respect of anything in respect of which the person has been convicted of an offence.

Notice of appeal

75   Notice of an appeal under this Schedule must specify the grounds of appeal.

Conclusiveness of amounts stated in interest restriction return

76   (1) This paragraph applies to an amount stated in an interest restriction return submitted under paragraph 7 or 8 ("the interest restriction return"), other than an amount that is also stated in a company tax return.

(2) If the amount can no longer be altered, it is taken to be conclusively determined for the purposes of the Corporation Tax Acts.

(3) An amount is regarded as one that can no longer be altered if—
   (a) the interest restriction return has not been superseded by a subsequent interest restriction return;
   (b) the applicable time limit has passed;
   (c) any enquiry into the interest restriction return has been completed;
   (d) if the closure notice in relation to an enquiry into the interest restriction return contained a statement under paragraph 49(2)(b), the period within which an appeal against the statement may be brought has ended; and
   (e) if such an appeal is brought, the appeal has been finally determined.

(4) For the purposes of sub-paragraph (3) the "applicable time limit" means the time limit in paragraph 8(3) or, in a case where paragraph 57(2) or (4) applies and imposes a later time limit for submission of the interest restriction return, that later time limit.

(5) Nothing in this paragraph affects—
   (a) the power under paragraph 42 (extended time limits for opening enquiries: discovery of errors), or
   (b) any power to make a determination under paragraph 56 or 58 (determinations by officers of Revenue and Customs)."

444   *Finance (No. 2) Act 2017 (c. 32)*
Schedule 5 – Corporate interest restriction
Part 3 – Consequential amendments

PART 3

CONSEQUENTIAL AMENDMENTS

TMA 1970

3   (1)   In section 98 of TMA 1970 (special returns, etc), in the table in subsection (5), in the first column, the entry relating to regulations under section 283, 284, 285, 295 or 297 of TIOPA 2010 is repealed.

      (2)   In consequence of sub-paragraph (1), paragraph 157(3) of Schedule 8 to TIOPA 2010 is repealed.

FA 1998

4   In paragraph 88 of Schedule 18 to FA 1998 (conclusiveness of amounts stated in company tax returns), at the end insert—

> "(9) Nothing in this paragraph affects the operation of any provision of Part 10 of TIOPA 2010 (corporate interest restriction)."

CTA 2009

5   In section A1 of CTA 2009 (overview of the Corporation Tax Acts), in subsection (2)—
       (a)   omit paragraph (i), and
       (b)   after paragraph (ja) insert—
> "(jb)   Part 10 of that Act (corporate interest restriction),".

CTA 2010

6   CTA 2010 is amended as follows.

7   After section 937N (risk transfer schemes) insert—

"937NA   Priority

> For the purposes of this Part, the provisions of Part 10 of TIOPA 2010 (corporate interest restriction) are to be treated as of no effect."

8   In section 938N (group mismatch schemes: priority), for paragraph (e) substitute—
> "(e)   Part 10 of that Act (corporate interest restriction)."

9   In section 938V (tax mismatch schemes: priority), for paragraph (d) substitute—
> "(d)   Part 10 of that Act (corporate interest restriction)."

TIOPA 2010: consequential renumbering

10   (1)   In consequence of the insertion of a new Part 10 of TIOPA 2010 by Part 1 of this Schedule, the existing Part 10 of that Act becomes a new Part 11.

      (2)   The following provisions of TIOPA 2010 are repealed—
       (a)   the existing sections 375 and 376 (which contain powers that are no longer exercisable), and
       (b)   the existing section 381(2)(e) and (f) (which refer to those sections);

but the repeals made by this sub-paragraph do not affect any orders made under section 375 or 376 before the passing of this Act.

(3) As a result of the provision made by sub-paragraphs (1) and (2), the following provisions of TIOPA 2010 are renumbered as follows –

    (a) the existing section 372 becomes section 499;

    (b) the existing section 373 becomes section 500;

    (c) the existing section 374 becomes section 501;

    (d) the existing section 377 becomes section 502;

    (e) the existing section 378 becomes section 503;

    (f) the existing section 379 becomes section 504;

    (g) the existing section 380 becomes section 505;

    (h) the existing section 381 becomes section 506;

    (i) the existing section 382 becomes section 507.

(4) Consequently –

    (a) in section 287(2A) of TCGA 1992, for "372" substitute "499";

    (b) in section 1014(2)(fa) of ITA 2007, for "372" substitute "499";

    (c) in section 1171(2)(f) of CTA 2010, for "372" substitute "499";

    (d) in section 1 of TIOPA 2010 –

        (i) in subsection (4), for "10" substitute "11";

        (ii) in subsection (5), for "373" substitute "500";

    (e) in section 381(2) of TIOPA 2010 –

        (i) in paragraph (a), for "372" substitute "499";

        (ii) in paragraph (b), for "373" substitute "500";

        (iii) in paragraph (d), for "374" substitute "501";

        (iv) in paragraph (g), for "377(2) and (3)" substitute "502(2) and (3)";

        (v) in paragraph (h), for "380" substitute "505";

        (vi) in paragraph (i), for "382" substitute "507".

(5) In section 379(1) and (2) of TIOPA 2010 (index of defined expressions), for "8" substitute "10".

TIOPA 2010: repeal of Part 7

11 (1) Part 7 of TIOPA 2010 (tax treatment of financing costs and income) is repealed; and accordingly the following provisions of that Act are also repealed –

    (a) section 1(1)(d) (overview);

    (b) in Schedule 9, Part 7 (transitional provision);

    (c) in Schedule 11, Part 5 (index of defined expressions).

(2) In consequence of sub-paragraph (1), the following enactments (which amend provisions repealed by that sub-paragraph) are repealed –

    (a) in F(No.3)A 2010, section 11 and Schedule 5;

    (b) in FA 2011, in Schedule 13, paragraphs 29 and 30;

    (c) in FA 2012 –

        (i) section 31 and Schedule 5;

        (ii) in Schedule 16, paragraphs 242 and 243(a);

        (iii) in Schedule 20, paragraphs 43 to 45;

    (d)   in FA 2013, section 44;

    (e)   in FA 2014, section 39.

(3) The following regulations were made under powers contained in Part 7 of TIOPA 2010 and are therefore revoked by virtue of sub-paragraph (1) –

    (a)   the Corporation Tax (Financing Costs and Income) Regulations 2009 (S.I. 2009/3173);

    (b)   the Corporation Tax (Tax Treatment of Financing Costs and Income) (Acceptable Financial Statements) Regulations 2009 (S.I. 2009/3217);

    (c)   the Corporation Tax (Exclusion from Short-Term Loan Relationships) Regulations 2009 (S.I. 2009/3313);

    (d)   the Tax Treatment of Financing Costs and Income (Available Amount) Regulations 2010 (S.I. 2010/2929);

    (e)   the Tax Treatment of Financing Costs and Income (Correction of Mismatches) Regulations 2010 (S.I. 2010/3025);

    (f)   the Taxation (International and Other Provisions) Act 2010 (Part 7) (Amendment) Regulations 2012 (S.I. 2012/3045);

    (g)   the Tax Treatment of Financing Costs and Income (Correction of Mismatches: Partnerships and Pensions) Regulations 2012 (S.I. 2012/3111);

    (h)   the Tax Treatment of Financing Costs and Income (Excluded Schemes) Regulations 2013 (S.I. 2013/2892);

    (i)   the Tax Treatment of Financing Costs and Income (Change of Accounting Standards: Investment Entities) Regulations 2015 (S.I. 2015/662).

TIOPA 2010: other amendments

12   TIOPA 2010 is amended as follows.

13   In section 1 (overview of Act), in subsection (1) –

    (a)   omit the "and" at the end of paragraph (d), and

    (b)   after paragraph (e) insert –

        "(f)   Part 9A (controlled foreign companies), and

        (g)   Part 10 (corporate interest restriction)."

14   In section 155 (transfer pricing: "potential advantage" in relation to United Kingdom taxation), in subsection (6), for paragraph (a) substitute –

        "(a)   Part 10 (corporate interest restriction),".

15   In section 157 (direct participation), in subsection (1) –

    (a)   omit the "and" at the end of paragraph (c), and

    (b)   after paragraph (d) insert ", and

        (e)   in Part 10, section 463(4)."

16   In section 159 (indirect participation: potential direct participant), in subsection (1) –

    (a)   omit the "and" at the end of paragraph (c), and

    (b)   after paragraph (d) insert ", and

        (e)   in Part 10, section 463(4)."

17   In section 160 (indirect participation: one of several major participants), in subsection (1) –

   (a) omit the "and" at the end of paragraph (c), and
   (b) after paragraph (d) insert ", and
     (e) in Part 10, section 463(4)."

18 In section 259CB (financial instruments: hybrid or otherwise impermissible deduction/non-inclusion mismatches and their extent), in subsection (6), for paragraph (e) substitute —
   "(e) Part 10 (corporate interest restriction)."

19 In section 259DC (hybrid transfer deduction/non-inclusion mismatches and their extent), in subsection (5), for paragraph (d) substitute —
   "(d) Part 10 (corporate interest restriction)."

20 After section 259NE (treatment of a person who is a member of a partnership) insert —

"Priority

259NEA Priority

   For the purposes of this Part, the provisions of Part 10 (corporate interest restriction) are to be treated as of no effect."

21 (1) Chapter 3 of Part 9A (CFCs: the CFC charge gateway) is amended as follows.

 (2) In section 371CE (which makes provision for determining whether Chapter 6 of Part 9A applies) —
   (a) in subsection (2)(a), after "period" insert "(see section 371CEA)", and
   (b) omit subsections (4) and (5).

 (3) After section 371CE insert —

"371CEA Section 371CE: meaning of "group treasury company"

  (1) This section makes provision for determining whether the CFC is a group treasury company in the accounting period for the purposes of section 371CE.

  (2) The CFC is a group treasury company in the accounting period if —
   (a) it is a member of a worldwide group in relation to a period of account in which the accounting period wholly or partly falls,
   (b) throughout the accounting period —
    (i) all, or substantially all, of the activities undertaken by it consist of treasury activities undertaken for the group, and
    (ii) all, or substantially all, of its assets and liabilities relate to such activities, and
   (c) at least 90% of its relevant income for the accounting period is group treasury revenue.

  (3) For the purposes of this section a company undertakes treasury activities for the group if it does one or more of the following in relation to, or on behalf of, the group or any of its members —
   (a) managing surplus deposits of money or overdrafts,
   (b) making or receiving deposits of money,
   (c) lending money,

      (d)   subscribing for or holding shares in a company which is a UK group company undertaking treasury activities for the group at least 90% of whose relevant income is group treasury revenue for its relevant accounting period,

      (e)   investing in debt securities, and

      (f)   hedging assets, liabilities, income or expenses.

    (4)   For the purposes of this section "group treasury revenue", in relation to a company, means revenue—

      (a)   arising from the treasury activities that the company undertakes for the group, and

      (b)   accounted for as such under generally accepted accounting practice,

before any deduction (whether for expenses or otherwise).

    (5)   But revenue consisting of a dividend or other distribution is not group treasury revenue of the company unless it is from a company that meets the conditions in subsection (3)(d).

    (6)   In this section—

        "debt security" has the same meaning as in the Handbook made by the Financial Conduct Authority or Prudential Regulation Authority under the Financial Services and Markets Act 2000 (as the Handbook in question has effect from time to time),

        "period of account" has the same meaning as in Part 10,

        "relevant accounting period" has the same meaning as in Part 10,

        "relevant income", in relation to a company, means income—

           (a)   arising from the activities of the company, and

           (b)   accounted for as such under generally accepted accounting practice,

        before any deduction (whether for expenses or otherwise),

        "UK group company" has the same meaning as in Part 10, and

        "worldwide group" has the same meaning as in Part 10."

  (4) In consequence of the amendments made by this paragraph, in Schedule 47 to FA 2013, omit paragraph 17.

22 (1) Chapter 9 of Part 9A (CFCs: exemption for profits from qualifying loan relationships) is amended as follows.

    (2) For section 371IE substitute—

"371IE The "matched interest profits" exemption

    (1)   This section applies if—

      (a)   there are profits of qualifying loan relationships which are not exempt after sections 371IB and 371ID have been applied to each qualifying loan relationship,

      (b)   the relevant corporation tax accounting period (as defined in section 371BC(3)) of company C is a relevant accounting period of it in relation to a period of account of a worldwide group,

      (c)   the CFC's accounting period ends in that period of account, and

(d) apart from this section, the profits mentioned in paragraph (a) would be included in the chargeable profits of the CFC.

(2) In this section "the matched interest profits" means so much of the profits mentioned in subsection (1)(a) as remain after excluded credits and excluded debits are left out of account.

(3) If the aggregate net tax-interest expense of the group for the period is nil, all of the matched interest profits are exempt.

(4) Otherwise, there is a more limited exemption if the relevant proportion of the matched interest profits apportioned to C or other relevant chargeable companies exceeds the aggregate net tax-interest expense of the group for the period.

(5) For the purposes of this section "the relevant proportion of the matched interest profits apportioned to C or other relevant chargeable companies" is determined as follows.

Step 1

For each relevant chargeable company (including C) determine the percentage (P%) of the CFC's chargeable profits that are apportioned to the company under step 5 of section 371BC(1).

Step 2

For each relevant chargeable company (including C) multiply P% by the matched interest profits.

Step 3

The sum of the amounts for each company found under step 2 is "the relevant proportion of the matched interest profits apportioned to C or other relevant chargeable companies".

(6) For the purposes of this section a company is a relevant chargeable company if the relevant corporation tax accounting period of the company is a relevant accounting period in relation to the period of account of the group.

(7) The limited exemption is given effect by treating the matched interest profits as equal to the amount found by multiplying the amount that they would otherwise be by—

$$\frac{E}{RPMIP}$$

where—

E is the amount of the excess mentioned in subsection (4), and

RPMIP is the relevant proportion of the matched interest profits apportioned to C or other relevant chargeable companies.

(8) For the purposes of this section the aggregate net tax-interest expense of a worldwide group for a period of account is determined in accordance with Part 10 (corporate interest restriction) but without regard to debits, credits or other amounts arising from—

(a) banking business carried on by a company within the charge to corporation tax, or

(b) insurance business carried on by a company within the charge to corporation tax.

(9) For the purposes of this section—

450   *Finance (No. 2) Act 2017 (c. 32)*
Schedule 5 – Corporate interest restriction
Part 3 – Consequential amendments

"excluded credit" has the meaning given by section 386(3),

"excluded debit" has the meaning given by section 383(3), and

"period of account", "relevant accounting period" and "worldwide group" have the same meanings as in Part 10."

(3) In section 371IJ (claims), in subsection (6), for "the tested income amount or the tested expense amount mentioned in section 371IE(2)" substitute "the aggregate net tax-interest expense that is mentioned in section 371IE".

23   (1) Chapter 19 of Part 9A (CFCs: assumed taxable total profits, assumed total profits and the corporation tax assumptions) is amended as follows.

(2) In section 371SL (group relief etc), at the end insert—

"(4)   This section is subject to section 371SLA (corporate interest restriction)."

(3) After section 371SL insert—

"371SLA   Corporate interest restriction

(1)   This section applies for the purpose of applying Part 10 (corporate interest restriction).

(2)   Assume—

    (a)   that the CFC is a member of a worldwide group for a period of account of which it would be a member if section 371SL were ignored, and

    (b)   that the CFC is the only UK group company in the period (within the meaning of that Part).

(3)   Assume also that Part 10 applies as if subsections (2) and (3) of section 392 (interest capacity of the group: the de minimis amount) were omitted."

24   In Schedule 11, at the end insert—

"PART 7

CORPORATE INTEREST RESTRICTION: INDEX OF DEFINED EXPRESSIONS USED IN PART 10

abbreviated interest restriction return (in Part 10)	paragraph 20 of Schedule 7A
abbreviated return election (in Part 10)	paragraph 19 of Schedule 7A
accounting period (in Part 10)	Chapter 2 of Part 2 of CTA 2009 (applied by section 1119 of CTA 2010)
adjusted net group-interest expense of a worldwide group (in Part 10)	section 413

aggregate net tax-interest expense of a worldwide group (in Part 10)	section 390
aggregate net tax-interest income of a worldwide group (in Part 10)	section 390
aggregate tax-EBITDA of a worldwide group (in Part 10)	section 405
allocated reactivation of company for period of account (in Part 10)	paragraph 25 of Schedule 7A
allowable loss (in Part 10)	TCGA 1992 (applied by section 1119 of CTA 2010)
associated (in Chapter 8 of Part 10)	section 449(2)
amount available for reactivation of company in period of account (in Part 10)	paragraph 26 of Schedule 7A
available, in relation to interest allowance (in Chapter 4 of Part 10)	section 393
balance sheet (in Chapter 8 of Part 10)	section 449(1)
chargeable gain (in Part 10)	TCGA 1992 (applied by section 1119 of CTA 2010)
the Commissioners (in Part 10)	section 494(1)
company (in Part 10)	section 1121 of CTA 2010
company tax return (in Schedule 7A)	paragraph 73 of Schedule 7A
consenting company (in Part 10)	paragraph 10 of Schedule 7A
consolidated partnership (in Part 10)	section 430
consolidated subsidiary of another entity (in Part 10)	section 475
derivative contract (in Part 10)	Part 7 of CTA 2009 (applied by section 1119 of CTA 2010)
disallowed, in relation to tax-interest expense amount (in Part 10)	section 378
drawn up on acceptable principles, in relation to financial statements (in Chapter 11 of Part 10)	section 481
fair value accounting (in Part 10)	section 494(1)

fair value (in Part 10)	section 494(1)
filing date, in relation to a period of account of a worldwide group (in Part 10)	paragraph 7(5) of Schedule 7A
finance lease (in Part 10)	section 494(1)
financial asset (in Chapter 8 of Part 10)	section 449(1)
financial statements of a worldwide group (in Part 10)	section 479
fixed ratio method (in Part 10)	section 397
for accounting purposes (in Part 10)	section 1127(4) of CTA 2010
full interest restriction return (in Part 10)	paragraph 20 of Schedule 7A
generally accepted accounting practice (in Part 10)	section 1127(1) and (3) of CTA 2010
group-EBITDA (chargeable gains) election (in Part 10)	paragraph 15 of Schedule 7A
group ratio election (in Part 10)	paragraph 13 of Schedule 7A
group ratio (blended) election (in Part 10)	paragraph 14 of Schedule 7A
group ratio method (in Part 10)	section 398
group ratio percentage (in Part 10)	section 399
IAS financial statements (in Part 10)	section 488
impairment loss (in Part 10)	section 391
income (in Part 10)	section 1119 of CTA 2010
insurance company (in Part 10)	section 141 of FA 2012
interest allowance of a worldwide group (in Part 10)	section 396
interest allowance (alternative calculation) election (in Part 10)	paragraph 16 of Schedule 7A
interest allowance (consolidated partnerships) election (in Part 10)	paragraph 18 of Schedule 7A
interest allowance (non-consolidated investment) election (in Part 10)	paragraph 17 of Schedule 7A
interest capacity of a worldwide group (in Part 10)	section 392
interest reactivation cap of a worldwide group (in Part 10)	section 373

interest restriction return (in Part 10)	section 494(1)
international accounting standards (in Part 10)	section 1127(5) of CTA 2010
investor in a worldwide group (in Part 10)	section 404
loan relationship (in Part 10)	Part 5 of CTA 2009 (applied by section 1119 of CTA 2010)
loan relationships or other financing arrangements (in Chapter 8 of Part 10)	section 449(1)
local authority (in Part 10)	section 1130 of CTA 2010
local authority association (in Part 10)	section 1131 of CTA 2010
member of a worldwide group (in Part 10)	section 473(4)(a)
multi-company worldwide group (in Part 10)	section 473(4)(d)
net group-interest expense of a worldwide group (in Part 10)	section 410
net tax-interest expense of a company (in Part 10)	section 389
net tax-interest income of a company (in Part 10)	section 389
non-consenting company (in Part 10)	paragraph 10 of Schedule 7A
non-consolidated associate of a worldwide group (in Part 10)	section 429
non-consolidated subsidiary of an entity (in Part 10)	section 475
notice (in Part 10)	section 1119 of CTA 2010
party to a loan relationship (in Part 10)	section 494(2)
period of account of a worldwide group (in Part 10)	section 480
profit before tax, of a worldwide group (in Chapter 7 of Part 10)	section 416
pro-rata share of company (of total disallowed amount) (in Part 10)	paragraph 23 of Schedule 7A
pro-rata share of accounting period (of total disallowed amount) (in Part 10)	paragraph 24 of Schedule 7A
provision (in relation to a public infrastructure asset) (in Chapter 8 of Part 10)	section 436
public infrastructure asset (in Chapter 8 of Part 10)	section 436

qualifying charitable donation (in Part 10)	Part 6 of CTA 2010 (applied by section 1119 of CTA 2010)
qualifying infrastructure company (in Chapter 8 of Part 10)	section 433
qualifying infrastructure activity (in Chapter 8 of Part 10)	section 436
qualifying net group-interest expense of a worldwide group (in Part 10)	section 414
recognised, in financial statements (in Part 10)	section 489
recognised stock exchange (in Part 10)	section 1137 of CTA 2010
registered pension scheme (in Part 10)	section 150(2) of FA 2004 (applied by section 1119 of CTA 2010)
related party (in Part 10)	sections 462 to 472
related party investor (in Part 10)	section 404
relevant asset (in Chapter 7 of Part 10)	section 417
relevant accounting period (in Part 10)	section 490
relevant expense amount (in Chapter 7 of Part 10)	section 411
relevant income amount (in Chapter 7 of Part 10)	section 411
relevant public body (in Part 10)	section 491
reporting company (in Part 10)	section 494(1)
the return period (in Part 10)	section 494(1)
service concession agreement (in Part 10)	section 494(1)
share, of an investor in a worldwide group (in Part 10)	section 404
single-company worldwide group (in Part 10)	section 473(4)(c)
subject to interest reactivations (in Part 10)	section 373
subject to interest restrictions (in Part 10)	section 373
tax (in Part 10)	section 1119 of CTA 2010
tax-EBITDA of a company (in Part 10)	section 406
tax-interest expense amount of a company (in Part 10)	section 382

tax-interest income amount of a company (in Part 10)	section 385
trade (in Part 10)	section 1119 of CTA 2010
total disallowed amount of a worldwide group (in Part 10)	section 373
UK generally accepted accounting practice (in Part 10)	section 1127(2) of CTA 2010
UK group company (in Part 10)	section 492
UK property business (in Part 10)	Chapter 2 of Part 4 of CTA 2009 (applied by section 1119 of CTA 2010)
the UK sector of the continental shelf (in Chapter 8 of Part 10)	section 449(1)
the ultimate parent, of a worldwide group (in Part 10)	section 473(4)(b)
unexpired (in Chapter 4 of Part 10)	section 395
United Kingdom (in Part 10)	section 1170 of CTA 2010
used (in Chapter 4 of Part 10)	section 394
within the charge to corporation tax (in Part 10)	section 1167 of CTA 2010
wholly-owned subsidiary (in Part 10)	section 494(1)
a worldwide group (in Part 10)	section 473"

Part 4

Commencement and transitional provision

Commencement: new Part 10 of TIOPA

25 (1) The corporate interest restriction amendments have effect in relation to periods of account of worldwide groups that begin on or after 1 April 2017.

(2) In this paragraph "the corporate interest restriction amendments" means the amendments made by Parts 1 to 3 of this Schedule, apart from those made by paragraph 11 (repeal of Part 7 of TIOPA 2010).

(3) Any regulations made by the Treasury or Commissioners under Part 10 of TIOPA 2010 before 1 April 2018 may have effect in relation to periods of account of worldwide groups that begin on or after 1 April 2017.

(4) Sub-paragraphs (6) to (11) apply if —

    (a) financial statements of a worldwide group are drawn up by or on behalf of the ultimate parent in respect of a period that begins before, and ends on or after, 1 April 2017,

456   *Finance (No. 2) Act 2017 (c. 32)*
Schedule 5 — Corporate interest restriction
Part 4 — Commencement and transitional provision

    (b)   the period in respect of which the financial statements are drawn up is 18 months or less, and

    (c)   the financial statements are drawn up before the end of the period of 30 months beginning with the beginning of the period in respect of which they are drawn up.

(5) In sub-paragraphs (6) to (11) —

    (a)   "the group's actual financial statements" means the financial statements mentioned in sub-paragraph (4);

    (b)   "the straddling period of account" means the period in respect of which those financial statements are drawn up.

(6) For the purposes of Part 10 of TIOPA 2010, the group's actual financial statements are treated as not having been drawn up.

(7) Instead, financial statements of the worldwide group are treated for those purposes as having been drawn up in respect of each of the following periods —

    (a)   the period beginning at the time the straddling period of account begins and ending with 31 March 2017, and

    (b)   the period beginning with 1 April 2017 and ending at the time the straddling period of account ends.

(8) Where condition C or D in section 481 of TIOPA 2010 is met in relation to the group's actual financial statements, the financial statements treated as drawn up by sub-paragraph (7) are treated as drawn up in accordance with the generally accepted accounting principles and practice with which the group's actual financial statements were drawn up.

(9) Where neither of those conditions is met in relation to the group's actual financial statements, the financial statements treated as drawn up by sub-paragraph (7) are IAS financial statements.

(10) Where, for the purpose of determining amounts recognised in the financial statements treated as drawn up by sub-paragraph (7), it is expedient to apportion any amount that is recognised in the group's actual financial statements, the apportionment is to be made in accordance with section 1172 of CTA 2010 (apportionment on a time basis).

(11) But if it appears that apportionment in accordance with that section would work unjustly or unreasonably, the apportionment is to be made on a just and reasonable basis.

(12) Expressions used in this paragraph and in Part 10 of TIOPA 2010 have the same meaning in this paragraph as they have in that Part.

Commencement: repeal of Part 7 of TIOPA 2010

26 (1) The repeals and revocations made by paragraph 11 of this Schedule have effect in relation to periods of account of the worldwide group that begin on or after 1 April 2017.

    (2) Sub-paragraphs (4) to (10) apply if financial statements of the worldwide group are drawn up in respect of a period that begins before, and ends on or after, 1 April 2017.

    (3) In sub-paragraphs (4) to (10) —

Finance (No. 2) Act 2017 (c. 32)
Schedule 5 — Corporate interest restriction
Part 4 — Commencement and transitional provision

457

    (a)   "the group's actual financial statements" means the financial statements mentioned in sub-paragraph (2);

    (b)   "the straddling period of account" means the period in respect of which those financial statements are drawn up.

(4) For the purposes of Part 7 of TIOPA 2010, the group's actual financial statements are treated as not having been drawn up.

(5) Instead, financial statements of the worldwide group are treated for those purposes as having been drawn up in respect of each of the following periods—

    (a)   the period beginning at the time the straddling period of account begins and ending with 31 March 2017, and

    (b)   the period beginning with 1 April 2017 and ending at the time the straddling period of account ends.

(6) Where condition B, C or D in regulation 2 of the Acceptable Financial Statements Regulations is met in relation to the group's actual financial statements, the financial statements treated as drawn up by sub-paragraph (5) are treated as drawn up in accordance with the generally accepted accounting principles and practice with which the group's actual financial statements were drawn up.

(7) Where none of those conditions is met in relation to the group's actual financial statements, the financial statements treated as drawn up by sub-paragraph (5) are IAS financial statements.

(8) Where, for the purpose of determining amounts recognised in the financial statements treated as drawn up by sub-paragraph (5), it is expedient to apportion any amount that is recognised in the group's actual financial statements, the apportionment is to be made in accordance with section 1172 of CTA 2010 (apportionment on a time basis).

(9) But if it appears that apportionment in accordance with that section would work unjustly or unreasonably, the apportionment is to be made on a just and reasonable basis.

(10) In sub-paragraph (6), "the Acceptable Financial Statements Regulations" means the Corporation Tax (Tax Treatment of Financing Costs and Income) (Acceptable Financial Statements) Regulations 2009 (S.I. 2009/3217).

(11) Expressions used in this paragraph and in Part 7 of TIOPA 2010 have the same meaning in this paragraph as they have in that Part.

Time limits for elections relating to financial statements of a worldwide group

27 (1) In section 484 of TIOPA 2010, subsection (5) (which requires the date specified in an election under subsection (3) of that section to be on or after the day on which the election is made) does not apply in relation to an election made on or before 31 March 2018.

(2) In section 486 of that Act, subsection (5)(a) (which requires an election under that section to be made before the end-day of the new period of account) does not apply in relation to an election made on or before 31 March 2018.

458   *Finance (No. 2) Act 2017 (c. 32)*
Schedule 5 — Corporate interest restriction
Part 4 — Commencement and transitional provision

Time limit relating to appointment of reporting company or filing interest restriction return

28   (1) Paragraph 1(4)(a) of Schedule 7A to TIOPA 2010 (notice of the appointment of reporting company ineffective if given outside the period specified in that provision) does not apply to a notice that—

        (a) is given on or before 31 March 2018, and

        (b) would otherwise be of no effect by reason only of the expiry of the period specified in that provision.

    (2) Paragraph 2(4)(a) of that Schedule (notice of the revocation of the appointment of reporting company ineffective if given outside the period specified in that provision) does not apply to a notice that—

        (a) is given on or before 31 March 2018, and

        (b) would otherwise be of no effect by reason only of the expiry of the period specified in that provision.

    (3) Where the date determined under paragraph 7(5) of that Schedule as the filing date in relation to a period of account of a worldwide group would (apart from this sub-paragraph) be a date before 30 June 2018, that provision has effect as if it provided for the filing date in relation to the period to be 30 June 2018.

Change of accounting policy

29   (1) For the purposes of Part 10 of TIOPA 2010 a debit or credit to which this paragraph applies is to be ignored.

    (2) This paragraph applies to a debit or credit if—

        (a) it is brought into account under the Loan Relationships and Derivative Contracts (Change of Accounting Practice) Regulations 2004 (S.I. 2004/3271), and

        (b) the later period, in relation to the change of accounting policy to which the debit or credit relates, begins before 1 April 2017.

    (3) In sub-paragraph (2) "the later period" has the same meaning as in the regulations mentioned in that sub-paragraph.

Adjustments under Schedule 7 to F(No.2)A 2015

30   (1) For the purposes of Part 10 of TIOPA 2010 a debit or credit to which this paragraph applies is to be ignored.

    (2) This paragraph applies to a debit or credit if—

        (a) it is brought into account for the purposes of Part 5 of CTA 2009 by virtue of paragraphs 115 and 116 of Schedule 7 to F(No.2)A 2015 (transitional adjustments relating to loan relationships), or

        (b) it is brought into account for the purposes of Part 7 of CTA 2009 by virtue of paragraphs 120 and 121 of that Schedule (transitional adjustments relating to derivative contracts).

Power to make elections under Disregard Regulations for pre-1 April 2020 derivative contracts

31   (1) A company which is a UK group company of a worldwide group on 1 April 2017 may elect for the Disregard Regulations to have effect as if—

Finance (No. 2) Act 2017 (c. 32)
Schedule 5 – Corporate interest restriction
Part 4 – Commencement and transitional provision

459

  (a) the company had made an election ("the disregard election") under regulation 6A of those Regulations for the purposes of regulation 6(1)(a) of those Regulations,

  (b) the disregard election applied to regulations 7, 8 and 9 of those Regulations, and

  (c) the disregard election had effect in relation to derivative contracts entered into by the company before 1 April 2020.

(2) The election has effect for the calculation under Part 10 of TIOPA 2010 of—

  (a) the tax-interest expense amounts and tax-interest income amounts of the company and any relevant transferee company, and

  (b) the adjusted corporation tax earnings under section 406 of that Act of the company and any relevant transferee company.

(3) A company is a "relevant transferee company" if regulation 6B or 6C of the Disregard Regulations applies in relation to the company as the transferee mentioned in the regulation (on the assumption that an election has been made before the transfer under this paragraph).

(4) An election under this paragraph has effect only if every company which was a UK group company of the worldwide group on 1 April 2017 (other than one which was dormant on that date or at the time the election is made) also makes an election under this paragraph.

(5) An election under this paragraph—

  (a) must be made before 1 April 2018, and

  (b) is irrevocable.

(6) Section 457 of TIOPA 2010 is to apply in relation to debits resulting from an election under this paragraph.

(7) In this paragraph "the Disregard Regulations" means the Loan Relationships and Derivative Contracts (Disregard and Bringing into Account of Profits and Losses) Regulations 2004 (S.I. 2004/3256).

(8) Expressions used in this paragraph and in Part 10 of TIOPA 2010 have the same meaning in this paragraph as they have in that Part.

Qualifying infrastructure companies

32 (1) In the case of an accounting period of a company beginning before 1 April 2018, the company may make an election under section 433 or 444 of TIOPA 2010 before that date.

(2) Companies making an election under section 435 of TIOPA 2010 before 1 April 2018 may specify a date in the election from which it has effect which is before the date on which the election is made.

33 (1) This paragraph applies in the case of an accounting period of a company beginning before 1 April 2018 ("the transitional accounting period") if—

  (a) the company does not meet the public infrastructure assets test, or the public infrastructure income test, for the transitional accounting period, but

  (b) in the case of each test that it does not meet as mentioned in paragraph (a), the company would meet the test for an accounting period that includes that date and is at least 3 months long.

460   *Finance (No. 2) Act 2017 (c. 32)*
Schedule 5 — Corporate interest restriction
Part 4 — Commencement and transitional provision

(2) For the purposes of section 433 of TIOPA 2010 the company is treated as meeting the test (or tests) for the transitional accounting period.

(3) For the purposes of sections 438 and 440 to 442 of TIOPA 2010 such adjustments to the relevant amounts are to be made as are just and reasonable, having regard to the extent to which, but for this paragraph, the company would not have met the public infrastructure assets test, or the public infrastructure income test, for the transitional accounting period.

(4) For this purpose "the relevant amounts" means—

    (a) amounts that would otherwise have qualified as exempt amounts under section 438,

    (b) amounts that would otherwise have been treated as mentioned in section 440,

    (c) the tax-EBITDA of the company, and

    (d) the amounts that would otherwise have been left of account as a result of section 442.

(5) Expressions used in this paragraph and in section 433 of TIOPA 2010 have the same meaning in this paragraph as they have in that section.

Counteracting effect of avoidance arrangements

34   (1) This paragraph applies in relation to section 461 of TIOPA 2010.

    (2) Section 461 applies in relation to arrangements whenever entered into.

    (3) Arrangements are not "relevant avoidance arrangements" for the purposes of section 461 so far as—

        (a) they secure that an amount paid before 1 April 2017 is brought into account in an accounting period ending before that date, and

        (b) directly in consequence of the amount being brought into account as mentioned in paragraph (a), there is a reduction in the tax-interest expense amounts that could otherwise have been left out of account under Part 10 of TIOPA 2010.

    (4) If an accounting period begins before 1 April 2017 and ends on or after that date, sub-paragraph (3) is to have effect as if so much of the accounting period as falls before that date, and so much of that period as falls on or after that date, were treated as separate accounting periods.

    (5) Arrangements are not "relevant avoidance arrangements" for the purposes of section 461 if the obtaining of any tax advantages that would otherwise arise from them can reasonably be regarded as arising wholly from commercial restructuring arrangements entered into in connection with the commencement of Part 10 of TIOPA 2010.

    (6) For this purpose "commercial restructuring arrangements" means—

        (a) arrangements that, but for that Part, would have resulted in significantly more corporation tax becoming payable as a result of one or more loan relationships being brought within the charge to corporation tax, or

        (b) arrangements that—

            (i) are designed to secure, in a way that is wholly consistent with its policy objectives, the benefit of a relief expressly conferred by a provision of that Part, and

Finance (No. 2) Act 2017 (c. 32)
Schedule 5 – Corporate interest restriction
Part 4 – Commencement and transitional provision

461

      (ii)   are effected by taking only ordinary commercial steps in accordance with a generally prevailing commercial practice.

(7)   This paragraph is to be read as if it formed part of section 461.

Commencement of orders or regulations containing consequential provision

35   (1)   This paragraph applies in relation to any order or regulations made before 1 April 2018 by the Treasury or Commissioners containing provision that is consequential on provision made by this Schedule.

    (2)   Any order or regulations to which this paragraph applies may contain provision (however expressed) for securing that the consequential provision made by the order or regulations has effect in accordance with paragraph 25 (commencement) as if the consequential provision were included in the corporate interest restriction amendments mentioned in that paragraph.

Interpretation

36   References in this Part of this Schedule to Part 10 of TIOPA 2010 are to Part 10 of that Act as inserted by Parts 1 and 2 of this Schedule.

SCHEDULE 6   Section 21

RELIEF FOR PRODUCTION OF MUSEUM AND GALLERY EXHIBITIONS

PART 1

AMENDMENT OF CTA 2009

1   After Part 15D of CTA 2009 insert—

"PART 15E

MUSEUMS AND GALLERIES EXHIBITION TAX RELIEF

CHAPTER 1

INTRODUCTION

Overview

1218ZA Overview

    (1)   This Part is about the production of museum and gallery exhibitions, and applies for corporation tax purposes.

    (2)   This Chapter explains what is meant by "exhibition" and "touring exhibition" and how a company comes to be treated as the primary production company or a secondary production company for an exhibition.

    (3)   Chapter 2 is about the taxation of the activities of a production company and includes—

462

Finance (No. 2) Act 2017 (c. 32)
Schedule 6 — Relief for production of museum and gallery exhibitions
Part 1 — Amendment of CTA 2009

(a) provision for the company's activities in relation to its exhibition to be treated as a separate trade, and

(b) provision about the calculation of the profits and losses of that trade.

(4) Chapter 3 is about relief (called "museums and galleries exhibition tax relief") which may be given to a production company in relation to an exhibition—

(a) by way of additional deductions to be made in calculating the profits or losses of the company's separate trade, or

(b) by way of a payment (a "museums and galleries exhibition tax credit") to be made on the company's surrender of losses from that trade,

and describes the conditions a company must meet to qualify for museums and galleries exhibition tax relief.

(5) Chapter 4 contains provision about the use of losses of the separate trade (including provision about relief for terminal losses).

(6) Chapter 5 provides—

(a) for relief under Chapters 3 and 4 to be given on a provisional basis, and

(b) for such relief to be withdrawn if it turns out that conditions that must be met for such relief to be given are not actually met.

Interpretation

1218ZAA "Exhibition"

(1) In this Part "exhibition" means a curated public display of an organised collection of objects or works (or of a single object or work) considered to be of scientific, historic, artistic or cultural interest.

(2) But a display is not an exhibition if—

(a) it is organised in connection with a competition of any kind,

(b) its main purpose, or one of its main purposes, is to sell anything displayed or to advertise or promote any goods or services,

(c) it includes a live performance by any person,

(d) anything displayed is for sale, or

(e) anything displayed is alive.

(3) Subsection (2) does not prevent a display being an exhibition if it includes a live performance by a person which is merely incidental to, or forms a merely incidental part of, the collection displayed.

(4) A display is "public" if the general public is admitted to it, whether or not the public is charged for admission.

(5) A display does not fall outside subsection (4) just because visitors other than the general public are admitted to it for a single session or a small number of sessions.

Finance (No. 2) Act 2017 (c. 32)
Schedule 6 — Relief for production of museum and gallery exhibitions
Part 1 — Amendment of CTA 2009

463

1218ZAB "Touring exhibition"

(1) In this Part an exhibition is a "touring exhibition" if conditions A to E are met.

(2) Condition A is that—
    (a) there is a primary production company for the exhibition (see section 1218ZAC), and
    (b) the primary production company is within the charge to corporation tax.

(3) Condition B is that the primary production company intends, when planning the exhibition, that conditions C, D and E should be met in relation to it.

(4) Condition C is that the exhibition is held at two or more venues.

(5) Condition D is that at least 25% of the objects or works displayed at the first venue at which the exhibition is held are also displayed at every subsequent venue at which the exhibition is held.

(6) Condition E is that the period between the deinstalling of the exhibition at one venue and the installation of the exhibition at the next venue does not exceed 6 months.

1218ZAC Primary production company

(1) In this Part a company is the primary production company for an exhibition if the company (acting otherwise than in partnership) meets conditions A and B.

(2) Condition A is that the company—
    (a) makes an effective creative, technical or artistic contribution to the exhibition, and
    (b) directly negotiates for, contracts for and pays for rights, goods and services in relation to the exhibition.

(3) Condition B is that—
    (a) where the exhibition is held at just one venue, the company is responsible for the production of the exhibition at that venue;
    (b) where the exhibition is held at two or more venues, the company is responsible for the production of the exhibition at (at least) the first of those venues.

(4) For the purposes of this section and section 1218ZAD, a company is responsible for the production of the exhibition at a venue if—
    (a) it is responsible for producing and running the exhibition at the venue,
    (b) where the exhibition is at the venue for a limited time, it is responsible for deinstalling and closing the exhibition at the venue, and
    (c) it is actively engaged in decision-making in relation to the exhibition at the venue.

(5) If more than one company meets conditions A and B in relation to the production of the exhibition, the company that most directly meets those conditions is the primary production company for the exhibition.

(6)　If no company meets conditions A and B in relation to the production of the exhibition, there is no primary production company for the exhibition.

1218ZAD Secondary production company

(1)　If an exhibition is held at two or more venues, there may be one or more secondary production companies for the exhibition.

(2)　In this Part a company is the secondary production company for an exhibition at a venue if the company meets conditions C and D.

(3)　Condition C is that the company (acting otherwise than in partnership) is responsible for the production of the exhibition at the venue.

(4)　Condition D is that the company is not the primary production company.

(5)　If more than one company meets conditions C and D in relation to the production of the exhibition at the venue, the company that is most directly responsible for the production of the exhibition at the venue is the secondary production company for the exhibition at the venue.

(6)　If no company meets conditions C and D in relation to the production of the exhibition at the venue, there is no secondary production company for the exhibition at the venue.

CHAPTER 2

TAXATION OF ACTIVITIES OF PRODUCTION COMPANY

Separate exhibition trade

1218ZB Separate exhibition trade

(1)　Subsection (2) applies to a company in relation to an exhibition if, and only for so long as, the company qualifies for museums and galleries exhibition tax relief in relation to the production of the exhibition (see section 1218ZCA).

(2)　The company's activities in relation to the production of the exhibition are treated as a trade separate from any other activities of the company (including activities in relation to the production of any other exhibition).

(3)　In this Part the separate trade mentioned in subsection (2) is called "the separate exhibition trade".

(4)　Subsections (5) and (6) apply where the company is the primary production company for the exhibition.

(5)　The company is treated as beginning to carry on the separate exhibition trade—

　　(a)　at the beginning of the production stage of the exhibition at the first venue at which it is held, or

Finance (No. 2) Act 2017 (c. 32)
Schedule 6 — Relief for production of museum and gallery exhibitions
Part 1 — Amendment of CTA 2009

465

(b) if earlier, at the time of the first receipt by the company of any income from the production of the exhibition.

(6) The company is treated as ceasing to carry on the separate trade when the exhibition closes at the last venue at which it is held.

(7) Subsections (8) and (9) apply where the company is a secondary production company for the exhibition.

(8) The company is treated as beginning to carry on the separate exhibition trade—

    (a) at the beginning of the production stage of the exhibition at the first venue for which the company is the secondary production company, or

    (b) if earlier, at the time of the first receipt by the company of any income from the production of the exhibition.

(9) The company is treated as ceasing to carry on the separate trade when the exhibition closes at the last venue for which the company is the secondary production company.

Profits and losses of separate exhibition trade

1218ZBA Calculation of profits or losses of separate exhibition trade

(1) This section applies for the purpose of calculating the profits or losses of the separate exhibition trade.

(2) For the first period of account during which the separate exhibition trade is carried on, the following are brought into account—

    (a) as a debit, the costs of the production of the exhibition incurred to date;

    (b) as a credit, the proportion of the estimated total income from that production treated as earned at the end of that period.

(3) For subsequent periods of account the following are brought into account—

    (a) as a debit, the difference between the amount ("C") of the costs of the production of the exhibition incurred to date and the amount corresponding to C for the previous period, and

    (b) as a credit, the difference between the proportion ("PI") of the estimated total income from that production treated as earned at the end of that period and the amount corresponding to PI for the previous period.

(4) The proportion of the estimated total income treated as earned at the end of a period of account is—

$$\frac{C}{T} \times I$$

where—

    C is the total to date of costs incurred;

    T is the estimated total cost of the production of the exhibition;

    I is the estimated total income from the production of the exhibition.

466

Finance (No. 2) Act 2017 (c. 32)
Schedule 6 — Relief for production of museum and gallery exhibitions
Part 1 — Amendment of CTA 2009

1218ZBB Income from the production

(1) References in this Chapter to income from a production of an exhibition are to any receipts by the company in connection with the production or exploitation of the exhibition.

(2) This includes—

    (a) receipts from the sale of tickets or of rights in the exhibition;

    (b) royalties or other payments in connection with the exploitation of the exhibition or aspects of it (such as a particular exhibit);

    (c) payments for rights to produce merchandise;

    (d) a grant designated as made for the purposes of the exhibition;

    (e) receipts by the company by way of a profit share agreement.

1218ZBC Costs of the production

(1) References in this Chapter to the costs of a production of an exhibition are to expenditure incurred by the company on—

    (a) activities involved in developing, producing, running, deinstalling and closing the exhibition, or

    (b) activities with a view to exploiting the exhibition.

(2) This is subject to any provision of the Corporation Tax Acts prohibiting the making of a deduction, or restricting the extent to which a deduction is allowed, in calculating the profits of a trade.

1218ZBD When costs are taken to be incurred

(1) For the purposes of this Chapter, the costs that have been incurred on a production of an exhibition at a given time do not include any amount that has not been paid unless it is the subject of an unconditional obligation to pay.

(2) Where an obligation to pay an amount is linked to income being earned from the production of the exhibition, the obligation is not treated as having become unconditional unless an appropriate amount of income is or has been brought into account under section 1218ZBA.

1218ZBE Pre-trading expenditure

(1) This section applies if, before the company begins to carry on the separate exhibition trade, it incurs expenditure on activities falling within section 1218ZBC(1)(a).

(2) The expenditure may be treated as expenditure of the separate exhibition trade and as if incurred immediately after the company begins to carry on that trade.

(3) If expenditure so treated has previously been taken into account for other tax purposes, the company must amend any relevant company tax return accordingly.

(4) Any amendment or assessment necessary to give effect to subsection (3) may be made despite any limitation on the time within which an amendment or assessment may normally be made.

Finance (No. 2) Act 2017 (c. 32)
Schedule 6 — Relief for production of museum and gallery exhibitions
Part 1 — Amendment of CTA 2009

467

1218ZBF Estimates

Estimates for the purposes of section 1218ZBA must be made as at the balance sheet date for each period of account, on a just and reasonable basis taking into consideration all relevant circumstances.

CHAPTER 3

MUSEUMS AND GALLERIES EXHIBITION TAX RELIEF

Introduction

1218ZC Overview of museums and galleries exhibition tax relief

(1) Relief under this Chapter ("museums and galleries exhibition tax relief") is given by way of—

    (a) additional deductions (see sections 1218ZCE to 1218ZCG), and

    (b) museums and galleries exhibition tax credits (see sections 1218ZCH to 1218ZCK).

(2) See Schedule 18 to FA 1998 (in particular, Part 9D) for provision about the procedure for making claims for museums and galleries exhibition tax relief.

Companies qualifying for museums and galleries exhibition tax relief

1218ZCA Companies qualifying for museums and galleries exhibition tax relief

(1) A company qualifies for museums and galleries exhibition tax relief in relation to the production of an exhibition if conditions A to D are met.

(2) Condition A is that the company is—

    (a) the primary production company for the exhibition, or

    (b) a secondary production company for the exhibition.

(3) Condition B is that the company is—

    (a) a charitable company which maintains a museum or gallery,

    (b) wholly owned by a charity which maintains a museum or gallery, or

    (c) wholly owned by a local authority which maintains a museum or gallery.

See section 1218ZCB for the interpretation of paragraphs (b) and (c).

(4) Condition C is that at the beginning of the planning stage, the company intends that the exhibition should be public (within the meaning given by section 1218ZAA).

(5) Condition D is that the EEA expenditure condition is met (see section 1218ZCC).

(6) For the purposes of subsection (3) "museum or gallery" includes—

    (a) a library or archive, and

468   *Finance (No. 2) Act 2017 (c. 32)*
Schedule 6 — Relief for production of museum and gallery exhibitions
Part 1 — Amendment of CTA 2009

    (b) a site where a collection of objects or works (or a single object or work) considered to be of scientific, historic, artistic or cultural interest is exhibited outdoors (or partly outdoors).

 (7) There is further related provision in section 1218ZCM (tax avoidance arrangements).

1218ZCB Interpretation of section 1218ZCA(3)(b) and (c)

 (1) For the purposes of section 1218ZCA(3)(b) a company is "wholly owned by a charity which maintains a museum or gallery" if condition A or B is met.

 (2) Condition A is that—

    (a) the company has an ordinary share capital, and

    (b) every part of that share capital is owned by—

      (i) a charity which maintains a museum or gallery, or

      (ii) two charities, each of which maintains a museum or gallery.

 (3) Condition B is that—

    (a) the company is limited by guarantee,

    (b) there are no more than two beneficiaries of the company, and

    (c) the beneficiary, or each beneficiary, is—

      (i) a charity which maintains a museum or gallery, or

      (ii) a company wholly owned by a charity which maintains a museum or gallery.

 (4) For the purposes of section 1218ZCA(3)(c) a company is "wholly owned by a local authority" if—

    (a) where the company has an ordinary share capital, every part of that share capital is owned by the local authority, or

    (b) where the company is limited by guarantee, the local authority is the sole beneficiary of the company.

 (5) Ordinary share capital of a company is treated as owned by a charity or a local authority if the charity or local authority (as the case may be)—

    (a) directly or indirectly owns that share capital within the meaning of Chapter 3 of Part 24 of CTA 2010, or

    (b) would be taken so to own it if references in that Chapter to a body corporate included references to a charity or local authority which is not a body corporate.

 (6) A beneficiary of a company is a person who—

    (a) is beneficially entitled to participate in the company's divisible profits, or

    (b) will be beneficially entitled to share in any of the company's net assets available for distribution on its winding up.

 (7) In this section "museum or gallery" has the same meaning it has for the purposes of section 1218ZCA.

Finance (No. 2) Act 2017 (c. 32)
Schedule 6 — Relief for production of museum and gallery exhibitions
Part 1 — Amendment of CTA 2009

469

1218ZCC The EEA expenditure condition

(1) The "EEA expenditure condition" is that at least 25% of the core expenditure on the production of the exhibition incurred by the company is EEA expenditure.

(2) In this Part "EEA expenditure" means expenditure on goods or services that are provided from within the European Economic Area.

(3) Any apportionment of expenditure as between EEA and non-EEA expenditure for the purposes of this Part is to be made on a just and reasonable basis.

(4) The Treasury may by regulations —
    (a) amend the percentage specified in subsection (1);
    (b) amend subsection (2).

(5) See also sections 1218ZE and 1218ZEA (which are about the giving of relief provisionally on the basis that the EEA expenditure condition will be met).

1218ZCD "Core expenditure"

(1) Subject to the following provisions of this section, in this Part "core expenditure", in relation to a company's production of an exhibition, means expenditure on the activities involved in producing, deinstalling and closing the exhibition at every relevant venue.

(2) For the purposes of subsection (1) a venue is a "relevant venue" in relation to a company if the company's activities in relation to the exhibition at the venue form part of the company's separate exhibition trade.

(3) Expenditure on the activities involved in deinstalling and closing the exhibition at a venue is core expenditure only if the period between the opening and closing of the exhibition at the venue is 12 months or less.

(4) Expenditure on the storage of exhibits for an exhibition which is held at just one venue is not core expenditure.

(5) Where a company incurs expenditure on the storage of exhibits for an exhibition which is held at two or more venues, the amount of such expenditure which is core expenditure is limited to the amount of relevant storage expenditure (if any) incurred by the company in respect of a period of 4 months or less.

(6) For the purposes of subsection (5) expenditure in relation to the exhibition is "relevant storage expenditure" if —
    (a) the expenditure is incurred in respect of the storage of exhibits between the deinstallation of the exhibition at one venue and the opening of the exhibition at the next venue, and
    (b) the exhibits are not stored at a venue at which the exhibition has been held or is to be held.

(7) Expenditure of the following kinds is not core expenditure —

470

Finance (No. 2) Act 2017 (c. 32)
Schedule 6 — Relief for production of museum and gallery exhibitions
Part 1 — Amendment of CTA 2009

- (a) expenditure on any matters not directly involved with putting on the exhibition (for instance, financing, marketing, legal services and promotional events),
- (b) speculative development expenditure on initial exhibition concepts and feasibility,
- (c) expenditure on the ordinary running of the exhibition (for instance, invigilation and the maintenance of exhibits),
- (d) expenditure in relation to any live performance,
- (e) expenditure on further development of the exhibition during the running stage,
- (f) expenditure on purchasing the exhibits, and
- (g) expenditure on infrastructure, unless that expenditure is incurred solely for the purposes of the exhibition.

Additional deduction

1218ZCE Claim for additional deduction

(1) A company which qualifies for museums and galleries exhibition tax relief in relation to the production of an exhibition may claim an additional deduction in relation to the production.

(2) A claim under subsection (1) is made with respect to an accounting period.

(3) Where a company has made a claim, the company is entitled to make an additional deduction, in accordance with section 1218ZCF, in calculating the profit or loss of the separate exhibition trade for the accounting period concerned.

(4) Where the company tax return in which a claim is made is for an accounting period later than that in which the company begins to carry on the separate exhibition trade, the company must make any amendments of company tax returns for earlier periods that may be necessary.

(5) Any amendment or assessment necessary to give effect to subsection (4) may be made despite any limitation on the time within which an amendment or assessment may normally be made.

1218ZCF Amount of additional deduction

(1) The amount of an additional deduction to which a company is entitled as a result of a claim under section 1218ZCE is calculated as follows.

(2) For the first period of account during which the separate exhibition trade is carried on, the amount of the additional deduction is E, where E is—

- (a) so much of the qualifying expenditure incurred to date as is EEA expenditure, or
- (b) if less, 80% of the total amount of qualifying expenditure incurred to date.

Finance (No. 2) Act 2017 (c. 32)
Schedule 6 — Relief for production of museum and gallery exhibitions
Part 1 — Amendment of CTA 2009

471

(3) For any period of account after the first, the amount of the additional deduction is—

$$E - P$$

where E is—

    (a) so much of the qualifying expenditure incurred to date as is EEA expenditure, or

    (b) if less, 80% of the total amount of qualifying expenditure incurred to date, and

P is the total amount of the additional deductions given for previous periods.

(4) The Treasury may by regulations amend the percentage specified in subsection (2) or (3).

(5) If a period of account of the separate exhibition trade does not coincide with an accounting period, any necessary apportionments are to be made by reference to the number of days in the periods concerned.

1218ZCG "Qualifying expenditure"

(1) In this Chapter "qualifying expenditure", in relation to the production of an exhibition, means core expenditure (see section 1218ZCD) on the production that—

    (a) falls to be taken into account under sections 1218ZBA to 1218ZBF in calculating the profit or loss of the separate exhibition trade for tax purposes,

    (b) is not expenditure which is otherwise relievable, and

    (c) is incurred on or before 31 March 2022.

(2) For the purposes of this section expenditure is "otherwise relievable" if it is expenditure in respect of which (assuming a claim were made) the company would be entitled to—

    (a) an R&D expenditure credit under Chapter 6A of Part 3,

    (b) relief under Part 13 (additional relief for expenditure on research and development),

    (c) film tax relief under Chapter 3 of Part 15,

    (d) television tax relief under Chapter 3 of Part 15A,

    (e) video games tax relief under Chapter 3 of Part 15B,

    (f) an additional deduction under Part 15C (theatrical productions),

    (g) a theatre tax credit under Part 15C, or

    (h) orchestra tax relief under Chapter 3 of Part 15D.

(3) The Treasury may by regulations amend paragraph (c) of subsection (1) so as to substitute a later date for the date for the time being specified in that paragraph.

472   *Finance (No. 2) Act 2017 (c. 32)*
Schedule 6 — Relief for production of museum and gallery exhibitions
Part 1 — Amendment of CTA 2009

Museums and galleries exhibition tax credits

1218ZCH Museums and galleries exhibition tax credit claimable if company has surrenderable loss

(1) A company which qualifies for museums and galleries exhibition tax relief in relation to the production of an exhibition may claim a museums and galleries exhibition tax credit in relation to the production for an accounting period in which the company has a surrenderable loss.

(2) Section 1218ZCI sets out how to calculate the amount of any surrenderable loss that the company has in the accounting period.

(3) A company making a claim may surrender the whole or part of its surrenderable loss in the accounting period.

(4) Subject to section 1218ZCK, the amount of the museums and galleries exhibition tax credit to which a company making a claim is entitled for the accounting period is—

    (a) 25% of the amount of the loss surrendered if the exhibition is a touring exhibition (see section 1218ZAB), or

    (b) 20% of the amount of the loss surrendered if the exhibition is not a touring exhibition.

(5) The company's available loss for the accounting period (see section 1218ZCI(2)) is reduced by the amount surrendered.

1218ZCI Amount of surrenderable loss

(1) The company's surrenderable loss in the accounting period is—

    (a) the company's available loss for the period in the separate exhibition trade (see subsections (2) and (3)), or

    (b) if less, the available qualifying expenditure for the period (see subsections (4) and (5)).

(2) The company's available loss for an accounting period is—

$$L + RUL$$

where—

    L is the amount of the company's loss for the period in the separate exhibition trade, and

    RUL is the amount of any relevant unused loss of the company (see subsection (3)).

(3) The "relevant unused loss" of a company is so much of any available loss of the company for the previous accounting period as has not been—

    (a) surrendered under section 1218ZCH, or

    (b) carried forward under section 45 or 45B of CTA 2010 and set against profits of the separate exhibition trade.

(4) For the first period of account during which the separate exhibition trade is carried on, the available qualifying expenditure is the amount that is E for that period for the purposes of section 1218ZCF(2).

Finance (No. 2) Act 2017 (c. 32)   473
Schedule 6 — Relief for production of museum and gallery exhibitions
Part 1 — Amendment of CTA 2009

(5) For any period of account after the first, the available qualifying expenditure is—

$$E - S$$

where—

     E is the amount that is E for that period for the purposes of section 1218ZCF(3), and

     S is the total amount previously surrendered under section 1218ZCH.

(6) If a period of account of the separate exhibition trade does not coincide with an accounting period, any necessary apportionments are to be made by reference to the number of days in the periods concerned.

1218ZCJ Payment in respect of museums and galleries exhibition tax credit

(1) If a company—

     (a) is entitled to a museums and galleries exhibition tax credit for an accounting period, and

     (b) makes a claim,

the Commissioners for Her Majesty's Revenue and Customs ("the Commissioners") must pay the amount of the credit to the company.

(2) An amount payable in respect of—

     (a) a museums and galleries exhibition tax credit, or

     (b) interest on a museums and galleries exhibition tax credit under section 826 of ICTA,

may be applied in discharging any liability of the company to pay corporation tax.

To the extent that it is so applied the Commissioners' liability under subsection (1) is discharged.

(3) If the company's company tax return for the accounting period is enquired into by the Commissioners, no payment in respect of a museums and galleries exhibition tax credit for that period need be made before the Commissioners' enquiries are completed (see paragraph 32 of Schedule 18 to FA 1998).

In those circumstances the Commissioners may make a payment on a provisional basis of such amount as they consider appropriate.

(4) No payment need be made in respect of a museums and galleries exhibition tax credit for an accounting period before the company has paid to the Commissioners any amount that it is required to pay for payment periods ending in that accounting period—

     (a) under PAYE regulations, or

     (b) in respect of Class 1 national insurance contributions under Part 1 of the Social Security Contributions and Benefits Act 1992 or Part 1 of the Social Security Contributions and Benefits (Northern Ireland) Act 1992.

(5) A payment in respect of a museums and galleries exhibition tax credit is not income of the company for any tax purpose.

474   *Finance (No. 2) Act 2017 (c. 32)*
Schedule 6 — Relief for production of museum and gallery exhibitions
Part 1 — Amendment of CTA 2009

1218ZCK Maximum museums and galleries exhibition tax credits payable

(1) Subsections (2) and (3) prescribe the maximum amount of museums and galleries exhibition tax credits which may be paid to a company under section 1218ZCJ in respect of the company's separate exhibition trade.

(2) Where the separate exhibition trade relates to the production of a touring exhibition, the maximum amount which may be paid to the company is £100,000.

(3) Where the separate exhibition trade relates to the production of an exhibition which is not a touring exhibition, the maximum amount which may be paid to the company is £80,000.

(4) In accordance with Commission Regulation (EU) No. 651/2014 of 17 June 2014 declaring certain categories of aid compatible with the internal market, the total amount of museums and galleries exhibition tax credits payable under section 1218ZCJ in the case of any undertaking is not to exceed 75 million euros per year.

1218ZCL No account to be taken of amount if unpaid

(1) In determining for the purposes of this Chapter the amount of costs incurred on a production of an exhibition at the end of a period of account, ignore any amount that has not been paid 4 months after the end of that period.

(2) This is without prejudice to the operation of section 1218ZBD (when costs are taken to be incurred).

Anti-avoidance etc

1218ZCM Tax avoidance arrangements

(1) A company does not qualify for museums and galleries exhibition tax relief in relation to the production of an exhibition if there are any tax avoidance arrangements relating to the production.

(2) Arrangements are "tax avoidance arrangements" if their main purpose, or one of their main purposes, is the obtaining of a tax advantage.

(3) In this section—

"arrangements" includes any scheme, agreement or understanding, whether or not legally enforceable;

"tax advantage" has the meaning given by section 1139 of CTA 2010.

1218ZCN Transactions not entered into for genuine commercial reasons

(1) A transaction is to be ignored for the purpose of determining museums and galleries exhibition tax relief so far as the transaction is attributable to arrangements (other than tax avoidance arrangements) entered into otherwise than for genuine commercial reasons.

(2) In this section "arrangements" and "tax avoidance arrangements" have the same meaning as in section 1218ZCM.

Finance (No. 2) Act 2017 (c. 32)
Schedule 6 — Relief for production of museum and gallery exhibitions
Part 1 — Amendment of CTA 2009

475

CHAPTER 4

LOSSES OF SEPARATE EXHIBITION TRADE

1218ZD Application of sections 1218ZDA to 1218ZDC

(1) Sections 1218ZDA to 1218ZDC apply to a company which is treated under section 1218ZB(2) as carrying on a separate trade in relation to the production of an exhibition.

(2) In those sections "the completion period" means the accounting period in which the company ceases to carry on the separate exhibition trade.

1218ZDA Restriction on use of losses before completion period

(1) This section applies if a loss is made by the company in the separate exhibition trade in an accounting period preceding the completion period.

(2) The loss is not available for loss relief, except to the extent that the loss may be carried forward under section 45 or 45B of CTA 2010 to be deducted from profits of the separate exhibition trade in a subsequent period.

(3) If the loss is carried forward under section 45 or 45B of CTA 2010 and deducted from profits of the separate exhibition trade in a subsequent period, the deduction is to be ignored for the purposes of section 269ZB of CTA 2010 (restriction on deductions from trading profits).

(4) In this section "loss relief" includes any means by which a loss might be used to reduce the amount in respect of which a company, or any other person, is chargeable to tax.

1218ZDB Use of losses in the completion period

(1) Subsection (2) applies if a loss made in the separate exhibition trade is carried forward under section 45 or 45B of CTA 2010 to the completion period.

(2) So much (if any) of the loss as is not attributable to museums and galleries exhibition tax relief (see subsection (4)) may be treated for the purposes of section 37 and Part 5 of CTA 2010 as if it were a loss made in the completion period.

(3) If a loss is made in the separate exhibition trade in the completion period, the amount of the loss that may be—
   (a) deducted from total profits of the same or an earlier period under section 37 of CTA 2010, or
   (b) surrendered as group relief under Part 5 of that Act,
   is restricted to the amount (if any) that is not attributable to museums and galleries exhibition tax relief (see subsection (4)).

(4) The amount of a loss in any period that is attributable to museums and galleries exhibition tax relief is found by—

476

Finance (No. 2) Act 2017 (c. 32)
Schedule 6 — Relief for production of museum and gallery exhibitions
Part 1 — Amendment of CTA 2009

> (a) calculating what the amount of the loss would have been if there had been no additional deduction under Chapter 3 in that or any earlier period, and
>
> (b) deducting that amount from the total amount of the loss.

(5) This section does not apply to a loss surrendered, or treated as carried forward, under section 1218ZDC (terminal losses).

1218ZDC Terminal losses

(1) This section applies if —

> (a) the company ceases to carry on the separate exhibition trade, and
>
> (b) if the company had not ceased to carry on that trade, it could have carried forward an amount under section 45 or 45B of CTA 2010 to be set against profits of that trade in a later period ("the terminal loss").

Below in this section the company is referred to as "company A" and the separate exhibition trade is referred to as "trade 1".

(2) If company A —

> (a) is treated under section 1218ZB(2) as carrying on a separate trade in relation to the production of another exhibition ("trade 2"), and
>
> (b) is carrying on trade 2 when it ceases to carry on trade 1,

company A may (on making a claim) make an election under subsection (3).

(3) The election is to have the terminal loss (or a part of it) treated —

> (a) in a case where the loss could have been carried forward under section 45 of CTA 2010 had trade 1 not ceased, as if it were a loss carried forward under that section to be set against the profits of trade 2 of the first accounting period beginning after the cessation and so on, and
>
> (b) in a case where the loss could have been carried forward under section 45B of CTA 2010 had trade 1 not ceased, as if it were a loss made in trade 2 which has been carried forward under that section to the first accounting period beginning after the cessation.

(4) Subsection (5) applies if —

> (a) another company ("company B") is treated under section 1218ZB(2) as carrying on a separate trade ("company B's trade") in relation to the production of —
>
>> (i) the exhibition which is the subject of trade 1, or
>>
>> (ii) another exhibition,
>
> (b) company B is carrying on company B's trade when company A ceases to carry on trade 1, and
>
> (c) company B is in the same group as company A for the purposes of Part 5 of CTA 2010 (group relief).

(5) Company A may surrender the loss (or a part of it) to company B.

(6) On the making of a claim by company B the amount surrendered is treated —

Finance (No. 2) Act 2017 (c. 32)
Schedule 6 — Relief for production of museum and gallery exhibitions
Part 1 — Amendment of CTA 2009

477

> (a) in a case where the amount could have been carried forward under section 45 of CTA 2010 had trade 1 not ceased, as if it were a loss carried forward by company B under that section to be set against the profits of company B's trade of the first accounting period beginning after the cessation and so on, and
>
> (b) in a case where the amount could have been carried forward under section 45B of CTA 2010 had trade 1 not ceased, as if it were a loss made in company B's trade which has been carried forward under that section to the first accounting period beginning after the cessation.

(7) The Treasury may by regulations make administrative provision in relation to the surrender of a loss under subsection (5) and the resulting claim under subsection (6).

(8) "Administrative provision" means provision corresponding, subject to such adaptations or other modifications as appear to the Treasury to be appropriate, to that made by Part 8 of Schedule 18 to FA 1998 (company tax returns: claims for group relief).

(9) A deduction under section 45 or 45B of CTA 2010 which is made in reliance on this section is to be ignored for the purposes of section 269ZB of that Act (restriction on deductions from trading profits).

CHAPTER 5

PROVISIONAL ENTITLEMENT TO RELIEF

1218ZE Provisional entitlement to relief

(1) In relation to a company and the production of an exhibition, "interim accounting period" means any accounting period that—
> (a) is one in which the company carries on the separate exhibition trade, and
> (b) precedes the accounting period in which it ceases to do so.

(2) A company is not entitled to museums and galleries exhibition tax relief for an interim accounting period unless—
> (a) its company tax return for the period states the amount of planned core expenditure on the production of the exhibition that is EEA expenditure (see section 1218ZCC(2)), and
> (b) that amount is such as to indicate that the EEA expenditure condition (see section 1218ZCC) will be met.

If those requirements are met, the company is provisionally treated in relation to that period as if the EEA expenditure condition were met.

1218ZEA Clawback of provisional relief

(1) If a statement is made under section 1218ZE(2) but it subsequently appears that the EEA expenditure condition will not be met on the company's ceasing to carry on the separate exhibition trade, the company—

478

Finance (No. 2) Act 2017 (c. 32)
Schedule 6 — Relief for production of museum and gallery exhibitions
Part 1 — Amendment of CTA 2009

     (a)   is not entitled to museums and galleries exhibition tax relief for any period for which its entitlement depended on such a statement, and

     (b)   must amend accordingly its company tax return for any such period.

(2)   When a company ceases to carry on the separate exhibition trade, the company's company tax return for the period in which that cessation occurs must—

     (a)   state that the company has ceased to carry on the separate exhibition trade, and

     (b)   be accompanied by a final statement of the amount of the core expenditure on the production of the exhibition that is EEA expenditure.

(3)   If that statement shows that the EEA expenditure condition is not met—

     (a)   the company is not entitled to museums and galleries exhibition tax relief or to relief under section 1218ZDC (transfer of terminal losses) for any period, and

     (b)   must amend accordingly its company tax return for any period for which such relief was claimed.

(4)   Any amendment or assessment necessary to give effect to this section may be made despite any limitation on the time within which an amendment or assessment may normally be made.

CHAPTER 6

INTERPRETATION

1218ZF Regulations about activities in relation to an exhibition

The Treasury may by regulations amend section 1218ZBC (costs of the production) or 1218ZCD ("core expenditure") for the purpose of providing that activities of a specified description are, or are not, to be regarded as activities involved in developing or (as the case may be) producing, running, deinstalling or closing—

     (a)   an exhibition, or

     (b)   an exhibition of a specified description.

1218ZFA Interpretation

In this Part—

    "company tax return" has the same meaning as in Schedule 18 to FA 1998 (see paragraph 3(1) of that Schedule);

    "core expenditure" has the meaning given by section 1218ZCD;

    "costs", in relation to an exhibition, has the meaning given by section 1218ZBC;

    "EEA expenditure" has the meaning given by section 1218ZCC(2);

    "EEA expenditure condition" has the meaning given by section 1218ZCC;

    "exhibition" has the meaning given by section 1218ZAA;

Finance (No. 2) Act 2017 (c. 32)
Schedule 6 — Relief for production of museum and gallery exhibitions
Part 1 — Amendment of CTA 2009

479

"income", in relation to an exhibition, has the meaning given by section 1218ZBB;

"museums and galleries exhibition tax relief" is to be read in accordance with Chapter 3 (see in particular section 1218ZC(1));

"primary production company" has the meaning given by section 1218ZAC;

"qualifying expenditure" has the meaning given by section 1218ZCG;

"secondary production company" has the meaning given by section 1218ZAD;

"the separate exhibition trade" is to be read in accordance with section 1218ZB;

"touring exhibition" has the meaning given by section 1218ZAB."

PART 2

CONSEQUENTIAL AMENDMENTS

ICTA

2   (1) Section 826 of ICTA (interest on tax overpaid) is amended as follows.

(2) In subsection (1), after paragraph (fd) insert—

"(fe)   a payment of museums and galleries exhibition tax credit falls to be made to a company; or".

(3) In subsection (3C), for "or orchestra tax credit" substitute ", orchestra tax credit or museums and galleries exhibition tax credit".

(4) In subsection (8A)—

(a)   in paragraph (a), for "or (fd)" substitute ", (fd) or (fe)", and

(b)   in paragraph (b)(ii), after "orchestra tax credit" insert "or museums and galleries exhibition tax credit".

(5) In subsection (8BA), after "orchestra tax credit" (in both places) insert "or museums and galleries exhibition tax credit".

FA 1998

3   Schedule 18 to FA 1998 (company tax returns, assessments and related matters) is amended in accordance with paragraphs 4 to 6.

4   In paragraph 10 (other claims and elections to be included in return), in sub-paragraph (4), for "or 15D" substitute ", 15D or 15E".

5   (1) Paragraph 52 (recovery of excessive repayments etc) is amended as follows.

(2) In sub-paragraph (2), after paragraph (bh) insert—

"(bi)   museums and galleries exhibition tax credit under Part 15E of that Act,".

(3) In sub-paragraph (5)—

480   *Finance (No. 2) Act 2017 (c. 32)*
Schedule 6 — Relief for production of museum and gallery exhibitions
Part 2 — Consequential amendments

        (a)   after paragraph (aj) insert—

                "(ak)   an amount of museums and galleries exhibition tax credit paid to a company for an accounting period,", and

        (b)   in the words after paragraph (b), after "(aj)" insert ", (ak)".

6   In Part 9D (certain claims for tax relief)—

        (a)   in the heading, for "or 15D" substitute ", 15D or 15E", and

        (b)   in paragraph 83S (introduction), after sub-paragraph (f) insert—

                "(g)   museums and galleries exhibition tax relief."

CAA 2001

7   In Schedule A1 to CAA 2001 (first-year tax credits), in paragraph 11(4), omit the "and" at the end of paragraph (f) and after paragraph (g) insert ", and

                (h)   Chapter 3 of Part 15E of that Act (museums and galleries exhibition tax credits)."

FA 2007

8   In Schedule 24 to FA 2007 (penalties for errors), in paragraph 28(fa) (meaning of "corporation tax credit"), omit the "or" at the end of paragraph (ivd) and after that paragraph insert—

                "(ive)   a museums and galleries exhibition tax credit under Chapter 3 of Part 15E of that Act, or".

CTA 2009

9   CTA 2009 is amended in accordance with paragraphs 10 to 14.

10   In section 104BA (restriction on claiming other tax reliefs), after subsection (4) insert—

        "(5)   For provision prohibiting an R&D expenditure credit being given under this Chapter and relief being given under Chapter 3 of Part 15E (museums and galleries exhibition tax relief), see section 1218ZCG(2)."

11   In Part 8 (intangible fixed assets), in Chapter 10 (excluded assets), after section 808D insert—

"808E Assets representing expenditure incurred in course of separate exhibition trade

        (1)   This Part does not apply to an intangible fixed asset held by a museums and galleries exhibition production company so far as the asset represents expenditure on an exhibition that is treated under Part 15E as expenditure of a separate trade (see particularly sections 1218ZB and 1218ZBE).

        (2)   In this section—

            "exhibition" has the same meaning as in Part 15E (see section 1218ZAA);

            "museums and galleries exhibition production company" means a company which, for the purposes of that Part, is the primary production company or a secondary production

Finance (No. 2) Act 2017 (c. 32)
Schedule 6 – Relief for production of museum and gallery exhibitions
Part 2 – Consequential amendments

481

company for an exhibition (see sections 1218ZAC and 1218ZAD)."

12   In section 1040ZA (restriction on claiming other tax reliefs), after subsection (4) insert—

"(5)   For provision prohibiting relief being given under this Part and under Chapter 3 of Part 15E (museums and galleries exhibition tax relief), see section 1218ZCG(2)."

13   In section 1310 (orders and regulations), in subsection (4), after paragraph (eo) insert—

"(ep)   section 1218ZCC (EEA expenditure condition),
 (eq)   section 1218ZCF (amount of additional deduction),
 (er)   section 1218ZF (regulations about activities in relation to exhibition),".

14   In Schedule 4 (index of defined expressions), insert at the appropriate places—

"company tax return (in Part 15E)	section 1218ZFA"
"core expenditure (in Part 15E)	section 1218ZCD"
"costs, in relation to an exhibition (in Part 15E)	section 1218ZBC"
"EEA expenditure (in Part 15E)	section 1218ZCC(2)"
"EEA expenditure condition (in Part 15E)	section 1218ZCC"
"exhibition (in Part 15E)	section 1218ZAA"
"income, in relation to an exhibition (in Part 15E)	section 1218ZBB"
"museums and galleries exhibition tax relief (in Part 15E)	section 1218ZC(1)"
"primary production company (in Part 15E)	section 1218ZAC"
"qualifying expenditure (in Part 15E)	section 1218ZCG"
"secondary production company (in Part 15E)	section 1218ZAD"
"separate exhibition trade (in Part 15E)	section 1218ZB"
"touring exhibition (in Part 15E)	section 1218ZAB".

FA 2009

15   In Schedule 54A to FA 2009 (which is prospectively inserted by F(No. 3)A 2010 and contains provision about the recovery of certain amounts of interest paid by HMRC), in paragraph 2—

(a)   in sub-paragraph (2), omit the "or" at the end of paragraph (h) and after paragraph (i) insert ", or

(j)   a payment of museums and galleries exhibition tax credit under Chapter 3 of Part 15E of CTA 2009 for an accounting period.";

482   *Finance (No. 2) Act 2017 (c. 32)*
Schedule 6 — Relief for production of museum and gallery exhibitions
Part 2 — Consequential amendments

(b)   in sub-paragraph (4), for "(i)" substitute "(j)".

CTA 2010

16   In Part 8B of CTA 2010 (trading profits taxable at Northern Ireland rate), in section 357H(7) (introduction), after "Chapter 14A for provision about orchestra tax relief;" insert "Chapter 14B for provision about museums and galleries exhibition tax relief;".

17   In Part 8B of CTA 2010, after section 357UQ insert—

"CHAPTER 14B

MUSEUMS AND GALLERIES EXHIBITION TAX RELIEF

Introductory

357UR Introduction and interpretation

(1)   This Chapter makes provision about the operation of Part 15E of CTA 2009 (museums and galleries exhibition tax relief) in relation to expenditure incurred by a company in an accounting period in which it is a Northern Ireland company.

(2)   In this Chapter—
     (a)   "Northern Ireland expenditure" means expenditure incurred in a trade to the extent that the expenditure forms part of the Northern Ireland profits or Northern Ireland losses of the trade;
     (b)   "the separate exhibition trade" has the same meaning as in Part 15E of CTA 2009 (see section 1218ZB(3) of that Act);
     (c)   "qualifying expenditure" has the same meaning as in Chapter 3 of that Part (see section 1218ZCG of that Act).

(3)   References in Part 15E of CTA 2009 to "museums and galleries exhibition tax relief" include relief under this Chapter.

Museums and galleries exhibition tax relief

357US Northern Ireland additional deduction

(1)   In this Chapter "a Northern Ireland additional deduction" means so much of a deduction under section 1218ZCE of CTA 2009 (claim for additional deduction) as is calculated by reference to qualifying expenditure that is Northern Ireland expenditure.

(2)   A Northern Ireland additional deduction forms part of the Northern Ireland profits or Northern Ireland losses of the separate exhibition trade.

357UT Northern Ireland supplementary deduction

(1)   This section applies where—
     (a)   a company is entitled under section 1218ZCE of CTA 2009 to an additional deduction in calculating the profit or loss of the separate exhibition trade in an accounting period,
     (b)   the company is a Northern Ireland company in the period,

      (c)   the additional deduction is wholly or partly a Northern Ireland additional deduction, and

      (d)   any of the following conditions is met—

          (i)   the company does not have a surrenderable loss in the accounting period;

          (ii)   the company has a surrenderable loss in the accounting period, but does not make a claim under section 1218ZCH of CTA 2009 (museums and galleries exhibition tax credit claimable if company has surrenderable loss) for the period;

          (iii)   the company has a surrenderable loss in the accounting period and makes a claim under that section for the period, but the amount of Northern Ireland losses surrendered on the claim is less than the Northern Ireland additional deduction.

(2)   The company is entitled to make another deduction ("a Northern Ireland supplementary deduction") in respect of qualifying expenditure.

(3)   See section 357UU for provision about the amount of the Northern Ireland supplementary deduction.

(4)   The Northern Ireland supplementary deduction—

      (a)   is made in calculating the profit or loss of the separate exhibition trade, and

      (b)   forms part of the Northern Ireland profits or Northern Ireland losses of the separate exhibition trade.

(5)   In this section "surrenderable loss" has the meaning given by section 1218ZCI of CTA 2009.

357UU Northern Ireland supplementary deduction: amount

(1)   This section contains provision for the purposes of section 357UT(2) about the amount of the Northern Ireland supplementary deduction.

(2)   If the accounting period falls within only one financial year, the amount of the Northern Ireland supplementary deduction is—

$$(A - B) \times \left(\frac{(MR - NIR)}{NIR} \right)$$

where—

A is the amount of the Northern Ireland additional deduction brought into account in the accounting period;

B is the amount of Northern Ireland losses surrendered in any claim under section 1218ZCH of CTA 2009 for the accounting period;

MR is the main rate for the financial year;

NIR is the Northern Ireland rate for the financial year.

(3)   If the accounting period falls within more than one financial year, the amount of the Northern Ireland supplementary deduction is determined by taking the following steps.

      Step 1

484   *Finance (No. 2) Act 2017 (c. 32)*
Schedule 6 — Relief for production of museum and gallery exhibitions
Part 2 — Consequential amendments

Calculate, for each financial year, the amount that would be the Northern Ireland supplementary deduction for the accounting period if it fell within only that financial year (see subsection (2)).

Step 2

Multiply each amount calculated under step 1 by the proportion of the accounting period that falls within the financial year for which it is calculated.

Step 3

Add together each amount found under step 2.

357UV Museums and galleries exhibition tax credit: Northern Ireland supplementary deduction ignored

For the purpose of determining the available loss of a company under section 1218ZCI of CTA 2009 (amount of surrenderable loss) for any accounting period, any Northern Ireland supplementary deduction made by the company in the period (and any Northern Ireland supplementary deduction made in any previous accounting period) is to be ignored.

Losses of separate exhibition trade

357UW Restriction on use of losses before completion period

(1) Section 1218ZDA of CTA 2009 (restriction on use of losses before completion period) has effect subject as follows.

(2) The reference in subsection (1) of that section to a loss made in the separate exhibition trade in an accounting period preceding the completion period is, if the company is a Northern Ireland company in that period, a reference to —

    (a) any Northern Ireland losses of the trade of the period, or

    (b) any mainstream losses of the trade of the period;

and references to losses in subsections (2) and (3) of that section are to be read accordingly.

(3) Subsection (4) applies if a Northern Ireland company has, in an accounting period preceding the completion period —

    (a) both Northern Ireland losses of the trade and mainstream profits of the trade, or

    (b) both mainstream losses of the trade and Northern Ireland profits of the trade.

(4) The company may make a claim under section 37 (relief for trade losses against total profits) for relief for the losses mentioned in subsection (3)(a) or (b).

(5) But relief on such a claim is available only —

    (a) in the case of a claim for relief for Northern Ireland losses, against mainstream profits of the trade of the same period;

    (b) in the case of a claim for relief for mainstream losses, against Northern Ireland profits of the trade of the same period.

(6) In this section "the completion period" has the same meaning as in section 1218ZDA of CTA 2009 (see section 1218ZD(2) of that Act).

Finance (No. 2) Act 2017 (c. 32)
Schedule 6 — Relief for production of museum and gallery exhibitions
Part 2 — Consequential amendments

485

357UX Use of losses in the completion period

(1) Section 1218ZDB of CTA 2009 (use of losses in the completion period) has effect subject as follows.

(2) The reference in subsection (1) of that section to a loss made in the separate exhibition trade is, in relation to a loss made in a period in which the company is a Northern Ireland company, a reference to —

    (a) any Northern Ireland losses of the trade of the period, or

    (b) any mainstream losses of the trade of the period;

and references to losses in subsections (2) and (4) of that section are to be read accordingly.

(3) The references in subsection (3) of that section to a loss made in the separate exhibition trade in the completion period are, where the company is a Northern Ireland company in the period, references to —

    (a) any Northern Ireland losses of the trade of the period, or

    (b) any mainstream losses of the trade of the period;

and references to losses in subsection (4) of that section are to be read accordingly.

(4) Subsection (4) of that section has effect, in relation to Northern Ireland losses, as if the reference to an additional deduction under Chapter 3 of Part 15E of CTA 2009 included a reference to a Northern Ireland supplementary deduction under this Chapter.

357UY Terminal losses

(1) Section 1218ZDC of CTA 2009 (terminal losses) has effect subject as follows.

(2) Where —

    (a) a company makes an election under subsection (3) of that section (election to treat terminal loss as loss brought forward of different trade) in relation to all or part of a terminal loss, and

    (b) the terminal loss is a Northern Ireland loss,

that subsection has effect as if the reference in it to a loss brought forward were to a Northern Ireland loss brought forward.

(3) Where —

    (a) a company makes a claim under subsection (6) of that section (claim to treat terminal loss as loss brought forward by different company) in relation to part or all of a terminal loss, and

    (b) the terminal loss is a Northern Ireland loss,

that subsection has effect as if the reference in it to a loss brought forward were to a Northern Ireland loss brought forward."

18 (1) Schedule 4 to CTA 2010 (index of defined expressions) is amended as follows.

(2) In the entry for "Northern Ireland expenditure" —

    (a) for "14A" substitute "14B", and

    (b) for "and 357UJ(2)" substitute ", 357UJ(2) and 357UR(2)".

486   *Finance (No. 2) Act 2017 (c. 32)*
Schedule 6 — Relief for production of museum and gallery exhibitions
Part 2 — Consequential amendments

(3) Insert at the appropriate places—

"qualifying expenditure (in Chapter 14B of Part 8B)	section 357UR(2)"
"the separate exhibition trade (in Chapter 14B of Part 8B)	section 357UR(2)"

FA 2016

19 In Schedule 24 to FA 2016 (tax advantages constituting the grant of state aid), in Part 1, in the table headed "*Creative tax reliefs*", after the entry for "Orchestra tax relief" insert—

"Museums and galleries exhibition tax relief	Part 15E of CTA 2009"

PART 3

COMMENCEMENT

20 Any power to make regulations conferred on the Treasury by virtue of this Schedule comes into force on the day on which this Act is passed.

21 (1) The amendments made by the following provisions of this Schedule have effect in relation to accounting periods beginning on or after 1 April 2017—

  (a) Part 1, and

  (b) in Part 2, paragraphs 2 to 15 and 19.

 (2) Sub-paragraph (3) applies where a company has an accounting period beginning before 1 April 2017 and ending on or after that date ("the straddling period").

 (3) For the purposes of Part 15E of CTA 2009—

  (a) so much of the straddling period as falls before 1 April 2017, and so much of that period as falls on or after that date, are separate accounting periods, and

  (b) any amounts brought into account for the purposes of calculating for corporation tax purposes the profits of a trade for the straddling period are apportioned to the two separate accounting periods on such basis as is just and reasonable.

22 (1) Section 4 of CT(NI)A 2015 (power to make consequential amendments) has effect as if paragraphs 16 to 18 of this Schedule were contained in that Act.

 (2) Section 5(4) to (6) of CT(NI)A 2015 (commencement) has effect as if—

  (a) references to Part 8B of CTA 2010 were to that Part as amended by paragraphs 16 and 17 of this Schedule, and

  (b) references to the amendments made by Schedules 1 and 2 to CT(NI)A 2015 included the amendments made by paragraph 18 of this Schedule.

Finance (No. 2) Act 2017 (c. 32)
Schedule 7 — Trading profits taxable at the Northern Ireland rate
Part 1 — Amendments relating to SMEs

487

SCHEDULE 7

Section 25

TRADING PROFITS TAXABLE AT THE NORTHERN IRELAND RATE

PART 1

AMENDMENTS RELATING TO SMEs

Amendments of CTA 2010

1   CTA 2010 is amended as follows.

2   (1) Section 357H (introduction) is amended as follows.

    (2) In subsection (5) —
         (a)   after "that is an SME" insert "and is a Northern Ireland employer";
         (b)   for "that is not an SME" substitute "that —
                    (a)   is an SME that is not a Northern Ireland employer and has made the requisite election, or
                    (b)   is not an SME."

3   (1) Section 357KA (meaning of "Northern Ireland company") is amended as follows.

    (2) In subsection (1)(b), for "the SME condition" substitute "the SME (Northern Ireland employer) condition, the SME (election) condition".

    (3) In subsection (2), for "SME condition" substitute "SME (Northern Ireland employer) condition".

    (4) After subsection (2) insert —

        "(2A)   The "SME (election) condition" is that —
                (a)   the company is an SME in relation to the period,
                (b)   the company is not a Northern Ireland employer in relation to the period,
                (c)   the company has a NIRE in the period,
                (d)   the company is not a disqualified close company in relation to the period, and
                (e)   an election by the company for the purposes of this subsection has effect in relation to the period."

    (5) In subsection (4), after the definition of "Northern Ireland employer" insert —

            "disqualified close company", see section 357KEA;".

    (6) After subsection (3) insert —

        "(3A)   An election for the purposes of subsection (2A) —
                (a)   must be made by notice to an officer of Revenue and Customs,
                (b)   must specify the accounting period in relation to which it is to have effect ("the specified accounting period"),
                (c)   must be made before the end of the period of 12 months beginning with the end of the specified accounting period, and

488   *Finance (No. 2) Act 2017 (c. 32)*
Schedule 7 — Trading profits taxable at the Northern Ireland rate
Part 1 — Amendments relating to SMEs

        (d)   if made in accordance with paragraphs (a) to (c) has effect in relation to the specified accounting period."

4   (1)   Section 357KE (Northern Ireland workforce conditions) is amended as follows.

    (2)   In subsection (2)—

        (a)   omit the "and" at the end of paragraph (b), and

        (b)   at the end of paragraph (c) insert ", and

            (d)   in the case of a close company, or of a company which would be a close company if it were UK resident, individuals who are participators in the company."

    (3)   After subsection (7) insert—

    "(7A)   In this section "participator" has the same meaning as in sections 1064 to 1067 (see sections 1068 and 1069).

    (7B)   In determining for the purposes of this section the amount of working time that is spent in any place by a participator in the company, time spent by the participator in that place is to be included where—

        (a)   the time is spent by the participator in providing services to a person other than the company ("the third party"), and

        (b)   condition A or B is met.

    (7C)   Condition A is that the provision of the services results in a payment being made (whether directly or indirectly) to the company by—

        (a)   the third party, or

        (b)   a person connected with the third party.

    (7D)   Condition B is that—

        (a)   the company holds a right that it acquired (whether directly or indirectly) from the participator, and

        (b)   any payment in connection with that right is made (whether directly or indirectly) to the company by—

            (i)   the third party, or

            (ii)   a person connected with the third party.

    (7E)   Section 1122 (connected persons) applies for the purposes of this section."

5   After section 357KE insert—

"Meaning of "disqualified close company"

357KEA "Disqualified close company"

    (1)   A company is a "disqualified close company" in relation to a period if—

        (a)   the company is a close company, or would be a close company if it were UK resident, at any time in the period, and

        (b)   conditions A and B are met.

    (2)   Condition A is that the company has a NIRE in the period as a result of tax-avoidance arrangements.

Finance (No. 2) Act 2017 (c. 32)   **489**
Schedule 7 — Trading profits taxable at the Northern Ireland rate
Part 1 — Amendments relating to SMEs

(3)   Condition B is that—

    (a)   50% or more of the working time that is spent in the United Kingdom during the period by members of the company's workforce is working time spent by participators in the company otherwise than in Northern Ireland, or

    (b)   50% or more of the company's workforce expenses that are attributable to working time spent in the United Kingdom during the period by members of the company's workforce are attributable to working time spent by participators in the company otherwise than in Northern Ireland.

(4)   For the purposes of this section "tax avoidance arrangements" means arrangements the sole or main purpose of which is to secure that any profits or losses of the company for the period are Northern Ireland profits or losses.

(5)   In subsection (4) "arrangements" includes any agreement, understanding, scheme, transaction or series of transactions (whether or not legally enforceable).

(6)   The following provisions apply for the purposes of this section as they apply for the purposes of section 357KE (Northern Ireland workforce conditions)—

    (a)   subsections (2) to (5) and (7A) to (7E) of that section;

    (b)   regulations made under that section.

(7)   In its application by virtue of subsection (6), subsection (5) of section 357KE has effect as if the reference in it to subsection (1)(b) of that section were to subsection (3)(b) of this section."

6   In the heading of Chapter 6 of Part 8B, at the end insert "that are Northern Ireland employers".

7   In section 357M (Chapter 6: introductory), in subsection (1), for "SME condition" substitute "SME (Northern Ireland employer) condition".

8   In the heading of Chapter 7 of Part 8B, after "losses etc:" insert "SMEs that are not Northern Ireland employers and".

9   In section 357N (Chapter 7: introductory), in subsection (1), after "by virtue of" insert "the SME (election) condition or".

10   (1)   Section 357OB (Northern Ireland intangibles credits and debits: SMEs) is amended as follows.

    (2)   In the heading, at the end, insert "that are Northern Ireland employers".

    (3)   In subsection (1)(a), for "SME condition" substitute "SME (Northern Ireland employer) condition".

11   (1)   Section 357OC (Northern Ireland intangibles credits and debits: large companies) is amended as follows.

    (2)   In the heading, after "debits:" insert "SMEs that are not Northern Ireland employers and".

    (3)   In subsection (1), after "by virtue of" insert "the SME (election) condition or".

490

Finance (No. 2) Act 2017 (c. 32)
Schedule 7 — Trading profits taxable at the Northern Ireland rate
Part 1 — Amendments relating to SMEs

12 (1) Section 357VB (relevant Northern Ireland IP profits: SMEs) is amended as follows.

(2) In the heading, at the end, insert "that are Northern Ireland employers".

(3) In subsection (1)(a), for "SME condition" substitute "SME (Northern Ireland employer) condition".

13 (1) Section 357VC (relevant Northern Ireland IP profits: large companies) is amended as follows.

(2) In the heading, after "profits:" insert "SMEs that are not Northern Ireland employers and".

(3) In subsection (1)(a), after "by virtue of" insert "the SME (election) condition or".

14 (1) Section 357WA (meaning of "Northern Ireland firm") is amended as follows.

(2) In subsection (1)(b), for "SME partnership condition" substitute "SME (Northern Ireland employer) partnership condition, the SME (election) partnership condition".

(3) In subsection (2), for "SME partnership condition" substitute "SME (Northern Ireland employer) partnership condition".

(4) After subsection (2) insert—

"(2A) The "SME (election) partnership condition" is that—
   (a) the firm is an SME in relation to the firm's accounting period,
   (b) the firm is not a Northern Ireland employer in relation to that period,
   (c) the firm has a NIRE in that period,
   (d) the firm is not a disqualified firm in relation to the period, and
   (e) an election by the firm for the purposes of this subsection has effect in relation to that period."

(5) After subsection (3) insert—

"(3A) An election for the purposes of subsection (2A)—
   (a) must be made by notice to an officer of Revenue and Customs,
   (b) must specify the accounting period in relation to which it is to have effect ("the specified accounting period"),
   (c) must be made before the end of the period of 12 months beginning with the end of the specified accounting period, and
   (d) if made in accordance with paragraphs (a) to (c) has effect in relation to the specified accounting period."

(6) In subsection (4)—
   (a) in the opening words, for "to subsections (2) and (3)" substitute "in relation to a firm";

Finance (No. 2) Act 2017 (c. 32)
Schedule 7 — Trading profits taxable at the Northern Ireland rate
Part 1 — Amendments relating to SMEs

491

      (b)   for paragraph (b) substitute —

            "(b)   references to the Northern Ireland workforce conditions were to the Northern Ireland workforce partnership conditions (see section 357WBA)."

  (7) In subsection (5) omit paragraph (c).

15   After section 357WB, insert —

"357WBA Northern Ireland workforce partnership conditions

  (1) The Northern Ireland workforce partnership conditions, in relation to a period, are —

      (a)   that 75% or more of the working time that is spent in the United Kingdom during the period by members of the firm's workforce is spent in Northern Ireland, and

      (b)   that 75% or more of the firm's workforce expenses that are attributable to working time spent in the United Kingdom during the period by members of the firm's workforce are attributable to time spent in Northern Ireland.

  (2) References in this section to members of the firm's workforce are to —

      (a)   employees of the firm,

      (b)   externally provided workers in relation to the firm, and

      (c)   individuals who are partners in the firm.

  (3) In subsection (2) "externally provided worker", in relation to a firm, has the same meaning as in Part 13 of CTA 2009 (see section 1128 of that Act).

      In the application of section 1128 of that Act for the purposes of subsection (2), references to a company are to be read as references to a firm and references to a director are to be treated as omitted.

  (4) References in this section to the working time spent by members of the firm's workforce in a place are to the total time spent by those persons in that place while providing services to the firm.

  (5) References in this section to "the firm's workforce expenses" are, where the period is an accounting period of the firm, to the total of the deductions made by the firm in the period in respect of members of the firm's workforce in calculating the profits of the firm's trade.

  (6) References in this section to "the firm's workforce expenses" are, where the period is not an accounting period of the firm, to the total of —

      (a)   the deductions made by the firm in any accounting period falling wholly within the period, and

      (b)   the appropriate proportion of the deductions made by the firm in any accounting period falling partly within the period,

      in respect of members of the firm's workforce in calculating the profits of the firm's trade.

  (7) For the purposes of subsection (6)(b), "the appropriate proportion" is to be determined by reference to the number of days in the periods concerned.

492

Finance (No. 2) Act 2017 (c. 32)
Schedule 7 — Trading profits taxable at the Northern Ireland rate
Part 1 — Amendments relating to SMEs

(8) The Commissioners for Her Majesty's Revenue and Customs may by regulations specify descriptions of deduction that are, or are not, to be regarded for the purposes of this section as made in respect of members of a firm's workforce.

(9) Regulations under this section—

   (a) may make different provision for different purposes;

   (b) may make incidental, supplemental, consequential and transitional provision and savings.

(10) Section 357WBB contains supplementary provision applying for the purposes of this section.

357WBB Section 357WBA: supplementary

(1) References in section 357WBA or this section to a partner in the firm include any person entitled to a share of income of the firm.

(2) In determining for the purposes of section 357WBA the amount of working time that is spent in any place by a partner in the firm, time spent by the partner in that place is to be included where—

   (a) the time is spent by the partner in providing services to a person other than the firm ("the third party"), and

   (b) condition A or B is met.

(3) Condition A is that the provision of the services results in a payment being made (whether directly or indirectly) to the firm by—

   (a) the third party, or

   (b) a person connected with the third party.

(4) Condition B is that—

   (a) the firm holds a right that it acquired (whether directly or indirectly) from the partner, and

   (b) any payment in connection with that right is made (whether directly or indirectly) to the firm by—

      (i) the third party, or

      (ii) a person connected with the third party.

(5) Section 1122 (connected persons) applies for the purposes of this section.

(6) References in section 357WBA to deductions made in respect of the members of the firm's workforce in calculating profits of the firm's trade include, in relation to a partner in the firm, the appropriate notional consideration for services provided by the partner (see subsections (7) and (8)).

(7) For the purposes of subsection (6), "the appropriate notional consideration for services" provided by a partner is—

   (a) the amount which the partner would receive in consideration for services provided to the firm by the partner during the period in question, were the consideration to be calculated on the basis mentioned in subsection (8), less

   (b) any amount actually received in consideration for such services which is not included in the partner's profit share.

Finance (No. 2) Act 2017 (c. 32)
Schedule 7 — Trading profits taxable at the Northern Ireland rate
Part 1 — Amendments relating to SMEs

493

(8) The consideration mentioned in subsection (7)(a) is to be calculated on the basis that the partner is not a partner in the firm and is acting at arm's length from the firm.

357WBC "Disqualified firm"

(1) For the purposes of this Chapter, a firm is a "disqualified firm" in relation to a period if conditions A and B are met.

(2) Condition A is that the firm has a NIRE in the period as a result of tax-avoidance arrangements.

(3) Condition B is that—
    (a) 50% or more of the working time that is spent in the United Kingdom during the period by members of the firm's workforce is working time spent by partners otherwise than in Northern Ireland, or
    (b) 50% or more of the firm's workforce expenses that are attributable to working time spent in the United Kingdom during the period by members of the firm's workforce are attributable to working time spent by partners otherwise than in Northern Ireland.

(4) For the purposes of this section "tax avoidance arrangements" means arrangements the sole or main purpose of which is to secure that any profits or losses of the firm for the period are Northern Ireland profits or losses.

(5) In subsection (4) "arrangements" includes any agreement, understanding, scheme, transaction or series of transactions (whether or not legally enforceable).

(6) The following provisions apply for the purposes of this section as they apply for the purposes of section 357WBA (Northern Ireland workforce partnership conditions)—
    (a) subsections (2) to (5) of that section;
    (b) regulations made under that section;
    (c) section 357WBB."

16 In section 357WC (Northern Ireland profits etc of firm determined under Chapter 6), in subsection (2), for "SME partnership condition" substitute "SME (Northern Ireland employer) partnership condition".

17 (1) Section 357WD (Northern Ireland profits etc of firm determined under Chapter 7) is amended as follows.

(2) For subsections (1) to (3) substitute—

"(1) This section applies where—
    (a) a company ("the corporate partner") is a partner in a firm at any time during an accounting period of the firm ("the firm's accounting period") and is within the charge to corporation tax in relation to the firm's trade, and
    (b) condition A or B is met.

(2) Condition A is that the firm is a Northern Ireland firm in the firm's accounting period by virtue of the SME (election) partnership condition or the large partnership condition in section 357WA.

494

Finance (No. 2) Act 2017 (c. 32)
Schedule 7 — Trading profits taxable at the Northern Ireland rate
Part 1 — Amendments relating to SMEs

    (3)   Condition B is that—

        (a)   the firm is a Northern Ireland firm in the firm's accounting period by virtue of the SME (Northern Ireland employer) partnership condition in section 357WA, and

        (b)   the corporate partner is not an SME in relation to an accounting period of the corporate partner which is the same as, or overlaps (to any extent), the firm's accounting period."

    (3)   In subsection (4), after "losses etc:" insert "SMEs that are not Northern Ireland employers and".

18   In section 357WE (sections 357WC and 357WD: interpretation), omit subsection (2).

19   (1)   Section 357WF (application of section 747 of CTA 2009 to Northern Ireland firm) is amended as follows.

    (2)   In paragraph (e)—

        (a)   for "SME condition" substitute "SME (Northern Ireland employer) condition";

        (b)   for "SME partnership condition" substitute "SME (Northern Ireland employer) partnership condition".

    (3)   After paragraph (e) insert—

        "(ea)   references to the SME (election) condition in section 357KA were to the SME (election) partnership condition in section 357WA;".

20   (1)   Section 357WG (application of Part 8A to Northern Ireland firm) is amended as follows.

    (2)   In paragraph (g)—

        (a)   for "SME condition" (in the first place it appears) substitute "SME (Northern Ireland employer) condition";

        (b)   for "SME condition" (in the second place it appears) substitute "SME (Northern Ireland employer) partnership condition".

    (3)   For paragraph (h) substitute—

        "(h)   references in section 357VC to—

            (i)   the SME (election) condition in section 357KA were to the SME (election) partnership condition in section 357WA;

            (ii)   the large company condition in section 357KA were to the large partnership condition in section 357WA;

            (iii)   a qualifying trade by virtue of section 357KB(1) were to a qualifying partnership trade by virtue of section 357WB(1)."

21   In Schedule 4 (index of defined expressions)—

        (a)   omit the entry for "SME condition (in Part 8B)";

        (b)   at the appropriate places, insert—

| "disqualified close company (in Part 8B) | section 357KEA" |

Finance (No. 2) Act 2017 (c. 32)
Schedule 7 — Trading profits taxable at the Northern Ireland rate
Part 1 — Amendments relating to SMEs

495

"SME (Northern Ireland employer) condition (in Part 8B) | section 357KA"

"SME (election) condition (in Part 8B) | section 357KA"

Amendments relating to capital allowances

22   CAA 2001 is amended in accordance with paragraphs 23 and 24.

23   (1) Section 6A ("NIRE company" and "Northern Ireland SME company") is amended as follows.

        (2) In the heading, for "Northern Ireland SME company" substitute "SME (Northern Ireland employer) company".

        (3) In the definition of "NIRE company", after "by virtue of" insert "the SME (election) condition or".

        (4) For "Northern Ireland SME company" substitute "SME (Northern Ireland employer) company".

        (5) For "SME condition" substitute "SME (Northern Ireland employer) condition".

24   In the following provisions, for "a Northern Ireland SME company" substitute "an SME (Northern Ireland employer) company"—
        (a)   section 6C(1)(a) and (c);
        (b)   section 6D(1);
        (c)   section 6E(1);
        (d)   section 61(4B)(a);
        (e)   section 66B(1)(a), (b) and (c);
        (f)   section 66C(b);
        (g)   section 66D(1)(a) and (b);
        (h)   section 66E(b);
        (i)   section 212ZE(b);
        (j)   Schedule 1.

25   In CT(NI)A 2015, in Schedule 1, in Part 6 (capital allowances: transitional provision), in paragraphs 20(1)(a) and 21(1)(a), for "a Northern Ireland SME company" substitute "an SME (Northern Ireland employer) company".

PART 2

MINOR AMENDMENTS

26   In section 357IA of CTA 2010 (power of Northern Ireland Assembly to set Northern Ireland rate), for "Minister of Finance and Personnel" substitute "Minister of Finance".

27   In section 357QB(5)(b) of that Act (tax credit: entitlement), for "Chapter 2" substitute "land remediation".

28   (1) Paragraph 2 of Schedule A1 to CAA 2001 (amount of first-year tax credit) is amended as follows.

        (2) For sub-paragraphs (3A) and (4) substitute—

                "(4) The Treasury may by regulations amend sub-paragraph (1)—

496

Finance (No. 2) Act 2017 (c. 32)
Schedule 7 — Trading profits taxable at the Northern Ireland rate
Part 2 — Minor amendments

    (a)   so as to provide for a different percentage to apply where the surrenderable loss relates to a qualifying activity that is an NI rate activity, or

    (b)   so as to substitute for any percentage for the time being specified in that sub-paragraph such other percentage as the Treasury thinks fit."

  (3) In sub-paragraph (5), for "An order" substitute "Regulations".

29   In consequence of paragraph 28, in the Corporation Tax (Northern Ireland) Act 2015, in Schedule 1, omit paragraph 10.

PART 3

COMMENCEMENT ETC

30 (1) Any power to make regulations under Part 8B of CTA 2010 by virtue of Part 1 or 2 of this Schedule may be exercised on or after the day on which this Act is passed.

  (2) Section 4 of CT(NI)A 2015 (power to make consequential amendments) has effect as if Parts 1 and 2 of this Schedule were contained in that Act.

  (3) Section 5(4) to (6) of CT(NI)A 2015 (commencement) has effect as if—

    (a)   references to Part 8B of CTA 2010 were to that Part as amended by Parts 1 and 2 of this Schedule, and

    (b)   references to the amendments made by Schedules 1 and 2 to CT(NI)A 2015 included the amendments made by paragraphs 21 to 24 of this Schedule.

SCHEDULE 8

Section 29

DEEMED DOMICILE: INCOME TAX AND CAPITAL GAINS TAX

PART 1

APPLICATION OF DEEMED DOMICILE RULE

ICTA

1 (1) In section 266A of ICTA (life assurance premiums paid by employer), after subsection (8) insert—

    "(8A) Section 835BA of ITA 2007 (deemed domicile) applies for the purposes of subsection (6)(b)."

  (2) The amendment made by this paragraph has effect in relation to the tax year 2017-18 and subsequent tax years.

TCGA 1992

2   TCGA 1992 is amended as follows.

3 (1) Section 16ZA (losses: non-UK domiciled individuals) is amended as follows.

Finance (No. 2) Act 2017 (c. 32)
Schedule 8 — Deemed domicile: income tax and capital gains tax
Part 1 — Application of deemed domicile rule

497

    (2) For subsections (1) to (3) substitute —

        "(1) An individual may make an election under this section in respect of —

            (a) the first tax year in which section 809B of ITA 2007 (claim for remittance basis) applies to the individual, or

            (b) the first tax year in which that section applies to the individual following a period in which the individual has been domiciled in the United Kingdom.

        (2) Where an individual makes an election under this section in respect of a tax year, the election has effect in relation to the individual for —

            (a) that tax year, and

            (b) all subsequent tax years.

      (2A) But if after making an election under this section an individual becomes domiciled in the United Kingdom at any time in a tax year, the election does not have effect in relation to the individual for —

            (a) that tax year, or

            (b) any subsequent tax year.

      (2B) Where an election made by an individual under this section in respect of a tax year ceases to have effect by virtue of subsection (2A), the fact that it has ceased to have effect does not prevent the individual from making another election under this section in respect of a later tax year.

        (3) If an individual does not make an election under this section in respect of a year referred to in subsection (1)(a) or (b), foreign losses accruing to the individual in —

            (a) that tax year, or

            (b) any subsequent tax year except one in which the individual is domiciled in the United Kingdom,

        are not allowable losses."

    (3) After subsection (6) insert —

        "(7) Section 835BA of ITA 2007 (deemed domicile) applies for the purposes of this section."

    (4) The amendments made by this paragraph have effect in relation to the tax year 2017-18 and subsequent tax years.

    (5) Where —

        (a) an individual makes an election under section 16ZA of TCGA 1992 as originally enacted for a tax year before the tax year 2017-18, but

        (b) after making the election the individual becomes domiciled in the United Kingdom at any time in a tax year,

    sections 16ZB and 16ZC of that Act do not have effect in relation to the individual by virtue of that election for that tax year or any subsequent tax year.

    (6) Section 835BA of ITA 2007 (deemed domicile) applies for the purposes of sub-paragraph (5).

4   (1) In section 16ZB (election under section 16ZA: foreign chargeable gains remitted in the tax year after that in which they accrue), in subsection (1), for

498   *Finance (No. 2) Act 2017 (c. 32)*
Schedule 8 — Deemed domicile: income tax and capital gains tax
Part 1 — Application of deemed domicile rule

paragraphs (a) and (b) substitute—

> "(a) the individual has made an election under section 16ZA in respect of a tax year before the applicable year,
>
> (aa) the election has effect in relation to the individual for the applicable year,
>
> (b) foreign chargeable gains accrued to the individual in or after the tax year in respect of which the election was made but before the applicable year, and".

    (2) The amendment made by this paragraph has effect in relation to the tax year 2017-18 and subsequent tax years.

5   (1) In section 16ZC (election under section 16ZA by individual to whom remittance basis applies), in subsection (1), for paragraphs (a) to (c) substitute—

> "(a) the individual has made an election under section 16ZA in respect of the tax year or any earlier tax year,
>
> (b) the election has effect in relation to the individual for the tax year, and
>
> (c) section 809B, 809D or 809E of ITA 2007 (remittance basis) applies to the individual for the tax year."

    (2) The amendment made by this paragraph has effect in relation to the tax year 2017-18 and subsequent tax years.

6   (1) In section 69 (trustees of settlements), after subsection (2E) insert—

> "(2F) Section 835BA of ITA 2007 (deemed domicile) applies for the purposes of subsection (2B)(c)."

    (2) The amendment made by this paragraph has effect in relation to a settlement—

> (a) in a case where the settlement arose on the settlor's death (whether by will, intestacy or otherwise), where the settlor died on or after 6 April 2017;
>
> (b) in any other case, where the settlor made the settlement (or was treated for the purposes of TCGA 1992 as making the settlement) on or after 6 April 2017.

7   (1) In section 86 (attribution of gains to settlors with interest in non-resident or dual resident settlements), after subsection (3) insert—

> "(3A) Section 835BA of ITA 2007 (deemed domicile) applies for the purposes of subsection (1)(c)."

    (2) The amendment made by this paragraph has effect in relation to the tax year 2017-18 and subsequent tax years.

8   (1) In section 275 (location of assets), after subsection (3) insert—

> "(3A) Section 835BA of ITA 2007 (deemed domicile) applies for the purposes of subsection (1)(l)(iii)."

    (2) The amendment made by this paragraph has effect for the purposes of determining for the purposes of TCGA 1992 the situation of any asset, or whether the situation of any asset is in the United Kingdom, at any time on or after 6 April 2017 (irrespective of when the asset was acquired by the person holding it).

Finance (No. 2) Act 2017 (c. 32)
Schedule 8 — Deemed domicile: income tax and capital gains tax
Part 1 — Application of deemed domicile rule

499

9   (1) In Schedule 5A (settlements with foreign element: information), in paragraph 3, after sub-paragraph (3) insert—

"(3A) Section 835BA of ITA 2007 (deemed domicile) applies for the purposes of sub-paragraph (3)."

(2) The amendment made by this paragraph has effect in relation to settlements created on or after 6 April 2017.

ITEPA 2003

10   (1) ITEPA 2003 is amended as follows.

(2) In section 355 (deductions for corresponding payments by non-domiciled employees with foreign employers), in subsection (2), at the end insert "(and section 835BA of ITA 2007 (deemed domicile) applies for the purposes of this subsection)".

(3) In section 373 (non-domiciled employee's travel costs and expenses where duties performed in UK), at the end insert—

"(7) Section 835BA of ITA 2007 (deemed domicile) applies for the purposes of subsection (1)."

(4) In section 374 (non-domiciled employee's spouse's etc travel costs and expenses where duties performed in UK), at the end insert —

"(10) Section 835BA of ITA 2007 (deemed domicile) applies for the purposes of subsection (1)."

(5) In section 376 (foreign accommodation and subsistence costs and expenses (overseas employment)), at the end insert —

"(6) Section 835BA of ITA 2007 (deemed domicile) applies for the purposes of subsection (1)(c)."

(6) The amendments made by this paragraph have effect in relation to the tax year 2017-18 and subsequent tax years.

ITA 2007

11   ITA 2007 is amended as follows.

12   (1) In section 476 (how to work out whether settlor meets condition C in section 475), after subsection (3) insert—

"(3A) Section 835BA (deemed domicile) applies for the purposes of subsections (2)(b) and (3)(b)."

(2) The amendment made by this paragraph has effect—
    (a) so far as relating to section 476(2)(b) of ITA 2007, in relation to a settlor who dies on or after 6 April 2017;
    (b) so far as relating to section 476(3)(b) of ITA 2007, in relation to a settlement made on or after 6 April 2017.

13   (1) In section 718 (meaning of "person abroad" etc), after subsection (2) insert—

"(3) Section 835BA (deemed domicile) applies for the purposes of subsection (1)(b)."

500
Finance (No. 2) Act 2017 (c. 32)
Schedule 8 — Deemed domicile: income tax and capital gains tax
Part 1 — Application of deemed domicile rule

(2) The amendment made by this paragraph has effect in relation to the tax year 2017-18 and subsequent tax years.

14 (1) Chapter A1 of Part 14 (remittance basis) is amended as follows.

(2) In section 809B (claim for remittance basis to apply), after subsection (1) insert—

"(1A) Section 835BA (deemed domicile) applies for the purposes of subsection (1)(b)."

(3) In section 809C (claim for remittance basis by long-term UK resident: nomination) omit the following—
   (a) in subsection (1)(b), "the 17-year residence test,";
   (b) subsection (1ZA);
   (c) subsection (1A)(a);
   (d) in subsection (1B)(a), "the 17-year residence test or";
   (e) subsection (4)(za).

(4) In section 809E (application of remittance basis without claim: other cases), after subsection (1) insert—

"(1A) Section 835BA (deemed domicile) applies for the purposes of subsection (1)(b)."

(5) In section 809H (claim for remittance basis by long-term UK resident: charge) omit the following—
   (a) in subsection (1)(c), "the 17-year residence test,";
   (b) in subsection (1A)—
       (i) "(1ZA)";
       (ii) "the 17-year residence test,";
   (c) subsection (5B)(za).

(6) The amendments made by this paragraph have effect in relation to the tax year 2017-18 and subsequent tax years.
   This is subject to paragraphs 15 and 16.

15 (1) This paragraph applies in a case where—
   (a) section 10A of TCGA 1992 (temporary non-residents) as originally enacted applies in relation to an individual, and
   (b) the year of return is 2017-18.

(2) For the purposes of capital gains tax in respect of foreign chargeable gains accruing to the individual during an intervening year, the amendment made by paragraph 14(2) does not have effect in relation to the year of return.

(3) Where by virtue of sub-paragraph (2) an individual makes a claim under section 809B of ITA 2007 for the tax year 2017-18, sections 809C, 809G and 809H of ITA 2007 do not apply to the individual for that tax year.

(4) In this paragraph—
   "intervening year" and "year of return" have the same meanings as in section 10A of TCGA 1992 as originally enacted;
   "foreign chargeable gain" has the meaning given by section 12(4) of TCGA 1992.

Finance (No. 2) Act 2017 (c. 32)
Schedule 8 — Deemed domicile: income tax and capital gains tax
Part 1 — Application of deemed domicile rule

501

16 (1) This paragraph applies in a case where section 10A of TCGA 1992 as substituted by paragraph 119 of Schedule 45 to FA 2013 applies in relation to an individual.

(2) For the purposes of capital gains tax in respect of foreign chargeable gains accruing to the individual during a temporary period of non-residence beginning before 8 July 2015, the amendment made by paragraph 14(2) does not have effect in relation to the tax year which consists of or includes the period of return.

(3) Where by virtue of sub-paragraph (2) an individual makes a claim under section 809B of ITA 2007 for any of the tax years 2017-18 to 2020-21 inclusive, sections 809C, 809G and 809H of ITA 2007 do not apply to the individual for that tax year.

(4) In this paragraph, "foreign chargeable gain" has the meaning given by section 12(4) of TCGA 1992.

(5) Part 4 of Schedule 45 to FA 2013 explains what "temporary period of non-residence" and "period of return" mean.

17 (1) In section 834 (residence of personal representatives), at the end insert—

"(5) Section 835BA (deemed domicile) applies for the purposes of subsection (3)."

(2) The amendment made by this paragraph has effect in relation to the tax year 2017-18 and subsequent tax years.

PART 2

PROTECTION OF OVERSEAS TRUSTS

TCGA 1992

18 In Schedule 5 to TCGA 1992 (provisions supplementing section 86 of TCGA 1992), after paragraph 5 insert—

"5A (1) Section 86 does not apply in relation to a year ("the particular year") if Conditions A to D are met.

(2) Condition A is that the particular year is—
(a) the tax year 2017-18, or
(b) a later tax year.

(3) Condition B is that when the settlement is created the settlor—
(a) is not domiciled in the United Kingdom, and
(b) if the settlement is created on or after 6 April 2017, is not deemed domiciled in the United Kingdom.

(4) Condition C is that there is no time in the particular year when the settlor is—
(a) domiciled in the United Kingdom, or
(b) deemed domiciled in the United Kingdom by virtue of Condition A in section 835BA of ITA 2007.

(5) Condition D is that no property or income is provided directly or indirectly for the purposes of the settlement by the settlor, or by

502   *Finance (No. 2) Act 2017 (c. 32)*
Schedule 8 — Deemed domicile: income tax and capital gains tax
Part 2 — Protection of overseas trusts

the trustees of another settlement of which the settlor is the settlor or a beneficiary, at a time in the relevant period when the settlor is—

 (a) domiciled in the United Kingdom, or

 (b) deemed domiciled in the United Kingdom.

(6) In sub-paragraph (5) "relevant period" means the period—

 (a) beginning with the start of 6 April 2017 or, if later, the creation of the settlement, and

 (b) ending with the end of the particular year.

(7) For the purposes of Condition D, the addition of value to property comprised in the settlement is to be treated as the direct provision of property for the purposes of the settlement.

(8) Paragraph 5B contains further provision for the purposes of Condition D.

(9) In this paragraph "deemed domiciled" means regarded for the purposes of section 86(1)(c) as domiciled in the United Kingdom as a result of section 835BA of ITA 2007 having effect.

5B (1) This paragraph applies for the purposes of Condition D in paragraph 5A.

(2) Ignore—

 (a) property or income provided under a transaction, other than a loan, where the transaction is entered into on arm's length terms,

 (b) property or income provided, otherwise than under a loan, without any intention by the person providing it to confer a gratuitous benefit on any person,

 (c) the principal of a loan which is made to the trustees of the settlement on arm's length terms,

 (d) the payment of interest to the trustees of the settlement under a loan made by them on arm's length terms,

 (e) repayment to the trustees of the settlement of the principal of a loan made by them,

 (f) property or income provided in pursuance of a liability incurred by any person before 6 April 2017, and

 (g) where the settlement's expenses relating to taxation and administration for a tax year exceed its income for that year, property or income provided towards meeting that excess if the value of any such property and income is not greater than the amount of—

  (i) the excess, or

  (ii) if greater, the amount by which such expenses exceed the amount of such expenses which may be paid out of the settlement's income.

(3) Where—

 (a) a loan is made to the trustees of the settlement by the settlor or the trustees of a settlement connected with the settlor, and

 (b) the loan is on arm's length terms, but

Finance (No. 2) Act 2017 (c. 32)
Schedule 8 — Deemed domicile: income tax and capital gains tax
Part 2 — Protection of overseas trusts

503

    (c)   a relevant event occurs,

the principal of the loan is to be regarded as having been provided to the trustees at the time of that event (despite sub-paragraph (2)).

(4) In sub-paragraph (3) "relevant event" means —

    (a)   capitalisation of interest payable under the loan,

    (b)   any other failure to pay interest in accordance with the terms of the loan, or

    (c)   variation of the terms of the loan such that they cease to be arm's length terms.

(5) Sub-paragraph (6) applies (subject to sub-paragraph (7)) where —

    (a)   the settlor becomes deemed domiciled in the United Kingdom on or after 6 April 2017,

    (b)   before the date on which the settlor becomes deemed domiciled in the United Kingdom ("the deemed domicile date"), a loan has been made to the trustees of the settlement by —

        (i)   the settlor, or

        (ii)   the trustees of a settlement connected with the settlor,

    (c)   the loan is not entered into on arm's length terms, and

    (d)   any amount that is outstanding under the loan on the deemed domicile date ("the outstanding amount") is payable or repayable on demand on or after that date.

(6) Where this sub-paragraph applies, the outstanding amount is to be regarded as property directly provided on the deemed domicile date by the lender for the purposes of the settlement (despite sub-paragraph (2)).

(7) But if the deemed domicile date is 6 April 2017, sub-paragraph (6) does not apply if —

    (a)   the principal of the loan is repaid, and all interest payable under the loan is paid, before 6 April 2018, or

    (b)   the loan becomes a loan on arm's length terms before 6 April 2018 and —

        (i)   before that date interest is paid to the lender in respect of the period beginning with 6 April 2017 and ending with 5 April 2018 as if those arm's length terms had been terms of the loan in relation to that period, and

        (ii)   interest continues to be payable from 6 April 2018 in accordance with those terms.

(8) For the purposes of this paragraph a loan is on "arm's length terms" —

    (a)   in the case of a loan made to the trustees of a settlement, only if interest at the official rate or more is payable at least annually under the loan;

    (b)   in the case of a loan made by the trustees of a settlement, only if any interest payable under the loan is payable at no more than the official rate.

504

Finance (No. 2) Act 2017 (c. 32)
Schedule 8 – Deemed domicile: income tax and capital gains tax
Part 2 – Protection of overseas trusts

(9) For the purposes of this paragraph—

a settlement is "connected" with a person if the person is the settlor or a beneficiary of it;

"deemed domiciled" has the same meaning as in paragraph 5A;

"official rate", in relation to interest, means the rate of interest applicable from time to time under section 178 of the Finance Act 1989 for the purposes of Chapter 7 of Part 3 of ITEPA 2003."

FA 2004

19   In paragraph 8 of Schedule 15 to FA 2004 (income tax on benefits received by former owner of property: intangible property comprised in settlement where settlor retains an interest), after sub-paragraph (3) insert—

"(4) For the purpose of deciding whether the condition in sub-paragraph (1)(a) is met, ignore section 628A of ITTOIA 2005 (which provides for section 624 of that Act not to apply to certain foreign income arising under a settlement)."

ITTOIA 2005

20   Chapter 5 of Part 5 of ITTOIA 2005 (settlements) is amended as follows.

21   In section 624 (income under a settlement where settlor retains an interest), in subsection (3) (which lists provisions containing exceptions)—
    (a)   omit the "and" at the end of the entry for section 627, and
    (b)   after the entry for section 628 insert ", and

            section 628A (exception for protected foreign-source income)."

22   After section 628 insert—

"628A Exception for protected foreign-source income

    (1)   The rule in section 624(1) does not apply to income which arises under a settlement if it is protected foreign-source income for a tax year.

    (2)   For this purpose, income arising under a settlement in a tax year is "protected foreign-source income" for the tax year if Conditions A to F are met.

    (3)   Condition A is that the income would be relevant foreign income if it were income of a UK resident individual.

    (4)   Condition B is that the income is from property originating from the settlor (see section 645).

    (5)   Condition C is that when the settlement is created the settlor—
        (a)   is not domiciled in the United Kingdom, and
        (b)   if the settlement is created on or after 6 April 2017, is not deemed domiciled in the United Kingdom.

    (6)   Condition D is that there is no time in the tax year when the settlor is—

Finance (No. 2) Act 2017 (c. 32)
Schedule 8 — Deemed domicile: income tax and capital gains tax
Part 2 — Protection of overseas trusts

505

        (a)   domiciled in the United Kingdom, or

        (b)   deemed domiciled in the United Kingdom by virtue of Condition A in section 835BA of ITA 2007.

(7)   Condition E is that the trustees of the settlement are not UK resident for the tax year.

(8)   Condition F is that no property or income is provided directly or indirectly for the purposes of the settlement by the settlor, or by the trustees of any other settlement of which the settlor is a beneficiary or settlor, at a time in the relevant period when the settlor is—

        (a)   domiciled in the United Kingdom, or

        (b)   deemed domiciled in the United Kingdom.

(9)   In subsection (8) "relevant period" means the period—

        (a)   beginning with the start of 6 April 2017 or, if later, the creation of the settlement, and

        (b)   ending with the end of the tax year.

(10)   For the purposes of Condition F, the addition of value to property comprised in the settlement is to be treated as the direct provision of property for the purposes of the settlement.

(11)   Section 628B (tainting) contains further provision for the purposes of Condition F.

(12)   In this section "deemed domiciled" means regarded for the purposes of section 809(1)(b) of ITA 2007 as domiciled in the United Kingdom as a result of section 835BA of ITA 2007 having effect.

(13)   Section 648(3) to (5) (relevant foreign income treated as arising under settlement only if and when remitted) do not apply for the purposes of this section.

628B Section 628A: tainting

(1)   This section applies for the purposes of Condition F in section 628A.

(2)   Ignore—

        (a)   property or income provided under a transaction, other than a loan, where the transaction is entered into on arm's length terms,

        (b)   property or income provided, otherwise than under a loan, without any intention by the person providing it to confer a gratuitous benefit on any person,

        (c)   the principal of a loan which is made to the trustees of the settlement on arm's length terms,

        (d)   the payment of interest to the trustees of the settlement under a loan made by them on arm's length terms,

        (e)   repayment to the trustees of the settlement of the principal of a loan made by them,

        (f)   property or income provided in pursuance of a liability incurred by any person before 6 April 2017, and

        (g)   where the settlement's expenses relating to taxation and administration for a tax year exceed its income for that year, property or income provided towards meeting that excess if the value of any such property and income is not greater than the amount of —

    (i)   the excess, or

    (ii)   if greater, the amount by which such expenses exceed the amount of such expenses which may be paid out of the settlement's income.

(3)   Where —

    (a)   a loan is made to the trustees of the settlement by the settlor or the trustees of a settlement connected with the settlor, and

    (b)   the loan is on arm's length terms, but

    (c)   a relevant event occurs,

the principal of the loan is to be regarded as having been provided to the trustees at the time of that event (despite subsection (2)).

(4)   In subsection (3) "relevant event" means —

    (a)   capitalisation of interest payable under the loan,

    (b)   any other failure to pay interest in accordance with the terms of the loan, or

    (c)   variation of the terms of the loan such that they cease to be arm's length terms.

(5)   Subsection (6) applies (subject to subsection (7)) where —

    (a)   the settlor becomes deemed domiciled in the United Kingdom on or after 6 April 2017,

    (b)   before the date on which the settlor becomes deemed domiciled in the United Kingdom ("the deemed domicile date"), a loan has been made to the trustees of the settlement by —

        (i)   the settlor, or

        (ii)   the trustees of a settlement connected with the settlor,

    (c)   the loan is not entered into on arm's length terms, and

    (d)   any amount that is outstanding under the loan on the deemed domicile date ("the outstanding amount") is payable or repayable on demand on or after that date.

(6)   Where this subsection applies, the outstanding amount is to be regarded as property directly provided on the deemed domicile date by the lender for the purposes of the settlement (despite subsection (2)).

(7)   But if the deemed domicile date is 6 April 2017, subsection (6) does not apply if —

    (a)   the principal of the loan is repaid, and all interest payable under the loan is paid, before 6 April 2018, or

    (b)   the loan becomes a loan on arm's length terms before 6 April 2018 and —

        (i)   before that date interest is paid to the lender in respect of the period beginning with 6 April 2017 and ending with 5 April 2018 as if those arm's length terms had been terms of the loan in relation to that period, and

        (ii)   interest continues to be payable from 6 April 2018 in accordance with those terms.

Finance (No. 2) Act 2017 (c. 32)
Schedule 8 — Deemed domicile: income tax and capital gains tax
Part 2 — Protection of overseas trusts

507

(8) For the purposes of this section, a loan is on "arm's length terms"—

(a) in the case of a loan made to the trustees of a settlement, only if interest at the official rate or more is payable at least annually under the loan;

(b) in the case of a loan made by the trustees of a settlement, only if any interest payable under the loan is payable at no more than the official rate.

(9) For the purposes of this section—

a settlement is "connected" with a person if the person is the settlor or a beneficiary of it;

"deemed domiciled" has the same meaning as in section 628A;

"official rate", in relation to interest, means the rate of interest applicable from time to time under section 178 of FA 1989 for the purposes of Chapter 7 of Part 3 of ITEPA 2003.

628C Foreign income arising before, but remitted on or after, 6 April 2017

(1) For the purposes of applying section 809L of ITA 2007 (meaning of remitted to the UK) in relation to transitional trust income, "relevant person" in that section does not include the trustees of the settlement concerned.

(2) "Transitional trust income" means income—

(a) that arises under a settlement in the period beginning with the tax year 2008-09 and ending with the tax year 2016-17 ("the protection period"),

(b) that would be protected foreign-source income for the purposes of section 628A(1) if section 628A(2)—

(i) had effect for the protection period, and

(ii) so had effect with a reference to conditions A to E (instead of A to F),

(c) that prior to 6 April 2017 has neither been distributed by the trustees of the settlement nor treated under section 624(1) as income of the settlor, and

(d) that would for the tax year in which it arose under the settlement have been treated under section 624(1) as income of the settlor if the settlor had been domiciled in the United Kingdom for that year.

(3) Section 648(3) to (5) (relevant foreign income treated as arising under settlement only if and when remitted), and corresponding earlier enactments, do not apply for the purposes of subsection (2)(a) and (d)."

23 (1) In section 629(5) (list of exceptions), at the end insert "or section 630A (exception for protected foreign-source income)."

(2) After section 630 insert—

"630A Exception for protected foreign-source income

(1) The rule in section 629(1) does not apply to income which arises under a settlement if it is protected foreign-source income for a tax year.

508

Finance (No. 2) Act 2017 (c. 32)
Schedule 8 – Deemed domicile: income tax and capital gains tax
Part 2 – Protection of overseas trusts

(2) Sections 628A(2) to (12) and 628B (meaning of "protected foreign-source income") have effect also for this purpose.

(3) Section 648(3) to (5) (relevant foreign income treated as arising under settlement only if and when remitted) do not apply for the purposes of this section."

24 (1) Section 635 (capital sums treated under section 633 as income: meaning of "available income") is amended as follows.

(2) In subsection (2), before "income" insert "unprotected".

(3) After subsection (4) insert—

"(5) In subsection (2) "unprotected income" means income which is not protected foreign-source income, and sections 628A(2) to (13) and 628B (meaning of "protected foreign-source income") have effect also for this purpose."

25 In section 636(1) (meaning in section 635 of "undistributed"), before "income", in both places it occurs, insert "unprotected".

26 In section 645(1) (meaning of property originating from the settlor), for "section" substitute "sections 628A and".

ITA 2007

27 Chapter 2 of Part 13 of ITA 2007 (transfer of assets abroad) is amended as follows.

28 In section 721 (income of a person abroad that is treated as arising to a UK resident individual), for subsection (3B) (amount treated as arising) substitute—

"(3B) The amount of the income treated as arising under subsection (1) is (subject to sections 724 and 725) given by the following rules—
Rule 1
The amount is equal to the amount of the income of the person abroad if the individual—
   (a) is domiciled in the United Kingdom at any time in the tax year, or
   (b) is at any time in the tax year regarded for the purposes of section 718(1)(b) as domiciled in the United Kingdom as a result of section 835BA having effect because of Condition A in that section being met.
Rule 2
In any other case, the amount is equal to so much of the income of the person abroad as is not protected foreign-source income (see section 721A).

(3BA) In a case in which rule 2 of subsection (3B) applies, so much of the income of the person abroad as is protected foreign-source income for the purposes of that rule counts as "protected income" for the purposes of section 733A(1)(b)(i)."

Finance (No. 2) Act 2017 (c. 32)
Schedule 8 — Deemed domicile: income tax and capital gains tax
Part 2 — Protection of overseas trusts

509

29   After section 721 insert—

"721A Meaning of "protected foreign-source income" in section 721

(1)   This section has effect for the purposes of rule 2 of section 721(3B) (cases where the individual is not UK domiciled and is not deemed domiciled by virtue of Condition A in section 835BA).

(2)   The income of the person abroad is "protected foreign-source income" so far as it is within subsection (3) or (4).

(3)   Income is within this subsection if—
    (a)   it would be relevant foreign income if it were the individual's,
    (b)   the person abroad is the trustees of a settlement,
    (c)   the trustees are non-UK resident for the tax year,
    (d)   when the settlement is created, the individual is—
        (i)   not domiciled in the United Kingdom, and
        (ii)   if the settlement is created on or after 6 April 2017, not deemed domiciled in the United Kingdom, and
    (e)   no property or income is provided directly or indirectly for the purposes of the settlement by the individual, or by the trustees of any other settlement of which the individual is a beneficiary or settlor, at a time in the period—
        (i)   beginning with the start of 6 April 2017 or, if later, the creation of the settlement, and
        (ii)   ending with the end of the tax year,
    when the individual is domiciled or deemed domiciled in the United Kingdom.

(4)   Income is within this subsection if—
    (a)   it would be relevant foreign income if it were the individual's,
    (b)   the person abroad is a company,
    (c)   the trustees of a settlement—
        (i)   are participators in the person abroad, or
        (ii)   are participators in the first in a chain of two or more companies where the last company in the chain is the person abroad and where each company in the chain (except the last) is a participator in the next company in the chain,
    (d)   the individual's power to enjoy the income results from the trustees being participators as mentioned in paragraph (c)(i) or (ii),
    (e)   the trustees are not UK resident for the tax year,
    (f)   when the settlement is created, the individual is—
        (i)   not domiciled in the United Kingdom, and
        (ii)   if the settlement is created on or after 6 April 2017, not deemed domiciled in the United Kingdom, and
    (g)   no property or income is provided directly or indirectly for the purposes of the settlement by the individual, or by the trustees of any other settlement of which the individual is a beneficiary or settlor, at a time in the period—

510   *Finance (No. 2) Act 2017 (c. 32)*
Schedule 8 — Deemed domicile: income tax and capital gains tax
Part 2 — Protection of overseas trusts

          (i)   beginning with the start of 6 April 2017 or, if later, the creation of the settlement, and

          (ii)   ending with the end of the tax year,

    when the individual is domiciled or deemed domiciled in the United Kingdom.

(5)   For the purposes of subsections (3)(e) and (4)(g), the addition of value to property comprised in the settlement is to be treated as the direct provision of property for the purposes of the settlement.

(6)   Section 721B (tainting) contains further provision for the purposes of subsections (3)(e) and (4)(g).

(7)   In this section—

    "participator", in relation to a company, has the meaning given by section 454 of CTA 2010;

    "deemed domiciled" means regarded for the purposes of section 718(1)(b) as domiciled in the United Kingdom as a result of section 835BA of ITA 2007 having effect.

721B Section 721A: tainting

(1)   This section applies for the purposes of subsections (3)(e) and (4)(g) of section 721A.

(2)   Ignore—

    (a)   property or income provided under a transaction, other than a loan, where the transaction is entered into on arm's length terms,

    (b)   property or income provided, otherwise than under a loan, without any intention by the person providing it to confer a gratuitous benefit on any person,

    (c)   the principal of a loan which is made to the trustees of the settlement on arm's length terms,

    (d)   the payment of interest to the trustees of the settlement under a loan made by them on arm's length terms,

    (e)   repayment to the trustees of the settlement of the principal of a loan made by them,

    (f)   property or income provided in pursuance of a liability incurred by any person before 6 April 2017, and

    (g)   where the settlement's expenses relating to taxation and administration for a tax year exceed its income for that year, property or income provided towards meeting that excess if the value of any such property and income is not greater than the amount of—

          (i)   the excess, or

          (ii)   if greater, the amount by which such expenses exceed the amount of such expenses which may be paid out of the settlement's income.

(3)   Where—

    (a)   a loan is made to the trustees of the settlement by the settlor or the trustees of a settlement connected with the settlor, and

    (b)   the loan is on arm's length terms, but

    (c)   a relevant event occurs,

Finance (No. 2) Act 2017 (c. 32)
Schedule 8 — Deemed domicile: income tax and capital gains tax
Part 2 — Protection of overseas trusts

511

the principal of the loan is to be regarded as having been provided to the trustees at the time of that event (despite subsection (2)).

(4) In subsection (3) "relevant event" means —
    (a) capitalisation of interest payable under the loan,
    (b) any other failure to pay interest in accordance with the terms of the loan, or
    (c) variation of the terms of the loan such that they cease to be arm's length terms.

(5) Subsection (6) applies (subject to subsection (7)) where —
    (a) the settlor becomes deemed domiciled in the United Kingdom on or after 6 April 2017,
    (b) before the date on which the settlor becomes deemed domiciled in the United Kingdom ("the deemed domicile date"), a loan has been made to the trustees of the settlement by —
        (i) the settlor, or
        (ii) the trustees of a settlement connected with the settlor,
    (c) the loan is not entered into on arm's length terms, and
    (d) any amount that is outstanding under the loan on the deemed domicile date ("the outstanding amount") is payable or repayable on demand on or after that date.

(6) Where this subsection applies, the outstanding amount is to be regarded as property directly provided on the deemed domicile date by the lender for the purposes of the settlement (despite subsection (2)).

(7) But if the deemed domicile date is 6 April 2017, subsection (6) does not apply if —
    (a) the principal of the loan is repaid, and all interest payable under the loan is paid, before 6 April 2018, or
    (b) the loan becomes a loan on arm's length terms before 6 April 2018 and —
        (i) before that date interest is paid to the lender in respect of the period beginning with 6 April 2017 and ending with 5 April 2018 as if those arm's length terms had been terms of the loan in relation to that period, and
        (ii) interest continues to be payable from 6 April 2018 in accordance with those terms.

(8) For the purposes of this section, a loan is on "arm's length terms" —
    (a) in the case of a loan made to the trustees of a settlement, only if interest at the official rate or more is payable at least annually under the loan;
    (b) in the case of a loan made by the trustees of a settlement, only if any interest payable under the loan is payable at no more than the official rate.

(9) For the purposes of this section —
    a settlement is "connected" with a person if the person is the settlor or a beneficiary of it;
    "deemed domiciled" has the same meaning as in section 721A;

512

Finance (No. 2) Act 2017 (c. 32)
Schedule 8 — Deemed domicile: income tax and capital gains tax
Part 2 — Protection of overseas trusts

"official rate", in relation to interest, means the rate of interest applicable from time to time under section 178 of FA 1989 for the purposes of Chapter 7 of Part 3 of ITEPA 2003."

30   In section 726 (individuals to whom remittance basis applies), after subsection (5) insert—

"(6)   In addition, where the tax year in which any foreign deemed income arises is earlier than the tax year 2017-18, section 832 of ITTOIA 2005 does not apply to the foreign deemed income so far as it—

(a)   is remitted to the United Kingdom in the tax year 2017-18 or a later tax year, and

(b)   is transitionally protected income.

(7)   In subsection (6)—

"remitted to the United Kingdom" is to be read in accordance with Chapter A1 of Part 14, and

"transitionally protected income" means any foreign deemed income where the income mentioned in section 721(2)—

(a)   arises in a tax year earlier than the tax year 2017-18,

(b)   would be protected foreign-source income as defined by section 721A if section 721A—

(i)   had effect for tax years earlier than the tax year 2017-18, and

(ii)   so had effect with the omission of its subsections (3)(e), (4)(g), (5) and (6), and

(c)   has not prior to 6 April 2017 been distributed by the trustees of the settlement concerned."

31   In section 728 (income of a person abroad that is treated as arising to a UK resident individual), for subsection (1A) (amount treated as arising) substitute—

"(1A)   The amount of the income treated as arising under subsection (1) is (subject to subsection (2)) given by the following rules—

Rule 1

The amount is equal to the amount of the income of the person abroad if the individual—

(a)   is domiciled in the United Kingdom at any time in the tax year, or

(b)   is at any time in the tax year regarded for the purposes of section 718(1)(b) as domiciled in the United Kingdom as a result of section 835BA having effect because of Condition A in that section being met.

Rule 2

In any other case, the amount is equal to so much of the income of the person abroad as is not protected foreign-source income (see section 729A).

(1B)   In a case in which rule 2 of subsection (1A) applies, so much of the income of the person abroad as is protected foreign-source income for the purposes of that rule counts as "protected income" for the purposes of section 733A(1)(b)(i)."

Finance (No. 2) Act 2017 (c. 32)   **513**
Schedule 8 — Deemed domicile: income tax and capital gains tax
Part 2 — Protection of overseas trusts

32   After section 729 insert—

"729A Meaning of "protected foreign-source income" in section 728

   (1)   This section has effect for the purposes of rule 2 of section 728(1A) (cases where the individual is not UK domiciled and is not deemed domiciled by virtue of Condition A in section 835BA).

   (2)   The income of the person abroad is "protected foreign-source income" so far as it is within subsection (3) or (4).

   (3)   Income is within this subsection if—
      (a)   it would be relevant foreign income if it were the individual's,
      (b)   the person abroad is the trustees of a settlement,
      (c)   the trustees are non-UK resident for the tax year,
      (d)   when the settlement is created, the individual is—
         (i)   not domiciled in the United Kingdom, and
        (ii)   if the settlement is created on or after 6 April 2017, not deemed domiciled in the United Kingdom, and
      (e)   no property or income is provided directly or indirectly for the purposes of the settlement by the individual, or by the trustees of any other settlement of which the individual is a beneficiary or settlor, at a time in the period—
         (i)   beginning with the start of 6 April 2017 or, if later, the creation of the settlement, and
        (ii)   ending with the end of the tax year,
       when the individual is domiciled or deemed domiciled in the United Kingdom.

   (4)   Income is within this subsection if—
      (a)   it would be relevant foreign income if it were the individual's,
      (b)   the person abroad is a company,
      (c)   the trustees of a settlement—
         (i)   are participators in the person abroad, or
        (ii)   are participators in the first in a chain of two or more companies where the last company in the chain is the person abroad and where each company in the chain (except the last) is a participator in the next company in the chain,
      (d)   the condition in paragraph (c) is met as a result of a relevant transaction (whether or not it is also met otherwise than as a result of a relevant transaction),
      (e)   the income has become the income of the person abroad as a result of that relevant transaction,
      (f)   the trustees are not UK resident for the tax year,
      (g)   when the settlement is created, the individual is—
         (i)   not domiciled in the United Kingdom, and
        (ii)   if the settlement is created on or after 6 April 2017, not deemed domiciled in the United Kingdom, and
      (h)   no property or income is provided directly or indirectly for the purposes of the settlement by the individual, or by the

514   *Finance (No. 2) Act 2017 (c. 32)*
Schedule 8 — Deemed domicile: income tax and capital gains tax
Part 2 — Protection of overseas trusts

trustees of any other settlement of which the individual is a beneficiary or settlor, at a time in the period—

    (i)   beginning with start of 6 April 2017 or, if later, the creation of the settlement, and

    (ii)   ending with the end of the tax year,

when the individual is domiciled or deemed domiciled in the United Kingdom.

(5)   For the purposes of subsections (3)(e) and (4)(h), the addition of value to property comprised in the settlement is to be treated as the direct provision of property for the purposes of the settlement.

(6)   Section 721B (tainting) applies for the purposes of subsections (3)(e) and (4)(h) as it applies for the purposes of section 721A(3)(e) and (4)(g).

(7)   In this section—

      "participator", in relation to a company, has the meaning given by section 454 of CTA 2010, and

      "deemed domiciled" means regarded for the purposes of section 718(1)(b) as domiciled in the United Kingdom as a result of section 835BA of ITA 2007 having effect."

33   In section 730 (individuals to whom remittance basis applies), after subsection (5) insert—

    "(6)   In addition, where the tax year in which any foreign deemed income arises is earlier than the tax year 2017-18, section 832 of ITTOIA 2005 does not apply to the foreign deemed income so far as it—

      (a)   is remitted to the United Kingdom in the tax year 2017-18 or a later tax year, and

      (b)   is transitionally protected income.

    (7)   In subsection (6)—

      "remitted to the United Kingdom" is to be read in accordance with Chapter A1 of Part 14, and

      "transitionally protected income" means any foreign deemed income where the income mentioned in section 728(1)(a)—

        (a)   arises in a tax year earlier than the tax year 2017-18,

        (b)   would be protected foreign-source income as defined by section 729A if section 729A—

          (i)   had effect for tax years earlier than the tax year 2017-18, and

          (ii)   so had effect with the omission of its subsections (3)(e), (4)(h), (5) and (6), and

        (c)   has not prior to 6 April 2017 been distributed by the trustees of the settlement concerned."

34   (1)   Section 731 (charge to tax on income treated as arising under section 732) is amended as follows.

    (2)   In subsection (1), for "non-transferors" substitute "individuals".

Finance (No. 2) Act 2017 (c. 32)
Schedule 8 — Deemed domicile: income tax and capital gains tax
Part 2 — Protection of overseas trusts

515

(3) After subsection (1) insert—

"(1A) But where the individual is non-UK resident for the tax year in which a benefit is received, there is a charge to tax under this section on any matched deemed income—

(a) only so far as that matched deemed income would under section 735A (if it applied also for this purpose) be matched with an amount of relevant income that is protected income for the purposes of section 733A(1)(b)(i) (see sections 721(3BA) and 728(1B)), and

(b) only if—

(i) the individual is the settlor of the settlement concerned, or

(ii) the benefit is received by the individual at a time when the individual is a close member of the family of the settlor of that settlement.

(1B) For the purposes of subsection (1A)—

(a) "matched deemed income" means income which—

(i) is treated by section 732 as arising to the individual, and

(ii) would, if section 735A applied also for this purpose, be matched under that section with the benefit, and

(b) a person is a close member of the family of the settlor of a settlement if the person is—

(i) the settlor's spouse or civil partner, or

(ii) a child of the settlor, or of a person within sub-paragraph (i), if the child has not reached the age of 18;

and section 733A(7) (persons living together) applies also for the purposes of paragraph (b)."

(4) In subsection (3) (person liable for tax is person to whom income is treated as arising), at the end insert ", but this is subject to section 733A."

35 (1) Section 732 (when income is treated as arising for the purposes of the charge under section 731) is amended in accordance with sub-paragraphs (2) to (4).

(2) In subsection (1) (cases in which tax can be charged under section 731)—

(a) in paragraph (b), for "who is UK resident for a tax year receives a benefit in that tax year" substitute "receives a benefit in a tax year", and

(b) for paragraph (d) substitute—

"(d) where there is a time in the year when the individual is relevantly domiciled, the individual is not liable to income tax under section 720 or 727 by reference to the transfer, and".

(3) After subsection (3) insert—

"(4) For the purposes of subsection (1)(d), the individual is "relevantly domiciled" at any time if at that time—

(a) the individual is domiciled in the United Kingdom, or

(b) the individual is regarded for the purposes of section 718(1)(b) as domiciled in the United Kingdom as a result of

516   *Finance (No. 2) Act 2017 (c. 32)*
Schedule 8 — Deemed domicile: income tax and capital gains tax
Part 2 — Protection of overseas trusts

section 835BA having effect because of Condition A in that section being met."

(4) In the heading, for "Non-transferors" substitute "Individuals".

(5) In section 733(1) (income charged under section 731), in the first sentence of Step 2, at the end insert "except that, where any of that income is matched deemed income for the purposes of section 731(1A), that matched deemed income is to be deducted only so far as it is matched deemed income on which tax has been charged under section 731 for an earlier tax year."

36   After section 733 insert—

"733A Settlor liable for section 731 charge on closely-related beneficiary

(1) Subsections (2) and (3) apply if—

    (a) an amount of income is treated as arising to an individual under section 732 for a tax year,

    (b) under section 735A (if it applied also for this purpose) that amount would be matched—

        (i) with an amount of relevant income that is protected income for the purposes of this sub-paragraph (see sections 721(3BA) and 728(1B)), and

        (ii) with a benefit received by the individual at a time when the individual was a close member (see subsection (7)) of the family of the settlor of the settlement concerned,

    (c) there is no time in the year when the trustees of the settlement are resident in the United Kingdom,

    (d) there is a time in the year when the settlor is resident in the United Kingdom,

    (e) there is no time in the year when the settlor is domiciled in the United Kingdom, and

    (f) there is no time in the year when the settlor is regarded for the purposes of section 718(1)(b) as domiciled in the United Kingdom as a result of section 835BA having effect because of Condition A in that section being met.

(2) If—

    (a) the individual is not resident in the United Kingdom at any time in the year, or

    (b) section 809B, 809D or 809E (remittance basis) applies to the individual for the year and none of the amount mentioned in subsection (1)(a) of this section is remitted to the United Kingdom in the year,

the settlor is liable for the tax charged under section 731 on that amount as if that amount were income arising to the settlor in the year (and the individual is not liable in any later year for income tax on that amount).

(3) If—

    (a) section 809B, 809D or 809E (remittance basis) applies to the individual for the year, and

    (b) part only of the amount mentioned in subsection (1)(a) of this section is remitted to the United Kingdom in the year,

Finance (No. 2) Act 2017 (c. 32)
Schedule 8 — Deemed domicile: income tax and capital gains tax
Part 2 — Protection of overseas trusts

517

the settlor is liable for the tax charged under section 731 on the remainder of that amount as if that remainder were income arising to the settlor in the year (and the individual is not liable in any later year for income tax on that remainder).

(4) The amount mentioned in subsection (1)(a) may be the whole, or part only, of the amount treated as arising to the individual under section 732 for the year in the case of the relevant transfer and its associated operations.

(5) Where any tax for which the settlor is liable as a result of subsection (2) or (3) is paid, the settlor is entitled to recover the amount of the tax from the individual.

(6) For the purpose of recovering that amount, the settlor is entitled to require an officer of Revenue and Customs to give the settlor a certificate specifying—

    (a)   the amount of the income concerned, and

    (b)   the amount of tax paid,

and any such certificate is conclusive evidence of the facts stated in it.

(7) For the purposes of subsection (1)(b)(ii), a person is a close member of the family of the settlor if the person is—

    (a)   the settlor's spouse or civil partner, or

    (b)   a child of the settlor, or of a person within paragraph (a), if the child has not reached the age of 18.

(8) For the purposes of subsection (7)—

    (a)   two people living together as if they were spouses of each other are treated as if they were spouses of each other, and

    (b)   two people of the same sex living together as if they were civil partners of each other are treated as if they were civil partners of each other.

(9) Sections 809L to 809Z6 (remittance basis: rules about when income is remitted, including rule treating pre-arising remittances of deemed income as made when the income arises) apply for the purposes of this section."

37   In section 735A(6) (matching of income on which individual charged under section 731), after "individual" insert ", or as a result of section 733A another person,".

38   After section 735A insert—

"735B Settlor liable under section 733A and remittance basis applies

(1) This section applies in relation to income if—

    (a)   the income is treated by section 732 as arising to an individual ("the beneficiary") for a tax year,

    (b)   another individual ("the settlor") is under section 733A(2) or (3) liable for tax on the income, and

    (c)   section 809B, 809D or 809E (remittance basis) applies to the settlor for that year.

(2) The income ("the transferred-liability deemed income") is treated as relevant foreign income of the settlor.

518

Finance (No. 2) Act 2017 (c. 32)
Schedule 8 — Deemed domicile: income tax and capital gains tax
Part 2 — Protection of overseas trusts

(3) If, for the purposes of section 735 as it applies in relation to the beneficiary, any benefit or relevant income relates to any part of the transferred-liability deemed income then, for the purposes of Chapter A1 of Part 14 as it applies in relation to the settlor, that benefit or relevant income is to be treated as deriving from that part of the transferred-liability deemed income.

(4) In the application of section 832 of ITTOIA 2005 in relation to the income, subsection (2) of that section has effect with the omission of its paragraph (b)."

Commencement of amendments in FA 2004, ITTOIA 2005 and ITA 2007

39 The amendments made by paragraphs 19 to 38 have effect for the tax year 2017-18 and subsequent tax years.

FA 2008

40 In Part 2 of Schedule 7 to FA 2008 (remittance basis: trusts etc), after paragraph 171 insert—

"172 (1) Sub-paragraph (2) has effect for the purposes of—
paragraphs 100(1)(b), 101(1)(c) and 102(1)(e),
paragraph (b) of paragraph 118(3) so far as having effect for the purposes of paragraph 118(1)(d), and
paragraphs 124(1)(b), 126(7)(b), 127(1)(e) and 151(1)(b).

(2) An individual not domiciled in the United Kingdom at a time in the tax year 2017-18, or a later tax year, is to be regarded as domiciled in the United Kingdom at that time if—
    (a) the individual was born in the United Kingdom,
    (b) the individual's domicile of origin was in the United Kingdom, and
    (c) the individual is resident in the United Kingdom for the tax year concerned."

PART 3

CAPITAL GAINS TAX REBASING

41 (1) This paragraph applies to the disposal of an asset by an individual ("P") where—
    (a) the asset was held by P on 5 April 2017,
    (b) the disposal is made on or after 6 April 2017,
    (c) the asset was not situated in the United Kingdom at any time in the relevant period, and
    (d) P is a qualifying individual.

(2) The relevant period is the period which—
    (a) begins with 16 March 2016 or, if later, the date on which P acquired the asset, and
    (b) ends with 5 April 2017.

(3) P is a qualifying individual if—

Finance (No. 2) Act 2017 (c. 32)
Schedule 8 – Deemed domicile: income tax and capital gains tax
Part 3 – Capital gains tax rebasing

519

(a) section 809H of ITA 2007 (claim for remittance basis by long-term UK resident: charge) applied in relation to P for any tax year before the tax year 2017-18,

(b) P is not an individual –

(i) who was born in the United Kingdom, and

(ii) whose domicile of origin was in the United Kingdom,

(c) P was not domiciled in the United Kingdom at any time in a relevant tax year, and

(d) P met condition B in section 835BA of ITA 2007 in relation to each relevant tax year.

(4) The relevant tax years are –

(a) the tax year 2017-18, and

(b) if the disposal was made after that tax year, all subsequent tax years up to and including that in which the disposal was made.

(5) In computing, for the purpose of TCGA 1992, the gain or loss accruing on the disposal, it is to be assumed that P acquired the asset on 5 April 2017 for a consideration equal to its market value on that date.

(6) Sub-paragraph (5) applies notwithstanding section 58(1) of TCGA 1992 (disposals between spouses).

(7) Where under section 127 of TCGA 1992 (including that section as applied by sections 132, 135 and 136 of that Act) an original and a new holding of shares or other securities are treated as the same asset, the condition in sub-paragraph (1)(c) applies to both the original and the new holding.

(8) This Part of this Schedule has effect as if it were included in TCGA 1992.

42 (1) This paragraph applies for the purposes of paragraph 41(1)(c) in the case of an asset which, having been situated outside the United Kingdom, becomes situated in the United Kingdom before the end of the relevant period.

(2) The asset is to be regarded as not situated in the United Kingdom at a time in the relevant period when –

(a) it meets the condition in section 809Z(3)(a), (b) or (c) of ITA 2007 (public access),

(b) it meets the condition in section 809Z3(3)(a), (b) or (c) of ITA 2007 (repairs),

(c) the sole or principal purpose of its being situated in the United Kingdom is to sell it or put it up for sale, or

(d) in the case of clothing, footwear, jewellery or a watch, it is for the personal use of –

(i) P or a husband, wife or civil partner of P, or

(ii) a child or grandchild of a person within sub-paragraph (i), if the child or grandchild has not reached the age of 18.

(3) The asset is to be regarded as not situated in the United Kingdom at any time in the relevant period if it is brought to, or received or used in, the United Kingdom in circumstances in which section 809L(2)(a) of ITA 2007 applies but –

(a) by virtue of section 809X(5)(c) of ITA 2007 (notional remitted amount less than £1000) it is treated as not remitted to the United Kingdom, or

520

Finance (No. 2) Act 2017 (c. 32)
Schedule 8 — Deemed domicile: income tax and capital gains tax
Part 3 — Capital gains tax rebasing

      (b)   by the end of the relevant period it has not failed to meet the temporary importation rule in section 809Z4 of ITA 2007.

    (4) Section 809M(3)(a) and (b) of ITA 2007 (persons living together) apply for the purposes of sub-paragraph (2)(d)(i).

43   (1) An individual may make an election for paragraph 41 not to apply to a disposal made by the individual.

    (2) Sections 42 and 43 of TMA 1970 (procedure and time limit for claims), except section 42(1A) of that Act, apply in relation to an election under this paragraph as they apply in relation to a claim for relief.

    (3) An election under this paragraph is irrevocable.

    (4) All such adjustments are to be made, whether by way of discharge or repayment of tax, the making of assessments or otherwise, as are required to give effect to an election under this paragraph.

PART 4

CLEANSING OF MIXED FUNDS

44   (1) This paragraph applies for the purposes of the application of section 809Q(3) of ITA 2007 in relation to an individual ("P").

    (2) Section 809R(4) of ITA 2007 does not apply to an offshore transfer from a mixed fund where—

      (a)   the transfer is made in the tax year 2017-18 or the tax year 2018-19,

      (b)   the transfer is a transfer of money,

      (c)   the mixed fund from which the transfer is made is an account (account A) and the transfer is made to another account (account B),

      (d)   the transfer is nominated by P for the purposes of this sub-paragraph,

      (e)   at the time of the nomination no other transfer from account A to account B has been so nominated, and

      (f)   P is a qualifying individual.

    (3) P is a qualifying individual if—

      (a)   section 809B, 809D or 809E of ITA 2007 (remittance basis) applied in relation to P for any tax year before the tax year 2017-18, and

      (b)   P is not an individual—

         (i)   who was born in the United Kingdom, and

        (ii)   whose domicile of origin was in the United Kingdom.

    (4) An offshore transfer to which sub-paragraph (2) applies is to be treated as containing such amount of such kind or kinds of income and capital in the mixed fund immediately before the transfer as may be specified in the nomination under sub-paragraph (2)(d).

    (5) An amount of a kind of income or capital specified under sub-paragraph (4) may not exceed the amount of that kind which is in the mixed fund immediately before the transfer.

    (6) In this paragraph "mixed fund" and "offshore transfer" have the same meanings as in section 809R(4) of ITA 2007.

Finance (No. 2) Act 2017 (c. 32)
Schedule 8 – Deemed domicile: income tax and capital gains tax
Part 4 – Cleansing of mixed funds

521

45   (1) This paragraph applies to a transfer made by a person ("P") from a mixed fund where—

    (a) the transfer is made in the tax year 2017-18 or the tax year 2018-19,

    (b) the transfer is a transfer of money,

    (c) the mixed fund from which the transfer is made is an overseas account (account A) containing pre-6 April 2008 income or chargeable gains,

    (d) the transfer is made to another overseas account (account B),

    (e) the transfer is nominated by the person for the purposes of this sub-paragraph,

    (f) at the time of the nomination no other transfer from account A to account B has been so nominated, and

    (g) P is a qualifying individual.

    (2) P is a qualifying individual if—

    (a) section 809B, 809D or 809E of ITA 2007 (remittance basis) applied in relation to P for any tax year before the tax year 2017-18, and

    (b) P is not an individual—

        (i) who was born in the United Kingdom, and

        (ii) whose domicile of origin was in the United Kingdom.

    (3) A transfer to which this paragraph applies is to be treated as containing such amount of such kind or kinds of income or capital in the mixed fund immediately before the transfer (for example, income or chargeable gains for a particular tax year) as may be specified in the nomination under sub-paragraph (1)(e).

    (4) An amount of a kind of income or capital specified under sub-paragraph (3) may not exceed the amount of that kind which is in the mixed fund immediately before the transfer.

    (5) In this paragraph and paragraph 46—

      "mixed fund" has the same meaning as in section 809R(4) of ITA 2007;

      "overseas account" means an account situated outside the United Kingdom;

      "pre-6 April 2008 income or chargeable gains" means income or chargeable gains for the tax year 2007-8 or any earlier tax year.

46   (1) This paragraph applies to determine, for the purposes of paragraph 45, the composition of the mixed fund referred to in paragraph 45(1).

    (2) Sub-paragraphs (3) to (5) apply where a transfer of money is made before 6 April 2008 from the mixed fund to another overseas account.

    (3) Take the following Steps—

      Step 1. Calculate the total amount of income and chargeable gains in the mixed fund immediately before the transfer ("the total income and gains").

      Step 2. Calculate what proportion of the total income and gains is income and what proportion is chargeable gains.

    (4) If the amount transferred does not exceed the total income and gains, the transfer is to be treated as if it consisted of income and chargeable gains in the proportions found under Step 2 in sub-paragraph (3).

522

Finance (No. 2) Act 2017 (c. 32)
Schedule 8 — Deemed domicile: income tax and capital gains tax
Part 4 — Cleansing of mixed funds

(5) If the amount transferred exceeds the total income and gains, the transfer is to be treated as if it consisted of—

    (a) all the income and chargeable gains that were in the mixed fund immediately before the transfer, and

    (b) in respect of the balance, other capital from the mixed fund.

(6) Sub-paragraphs (7) and (8) apply where—

    (a) a transfer of money is made before 6 April 2008 from another overseas account to the mixed fund, and

    (b) there is insufficient evidence to determine the composition of the transfer.

(7) Take the following Steps—

    Step 1. Calculate the total amount of income and chargeable gains in the other overseas account immediately before the transfer ("the total income and gains").

    Step 2. Calculate what proportion of the total income and gains is income and what proportion is chargeable gains.

(8) The transfer is to be presumed to consist of income and chargeable gains in the proportions found under Step 2 in sub-paragraph (7).

(9) For the purposes of Steps 1 and 2 in sub-paragraph (7), if there is insufficient evidence to say that an amount is income or that it is chargeable gains, treat it as income.

SCHEDULE 9

Section 31

SETTLEMENTS AND TRANSFER OF ASSETS ABROAD: VALUE OF BENEFITS

Capital gains tax: settlements: value of benefit conferred by certain capital payments

1   (1) In section 97(4) of TCGA 1992 (supplementary provisions in relation to settlements), at the end insert "(see sections 97A to 97C for the value of benefits conferred by a capital payment made by way of loan or by way of making movable property or land available)".

    (2) After section 97 of TCGA 1992 insert—

"97A Value of benefit conferred by capital payment made by way of loan

    (1) For the purposes of section 97(4), the value of the benefit conferred on a person (P) by a capital payment made by way of loan to P is, for each tax year in which the loan is outstanding, the amount (if any) by which—

        (a) the amount of interest that would have been payable in that year on the loan if interest had been payable on the loan at the official rate, exceeds

        (b) the amount of interest (if any) actually paid by P in that year on the loan.

    (2) In this section and section 97B the "official rate", in relation to interest, means the rate applicable from time to time under section

178 of the Finance Act 1989 for the purposes of Chapter 7 of Part 3 of ITEPA 2003.

97B Value of benefit conferred by capital payment made by way of making movable property available

(1) For the purposes of section 97(4), the value of the benefit conferred by a capital payment consisting of making movable property available, without any transfer of the property in it, to a person (P) is, for each tax year in which the benefit is conferred on P—

$$\left(\frac{CC \times R \times D}{Y} \right) - T$$

where—

CC is the capital cost of the movable property on the date when the property is first made available to P in the tax year,

D is the number of days in the tax year on which the property is made available to P (the relevant period),

R is the official rate of interest for the relevant period (but see subsection (3)),

T is the total of the amounts (if any) paid in the tax year by P—

(a) to the person conferring the benefit, in respect of the availability of the movable property, or

(b) so far as not within paragraph (a), in respect of the repair, insurance, maintenance or storage of the movable property, and

Y is the number of days in the tax year.

(2) In subsection (1), in the meaning of CC, the "capital cost" of movable property means an amount equal to the total of—

(a) the amount which is the greater of—

(i) the amount or value of the consideration given for the acquisition of the movable property by, or on behalf of, the person (A) conferring the benefit, and

(ii) its market value at the time of that acquisition, and

(b) the amount of any expenditure wholly and exclusively incurred by, or on behalf of, A for the purpose of enhancing the value of the movable property.

(3) If the official rate of interest changes during the relevant period, then in subsection (1) R is the average official rate of interest for the period calculated as follows.

Step 1

Multiply each official rate of interest in force during the relevant period by the number of days when it is in force.

Step 2

Add together the products found in Step 1.

Step 3

Divide the total found in Step 2 by the number of days in the relevant period.

(4) In subsections (1) and (2), "movable property" means any tangible movable property other than money.

97C Value of benefit conferred by capital payment made by way of making land available

(1) For the purposes of section 97(4), the value of the benefit conferred by a capital payment consisting of making land available for the use of a person (P) is, for each tax year in which the benefit is conferred on P, the amount by which—

   (a) the rental value of the land for the period of the tax year during which the land is made available to P, exceeds

   (b) the total of the amounts (if any) paid in the tax year by P—

      (i)   to the person conferring the benefit, in respect of the availability of the land, or

      (ii) so far as not within sub-paragraph (i), in respect of costs of repair, insurance or maintenance relating to the land.

(2) Subsection (1) does not apply in the case where the person conferring the benefit transfers the whole of the person's interest in the land to P.

(3) In subsection (1) "the rental value" of the land for a period means the rent which would have been payable for the period if the land had been let to P at an annual rent equal to the annual value.

(4) For the purposes of subsection (3) "the annual value" of land is the rent that might reasonably be expected to be obtained on a letting from year to year if—

   (a) the tenant undertook to pay all taxes, rates and charges usually paid by a tenant, and

   (b) the landlord undertook to bear the costs of the repairs and insurance and the other expenses (if any) necessary for maintaining the property in a state to command that rent.

(5) For the purposes of subsection (4) that rent—

   (a) is to be taken to be the amount that might reasonably be expected to be so obtained in respect of a letting of the land, and

   (b) is to be calculated on the basis that the only amounts that may be deducted in respect of services provided by the landlord are amounts in respect of the costs to the landlord of providing any relevant services.

(6) In subsection (5) "relevant service" means a service other than the repair, insurance or maintenance of the property."

Income tax: transfer of assets abroad: value of certain benefits

2   After section 742A of ITA 2007 insert—

"Value of certain benefits

742B Value of certain benefits

Sections 742C to 742E apply where it is necessary, for the purpose of calculating a charge to income tax under the preceding provisions of this Chapter, to determine the value of a benefit provided to a person by way of—

    (a)   a payment by way of loan (see section 742C),

    (b)   making available movable property without any transfer of the property in it (see section 742D), or

    (c)   making available land for use without transferring the whole interest in it (see section 742E).

742C Value of benefit provided by a payment by way of loan

    (1)   The value of the benefit provided to a person (P) by a payment by way of loan to P is, for each tax year in which the loan is outstanding, the amount (if any) by which—

        (a)   the amount of interest that would have been payable in that year on the loan if interest had been payable on the loan at the official rate, exceeds

        (b)   the amount of interest (if any) actually paid by P in that year on the loan.

    (2)   In this section and section 742D the "official rate", in relation to interest, means the rate applicable from time to time under section 178 of the Finance Act 1989 for the purposes of Chapter 7 of Part 3 of ITEPA 2003.

742D Value of benefit provided by making movable property available

    (1)   The value of the benefit provided by making movable property available, without any transfer of the property in it, to a person (P) is, for each tax year in which the benefit is provided to P—

$$\left(\frac{CC \times R \times D}{Y}\right) - T$$

where—

    CC is the capital cost of the movable property on the date when the property is first made available to P in the tax year,

    D is the number of days in the tax year on which the property is made available to P (the relevant period),

    R is the official rate of interest for the relevant period (but see subsection (3)),

    T is the total of the amounts (if any) paid in the tax year by P—

        (a)   to the person providing the benefit, in respect of the availability of the movable property, or

        (b)   so far as not within paragraph (a), in respect of the repair, insurance, maintenance or storage of the movable property, and

    Y is the number of days in the tax year.

    (2)   In subsection (1), in the meaning of CC, the "capital cost" of the movable property means an amount equal to the total of—

        (a)   the amount which is the greater of—

            (i)   the amount or value of the consideration given for the acquisition of the movable property by, or on behalf of, the person (A) providing the benefit, and

           (ii)   its market value at the time of that acquisition, and

  (b) the amount of any expenditure wholly and exclusively incurred by, or on behalf of, A for the purpose of enhancing the value of the movable property.

(3) If the official rate of interest changes during the relevant period, then in subsection (1) R is the average official rate of interest for the period calculated as follows.

Step 1

Multiply each official rate of interest in force during the relevant period by the number of days when it is in force.

Step 2

Add together the products found in Step 1.

Step 3

Divide the total found in Step 2 by the number of days in the relevant period.

(4) In subsections (1) and (2), "movable property" means any tangible movable property other than money.

742E Value of benefit provided by making land available

(1) The value of the benefit provided by making land available for the use of a person (P) is, for each tax year in which the benefit is provided to P, the amount by which—

  (a) the rental value of the land for the period of the tax year during which the land is made available to P, exceeds

  (b) the total of the amounts (if any) paid in the tax year by P—

    (i) to the person providing the benefit, in respect of the availability of the land, or

    (ii) so far as not within sub-paragraph (i), in respect of costs of repair, insurance or maintenance relating to the land.

(2) Subsection (1) does not apply in the case where the person providing the benefit transfers the whole of the person's interest in the land to P.

(3) In subsection (1) "the rental value" of the land for a period means the rent which would have been payable for the period if the land had been let to P at an annual rent equal to the annual value.

(4) For the purposes of subsection (3) "the annual value" of land is the rent that might reasonably be expected to be obtained on a letting from year to year if—

  (a) the tenant undertook to pay all taxes, rates and charges usually paid by a tenant, and

  (b) the landlord undertook to bear the costs of the repairs and insurance and the other expenses (if any) necessary for maintaining the property in a state to command that rent.

(5) For the purposes of subsection (4) that rent—

  (a) is to be taken to be the amount that might reasonably be expected to be so obtained in respect of a letting of the land, and

     (b) is to be calculated on the basis that the only amounts that may be deducted in respect of services provided by the landlord are amounts in respect of the costs to the landlord of providing any relevant services."

    (6) In subsection (5) "relevant service" means a service other than the repair, insurance or maintenance of the property."

Commencement

3   The amendments made by this Schedule have effect in relation to capital payments or benefits received in the tax year 2017-18 and subsequent tax years.

SCHEDULE 10

Section 33

INHERITANCE TAX ON OVERSEAS PROPERTY REPRESENTING UK RESIDENTIAL PROPERTY

Non-excluded overseas property

1   In IHTA 1984, before Schedule 1 insert—

"SCHEDULE A1

NON-EXCLUDED OVERSEAS PROPERTY

PART 1

OVERSEAS PROPERTY WITH VALUE ATTRIBUTABLE TO UK RESIDENTIAL PROPERTY

Introductory

1   Property is not excluded property by virtue of section 6(1) or 48(3)(a) if and to the extent that paragraph 2 or 3 applies to it.

Close company and partnership interests

2   (1) This paragraph applies to an interest in a close company or in a partnership, if and to the extent that the interest meets the condition in sub-paragraph (2).

    (2) The condition is that the value of the interest is—

        (a) directly attributable to a UK residential property interest, or

        (b) attributable to a UK residential property interest by virtue only of one or more of the following—

           (i) an interest in a close company;

          (ii) an interest in a partnership;

         (iii) property to which paragraph 3 (loans) applies.

    (3) For the purposes of sub-paragraphs (1) and (2) disregard—

   (a) an interest in a close company, if the value of the interest is less than 5% of the total value of all the interests in the close company;

   (b) an interest in a partnership, if the value of the interest is less than 5% of the total value of all the interests in the partnership.

(4) In determining under sub-paragraph (3) whether to disregard a person's interest in a close company or partnership, treat the value of the person's interest as increased by the value of any connected person's interest in the close company or partnership.

(5) In determining whether or to what extent the value of an interest in a close company or in a partnership is attributable to a UK residential property interest for the purposes of sub-paragraph (1), liabilities of a close company or partnership are to be attributed rateably to all of its property, whether or not they would otherwise be attributed to any particular property.

Loans

3 This paragraph applies to —

   (a) the rights of a creditor in respect of a loan which is a relevant loan (see paragraph 4), and

   (b) money or money's worth held or otherwise made available as security, collateral or guarantee for a loan which is a relevant loan, to the extent that it does not exceed the value of the relevant loan.

4 (1) For the purposes of this Schedule a loan is a relevant loan if and to the extent that money or money's worth made available under the loan is used to finance, directly or indirectly —

   (a) the acquisition by an individual, a partnership or the trustees of a settlement of —

     (i) a UK residential property interest, or

     (ii) property to which paragraph 2 to any extent applies, or

   (b) the acquisition by an individual, a partnership or the trustees of a settlement of an interest in a close company or a partnership ("the intermediary") and the acquisition by the intermediary of property within paragraph (a)(i) or (ii).

(2) In this paragraph references to money or money's worth made available under a loan or sale proceeds being used "indirectly" to finance the acquisition of something include the money or money's worth or sale proceeds being used to finance —

   (a) the acquisition of any property the proceeds of sale of which are used directly or indirectly to finance the acquisition of that thing, or

   (b) the making, or repayment, of a loan to finance the acquisition of that thing.

(3) In this paragraph references to the acquisition of a UK residential property interest by an individual, a partnership, the trustees of a settlement or a close company include the maintenance, or an

Finance (No. 2) Act 2017 (c. 32)
Schedule 10 — Inheritance tax on overseas property representing UK residential property

529

enhancement, of the value of a UK residential property interest which is (as the case may be) the property of the individual, property comprised in the settlement or property of the partnership or close company.

(4) Where the UK residential property interest by virtue of which a loan is a relevant loan is disposed of, the loan ceases to be a relevant loan.

(5) Where a proportion of the UK residential property interest by virtue of which a loan is a relevant loan is disposed of, the loan ceases to be a relevant loan by the same proportion.

(6) In this Schedule, references to a loan include an acknowledgment of debt by a person or any other arrangement under which a debt arises; and in such a case references to money or money's worth made available under the loan are to the amount of the debt.

PART 2

SUPPLEMENTARY

Disposals and repayments

5   (1) This paragraph applies to —
    (a) property which constitutes consideration in money or money's worth for the disposal of property to which paragraph 2 or paragraph 3(a) applies;
    (b) any money or money's worth paid in respect of a creditor's rights falling within paragraph 3(a);
    (c) any property directly or indirectly representing property within paragraph (a) or (b).

(2) If and to the extent that this paragraph applies to any property —
    (a) for the two-year period it is not excluded property by virtue of section 6(1), (1A) or (2) or 48(3)(a), (3A) or (4), and
    (b) if it is held in a qualifying foreign currency account within the meaning of section 157 (non-residents' bank accounts), that section does not apply to it for the two-year period.

(3) The two-year period is the period of two years beginning with the date of —
    (a) the disposal referred to in sub-paragraph (1)(a), or
    (b) the payment referred to in sub-paragraph (1)(b).

(4) The value of any property within sub-paragraph (1)(c) is to be treated as not exceeding the relevant amount.

(5) The relevant amount is —
    (a) where the property within sub-paragraph (1)(c) directly or indirectly represents property within sub-paragraph (1)(a) ("the consideration"), the value of the consideration at the time of the disposal referred to in that sub-paragraph, and
    (b) where the property within sub-paragraph (1)(c) directly or indirectly represents property within sub-paragraph

(1)(b), the amount of the money or money's worth paid as mentioned in that sub-paragraph.

Tax avoidance arrangements

6 (1) In determining whether or to what extent property situated outside the United Kingdom is excluded property, no regard is to be had to any arrangements the purpose or one of the main purposes of which is to secure a tax advantage by avoiding or minimising the effect of paragraph 1 or 5.

 (2) In this paragraph —

   "tax advantage" has the meaning given in section 208 of the Finance Act 2013;

   "arrangements" includes any scheme, transaction or series of transactions, agreement or understanding (whether or not legally enforceable and whenever entered into) and any associated operations.

Double taxation relief arrangements

7 (1) Nothing in any double taxation relief arrangements made with the government of a territory outside the United Kingdom is to be read as preventing a person from being liable for any amount of inheritance tax by virtue of paragraph 1 or 5 in relation to any chargeable transfer if under the law of that territory —

  (a) no tax of a character similar to inheritance tax is charged on that chargeable transfer, or

  (b) a tax of a character similar to inheritance tax is charged in relation to that chargeable transfer at an effective rate of 0% (otherwise than by virtue of a relief or exemption).

 (2) In this paragraph —

   "double taxation relief arrangements" means arrangements having effect under section 158(1);

   "effective rate" means the rate found by expressing the tax chargeable as a percentage of the amount by reference to which it is charged.

PART 3

INTERPRETATION

UK residential property interest

8 (1) In this Schedule "UK residential property interest" means an interest in UK land —

  (a) where the land consists of a dwelling,

  (b) where and to the extent that the land includes a dwelling, or

  (c) where the interest subsists under a contract for an off-plan purchase.

Finance (No. 2) Act 2017 (c. 32)
Schedule 10 — Inheritance tax on overseas property representing UK residential property

531

(2) For the purposes of sub-paragraph (1)(b), the extent to which land includes a dwelling is to be determined on a just and reasonable basis.

(3) In this paragraph—

"interest in UK land" has the meaning given by paragraph 2 of Schedule B1 to the 1992 Act (and the power in sub-paragraph (5) of that paragraph applies for the purposes of this Schedule);

"the land", in relation to an interest in UK land which is an interest subsisting for the benefit of land, is a reference to the land for the benefit of which the interest subsists;

"dwelling" has the meaning given by paragraph 4 of Schedule B1 to the 1992 Act (and the power in paragraph 5 of that Schedule applies for the purposes of this Schedule);

"contract for an off-plan purchase" has the meaning given by paragraph 1(6) of Schedule B1 to the 1992 Act.

Close companies

9   (1) In this Schedule—

"close company" means a company within the meaning of the Corporation Tax Acts which is (or would be if resident in the United Kingdom) a close company for the purposes of those Acts;

references to an interest in a close company are to the rights and interests that a participator in a close company has in that company.

(2) In this paragraph—

"participator", in relation to a close company, means any person who is (or would be if the company were resident in the United Kingdom) a participator in relation to that company within the meaning given by section 454 of the Corporation Tax Act 2010;

references to rights and interests in a close company include references to rights and interests in the assets of the company available for distribution among the participators in the event of a winding-up or in any other circumstances.

Partnerships

10   In this Schedule "partnership" means—

(a) a partnership within the Partnership Act 1890,

(b) a limited partnership registered under the Limited Partnerships Act 1907,

(c) a limited liability partnership formed under the Limited Liability Partnerships Act 2000 or the Limited Liability Partnerships Act (Northern Ireland) 2002, or

(d) a firm or entity of a similar character to either of those mentioned in paragraph (a) or (b) formed under the law of a country or territory outside the United Kingdom."

Consequential and supplementary amendments

2   IHTA 1984 is amended as follows.

3   In section 6 (excluded property), at the end insert—

         "(5)   This section is subject to Schedule A1 (non-excluded overseas property)."

4   In section 48 (excluded property)—
         (a)   in subsections (3) and (3A), at the end insert "and to Schedule A1";
         (b)   in subsection (4), at the end (but on a new line) insert "This subsection is subject to Schedule A1."

5   In section 65 (charge at other times), after subsection (7B) (as inserted by section 30) insert—

         "(7C)   Tax shall not be charged under this section by reason only that property comprised in a settlement ceases to any extent to be property to which paragraph 2 or 3 of Schedule A1 applies and thereby becomes excluded property by virtue of section 48(3)(a) above.

         (7D)   Tax shall not be charged under this section where property comprised in a settlement or any part of that property—
                 (a)   is, by virtue of paragraph 5(2)(a) of Schedule A1, not excluded property for the two year period referred to in that paragraph, but
                 (b)   becomes excluded property at the end of that period."

6   In section 157 (non-residents' bank accounts), after subsection (3) insert—

         "(3A)   This section is subject to paragraph 5 of Schedule A1 (non-excluded overseas property)."

7   In section 237 (imposition of charge), after subsection (2) insert—

         "(2A)   Where tax is charged by virtue of Schedule A1 on the value transferred by a chargeable transfer, the reference in subsection (1)(a) to property to the value of which the value transferred is wholly or partly attributable includes the UK residential property interest (within the meaning of that Schedule) to which the charge to tax relates."

8   In section 272 (general interpretation), in the definition of "excluded property", after "above" insert "and Schedule A1".

Commencement

9   (1) The amendments made by this Schedule have effect in relation to times on or after 6 April 2017.

     (2) But for the purposes of paragraph 5(1) of Schedule A1 to IHTA 1984 as inserted by this Schedule—
         (a)   paragraph (a) of that paragraph does not apply in relation to a disposal of property occurring before 6 April 2017, and
         (b)   paragraph (b) of that paragraph does not apply in relation to a payment of money or money's worth occurring before 6 April 2017.

Transitional provision

10 (1) Sub-paragraphs (2) and (3) apply if an amount of inheritance tax−

    (a) would not be charged but for the amendments made by this Schedule, or

    (b) is, because of those amendments, greater than it would otherwise have been.

(2) Section 233 of IHTA 1984 (interest on unpaid inheritance tax) applies in relation to the amount of inheritance tax as if the reference, in the closing words of subsection (1) of that section, to the end of the period mentioned in paragraph (a), (aa), (b) or (c) of that subsection were a reference to−

    (a) the end of that period, or

    (b) if later, the end of the month immediately following the month in which this Act is passed.

(3) Subsection (1) of section 234 of IHTA 1984 (cases where inheritance tax payable by instalments carries interest only from instalment dates) applies in relation to the amount of inheritance tax as if the reference, in the closing words of that subsection, to the date at which an instalment is payable were a reference to−

    (a) the date at which the instalment is payable, or

    (b) if later, the end of the month immediately following the month in which this Act is passed.

11 (1) Sub-paragraph (2) applies if−

    (a) a person is liable as mentioned in section 216(1)(c) of IHTA 1984 (trustee liable on 10-year anniversary, and other trust cases) for an amount of inheritance tax charged on an occasion, and

    (b) but for the amendments made by this Schedule−

        (i) no inheritance tax would be charged on that occasion, or

        (ii) a lesser amount of inheritance tax would be charged on that occasion.

(2) Section 216(6)(ad) of IHTA 1984 (delivery date for accounts required by section 216(1)(c)) applies in relation to the account to be delivered in connection with the occasion as if the reference to the expiration of the period of 6 months from the end of the month in which the occasion occurs were a reference to−

    (a) the expiration of that period, or

    (b) if later, the end of the month immediately following the month in which this Act is passed.

Finance (No. 2) Act 2017 (c. 32)

534   *Schedule 11 — Employment income provided through third parties: loans etc outstanding on 5 April 2019*
       Part 1 — Application of Part 7A of ITEPA 2003

SCHEDULE 11   Section 34

EMPLOYMENT INCOME PROVIDED THROUGH THIRD PARTIES: LOANS ETC OUTSTANDING ON 5 APRIL 2019

PART 1

APPLICATION OF PART 7A OF ITEPA 2003

Relevant step

1   (1) A person ("P") is treated as taking a relevant step for the purposes of Part 7A of ITEPA 2003 if—
         (a) P has made a loan, or a quasi-loan, to a relevant person,
         (b) the loan or quasi-loan was made on or after 6 April 1999, and
         (c) an amount of the loan or quasi-loan is outstanding immediately before the end of 5 April 2019.

     (2) P is treated as taking the step immediately before—
         (a) the end of the approved repayment date, if P has made a loan which is an approved fixed term loan on 5 April 2019, or
         (b) the end of 5 April 2019, in any other case.

     (3) Where P is treated by this paragraph as taking a relevant step, references to "the relevant step" in section 554A(1)(e)(i) and (ii) of ITEPA 2003 have effect as if they were references to the step of making the loan or, as the case may be, quasi-loan.

     (4) For the purposes of section 554Z3(1) of ITEPA 2003 (value of relevant step), the step is to be treated as involving a sum of money equal to the amount of the loan or quasi-loan that is outstanding at the time P is treated as taking the step.

     (5) Subsections (2) and (3) of section 554C of ITEPA 2003 ("relevant person") apply for the purposes of this Schedule as they apply for the purposes of that section.

     (6) Sub-paragraph (1) is subject to paragraphs 23 and 24 (accelerated payments).

     (7) For the purposes of this paragraph, whether an amount of a loan or quasi-loan is outstanding at a particular time—
         (a) is to be determined in accordance with the following provisions of this Schedule, and
         (b) does not depend on the loan or quasi-loan subsisting at that time.

     (8) References in this Schedule and in Part 7A of ITEPA 2003 to a relevant step within paragraph 1 of this Schedule are to be read as references to a relevant step which a person is treated by this paragraph as taking.

Meaning of "loan", "quasi-loan" and "approved repayment date"

2   (1) In this Part of this Schedule "loan" includes—
         (a) any form of credit;
         (b) a payment that is purported to be made by way of a loan.

Finance (No. 2) Act 2017 (c. 32)   535
Schedule 11 — Employment income provided through third parties: loans etc outstanding on 5 April 2019
Part 1 — Application of Part 7A of ITEPA 2003

(2) For the purposes of paragraph 1, P makes a "quasi-loan" to a relevant person if (and when) P acquires a right (the "acquired debt") —

    (a) which is a right to a payment or a transfer of assets, and

    (b) in respect of which the condition in sub-paragraph (3) is met.

(3) The condition is met in relation to a right if there is a connection (direct or indirect) between the acquisition of the right and —

    (a) a payment made, by way of a loan or otherwise, to the relevant person, or

    (b) a transfer of assets to the relevant person.

(4) Where a quasi-loan or a loan made by P to a relevant person is replaced, directly or indirectly, by a loan or another loan (the "replacement loan"), references in paragraph 1 to the loan are references to the replacement loan.

(5) Where a loan or a quasi-loan made by P to a relevant person is replaced, directly or indirectly, by a quasi-loan or another quasi-loan (the "replacement quasi-loan"), references in paragraph 1 to the quasi-loan are references to the replacement quasi-loan.

(6) In this Part of this Schedule, "approved repayment date", in relation to an approved fixed term loan, means the date by which, under the terms of the loan at the time of making the application for approval under paragraph 20, the whole of the loan must be repaid.

Meaning of "outstanding": loans

3   (1) An amount of a loan is "outstanding" for the purposes of paragraph 1 if the relevant principal amount exceeds the repayment amount.

(2) In sub-paragraph (1) "relevant principal amount", in relation to a loan, means the total of —

    (a) the initial principal amount lent, and

    (b) any sums that have become principal under the loan, otherwise than by capitalisation of interest.

(3) In sub-paragraph (1) "repayment amount", in relation to a loan, means the total of —

    (a) the amount of principal under the loan that has been repaid before 17 March 2016, and

    (b) payments in money made by the relevant person on or after 17 March 2016 by way of repayment of principal under the loan.

4   (1) A payment is to be disregarded for the purposes of paragraph 3(3)(b) if —

    (a) there is any connection (direct or indirect) between the payment and a tax avoidance arrangement (other than the arrangement under which the loan was made), or

    (b) the payment, or a sum or asset directly or indirectly representing the payment, is the subject of a relevant step (as defined in section 554A(2) of ITEPA 2003) that is taken —

        (i) after the payment is made, but

        (ii) before the end of the relevant date.

(2) But a payment is not to be disregarded under sub-paragraph (1)(b) if, by the end of the relevant date, each relevant tax liability has been paid in full.

536

Finance (No. 2) Act 2017 (c. 32)
Schedule 11 — Employment income provided through third parties: loans etc outstanding on 5 April 2019
Part 1 — Application of Part 7A of ITEPA 2003

(3) For the purposes of this paragraph, each of the following is a "relevant tax liability"—

    (a) any liability for income tax arising by virtue of the application of Chapter 2 by reason of the relevant step mentioned in sub-paragraph (1)(b), and

    (b) where section 554Z6 of ITEPA 2003 (overlap with certain earnings) applies because that relevant step gives rise to relevant earnings for the purposes of that section, any liability for income tax in respect of those relevant earnings.

(4) In this paragraph, "relevant date" means—

    (a) the approved repayment date, if P has made a loan which is an approved fixed term loan on 5 April 2019, or

    (b) 5 April 2019, in any other case.

(5) Sub-paragraph (6) applies if a payment is disregarded under sub-paragraph (1)(b).

(6) The value of the relevant step treated as taken by paragraph 1 is not reduced under section 554Z5(3) of ITEPA 2003 (overlap with money or asset subject to earlier tax liability) by the amount of the sum, or the value of the asset, which is the subject of the relevant step mentioned in sub-paragraph (1)(b) unless the payment condition is met by reason of section 554Z5(4)(a) and (b)(ii) being met.

5 (1) This paragraph applies where—

    (a) a person ("P") has made a loan to a relevant person,

    (b) the loan was made on or after 6 April 1999, and

    (c) before the end of 5 April 2019, A or B acquires (whether or not for consideration) a right to payment of the whole or part of the loan.

(2) The amount of the loan in respect of which A or B acquires a right to payment is to be treated—

    (a) for the purposes of paragraph 1(1) as an amount, of the loan made by P to the relevant person, that is outstanding immediately before the end of 5 April 2019;

    (b) for the purposes of paragraph 1(4) and section 554Z3(1) of ITEPA 2003, as an amount of the loan that is outstanding at the time P is treated as taking the relevant step under paragraph 1(1).

(3) Where a quasi-loan or a loan made by P to a relevant person is replaced, directly or indirectly, by a loan or another loan (the "replacement loan"), references in sub-paragraphs (1) and (2) to the loan are references to the replacement loan.

Meaning of "outstanding": loans in currencies other than sterling

6 (1) In paragraphs 7 to 10 "the loan currency", in relation to a loan, means the currency in which the initial principal amount of the loan is denominated (whether or not that amount is paid in that currency).

(2) For the purposes of paragraphs 7 to 10, the value of an amount in a particular currency is to be determined by reference to an appropriate spot rate of exchange.

Finance (No. 2) Act 2017 (c. 32) 537
Schedule 11 — Employment income provided through third parties: loans etc outstanding on 5 April 2019
Part 1 — Application of Part 7A of ITEPA 2003

7   (1) This paragraph applies in relation to a loan where the loan currency is a currency other than sterling.

(2) But this paragraph does not apply if paragraph 10 applies in relation to the loan.

(3) The amount of the loan that is outstanding, at the time P is treated as taking the relevant step, is to be calculated in sterling as follows —

Step 1
Calculate, in the loan currency, the amount that is outstanding at that time.

Step 2
Take the value in sterling, at that time, of that amount.

(4) See paragraph 8 for provision about repayments made in a currency other than the loan currency.

Repayments in currencies other than the loan currency

8   (1) This paragraph applies in relation to a loan where —
    (a) payments in money are made by way of repayment of principal under the loan, and
    (b) some or all of the payments are made in a currency other than the loan currency.

(2) But this paragraph does not apply if paragraph 10 applies in relation to the loan.

(3) For the purposes of calculating the repayment amount in relation to the loan, the amount of each of the payments referred to in sub-paragraph (1)(b) is an amount equal to its value in the loan currency on the date it is made.

Loans made in a depreciating currency

9   (1) Paragraph 10 applies in relation to a loan where —
    (a) the loan currency is a currency other than sterling, and
    (b) it is reasonable to suppose that the main reason, or one of the main reasons, for the loan being made in that currency is that the loan currency is expected to depreciate as against sterling during the loan period.

(2) The "loan period", in relation to a loan, is the period —
    (a) beginning at the time the loan is made, and
    (b) ending with the time by which, under the terms of the loan, the whole of the loan is to be repaid.

10   (1) Where this paragraph applies in relation to a loan —
    (a) paragraphs 7 and 8 do not apply in relation to the loan, and
    (b) sub-paragraphs (2) to (5) apply for the purposes of calculating the amount of the loan that is outstanding at the time P is treated as taking the relevant step.

(2) The relevant principal amount, in relation to the loan, is an amount equal to the total of —

538   *Finance (No. 2) Act 2017 (c. 32)*

Schedule 11 — Employment income provided through third parties: loans etc outstanding on 5 April 2019
Part 1 — Application of Part 7A of ITEPA 2003

     (a)   the value in sterling, at the reference date, of the initial principal amount lent, and

     (b)   the value in sterling, at the reference date, of any sums that become principal under the loan, otherwise than by capitalisation of interest.

(3) The "reference date" —

     (a)   in relation to an amount within sub-paragraph (2)(a), means the date on which the loan is made, and

     (b)   in relation to a sum within sub-paragraph (2)(b), means the date on which the sum becomes principal.

(4) The repayment amount, in relation to the loan, is an amount equal to the total of —

     (a)   the amount of principal under the loan that has been repaid in sterling, and

     (b)   where payments are made, in a currency other than sterling, by way of repayment of principal under the loan, the amount equal to the sterling value of the payments.

(5) The "sterling value" of a payment is its value in sterling on the date it is made.

Meaning of "outstanding": quasi-loans

11   (1) An amount of a quasi-loan is outstanding for the purposes of paragraph 1 if the initial debt amount exceeds the repayment amount.

    (2) In sub-paragraph (1) "initial debt amount", in relation to a quasi-loan, means the total of —

       (a)   an amount equal to the value of the acquired debt (see paragraph 2(2)), and

       (b)   where P subsequently acquires a further right (an "additional debt") to a payment, or transfer of assets, in connection with the payment mentioned in paragraph 2(3)(a) or (as the case may be) the transfer mentioned in paragraph 2(3)(b), an amount equal to the value of the additional debt.

    (3) For the purposes of sub-paragraph (2) —

       (a)   where the acquired debt is a right to payment of an amount, the "value" of the debt is that amount,

       (b)   where the additional debt is a right to payment of an amount, the "value" of the debt is that amount, but is nil if the additional debt accrued to P by the capitalisation of interest on the acquired debt or another additional debt, and

       (c)   where the acquired debt or additional debt is a right to a transfer of assets, the "value" of the debt is an amount equal to —

          (i)   the market value of the assets at the time the right is acquired (or the value of the right at that time if the assets are non-fungible and not in existence at that time), or

         (ii)   if higher, the cost of the assets at that time.

    (4) In sub-paragraph (1) "repayment amount", in relation to a quasi-loan, means the total of —

       (a)   the amount (if any) by which the initial debt amount has been reduced (by way of repayment) before 17 March 2016,

Finance (No. 2) Act 2017 (c. 32)   539
Schedule 11 — Employment income provided through third parties: loans etc outstanding on 5 April 2019
Part 1 — Application of Part 7A of ITEPA 2003

(b)   payments in money (if any) made by the relevant person on or after 17 March 2016 by way of repayment of the initial debt amount, and

(c)   if the acquired debt or an additional debt is a right to a transfer of assets, and the assets have been transferred, an amount equal to the market value of the assets at the time of the transfer.

12   (1)   A payment or transfer is to be disregarded for the purposes of paragraph 11(4)(b) or (c) if—

(a)   there is any connection (direct or indirect) between the payment or transfer and a tax avoidance arrangement (other than the arrangement under which the quasi-loan was made), or

(b)   the payment or the asset transferred, or a sum or asset directly or indirectly representing the payment or asset, is the subject of a relevant step (as defined in section 554A(2) of ITEPA 2003) that is taken—

(i)   after the payment is made or the asset transferred, but

(ii)   before the end of 5 April 2019.

(2)   But a payment or transfer is not to be disregarded under sub-paragraph (1)(b) if, by the end of 5 April 2019, each relevant tax liability has been paid in full.

(3)   For the purposes of this paragraph, each of the following is a "relevant tax liability"—

(a)   any liability for income tax arising by virtue of the application of Chapter 2 by reason of the relevant step mentioned in sub-paragraph (1)(b), and

(b)   where section 554Z6 of ITEPA 2003 (overlap with certain earnings) applies because that relevant step gives rise to relevant earnings for the purposes of that section, any liability for income tax in respect of those relevant earnings.

(4)   Sub-paragraph (5) applies if a payment is disregarded under sub-paragraph (1)(b).

(5)   The value of the relevant step treated as taken by paragraph 1 is not reduced under section 554Z5(3) of ITEPA 2003 (overlap with money or asset subject to earlier tax liability) by the amount of the sum, or the value of the asset, which is the subject of the relevant step mentioned in sub-paragraph (1)(b) unless the payment condition is met by reason of section 554Z5(4)(a) and (b)(ii) being met.

13   (1)   This paragraph applies where—

(a)   a person ("P") has made a quasi-loan to a relevant person,

(b)   the quasi-loan was made on or after 6 April 1999, and

(c)   before the end of 5 April 2019, A or B acquires (whether or not for consideration) a right to the payment or transfer of assets mentioned in paragraph 2(2)(a).

(2)   The amount equal to the value of the right acquired by A or B is to be treated—

(a)   for the purposes of paragraph 1(1) as an amount, of the quasi-loan made by P to the relevant person, that is outstanding immediately before the end of 5 April 2019;

540   *Finance (No. 2) Act 2017 (c. 32)*
Schedule 11 — Employment income provided through third parties: loans etc outstanding on 5 April 2019
Part 1 — Application of Part 7A of ITEPA 2003

(b) for the purposes of paragraph 1(4) and section 554Z3(1) of ITEPA 2003, as an amount of the quasi-loan that is outstanding at the time P is treated as taking the relevant step under paragraph 1(1).

(3) For the purposes of sub-paragraph (2) —

(a) where the right acquired by A or B is a right to payment of an amount, the "value" of the right is that amount;

(b) where the right acquired by A or B is a right to a transfer of assets, the "value" of the right is an amount equal to —

(i) the market value of the assets at the time the right is acquired (or the value of the right at that time if the assets are non-fungible and not in existence at that time), or

(ii) if higher, the cost of the assets at that time.

(4) Where a loan or a quasi-loan made by P to a relevant person is replaced, directly or indirectly, by a quasi-loan or another quasi-loan (the "replacement quasi-loan"), references in sub-paragraphs (1) and (2) to the quasi-loan are references to the replacement quasi-loan.

Meaning of "outstanding": quasi-loans in currencies other than sterling

14 (1) Paragraphs 15 to 18 apply where P makes a quasi-loan to a relevant person by reason of acquiring a right to a payment in a particular currency (the "quasi-loan currency").

(2) For the purposes of paragraphs 15 to 18, the value of an amount in a particular currency is to be determined by reference to an appropriate spot rate of exchange.

15 (1) This paragraph applies in relation to the quasi-loan if the quasi-loan currency is a currency other than sterling.

(2) But this paragraph does not apply if paragraph 18 applies in relation to the quasi-loan.

(3) The amount of the quasi-loan that is outstanding, at the time P is treated as taking the relevant step, is to be calculated in sterling as follows —

Step 1
Calculate, in the quasi-loan currency, the amount that is outstanding at that time.

Step 2
Take the value in sterling, at that time, of that amount.

(4) See paragraph 16 for provision about repayments made in a currency other than the quasi-loan currency.

Repayments in currencies other than the quasi-loan currency

16 (1) This paragraph applies in relation to the quasi-loan if —

(a) payments in money are made by way of repayment of the initial debt amount, and

(b) some or all of the payments are made in a currency other than the quasi-loan currency.

Finance (No. 2) Act 2017 (c. 32)
541
Schedule 11 – Employment income provided through third parties: loans etc outstanding on 5 April 2019
Part 1 – Application of Part 7A of ITEPA 2003

(2) But this paragraph does not apply if paragraph 18 applies in relation to the quasi-loan.

(3) For the purposes of calculating the repayment amount in relation to the quasi-loan, the amount of each of the payments referred to in sub-paragraph (1)(b) is an amount equal to its value in the quasi-loan currency on the date it is made.

Quasi-loans made in a depreciating currency

17 (1) Paragraph 18 applies in relation to the quasi-loan if –
  (a) the quasi-loan currency is a currency other than sterling, and
  (b) it is reasonable to suppose that the main reason, or one of the main reasons, for the quasi-loan being made in that currency is that the quasi-loan currency is expected to depreciate during the quasi-loan period.

(2) The "quasi-loan period", in relation to a quasi-loan, is the period –
  (a) beginning at the time the quasi-loan is made, and
  (b) ending with the time by which, under the terms of the quasi-loan, the whole of the quasi-loan is to be repaid.

18 (1) Where this paragraph applies in relation to the quasi-loan –
  (a) paragraphs 15 and 16 do not apply in relation to the quasi-loan, and
  (b) sub-paragraphs (2) to (5) apply for the purposes of calculating the amount of the quasi-loan that is outstanding at the time P is treated as taking the relevant step.

(2) The initial debt amount, in relation to the quasi-loan, is an amount equal to the total of –
  (a) the value in sterling, at the reference date, of the acquired debt, and
  (b) the value in sterling, at the reference date, of any additional debt.

(3) The "reference date" –
  (a) in relation to a right within sub-paragraph (2)(a), means the date on which P acquires it, and
  (b) in relation to a right within sub-paragraph (2)(b), means the date on which P acquires it.

(4) The repayment amount, in relation to the quasi-loan, is an amount equal to the total of –
  (a) the amount of the initial debt amount that has been repaid in sterling, and
  (b) where payments are made, in a currency other than sterling, by way of repayment of the initial debt amount, the amount equal to the sterling value of the payments.

(5) The "sterling value" of a payment is its value in sterling on the date it is made.

Meaning of "approved fixed term loan"

19 (1) A loan is an "approved fixed term loan" on 5 April 2019 if, at any time on that day, it is a qualifying loan which has been approved by an officer of Revenue and Customs in accordance with paragraph 20.

542 Finance (No. 2) Act 2017 (c. 32)
Schedule 11 — Employment income provided through third parties: loans etc outstanding on 5 April 2019
Part 1 — Application of Part 7A of ITEPA 2003

(2) A loan is a "qualifying loan" if —
    (a)   the loan was made before 9 December 2010,
    (b)   the term of the loan cannot exceed 10 years, and
    (c)   it is not an excluded loan under sub-paragraph (3).

(3) A loan is an excluded loan if, at any time after the loan was made —
    (a)   the loan has been replaced, directly or indirectly, by another loan, or
    (b)   the terms of the loan have been altered so as —
        (i)   to meet the condition in sub-paragraph (2)(b), or
        (ii)   to postpone the date by which, under the terms of the loan, the whole of the loan must be repaid.

PART 2

APPROVAL OF A QUALIFYING LOAN ETC.

Application to HMRC

20 (1) The liable person in relation to a qualifying loan may make an application to the Commissioners for Her Majesty's Revenue and Customs for approval of the loan.

(2) An officer of Revenue and Customs may grant such an application if satisfied that, in relation to the loan —
    (a)   the qualifying payments condition is met (see paragraph 21), or
    (b)   the commercial terms condition is met (see paragraph 22).

(3) Subject to sub-paragraph (4), an application may be made in 2018.

(4) An application may be made after 2018 if an officer of Revenue and Customs considers it is reasonable in all the circumstances for the liable person to make a late application.

(5) An application for an approval must be made in such form and manner, and contain such information, as may be specified by, or on behalf of, the Commissioners for Her Majesty's Revenue and Customs.

(6) An officer of Revenue and Customs must notify the applicant of the decision on an application.

(7) Where on an application under this paragraph a loan is approved, the approval may be revoked by an officer of Revenue and Customs if the officer considers that —
    (a)   information provided in making the application contained an inaccuracy, and
    (b)   the inaccuracy was deliberate on the applicant's part.

(8) Where approval is revoked under sub-paragraph (7), approval is to be treated as having been refused at the outset.

(9) In this paragraph "liable person", in relation to a loan, means the person who is liable for any tax on the value of the relevant step in relation to the loan under paragraph 1.

Finance (No. 2) Act 2017 (c. 32)
Schedule 11 — Employment income provided through third parties: loans etc outstanding on 5 April 2019
Part 2 — Approval of a qualifying loan etc.

543

Qualifying payments condition

21 (1) The qualifying payments condition is met in relation to a qualifying loan if, during the relevant period —

    (a) payments have been made to the lender in respect of the repayment of the principal of the loan, and

    (b) the payments have been made at intervals not exceeding 53 weeks.

(2) The "relevant period" in relation to a loan is the period beginning with the making of the loan and ending with the making of the application.

Commercial terms condition

22 (1) The commercial terms condition is met in relation to a qualifying loan if —

    (a) either —

        (i) it is reasonable to assume that, had the qualifying loan been made in the ordinary course of a lending business, loans on terms comparable to those of the qualifying loan would have been available to members of the public, or

        (ii) the qualifying loan was made in the ordinary course of a lending business, and

    (b) the borrower has, in all material respects, complied with the terms of the loan.

(2) For the purposes of sub-paragraph (1), a loan is made in the ordinary course of a lending business if it is made by a person in the ordinary course of a business carried on by the person which includes —

    (a) the lending of money, or

    (b) the supplying of goods or services on credit.

Accelerated payments

23 (1) Paragraph 24(1) applies where —

    (a) a person ("P") would (ignoring paragraph 24) be treated as taking a relevant step within paragraph 1 by reason of making a loan, or a quasi-loan, to a relevant person,

    (b) an accelerated payment notice, or a partner payment notice, relating to a relevant charge (the "accelerated payment notice") has been given under Chapter 3 of Part 4 of FA 2014,

    (c) the relevant person makes a payment (the "accelerated payment") in respect of the understated or disputed tax to which the notice relates,

    (d) the accelerated payment is made on or before the relevant date, and

    (e) the amount of the loan or quasi-loan that, at the end of the relevant date, is outstanding for the purposes of paragraph 1 (see paragraphs 3 to 18) is equal to or less than the amount of the accelerated payment.

(2) In sub-paragraph (1)(b), "relevant charge" means a charge to tax arising by reason of a step taken pursuant to the relevant arrangement concerned.

(3) The reference in sub-paragraph (2) to the relevant arrangement concerned is a reference to the relevant arrangement in pursuance of which, or in connection with which, the loan or quasi-loan mentioned in sub-paragraph (1)(a) is made.

544

*Finance (No. 2) Act 2017 (c. **32**)*
Schedule 11 — Employment income provided through third parties: loans etc outstanding on 5 April 2019
Part 2 — Approval of a qualifying loan etc.

(4) In sub-paragraph (1)(d) and (e), "the relevant date" means —

    (a) the approved repayment date, if P has made a loan which is an approved fixed term loan on 5 April 2019, or

    (b) 5 April 2019, in any other case.

(5) In sub-paragraphs (1)(c) and (2) —

    (a) the reference to tax includes a reference to relevant contributions, and

    (b) the reference to a charge to tax includes a reference to a liability to pay relevant contributions;

and for those purposes "relevant contributions" has the same meaning as in Schedule 2 to the National Insurance Contributions Act 2015 (application of Part 4 of FA 2014 to national insurance contributions).

(6) If more than one notice relating to a particular relevant charge has been given —

    (a) the reference in sub-paragraph (1)(e) to the amount of the accelerated payment is to be treated as a reference to the aggregate of the amounts of each accelerated payment in respect of which the conditions in sub-paragraph (1)(c) and (d) are met, and

    (b) the reference in paragraph 24(2) to the accelerated payment notice is to be treated as a reference to the accelerated payment notices or any of them.

24 (1) The relevant person may make an application to the Commissioners for Her Majesty's Revenue and Customs for P to be treated —

    (a) as taking the relevant step only if the condition in sub-paragraph (2) is met, and

    (b) as doing so not at the time given by paragraph 1(2) but immediately before —

        (i) the end of the 30 days beginning with the date on which the condition in sub-paragraph (2) becomes met, or

        (ii) if later, the end of 5 April 2019.

(2) The condition is that, on the withdrawal of the accelerated payment notice or on the determination of an appeal, any part of the accelerated payment is repaid.

(3) Subject to sub-paragraph (4), an application under sub-paragraph (1) may be made in 2018.

(4) An application may be made after 2018 if an officer of Revenue and Customs considers it is reasonable in all the circumstances for the relevant person to make a late application.

(5) An application must be made in such form and manner, and contain such information, as may be specified by, or on behalf of, the Commissioners for Her Majesty's Revenue and Customs.

(6) An officer of Revenue and Customs must notify the applicant of the decision on an application under this paragraph.

(7) A favourable decision on an application under this paragraph may be revoked by an officer of Revenue and Customs if the officer considers that —

    (a) information provided in making the application contained an inaccuracy, and

> (b)   the inaccuracy was deliberate on the applicant's part.

(8) Where the decision on an application is revoked under sub-paragraph (7), the application is to be treated as having been refused at the outset.

PART 3

EXCLUSIONS

Commercial transactions

25   Chapter 2 of Part 7A of ITEPA 2003 does not apply by reason of a relevant step within paragraph 1 which is treated as being taken by a person ("P") if —

> (a)   P is treated as taking a relevant step by that paragraph by reason of the payment of a sum of money by way of a loan,
>
> (b)   the loan is (at the time it is made) a loan on ordinary commercial terms within the meaning of section 176 of ITEPA 2003, ignoring conditions B and C in that section, and
>
> (c)   there is no connection (direct or indirect) between the relevant step and a tax avoidance arrangement.

26   In section 554F of ITEPA 2003 (exclusions: commercial transactions), at the end insert —

> "(6)   See paragraph 25 of Schedule 11 to F(No. 2)A 2017 for provision about exclusions where a loan is made on ordinary commercial terms and the relevant step is within paragraph 1 of that Schedule."

Transfer of employment-related loans

27   (1) Chapter 2 of Part 7A of ITEPA 2003 does not apply by reason of a relevant step within paragraph 1 which is treated as being taken by a person ("P") if —

> (a)   P is treated as taking a relevant step within that paragraph by reason of making a quasi-loan by acquiring a right to payment of an amount equal to the whole or part of a payment made by way of a loan to a relevant person (the "borrower"),
>
> (b)   the loan, at the time it was made, was an employment-related loan,
>
> (c)   at the time the right is acquired, the section 180 threshold is not exceeded in relation to the loan,
>
> (d)   at the time the right is acquired, the borrower is an employee, or a prospective employee, of P, and
>
> (e)   there is no connection (direct or indirect) between the acquisition of the right and a tax avoidance arrangement.

(2) Subsections (2) to (5) of section 554OA of ITEPA 2003 (section 180 threshold) apply for the purposes of this paragraph as they apply for the purposes of that section.

(3) In this paragraph, "employment-related loan" has the same meaning as it has for the purposes of Chapter 7 of Part 3.

28   In section 554OA of ITEPA 2003 (exclusions: transfer of employment-related

546

Finance (No. 2) Act 2017 (c. 32)
Schedule 11 — Employment income provided through third parties: loans etc outstanding on 5 April 2019
Part 3 — Exclusions

loans), at the end insert—

"(6)　See paragraph 27 of Schedule 11 to F(No. 2)A 2017 for provision about exclusions where a loan is an employment-related loan and the relevant step is within paragraph 1 of that Schedule."

Transactions under employee benefit packages

29　(1)　Chapter 2 of Part 7A of ITEPA 2003 does not apply by reason of a relevant step within paragraph 1 which is treated as being taken by a person ("P") if—

(a)　P is treated as taking a relevant step by that paragraph by reason of the payment of a sum of money by way of a loan,

(b)　the step is not taken under a pension scheme,

(c)　the loan was made for the sole purpose of a transaction of P's with A and which P entered into in the ordinary course of P's business,

(d)　at the time the loan was made (the "relevant time")—

(i)　a substantial proportion of P's business involved making similar loans to members of the public,

(ii)　the transaction with A was part of a package of benefits which was available to a substantial proportion of B's employees, and

(iii)　sub-paragraph (3) does not apply,

(e)　the terms on which similar transactions were offered by P under the package of benefits mentioned in paragraph (d)(ii) were generous enough to enable substantially all of the employees of B to whom the package was available at or around the relevant time to take advantage of what was offered (if they wanted to),

(f)　the terms on which P entered into the transaction with A were substantially the same as the terms on which at or around the relevant time P normally entered into similar transactions with employees of B under the package of benefits,

(g)　if B is a company, a majority of B's employees to whom the package of benefits was available at the relevant time did not have a material interest (as defined in section 68 of ITEPA 2003) in B, and

(h)　there is no connection (direct or indirect) between the relevant step and a tax avoidance arrangement.

(2)　For the purposes of sub-paragraph (1)(d)(i)—

(a)　a loan is "similar" if it is made for the same or similar purposes as the loan which is the subject of the relevant step, and

(b)　"members of the public" means members of the public at large with whom P deals at arm's length.

(3)　This sub-paragraph applies if any feature of the package of benefits mentioned in sub-paragraph (1)(d)(ii) had or would have been likely to have had the effect that, of the employees of B to whom the package was available, it is employees within sub-paragraph (4) on whom benefits under the package will be wholly or mainly conferred.

(4)　The employees within this sub-paragraph are—

(a)　directors,

(b)　senior employees,

(c)   employees who at the relevant time received, or as a result of the package of benefits would have been likely to have received, the higher or highest levels of remuneration, and

(d)   if, at the relevant time, B was a company and was a member of a group of companies, any employees not within paragraph (b) or (c) who—

     (i)   were senior employees in the group, or

     (ii)   received, or as a result of the package of benefits would have been likely to have received, the higher or highest levels of remuneration in the group.

(5)   For the purposes of sub-paragraph (1)(d) and (e) a transaction is "similar" if it is of the same or a similar type to the transaction which P has or had with A.

(6)   In this paragraph references to A include references to any person linked with A.

(7)   In this paragraph "pension scheme" has the same meaning as in Part 4 of FA 2004 (see section 150(1) of that Act).

30   In section 554G of ITEPA 2003 (exclusions: transactions under employee benefit packages), at the end insert—

     "(8)   See paragraph 29 of Schedule 11 to F(No. 2)A 2017 for provision about exclusions for transactions under employee benefit packages in a case in which the relevant step is within paragraph 1 of that Schedule."

Cases involving employment-related securities

31   Chapter 2 of Part 7A of ITEPA 2003 does not apply by reason of a relevant step within paragraph 1 which is treated as being taken by a person ("P") if—

(a)   P is treated as taking a relevant step by that paragraph by reason of the payment of a sum of money by way of a loan (the "relevant loan"),

(b)   the relevant loan is made and used solely for the purpose of enabling A to exercise an employment-related securities option (within the meaning of Chapter 5 of Part 7 of ITEPA 2003),

(c)   the exercise of the option by A gives rise to employment income of A in respect of A's employment with B—

     (i)   which is chargeable to income tax or would be chargeable apart from Chapter 5B of Part 2 of ITEPA 2003, or

     (ii)   which is exempt income, and

(d)   there is no connection (direct or indirect) between the relevant step and a tax avoidance arrangement.

32   In section 554N of ITEPA 2003 (exclusions: other cases involving employment-related securities etc.), at the end insert—

     "(17)   See paragraph 31 of Schedule 11 to F(No. 2)A 2017 for provision about exclusions where a loan is made for the purpose of enabling the exercise of an employment-related securities option and the relevant step is within paragraph 1 of that Schedule."

548   *Finance (No. 2) Act 2017 (c. 32)*
Schedule 11 — Employment income provided through third parties: loans etc outstanding on 5 April 2019
Part 3 — Exclusions

Employee car ownership schemes

33   (1)   This paragraph applies if—

      (a)   there is an arrangement ("the car ownership arrangement") which—

          (i)   provides for A to purchase a new car from another person ("S") using a loan ("the car loan") to be made to A by an authorised lender,

          (ii)   specifies the date ("the repayment date") by which the car loan must be fully repaid which must be no later than four years after the date on which the car loan is made, and

          (iii)   permits A, in order to obtain funds to repay the car loan, to sell the car back to S on a specified date at a specified price based on an estimate (made at the time the car ownership arrangement is made) of the likely outstanding amount of the car loan on the specified date, and

          (iv)   as provided for by the car ownership arrangement, A purchases the car using the car loan.

   (2)   Chapter 2 does not apply by reason of a relevant step within paragraph 1 which is treated as being taken by a person if—

      (a)   the person is treated as taking a relevant step by that paragraph by reason of making the car loan, and

      (b)   the car ownership arrangement is not a tax avoidance arrangement and there is no other connection (direct or indirect) between the relevant step and a tax avoidance arrangement.

   (3)   In this paragraph—

     "car" has the meaning given by section 235(2) of ITEPA 2003, and

     "authorised lender" means a person who—

      (a)   has permission under Part 4A of the Financial Services and Markets Act 2000 to enter into, or to exercise or have the right to exercise rights and duties under, a contract of the kind mentioned in paragraph 23 of Schedule 2 to that Act, and

      (b)   is not acting as a trustee.

   (4)   The definition of "authorised lender" must be read with—

      (a)   section 22 of the Financial Services and Markets Act 2000,

      (b)   any relevant order under that section, and

      (c)   Schedule 2 to that Act.

34   In section 554O of ITEPA 2003 (exclusions: employee car ownership schemes), at the end insert—

     "(7)   See paragraph 33 of Schedule 11 to F(No. 2)A 2017 for provision about exclusions for car loans in a case in which the relevant step is within paragraph 1 of that Schedule."

Acquisition of unlisted employer shares

35   (1)   Chapter 2 of Part 7A of ITEPA 2003 does not apply by reason of a relevant step within paragraph 1 which is treated as being taken by a person ("P") if the conditions in sub-paragraph (2) are met.

   (2)   The conditions are that—

      (a)   the loan or quasi-loan concerned was made before 9 December 2010,

(b) if P is treated as taking a relevant step by paragraph 1 by reason of the payment of a sum of money by way of loan, the sum is used by A solely to acquire employer shares,

(c) if P is treated as taking a relevant step by paragraph 1 by reason of making a quasi-loan, the transfer of assets mentioned in paragraph 2(3)(b) is the transfer of employer shares to A,

(d) the employer shares are acquired, or transferred, before the end of the period of one year beginning with the day on which the loan, or quasi-loan, is made, and

(e) the employer shares are not listed on a recognised stock exchange at any time during the period beginning with the day on which the loan, or quasi-loan, is made and ending with the earlier of —

   (i) the day on which A ceases to hold the shares, or

   (ii) the day on which the loan, or quasi-loan, is repaid.

(3) In this paragraph "employer shares" means shares that form part of the ordinary share capital of —

   (a) B, or

   (b) if B is a company and is a member of a group of companies at the time the shares are acquired, any other company which is a member of that group at that time.

(4) Sub-paragraph (6) applies if —

   (a) apart from sub-paragraph (1), Chapter 2 of Part 7A would apply by reason of the relevant step mentioned in sub-paragraph (1), and

   (b) at the end of the relevant period, an amount of the loan, or quasi-loan, is outstanding.

(5) In this paragraph "the relevant period" means the period of 12 months beginning with the day on which A ceases to hold the shares.

(6) Part 7A of ITEPA 2003 has effect as if —

   (a) a relevant step within paragraph 1 were taken by reason of making a loan, or quasi-loan, of an amount equal to the amount of the loan, or quasi-loan, outstanding at the end of the relevant period, and

   (b) the relevant step were taken on the day after the end of the relevant period.

PART 4

SUPPLEMENTARY PROVISION

Duty to provide loan balance information to B

36 (1) This paragraph applies where —

   (a) a person ("P") has made a loan, or a quasi-loan, to a relevant person,

   (b) the loan or quasi-loan was made on or after 6 April 1999, and

   (c) an amount of the loan or quasi-loan is outstanding at any time —

      (i) on or after 17 March 2016, and

      (ii) before the end of 5 April 2019.

(2) Each of A and P must ensure that the loan balance information in relation to the loan or quasi-loan is provided to B before the end of the period of 10 days beginning with the day after the loan charge date.

550

Finance (No. 2) Act 2017 (c. 32)
Schedule 11 — Employment income provided through third parties: loans etc outstanding on 5 April 2019
Part 4 — Supplementary provision

(3) The "loan balance information" is —

 (a) the information that is necessary for B to ascertain the amount of the loan or quasi-loan concerned that is outstanding immediately before the end of the loan charge date, and

 (b) such other information about the loan or quasi-loan as B may reasonably require for the purpose of compliance with B's obligations under PAYE regulations.

(4) In this paragraph "loan charge date" means —

 (a) the approved repayment date, if the loan is an approved fixed term loan on 5 April 2019, or

 (b) 5 April 2019, in any other case.

(5) If, despite taking reasonable steps, A and P have failed to contact B to provide the loan balance information, each of them is responsible for ensuring that the Commissioners for Her Majesty's Revenue and Customs are notified of that fact.

(6) A notification under sub-paragraph (5) must be made in such form and manner, and contain such information, as may be specified by, or on behalf of, the Commissioners for Her Majesty's Revenue and Customs.

(7) "Loan", "quasi-loan" and "outstanding" have the same meaning for the purposes of this paragraph as they have for the purposes of paragraph 1.

Double taxation

37 (1) Sub-paragraph (2) applies where —

 (a) P is treated as taking a relevant step by paragraph 1 by reason of a loan made to a relevant person, and

 (b) the loan is an employment-related loan (within the meaning of Chapter 7 of Part 3 of ITEPA 2003).

(2) The effect of section 554Z2(2)(a) of ITEPA 2003 (value of relevant step to count as employment income: application of Part 7A instead of the benefits code) is that the loan is not be treated as a taxable cheap loan for the purposes of Chapter 7 of Part 3 of that Act for —

 (a) the tax year in which the relevant step is treated as being taken, and

 (b) any subsequent tax year.

38   In section 554Z2 of ITEPA 2003, at the end insert —

 "(4) See paragraph 37 of Schedule 11 to F(No. 2)A 2017 for provision about the effect of subsection (2)(a) in a case in which the relevant step is within paragraph 1 of that Schedule."

Remittance basis

39   Part 7A of ITEPA 2003 is amended as follows.

40 (1) Section 554Z9 (remittance basis: A does not meet section 26A requirement) is amended in accordance with this paragraph.

(2) In subsection (1), for "Subsection (2) applies" substitute "Subsections (2) and (2A) apply".

(3)   In subsection (1A), for "subsection (2) does not apply" substitute "subsections (2) and (2A) do not apply".

(4)   At the beginning of subsection (2) insert "Except in a case within subsection (2A),".

(5)   After subsection (2) insert—

"(2A)   Where the relevant step is within paragraph 1 of Schedule 11 to F(No. 2)A 2017, A's employment income by virtue of section 554Z2(1), or the relevant part of it, is "taxable specific income" in the tax year in which the relevant step is treated as being taken so far as the income is remitted to the United Kingdom in that tax year or in any previous tax year."

(6)   In subsection (3) for "this purpose" substitute "the purposes of subsections (2) and (2A)".

(7)   In subsection (5)—

(a)   in the words before paragraph (a), for "subsection (2)" substitute "subsection (2) or (2A)";

(b)   in the words after paragraph (d)—

(i)   for "subsection (2)" substitute "subsection (2) or (2A)";

(ii)   for "that subsection" substitute "subsection (2) or (2A) (as the case may be)".

41   (1)   Section 554Z10 (remittance basis: A meets section 26A requirement) is amended in accordance with this paragraph.

(2)   In subsection (1) for "Subsection (2) applies" substitute "Subsections (2) and (2A) apply".

(3)   At the beginning of subsection (2) insert "Except in a case within subsection (2AA),".

(4)   After subsection (2) insert—

"(2AA)   Where the relevant step is within paragraph 1 of Schedule 11 to F(No. 2)A 2017, the overseas portion of (as the case may be)—

(a)   A's employment income by virtue of section 554Z2(1), or

(b)   the relevant part of A's employment income by virtue of that section,

is "taxable specific income" in the tax year in which the relevant step is treated as being taken so far as the overseas portion is remitted to the United Kingdom in that tax year or in any previous tax year."

42   (1)   Section 554Z11 (remittance basis: supplementary) is amended in accordance with this paragraph.

(2)   In subsection (4), for "554Z9(2) or 554Z10(2)" substitute "554Z9(2) or (2A) or 554Z10(2) or (2AA)".

(3)   In subsection (5), for "554Z9(2) or 554Z10(2)" substitute "554Z9(2) or (2A) or 554Z10(2) or (2AA)".

(4)   In subsection (6), for "554Z9(2) or 554Z10(2)" substitute "554Z9(2) or (2A) or 554Z10(2) or (2AA)".

552   *Finance (No. 2) Act 2017 (c. 32)*
Schedule 11 — Employment income provided through third parties: loans etc outstanding on 5 April 2019
Part 4 — Supplementary provision

43   (1) Section 554Z11A (temporary non-residents) is amended in accordance with this paragraph.

     (2) In subsection (2) —

        (a) after "554Z9(2)" insert "or (2A)";

        (b) after "554Z10(2)" insert "or (2AA)".

     (3) In subsection (3)(d)(i), for "554Z9(2) or 554Z10(2)" substitute "554Z9(2) or (2A) or 554Z10(2) or (2AA)".

Interpretation

44   (1) In this Schedule, "tax avoidance arrangement" has the same meaning as it has for the purposes of Part 7A of ITEPA 2003 (see section 554Z(13) to (15) of that Act).

     (2) Section 554Z(16) (determining whether a step is connected with a tax avoidance arrangement) applies for the purposes of this Schedule as it applies for the purposes of Part 7A of ITEPA 2003.

45   See section 554A(1)(a) of ITEPA 2003 for the meaning of "A" and "B".

PART 5

CONSEQUENTIAL AMENDMENTS

ITEPA 2003

46   (1) ITEPA 2003 is amended in accordance with this paragraph.

     (2) In section 554A(2) (meaning of "relevant step"), after "or 554D" insert ", or paragraph 1 of Schedule 11 to F(No. 2)A 2017".

     (3) In section 554A(4) (relevant step taken on or after A's death), in paragraph (a) after "section 554B taken" insert ", or a relevant step within paragraph 1 of Schedule 11 to F(No.2)A 2017 which is treated as being taken,".

     (4) In section 554Z(9) (interpretation: reference to definition of "relevant step"), at the end insert ", but see also Schedule 11 to F(No. 2)A 2017".

     (5) In section 554Z(10) (interpretation: relevant step which involves a sum of money) omit "or" at the end of paragraph (b) and after paragraph (c) insert ", or

        (d) a step within paragraph 1 of Schedule 11 to F(No. 2)A 2017."

     (6) In section 554Z5 of ITEPA 2003 (overlap with money or asset subject to earlier tax liability), at the end insert —

        "(12) See paragraphs 4(5) and (6) and 12(4) and (5) of Schedule 11 of F(No. 2)A 2017) for provision about the effect of subsection (3) in certain cases where the relevant step is within paragraph 1 of that Schedule."

FA 2011

47   In paragraph 59 of Schedule 2 to FA 2011 (transitional provision relating to Part 7A of ITEPA 2003), in sub-paragraph (1)(a), after "ITEPA 2003" insert "or paragraph 1 of Schedule 11 to F(No. 2)A 2017".

Finance (No. 2) Act 2017 (c. 32)
Schedule 12 — Trading income provided through third parties: loans etc outstanding on 5 April 2019

553

SCHEDULE 12   Section 35

TRADING INCOME PROVIDED THROUGH THIRD PARTIES: LOANS ETC OUTSTANDING ON 5
APRIL 2019

Application of sections 23A to 23H of ITTOIA 2005 in relation to loans etc. outstanding on 5 April 2019

1   (1) A loan or quasi-loan in relation to which sub-paragraph (2) applies is to be treated as a "relevant benefit" for the purposes of sections 23A to 23H of ITTOIA 2005.

     (2) This sub-paragraph applies in relation to a loan or a quasi-loan if—
         (a)   the loan or quasi-loan was made—
               (i)   on or after 6 April 1999, and
               (ii)   before 6 April 2017, and
         (b)   an amount of the loan or quasi-loan is outstanding immediately before the end of 5 April 2019.

     (3) Where section 23E of ITTOIA 2005 applies in relation to a relevant benefit which is a loan or quasi-loan in relation to which sub-paragraph (2) applies, section 23E has effect—
         (a)   as if the "relevant benefit amount" were the amount of the loan or quasi-loan that is outstanding immediately before—
               (i)   the end of the approved repayment date, if the relevant benefit is an approved fixed term loan on 5 April 2019, or
               (ii)   the end of 5 April 2019 in any other case,
         (b)   as if section 23E(1)(a) specified—
               (i)   the tax year in which the approved repayment date falls, if the relevant benefit is an approved fixed term loan on 5 April 2019, or
               (ii)   the tax year 2018-2019 in any other case, and
         (c)   where T ceases to carry on the relevant trade in a tax year before the tax year so specified in section 23E(1)(a), as if section 23E(1)(b) were omitted and as if section 23E(1) provided that the relevant benefit amount is to be treated for income tax purposes as a post-cessation receipt of the trade received in the tax year so specified in section 23E(1)(a).

     (4) This paragraph is subject to paragraphs 19 and 20 (accelerated payments).

     (5) For the purposes of this paragraph, whether an amount of a loan or quasi-loan is outstanding at a particular time—
         (a)   is to be determined in accordance with the following provisions of this Schedule, and
         (b)   does not depend on the loan or quasi-loan subsisting at that time.

Meaning of "loan", "quasi-loan" and "approved repayment date"

2   (1) In this Schedule "loan" includes—
         (a)   any form of credit;
         (b)   a payment that is purported to be made by way of a loan.

(2) For the purposes of paragraph 1, a person ("P") makes a "quasi-loan" to T if (and when) P acquires a right (the "acquired debt") —

  (a) which is a right to a payment or a transfer of assets, and

  (b) in respect of which the condition in sub-paragraph (3) is met.

(3) The condition is met in relation to a right if there is a connection (direct or indirect) between the acquisition of the right and —

  (a) a payment made, by way of a loan or otherwise, to T, or

  (b) a transfer of assets to T.

(4) Where a loan or a quasi-loan made to T is replaced, directly or indirectly, by another loan (the "replacement loan"), references in paragraph 1 to the loan are references to the replacement loan.

(5) Where a loan or a quasi-loan made to T is replaced, directly or indirectly, by another quasi-loan (the "replacement quasi-loan"), references in paragraph 1 to the quasi-loan are references to the replacement quasi-loan.

(6) In this Schedule, "approved repayment date", in relation to an approved fixed term loan, means the date by which, under the terms of the loan at the time of making the application for approval under paragraph 16, the whole of the loan must be repaid.

(7) In this paragraph and in paragraphs 3, 9, 10, 19 and 20 —

  (a) "T" is the person mentioned in section 23A(2) of ITTOIA 2005,

  (b) references to T include references to a person who is or has been connected with T, and

  (c) for that purpose, section 993 of ITA 2007 (meaning of "connected") applies for the purposes of this Schedule but as if subsection (4) of that section were omitted.

Meaning of "outstanding": loans

3 (1) An amount of a loan is "outstanding" for the purposes of paragraph 1 if the relevant principal amount exceeds the repayment amount.

(2) In sub-paragraph (1) "relevant principal amount", in relation to a loan, means the total of —

  (a) the initial principal amount lent, and

  (b) any sums that have become principal under the loan, otherwise than by capitalisation of interest.

(3) In sub-paragraph (1) "repayment amount", in relation to a loan, means the total of —

  (a) the amount of principal under the loan that has been repaid before 5 December 2016, and

  (b) payments in money made by T on or after 5 December 2016 by way of repayment of principal under the loan.

(4) A payment is to be disregarded for the purposes of sub-paragraph (3)(b) if there is any connection (direct or indirect) between the payment and a tax avoidance arrangement (other than the arrangement in pursuance of which the loan was made).

(5) In this paragraph and in paragraph 9, "tax avoidance arrangement" means an arrangement which has a tax avoidance purpose.

(6) For the purposes of sub-paragraph (5), an arrangement has a tax avoidance purpose if sub-paragraph (7) applies to a person who is a party to the arrangement.

(7) This sub-paragraph applies to a person if the main purpose, or one of the main purposes, of the person entering into the arrangement is the avoidance of tax.

(8) The following paragraphs apply for the purpose of determining whether any payment is connected with a tax avoidance arrangement—

    (a) a payment is connected with a tax avoidance arrangement if (for example) the payment is made (wholly or partly) in pursuance of—

        (i) the tax avoidance arrangement, or

        (ii) an arrangement at one end of a series of arrangements with the tax avoidance arrangement being at the other end, and

    (b) it does not matter whether the person making the payment is unaware of the tax avoidance arrangement.

Meaning of "outstanding": loans in currencies other than sterling

4 (1) In paragraphs 5 to 8 "the loan currency", in relation to a loan, means the currency in which the initial principal amount of the loan is denominated (whether or not that amount is paid in that currency).

(2) For the purposes of paragraphs 5 to 8, the value of an amount in a particular currency is to be determined by reference to an appropriate spot rate of exchange.

5 (1) This paragraph applies in relation to a loan where the loan currency is a currency other than sterling.

(2) But this paragraph does not apply if paragraph 8 applies in relation to the loan.

(3) The amount of the loan that is outstanding, at the relevant time, is to be calculated in sterling as follows—

Step 1
Calculate, in the loan currency, the amount that is outstanding at that time.

Step 2
Take the value in sterling, at that time, of that amount.

(4) For the purposes of this paragraph and paragraph 8, the "relevant time" in relation to a loan is the time immediately before—

    (a) the end of the approved repayment date, if the loan is an approved fixed term loan on 5 April 2019, or

    (b) the end of 5 April 2019 in any other case.

(5) See paragraph 6 for provision about repayments made in a currency other than the loan currency.

Repayments in currencies other than the loan currency

6 (1) This paragraph applies in relation to a loan where—

     (a)   payments in money are made by way of repayment of principal under the loan, and

     (b)   some or all of the payments are made in a currency other than the loan currency.

(2) But this paragraph does not apply if paragraph 8 applies in relation to the loan.

(3) For the purposes of calculating the repayment amount in relation to the loan, the amount of each of the payments referred to in sub-paragraph (1)(b) is an amount equal to its value in the loan currency on the date it is made.

Loans made in a depreciating currency

7   (1) Paragraph 8 applies in relation to a loan where—

     (a)   the loan currency is a currency other than sterling, and

     (b)   it is reasonable to suppose that the main reason, or one of the main reasons, for the loan being made in that currency is that the loan currency is expected to depreciate as against sterling during the loan period.

(2) The "loan period", in relation to a loan, is the period—

     (a)   beginning at the time the loan is made, and

     (b)   ending with the time by which, under the terms of the loan, the whole of the loan is to be repaid.

8   (1) Where this paragraph applies in relation to a loan—

     (a)   paragraphs 5 and 6 do not apply in relation to the loan, and

     (b)   sub-paragraphs (2) to (5) apply for the purposes of calculating the amount of the loan that is outstanding at the relevant time (as defined in paragraph 5(4)).

(2) The relevant principal amount, in relation to the loan, is an amount equal to the total of—

     (a)   the value in sterling, at the reference date, of the initial principal amount lent, and

     (b)   the value in sterling, at the reference date, of any sums that become principal under the loan, otherwise than by capitalisation of interest.

(3) The "reference date"—

     (a)   in relation to an amount within sub-paragraph (2)(a), means the date on which the loan is made, and

     (b)   in relation to a sum within sub-paragraph (2)(b), means the date on which the sum becomes principal.

(4) The repayment amount, in relation to the loan, is an amount equal to the total of—

     (a)   the amount of principal under the loan that has been repaid in sterling, and

     (b)   where payments are made, in a currency other than sterling, by way of repayment of principal under the loan, the amount equal to the sterling value of the payments.

(5) The "sterling value" of a payment is its value in sterling on the date it is made.

Meaning of outstanding: "quasi-loans"

9 (1) An amount of a quasi-loan is outstanding for the purposes of paragraph 1 if the initial debt amount exceeds the repayment amount.

  (2) In sub-paragraph (1), "initial debt amount" means the total of —
    (a) an amount equal to the value of the acquired debt (see paragraph 2(2)), and
    (b) where P subsequently acquires a further right (the "additional debt") to a payment, or transfer of assets, in connection with the payment mentioned in paragraph 2(3)(a) or (as the case may be) the transfer mentioned in paragraph 2(3)(b), an amount equal to the value of the additional debt.

  (3) For the purposes of sub-paragraph (2) —
    (a) where the acquired debt is a right to payment of an amount, the "value" of the debt is that amount,
    (b) where the additional debt is a right to payment of an amount, the "value" of the debt is that amount, but is nil if the additional debt accrued to P by the capitalisation of interest on the acquired debt or another additional debt, and
    (c) where the acquired debt or additional debt is a right to a transfer of assets, the "value" of the debt is an amount equal to —
      (i) the market value of the assets at the time the right is acquired (or the value of the right at that time if the assets are non-fungible and not in existence at that time), or
      (ii) if higher, the cost of the assets at that time.

  (4) In sub-paragraph (1), "repayment amount", in relation to a quasi-loan, means the total of —
    (a) the amount (if any) by which the initial debt amount has been reduced (by way of repayment) before 5 December 2016,
    (b) payments in money (if any) made by T on or after 5 December 2016 by way of repayment of the initial debt amount, and
    (c) if the acquired debt or additional debt is a right to a transfer of assets, and the assets have been transferred, an amount equal to the market value of the assets at the time of the transfer.

  (5) A payment or transfer is to be disregarded for the purposes of sub-paragraph (4)(b) or (c) if there is any connection (direct or indirect) between the payment or transfer and a tax avoidance arrangement (other than the arrangement under which the quasi-loan was made).

  (6) In this paragraph, "market value" has the same meaning as it has for the purposes of TCGA 1992 by virtue of Part 8 of that Act.

Meaning of "outstanding": quasi-loans in currencies other than sterling

10 (1) Paragraphs 11 to 14 apply where P makes a quasi-loan to T by reason of acquiring a right to a payment in a particular currency (the "quasi-loan currency").

  (2) For the purposes of paragraphs 11 to 14, the value of an amount in a particular currency is to be determined by reference to an appropriate spot rate of exchange.

11 (1) This paragraph applies in relation to the quasi-loan if the quasi-loan currency is a currency other than sterling.

   (2) But this paragraph does not apply if paragraph 14 applies in relation to the quasi-loan.

   (3) The amount of the quasi-loan that is outstanding, at the relevant time, is to be calculated in sterling as follows —

   Step 1
   Calculate, in the quasi-loan currency, the amount that is outstanding at that time.

   Step 2
   Take the value in sterling, at that time, of that amount.

   (4) For the purposes of this paragraph and paragraph 14, the "relevant time" in relation to a quasi-loan is the time immediately before the end of 5 April 2019.

   (5) See paragraph 12 for provision about repayments made in a currency other than the quasi-loan currency.

Repayments in currencies other than the quasi-loan currency

12 (1) This paragraph applies in relation to the quasi-loan if —
       (a) payments in money are made by way of repayment of the initial debt amount, and
       (b) some or all of the payments are made in a currency other than the quasi-loan currency.

   (2) But this paragraph does not apply if paragraph 14 applies in relation to the quasi-loan.

   (3) For the purposes of calculating the repayment amount in relation to the quasi-loan, the amount of each of the payments referred to in sub-paragraph (1)(b) is an amount equal to its value in the quasi-loan currency on the date it is made.

Quasi-loans made in a depreciating currency

13 (1) Paragraph 14 applies in relation to the quasi-loan if —
       (a) the quasi-loan currency is a currency other than sterling, and
       (b) it is reasonable to suppose that the main reason, or one of the main reasons, for the quasi-loan being made in that currency is that the quasi-loan currency is expected to depreciate as against sterling during the quasi-loan period.

   (2) The "quasi-loan period", in relation to a quasi-loan, is the period —
       (a) beginning at the time the quasi-loan is made, and
       (b) ending with the time by which, under the terms of the quasi-loan, the whole of the quasi-loan is to be repaid.

14 (1) Where this paragraph applies in relation to the quasi-loan —
       (a) paragraphs 11 and 12 do not apply in relation to the quasi-loan, and

    (b)   sub-paragraphs (2) to (5) apply for the purposes of calculating the amount of the quasi-loan that is outstanding at the relevant time (as defined in paragraph 11(4)).

(2) The initial debt amount, in relation to the quasi-loan, is an amount equal to the total of —

    (a)   the value in sterling, at the reference date, of the acquired debt, and

    (b)   the value in sterling, at the reference date, of any additional debt.

(3) The "reference date", in relation to a right within sub-paragraph (2)(a) or (2)(b), means the date on which P acquires it.

(4) The repayment amount, in relation to the quasi-loan, is an amount equal to the total of —

    (a)   the amount of the initial debt amount that has been repaid in sterling, and

    (b)   where payments are made, in a currency other than sterling, by way of repayment of the initial debt amount, the amount equal to the sterling value of the payments.

(5) The "sterling value" of a payment is its value in sterling on the date it is made.

Meaning of "approved fixed term loan"

15   (1) A loan is an "approved fixed term loan" on 5 April 2019 if, at any time on that day, it is a qualifying loan which has been approved by an officer of Revenue and Customs in accordance with paragraph 16.

    (2) A loan is a "qualifying loan" if —

       (a)   the loan was made before 9 December 2010,

       (b)   the term of the loan cannot exceed 10 years, and

       (c)   it is not an excluded loan under sub-paragraph (3).

    (3) A loan is an excluded loan if, at any time after the loan was made —

       (a)   the loan has been replaced, directly or indirectly, by another loan, or

       (b)   the terms of the loan have been altered so as —

          (i)   to meet the condition in sub-paragraph (2)(b), or

          (ii)   to postpone the date by which, under the terms of the loan, the whole of the loan must be repaid.

Approval: application to HMRC

16   (1) A person may make an application to the Commissioners for Her Majesty's Revenue and Customs for approval of a qualifying loan made to T.

    (2) An officer of Revenue and Customs may grant such an application if satisfied that, in relation to the loan —

       (a)   the qualifying payments condition is met (see paragraph 17), or

       (b)   the commercial terms condition is met (see paragraph 18).

    (3) Subject to sub-paragraph (4), an application may be made in 2018.

    (4) An application may be made after 2018 if an officer of Revenue and Customs considers it reasonable in all the circumstances for a late application to be made.

    (5) An application for an approval must be made in such form and manner, and contain such information, as may be specified by, or on behalf of, the Commissioners for Her Majesty's Revenue and Customs.

    (6) An officer of Revenue and Customs must notify the applicant of the decision on an application.

Approval: qualifying payments condition

17 (1) The qualifying payments condition is met in relation to a qualifying loan if, during the relevant period —

    (a) payments have been made in respect of the repayment of the principal of the loan, and

    (b) the payments have been made at intervals not exceeding 53 weeks.

    (2) The "relevant period" in relation to a loan is the period beginning with the making of the loan and ending with the making of the application.

Approval: commercial terms condition

18 (1) The commercial terms condition is met in relation to a qualifying loan if —

    (a) either —

       (i) it is reasonable to assume that, had the qualifying loan been made in the ordinary course of a lending business, loans on terms comparable to those of the qualifying loan would have been available to members of the public, or

       (ii) the qualifying loan was made in the ordinary course of a lending business; and

    (b) the borrower has, in all material respects, complied with the terms of the loan.

    (2) For the purposes of sub-paragraph (1), a loan is made in the ordinary course of a lending business if it is made by a person in the ordinary course of a business carried on by the person which includes —

    (a) the lending of money, or

    (b) the supplying of goods or services on credit.

Accelerated payments

19 (1) Paragraph 20(1) applies where —

    (a) section 23E of ITTOIA 2005 would (ignoring paragraph 20) apply in relation to a relevant benefit arising to T,

    (b) the relevant benefit is a loan or quasi-loan in relation to which paragraph 1(2) applies,

    (c) an accelerated payment notice, or a partner payment notice, relating to a relevant charge (the "accelerated payment notice") has been given under Chapter 3 of Part 4 of FA 2014,

    (d) T makes a payment (the "accelerated payment") in respect of the understated or disputed tax to which the notice relates,

    (e) the accelerated payment is made on or before the relevant date, and

    (f) the amount of the loan or quasi-loan that, at the end of the relevant date, is outstanding for the purposes of paragraph 1 (see paragraphs 3 to 14) is equal to or less than the amount of the accelerated payment.

Finance (No. 2) Act 2017 (c. 32)
Schedule 12 − Trading income provided through third parties: loans etc outstanding on 5 April 2019

561

(2) In sub-paragraph (1)(c), "relevant charge" means a charge to tax under section 23E of ITTOIA 2005 arising by reason of a relevant benefit which arises to T in pursuance of the relevant arrangement in pursuance of which the relevant benefit mentioned in sub-paragraph (1)(a) and (b) arises.

(3) In sub-paragraph (1)(e) and (f), "the relevant date" means −
   (a) the approved repayment date, if the relevant benefit is an approved fixed term loan on 5 April 2019, or
   (b) 5 April 2019, in any other case.

20 (1) T may make an application to the Commissioners for Her Majesty's Revenue and Customs to be treated −
   (a) as if the relevant benefit mentioned in paragraph 19(1)(a) and (b) arises only if the condition in sub-paragraph (2) is met, and
   (b) as if it arises immediately before the end of the 30 days beginning with the date on which the condition in sub-paragraph (2) becomes met.

(2) The condition is that, on the withdrawal of the accelerated payment notice or on the determination of an appeal, any part of the accelerated payment is repaid.

(3) Subject to sub-paragraph (4), an application under sub-paragraph (1) may be made in 2018.

(4) An application may be made after 2018 if an officer of Revenue and Customs considers it reasonable in all the circumstances for a late application to be made.

(5) An application must be made in such form and manner, and contain such information, as may be specified by, or on behalf of, the Commissioners for Her Majesty's Revenue and Customs.

(6) An officer of Revenue and Customs must notify the applicant of the decision on an application under this paragraph.

SCHEDULE 13   Section 55

THIRD COUNTRY GOODS FULFILMENT BUSINESSES: PENALTY

Liability to penalty

1 (1) A penalty is payable by a person ("P") who −
   (a) carries on a third country goods fulfilment business, and
   (b) is not an approved person.

(2) In this Schedule references to a "contravention" are to acting as mentioned in sub-paragraph (1).

Amount of penalty

2 (1) If the contravention is deliberate and concealed, the amount of the penalty is the maximum amount (see paragraph 10).

    (2) If the contravention is deliberate but not concealed, the amount of the penalty is 70% of the maximum amount.

    (3) In any other case, the amount of the penalty is 30% of the maximum amount.

    (4) The contravention is —

        (a) "deliberate and concealed" if the contravention is deliberate and P makes arrangements to conceal the contravention, and

        (b) "deliberate but not concealed" if the contravention is deliberate but P does not make arrangements to conceal the contravention.

Reductions for disclosure

3   (1) Paragraph 4 provides for reductions in penalties under this Schedule where P discloses a contravention.

    (2) P discloses a contravention by —

        (a) telling the Commissioners about it,

        (b) giving the Commissioners reasonable help in identifying any other contraventions of which P is aware, and

        (c) allowing the Commissioners access to records for the purpose of identifying such contraventions.

    (3) Disclosure of a contravention —

        (a) is "unprompted" if made at a time when P has no reason to believe that the Commissioners have discovered or are about to discover the contravention, and

        (b) otherwise, is "prompted".

    (4) In relation to disclosure, "quality" includes timing, nature and extent.

4   (1) Where P discloses a contravention, the Commissioners must reduce the penalty to one that reflects the quality of the disclosure.

    (2) If the disclosure is prompted, the penalty may not be reduced below —

        (a) in the case of a contravention that is deliberate and concealed, the maximum amount,

        (b) in the case of a contravention that is deliberate but not concealed, 35% of the maximum amount, and

        (c) in any other case, 20% of the maximum amount.

    (3) If the disclosure is unprompted, the penalty may not be reduced below —

        (a) in the case of a contravention that is deliberate and concealed, 30% of the maximum amount,

        (b) in the case of a contravention that is deliberate but not concealed, 20% of the maximum amount, and

        (c) in any other case, 10% of the maximum amount.

Special reduction

5   (1) If the Commissioners think it right because of special circumstances, they may reduce a penalty under this Schedule.

    (2) In sub-paragraph (1) "special circumstances" does not include ability to pay.

(3) In sub-paragraph (1) the reference to reducing a penalty includes a reference to—

     (a) staying a penalty, and

     (b) agreeing a compromise in relation to proceedings for a penalty.

Assessment

6   (1) Where P becomes liable for a penalty under this Schedule, the Commissioners must—

     (a) assess the penalty,

     (b) notify P, and

     (c) state in the notice the contravention in respect of which the penalty is assessed.

   (2) A penalty under this Schedule must be paid before the end of the period of 30 days beginning with the day on which notification of the penalty is issued.

   (3) A penalty under this Schedule is recoverable as a debt due to the Crown.

   (4) An assessment of a penalty under this Schedule may not be made later than one year after evidence of facts sufficient in the opinion of the Commissioners to indicate the contravention comes to their knowledge.

   (5) Two or more contraventions may be treated by the Commissioners as a single contravention for the purposes of assessing a penalty under this Schedule.

Reasonable excuse

7   (1) Liability to a penalty does not arise under this Schedule in respect of a contravention which is not deliberate if P satisfies the Commissioners or (on an appeal made to the appeal tribunal) the tribunal that there is a reasonable excuse for the contravention.

   (2) For the purposes of sub-paragraph (1), where P relies on any other person to do anything, that is not a reasonable excuse unless P took reasonable care to avoid the contravention.

Companies: officer's liability

8   (1) Where a penalty under this Schedule is payable by a company in respect of a contravention which was attributable to an officer of the company, the officer is liable to pay such portion of the penalty (which may be 100%) as the Commissioners may specify by written notice to the officer.

   (2) Sub-paragraph (1) does not allow the Commissioners to recover more than 100% of a penalty.

   (3) In the application of sub-paragraph (1) to a body corporate other than a limited liability partnership, "officer" means—

     (a) a director (including a shadow director within the meaning of section 251 of the Companies Act 2006),

     (b) a manager, and

     (c) a secretary.

(4) In the application of sub-paragraph (1) to a limited liability partnership, "officer" means a member.

(5) In the application of sub-paragraph (1) in any other case, "officer" means —

    (a) a director,

    (b) a manager,

    (c) a secretary, and

    (d) any other person managing or purporting to manage any of the company's affairs.

(6) Where the Commissioners have specified a portion of a penalty in a notice given to an officer under sub-paragraph (1) —

    (a) paragraph 5 applies to the specified portion as to a penalty,

    (b) the officer must pay the specified portion before the end of the period of 30 days beginning with the day on which the notice is given,

    (c) sub-paragraphs (3) to (5) of paragraph 6 apply as if the notice were an assessment of a penalty, and

    (d) paragraph 9 applies as if the officer were liable to a penalty.

(7) In this paragraph "company" means any body corporate or unincorporated association, but does not include a partnership.

Double jeopardy

9   P is not liable to a penalty under this Schedule in respect of a contravention in respect of which P has been convicted of an offence.

The maximum amount

10   (1) In this Schedule "the maximum amount" means £10,000.

    (2) If it appears to the Treasury that there has been a change in the value of money since the last relevant date, they may by regulations substitute for the sum for the time being specified in sub-paragraph (1) such other sum as appears to them to be justified by the change.

    (3) In sub-paragraph (2), "relevant date" means —

        (a) the date on which this Act is passed, and

        (b) each date on which the power conferred by that sub-paragraph has been exercised.

    (4) Regulations under this paragraph do not apply to any contravention which occurs wholly before the date on which they come into force.

Appeal tribunal

11   In this Schedule "appeal tribunal" has the same meaning as in Chapter 2 of Part 1 of the Finance Act 1994.

Finance (No. 2) Act 2017 (c. 32)
Schedule 14 — Digital reporting and record-keeping for income tax etc: further amendments
Part 1 — Amendments of TMA 1970

565

SCHEDULE 14

Section 61

DIGITAL REPORTING AND RECORD-KEEPING FOR INCOME TAX ETC: FURTHER AMENDMENTS

PART 1

AMENDMENTS OF TMA 1970

1   TMA 1970 is amended as follows.

2   (1) Section 7 (notice of liability) is amended as follows.

    (2) In subsection (1A) for the words from "under section 8" to the end substitute "to file under section 8 for the year of assessment".

    (3) In subsection (1B)(a) for the words from "under section 8" to "gains" substitute "to file under section 8 for the year of assessment".

    (4) In subsection (7) for "section 9" substitute "section 8 or 8A".

3   (1) Section 8 (personal return) is amended as follows.

    (2) For the heading substitute "Notices to file: persons other than trustees".

    (3) For subsection (1) substitute—

> "(1) For the purpose of establishing—
>> (a) the amounts in which a person is chargeable to income tax and capital gains tax for a year of assessment, and
>> (b) the amount payable by the person by way of income tax for the year,
>
> an officer of Revenue and Customs may give the person a notice to file for the year of assessment."

    (4) In subsection (1AA)(a) for "return" substitute "information filed in response to the notice to file or in any end of period statement for the year of assessment provided to HMRC by the person".

    (5) After subsection (1AA) insert—

> "(1AB) A notice to file for a year of assessment is a notice requiring the person concerned—
>> (a) to file the following for that year (in addition to any end of period statement for the year that may be required by regulations under paragraph 8 of Schedule A1)—
>>> (i) such information as may reasonably be required in pursuance of the notice for the purpose mentioned in subsection (1),
>>> (ii) a self-assessment (but see section 9(2)), and
>>> (iii) a final declaration, and
>> (b) to deliver to HMRC such accounts, statements, or other documents (relating to the information filed as mentioned in paragraph (a)(i) and (ii)) as may reasonably be required for the purpose mentioned in subsection (1).
>
> (1AC) The duty to file the things mentioned in subsection (1AB)(a) is to be complied with—

566

Finance (No. 2) Act 2017 (c. 32)
Schedule 14 — Digital reporting and record-keeping for income tax etc: further amendments
Part 1 — Amendments of TMA 1970

      (a)   where the person is not required to provide an end of period statement for the year, by making and delivering to HMRC a return containing those things, and

      (b)   where the person is required to provide such a statement, by —

           (i)   making and delivering to HMRC a return containing those things, or

           (ii)   providing those things to HMRC using the facility to file mentioned in paragraph 9 of Schedule A1.

(1AD)   It is immaterial that any of the information required as mentioned in subsection (1AB)(a)(i) in response to a notice to file has been provided to HMRC before the date of the notice."

(6) In subsection (1B) —

      (a)   for "a return under this section" substitute "the information filed in response to a notice to file";

      (b)   after "relevant" insert "partnership".

(7) In subsection (1C) —

      (a)   after ""relevant" insert "partnership";

      (b)   after "means a" insert "partnership";

      (c)   for "of this Act" substitute ", or under regulations under paragraph 10 of Schedule A1,".

(8) For subsection (1D) substitute —

  "(1D)   Where the method to be used for complying with a notice to file for a year of assessment (Year 1) is filing a return —

      (a)   if the return is a non-electronic return, the person must comply with the notice on or before 31 October in Year 2, and

      (b)   if the return is an electronic return, the person must comply with the notice on or before 31 January in Year 2."

(9) In subsection (1F) for "a return" substitute "the return".

(10) In subsection (1G) for "a return" substitute "the return".

(11) After subsection (1H) insert —

  "(1HA)   Where the method to be used for complying with a notice to file for a year of assessment (Year 1) is using the facility mentioned in paragraph 9 of Schedule A1, the person must comply with the notice on or before —

      (a)   31 January in Year 2, or

      (b)   if later, the last day of the period of 3 months beginning with the date of the notice."

(12) For subsection (2) substitute —

  "(2)   The final declaration required by a notice to file is a declaration by the person concerned to the effect that to the best of the person's knowledge the information and self-assessment filed in response to the notice are (taken together) correct and complete."

(13) In subsections (3), (4) and (4A) for "under this section" substitute "to file".

(14) In subsection (4B) for the words from "may" to "income" substitute "to file may require the information filed in response".

(15) After subsection (5) insert—

"(6) In this section "notice to file" means a notice to file under this section.

(7) In the Taxes Acts, unless the contrary intention appears, a reference (whether specific or general)—

(a) to a return under this section for a year of assessment, is to—

(i) the information, self-assessment and final declaration filed for the year under this section, and

(ii) any end of period statement for the year provided to HMRC;

(b) to anything required to be included in a return under this section for a year of assessment, is to—

(i) the information, self-assessment and final declaration required to be filed for the year under this section, and

(ii) any end of period statement for the year required to be provided to HMRC, and

(c) to making or delivering a return under this section, is to—

(i) making or delivering a return as mentioned in subsection (1AC)(a) or (b)(i), or

(ii) if the response to a notice to file is made using the facility mentioned in paragraph 9 of Schedule A1, making the final declaration required by the notice."

4 (1) Section 8A (trustee's return) is amended as follows.

(2) For the heading substitute "Notices to file: trustees".

(3) For subsection (1) substitute—

"(1) For the purpose of establishing—

(a) the amounts in which the relevant trustees of a settlement, and the settlors and beneficiaries, are chargeable to income tax and capital gains tax for a year of assessment, and

(b) the amount payable by them by way of income tax for the year,

an officer of Revenue and Customs may give any relevant trustee a notice to file for the year of assessment.

(1ZA) A notice to file may be given to any one trustee or separate notices may be given to each trustee or to such trustees as the officer giving the notice thinks fit."

(4) In subsection (1AA)(a) for "return" substitute "information filed in response to the notice to file or in any end of period statement for the year of assessment provided to HMRC by the relevant trustees".

(5) After subsection (1AA) insert—

"(1AB) A notice to file for a year of assessment is a notice requiring the trustee to whom it is given—

  (a) to file the following for that year (in addition to any end of
       period statement for the year that may be required by
       regulations under paragraph 8 of Schedule A1) —
       (i)   such information as may reasonably be required in
             pursuance of the notice for the purpose mentioned in
             subsection (1),
       (ii) a self-assessment (but see section 9(2)), and
       (iii) a final declaration, and
  (b) to deliver to HMRC such accounts, statements, or other
       documents (relating to the information filed as mentioned in
       paragraph (a)(i) and (ii)) as may reasonably be required for
       the purpose mentioned in subsection (1).

(1AC) The duty to file the things mentioned in subsection (1AB)(a) is to be
       complied with —
  (a) where the relevant trustees are not required to provide an
       end of period statement for the year, by the trustee making
       and delivering to HMRC a return containing those things,
       and
  (b) where the relevant trustees are required to provide such a
       statement, by the trustee —
       (i)   making and delivering to HMRC a return containing
             those things, or
       (ii) providing those things to HMRC using the facility to
             file mentioned in paragraph 9 of Schedule A1.

(1AD) It is immaterial that any of the information required as mentioned in
       subsection (1AB)(a)(i) in response to a notice to file has been
       provided to HMRC before the date of the notice."

(6) For subsection (1B) substitute —

  "(1B) Where the method to be used by the trustee for complying with a
         notice to file for a year of assessment (Year 1) is filing a return —
    (a) if the return is a non-electronic return, the trustee must
         comply with the notice on or before 31 October in Year 2, and
    (b) if the return is an electronic return, the trustee must comply
         with the notice on or before 31 January in Year 2."

(7) In subsection (1D) for "a return" substitute "the return".

(8) In subsection (1E) for "a return" substitute "the return".

(9) After subsection (1F) insert —

  "(1FA) Where the method to be used for complying with a notice to file for
          a year of assessment (Year 1) is using the facility mentioned in
          paragraph 9 of Schedule A1, the trustee must comply with the notice
          on or before —
    (a) 31 January in Year 2, or
    (b) if later, the last day of the period of 3 months beginning with
         the date of the notice."

(10) For subsection (2) substitute—

"(2)   The final declaration required by a notice to file is a declaration by the trustee to the effect that to the best of the trustee's knowledge the information and self-assessment filed in response to the notice are (taken together) correct and complete."

(11) In subsections (3) and (4) for "under this section" substitute "to file".

(12) After subsection (5) insert—

"(6)   In this section "notice to file" means a notice to file under this section.

(7)   In the Taxes Acts, unless the contrary intention appears, a reference (whether specific or general)—
  (a)   to a return under this section for a year of assessment, is to—
      (i)   the information, self-assessment and final declaration filed for the year under this section, and
      (ii)   any end of period statement for the year provided to HMRC,
  (b)   to anything required to be included in a return under this section for a year of assessment, is to—
      (i)   the information, self-assessment and final declaration required to be filed for the year under this section, and
      (ii)   any end of period statement for the year required to be provided to HMRC, and
  (c)   to making or delivering a return under this section, is to—
      (i)   making or delivering a return as mentioned in subsection (1AC)(a) or (b)(i), or
      (ii)   if the response to a notice to file is made using the facility mentioned in paragraph 9 of Schedule A1, making the final declaration required by the notice."

5   In section 8B (withdrawal of notice under section 8 or 8A)—
  (a)   in the heading after "notice" insert "to file";
  (b)   in subsection (1) after "notice" insert "to file".

6   (1) Section 9 (returns to include self-assessment) is amended as follows.

(2) For the heading substitute "Self-assessment required by a notice to file".

(3) In subsection (1) for the words from the beginning to "say—" substitute "Subject to subsection (1A), the self-assessment required by virtue of subsection (1AB)(a) of section 8 or 8A from a person given a notice to file for a year of assessment is—".

(4) In subsection (2) for "to comply with subsection (1) above" substitute "by virtue of section 8 or 8A to make and file a self-assessment".

(5) In subsection (3) for the words from ", a person" to "above" substitute "required by virtue of section 8 or 8A, a person does not include a self-assessment".

(6) In subsection (3A) after "self-assessment" insert "under section 8 or 8A".

7   (1) Section 12ZH (NRCGT returns and self-assessment: section 8) is amended as follows.

570   *Finance (No. 2) Act 2017 (c. 32)*
Schedule 14 — Digital reporting and record-keeping for income tax etc: further amendments
Part 1 — Amendments of TMA 1970

(2) In subsection (3) for the words from "required" to "return" substitute "given a notice to file".

(3) In subsection (4) after "(1G)" insert "and (1HA)".

(4) In subsections (5) and (6) omit ", for the purposes set out in section 9(1),".

(5) In subsection (8)(b) for "section 9" substitute "section 8".

(6) In subsection (10) for "section 9" substitute "section 8".

(7) In subsection (11) for "section 9" substitute "section 8".

8 (1) Section 12ZI (NRCGT returns and self-assessment: section 8A) is amended as follows.

(2) In subsection (3) for the words from "required" to "return" substitute "given a notice to file".

(3) In subsection (4)(b) after "(1E)" insert "and (1FA)".

(4) In subsections (5) and (6) omit ", for the purposes set out in section 9(1),".

(5) In subsection (8)(b) for "section 9" substitute "section 8A".

(6) In subsection (10) for "section 9" substitute "section 8A".

(7) In subsection (11) for "section 9" substitute "section 8A".

9 In section 12AA(10A) (definitions) for ""partnership return"" substitute ""section 12AA partnership return"".

10 In section 12AB(1) (partnership return to include partnership statement) in the words before paragraph (a) after "Every" insert "section 12AA".

11 (1) Section 12ABA (amendment of partnership return by taxpayer) is amended as follows.

(2) In subsection (1)—
    (a) omit the words from "by the" to "successor,";
    (b) at the end insert "given by—
          (a) in the case of a section 12AA partnership return, the partner who made and delivered the return or his successor, and
          (b) in the case of a Schedule A1 partnership return, the nominated partner."

(3) In subsection (4) after "date"" insert ", in relation to a section 12AA partnership return,".

(4) After subsection (4) insert—

    "(5) In this section "the filing date", in relation to a Schedule A1 partnership return for a year of assessment (Year 1), means 31 January of Year 2."

12 (1) Section 12ABB (HMRC power to correct partnership return) is amended as follows.

Finance (No. 2) Act 2017 (c. 32)   571
Schedule 14 — Digital reporting and record-keeping for income tax etc: further amendments
Part 1 — Amendments of TMA 1970

(2) In subsection (2), for the words from "by notice" to the end substitute—

    "(a) in the case of a section 12AA partnership return, by notice to the partner who made and delivered the return, or his successor, and

    (b) in the case of a Schedule A1 partnership return, by notice to the nominated partner."

(3) In subsection (4) for the words from "the person" to the end substitute "notice rejecting the correction is given—

    (a) in the case of a section 12AA partnership return, by the person to whom the notice of correction was given or his successor, and

    (b) in the case of a Schedule A1 partnership return, by the nominated partner."

13 (1) Section 12AC (notice of enquiry into partnership return) is amended as follows.

(2) In subsection (1)—

    (a) after "return if" insert ", within the time allowed,";

    (b) at the beginning of paragraph (a) insert "in the case of a section 12AA partnership return,";

    (c) after that paragraph insert—

        "(aa) in the case of a Schedule A1 partnership return, to the nominated partner.";

    (d) omit paragraph (b).

(3) In subsection (7)—

    (a) the words from "the day" to the end become paragraph (a);

    (b) at the beginning of that paragraph insert "in relation to a section 12AA partnership return,";

    (c) after that paragraph insert—

        "(b) in relation to a Schedule A1 partnership return for a year of assessment (Year 1), means 31 January of Year 2."

14 (1) Section 12B (records to be kept for purposes of returns) is amended as follows.

(2) For subsection (1) substitute—

    "(1) This section applies to any person who may—

        (a) be given a notice to file under section 8 or 8A in respect of a year of assessment,

        (b) be required by a notice under section 12AA to make and deliver a partnership return in respect of a year of assessment or other period, or

        (c) be required by regulations under paragraph 10 of Schedule A1 to provide a partnership return for a year of assessment.

    (1A) The person must—

        (a) keep all such records as may be requisite for the purpose of enabling the person to make and deliver a correct and complete return, under that section or those regulations, for that year of assessment or period, and

572

Finance (No. 2) Act 2017 (c. 32)
Schedule 14 — Digital reporting and record-keeping for income tax etc: further amendments
Part 1 — Amendments of TMA 1970

     (b)   preserve those records until the end of the relevant day (see subsections (2) to (2ZB))."

(3) In subsection (2) for "day referred to in subsection (1) above is" substitute "relevant day is (subject to subsection (2ZB))".

(4) After subsection (2) insert—

  "(2ZA) Subsection (2ZB) applies where, before the day mentioned in subsection (2), the person—

     (a)   is given a notice under section 8, 8A or 12AA, or

     (b)   becomes subject to a requirement imposed by regulations under paragraph 10 of Schedule A1.

  (2ZB) Where this subsection applies the relevant day is the later of the day mentioned in subsection (2), and—

     (a)   if enquiries are made into the return, the day on which under section 28A(1B) or 28B(1B) those enquiries are completed, or

     (b)   if no such enquiries are made, the day on which an officer no longer has power to make them."

(5) In subsection (2A)—

     (a)   in paragraph (a) for "(1)" substitute "(1)(a) or (b)";

     (b)   in the words after paragraph (b)—

         (i)   omit "the relevant day, that is to say,";

        (ii)   for "(1)" substitute "(1A)".

(6) In subsection (3)(a) for "(1)" substitute "(1A)".

(7) In subsection (4)—

     (a)   for "(1)" substitute "(1A)";

     (b)   at the end insert "and regulations under paragraph 11 of Schedule A1".

(8) In subsection (5) for "(1)" substitute "(1A)".

15   In section 28ZA(6) (referral of questions during enquiry)—

     (a)   in paragraph (b) after "of this Act" insert "into a section 12AA partnership return";

     (b)   after paragraph (b) insert—

         "(c)   in relation to an enquiry under section 12AC(1) of this Act into a Schedule A1 partnership return, the nominated partner."

16   In section 28B(8) (completion of enquiry into partnership return) for the words from "the person" to the end substitute—

     "(a)   in relation to a section 12AA partnership return, the person to whom notice of enquiry was given or his successor, and

     (b)   in relation to a Schedule A1 partnership return, the nominated partner."

17   In section 28C(3) (determination of tax where no return delivered) for "section 9" substitute "section 8 or 8A".

18   In section 28H(2)(b) (simple assessments)—

       (a)   for the words "to make and deliver such a return" substitute "imposed";

       (b)   after "notice" insert "to file".

19   In section 28I(2)(b) (simple assessments for trustees) —

       (a)   for the words "to make and deliver such a return" substitute "imposed";

       (b)   after "notice" insert "to file".

20   (1) Section 29 (assessment where loss of tax discovered) is amended as follows.

     (2) In subsection (2) at the end insert "(or, where the error or mistake is in an end of period statement forming part of the return, if that statement was provided on the basis of or in accordance with the practice generally prevailing at the time when it was provided)."

     (3) In subsection (6) after paragraph (a) insert —

        "(aa)   it is contained in any information provided by the taxpayer to HMRC under regulations under paragraph 7 of Schedule A1 (periodic updates);".

21   In section 30B(10) (amendment of partnership statement where loss of tax discovered) at the end insert "or (in relation to a Schedule A1 partnership return) the nominated partner".

22   (1) Section 42 (procedure for making claims) is amended as follows.

     (2) In subsection (2) —

       (a)   after "of this Act" insert ", or where a partnership is required to provide a return by regulations under paragraph 10 of Schedule A1,";

       (b)   after "that section" insert "or those regulations".

     (3) In subsection (9) after "of this Act" insert "or a Schedule A1 partnership return".

     (4) In subsection (11)(a) after "of this Act" insert "or a Schedule A1 partnership return".

23   (1) Section 59A (payments on account of income tax) is amended as follows.

     (2) In subsection (1)(a) for "section 9" substitute "section 8 or 8A".

     (3) In subsection (4A)(a) for "section 9" substitute "section 8 or 8A".

24   (1) Section 59B (payment of income tax and capital gains tax: assessments other than simple assessments) is amended as follows.

     (2) In subsection (1)(a) for "section 9" substitute "section 8 or 8A".

     (3) In subsection (4A) for "section 9" substitute "section 8 or 8A".

     (4) In subsection (5A) for "section 9" substitute "section 8 or 8A".

     (5) In subsection (6) for "section 9" substitute "section 8 or 8A".

25   (1) Section 106C (offence of failing to deliver a return) is amended as follows.

     (2) In subsection (1) —

574   *Finance (No. 2) Act 2017 (c. 32)*
Schedule 14 — Digital reporting and record-keeping for income tax etc: further amendments
Part 1 — Amendments of TMA 1970

    (a)   for "required by a notice under section 8 to make and deliver a return" substitute "given a notice to file under section 8";

    (b)   in paragraph (a) for "the return" substitute "a return under that section".

  (3) In subsection (2) for "the return" substitute "a return under section 8".

26   In section 106D(1) (offence of making inaccurate return) —

    (a)   for "required by a notice under section 8 to make and deliver a return" substitute "given a notice to file under section 8";

    (b)   in paragraph (a) after "return" insert "under that section".

27   In section 106E (exclusions from offences under sections 106B to 106D) for "or make and deliver the return" substitute "under section 7, or is given the notice to file under section 8,".

28   In section 107A(2)(a) (trustee liability for penalties) after "section 12B of this Act" insert "or paragraph 12 of Schedule A1 to this Act".

29   In section 118(1) (interpretation) —

    (a)   after the definition of "CTA 2010" insert —

          ""end of period statement" has the meaning given by paragraph 8(6) of Schedule A1, and references to an end of period statement for a tax year are to be read in accordance with that paragraph;";

    (b)   after the definition of "ITA 2007" insert —

          ""nominated partner" has the meaning given by paragraph 5(5) of Schedule A1;"

    (c)   in the definition of "partnership return" for the words from "has the" to the end substitute "means (unless the context otherwise requires) —

          (a)   a section 12AA partnership return, or

          (b)   a Schedule A1 partnership return;";

    (d)   after the definition of "partnership return" insert —

          ""partnership statement" —

          (a)   in relation to a section 12AA partnership return, means the statement required by section 12AB;

          (b)   in relation to a Schedule A1 partnership return, has the meaning given by paragraph 10(6) of that Schedule;"

    (e)   after the definition of "return" insert —

          ""Schedule A1 partnership return" has the meaning given by paragraph 10(6) of Schedule A1;

          "section 12AA partnership return" has the meaning given by section 12AA(10A) of this Act;";

    (f)   in the definition of "successor" after "delivered, a" insert "section 12AA".

30 (1) Paragraph 3 of Schedule 1AB (recovery of overpaid tax) is amended as follows.

  (2) In sub-paragraph (2)(a) after "of this Act" insert "or a Schedule A1 partnership return".

Finance (No. 2) Act 2017 (c. 32)
Schedule 14 — Digital reporting and record-keeping for income tax etc: further amendments
Part 1 — Amendments of TMA 1970

575

(3) In sub-paragraph (3)(a) after "12AA" insert "or a Schedule A1 partnership return".

(4) In sub-paragraph (4) at the end insert "or a Schedule A1 partnership return".

PART 2

AMENDMENTS OF OTHER ACTS

TCGA 1992

31   In section 188J(2) of TCGA 1992 (the representative company of an NRCGT group) for "section 9(2)" substitute "section 8(1AB)(a)(iii)".

FA 1998

32   In paragraph 12(2) of Schedule 18 to FA 1998 (information about business carried on in partnership) for "statement under section 12AB of" substitute "partnership statement within the meaning of".

CAA 2001

33   In section 201(6) of CAA 2001 (elections) after "section 12AA of" insert "or regulations under paragraph 10 of Schedule A1 to".

Tax Credits Act 2002

34   In section 19(4)(a) of the Tax Credits Act 2002 (power to enquire) for "by section 8 of the Taxes Management Act 1970 (c. 9) to make a return" substitute "to make a return under section 8 of the Taxes Management Act 1970".

ITTOIA 2005

35   In section 217(2) of ITTOIA 2005 (conditions for basis period to end with new accounting date) —
    (a)   in paragraph (a) —
        (i)   after "TMA 1970" insert ", or of regulations under that Act," and
        (ii)   after "or 12AA of" insert ", or regulations under paragraph 10 of Schedule A1 to,";
    (b)   in paragraph (b) for "provision" substitute "section or paragraph".

ITA 2007

36   In section 964(4)(b) (collection through self-assessment return) for "section 9 of that Act" substitute "that section".

Crossrail Act 2008

37   In paragraph 44(1)(a) of Schedule 13 to the Crossrail Act 2008 (modification of transfer schemes: other persons and partnerships) after "12AA of" insert ", or regulations under paragraph 10 of Schedule A1 to,".

576

Finance (No. 2) Act 2017 (c. 32)
Schedule 14 — Digital reporting and record-keeping for income tax etc: further amendments
Part 2 — Amendments of other Acts

FA 2008

38 (1) Schedule 36 to FA 2008 (information and inspection powers) is amended as follows.

    (2) In paragraph 21(1) (taxpayer notices) after "12AA of" insert ", or regulations under paragraph 10 of Schedule A1 to,".

    (3) In paragraph 37(2)(a) (partnerships) after "section 12AA of" insert ", or regulations under paragraph 10 of Schedule A1 to,".

TIOPA 2010

39 TIOPA 2010 is amended as follows.

40 In section 94(3) (information made available) in each of paragraphs (a) and (b) after "section 12AA of" insert ", or regulations under paragraph 10 of Schedule A1 to,".

41 In section 95(8)(a) (interpretation of "tax return") after "12AA of" insert ", or regulations under paragraph 10 of Schedule A1 to,".

42 In section 171(5) (tax returns where transfer pricing notice given), in paragraph (a) of the definition of "tax return", after "12AA of" insert ", or regulations under paragraph 10 of Schedule A1 to,".

FA 2014

43 FA 2014 is amended as follows.

44 In section 253(6)(c) (definition of "tax return") after "section 12AA of" insert ", or regulations under paragraph 10 of Schedule A1 to,".

45 (1) Schedule 31 (follower notices and partnerships) is amended as follows.

    (2) In paragraph 2 (interpretation)—
        (a) in sub-paragraph (3)—
            (i)   the words from "in pursuance" to the end become paragraph (a);
            (ii) at the end of that paragraph insert "(a "section 12AA partnership return"), or";
            (iii) after that paragraph insert—
                  "(b) required by regulations under paragraph 10 of Schedule A1 to TMA 1970 (a "Schedule A1 partnership return").";
        (b) in sub-paragraph (4) after "in relation to a" insert "section 12AA";
        (c) after sub-paragraph (4) insert—
                  "(4A) "The nominated partner", in relation to a Schedule A1 partnership return, has the meaning given by paragraph 5 of Schedule A1 to TMA 1970."

    (3) In paragraph 3 (giving of follower notices in relation to partnership returns)—
        (a) in sub-paragraph (1), after "in relation to a" insert "section 12AA";

Finance (No. 2) Act 2017 (c. 32) 577
Schedule 14 — Digital reporting and record-keeping for income tax etc: further amendments
Part 2 — Amendments of other Acts

    (b)   after sub-paragraph (1) insert—

> "(1A)   For the purposes of section 204 a Schedule A1 partnership return, or an appeal in respect of the return, is to be regarded as made by the person who is for the time being the nominated partner (if that would not otherwise be the case).";

    (c)   in sub-paragraph (2), at the end insert ", or the nominated partner (as the case may be).";

    (d)   in sub-paragraph (4)—

        (i)   in paragraph (a), after "or a successor of that partner," insert "or as the nominated partner of a partnership,";

        (ii)   in paragraph (b) after "successors of that partner" insert "or to a nominated partner".

(4) In paragraph 5 (calculation of penalty etc) in sub-paragraph (10)—

    (a)   the words from "the representative partner" to the end become paragraph (a);

    (b)   at the end of that paragraph insert "(in relation to a section 12AA partnership return), or";

    (c)   after that paragraph insert—

> "(b)   the nominated partner (in relation to a Schedule A1 partnership return)."

46   (1) Schedule 32 (accelerated payments and partnerships) is amended as follows.

   (2) In paragraph 1 (interpretation)—

    (a)   in sub-paragraph (2)—

        (i)   the words from "in pursuance" to the end become paragraph (a);

        (ii)   at the end of that paragraph insert "(a "section 12AA partnership return"), or";

        (iii)   after that paragraph insert—

> "(b)   required by regulations under paragraph 10 of Schedule A1 to TMA 1970 (a "Schedule A1 partnership return").";

    (b)   in sub-paragraph (3) after "in relation to a" insert "section 12AA";

    (c)   after sub-paragraph (3) insert—

> "(3A)   "The nominated partner", in relation to a Schedule A1 partnership return, has the meaning given by paragraph 5 of Schedule A1 to TMA 1970."

   (3) In paragraph 2(2) (restriction on circumstances when accelerated payment notices can be given) after "a successor of that partner" insert "(in relation to a section 12AA partnership return), or to the nominated partner of the partnership (in relation to a Schedule A1 partnership return)".

   (4) In paragraph 3(5)(a) (circumstances in which partner payment notices can be given) after "or a successor of that partner" insert "(in relation to a section 12AA partnership return), or the nominated partner (in relation to a Schedule A1 partnership return)".

578   *Finance (No. 2) Act 2017 (c. 32)*
Schedule 14 — Digital reporting and record-keeping for income tax etc: further amendments
Part 2 — Amendments of other Acts

FA 2016

47   FA 2016 is amended as follows.

48   (1) Schedule 18 (serial tax avoidance) is amended as follows.

      (2) In paragraph 51(8)(b) (partnerships: information) after "TMA 1970" insert ", or under equivalent provision made by regulations under paragraph 10 of Schedule A1 to that Act,".

      (3) In paragraph 52 (partnerships: special provision about taxpayer emendations) —
         (a) in sub-paragraph (1) for "subsection (1)(b) of section 12AB of that Act (partnership statement)" substitute "section 12AB(1)(b) of that Act or under equivalent provision made by regulations under paragraph 10 of Schedule A1 to that Act (partnership statement)";
         (b) in sub-paragraph (3) —
              (i) in the words before paragraph (a), after "that person's successor" insert "(in the case of a section 12AA partnership return) or the nominated partner (in the case of a Schedule A1 partnership return)";
             (ii) for "subsection (1)(b) of section 12AB of TMA 1970 (partnership statement)" substitute "section 12AB(1)(b) of TMA 1970 or under equivalent provision made by regulations under paragraph 10 of Schedule A1 to that Act (partnership statement)".

      (4) In paragraph 53(1) (supplementary provision relating to partnerships) —
         (a) in the definition of "the representative partner" after "in relation to a" insert "section 12AA";
         (b) after the definition of "successor" insert —
                ""the nominated partner", in relation to a Schedule A1 partnership return, has the meaning given by paragraph 5 of Schedule A1 to TMA 1970."

      (5) In paragraph 58(1) (general interpretation), for the definition of "partnership return" substitute —
                ""partnership return" means a return —
                   (a) under section 12AA of TMA 1970 (a "section 12AA partnership return"), or
                   (b) required by regulations made under paragraph 10 of Schedule A1 to TMA 1970 (a "Schedule A1 partnership return");".

49   (1) Schedule 19 (large businesses: tax strategies and sanctions) is amended as follows.

      (2) In paragraph 12(5) (definition of "representative partner") —
         (a) the words from "the partner" to the end become paragraph (a);
         (b) at the end of that paragraph insert ", or";
         (c) after that paragraph insert —
                "(b) the nominated partner within the meaning of paragraph 5 of Schedule A1 to TMA 1970."

Finance (No. 2) Act 2017 (c. 32)
Schedule 14 — Digital reporting and record-keeping for income tax etc: further amendments
Part 2 — Amendments of other Acts

579

(3) In paragraph 13 (definition of "financial year") in paragraph (c) for "under a return issued under section 12AB" substitute "within the meaning of".

SCHEDULE 15

Section 63

PARTIAL CLOSURE NOTICES

TMA 1970

1 TMA 1970 is amended as follows.

2 In section 9A (notice of enquiry), in subsection (5) —

  (a) in paragraph (a), omit the final "or";

  (b) for paragraph (b) substitute —

> "(b) after a final closure notice has been issued in relation to an enquiry into the return, or
>
> (c) after a partial closure notice has been issued in such an enquiry in relation to the matters to which the amendment relates or which are affected by the amendment,".

3 (1) Section 9B (amendment of return by taxpayer during enquiry) is amended as follows.

  (2) In subsection (1), for "is in progress into the return" substitute "into the return is in progress in relation to any matter to which the amendment relates or which is affected by the amendment".

  (3) In subsection (3) —

    (a) after "in progress" insert "in relation to any matter to which the amendment relates or which is affected by the amendment";

    (b) in paragraph (a), for "the closure notice" substitute "a partial or final closure notice";

    (c) in paragraph (b), for "the closure notice is issued" substitute "a partial closure notice is issued in relation to the matters to which the amendment relates or which are affected by the amendment or, if no such notice is issued, a final closure notice is issued".

  (4) In subsection (4) —

    (a) after "in progress" insert "in relation to any matter";

    (b) for "the enquiry is completed" substitute "a partial closure notice is issued in relation to the matter or, if no such notice is issued, a final closure notice is issued".

4 (1) Section 9C (amendment of self-assessment during enquiry to prevent loss of tax) is amended as follows.

  (2) In subsection (1), for "is in progress into a return" substitute "into a return is in progress in relation to any matter".

  (3) In subsection (2), after "deficiency" insert "so far as it relates to the matter".

  (4) In subsection (4) —

    (a) after "in progress" insert "in relation to any matter";

        (b)   for "the enquiry is completed" substitute "a partial closure notice is issued in relation to the matter or, if no such notice is issued, a final closure notice is issued".

5   In section 12ZM (NRCGT returns: notice of enquiry), in subsection (4) —

        (a)   in paragraph (a), omit the final "or";

        (b)   for paragraph (b) substitute —

                "(b)   after a final closure notice has been issued in relation to an enquiry into the return, or

                (c)   after a partial closure notice has been issued in such an enquiry in relation to the matters to which the amendment relates or which are affected by the amendment,".

6   (1)   Section 12ZN (NRCGT returns: amendment of return by taxpayer during enquiry) is amended as follows.

    (2)   In subsection (1), for "is in progress into the return" substitute "into the return is in progress in relation to any matter to which the amendment relates or which is affected by the amendment".

    (3)   In subsection (3) —

        (a)   after "in progress" insert "in relation to any matter to which the amendment relates or which is affected by the amendment";

        (b)   in paragraph (a), for "the closure notice" substitute "a partial or final closure notice";

        (c)   in paragraph (b), for "the closure notice is issued" substitute "a partial closure notice is issued in relation to the matters to which the amendment relates or which are affected by the amendment or, if no such notice is issued, a final closure notice is issued".

    (4)   In subsection (4) —

        (a)   after "in progress" insert "in relation to any matter";

        (b)   for "the enquiry is completed" substitute "a partial closure notice is issued in relation to the matter or, if no such notice is issued, a final closure notice is issued".

7   In section 12AC (partnership return: notice of enquiry), in subsection (5) —

        (a)   in paragraph (a), omit the final "or";

        (b)   for paragraph (b) substitute —

                "(b)   after a final closure notice has been issued in relation to an enquiry into the return, or

                (c)   after a partial closure notice has been issued in such an enquiry in relation to the matters to which the amendment relates or which are affected by the amendment,".

8   (1)   Section 12AD (amendment of partnership return by taxpayer during enquiry) is amended as follows.

    (2)   In subsection (1), for "is in progress into the return" substitute "into the return is in progress in relation to any matter to which the amendment relates or which is affected by the amendment".

    (3)   In subsection (3) —

     (a)   after "in progress" insert "in relation to any matter to which the amendment relates or which is affected by the amendment";

     (b)   in paragraph (a), for "the closure notice" substitute "a partial or final closure notice";

     (c)   in paragraph (b), for "the closure notice is issued" substitute "a partial closure notice is issued in relation to the matters to which the amendment relates or which are affected by the amendment or, if no such notice is issued, a final closure notice is issued".

  (4) In subsection (4)(a), after "in progress" insert "in relation to any matter to which the amendment relates or which is affected by the amendment".

  (5) In subsection (5) —

     (a)   after "in progress" insert "in relation to any matter";

     (b)   for "the enquiry is completed" substitute "a partial closure notice is issued in relation to the matter or, if no such notice is issued, a final closure notice is issued".

9   In section 12B (records), in subsection (1)(b)(i), for "28A(1) or 28B(1)" substitute "28A(1B) or 28B(1B)".

10   (1) Section 28ZA (referral of questions during enquiry) is amended as follows.

  (2) In subsection (1), after "of this Act" insert "in relation to any matter".

  (3) In subsection (5) —

     (a)   after "in progress" insert "in relation to any matter";

     (b)   for "the enquiry is completed" substitute "a partial closure notice is issued in relation to the matter or, if no such notice is issued, a final closure notice is issued".

11   In section 28ZD (effect of referral on enquiry), in subsection (1) —

     (a)   for paragraph (a) substitute —

         "(a)   no partial closure notice relating to the question referred shall be given,

        (aa)   no final closure notice shall be given in relation to the enquiry, and";

     (b)   in paragraph (b), for "such a notice" substitute "a notice referred to in paragraph (a) or (aa)".

12   (1) Section 28A (completion of enquiry into personal, trustee or NRCGT return) is amended as follows.

  (2) For subsection (1) substitute —

     "(1)   This section applies in relation to an enquiry under section 9A(1) or 12ZM of this Act.

    (1A)   Any matter to which the enquiry relates is completed when an officer of Revenue and Customs informs the taxpayer by notice (a "partial closure notice") that the officer has completed his enquiries into that matter.

    (1B)   The enquiry is completed when an officer of Revenue and Customs informs the taxpayer by notice (a "final closure notice") —

       (a)   in a case where no partial closure notice has been given, that the officer has completed his enquiries, or

      (b)   in a case where one or more partial closure notices have been given, that the officer has completed his remaining enquiries."

(3) In subsection (2) —

      (a)   for "closure notice" substitute "partial or final closure notice";

      (b)   for "either" substitute "state the officer's conclusions and".

(4) In subsections (3) and (4), for "closure notice" substitute "partial or final closure notice".

(5) In subsection (6), for "a closure notice" substitute "the partial or final closure notice".

(6) After subsection (6) insert—

    "(7)   In this section "the taxpayer" means the person to whom notice of enquiry was given.

     (8)   In the Taxes Acts, references to a closure notice under this section are to a partial or final closure notice under this section."

13 (1) Section 28B (completion of enquiry into partnership return) is amended as follows.

(2) For subsection (1) substitute—

    "(1)   This section applies in relation to an enquiry under section 12AC of this Act.

    (1A)   Any matter to which the enquiry relates is completed when an officer of Revenue and Customs informs the taxpayer by notice (a "partial closure notice") that the officer has completed his enquiries into that matter.

    (1B)   The enquiry is completed when an officer of Revenue and Customs informs the taxpayer by notice (a "final closure notice") —

        (a)   in a case where no partial closure notice has been given, that the officer has completed his enquiries, or

        (b)   in a case where one or more partial closure notices have been given, that the officer has completed his remaining enquiries."

(3) In subsection (2) —

      (a)   for "closure notice" substitute "partial or final closure notice";

      (b)   for "either" substitute "state the officer's conclusions and".

(4) In subsections (3) and (5), for "closure notice" substitute "partial or final closure notice".

(5) In subsection (7), for "a closure notice" substitute "the partial or final closure notice".

(6) After subsection (7) insert—

    "(8)   In this section "the taxpayer" means the person to whom notice of enquiry was given or his successor.

     (9)   In the Taxes Acts, references to a closure notice under this section are to a partial or final closure notice under this section."

14   In section 29 (assessment where loss of tax discovered), in subsection (5), for paragraph (b) substitute—

        "(b)   in a case where a notice of enquiry into the return was given—

            (i)   issued a partial closure notice as regards a matter to which the situation mentioned in subsection (1) above relates, or

            (ii)   if no such partial closure notice was issued, issued a final closure notice,".

15   In section 29A (NRCGT disposals: determination of amount which should have been assessed), in subsection (5), for paragraph (b) substitute—

        "(b)   in a case where a notice of enquiry into the return was given—

            (i)   issued a partial closure notice as regards a matter to which the situation mentioned in subsection (1) relates, or

            (ii)   if no such partial closure notice was issued, issued a final closure notice,".

16   In section 30 (recovery of overpayment of tax etc), in subsection (5)(b), for "28A(1)" substitute "28A(1B)".

17   In section 30B (amendment of partnership statement where loss of tax discovered), in subsection (6), for paragraph (b) substitute—

        "(b)   in a case where a notice of enquiry into that return was given—

            (i)   issued a partial closure notice as regards a matter to which the situation mentioned in subsection (1) above relates, or

            (ii)   if no such partial closure notice was issued, issued a final closure notice,".

18   In section 31 (appeals: right of appeal), in subsection (2)—

        (a)   after "in progress" insert "in relation to any matter to which the amendment relates or which is affected by the amendment";

        (b)   for "the enquiry is completed" substitute "a partial closure notice is issued in relation to the matter or, if no such notice is issued, a final closure notice is issued".

19   In section 59AA (NRCGT disposals: payments on account of CGT), in subsection (8)(a), for "28A(1)" substitute "28A(1B)".

20   In section 59B (payment of income tax and capital gains tax), in subsection (4A)(a), for "28A(1)" substitute "28A(1B)".

21 (1) In Schedule 3ZA (date by which payment to be made after amendment etc of self-assessment), paragraph 2 is amended as follows.

    (2) In sub-paragraph (3)(b)—

        (a)   for the first "the closure notice" substitute "a partial or final closure notice";

        (b)   for "the day on which the closure notice was given" substitute "the relevant day".

(3) After sub-paragraph (3) insert—

"(4) In sub-paragraph (3)(b), "the relevant day" means—
  (a) in the case of an amount of tax that is payable, the day on which the partial or final closure notice was given;
  (b) in the case of an amount of tax that is repayable—
    (i) if the closure notice was a final closure notice, the day on which that notice was given, and
    (ii) if the closure notice was a partial closure notice, the day on which the final closure notice relating to the enquiry was given."

TCGA 1992

22 (1) Section 184I of TCGA 1992 (notices under sections 184G and 184H) is amended as follows.

(2) In subsection (4)—
  (a) after "completed" insert "in relation to any matters";
  (b) after "relevant notice" insert "relating to those matters".

(3) In subsection (5), for "into the return" substitute "referred to in subsection (4)".

(4) In subsection (7)(a), after "period" insert "(so far as relating to the matters in question)".

(5) After subsection (9) insert—

"(9A) Subsection (9) does not apply to a partial closure notice which does not relate to any matter to which the relevant notice relates."

(6) In subsection (10), after "completed," insert "so far as relating to the matters to which the relevant notice relates,".

FA 1998

23 Schedule 18 to FA 1998 (company tax returns, assessments and related matters) is amended as follows.

24 (1) Paragraph 30 (amendment of self-assessment during enquiry to prevent loss of tax) is amended as follows.

(2) In sub-paragraph (1)—
  (a) for "before the enquiry is completed" substitute "while the enquiry is in progress in relation to a matter";
  (b) after "deficiency" insert "so far as it relates to the matter".

(3) After sub-paragraph (5) insert—

"(6) For the purposes of this paragraph, the period during which an enquiry is in progress in relation to any matter is the whole of the period—
  (a) beginning with the day on which notice of enquiry is given, and

        (b)   ending with the day on which a partial closure notice is issued in relation to the matter or, if no such notice is issued, a final closure notice is issued."

25 (1) Paragraph 31 (amendment of return by company during enquiry) is amended as follows.

    (2) In sub-paragraph (1), for "is in progress into the return" substitute "into the return is in progress in relation to any matter to which the amendment relates or which is affected by the amendment".

    (3) In sub-paragraph (3) for "until after the enquiry is completed" substitute "while the enquiry is in progress in relation to any matter to which the amendment relates or which is affected by the amendment".

    (4) In sub-paragraph (4)(a) —

        (a)   for "the closure notice" substitute "a partial or final closure notice";

        (b)   for "on the completion of the enquiry" substitute "when a partial closure notice is issued in relation to the matters to which the amendment relates or which are affected by the amendment or, if no such notice is issued, a final closure notice is issued".

    (5) In sub-paragraph (5) —

        (a)   after "in progress" insert "in relation to any matter";

        (b)   for "the enquiry is completed" substitute "a partial closure notice is issued in relation to the matter or, if no such notice is issued, a final closure notice is issued".

26 (1) Paragraph 31A (referral of questions to the tribunal during enquiry) is amended as follows.

    (2) In sub-paragraph (1), for "into" substitute "in relation to any matter relating to".

    (3) In sub-paragraph (5) —

        (a)   after "in progress" insert "in relation to any matter";

        (b)   for "the enquiry is completed" substitute "a partial closure notice is issued in relation to the matter or, if no such notice is issued, a final closure notice is issued".

27   In paragraph 31C (effect of referral on enquiry), in sub-paragraph (1) —

        (a)   for paragraph (a) substitute —

                "(a)   no partial closure notice relating to the question referred shall be given,

                (aa)   no final closure notice shall be given in relation to the enquiry, and";

        (b)   in paragraph (b), for "such a notice" substitute "a notice referred to in paragraph (a) or (aa)".

28 (1) Paragraph 32 (completion of enquiry) is amended as follows.

    (2) For sub-paragraph (1) substitute —

        "(1) Any matter to which an enquiry relates is completed when an officer of Revenue and Customs informs the company by notice (a "partial closure notice") that they have completed their enquiries into that matter.

> > (1A) An enquiry is completed when an officer of Revenue and Customs informs the company by notice (a "final closure notice") —
> >
> > > (a) in a case where no partial closure notice has been given, that they have completed their enquiries, or
> > >
> > > (b) in a case where one or more partial closure notices have been given, that they have completed their remaining enquiries.
> >
> > (1B) A partial or final closure notice takes effect when it is issued."
>
> (3) In subsection (2), after "concludes" insert "in a partial or final closure notice".
>
> (4) After sub-paragraph (3) insert—
>
> > "(4) In the Taxes Acts, references to a closure notice under this paragraph are to a partial or final closure notice under this paragraph."

29   In paragraph 33 (direction to complete enquiry), in sub-paragraphs (1) and (3), for "closure notice" substitute "partial or final closure notice".

30   (1) Paragraph 34 (amendment of return after enquiry) is amended as follows.

> (2) In sub-paragraph (1), for "closure notice" substitute "partial or final closure notice".
>
> (3) In sub-paragraph (2) —
>
> > (a) for "closure notice" substitute "partial or final closure notice";
> >
> > (b) after "must" insert "state the officer's conclusions and".
>
> (4) In sub-paragraphs (2A), (4)(c) and (5), for "closure notice" substitute "partial or final closure notice".

31   In paragraph 42 (restriction on power to make discovery assessment or determination), in sub-paragraph (2A), for the words from "after any" to the end substitute "a notice within sub-paragraph (4) after any enquiries have been completed into the return (so far as relating to the matters to which the notice relates)".

32   In paragraph 44 (situation not disclosed by return or related document etc), in sub-paragraph (1), for paragraph (b) substitute—

> > "(b) in a case where a notice of enquiry into the return was given—
> >
> > > (i) issued a partial closure notice as regards a matter to which the situation mentioned in paragraph 41(1) or (2) relates, or
> > >
> > > (ii) if no such partial closure notice was issued, issued a final closure notice,".

33   In paragraph 61 (consequential claims etc), in sub-paragraphs (1)(a) and (3)(a), for "closure notice" substitute "partial or final closure notice".

34   (1) Paragraph 88 (conclusiveness) is amended as follows.

> (2) In sub-paragraph (3)(b), at the end insert "(or is completed so far as relating to the matters to which the amount relates by the issue of a partial closure notice)".

(3) In sub-paragraph (4)(b), at the end insert "(or the completion of the enquiry so far as relating to the matters to which the amount relates by the issue of a partial closure notice)".

Tax Credits Act 2002

35 (1) Section 20 of the Tax Credits Act 2002 (decisions on discovery) is amended as follows.

(2) In subsection (2)(f), for "a closure notice" substitute "a partial or final closure notice".

(3) In subsection (3)(b), at the end insert "as specified in subsection (1)".

FA 2008

36 In Schedule 36 to FA 2008 (information and inspection powers), in paragraphs 21(4) and 21ZA(3), at the end insert "so far as relating to the matters to which the taxpayer notice relates".

TIOPA 2010

37 TIOPA 2010 is amended as follows.

38 (1) Section 92 (counteraction notices given after tax return made) is amended as follows.

(2) In subsection (3) —
   (a) after "completed" insert "in relation to any matters";
   (b) after "counteraction notice" insert "relating to those matters".

(3) In subsection (4), after "enquiries" insert "referred to in subsection (3)".

(4) In subsection (5)(a), after "return" insert "(so far as relating to the matters in question)".

39 (1) Section 93 (amendment, closure notices and discovery assessments in section 92 cases) is amended as follows.

(2) After subsection (3) insert —

   "(3A) Subsection (3) does not apply to a partial closure notice which does not relate to any matter to which the counteraction notice relates."

(3) In subsection (4), after "completed," insert "so far as relating to the matters to which the counteraction notice relates,".

40 In section 171 (tax returns where transfer pricing notice given), after subsection (2) insert —

   "(2A) Subsection (2) does not apply to a partial closure notice which does not relate to any matter to which the transfer pricing notice relates."

41 (1) Section 256 (notices given after tax return made), so far as continuing to have effect, is amended as follows.

(2) In subsection (2) —
   (a) after "completed" insert "in relation to any matters";
   (b) after "receipt notice" insert "relating to those matters".

588
Finance (No. 2) Act 2017 (c. 32)
Schedule 16 — Penalties for enablers of defeated tax avoidance
Part 1 — Liability to penalty

(3) In subsection (6)(a), after "return" insert "(so far as relating to the matters in question)".

42 (1) Section 257 (amendments, closure notices etc), so far as continuing to have effect, is amended as follows.

(2) After subsection (4) insert—

"(4A) Subsection (4) does not apply to a partial closure notice which does not relate to any matter to which the Part 6 notice relates."

(3) In subsection (5), after "completed," insert "so far as relating to the matters to which the Part 6 notice relates,".

43 In section 371IJ (claims), in subsection (4)(b), after "completed" insert "so far as relating to the matters to which the claim relates".

Commencement

44 The amendments made by this Schedule have effect in relation to an enquiry under section 9A, 12ZM or 12AC of TMA 1970 or Schedule 18 to FA 1998 where—

(a) notice of the enquiry is given on or after the day on which this Act is passed, or

(b) the enquiry is in progress immediately before that day.

SCHEDULE 16   Section 65

PENALTIES FOR ENABLERS OF DEFEATED TAX AVOIDANCE

PART 1

LIABILITY TO PENALTY

1 Where—

(a) a person ("T") has entered into abusive tax arrangements, and

(b) T incurs a defeat in respect of the arrangements,

a penalty is payable by each person who enabled the arrangements.

2 (1) Parts 2 to 4 of this Schedule define—

"abusive tax arrangements";

a "defeat in respect of the arrangements";

a "person who enabled the arrangements".

(2) The other Parts of this Schedule make provision supplementing paragraph 1 as follows—

(a) Part 5 makes provision about the amount of a penalty;

(b) Parts 6 to 8 provide for the assessment of penalties, referrals to the GAAR Advisory Panel and appeals against assessments;

(c) Part 9 applies information and inspection powers, and makes provision about declarations relating to legally privileged communications;

Finance (No. 2) Act 2017 (c. 32)
Schedule 16 — Penalties for enablers of defeated tax avoidance
Part 1 — Liability to penalty

589

      (d)   Part 10 confers power to publish details of persons who have incurred penalties;

      (e)   Parts 11 and 12 contain miscellaneous and general provisions.

PART 2

"ABUSIVE" AND "TAX ARRANGEMENTS": MEANING

3   (1)   Arrangements are "tax arrangements" for the purposes of this Schedule if, having regard to all the circumstances, it would be reasonable to conclude that the obtaining of a tax advantage was the main purpose, or one of the main purposes, of the arrangements.

    (2)   Tax arrangements are "abusive" for the purposes of this Schedule if they are arrangements the entering into or carrying out of which cannot reasonably be regarded as a reasonable course of action in relation to the relevant tax provisions, having regard to all the circumstances.

    (3)   The circumstances to which regard must be had under sub-paragraph (2) include—

      (a)   whether the substantive results, or the intended substantive results, of the arrangements are consistent with any principles on which the relevant tax provisions are based (whether express or implied) and the policy objectives of those provisions,

      (b)   whether the means of achieving those results involves one or more contrived or abnormal steps, and

      (c)   whether the arrangements are intended to exploit any shortcomings in those provisions.

    (4)   Where the tax arrangements form part of any other arrangements regard must also be had to those other arrangements.

    (5)   Each of the following is an example of something which might indicate that tax arrangements are abusive—

      (a)   the arrangements result in an amount of income, profits or gains for tax purposes that is significantly less than the amount for economic purposes;

      (b)   the arrangements result in deductions or losses of an amount for tax purposes that is significantly greater than the amount for economic purposes;

      (c)   the arrangements result in a claim for the repayment or crediting of tax (including foreign tax) that has not been, and is unlikely to be, paid;

but a result mentioned in paragraph (a), (b) or (c) is to be taken to be such an example only if it is reasonable to assume that such a result was not the anticipated result when the relevant tax provisions were enacted.

    (6)   The fact that tax arrangements accord with established practice, and HMRC had, at the time the arrangements were entered into, indicated their acceptance of that practice, is an example of something which might indicate that the arrangements are not abusive.

    (7)   The examples given in sub-paragraphs (5) and (6) are not exhaustive.

    (8)   In sub-paragraph (5) the reference to income includes earnings, within the meaning of Part 1 of the Social Security Contributions and Benefits Act 1992

590

Finance (No. 2) Act 2017 (c. 32)
Schedule 16 — Penalties for enablers of defeated tax avoidance
Part 2 — "Abusive" and "tax arrangements": meaning

or Part 1 of the Social Security Contributions and Benefits (Northern Ireland) Act 1992.

PART 3

"DEFEAT" IN RESPECT OF ABUSIVE TAX ARRANGEMENTS

"Defeat" in respect of abusive tax arrangements

4   T (within the meaning of paragraph 1) incurs a "defeat" in respect of abusive tax arrangements entered into by T ("the arrangements concerned") if —

    (a)   Condition A (in paragraph 5) is met, or

    (b)   Condition B (in paragraph 6) is met.

Condition A

5   (1)   Condition A is that—

    (a)   T, or a person on behalf of T, has given HMRC a document of a kind listed in the Table in paragraph 1 of Schedule 24 to FA 2007 (returns etc),

    (b)   the document was submitted on the basis that a tax advantage ("the relevant tax advantage") arose from the arrangements concerned,

    (c)   the relevant tax advantage has been counteracted, and

    (d)   the counteraction is final.

(2)   For the purposes of this paragraph the relevant tax advantage has been "counteracted" if adjustments have been made in respect of T's tax position on the basis that the whole or part of the relevant tax advantage does not arise.

(3)   For the purposes of this paragraph a counteraction is "final" when the adjustments in question, and any amounts arising from the adjustments, can no longer be varied, on appeal or otherwise.

(4)   In this paragraph "adjustments" means any adjustments, whether by way of an assessment, the modification of an assessment or return, the amendment or disallowance of a claim, a payment, the entering into of a contract settlement or otherwise.

Accordingly, references to "making" adjustments include securing that adjustments are made by entering into a contract settlement.

(5)   Any reference in this paragraph to giving HMRC a document includes —

    (a)   communicating information to HMRC in any form and by any method;

    (b)   making a statement or declaration in a document.

(6)   Any reference in this paragraph to a document of a kind listed in the Table in paragraph 1 of Schedule 24 to FA 2007 includes —

    (a)   a document amending a document of a kind so listed, and

    (b)   a document which —

        (i)   relates to national insurance contributions, and

        (ii)   is a document in relation to which that Schedule applies.

Finance (No. 2) Act 2017 (c. 32)
591
Schedule 16 — Penalties for enablers of defeated tax avoidance
Part 3 — "Defeat" in respect of abusive tax arrangements

Condition B

6   (1)   Condition B is that (in a case not falling within Condition A) —

    (a)   HMRC have made an assessment in relation to tax,

    (b)   the assessment counteracts a tax advantage that it is reasonable to assume T expected to obtain from the arrangements concerned ("the expected tax advantage"), and

    (c)   the counteraction is final.

    (2)   For the purposes of this paragraph an assessment "counteracts" the expected tax advantage if the assessment is on a basis which prevents T from obtaining (or obtaining the whole of) the expected tax advantage.

    (3)   For the purposes of this paragraph a counteraction is "final" —

    (a)   when a relevant contract settlement is made, or

    (b)   if no contract settlement has been made, when the assessment in question and any amounts arising from the assessment can no longer be varied, on appeal or otherwise.

    (4)   In sub-paragraph (3) a "relevant contract settlement" means a contract settlement on a basis which prevents T from obtaining (or obtaining the whole of) the expected tax advantage.

PART 4

PERSONS WHO "ENABLED" THE ARRANGEMENTS

Persons who "enabled" the arrangements

7   (1)   A person is a person who "enabled" the arrangements mentioned in paragraph 1 if that person is —

    (a)   a designer of the arrangements (see paragraph 8),

    (b)   a manager of the arrangements (see paragraph 9),

    (c)   a person who marketed the arrangements to T (see paragraph 10),

    (d)   an enabling participant in the arrangements (see paragraph 11), or

    (e)   a financial enabler in relation to the arrangements (see paragraph 12).

    (2)   This paragraph is subject to paragraph 13 (excluded persons).

Designers of arrangements

8   (1)   For the purposes of paragraph 7 a person is a "designer" of the arrangements if that person was, in the course of a business carried on by that person, to any extent responsible for the design of —

    (a)   the arrangements, or

    (b)   a proposal which was implemented by the arrangements;

but this is subject to sub-paragraph (2).

    (2)   Where a person would (in the absence of this sub-paragraph) fall within sub-paragraph (1) because of having provided advice which was used in the design of the arrangements or of a proposal, that person does not because of that advice fall within that sub-paragraph unless —

    (a)   the advice is relevant advice, and

592

Finance (No. 2) Act 2017 (c. 32)
Schedule 16 — Penalties for enablers of defeated tax avoidance
Part 4 — Persons who "enabled" the arrangements

    (b)   the knowledge condition is met.

(3) Advice is "relevant advice" if—

    (a)   the advice or any part of it suggests arrangements or an alteration of proposed arrangements, and

    (b)   it is reasonable to assume that the suggestion was made with a view to arrangements being designed in such a way that a tax advantage (or a greater tax advantage) might be expected to arise from them.

(4) The knowledge condition is that, when the advice was provided, the person providing it knew or could reasonably be expected to know—

    (a)   that the advice would be used in the design of abusive tax arrangements or of a proposal for such arrangements, or

    (b)   that it was likely that the advice would be so used.

(5) For the purposes of sub-paragraph (3), advice is not to be taken to "suggest" anything—

    (a)   which is put forward by the advice for consideration, but

    (b)   which the advice can reasonably be read as recommending against.

(6) In sub-paragraph (3)—

    (a)   the reference in paragraph (a) to arrangements or an alteration of proposed arrangements includes a proposal for arrangements or an alteration of a proposal for arrangements, and

    (b)   the reference in paragraph (b) to arrangements includes arrangements proposed by a proposal.

(7) For the purposes of this paragraph—

    (a)   references to advice include an opinion;

    (b)   advice is "used" in a design if the advice is taken account of in that design.

Managers of arrangements

9   (1) For the purposes of paragraph 7 a person is a "manager" of the arrangements if that person—

    (a)   was, in the course of a business carried on by that person, to any extent responsible for the organisation or management of the arrangements, and

    (b)   when carrying out any functions in relation to the organisation or management of the arrangements, knew or could reasonably be expected to know that the arrangements involved were abusive tax arrangements.

(2) Where—

    (a)   a person is, in the course of a business carried on by the person, to any extent responsible for facilitating T's withdrawal from the arrangements, and

    (b)   it is reasonable to assume that the obtaining of a tax advantage is not T's purpose (or one of T's purposes) in withdrawing from the arrangements,

that person is not because of anything done in the course of facilitating that withdrawal to be regarded as to any extent responsible for the organisation or management of the arrangements.

Finance (No. 2) Act 2017 (c. **32**)   593
Schedule 16 – Penalties for enablers of defeated tax avoidance
Part 4 – Persons who "enabled" the arrangements

Marketers of arrangements

10   For the purposes of paragraph 7 a person "marketed" the arrangements to T if, in the course of a business carried on by that person—

(a)   that person made available for implementation by T a proposal which has since been implemented, in relation to T, by the arrangements, or

(b)   that person—

(i)   communicated information to T or another person about a proposal which has since been implemented, in relation to T, by the arrangements, and

(ii)   did so with a view to T entering into the arrangements or transactions forming part of the arrangements.

Enabling participants

11   For the purposes of paragraph 7 a person is "an enabling participant" in the arrangements if—

(a)   that person is a person (other than T) who enters into the arrangements or a transaction forming part of the arrangements,

(b)   without that person's participation in the arrangements or transaction (or the participation of another person in the arrangements or transaction in the same capacity as that person), the arrangements could not be expected to result in a tax advantage for T, and

(c)   when that person entered into the arrangements or transaction, that person knew or could reasonably be expected to know that what was being entered into was abusive tax arrangements or a transaction forming part of such arrangements.

Financial enablers

12   (1) For the purposes of paragraph 7 a person is a "financial enabler" in relation to the arrangements if—

(a)   in the course of a business carried on by that person, that person provided a financial product (directly or indirectly) to a relevant party,

(b)   it is reasonable to assume that the purpose (or a purpose) of the relevant party in obtaining the financial product was to participate in the arrangements, and

(c)   when the financial product was provided, the person providing it knew or could reasonably be expected to know that the purpose (or a purpose) of obtaining it was to participate in abusive tax arrangements.

(2) In this paragraph "a relevant party" means T or an enabling participant in the arrangements within the meaning given by paragraph 11.

(3) Any reference in this paragraph to a person's providing a financial product to a relevant party includes (but is not limited to) the person's doing any of the following—

(a)   providing a loan to a relevant party;

(b)   issuing or transferring a share to a relevant party;

(c)   entering into arrangements with a relevant party such that—

594   *Finance (No. 2) Act 2017 (c. 32)*
Schedule 16 — Penalties for enablers of defeated tax avoidance
Part 4 — Persons who "enabled" the arrangements

        (i)   the person becomes a party to a relevant contract within the meaning of section 577 of CTA 2009 (derivative contracts);

        (ii)   there is a repo in respect of securities within the meaning of section 263A(A1) of TCGA 1992;

        (iii) the person or the relevant party has a creditor repo, creditor quasi-repo, debtor repo or debtor quasi-repo within the meaning of sections 543, 544, 548 and 549 of CTA 2009;

(d)   entering into a stock lending arrangement, within the meaning of section 263B(1) of TCGA 1992, with a relevant party;

(e)   entering into an alternative finance arrangement, within the meaning of Chapter 6 of Part 6 of CTA 2009 or Part 10A of ITA 2007, with a relevant party;

(f)   entering into a contract with a relevant party which, whether alone or in combination with one or more other contracts —

        (i)   is in accordance with generally accepted accounting practice required to be treated as a loan, deposit or other financial asset or obligation, or

        (ii)   would be required to be so treated by the person if the person were a company to which the Companies Act 2006 applies;

and references to obtaining a financial product are to be read accordingly.

(4)   The Treasury may by regulations amend sub-paragraph (3).

Excluded persons

13   (1)   A person who —

      (a)   would (in the absence of this paragraph) be regarded for the purposes of this Schedule as having enabled particular arrangements mentioned in paragraph 1, but

      (b)   is a person within sub-paragraph (2),

    is not to be regarded as having enabled those arrangements.

  (2)   The persons within this sub-paragraph are —

      (a)   T;

      (b)   where T is a company, any company in the same group as T.

Powers to add categories of enabler and to provide exceptions

14   (1)   The Treasury may by regulations add to the categories of persons who, in relation to arrangements mentioned in paragraph 1, are for the purposes of this Schedule persons who enabled the arrangements.

  (2)   The Treasury may by regulations provide that a person who would otherwise be regarded for the purposes of this Schedule as having enabled arrangements is not to be so regarded where conditions prescribed by the regulations are met.

  (3)   Regulations under this paragraph may —

      (a)   amend this Part of this Schedule;

      (b)   make supplementary, incidental, and consequential provision, including provision amending any other Part of this Schedule;

      (c)   make transitional provision.

Finance (No. 2) Act 2017 (c. 32)
Schedule 16 — Penalties for enablers of defeated tax avoidance
Part 5 — Amount of penalty

595

PART 5

AMOUNT OF PENALTY

Amount of penalty

15 (1) For each person who enabled the arrangements mentioned in paragraph 1, the penalty payable under paragraph 1 is the total amount or value of all the relevant consideration received or receivable by that person ("the person in question").

    (2) Particular consideration is "relevant" for the purposes of this paragraph if—
       (a) it is consideration for anything done by the person in question which enabled the arrangements mentioned in paragraph 1, and
       (b) it has not previously been taken into account in calculating the amount of a penalty payable under paragraph 1.

    (3) For the purposes of this paragraph a thing done by a person "enabled" the arrangements mentioned in paragraph 1 if, by doing that thing (alone or with anything else), the person fell within the definition in Part 4 of this Schedule of a person who enabled those arrangements.

16 (1) This paragraph applies for the purposes of paragraph 15.

    (2) Where consideration for anything done by a person ("A") is, under any arrangements with A, paid or payable to a person other than A, it is to be taken to be received or receivable by A.

    (3) The "consideration" for anything done by a person does not include any amount charged by that person in respect of value added tax.

    (4) Consideration attributable to two or more transactions is to be apportioned on a just and reasonable basis.

    (5) Any consideration given for what is in substance one bargain is to be treated as attributable to all elements of the bargain, even though—
       (a) separate consideration is, or purports to be, given for different elements of the bargain, or
       (b) there are, or purport to be, separate transactions in respect of different elements of the bargain.

Reduction of penalty where other penalties incurred

17 (1) The amount of a penalty for which a person is liable under paragraph 1 is to be reduced by the amount of any other penalty incurred by the person in respect of conduct for which the person is liable to the penalty under paragraph 1.

    (2) In this paragraph "any other penalty" means a penalty—
       (a) which is a penalty under a provision other than paragraph 1, and
       (b) which has been assessed.

Mitigation of penalty

18 (1) HMRC may in their discretion reduce a penalty under paragraph 1.

596

Finance (No. 2) Act 2017 (c. 32)
Schedule 16 — Penalties for enablers of defeated tax avoidance
Part 5 — Amount of penalty

(2) In this paragraph the reference to reducing a penalty includes a reference to—

    (a) entirely remitting the penalty, or

    (b) staying, or agreeing a compromise in relation to, proceedings for the recovery of a penalty.

PART 6

ASSESSMENT OF PENALTY

Assessment of penalty

19 (1) Where a person is liable for a penalty under paragraph 1 HMRC must—

    (a) assess the penalty, and

    (b) notify the person.

(2) If—

    (a) HMRC do not have all the information required to determine the amount or value of the relevant consideration within the meaning of paragraph 15, and

    (b) HMRC have taken all reasonable steps to obtain that information,

HMRC may assess the penalty on the basis of a reasonable estimate by HMRC of that consideration.

(3) This paragraph is subject to—

    (a) paragraphs 21 and 22 (limits on when penalty may be assessed); and

    (b) Part 7 of this Schedule (requirement for opinion of GAAR Advisory Panel before penalty may be assessed).

20 (1) A penalty under paragraph 1 must be paid before the end of the period of 30 days beginning with the day on which notification of the penalty is issued.

(2) An assessment of a penalty under paragraph 1—

    (a) is to be treated for procedural purposes in the same way as an assessment to tax (except in respect of a matter expressly provided for by this Schedule), and

    (b) may be enforced as if it were an assessment to tax.

Special provision about assessment for multi-user schemes

21 (1) This paragraph applies where—

    (a) a proposal for arrangements is implemented more than once, by a number of tax arrangements which are substantially the same as each other ("related arrangements"),

    (b) paragraph 1 applies in relation to particular arrangements ("the arrangements concerned") which are one of the number of related arrangements implementing the proposal, and

    (c) at the time when the person who entered into the arrangements concerned incurs a defeat in respect of them, the required percentage of relevant defeats has not been reached.

(2) HMRC may not assess any penalty payable under paragraph 1 in respect of the arrangements concerned until the required percentage of relevant defeats is reached.

Finance (No. 2) Act 2017 (c. 32)
Schedule 16 — Penalties for enablers of defeated tax avoidance
Part 6 — Assessment of penalty

597

(3) For the purposes of this paragraph the "required percentage of relevant defeats" is reached when HMRC reasonably believe that defeats have been incurred in the case of more than 50% of the related arrangements implementing the proposal.

(4) Sub-paragraph (2) does not apply in relation to a penalty if the person liable to the penalty requests assessment of the penalty sooner than the time allowed by sub-paragraph (2).

Time limit for assessment

22 (1) An assessment of a person as liable to a penalty under paragraph 1 may not take place after the relevant time.

(2) In this paragraph "the relevant time" means, subject to sub-paragraphs (3) to (6) —

    (a) where a GAAR final decision notice within the meaning of paragraph 24(1) has been given in relation to the arrangements to which the penalty relates, the end of 12 months beginning with the date on which T incurs the defeat mentioned in paragraph 1;

    (b) where a notice under paragraph 25 has been given to the person mentioned in sub-paragraph (1) above in respect of the arrangements to which the penalty relates, the end of 12 months beginning with the end of the time allowed for making representations in respect of that notice;

    (c) where —

        (i) a referral has been made under paragraph 26 in respect of the arrangements to which the penalty relates, and

        (ii) paragraph (d) does not apply,

    the end of 12 months beginning with the date on which the opinion of the GAAR Advisory Panel is given on the referral (within the meaning given by paragraph 34(6));

    (d) where a notice under paragraph 35 has been given to the person mentioned in sub-paragraph (1) above in respect of the arrangements to which the penalty relates, the end of 12 months beginning with the end of the time allowed for making representations in respect of that notice.

(3) Where —

    (a) paragraph 21 prevented a penalty from being assessed before the required percentage of relevant defeats was reached, and

    (b) the required percentage of relevant defeats (within the meaning of paragraph 21) has been reached,

the relevant time in relation to that penalty is whichever is the later of —

    (i) the relevant time given by sub-paragraph (2), and

    (ii) the end of 12 months beginning with the date on which that required percentage was reached.

(4) Where under paragraph 21(4) a person requests assessment of a penalty, the relevant time in relation to that penalty is whichever is the later of —

    (a) the relevant time given by sub-paragraph (2), and

    (b) the end of 12 months beginning with the date on which the request is made,

598

Finance (No. 2) Act 2017 (c. 32)
Schedule 16 — Penalties for enablers of defeated tax avoidance
Part 6 — Assessment of penalty

and sub-paragraph (3) does not apply to the penalty even if the required percentage of relevant defeats is reached.

(5) Sub-paragraph (6) applies where —

    (a) at any time a declaration has been made under paragraph 44 for the purposes of any determination of whether a person is liable to a penalty under paragraph 1 in relation to particular arrangements ("the arrangements concerned"), and

    (b) subsequently, facts that in the Commissioners' opinion are sufficient to indicate that the declaration contains a material inaccuracy have come to the Commissioners' knowledge.

(6) The relevant time in respect of any penalty under paragraph 1 payable by that person in relation to the arrangements concerned is whichever is the later of —

    (a) the relevant time given by the preceding provisions of this paragraph, and

    (b) the end of 12 months beginning with the date on which such facts came to the Commissioners' knowledge.

PART 7

GAAR ADVISORY PANEL OPINION, AND REPRESENTATIONS

Requirement for opinion of GAAR Advisory Panel

23 (1) A penalty under paragraph 1 may not be assessed unless —

    (a) the decision that it should be assessed is taken by a designated HMRC officer, and

    (b) either the condition in sub-paragraph (2) or the condition in sub-paragraph (3) is met.

(2) The condition in this sub-paragraph is that, when the assessment is made —

    (a) a GAAR final decision notice has been given in relation to —

        (i) the arrangements to which the penalty relates ("the relevant arrangements"), or

        (ii) arrangements that are equivalent to the relevant arrangements,

    (b) where a notice is required by paragraph 25 to be given to the person liable to the penalty, that notice has been given and the time allowed for making representations under that paragraph has expired, and

    (c) a designated HMRC officer has, in deciding whether the penalty should be assessed, considered —

        (i) the opinion of the GAAR Advisory Panel which was considered by HMRC in preparing that GAAR final decision notice, and

        (ii) any representations made under paragraph 25.

(3) The condition in this sub-paragraph is that, when the assessment is made —

    (a) an opinion of the GAAR Advisory Panel which applies to the relevant arrangements has been given on a referral under paragraph 26,

Finance (No. 2) Act 2017 (c. 32)   599
Schedule 16 — Penalties for enablers of defeated tax avoidance
Part 7 — GAAR Advisory Panel opinion, and representations

(b) where a notice is required by paragraph 35 to be given to the person liable to the penalty, that notice has been given and the time allowed for making representations under that paragraph has expired, and

(c) a designated HMRC officer has, in deciding whether the penalty should be assessed, considered —

    (i) that opinion of the GAAR Advisory Panel, and

    (ii) any representations made under paragraph 35.

(4) Where a notification of a penalty under paragraph 1 is given, the notification must be accompanied by a report prepared by HMRC of —

(a) if the condition in sub-paragraph (2) is met, the opinion of the GAAR Advisory Panel which was considered by HMRC in preparing the GAAR final decision notice;

(b) if the condition in sub-paragraph (3) is met, the opinion of the GAAR advisory panel mentioned in that sub-paragraph.

(5) Paragraph 24 contains definitions of terms used in this paragraph.

24 (1) In this Schedule a "GAAR final decision notice" means a notice under —

(a) paragraph 12 of Schedule 43 to FA 2013 (notice of final decision after considering opinion of GAAR Advisory Panel on referral under Schedule 43),

(b) paragraph 8 or 9 of Schedule 43A to FA 2013 (notice of final decision after considering opinion of GAAR Advisory Panel), or

(c) paragraph 8 of Schedule 43B to FA 2013 (notice of final decision after considering opinion of GAAR Advisory Panel on referral under Schedule 43B).

(2) For the purposes of this Part of this Schedule, where the GAAR Advisory Panel gives an opinion on a referral under paragraph 26 the arrangements to which the opinion "applies" are —

(a) the arrangements in respect of which the referral was made (that is, "the arrangements in question" within the meaning given by paragraph 26(1)), and

(b) any arrangements that are equivalent to those arrangements.

(3) For the purposes of this Part of this Schedule, arrangements are "equivalent" to one another if they are substantially the same as one another having regard to —

(a) their substantive results or intended substantive results,

(b) the means of achieving those results, and

(c) the characteristics on the basis of which it could reasonably be argued, in each case, that the arrangements are abusive tax arrangements.

Notice where Panel opinion already obtained in relation to equivalent arrangements

25 (1) This paragraph applies where a designated HMRC officer is of the view that —

(a) a person is liable to a penalty under paragraph 1 in relation to particular arrangements ("the arrangements concerned"),

(b) no GAAR final decision notice has been given in relation to those arrangements, but those arrangements are equivalent to

600

Finance (No. 2) Act 2017 (c. 32)
Schedule 16 — Penalties for enablers of defeated tax avoidance
Part 7 — GAAR Advisory Panel opinion, and representations

arrangements in relation to which a GAAR final decision notice has been given ("the GAAR decision arrangements"), and

(c) accordingly, the opinion of the GAAR Advisory Panel which was considered by HMRC in preparing that GAAR final decision notice is relevant to the arrangements concerned.

(2) A designated HMRC officer must give the person mentioned in sub-paragraph (1) a notice in writing—

(a) explaining that the officer is of the view mentioned there,

(b) specifying the arrangements concerned,

(c) describing the material characteristics of the GAAR decision arrangements,

(d) setting out a report prepared by HMRC of the opinion of the GAAR Advisory Panel which was considered by HMRC in preparing the GAAR final decision notice, and

(e) explaining the effect of sub-paragraphs (3) and (4).

(3) A person to whom a notice under this paragraph is given has 30 days, beginning with the day on which the notice is given, to send to the designated HMRC officer (in writing) any representations that that person wishes to make as to why the arrangements concerned are not equivalent to the GAAR decision arrangements.

(4) A designated HMRC officer may, on a written request by that person, extend the period during which representations may be made by that person.

(5) Paragraph 24 contains definitions of the following terms used in this paragraph—

"GAAR final decision notice";

"equivalent", in relation to arrangements.

Referral to GAAR Advisory Panel

26 (1) A designated HMRC officer may make a referral under this paragraph if—

(a) the officer considers that a person is liable to a penalty under paragraph 1 in relation to particular arrangements ("the arrangements in question"), and

(b) the requirements of paragraph 28 (procedure before making of referral) have been complied with.

(2) But a referral may not be made under this paragraph if a GAAR final decision notice (within the meaning of paragraph 24(1)) has already been given in relation to—

(a) the arrangements in question, or

(b) arrangements that are equivalent to those arrangements.

(3) A referral under this paragraph is a referral to the GAAR Advisory Panel of the question whether the entering into and carrying out of tax arrangements such as are described in the referral statement (see paragraph 27) is a reasonable course of action in relation to the relevant tax provisions.

27 (1) In this Part of this Schedule "the referral statement", in relation to a referral under paragraph 26, means a statement made by a designated HMRC officer which—

(a) accompanies the referral,

Finance (No. 2) Act 2017 (c. 32)
601
Schedule 16 — Penalties for enablers of defeated tax avoidance
Part 7 — GAAR Advisory Panel opinion, and representations

    (b)   is a general statement of the material characteristics of the arrangements in question (within the meaning given by paragraph 26(1)), and

    (c)   complies with sub-paragraph (2).

(2) A statement under this paragraph must—

    (a)   contain a factual description of the arrangements in question,

    (b)   set out HMRC's view as to whether those arrangements accord with established practice (as it stood when those arrangements were entered into),

    (c)   explain why it is the designated HMRC officer's view that a tax advantage of the nature described in the statement and arising from tax arrangements having the characteristics described in the statement would be a tax advantage arising from arrangements that are abusive,

    (d)   set out any matters the designated HMRC officer is aware of which may suggest that any view of HMRC or the designated HMRC officer expressed in the statement is not correct, and

    (e)   set out any other matters which the designated HMRC officer considers are required for the purposes of the exercise of the GAAR Advisory Panel's functions under paragraphs 33 and 34.

Notice before decision whether to refer

28   (1) A referral must not be made under paragraph 26 unless—

    (a)   a designated HMRC officer has given each relevant person a notice under this paragraph,

    (b)   in the case of each relevant person, the time allowed for making representations has expired, and

    (c)   in deciding whether to make the referral, a designated HMRC officer has considered any representations made by a relevant person within the time allowed.

(2) In this paragraph a "relevant person" means any person who at the time of the referral is considered by the officer making the referral to be liable to a penalty under paragraph 1 in relation to the arrangements in question (within the meaning given by paragraph 26(1)).

(3) A notice under this paragraph is a notice in writing which—

    (a)   explains that the officer giving the notice considers that the person to whom the notice is given is liable to a penalty under paragraph 1 in relation to the arrangements in question (specifying those arrangements),

    (b)   explains why the officer considers those arrangements to be abusive tax arrangements,

    (c)   explains that HMRC are proposing to make a referral under paragraph 26 of the question whether the entering into and carrying out of tax arrangements that have the characteristics of the arrangements in question is a reasonable course of action in relation to the relevant tax provisions, and

    (d)   explains the effect of sub-paragraphs (4) and (5).

(4) Each person to whom a notice under this paragraph is given has 45 days, beginning with the day on which the notice is given to that person, to send

602

Finance (No. 2) Act 2017 (c. 32)
Schedule 16 — Penalties for enablers of defeated tax avoidance
Part 7 — GAAR Advisory Panel opinion, and representations

written representations to the designated HMRC officer in response to the notice.

(5) A designated HMRC officer may, on a written request by a person to whom a notice is given, extend the period during which representations may be made by that person.

Notice of decision whether to refer

29   Where a designated HMRC officer decides whether to make a referral under paragraph 26, the officer must, as soon as reasonably practicable, give written notice of that decision to each person to whom notice under paragraph 28 was given.

Information to accompany referral

30   A referral under paragraph 26 must (as well as being accompanied by the referral statement under paragraph 27) be accompanied by —
    (a) a declaration that, as far as HMRC are aware, nothing which is material to the GAAR Advisory Panel's consideration of the matter has been omitted from that statement,
    (b) a copy of each notice given under paragraph 28 by HMRC in relation to the referral,
    (c) a copy of any representations received under paragraph 28 and any comments that HMRC wish to make in respect of those representations, and
    (d) a copy of each notice given under paragraph 31 by HMRC.

Notice on making of referral

31   (1) Where a referral is made under paragraph 26, a designated HMRC officer must at the same time give to each relevant person a notice in writing which —
    (a) notifies the person of the referral,
    (b) is accompanied by a copy of the referral statement,
    (c) is accompanied by a copy of any comments provided to the GAAR Advisory Panel under paragraph 30(c) in respect of representations made by the person,
    (d) notifies the person of the period under paragraph 32 for making representations, and
    (e) notifies the person of the requirement under that paragraph to send any representations to the officer.

    (2) In this paragraph "relevant person" has the same meaning as in paragraph 28 (see sub-paragraph (2) of that paragraph).

Right to make representations to GAAR Advisory Panel

32   (1) A person who has received a notice under paragraph 31 has 21 days, beginning with the day on which that notice is given, to send to the GAAR Advisory Panel written representations about —
    (a) the notice given to the person under paragraph 28, or
    (b) any comments provided to the GAAR Advisory Panel under paragraph 30(c) in respect of representations made by the person.

Finance (No. 2) Act 2017 (c. 32)
Schedule 16 – Penalties for enablers of defeated tax avoidance
Part 7 – GAAR Advisory Panel opinion, and representations

603

(2) The GAAR Advisory Panel may, on a written request made by the person, extend the period during which representations may be made.

(3) If a person sends representations to the GAAR Advisory Panel under this paragraph, the person must at the same time send a copy of the representations to the designated HMRC officer.

(4) If a person sends representations to the GAAR Advisory Panel under this paragraph and that person made no representations under paragraph 28, a designated HMRC officer –

    (a) may provide the GAAR Advisory Panel with comments on that person's representations under this paragraph, and

    (b) if such comments are provided, must at the same time send a copy of them to that person.

Decision of GAAR Advisory Panel and opinion notices

33 (1) Where a referral is made to the GAAR Advisory Panel under paragraph 26, the Chair must arrange for a sub-panel consisting of 3 members of the GAAR Advisory Panel (one of whom may be the Chair) to consider it.

(2) The sub-panel may invite –

    (a) any person to whom notice under paragraph 28 was given, or

    (b) the designated HMRC officer,

(or both) to supply the sub-panel with further information within a period specified in the invitation.

(3) Invitations must explain the effect of sub-paragraph (4) or (5) (as appropriate).

(4) If a person invited under sub-paragraph (2)(a) supplies information to the sub-panel under this paragraph, that person must at the same time send a copy of the information to the designated HMRC officer.

(5) If a designated HMRC officer supplies information to the sub-panel under this paragraph, the officer must at the same time send a copy of the information to each person to whom notice under paragraph 28 was given.

34 (1) The sub-panel must produce –

    (a) one opinion notice stating the joint opinion of all the members of the sub-panel, or

    (b) two or three opinion notices which taken together state the opinions of all the members.

(2) The sub-panel must give a copy of the opinion notice or notices to the designated HMRC officer.

(3) An opinion notice is a notice which states that in the opinion of the members of the sub-panel, or one or more of those members –

    (a) the entering into and carrying out of tax arrangements such as are described in the referral statement is a reasonable course of action in relation to the relevant tax provisions,

    (b) the entering into or carrying out of such tax arrangements is not a reasonable course of action in relation to the relevant tax provisions, or

604

Finance (No. 2) Act 2017 (c. 32)
Schedule 16 — Penalties for enablers of defeated tax avoidance
Part 7 — GAAR Advisory Panel opinion, and representations

    (c)   it is not possible, on the information available, to reach a view on that matter,

and the reasons for that opinion.

(4) In forming their opinions for the purposes of sub-paragraph (3) members of the sub-panel must —

    (a)   have regard to all the matters set out in the referral statement,

    (b)   have regard to the matters mentioned in paragraphs (a) to (c) of paragraph 3(3) and paragraph 3(4), and

    (c)   take account of paragraph 3(5) to (7).

(5) For the purposes of the giving of an opinion under this paragraph, the arrangements are to be assumed to be tax arrangements.

(6) For the purposes of this Schedule —

    (a)   an opinion of the GAAR Advisory Panel is to be treated as having been given on a referral under paragraph 26 when an opinion notice (or notices) has been given under this paragraph in respect of the referral, and

    (b)   any requirement to consider the opinion of the GAAR Advisory Panel given on such a referral is a requirement to consider the contents of the opinion notice (or notices) given on the referral.

Notice before deciding that arrangements are ones to which Panel opinion applies

35   (1) This paragraph applies where —

    (a)   an opinion of the GAAR Advisory Panel has been given on a referral under paragraph 26,

    (b)   a designated HMRC officer is of the view that a person is liable to a penalty under paragraph 1 in relation to particular arrangements ("the arrangements concerned") and that that opinion of the GAAR Advisory Panel applies to those arrangements, and

    (c)   that person is not a person to whom notice under paragraph 28 was given in connection with the referral.

(2) A designated HMRC officer must give the person mentioned in sub-paragraph (1)(b) a notice in writing —

    (a)   explaining that the officer is of the view mentioned in that paragraph,

    (b)   specifying the arrangements concerned,

    (c)   setting out a report prepared by HMRC of the opinion mentioned in sub-paragraph (1)(a), and

    (d)   explaining the effect of sub-paragraphs (3) and (4).

(3) A person to whom a notice under this paragraph is given has 30 days, beginning with the day on which the notice is given, to send the designated HMRC officer (in writing) any representations as to why the opinion does not apply to the arrangements concerned.

(4) A designated HMRC officer may, on a written request by that person, extend the period during which representations may be made by that person.

(5) Paragraph 24(2) defines the arrangements that an opinion given on a referral under paragraph 26 "applies to".

Finance (No. 2) Act 2017 (c. 32)
Schedule 16 — Penalties for enablers of defeated tax avoidance
Part 7 — GAAR Advisory Panel opinion, and representations

605

Requirement for court or tribunal to take Panel opinion into account

36 (1) In this paragraph "enabler penalty proceedings" means proceedings before a court or tribunal in connection with a penalty under paragraph 1.

(2) In determining in enabler penalty proceedings any question whether tax arrangements to which the penalty relates were abusive, the court or tribunal—

(a) must take into account the relevant Panel opinion, and

(b) may also take into account any matter mentioned in sub-paragraph (4).

(3) In sub-paragraph (2)(a) "the relevant Panel opinion" means the opinion of the GAAR Advisory Panel which under this Part of this Schedule was required to be considered by a designated HMRC officer in deciding whether the penalty should be assessed.

(4) The matters mentioned in sub-paragraph (2)(b) are—

(a) guidance, statements or other material (whether of HMRC, a Minister of the Crown or anyone else) that was in the public domain at the time the arrangements were entered into, and

(b) evidence of established practice at that time.

PART 8

APPEALS

37 A person may appeal against—

(a) a decision of HMRC that a penalty under paragraph 1 is payable by that person, or

(b) a decision of HMRC as to the amount of a penalty under paragraph 1 payable by the person.

38 (1) An appeal under paragraph 37 is to be treated in the same way as an appeal against an assessment to the tax to which the arrangements concerned relate (including by the application of any provision about bringing the appeal by notice to HMRC, about HMRC review of the decision or about determination of the appeal by the First-tier Tribunal or Upper Tribunal).

(2) Sub-paragraph (1) does not apply—

(a) so as to require a person to pay a penalty under paragraph 1 before an appeal against the assessment of the penalty is determined;

(b) in respect of any other matter expressly provided for by this Schedule.

(3) In this paragraph "the arrangements concerned" means the arrangements to which the penalty relates.

39 (1) On an appeal under paragraph 37(a) that is notified to the tribunal, the tribunal may affirm or cancel HMRC's decision.

(2) On an appeal under paragraph 37(b) that is notified to the tribunal, the tribunal may—

(a) affirm HMRC's decision, or

(b) substitute for that decision another decision that HMRC had power to make.

(3) If the tribunal substitutes its decision for HMRC's, the tribunal may rely on paragraph 18—

    (a) to the same extent as HMRC (which may mean applying the same percentage reduction as HMRC to a different starting point), or

    (b) to a different extent, but only if the tribunal thinks that HMRC's decision in respect of the application of paragraph 18 was flawed.

(4) In sub-paragraph (3)(b) "flawed" means flawed when considered in the light of the principles applicable in proceedings for judicial review.

(5) In this paragraph "tribunal" means the First-tier Tribunal or Upper Tribunal (as appropriate by virtue of paragraph 38(1)).

PART 9

INFORMATION

Information and inspection powers: application of Schedule 36 to FA 2008

40 (1) Schedule 36 to FA 2008 (information and inspection powers) applies for the purpose of checking a relevant person's position as regards liability for a penalty under paragraph 1 as it applies for checking a person's tax position, subject to the modifications in paragraphs 41 to 43.

(2) In this paragraph and paragraphs 41 to 43—

    "relevant person" means a person an officer of Revenue and Customs has reason to suspect is or may be liable to a penalty under paragraph 1;

    "the Schedule" means Schedule 36 to FA 2008.

General modifications of Schedule 36 to FA 2008 as applied

41 In its application for the purpose mentioned in paragraph 40(1) above, the Schedule has effect as if—

    (a) any provisions which can have no application for that purpose were omitted,

    (b) references to "the taxpayer" were references to the relevant person whose position as regards liability for a penalty under paragraph 1 is to be checked, and references to "a taxpayer" were references to a relevant person,

    (c) references to a person's "tax position" were to the relevant person's position as regards liability for a penalty under paragraph 1,

    (d) references to prejudice to the assessment or collection of tax included prejudice to the investigation of the relevant person's position as regards liability for a penalty under paragraph 1, and

    (e) references to a pending appeal relating to tax were to a pending appeal relating to an assessment of liability for a penalty under paragraph 1.

Specific modifications of Schedule 36 to FA 2008 as applied

42 (1) The Schedule as it applies for the purpose mentioned in paragraph 40(1) above has effect with the modifications in sub-paragraphs (2) to (6).

(2) Paragraph 10A (power to inspect business premises of involved third parties) has effect as if the reference in sub-paragraph (1) to the position of any person or class of persons as regards a relevant tax were to the position of a relevant person as regards liability for a penalty under paragraph 1.

(3) Paragraph 47 (right to appeal against penalties under the Schedule) has effect as if after paragraph (b) (but not as part of that paragraph) there were inserted the words "but paragraph (b) does not give a right of appeal against the amount of an increased daily penalty payable by virtue of paragraph 49A."

(4) Paragraph 49A (increased daily default penalty) has effect as if—

    (a) in sub-paragraphs (1)(c) and (2) for "imposed" there were substituted "assessable";

    (b) for sub-paragraphs (3) and (4) there were substituted—

> "(3) If the tribunal decides that an increased daily penalty should be assessable—
>
>   (a) the tribunal must determine the day from which the increased daily penalty is to apply and the maximum amount of that penalty ("the new maximum amount");
>
>   (b) from that day, paragraph 40 has effect in the person's case as if "the new maximum amount" were substituted for "£60".
>
> (4) The new maximum amount may not be more than £1,000.";

    (c) in sub-paragraph (5) for "the amount" there were substituted "the new maximum amount".

(5) Paragraph 49B (notification of increased daily default penalty) has effect as if—

    (a) in sub-paragraph (1) for "a person becomes liable to a penalty" there were substituted "the tribunal makes a determination";

    (b) in sub-paragraph (2) for "the day from which the increased penalty is to apply" there were substituted "the new maximum amount and the day from which it applies";

    (c) sub-paragraph (3) were omitted.

(6) Paragraph 49C is treated as omitted.

43   Paragraphs 50 and 51 are excluded from the application of the Schedule for the purpose mentioned in paragraph 40(1) above.

Declarations about contents of legally privileged communications

44   (1) Subject to sub-paragraph (5), a declaration under this paragraph is to be treated by—

    (a) HMRC, or

    (b) in any proceedings before a court or tribunal in connection with a penalty under paragraph 1, the court or tribunal,

as conclusive evidence of the things stated in the declaration.

(2) A declaration under this paragraph is a declaration which—

    (a) is made by a relevant lawyer,

608

Finance (No. 2) Act 2017 (c. 32)
Schedule 16 — Penalties for enablers of defeated tax avoidance
Part 9 — Information

      (b)   relates to one or more communications falling within sub-paragraph (3), and

      (c)   meets such requirements as may be prescribed by regulations under sub-paragraph (4).

(3)   A communication falls within this sub-paragraph if —

      (a)   it was made by a relevant lawyer (whether or not the one making the declaration),

      (b)   it is legally privileged, and

      (c)   if it were not legally privileged, it would be relied on by a person for the purpose of establishing that that person is not liable to a penalty under paragraph 1 (whether or not that person is the person who made the communication or is making the declaration).

(4)   The Treasury may by regulations impose requirements as to the form and contents of declarations under this paragraph.

(5)   Sub-paragraph (1) does not apply where HMRC or (as the case may be) the court or tribunal is satisfied that the declaration contains information which is incorrect.

(6)   In this paragraph "a relevant lawyer" means a barrister, advocate, solicitor or other legal representative communications with whom may be the subject of a claim to legal professional privilege or, in Scotland, protected from disclosure in legal proceedings on the grounds of confidentiality of communication.

(7)   For the purpose of this paragraph, a communication is "legally privileged" if it is a communication in respect of which a claim to legal professional privilege, or (in Scotland) to confidentiality of communications as between client and professional legal adviser, could be maintained in legal proceedings.

45   (1)   Where a person carelessly or deliberately gives any incorrect information in a declaration under paragraph 44, the person is liable to a penalty not exceeding £5,000.

(2)   For the purposes of this paragraph, incorrect information is carelessly given by a person if the information is incorrect because of a failure by the person to take reasonable care.

(3)   Paragraphs 19(1), 20, 22(1), 37, 38 and 39(1), (2) and (5) apply in relation to a penalty under this paragraph as they apply in relation to a penalty under paragraph 1, subject to the modifications in sub-paragraphs (4) and (5).

(4)   In its application to a penalty under this paragraph, paragraph 22(1) has effect as if for "the relevant time" there were substituted "the end of 12 months beginning with the date on which facts sufficient to indicate that the person is liable to the penalty came to the Commissioners' knowledge".

(5)   In its application to a penalty under this paragraph, paragraph 38(3) has effect as if the reference to the arrangements to which the penalty relates were to the arrangements to which the declaration under paragraph 44 relates.

(6)   In paragraph 44 any reference to a penalty under paragraph 1 includes a reference to a penalty under this paragraph.

Finance (No. 2) Act 2017 (c. 32) 609
Schedule 16 — Penalties for enablers of defeated tax avoidance
Part 10 — Publishing details of persons who have incurred penalties

PART 10

PUBLISHING DETAILS OF PERSONS WHO HAVE INCURRED PENALTIES

Power to publish details

46 (1) The Commissioners may publish information about a person where—
  (a) the person has incurred a penalty under paragraph 1,
  (b) the penalty has become final, and
  (c) either the condition in sub-paragraph (2) or the condition in sub-paragraph (3) is met.

  (2) The condition in this sub-paragraph is that, at the time when the penalty mentioned in sub-paragraph (1) becomes final, 50 or more other penalties which are reckonable penalties have been incurred by the person.

  (3) The condition in this sub-paragraph is that—
  (a) the amount of the penalty mentioned in sub-paragraph (1), or
  (b) the total amount of that penalty and any other penalties incurred by that person which are reckonable penalties,
  is more than £25,000.

  (4) The information that may be published under this paragraph is—
  (a) the person's name (including any trading name, previous name or pseudonym),
  (b) the person's address (or registered office),
  (c) the nature of any business carried on by the person,
  (d) the total number of the penalties in question (that is, the penalty mentioned in sub-paragraph (1) and any penalties that are reckonable penalties in relation to that penalty),
  (e) the total amount of the penalties in question, and
  (f) any other information that the Commissioners consider it appropriate to publish in order to make clear the person's identity.

  (5) The information may be published in any way that the Commissioners consider appropriate.

  (6) For the purposes of this Part of this Schedule a penalty becomes "final"—
  (a) if the penalty has been assessed and paragraph (b) does not apply, at the time when the period for any appeal or further appeal relating to the penalty expires or, if later, when any appeal or final appeal relating to it is finally determined;
  (b) if a contract settlement has been made in relation to the penalty, at the time when the contract is made;
  and "contract settlement" here means a contract between the Commissioners and the person under which the Commissioners undertake not to assess the penalty or (if it has been assessed) not to take proceedings to recover it.

  (7) "Reckonable penalty" has the meaning given by paragraph 47.

  (8) This paragraph is subject to paragraphs 48 to 50.

47 (1) A penalty is a "reckonable penalty" for the purposes of paragraph 46 if—
  (a) it is a penalty under paragraph 1 which becomes final at the same time as, or before, the penalty mentioned in paragraph 46(1),

610

Finance (No. 2) Act 2017 (c. 32)
Schedule 16 — Penalties for enablers of defeated tax avoidance
Part 10 — Publishing details of persons who have incurred penalties

(b)   its entry date and the entry date of the penalty mentioned in paragraph 46(1) are not more than 12 months apart, and

(c)   it is not a penalty which under paragraph 48(1) is to be disregarded.

(2)   For the purposes of this paragraph the "entry date" of a penalty under paragraph 1 is the date (or, if more than one, the latest date) on which the arrangements concerned or any agreement or transaction forming part of those arrangements was entered into by the taxpayer.

(3)   In sub-paragraph (2) —

"the arrangements concerned" means the arrangements to which the penalty relates, and

"the taxpayer" means the person whose defeat in respect of those arrangements resulted in the penalty being payable.

(4)   For the purposes of this paragraph, the entry date of a penalty is not more than 12 months apart from the entry date of another penalty if —

(a)   the entry dates of those penalties are the same, or

(b)   the period beginning with whichever of the entry dates is the earlier and ending with whichever of the entry dates is the later is 12 months or less.

Restrictions on power

48   (1)   In determining at any time whether or what information may be published in relation to a person under paragraph 46, the following penalties incurred by the person are to be disregarded —

(a)   a penalty which has been reduced to nil or stayed;

(b)   a penalty by reference to which information has previously been published under paragraph 46;

(c)   a penalty where —

(i)   the arrangements to which the penalty relates ("the arrangements concerned") are related to other arrangements, and

(ii)   the condition in sub-paragraph (3) is not met;

(d)   a penalty that relates to arrangements which are related to arrangements that have already been dealt with (within the meaning given by sub-paragraph (4)).

(2)   For the purposes of sub-paragraph (1)(c) and (d) arrangements are "related to" each other if they —

(a)   implement the same proposal for tax arrangements, and

(b)   are substantially the same as each other.

(3)   The condition referred to in sub-paragraph (1)(c) is that HMRC reasonably believe that —

(a)   defeats have been incurred in the case of all the arrangements that are related to the arrangements concerned ("the related arrangements"), and

(b)   each penalty under paragraph 1 which relates to the arrangements concerned or to any of the related arrangements has become final.

(4)   For the purposes of sub-paragraph (1)(d) arrangements have "already been dealt with" if information about the person has already been published

Finance (No. 2) Act 2017 (c. 32)
Schedule 16 — Penalties for enablers of defeated tax avoidance
Part 10 — Publishing details of persons who have incurred penalties

611

under paragraph 46 by reference to a penalty that relates to those arrangements.

49 (1) Publication of information under paragraph 46 on the basis of a penalty or penalties incurred by a person may not take place after the relevant time.

(2) In this paragraph "the relevant time" means the end of 12 months beginning with the date on which the penalty became final or, where more than one penalty is involved, the latest date on which any of them became final.

(3) Sub-paragraph (1) is not to be taken to prevent the re-publishing, or continued publishing, after the relevant time of a set of information published under paragraph 46 before that time.

(4) Information published under paragraph 46 may not be re-published, or continue to be published, after the end of 12 months beginning with the date on which it was first published.

(5) Nothing in paragraph 48 applies in relation to determining whether to re-publish (or continue to publish) a set of information already published under paragraph 46.

50 Before publishing information under paragraph 46 the Commissioners must—

(a) inform the person that they are considering doing so, and

(b) afford the person the opportunity to make representations about whether it should be published.

Power to amend

51 The Treasury may by regulations amend this Part of this Schedule so as to alter any of the following—

(a) the figure for the time being specified in paragraph 46(2);

(b) the sum for the time being specified in paragraph 46(3);

(c) any period for the time being specified in paragraph 47(1)(b) or (4).

PART 11

MISCELLANEOUS

Double jeopardy

52 A person is not liable to a penalty under paragraph 1 in respect of conduct for which the person has been convicted of an offence.

Application of provisions of TMA 1970

53 Subject to the provisions of this Schedule, the following provisions of TMA 1970 apply for the purposes of this Schedule as they apply for the purposes of the Taxes Acts—

(a) section 108 (responsibility of company officers),

(b) section 114 (want of form), and

(c) section 115 (delivery and service of documents).

PART 12

GENERAL

Meaning of "tax"

54 (1) In this Schedule "tax" includes any of the following taxes —

    (a) income tax,

    (b) corporation tax, including any amount chargeable as if it were corporation tax or treated as if it were corporation tax,

    (c) capital gains tax,

    (d) petroleum revenue tax,

    (e) diverted profits tax,

    (f) apprenticeship levy,

    (g) inheritance tax,

    (h) stamp duty land tax, and

    (i) annual tax on enveloped dwellings,

and also includes national insurance contributions.

(2) The Treasury may by regulations amend sub-paragraph (1) so as to —

    (a) add a tax to the list of taxes for the time being set out in that sub-paragraph;

    (b) remove a tax for the time being set out in that sub-paragraph;

    (c) remove the reference to national insurance contributions;

    (d) substitute for that reference a reference to national insurance contributions of a particular class or classes;

    (e) where provision has been made under paragraph (d) —

        (i) add a class or classes of national insurance contributions to those for the time being specified in that sub-paragraph;

        (ii) remove a class or classes of national insurance contributions for the time being so specified.

(3) Regulations under this paragraph may —

    (a) make supplementary, incidental, and consequential provision, including provision amending or repealing any provision of this Schedule;

    (b) make transitional provision.

Meaning of "tax advantage"

55 In this Schedule "tax advantage" includes —

    (a) relief or increased relief from tax,

    (b) repayment or increased repayment of tax,

    (c) receipt, or advancement of a receipt, of a tax credit,

    (d) avoidance or reduction of a charge to tax, an assessment of tax or a liability to pay tax,

    (e) avoidance of a possible assessment to tax or liability to pay tax,

    (f) deferral of a payment of tax or advancement of a repayment of tax, and

    (g) avoidance of an obligation to deduct or account for tax.

Other definitions

56　(1)　In this Schedule —

　　　"abusive tax arrangements" has the meaning given by paragraph 3;

　　　"arrangements" includes any agreement, understanding, scheme, transaction or series of transactions (whether or not legally enforceable);

　　　"business" includes any trade or profession;

　　　"the Commissioners" means the Commissioners for Her Majesty's Revenue and Customs;

　　　"company" has the same meaning as in the Corporation Tax Acts (see section 1121 of CTA 2010);

　　　"contract settlement" (except in paragraph 46(6)) means an agreement in connection with a person's liability to make a payment to the Commissioners under or by virtue of an enactment;

　　　"a defeat", in relation to arrangements, is to be read in accordance with paragraph 4;

　　　a "designated HMRC officer" means an officer of Revenue and Customs who has been designated by the Commissioners for the purposes of this Schedule;

　　　"the GAAR Advisory Panel" has the meaning given by paragraph 1 of Schedule 43 to FA 2013;

　　　"group" is to be read in accordance with sub-paragraph (2);

　　　"HMRC" means Her Majesty's Revenue and Customs;

　　　"national insurance contributions" means contributions under Part 1 of the Social Security Contributions and Benefits Act 1992 or Part 1 of the Social Security Contributions and Benefits (Northern Ireland) Act 1992;

　　　a "NICs decision" means a decision under section 8 of the Social Security Contributions (Transfer of Functions, etc.) Act 1999 or Article 7 of the Social Security Contributions (Transfer of Functions, etc.) (Northern Ireland) Order 1999 (SI 1999/671) relating to a person's liability for relevant contributions;

　　　"relevant contributions" means any of the following contributions under Part 1 of the Social Security Contributions and Benefits Act 1992 or Part 1 of the Social Security Contributions and Benefits (Northern Ireland) Act 1992 —

　　　　　(a)　Class 1 contributions;

　　　　　(b)　Class 1A contributions;

　　　　　(c)　Class 1B contributions;

　　　　　(d)　Class 2 contributions which must be paid but in relation to which section 11A of the Act in question (application of certain provisions of the Income Tax Acts) does not apply;

　　　"tax" is to be read in accordance with paragraph 54;

　　　"tax advantage" is to be read in accordance with paragraph 55.

　　(2)　For the purposes of this Schedule two companies are members of the same group if —

　　　　(a)　one is a 75% subsidiary of the other, or

　　　　(b)　both are 75% subsidiaries of a third company;

　　and in this paragraph "75% subsidiary" has, subject to sub-paragraph (3), the meaning given by section 1154 of CTA 2010.

614   *Finance (No. 2) Act 2017 (c. 32)*
Schedule 16 — Penalties for enablers of defeated tax avoidance
Part 12 — General

(3) So far as relating to 75% subsidiaries, section 151(4) of CTA 2010 (requirements relating to beneficial ownership) applies for the purposes of this Schedule as it applies for the purposes of Part 5 of that Act.

(4) In this Schedule references to an assessment to tax, however expressed —

    (a) in relation to inheritance tax and petroleum revenue tax, include a determination;

    (b) in relation to relevant contributions, include a NICs decision.

Regulations

57   (1) Any regulations under this Schedule must be made by statutory instrument.

    (2) A statutory instrument which contains (alone or with other provision) any regulations within sub-paragraph (3) may not be made unless a draft of the instrument has been laid before, and approved by a resolution of, the House of Commons.

    (3) Regulations within this sub-paragraph are —

        (a) regulations under paragraph 12;

        (b) regulations under paragraph 14(1);

        (c) regulations under paragraph 14(2) which amend or repeal any provision of this Schedule;

        (d) regulations under paragraph 51;

        (e) regulations under paragraph 54.

    (4) A statutory instrument containing only —

        (a) regulations under paragraph 14(2) which do not amend or repeal any provision of this Schedule, or

        (b) regulations under paragraph 44,

is subject to annulment in pursuance of a resolution of the House of Commons.

Consequential amendments

58   In section 103ZA of TMA 1970 (disapplication of sections 100 to 103 of that Act in the case of certain penalties) —

    (a) omit "or" at the end of paragraph (i), and

    (b) after paragraph (j) insert "or

        "(k) paragraph 1 or 45 of Schedule 16 to the Finance (No. 2) Act 2017 (enablers of defeated tax avoidance etc)."

59   In section 54 of ITTOIA 2005 (no deduction allowed for certain penalties etc) at the end of the table in subsection (2) insert —

"Penalty under Schedule 16 to F(No. 2)A 2017	Various taxes"

60   In section 1303 of CTA 2009 (no deduction allowed for certain penalties etc)

at the end of the table in subsection (2) insert—

| "Penalty under Schedule 16 to F(No. 2)A 2017 | Various taxes" |

61   In Schedule 34 to FA 2014 (promoters of tax avoidance schemes: threshold conditions), in paragraph 7—

(a)   in paragraph (a), for the words after "promoter" substitute "—

(i)   have been referred to the GAAR Advisory Panel under Schedule 43 to FA 2013 (referrals of single schemes),

(ii)   are in a pool in respect of which a referral has been made to that Panel under Schedule 43B to that Act (generic referrals), or

(iii) have been referred to that Panel under paragraph 26 of Schedule 16 to F(No. 2)A 2017 (referrals in relation to penalties for enablers of defeated tax avoidance),";

(b)   in paragraph (b), for the words after "referral" substitute "under (as the case may be)—

(i)   paragraph 11(3)(b) of Schedule 43 to FA 2013,

(ii)   paragraph 6(4)(b) of Schedule 43B to that Act, or

(iii) paragraph 34(3)(b) of Schedule 16 to F(No. 2)A 2017,

(opinion of sub-panel of GAAR Advisory Panel that arrangements are not reasonable), and".

Commencement

62   (1) Subject to sub-paragraphs (2) and (3), paragraphs 1 to 61 of this Schedule have effect in relation to arrangements entered into on or after the day on which this Act is passed.

(2) In determining in relation to any particular arrangements whether a person is a person who enabled the arrangements, any action of the person carried out before the day on which this Act is passed is to be disregarded.

(3) The amendments made by paragraph 61 do not apply in relation to a person who is a promoter in relation to arrangements if by virtue of sub-paragraph (2) above that person is not a person who enabled the arrangements.

616

Finance (No. 2) Act 2017 (c. 32)
Schedule 17 — Disclosure of tax avoidance schemes: VAT and other indirect taxes
Part 1 — Duties to disclose avoidance schemes etc

SCHEDULE 17   Section 66

DISCLOSURE OF TAX AVOIDANCE SCHEMES: VAT AND OTHER INDIRECT TAXES

PART 1

DUTIES TO DISCLOSE AVOIDANCE SCHEMES ETC

Preliminary: application of definitions

1   The definitions in paragraphs 2, 3, and 7 to 10 apply for the purposes of this Schedule.

"Indirect tax"

2   (1) "Indirect tax" means any of the following —
            VAT
            insurance premium tax
            general betting duty
            pool betting duty
            remote gaming duty
            machine games duty
            gaming duty
            lottery duty
            bingo duty
            air passenger duty
            hydrocarbon oils duty
            tobacco products duty
            duties on spirits, beer, wine, made-wine and cider
            soft drinks industry levy
            aggregates levy
            landfill tax
            climate change levy
            customs duties.

     (2) The Treasury may by regulations amend the list in sub-paragraph (1) by adding, varying or omitting an entry for a tax.

"Notifiable arrangements" and "notifiable proposal"

3   (1) "Notifiable arrangements" means any arrangements not excluded by sub-paragraph (2) which —
          (a) fall within any description prescribed by the Treasury by regulations,
          (b) enable, or might be expected to enable, any person to obtain a tax advantage in relation to any indirect tax that is so prescribed in relation to arrangements of that description, and
          (c) are such that the main benefit, or one of the main benefits, that might be expected to arise from the arrangements is the obtaining of that tax advantage.

Finance (No. 2) Act 2017 (c. 32)
Schedule 17 — Disclosure of tax avoidance schemes: VAT and other indirect taxes
Part 1 — Duties to disclose avoidance schemes etc

617

    (2) Arrangements that meet the requirements in paragraphs (a) to (c) of sub-paragraph (1) are not notifiable arrangements if they implement a proposal which is excluded from being a notifiable proposal by sub-paragraph (4).

    (3) "Notifiable proposal" means a proposal for arrangements which, if entered into, would be notifiable arrangements (whether the proposal relates to a particular person or to any person who may seek to take advantage of it).

    (4) A proposal is not a notifiable proposal if any of the following occur before 1 January 2018—

        (a) a promoter first makes a firm approach to another person in relation to the proposal,

        (b) a promoter makes the proposal available for implementation by any other person, or

        (c) a promoter first becomes aware of any transaction forming part of arrangements implementing the proposal.

4   (1) HMRC may apply to the tribunal for an order that—

        (a) a proposal is notifiable, or

        (b) arrangements are notifiable.

    (2) An application must specify—

        (a) the proposal or arrangements in respect of which the order is sought, and

        (b) the promoter.

    (3) On an application the tribunal may make the order only if satisfied that paragraph 3(1)(a) to (c) applies to the relevant arrangements and that they are not excluded from being notifiable by paragraph 3(2).

5   (1) HMRC may apply to the tribunal for an order that—

        (a) a proposal is to be treated as notifiable, or

        (b) arrangements are to be treated as notifiable.

    (2) An application must specify—

        (a) the proposal or arrangements in respect of which the order is sought, and

        (b) the promoter.

    (3) On an application the tribunal may make the order only if satisfied that HMRC—

        (a) have taken all reasonable steps to establish whether the proposal or arrangements are notifiable, and

        (b) have reasonable grounds for suspecting that the proposal or arrangements may be notifiable.

    (4) Reasonable steps under sub-paragraph (3)(a) may (but need not) include taking action under paragraph 29 or 30.

    (5) Grounds for suspicion under sub-paragraph (3)(b) may include—

        (a) the fact that the relevant arrangements fall within a description prescribed under paragraph 3(1)(a),

        (b) an attempt by the promoter to avoid or delay providing information or documents about the proposal or arrangements under or by virtue of paragraph 29 or 30,

618

Finance (No. 2) Act 2017 (c. 32)
Schedule 17 — Disclosure of tax avoidance schemes: VAT and other indirect taxes
Part 1 — Duties to disclose avoidance schemes etc

      (c)   the promoter's failure to comply with a requirement under or by virtue of paragraph 29 or 30 in relation to another proposal or other arrangements.

  (6) Where an order is made under this paragraph in respect of a proposal or arrangements, the relevant period for the purposes of sub-paragraph (1) of paragraph 11 or 12 in so far as it applies by virtue of the order is the period of 11 days beginning with the day on which the order is made.

  (7) An order under this paragraph in relation to a proposal or arrangements is without prejudice to the possible application of any of paragraphs 11 to 15, other than by virtue of this paragraph, to the proposal or arrangements.

"Tax advantage" in relation to VAT

6   (1) A person (P) obtains a tax advantage in relation to VAT if—

      (a)   in any prescribed accounting period, the amount by which the output tax accounted for by P exceeds the input tax deducted by P is less than it would otherwise be;

      (b)   P obtains a VAT credit when P would otherwise not do so, or obtains a larger credit or obtains a credit earlier than would otherwise be the case;

      (c)   in a case where P recovers input tax as a recipient of a supply before the supplier accounts for the output tax, the period between the time when the input tax is recovered and the time when the output tax is accounted for is greater than would otherwise be the case;

      (d)   in any prescribed accounting period, the amount of P's non-deductible tax is less than it otherwise would be;

      (e)   P avoids an obligation to account for tax.

  (2) In sub-paragraph (1)(d) "non-deductible tax", in relation to a taxable person, means—

      (a)   input tax for which the person is not entitled to credit under section 25 of VATA 1994,

      (b)   any VAT incurred by the person which is not input tax and in respect of which the person is not entitled to a refund from the Commissioners by virtue of any provision of VATA 1994.

  (3) For the purposes of sub-paragraph (2)(b), the VAT "incurred" by a taxable person is—

      (a)   VAT on the supply to the person of any goods or services,

      (b)   VAT on the acquisition by the person from another member State of any goods,

      (c)   VAT paid or payable by the person on the importation of any goods from a place outside the member States.

  (4) A person who is not a taxable person obtains a tax advantage in relation to VAT if that person's non-refundable tax is less that it otherwise would be.

  (5) In sub-paragraph (4) "non-refundable tax" means—

      (a)   VAT on the supply to the person of any goods or services,

      (b)   VAT on the acquisition by the person from another member State of goods,

      (c)   VAT paid or payable by the person on the importation of any goods from a place outside the member States,

Finance (No. 2) Act 2017 (c. 32) 619
Schedule 17 – Disclosure of tax avoidance schemes: VAT and other indirect taxes
Part 1 – Duties to disclose avoidance schemes etc

but excluding (in each case) any VAT in respect of which the person is entitled to a refund from the Commissioners by virtue of any provision of VATA 1994.

(6) Terms used in this paragraph which are defined in section 96 of VATA 1994 have the meanings given by that section.

"Tax advantage" in relation to taxes other than VAT

7   "Tax advantage", in relation to an indirect tax other than VAT, means—
    (a) relief or increased relief from tax,
    (b) repayment or increased repayment of tax,
    (c) avoidance or reduction of a charge to tax, an assessment of tax or a liability to pay tax,
    (d) avoidance of a possible assessment to tax or liability to pay tax,
    (e) deferral of a payment of tax or advancement of a repayment of tax, or
    (f) avoidance of an obligation to deduct or account for tax.

"Promoter"

8   (1) This paragraph describes when a person (P) is a promoter in relation to a notifiable proposal or notifiable arrangements.

(2) P is a promoter in relation to a notifiable proposal if, in the course of a relevant business, P—
    (a) is to any extent responsible for the design of the proposed arrangements,
    (b) makes a firm approach to another person (C) in relation to the proposal with a view to P making the proposal available for implementation by C or any other person, or
    (c) makes the proposal available for implementation by other persons.

(3) P is a promoter in relation to notifiable arrangements if—
    (a) P is by virtue of sub-paragraph (2)(b) or (c) a promoter in relation to a notifiable proposal which is implemented by the arrangements, or
    (b) if in the course of a relevant business, P is to any extent responsible for—
        (i) the design of the arrangements, or
        (ii) the organisation or management of the arrangements.

(4) In this paragraph "relevant business" means any trade, profession or business which—
    (a) involves the provision to other persons of services relating to taxation, or
    (b) is carried on by a bank or securities house.

(5) In sub-paragraph (4)(b)—
    "bank" has the meaning given by section 1120 of CTA 2010, and
    "securities house" has the meaning given by section 1009(3) of that Act.

(6) For the purposes of this paragraph anything done by a company is to be taken to be done in the course of a relevant business if it is done for the purposes of a relevant business falling within sub-paragraph (4)(b) carried on by another company which is a member of the same group.

620   *Finance (No. 2) Act 2017 (c. 32)*
Schedule 17 – Disclosure of tax avoidance schemes: VAT and other indirect taxes
Part 1 – Duties to disclose avoidance schemes etc

(7) Section 170 of the TCGA 1992 has effect for determining for the purposes of sub-paragraph (6) whether two companies are members of the same group, but as if in that section—

    (a) for each of the references to a 75 per cent subsidiary there were substituted a reference to a 51 per cent subsidiary, and

    (b) subsection (3)(b) and subsections (6) to (8) were omitted.

(8) A person is not to be treated as a promoter by reason of anything done in prescribed circumstances.

(9) In the application of this Schedule to a proposal or arrangements which are not notifiable, a reference to a promoter is a reference to a person who would be a promoter under this paragraph if the proposal or arrangements were notifiable.

"Introducer"

9   (1) A person is an introducer in relation to a notifiable proposal if the person makes a marketing contact with another person in relation to the proposal.

    (2) A person is not to be treated as an introducer by reason of anything done in prescribed circumstances.

    (3) In the application of this Schedule to a proposal or arrangements which are not notifiable, a reference to an introducer is a reference to a person who would be an introducer under this paragraph if the proposal or arrangements were notifiable.

"Makes a firm approach" and "marketing contact"

10   (1) A person makes a firm approach to another person in relation to a notifiable proposal if the person makes a marketing contact with the other person in relation to the proposal at a time when the proposed arrangements have been substantially designed.

    (2) A person makes a marketing contact with another person in relation to a notifiable proposal if—

    (a) the person communicates information about the proposal to the other person,

    (b) the communication is made with a view to that other person, or any other person, entering into transactions forming part of the proposed arrangements, and

    (c) the information communicated includes an explanation of the tax advantage that might be expected to be obtained from the proposed arrangements.

    (3) For the purposes of sub-paragraph (1) proposed arrangements have been substantially designed at any time if by that time the nature of the transactions to form part of them has been sufficiently developed for it to be reasonable to believe that a person who wished to obtain the tax advantage mentioned in sub-paragraph (2)(c) might enter into—

    (a) transactions of the nature developed, or

    (b) transactions not substantially different from transactions of that nature.

Finance (No. 2) Act 2017 (c. 32)   621
Schedule 17 — Disclosure of tax avoidance schemes: VAT and other indirect taxes
Part 1 — Duties to disclose avoidance schemes etc

Duties of promoter in relation to notifiable proposals or notifiable arrangements

11 (1) A person who is a promoter in relation to a notifiable proposal must, within the relevant period, provide HMRC with prescribed information relating to the proposal.

    (2) In sub-paragraph (1) "the relevant period" is the period of 31 days beginning with the relevant date.

    (3) In sub-paragraph (2) "the relevant date" is the earliest of the following —
        (a) the date on which the promoter first makes a firm approach to another person in relation to the proposal,
        (b) the date on which the promoter makes the proposal available for implementation by any other person, or
        (c) the date on which the promoter first becomes aware of any transaction forming part of notifiable arrangements implementing the proposal.

12 (1) A person who is a promoter in relation to notifiable arrangements must, within the relevant period after the date on which the person first becomes aware of any transaction forming part of the arrangements, provide HMRC with prescribed information relating to the arrangements.

    (2) In sub-paragraph (1) "the relevant period" is the period of 31 days beginning with that date.

    (3) The duty under sub-paragraph (1) does not apply if the notifiable arrangements implement a proposal in respect of which notice has been given to HMRC under paragraph 11(1).

13 (1) This paragraph applies where a person complies with paragraph 11(1) in relation to a notifiable proposal for arrangements and another person is —
        (a) also a promoter in relation to the proposal or is a promoter in relation to a notifiable proposal for arrangements which are substantially the same as the proposed arrangements (whether they relate to the same or different parties), or
        (b) a promoter in relation to notifiable arrangements implementing the proposal or notifiable arrangements which are substantially the same as notifiable arrangements implementing the proposal (whether they relate to the same or different parties).

    (2) Any duty of the other person under paragraph 11(1) or 12(1) in relation to the notifiable proposal or notifiable arrangements is discharged if —
        (a) the person who complied with paragraph 11(1) has notified the identity and address of the other person to HMRC or the other person holds the reference number allocated to the proposed notifiable arrangements under paragraph 22(1), and
        (b) the other person holds the information provided to HMRC in compliance with paragraph 11(1).

14 (1) This paragraph applies where a person complies with paragraph 12(1) in relation to notifiable arrangements and another person is —
        (a) a promoter in relation to a notifiable proposal for arrangements which are substantially the same as the notifiable arrangements (whether they relate to the same or different parties), or

622

Finance (No. 2) Act 2017 (c. 32)
Schedule 17 — Disclosure of tax avoidance schemes: VAT and other indirect taxes
Part 1 — Duties to disclose avoidance schemes etc

(b)   also a promoter in relation to the notifiable arrangements or notifiable arrangements which are substantially the same (whether they relate to the same or different parties).

(2)   Any duty of the other person under paragraph 11(1) or 12(1) in relation to the notifiable proposal or notifiable arrangements is discharged if—

(a)   the person who complied with paragraph 12(1) has notified the identity and address of the other person to HMRC or the other person holds the reference number allocated to the notifiable arrangements under paragraph 22(1), and

(b)   the other person holds the information provided to HMRC in compliance with paragraph 12(1).

15   Where a person is a promoter in relation to two or more notifiable proposals or sets of notifiable arrangements which are substantially the same (whether they relate to the same parties or different parties) the person need not provide information under paragraph 11(1) or 12(1) if the person has already provided information under either of those paragraphs in relation to any of the other proposals or arrangements.

Duty of promoter: supplemental information

16   (1)   This paragraph applies where—

(a)   a promoter (P) has provided information in purported compliance with paragraph 11(1) or 12(1), but

(b)   HMRC believe that P has not provided all the prescribed information.

(2)   HMRC may apply to the tribunal for an order requiring P to provide specified information about, or documents relating to, the notifiable proposal or arrangements.

(3)   The tribunal may make an order under sub-paragraph (2) in respect of information or documents only if satisfied that HMRC have reasonable grounds for suspecting that the information or documents—

(a)   form part of the prescribed information, or

(b)   will support or explain the prescribed information.

(4)   A requirement by virtue of sub-paragraph (2) is to be treated as part of P's duty under paragraph 11(1) or 12(1).

(5)   In so far as P's duty under sub-paragraph (1) of paragraph 11 or 12 arises out of an order made by virtue of sub-paragraph (2) above the relevant period for the purposes of that sub-paragraph (1) is—

(a)   the period of 11 days beginning with the date of the order, or

(b)   such longer period as HMRC may direct.

Duty of person dealing with promoter outside United Kingdom

17   (1)   This paragraph applies where a person enters into any transaction forming part of any notifiable arrangements in relation to which—

(a)   a promoter is resident outside the United Kingdom, and

(b)   no promoter is resident in the United Kingdom.

(2)   The person must, within the relevant period, provide HMRC with prescribed information relating to the arrangements.

Finance (No. 2) Act 2017 (c. 32)
623
Schedule 17 – Disclosure of tax avoidance schemes: VAT and other indirect taxes
Part 1 – Duties to disclose avoidance schemes etc

(3) In sub-paragraph (2) "the relevant period" is the period of 6 days beginning with the day on which the person enters into the first transaction forming part of the arrangements.

(4) Compliance with paragraph 11(1) or 12(1) by any promoter in relation to the arrangements discharges the person's duty under sub-paragraph (1).

Duty of parties to notifiable arrangements not involving promoter

18 (1) This paragraph applies to any person who enters into any transaction forming part of notifiable arrangements as respects which neither that person nor any other person in the United Kingdom is liable to comply with paragraph 11(1), 12(1) or 17(2).

(2) The person must at the prescribed time provide HMRC with prescribed information relating to the arrangements.

Duty to provide further information requested by HMRC

19 (1) This paragraph applies where—
   (a) a person has provided the prescribed information about notifiable proposals or arrangements in compliance with paragraph 11(1), 12(1), 17(2) or 18(2), or
   (b) a person has provided information in purported compliance with paragraph 17(2) or 18(2) but HMRC believe that the person has not provided all the prescribed information.

(2) HMRC may require the person to provide—
   (a) further specified information about the notifiable proposals or arrangements (in addition to the prescribed information under paragraph 11(1), 12(1), 17(2) or 18(2));
   (b) documents relating to the notifiable proposals or arrangements.

(3) Where HMRC impose a requirement on a person under this paragraph, the person must comply with the requirement within—
   (a) the period of 10 working days beginning with the day on which HMRC imposed the requirement, or
   (b) such longer period as HMRC may direct.

20 (1) This paragraph applies where HMRC—
   (a) have required a person to provide information or documents under paragraph 19, but
   (b) believe that the person has failed to provide the information or documents required.

(2) HMRC may apply to the tribunal for an order requiring the person to provide the information or documents required.

(3) The tribunal may make an order imposing such a requirement only if satisfied that HMRC have reasonable grounds for suspecting that the information or documents will assist HMRC in considering the notifiable proposals or arrangements.

(4) Where the tribunal makes an order imposing such a requirement, the person must comply with the requirement within—

624

Finance (No. 2) Act 2017 (c. 32)
Schedule 17 — Disclosure of tax avoidance schemes: VAT and other indirect taxes
Part 1 — Duties to disclose avoidance schemes etc

(a) the period of 10 working days beginning with the day on which the tribunal made the order, or

(b) such longer period as HMRC may direct.

Duty of promoters to provide updated information

21 (1) This paragraph applies where—

(a) information has been provided under paragraph 11(1), or 12(1) about any notifiable arrangements, or proposed notifiable arrangements, to which a reference number is allocated under paragraph 22, and

(b) after the provision of the information, there is a change in relation to the arrangements of a kind mentioned in sub-paragraph (2).

(2) The changes referred to in sub-paragraph (1)(b) are—

(a) a change in the name by which the notifiable arrangements, or proposed notifiable arrangements, are known;

(b) a change in the name or address of any person who is a promoter in relation to the arrangements or, in the case of proposed arrangements, the notifiable proposal.

(3) A person who is a promoter in relation to the notifiable arrangements or, in the case of proposed notifiable arrangements, the notifiable proposal must inform HMRC of the change mentioned in sub-paragraph (1)(b) within 30 days after it is made.

(4) Sub-paragraphs (5) and (6) apply for the purposes of sub-paragraph (3) where there is more than one person who is a promoter in relation to the notifiable arrangements or proposal.

(5) If the change in question is a change in the name or address of a person who is a promoter in relation to the notifiable arrangements or proposal, it is the duty of that person to comply with sub-paragraph (3).

(6) If a person provides information in compliance with sub-paragraph (3), the duty imposed by that sub-paragraph on any other person, so far as relating to the provision of that information, is discharged.

Arrangements to be given reference number

22 (1) Where a person (P) complies or purports to comply with paragraph 11(1), 12(1), 17(2) or 18(2) in relation to any notifiable proposal or notifiable arrangements, HMRC may within 90 days allocate a reference number to the notifiable arrangements or, in the case of a notifiable proposal, to the proposed notifiable arrangements.

(2) If HMRC do so it must notify the number to P and (where the person is one who has complied or purported to comply with paragraph 11(1) or 12(1)), to any other person—

(a) who is a promoter in relation to—

(i) the notifiable proposal (or arrangements implementing the notifiable proposal), or

(ii) the notifiable arrangements (or proposal implemented by the notifiable arrangements), and

(b) whose identity and address has been notified to HMRC by P.

Finance (No. 2) Act 2017 (c. 32) 625
Schedule 17 — Disclosure of tax avoidance schemes: VAT and other indirect taxes
Part 1 — Duties to disclose avoidance schemes etc

(3) The allocation of a reference number to any notifiable arrangements (or proposed notifiable arrangements) is not to be regarded as constituting any indication by HMRC that the arrangements would or could as a matter of law result in the obtaining by any person of a tax advantage.

(4) In this Part of this Schedule "reference number", in relation to any notifiable arrangements, means the reference number allocated under this paragraph.

Duty of promoter to notify client of number

23 (1)   This paragraph applies where a person who is a promoter in relation to notifiable arrangements is providing (or has provided) services to any person ("the client") in connection with the arrangements.

(2) The promoter must, within 30 days after the relevant date, provide the client with prescribed information relating to any reference number (or, if more than one, any one reference number) that has been notified to the promoter (whether by HMRC or any other person) in relation to —
   (a)   the notifiable arrangements, or
   (b)   any arrangements substantially the same as the notifiable arrangements (whether involving the same or different parties).

(3)   In sub-paragraph (2) "the relevant date" means the later of —
   (a)   the date on which the promoter becomes aware of any transaction which forms part of the notifiable arrangements, and
   (b)   the date on which the reference number is notified to the promoter.

(4) But where the conditions in sub-paragraph (5) are met the duty imposed on the promoter under sub-paragraph (2) to provide the client with information in relation to notifiable arrangements is discharged

(5) Those conditions are —
   (a)   that the promoter is also a promoter in relation to a notifiable proposal and provides services to the client in connection with them both,
   (b)   the notifiable proposal and the notifiable arrangements are substantially the same, and
   (c)   the promoter has provided to the client, in a form and manner specified by HMRC, prescribed information relating to the reference number that has been notified to the promoter in relation to the proposed notifiable arrangements.

(6) HMRC may give notice that, in relation to notifiable arrangements specified in the notice, promoters are not under the duty under sub-paragraph (2) after the date specified in the notice.

Duty of client to notify parties of number

24 (1) In this paragraph "client" means a person to whom a person who is a promoter in relation to notifiable arrangements or a notifiable proposal is providing (or has provided) services in connection with the arrangements or proposal.

(2) Sub-paragraph (3) applies where the client receives prescribed information relating to the reference number allocated to the arrangements or proposed arrangements,

626

Finance (No. 2) Act 2017 (c. 32)
Schedule 17 — Disclosure of tax avoidance schemes: VAT and other indirect taxes
Part 1 — Duties to disclose avoidance schemes etc

(3) The client must, within the relevant period, provide prescribed information relating to the reference number to any other person—

    (a) who the client might reasonably be expected to know is or is likely to be a party to the arrangements or proposed arrangements, and

    (b) who might reasonably be expected to gain a tax advantage in relation to any relevant tax by reason of the arrangements or proposed arrangements.

(4) In sub-paragraph (3) "the relevant period" is the period of 30 days beginning with the later of—

    (a) the day on which the client first becomes aware of any transaction forming part of the notifiable arrangements or proposed notifiable arrangements, and

    (b) the day on which the prescribed information is notified to the client by the promoter under paragraph 23.

(5) HMRC may give notice that, in relation to notifiable arrangements or a notifiable proposal specified in the notice, persons are not under the duty under sub-paragraph (3) after the date specified in the notice.

(6) The duty under sub-paragraph (3) does not apply in prescribed circumstances.

(7) For the purposes of this paragraph a tax is a "relevant tax", in relation to arrangements or arrangements proposed in a proposal of any description, if it is prescribed in relation to arrangements or proposals of that description by regulations under paragraph 3(1).

Duty of client to provide information to promoter

25 (1) This paragraph applies where a person who is a promoter in relation to notifiable arrangements has provided a person ("the client") with the information prescribed under paragraph 23(2).

(2) The client must, within the relevant period, provide the promoter with prescribed information relating to the client.

(3) In sub-paragraph (2) "the relevant period" is the period of 11 days beginning with the later of—

    (a) the date the client receives the reference number for the arrangements, and

    (b) the date the client first enters into a transaction which forms part of the arrangements.

(4) The duty under sub-paragraph (2) is subject to any exceptions that may be prescribed.

Duty of parties to notifiable arrangements to notify HMRC of number, etc

26 (1) Any person (P) who is a party to any notifiable arrangements must provide HMRC with prescribed information relating to—

    (a) any reference number notified to P under paragraph 23 or 24, and

    (b) the time when P obtains or expects to obtain by virtue of the arrangements a tax advantage in relation to any relevant tax.

Finance (No. 2) Act 2017 (c. 32)
Schedule 17 — Disclosure of tax avoidance schemes: VAT and other indirect taxes
Part 1 — Duties to disclose avoidance schemes etc

627

(2) For the purposes of sub-paragraph (1) a tax is a "relevant tax" in relation to any notifiable arrangements if it is prescribed in relation to arrangements of that description by regulations under paragraph 3(1).

(3) Regulations made by the Commissioners may —
    (a) in prescribed cases, require the information prescribed under sub-paragraph (1) to be given to HMRC—
        (i) in the prescribed manner,
        (ii) in the prescribed form,
        (iii) at the prescribed time, and
    (b) in prescribed cases, require the information prescribed under sub-paragraph (1) and such other information as is prescribed to be provided separately to HMRC at the prescribed time or times.

(4) In sub-paragraph (3) "prescribed" includes being prescribed in a document made under a power conferred by regulations made by the Commissioners.

(5) HMRC may give notice that, in relation to notifiable arrangements specified in the notice, persons are not under the duty under sub-paragraph (1) after the date specified in the notice.

(6) The duty under sub-paragraph (1) does not apply in prescribed circumstances.

Duty of promoter to provide details of clients

27 (1) This paragraph applies where a person who is a promoter in relation to notifiable arrangements is providing (or has provided) services to any person ("the client") in connection with the arrangements and either—
    (a) the promoter is subject to the reference number information requirement, or
    (b) the promoter has failed to comply with paragraph 11(1) or 12(1) in relation to the arrangements (or the notifiable proposal for them) but would be subject to the reference number information requirement if a reference number had been allocated to the arrangements.

(2) For the purposes of this paragraph "the reference number information requirement" is the requirement under paragraph 23(2) to provide to the client prescribed information relating to the reference number allocated to the notifiable arrangements.

(3) The promoter must, within the prescribed period after the end of the relevant period, provide HMRC with prescribed information in relation to the client.

(4) In sub-paragraph (3) "the relevant period" means such period (during which the promoter is or would be subject to the reference number information requirement) as is prescribed.

(5) The promoter need not comply with sub-paragraph (3) in relation to any notifiable arrangements at any time after HMRC have given notice under paragraph 23(6) in relation to the arrangements.

Enquiry following disclosure of client details

28 (1) This paragraph applies where—

628

Finance (No. 2) Act 2017 (c. 32)
Schedule 17 — Disclosure of tax avoidance schemes: VAT and other indirect taxes
Part 1 — Duties to disclose avoidance schemes etc

(a) a person who is a promoter in relation to notifiable arrangements has provided HMRC with information in relation to a person ("the client") under paragraph 27(3) (duty to provide client details), and

(b) HMRC suspect that a person other than the client is or is likely to be a party to the arrangements.

(2) HMRC may by written notice require the promoter to provide prescribed information in relation to any person other than the client who the promoter might reasonably be expected to know is or is likely to be a party to the arrangements.

(3) The promoter must comply with a requirement under or by virtue of sub-paragraph (2) within—

(a) the relevant period, or

(b) such longer period as HMRC may direct.

(4) In sub-paragraph (3) "the relevant period" is the period of 11 days beginning with the day on which the promoter receives the notice under sub-paragraph (2).

Pre-disclosure enquiry

29 (1) Where HMRC suspect that a person (P) is the promoter or introducer of a proposal, or the promoter of arrangements, which may be notifiable, they may by written notice require P to state—

(a) whether in P's opinion the proposal or arrangements are notifiable by P, and

(b) if not, the reasons for P's opinion.

(2) The notice must specify the proposal or arrangements to which it relates.

(3) For the purposes of sub-paragraph (1)(b)—

(a) it is not sufficient to refer to the fact that a lawyer or other professional has given an opinion,

(b) the reasons must show, by reference to this Part of this Schedule and regulations under it, why P thinks the proposal or arrangements are not notifiable by P, and

(c) in particular, if P asserts that the arrangements do not fall within any description prescribed under paragraph 3(1)(a), the reasons must provide sufficient information to enable HMRC to confirm the assertion.

(4) P must comply with a requirement under or by virtue of sub-paragraph (1) within—

(a) the relevant period, or

(b) such longer period as HMRC may direct.

(5) In sub-paragraph (4) "the relevant period" is the period of 11 days beginning with the day on which the notice under sub-paragraph (1) is issued.

Reasons for non-disclosure: supporting information

30 (1) Where HMRC receive from a person (P) a statement of reasons why a proposal or arrangements are not notifiable by P, HMRC may apply to the tribunal for an order requiring P to provide specified information or documents in support of the reasons.

Finance (No. 2) Act 2017 (c. 32)   629
Schedule 17 — Disclosure of tax avoidance schemes: VAT and other indirect taxes
Part 1 — Duties to disclose avoidance schemes etc

(2) P must comply with a requirement under or by virtue of sub-paragraph (1) within—

    (a)   the relevant period, or

    (b)   such longer period as HMRC may direct.

(3) In sub-paragraph (2) "the relevant period" is the period of 15 days beginning with the day on which the order concerned is made.

(4) The power under sub-paragraph (1)—

    (a)   may be exercised more than once, and

    (b)   applies whether or not the statement of reasons was received under paragraph 29(1)(b).

Provision of information to HMRC by introducers

31   (1) This paragraph applies where HMRC suspect—

    (a)   that a person (P) is an introducer in relation to a proposal, and

    (b)   that the proposal may be notifiable.

(2) HMRC may by written notice require P to provide HMRC with one or both of the following—

    (a)   prescribed information in relation to each person who has provided P with any information relating to the proposal,

    (b)   prescribed information in relation to each person with whom P has made a marketing contact in relation to the proposal.

(3) A notice must specify the proposal to which it relates.

(4) P must comply with a requirement under or sub-paragraph(2) within—

    (a)   the relevant period, or

    (b)   such longer period as HMRC may direct.

(5) In sub-paragraph (4) "the relevant period" is the period of 11 days beginning with the day on which the notice under sub-paragraph (2) is given.

Legal professional privilege

32   (1) Nothing in this Part of this Schedule requires any person to disclose to HMRC any privileged information.

(2) In this Part of this Schedule "privileged information" means information with respect to which a claim to legal professional privilege, or, in Scotland, to confidentiality of communications, could be maintained in legal proceedings.

Information

33   (1) This paragraph applies where a person is required to provide information under paragraph 23(2) or 24(3).

(2) HMRC may specify additional information which must be provided by that person to the recipients under paragraph 23(2) or 24(3) at the same time as the information referred to in sub-paragraph (1).

(3) HMRC may specify the form and manner in which the additional information is to be provided.

630

Finance (No. 2) Act 2017 (c. 32)
Schedule 17 — Disclosure of tax avoidance schemes: VAT and other indirect taxes
Part 1 — Duties to disclose avoidance schemes etc

(4) For the purposes of this paragraph "additional information" means information supplied by HMRC which relates to notifiable proposals or notifiable arrangements in general.

34 (1) HMRC may specify the form and manner in which information required to be provided by or under any of the information provisions must be provided if the provision is to be complied with.

(2) The "information provisions" are paragraphs 11(1), 12(1), 17(2), 18(2), 19(2), 21(3), 23(2), 24(3), 26(1) and (3), 27(3), 28(2), 29(1), 31(2) and 33(2).

35 No duty of confidentiality or other restriction on disclosure (however imposed) prevents the voluntary disclosure by any person to HMRC of information or documents which the person has reasonable grounds for suspecting will assist HMRC in determining whether there has been a breach of any requirement imposed by or under this Part of this Schedule.

36 (1) HMRC may publish information about—

    (a) any notifiable arrangements, or proposed notifiable arrangements, to which a reference number is allocated under paragraph 22;

    (b) any person who is a promoter in relation to the notifiable arrangements or, in the case of proposed notifiable arrangements, the notifiable proposal.

(2) The information that may be published is (subject to sub-paragraph (4))—

    (a) any information relating to arrangements within sub-paragraph (1)(a), or a person within sub-paragraph (1)(b), that is prescribed information for the purposes of paragraph 11, 12, 17 or 18;

    (b) any ruling of a court or tribunal relating to any such arrangements or person (in that person's capacity as a promoter in relation to a notifiable proposal or arrangements);

    (c) the number of persons in any period who enter into transactions forming part of notifiable arrangements within sub-paragraph (1)(a);

    (d) any other information that HMRC considers it appropriate to publish for the purpose of identifying arrangements within sub-paragraph (1)(a) or a person within sub-paragraph (1)(b).

(3) The information may be published in any manner that HMRC considers appropriate.

(4) No information may be published under this paragraph that identifies a person who enters into a transaction forming part of notifiable arrangements within sub-paragraph (1)(a).

(5) But where a person who is a promoter within sub-paragraph (1)(b) is also a person mentioned in sub-paragraph (4), nothing in sub-paragraph (4) is to be taken as preventing the publication under this paragraph of information so far as relating to the person's activities as a promoter.

(6) Before publishing any information under this paragraph that identifies a person as a promoter within sub-paragraph (1)(b), HMRC must—

    (a) inform the person that they are considering doing so, and

    (b) give the person reasonable opportunity to make representations about whether it should be published.

37 (1) This paragraph applies if—

Finance (No. 2) Act 2017 (c. 32)
Schedule 17 — Disclosure of tax avoidance schemes: VAT and other indirect taxes
Part 1 — Duties to disclose avoidance schemes etc

631

(a) information about notifiable arrangements, or proposed notifiable arrangements, is published under paragraph 36,

(b) at any time after the information is published, a ruling of a court or tribunal is made in relation to tax arrangements, and

(c) HMRC is of the opinion that the ruling is relevant to the arrangements mentioned in paragraph (a)

(2) A ruling is "relevant" to the arrangements if—

(a) the principles laid down, or reasoning given, in the ruling would, if applied to the arrangements, allow the purported advantage arising from the arrangements in relation to tax, and

(b) the ruling is final.

(3) HMRC must publish information about the ruling.

(4) The information must be published in the same manner as HMRC published the information mentioned in sub-paragraph (1)(a) (and may also be published in any other manner that HMRC considers appropriate).

(5) A ruling is "final" if it is—

(a) a ruling of the Supreme Court, or

(b) a ruling of any other court or tribunal in circumstances where—

(i) no appeal may be made against the ruling,

(ii) if an appeal may be made against the ruling with permission, the time limit for applications has expired and either no application has been made or permission has been refused,

(iii) if such permission to appeal against the ruling has been granted or is not required, no appeal has been made within the time limit for appeals, or

(iv) if an appeal was made, it was abandoned or otherwise disposed of before it was determined by the court or tribunal to which it was addressed.

(6) Where a ruling is final by virtue of sub-paragraph (ii), (iii) or (iv) of sub-paragraph (5)(b), the ruling is to be treated as made at the time when the sub-paragraph in question is first satisfied.

(7) In this paragraph "tax arrangements" means arrangements in respect of which it would be reasonable to conclude (having regard to all the circumstances) that the main purpose, or one of the main purposes, was the obtaining of a tax advantage.

Power to vary certain relevant periods

38   The Commissioners may by regulations amend this Part of this Schedule with a view to altering the definition of "the relevant period" for the purposes of—

paragraph 5(6)
paragraph 11(1)
paragraph 12(1)
paragraph 16(5)
paragraph 17(2)
paragraph 24(3)
paragraph 25(2)

632

Finance (No. 2) Act 2017 (c. 32)
Schedule 17 — Disclosure of tax avoidance schemes: VAT and other indirect taxes
Part 1 — Duties to disclose avoidance schemes etc

paragraph 27(3)
paragraph 28(3)
paragraph 29(4)
paragraph 30(2))
paragraph 31(4).

PART 2

PENALTIES

Penalty for failure to comply with duties under Part 1 (apart from paragraph 26)

39 (1) A person who fails to comply with any of the provisions of Part 1 of this Schedule mentioned in sub-paragraph (2) is liable —

    (a) to a penalty not exceeding —

        (i) in the case of a failure to comply with paragraph 11(1), 12(1), 17(2), 18(2) or 19, £600 for each day during the initial period for which the failure continues (but see also paragraphs 40(4) and 41), and

        (ii) in any other case, £5,000, and

    (b) if the failure continues after a penalty is imposed under paragraph (a), to a further penalty or penalties not exceeding £600 for each day on which the failure continues after the day on which the penalty under paragraph (a) was imposed (but excluding any day for which a penalty under this paragraph has already been imposed).

(2) Those provisions are —

    (a) paragraph 11(1) (duty of promoter in relation to notifiable proposal),

    (b) paragraph 12(1) (duty of promoter in relation to notifiable arrangements),

    (c) paragraph 17(2) (duty of person dealing with promoter outside United Kingdom),

    (d) paragraph 18(2) (duty of parties to notifiable arrangements not involving promoter),

    (e) paragraph 19 (duty to provide further information requested by HMRC),

    (f) paragraph 21 (duty of promoters to provide updated information),

    (g) paragraph 23(2) (duty of promoter to notify client of reference number),

    (h) paragraph 24(3) (duty of client to notify parties of reference number),

    (i) paragraph 25(2) (duty of client to provide information to promoter),

    (j) paragraph 27(3) (duty of promoter to provide details of clients),

    (k) paragraph 28(3) (enquiry following disclosure of client details),

    (l) paragraphs 29(4) and 30(2) (duty of promoter to respond to inquiry)

    (m) paragraph 31(4) (duty of introducer to give details of persons who have provided information or have been provided with information, and

    (n) paragraph 33 (duty to provide additional information).

(3) In this paragraph "the initial period" means the period —

    (a) beginning with the relevant day, and

(b)   ending with the earlier of the day on which the penalty under sub-paragraph (1)(a)(i) is determined and the last day before the failure ceases.

(4)   For the purposes of sub-paragraph (3)(a) "the relevant day" is the day specified in relation to the failure in the following table—

Failure	*Relevant day*
A failure to comply with paragraph 11(1) or 12(1) in so far as it applies by virtue of an order under paragraph 5	The first day after the end of the relevant period described in paragraph 5(6)
A failure to comply with paragraph 11(1) or 12(1) in so far as it applies by virtue of an order under paragraph 16(2)	The first day after the end of the relevant period (whether that is the period described in sub-paragraph 16(5)(a) or that period as extended by a direction under paragraph 16(5)(b))
Any other failure to comply with sub-paragraph (1) of paragraph 11	The first day after the end of the relevant period described in paragraph 11(2)
Any other failure to comply with sub-paragraph (1) of paragraph 12	The first day after the end of the relevant period described in paragraph 12(2)
A failure to comply with paragraph 17(2)	The first day after the end of the relevant period described in paragraph 17(3)
A failure to comply with paragraph 18(2)	The first day after the latest time by which paragraph 18(2) should have been complied with in the case concerned
A failure to comply with paragraph 19	The first day after the end of the period within which the person must comply with paragraph 19

40   (1)   In the case of a failure to comply with paragraph 11(1), 12(1), 17(2), 18(2) or 19, the amount of the penalty under paragraph 39(1)(a)(i) is to be arrived at after taking account of all relevant considerations.

(2)   Those considerations include the desirability of the penalty being set at a level which appears appropriate for deterring the person, or other persons, from similar failures to comply on future occasions having regard (in particular)—

(a)   in the case of a penalty for a promoter's failure to comply with paragraph 11(1), 12(1) or 19, to the amount of any fees received, or likely to have been received, by the promoter in connection with the notifiable proposal (or arrangements implementing the notifiable proposal), or with the notifiable arrangements, and

634

Finance (No. 2) Act 2017 (c. 32)
Schedule 17 — Disclosure of tax avoidance schemes: VAT and other indirect taxes
Part 2 — Penalties

(b)   in the case of a penalty for a relevant person's failure to comply with paragraph 17(2), 18(2) or 19, to the amount of any advantage gained, or sought to be gained, by the person in relation to any tax prescribed under paragraph 3(1)(b) in relation to the notifiable arrangements

(3)   In sub-paragraph (2)(b) "relevant person" means a person who enters into any transaction forming part of notifiable arrangements.

(4)   If the maximum penalty under paragraph 39(1)(a)(i) appears inappropriately low after taking account of all relevant considerations, the penalty is to be of such amount not exceeding £1 million as appears appropriate having regard to those considerations.

41   (1)   This paragraph applies where a failure to comply with a provision mentioned in paragraph 39(2) concerns a proposal or arrangements in respect of which an order has been made under paragraph 4 or 5.

(2)   The amounts specified in paragraph 39(1)(a)(i) and (b) are increased to £5,000 in relation to days falling after the end of the period of 11 days beginning with the day on which the order is made.

42   (1)   The Treasury may by regulations vary—
   (a)   any of the sums for the time being specified in paragraph 39(1);
   (b)   the sum for the time being specified in paragraph 40(4);
   (c)   the period for the time being specified in paragraph 41(2);
   (d)   the sum for the time being specified in paragraph 41(2).

(2)   Regulations under this paragraph may include incidental or transitional provision.

43   Where it appears to an officer of Revenue and Customs that—
   (a)   a penalty under paragraph 39(1)(a) has been imposed in a case where the maximum penalty is set by paragraph 39(1)(a)(i), and
   (b)   the maximum penalty was calculated on the basis that the initial period began with a day later than that which the officer considers to be the relevant day,
an officer of Revenue and Customs may commence proceedings for a re-determination of the penalty.

Penalty for failure to comply with duties under paragraph 26

44   (1)   A person who fails to comply with—
   (a)   paragraph 26(1), or
   (b)   regulations under paragraph 26(3),
is liable to a penalty not exceeding the relevant sum.

(2)   The relevant sum is £5,000 in respect of each scheme to which the failure relates unless the person falls within sub-paragraph (3) or (4).

(3)   If the person has previously failed to comply with paragraph 26(1) or regulations under paragraph 26(3) on one (and only one) occasion during the period of 36 months ending with the date on which the current failure began, the relevant sum is £7,500 in respect of each scheme to which the current failure relates (whether or not the same as any scheme to which the previous failure relates).

Finance (No. 2) Act 2017 (c. 32)
Schedule 17 — Disclosure of tax avoidance schemes: VAT and other indirect taxes
Part 2 — Penalties

635

(4) If the person has previously failed to comply with paragraph 26(1) or regulations under paragraph 26(3) on two or more occasions during the period of 36 months ending with the date on which the current failure began, the relevant sum is £10,000 in respect of each scheme to which the current failure relates (whether or not the same as any scheme to which any of the previous failures relates).

(5) In this paragraph "scheme" means any notifiable arrangements.

Penalty proceedings before First-tier tribunal

45 (1) An authorised officer may commence proceedings before the First-tier Tribunal for any penalty under paragraph 39(1)(a).

(2) In sub-paragraph (1) "authorised officer" means an officer of Revenue and Customs authorised by HMRC for the purposes of this paragraph.

(3) Proceedings for a penalty may not be commenced more than 12 months after evidence of facts sufficient to justify the bringing of proceedings comes to the knowledge of HMRC.

(4) If the First-tier Tribunal decide that the penalty is payable by the person —
   (a) the penalty is for all purposes to be treated as if it were tax charged in an assessment and due and payable,
   (b) the person may appeal to the Upper Tribunal against the decision that the penalty is payable, and
   (c) the person may appeal to the Upper Tribunal against the decision as to the amount of the penalty.

(5) On an appeal under sub-paragraph (4)(b) the Upper Tribunal may, if it appears that no penalty has been incurred, cancel the decision of the First-tier Tribunal.

(6) On an appeal under sub-paragraph (4)(c) the Upper Tribunal may —
   (a) affirm the decision of the First-tier Tribunal as to the amount of the penalty, or
   (b) substitute for that decision a decision that the First-tier Tribunal had power to make.

Assessment of penalties under paragraph 39(1)(b) or 44

46 (1) Where a person is liable to a penalty under paragraph 39(1)(b) or 44 an authorised officer may assess the amount due by way of a penalty.

(2) An assessment may not be made more than 12 months after evidence of facts sufficient to justify the making of the assessment first comes to the knowledge of HMRC.

(3) A notice of an assessment under sub-paragraph (1) stating —
   (a) the date on which it is issued, and
   (b) the time within which an appeal against the assessment may be made,
must be served on the person liable to the penalty.

(4) After the notice has been served the assessment may not be altered except in accordance with this paragraph or on appeal.

636

Finance (No. 2) Act 2017 (c. 32)
Schedule 17 — Disclosure of tax avoidance schemes: VAT and other indirect taxes
Part 2 — Penalties

(5) If it is discovered by an authorised officer that the amount of a penalty assessed under this paragraph is or has become insufficient the officer may make an assessment in a further amount so that the penalty is set at the amount which, in the officer's opinion, is correct or appropriate.

(6) A penalty imposed by a decision under this paragraph—

    (a) is due and payable at the end of the period of 30 days beginning with the date of the issue of the notice of the decision, and

    (b) is to be treated for all purposes as if it were tax charged in an assessment and due and payable.

(7) In this paragraph "authorised officer" means an officer of Revenue and Customs authorised by HMRC for the purposes of this paragraph.

47 (1) Where a person (P) is served with notice of an assessment under paragraph 46—

    (a) P may appeal against the decision that a penalty is payable by P, and

    (b) P may appeal against the decision as to the amount of the penalty.

(2) An appeal under sub-paragraph (1) is to be treated for procedural purposes in the same way as an appeal against an assessment to the relevant tax (including by the application of any provision about the bringing of an appeal by notice to HMRC, about HMRC review of the decision or about determination of the appeal by the First-tier Tribunal or Upper Tribunal)

(3) Sub-paragraph (2) does not apply—

    (a) so as to require P to pay a penalty before an appeal under sub-paragraph (1) is determined, or

    (b) in respect of any other matter expressly provided for by this Schedule.

(4) On an appeal under sub-paragraph (1)(a) the tribunal may affirm or cancel the decision that a penalty is payable by P.

(5) On an appeal under sub-paragraph (1)(b) the tribunal may—

    (a) affirm the decision as to the amount of the penalty, or

    (b) substitute for that decision another decision that the authorised officer had power to make.

(6) In this paragraph "tribunal" means the First-tier Tribunal or Upper Tribunal (as appropriate by virtue of sub-paragraph (2)).

Reasonable excuse

48 (1) Liability to a penalty under this Part of this Schedule does not arise in relation to a particular failure to comply if the person concerned (P) satisfies HMRC or the relevant tribunal (as the case may be) that there is a reasonable excuse for the failure.

(2) For this purpose—

    (a) an insufficiency of funds is not a reasonable excuse, unless attributable to events outside P's control,

    (b) where P relied on any other person to do anything, that cannot be a reasonable excuse unless P took reasonable care to avoid the failure,

      (c)   where P had a reasonable excuse but the excuse has ceased, P is to be treated as continuing to have the excuse if the failure is remedied without unreasonable delay after the excuse ceased, and

      (d)   reliance on advice is to be taken automatically not to be a reasonable excuse if the advice was addressed to, or was given to, a person other than P or takes no account of P's individual circumstances.

49   (1)   The making of an order under paragraph 4 or 5 against P does not of itself mean that P either did or did not have a reasonable excuse for non-compliance before the order was made.

      (2)   Where an order is made under paragraph 4 or 5 then for the purposes of paragraph 48 —

          (a)   the person identified in the order as the promoter of the proposal or arrangements cannot, in respect of any time after the end of the prescribed period mentioned in paragraph 41, rely on doubt as to notifiability as a reasonable excuse for failure to comply with paragraph 11(1) or 12(1), and

          (b)   any delay in compliance with that provision after the end of that period is not capable of being a reasonable excuse unless attributable to something other than doubt as to notifiability.

50   (1)   Where a person fails to comply with —

          (a)   paragraph 17(2) and the promoter for the purposes of paragraph 17 is a monitored promoter, or

          (b)   paragraph 18(2) and the arrangements for the purposes of paragraph 18 are arrangements of a monitored promoter,

      then for the purposes of paragraph 48 legal advice which the person took into account is to be disregarded in determining whether the person had a reasonable excuse, if the advice was given or procured by that monitored promoter.

      (2)   In determining for the purpose of paragraph 48 whether or not a person who is a monitored promoter had a reasonable excuse for a failure to do something, reliance on legal advice is to be taken automatically not to constitute a reasonable excuse if either —

          (a)   the advice was not based on a full and accurate description of the facts, or

          (b)   the conclusions in the advice that the person relied on were unreasonable.

      (3)   In this paragraph "monitored promoter" means a person who is a monitored promoter for the purposes of Part 5 of FA 2014

PART 3

CONSEQUENTIAL AMENDMENTS

VATA 1994

51   In section 77(4A) of VATA 1994 (cases in which the time allowed for assessment is 20 years), in paragraph (d) after "11A" insert "or an obligation under paragraph 17(2) or 18(2) of Schedule 17 to FA 2017".

638

Finance (No. 2) Act 2017 (c. 32)
Schedule 17 — Disclosure of tax avoidance schemes: VAT and other indirect taxes
Part 3 — Consequential amendments

Promoters of tax avoidance schemes

52   Part 5 of FA 2014 (promoters of tax avoidance schemes) is amended as follows.

53   (1) Section 281A (VAT: meaning of "tax advantage") is amended as follows.

     (2) In the heading after "VAT" insert "and other indirect taxes".

     (3) In subsection (1) —
         (a)   in paragraph (a) after "VAT" insert "and other indirect taxes", and
         (b)   in paragraph (b) for the words from "in paragraph 1" to the end substitute "for VAT in paragraph 6, and for other indirect taxes in paragraph 7, of Schedule 17 to FA 2017 (disclosure of tax avoidance schemes: VAT and other indirect taxes)."

     (4) In subsection (3) after "value added tax" (in both places) insert "or other indirect taxes".

     (5) After subsection (3) insert —

         "(4)   In this section "indirect tax" has the same meaning as in Schedule 17 to FA 2017."

54   (1) Schedule 34A (defeated arrangements) is amended as follows.

     (2) In paragraph 2(4) after ""schemes)" insert "or paragraph 22 of Schedule 17 to FA 2017 (disclosure of avoidance schemes: VAT and other indirect taxes).

     (3) In paragraph 14 —
         (a)   in sub-paragraph (1)(a) after "VAT" insert "or other indirect tax", and
         (b)   in sub-paragraphs (1)(a) and (b), (2) and (3) omit "taxable".

     (4) After paragraph 26 insert —

     "Disclosable VAT or other indirect tax arrangements"

         26A (1) For the purposes of this Schedule arrangements are "disclosable VAT or other indirect tax arrangements" at any time if at that time —
             (a)   the arrangements are disclosable Schedule 11A arrangements, or
             (b)   sub-paragraph (2) applies.

             (2) This sub-paragraph applies if a person —
             (a)   has provided information in relation to the arrangements under paragraph 12(1), 17(2) or 18(2) of Schedule 17 to FA 2017, or
             (b)   has failed to comply with any of those provisions in relation to the arrangements.

             (3) But for the purposes of this Schedule arrangements in respect of which HMRC have given notice under paragraph 23(6) of that Schedule (notice that promoters not under duty to notify client of reference number) are not to be regarded as disclosable VAT or other indirect tax arrangements.

Finance (No. 2) Act 2017 (c. 32)
Schedule 17 — Disclosure of tax avoidance schemes: VAT and other indirect taxes
Part 3 — Consequential amendments

639

(4) For the purposes of sub-paragraph (2) a person who would be required to provide information under paragraph 12(1) of that Schedule—

    (a) but for the fact that the arrangements implement a proposal in respect of which notice has been given under paragraph 11(1) of that Schedule, or

    (b) but for paragraph 13, 14 or 15 of that Schedule,

is treated as providing the information at the end of the period referred to in paragraph 12(1)."

(5) In the heading before paragraph 27, after ""disclosable" insert "Schedule 11A".

(6) In paragraph 27—

    (a) for "this Schedule" substitute "paragraph 26A", and

    (b) after ""disclosable" insert "Schedule 11A".

(7) In the heading before paragraph 28 for "and 27" substitute "to 27".

(8) In paragraph 28(1) after "26(1)(a)" insert "26A(2)(a)"

Serial tax avoidance

55 (1) Schedule 18 to FA 2016 (serial tax avoidance) is amended as follows.

(2) In paragraph 4 (meaning of "tax")—

    (a) number the current text as sub-paragraph (1) of that paragraph,

    (b) in that sub-paragraph (1), in paragraph (j) after "VAT" insert" "and indirect taxes", and

    (c) after that sub-paragraph (1) insert—

        "(2) For the purposes of this Schedule "indirect tax" means any of the following—

            insurance premium tax
            general betting duty
            pool betting duty
            remote gaming duty
            machine games duty
            gaming duty
            lottery duty
            bingo duty
            air passenger duty
            hydrocarbon oils duty
            tobacco products duty
            duties on spirits, beer, wine, made-wine and cider
            soft drinks industry levy
            aggregates levy
            landfill tax
            climate change levy
            customs duties.

640

Finance (No. 2) Act 2017 (c. 32)
Schedule 17 — Disclosure of tax avoidance schemes: VAT and other indirect taxes
Part 3 — Consequential amendments

(3) Before paragraph 9 (meaning of "disclosable VAT arrangements") insert—

"8A (1) For the purposes of this Schedule arrangements are "disclosable VAT arrangements" at any time if at that time sub-paragraph (2) or (3) applies.

(2) This sub-paragraph applies if the arrangements are disclosable Schedule 11A VAT arrangements (see paragraph 9).

(3) This paragraph applies if—

   (a)   the arrangements are notifiable arrangements for the purposes of Schedule 17 to FA 2017,

   (b)   the main benefit, or one of the main benefits that might be expected to arise from the arrangements is the obtaining of a tax advantage in relation to VAT (within the meaning of paragraph 6 of that Schedule), and

   (c)   a person—

      (i)   has provided information about the arrangements under paragraph 12(1), 17(2) or 18(2) of that Schedule, or

      (ii) has failed to comply with any of those provisions in relation to the arrangements.

(4) But for the purposes of this Schedule arrangements in respect of which HMRC have given notice under paragraph 23(6) of Schedule 17 (notice that promoters not under duty to notify client of reference number) are not to be regarded as "disclosable VAT arrangements".

(5) For the purposes of sub-paragraph (3)(c) a person who would be required to provide information under paragraph 12(1) of Schedule 17 to FA 2017—

   (a)   but for the fact that the arrangements implement a proposal in respect of which notice has been given under paragraph 11(1) of that Schedule, or

   (b)   but for paragraph 13, 14 or 15 of that Schedule,

   is treated as providing the information at the end of the period referred to in paragraph 12(1)."

(4) In the heading before paragraph 9 after ""Disclosable" insert "Schedule 11A".

(5) In paragraph 9—

   (a)   for "this Schedule" substitute "paragraph 8A", and

   (b)   after ""disclosable" insert "Schedule 11A".

(6) After paragraph 9 insert—

"Disclosable indirect tax arrangements"

"9A (1) For the purposes of this Schedule arrangements are "disclosable indirect tax arrangements" at any time if at that time—

   (a)   the arrangements are notifiable arrangements for the purposes of Schedule 17 to FA 2017,

   (b)   the main benefit, or one of the main benefits that might be expected to arise from the arrangements is the obtaining of

Finance (No. 2) Act 2017 (c. 32)
Schedule 17 – Disclosure of tax avoidance schemes: VAT and other indirect taxes
Part 3 – Consequential amendments

641

a tax advantage in relation to an indirect tax other than VAT (within the meaning of paragraph 7 of that Schedule), and

(c) a person —

(i) has provided information about the arrangements under paragraph 12(1), 17(2) or 18(2) of that Schedule, or

(ii) has failed to comply with any of those provisions in relation to the arrangements.

(2) But for the purposes of this Schedule arrangements in respect of which HMRC have given notice under paragraph 23(6) of Schedule 17 to FA 2016 (notice that promoters not under duty to notify client of reference number) are not to be regarded as "disclosable indirect tax arrangements".

(3) For the purposes of sub-paragraph (1)(c) a person who would be required to provide information under paragraph 12(1) of Schedule 17 —

(a) but for the fact that the arrangements implement a proposal in respect of which notice has been given under paragraph 11(1) of that Schedule, or

(b) but for paragraph 13, 14 or 15 of that Schedule,

is treated as providing the information at the end of the period referred to in paragraph 12(1)."

(7) In the heading before paragraph 10 (meaning of "failure to comply") for "and 9" substitute "to 9A".

(8) In paragraph 10(1) for "or 9(a)" substitute ", 8A(2)(c), 9(a) or 9A(1)(c)".

(9) In paragraph 11(1) (meaning of "relevant defeat") for "E" substitute "F".

(10) After paragraph 16 (condition E) insert —

"Condition F

16A (1) Condition F is that —

(a) the arrangements are indirect tax arrangements,

(b) P has relied on the arrangements (see sub-paragraph (2),

(c) the arrangements have been counteracted, and

(d) the counteraction is final.

(2) For the purpose of sub-paragraph (1) P relies on the arrangements if —

(a) P makes a return, claim, declaration or application for approval on the basis that a relevant tax advantage arises, or

(b) P fails to discharge a relevant obligation ("the disputed obligation") and there is reason to believe that P's failure to discharge that obligation is connected with the arrangements.

(3) For the purposes of sub-paragraph (2) "relevant tax advantage" means a tax advantage which the arrangements might be expected to enable P to obtain.

642

Finance (No. 2) Act 2017 (c. 32)
Schedule 17 — Disclosure of tax avoidance schemes: VAT and other indirect taxes
Part 3 — Consequential amendments

(4) For the purposes of sub-paragraph (2) an obligation is a relevant obligation if the arrangements might be expected to have the result that the obligation does not arise.

(5) For the purposes of this paragraph the arrangements are "counteracted" if —

    (a) adjustments, other than taxpayer emendations, are made in respect of P's tax position —

        (i) on the basis that the whole or part of the relevant tax advantage mentioned in sub-paragraph (2)(a) does not arise, or

        (ii) on the basis that the disputed obligation does (or did) arise, or

    (b) an assessment to tax is made, or any other action is taken by HMRC, on the basis mentioned in paragraph (a)(i) or (ii) (otherwise than by way of an adjustment).

(6) For the purposes of this paragraph a "counteraction" is final when the adjustments, assessment or action in question, and any amounts arising from the adjustments, assessment or action, can no longer be varied, on appeal or otherwise.

(7) For the purposes of sub-paragraph (1) the time at which it falls to be determined whether or not the arrangements are disclosable indirect tax arrangements is when the counteraction becomes final.

(8) The following are "taxpayer emendations" for the purposes of sub-paragraph (5) —

    (a) an adjustment made by P at a time when P had no reason to believe that HMRC had begun or were about to begin enquiries into P's affairs in relation to the tax in question;

    (b) an adjustment made by HMRC with respect to P's tax position (whether by way of an assessment or otherwise) as a result of a disclosure by P which meets the conditions in sub-paragraph (9).

(9) The conditions are that the disclosure —

    (a) is a full and explicit disclosure of an inaccuracy in a return or other document or of a failure to comply with an obligation, and

    (b) was made at a time when P had no reason to believe that HMRC were about to begin enquiries into P's affairs in relation to the tax in question."

(11) In paragraph 17 (annual information notices) —

    (a) in sub-paragraph (3)(a) for "or election," insert "election, declaration or application for approval,",

    (b) in sub-paragraphs (3)(b), (4) and (5)(a) for "DOTAS arrangements or VAT" substitute "disclosable",

    (c) in sub-paragraph (5) for "or election" insert "election, declaration or application for approval", and

Finance (No. 2) Act 2017 (c. 32)
Schedule 17 — Disclosure of tax avoidance schemes: VAT and other indirect taxes
Part 3 — Consequential amendments

643

    (d)   after sub-paragraph (11) insert —

> "(12) In this paragraph "disclosable arrangements" means any of the following —
>> (a)   DOTAS arrangements,
>> (b)   disclosable VAT arrangements, and
>> (c)   disclosable indirect tax arrangements.

(12) In the heading before paragraph 28 (exclusion of VAT from Part 4 of Schedule) after "VAT" insert "and indirect taxes".

(13) In paragraph 28 after "VAT" insert "or any other indirect tax".

(14) In paragraph 32 (value of counteracted advantage: basic rule for taxes other than VAT) —

    (a)   in sub-paragraph (1) for "or C" substitute "C or F" and after paragraph (c) insert ";

>> (d)   in the case of a relevant defeat incurred by virtue of Condition F, the additional amount due or payable in respect of tax as a result of the counteraction mentioned in paragraph 16A(1)(d).", and

    (b)   in sub-paragraph (2)(b) for "or (c)" substitute "(c) or (d)".

(15) In paragraph 35 (meaning of "the counteracted advantage" in paragraphs 33 and 34) in sub-paragraph (1) after paragraph (c) insert ";

> "(d)   in relation to a relevant defeat incurred by virtue of Condition F, means any tax advantage in respect of which the counteraction mentioned in paragraph 16A(1)(c) is made."

(16) In paragraph 43 (paragraph 42: meaning of "the relevant failure") after sub-paragraph (7) insert —

> "(8) In relation to a relevant defeat incurred by virtue of Condition F, "the relevant failure" means the failures or inaccuracies as a result of which the adjustments, assessments, or other actions mentioned in paragraph 16A(5) are required."

(17) In paragraph 55 (time of "use" of defeated arrangements) after sub-paragraph (8) insert —

> "(8A) If the person incurs the relevant defeat by virtue of Condition F, the person is treated as having "used" the arrangements on the following dates —
>> (a)   the filing date of any return made by the person on the basis mentioned in paragraph 16A(2)(a);
>> (b)   the date on which the person makes any claim, declaration or application for approval;
>> (c)   the date of any failure by the person to comply with a relevant obligation (as defined in paragraph 16A(4))."

(18) In paragraph 58(1) (interpretation) —
    (a)   after the definition of "contract settlement" insert —

>> ""disclosable indirect tax arrangements" is to be interpreted in accordance with paragraph 9A;

644

Finance (No. 2) Act 2017 (c. 32)
Schedule 17 — Disclosure of tax avoidance schemes: VAT and other indirect taxes
Part 3 — Consequential amendments

"disclosable Schedule 11A VAT arrangements is to be interpreted in accordance with paragraph 9;",

(b) after the definition of "HMRC" insert—

""indirect tax" has the meaning given by paragraph 4(2);",

(c) in the definition of "disclosable VAT arrangements" for "9" substitute "8A", and

(d) in the definition of "tax" for "4" substitute "4(1)".

PART 4

SUPPLEMENTAL

Regulations

56 (1) Any power of the Treasury or the Commissioners to make regulations under this Schedule is exercisable by statutory instrument.

(2) Regulations made under any such power may make different provision for different cases and may contain transitional provisions and savings.

(3) A statutory instrument containing regulations made by the Treasury under paragraph 2(2) or 42(1) may not be made unless a draft of the instrument has been laid before and approved by a resolution of the House of Commons.

(4) Any other statutory instrument containing regulations made under this Schedule, if made without a draft having been approved by a resolution of the House of Commons, is subject to annulment in pursuance of a resolution of the House of Commons.

Interpretation

57 In this Schedule—

"arrangements" includes any scheme, transaction or series of transactions;

"the Commissioners" means the Commissioners for Her Majesty's Revenue and Customs;

"company" has the meaning given by section 1121 of the Corporation Tax Act 2010;

"HMRC" means Her Majesty's Revenue and Customs;

"indirect tax" has the meaning given by paragraph 2(1);

"introducer" is to be construed in accordance with paragraph 9;

"makes a firm approach" has the meaning given by paragraph 10(1);

"makes a marketing contact" has the meaning given by paragraph 10(2);

"marketing contact" has the meaning give by paragraph 10(2);

"notifiable arrangements" has the meaning given by paragraph 3(1);

"notifiable proposal" has the meaning given by paragraph 3(3);

"prescribed" (except in or in references to paragraph 3(1)(a)), means prescribed by regulations made by HMRC;

"promoter" is to be construed in accordance with paragraph 8;

"reference number", in relation to notifiable arrangements, has the meaning given by paragraph 22(4);

"TCEA 2007" means the Tribunals, Courts and Enforcement Act 2007;

"tax advantage" means a tax advantage within the meaning of—

    (a)   paragraph 6 (in relation to VAT), or

    (b)   paragraph 7 (in relation to indirect taxes other than VAT);

"trade" includes every venture in the nature of a trade;

"tribunal" means the First-tier tribunal, or where determined by or under Tribunal Procedure Rules, the Upper Tribunal;

"working day" means a day which is not a Saturday or a Sunday, Christmas Day, Good Friday or a bank holiday under the Banking and Financial Dealings Act 1971 in any part of the United Kingdom.

SCHEDULE 18 Section 67

REQUIREMENT TO CORRECT CERTAIN OFFSHORE TAX NON-COMPLIANCE

PART 1

LIABILITY FOR PENALTY FOR FAILURE TO CORRECT

Failure to correct relevant offshore tax non-compliance

1   A penalty is payable by a person who—

    (a)   has any relevant offshore tax non-compliance to correct at the end of the tax year 2016-17, and

    (b)   fails to correct the relevant offshore tax non-compliance within the period beginning with 6 April 2017 and ending with 30 September 2018 (referred to in this Schedule as "the RTC period").

Main definitions: general

2   Paragraphs 3 to 13 have effect for the purposes of this Schedule.

"Relevant offshore tax non-compliance"

3   (1)   At the end of the 2016-17 tax year a person has "relevant offshore tax non-compliance" to correct if—

    (a)   Conditions A and B are satisfied in respect of any offshore tax non-compliance committed by that person on or before 5 April 2017 ("the original offshore tax non-compliance"), and

    (b)   Condition C will be satisfied on the relevant date (see paragraph 6).

    (2)   Where the original offshore tax non-compliance committed by a person has been corrected in part by the end of the tax year 2016-17, the person's "relevant offshore tax non-compliance" is the uncorrected part of the original offshore tax non-compliance.

4   Condition A is that the original offshore tax non-compliance has not been fully corrected before the end of the tax year 2016-17 (see paragraph 13).

5   Condition B is that—

    (a)   the original offshore tax non-compliance involved a potential loss of revenue when it was committed, and

646   *Finance (No. 2) Act 2017 (c. 32)*
Schedule 18 — Requirement to correct certain offshore tax non-compliance
Part 1 — Liability for penalty for failure to correct

     (b)   if the original offshore tax non-compliance has been corrected in part by the end of the tax year 2016-17, the uncorrected part at that time involved a potential loss of revenue.

6   (1)   Condition C is that on the relevant date it is lawful, on the assumptions set out in sub-paragraph (2), for HMRC to assess the person concerned to any tax the liability to which would have been disclosed to or discovered by HMRC if on that date—

    (a)   where none of the original offshore tax non-compliance was corrected before the end of the 2016-17 tax year, HMRC were aware of the information missing as a result of the failure to correct that tax non-compliance, or

    (b)   where the original offshore tax non compliance was corrected in part before that time, HMRC were aware of the information missing as a result of the failure to correct the rest of that tax non-compliance.

    (2)   The assumptions are—

    (a)   that paragraph 26 is to be disregarded, and

    (b)   where the tax at stake is inheritance tax, that the relevant offshore tax non-compliance is not corrected before the relevant date

    (3)   In this paragraph "the relevant date" is—

    (a)   where the tax at stake is income tax or capital gains tax, 6 April 2017, and

    (b)   where the tax at stake is inheritance tax, the day after the day on which this Act is passed.

"Offshore tax-non compliance" etc

7   (1)   "Offshore tax non-compliance" means tax non-compliance which involves an offshore matter or an offshore transfer, whether or not it also involves an onshore matter.

    (2)   Tax non-compliance "involves an onshore matter" if and to the extent that it does not involve an offshore matter or an offshore transfer.

    (3)   For the meaning of "involves an offshore matter or an offshore transfer" (in relation to the different descriptions of tax non-compliance) see paragraphs 9 to 11.

"Tax non-compliance"

8   (1)   "Tax non-compliance" means any of the following—

    (a)   a failure to comply on or before the filing date with an obligation under section 7 of TMA 1970 to give notice of chargeability to income tax or capital gains tax,

    (b)   a failure to comply on or before the filing date with an obligation to deliver to HMRC a return or other document which is listed in sub-paragraph (3), or

    (c)   delivering to HMRC a return or other document which is listed in sub-paragraph (3) or (4) and contains an inaccuracy which amounts to, or leads to—

        (i)   an understatement of a liability to tax,

        (ii)   a false or inflated statement of a loss, or

       (iii)   a false or inflated claim to repayment of tax.

Finance (No. 2) Act 2017 (c. 32)
Schedule 18 — Requirement to correct certain offshore tax non-compliance
Part 1 — Liability for penalty for failure to correct

647

(2) In sub-paragraph (1) —

    (a) "filing date", in relation to a notice of chargeability or a return or other document, means the date by which it is required to be given, made or delivered to HMRC,

    (b) "loss" includes a charge, expense, deficit and any other amount which may be available for, or relied on to claim, a deduction or relief, and

    (c) "repayment of tax" includes a reference to allowing a credit against tax.

(3) The documents relevant for the purposes of both of paragraphs (b) and (c) of sub-paragraph (1) are (so far as they relate to the tax or taxes shown in the first column) —

Tax to which document relates	Document
Income tax or capital gains tax	Return, accounts, statement or document required under section 8(1) of TMA 1970 (personal return)
Income tax or capital gains tax	Return, accounts, statement or document required under section 8A(1) of TMA 1970 (trustee's return)
Income tax	Return, accounts, statement or document required under section 12AA(2) or (3) of TMA 1970 (partnership return)
Income tax	Return under section 254 of FA 2004 (pension schemes)
Income tax	Particulars or documents required under regulation 12 of the Retirement Benefits Schemes (Information Powers) Regulations 1995 (SI 1995/3101) (information relating to pension schemes)
Capital gains tax	NRCGT return under section 12ZB of TMA 1970
Inheritance tax	Account under section 216 or 217 of IHTA 1984.

(4) The documents relevant for the purposes only of paragraph (c) of sub-paragraph (1) are (so far as they relate to the tax or taxes shown in the first column) —

648

Finance (No. 2) Act 2017 (c. 32)
Schedule 18 — Requirement to correct certain offshore tax non-compliance
Part 1 — Liability for penalty for failure to correct

Tax to which document relates	*Document*
Income tax or capital gains tax	Return, statement or declaration in connection with a claim for an allowance, deduction or relief
Income tax or capital gains tax	Accounts in connection with ascertaining liability to tax
Income tax or capital gains tax	Statement or declaration in connection with a partnership return
Income tax or capital gains tax	Accounts in connection with a partnership return
Inheritance tax	Information or document under regulations under section 256 of IHTA 1984
Inheritance tax	Statement or declaration in connection with a deduction, exemption or relief.
Income tax, capital gains tax or inheritance tax	Any other document given to HMRC by a person ("P") which is likely to be relied on by HMRC to determine, without further inquiry, a question about— (a) P's liability to tax; (b) payments by P by way of or in connection with tax; (c) any other payment by P (including penalties); (d) repayments, or any other kind of payment or credit, to P.

"Involves an offshore matter" and "involves an offshore transfer"

9   (1) This paragraph applies to any tax non-compliance consisting of a failure to comply with an obligation under section 7 of TMA 1970 to notify chargeability to income tax or capital gains tax.

      (2) The tax non-compliance "involves an offshore matter" if the potential loss of revenue is charged on or by reference to—

            (a) income arising from a source in a territory outside the UK,

            (b) assets situated or held in a territory outside the UK,

            (c) activities carried on wholly or mainly in a territory outside the UK, or

            (d) anything having effect as if it were income, assets or activities of a kind described above.

      (3) The tax non-compliance "involves an offshore transfer" if—

            (a) it does not involve an offshore matter, and

            (b) the applicable condition is satisfied (see sub-paragraphs (4) and (5)).

Finance (No. 2) Act 2017 (c. 32)
649
Schedule 18 — Requirement to correct certain offshore tax non-compliance
Part 1 — Liability for penalty for failure to correct

(4) Where the tax at stake is income tax the applicable condition is satisfied if the income on or by reference to which tax is charged, or any part of the income —

   (a) was received in a territory outside the UK, or

   (b) was transferred on or before 5 April 2017 to a territory outside the UK.

(5) Where the tax at stake is capital gains tax, the applicable condition is satisfied if the proceeds of the disposal on or by reference to which the tax is charged, or any part of the proceeds —

   (a) were received in a territory outside the UK, or

   (b) were transferred on or before 5 April 2017 to a territory outside the UK.

(6) In the case of a transfer falling within sub-paragraph (4)(b) or (5)(b), references to the income or proceeds transferred are to be read as including references to any assets derived from or representing the income or proceeds.

(7) In this paragraph and paragraphs 10 and 11 "assets" has the meaning given in section 21(1) of TCGA 1992, but also includes sterling.

10 (1) This paragraph applies where —

   (a) any tax non-compliance by a person consists of a failure to comply with an obligation to deliver a return or other document, and

   (b) a complete and accurate return or other document would have included information that would have enabled or assisted HMRC to assess the person's liability to tax.

(2) The tax non-compliance "involves an offshore matter" if the liability to tax that would have been shown in the return or other document is or includes a liability to tax charged on or by reference to —

   (a) income arising from a source in a territory outside the UK,

   (b) assets situated or held in a territory outside the UK,

   (c) activities carried on wholly or mainly in a territory outside the UK, or

   (d) anything having effect as if it were income, assets or activities of a kind described above.

(3) Where the tax at stake is inheritance tax, assets are treated for the purposes of sub-paragraph (2) as situated or held in a territory outside the UK if they are so situated or held immediately after the transfer of value by reason of which inheritance tax becomes chargeable.

(4) The tax non-compliance "involves an offshore transfer" if —

   (a) it does not involve an offshore matter, and

   (b) the applicable condition is satisfied in respect of the liability to tax that would have been shown by the return or other document (see sub-paragraphs (5) to (7)).

(5) Where the tax at stake is income tax the applicable condition is satisfied if the income on or by reference to which tax is charged, or any part of the income —

   (a) was received in a territory outside the UK, or

   (b) was transferred on or before 5 April 2017 to a territory outside the UK.

650

Finance (No. 2) Act 2017 (c. 32)
Schedule 18 — Requirement to correct certain offshore tax non-compliance
Part 1 — Liability for penalty for failure to correct

(6) Where the tax at stake is capital gains tax, the applicable condition is satisfied if the proceeds of the disposal on or by reference to which the tax is charged, or any part of the proceeds —

    (a)   was received in a territory outside the UK, or

    (b)   was transferred on or before 5 April 2017 to a territory outside the UK.

(7) Where the liability to tax which would have been shown in the document is a liability to inheritance tax, the applicable condition is satisfied if —

    (a)   the disposition that gives rise to the transfer of value by reason of which the tax becomes chargeable involves a transfer of assets, and

    (b)   after that disposition but on or before 5 April 2017 the assets, or any part of the assets, are transferred to a territory outside the UK.

(8) In the case of a transfer falling within sub-paragraph (5)(b), (6)(b) or (7)(b), references to the income or proceeds transferred are to be read as including references to any assets derived from or representing the income or proceeds.

11 (1) This paragraph applies to any tax non-compliance by a person if —

    (a)   the tax non-compliance consists of delivering or giving HMRC a return or other document which contains an inaccuracy, and

    (b)   the inaccuracy relates to information that would have enabled or assisted HMRC to assess the person's liability to tax.

(2) The tax non-compliance to which this paragraph applies "involves an offshore matter" if the information that should have been given in the tax document relates to —

    (a)   income arising from a source in a territory outside the UK,

    (b)   assets situated or held in a territory outside the UK,

    (c)   activities carried on wholly or mainly in a territory outside the UK, or

    (d)   anything having effect as if it were income, assets or activities of a kind described above.

(3) Where the tax at stake is inheritance tax, assets are treated for the purposes of sub-paragraph (2) as situated or held in a territory outside the UK if they are so situated or held immediately after the transfer of value by reason of which inheritance tax becomes chargeable.

(4) Tax non-compliance to which this paragraph applies "involves an offshore transfer" if —

    (a)   it does not involve an offshore matter, and

    (b)   the applicable condition is satisfied in respect of the liability to tax that would have been shown by the return or other document (see sub-paragraphs (5) to (7)).

(5) Where the tax at stake is income tax the applicable condition is satisfied if the income on or by reference to which the tax is charged, or any part of the income —

    (a)   was received in a territory outside the UK, or

    (b)   was transferred on or before 5 April 2017 to a territory outside the UK.

(6) Where the tax at stake is capital gains tax, the applicable condition is satisfied if —

Finance (No. 2) Act 2017 (c. 32)
651
Schedule 18 — Requirement to correct certain offshore tax non-compliance
Part 1 — Liability for penalty for failure to correct

    (a)   the information that should have been given in the tax document relates to the proceeds of the disposal on or by reference to which the tax is charged, and

    (b)   the proceeds, or any part of the proceeds—

        (i)   were received in a territory outside the UK, or

        (ii) were transferred on or before 5 April 2017 to a territory outside the UK.

(7)   Where the tax at stake is inheritance tax, the applicable condition is satisfied if—

    (a)   the information that should have been given in the tax document relates to the disposition that gives rise to the transfer of value by reason of which the tax becomes payable relates to a transfer of assets, and

    (b)   after that disposition but on or before 5 April 2017 the assets or any part of the assets are transferred to a territory outside the UK.

(8)   In the case of a transfer falling within sub-paragraph (5)(b), (6)(b) or (7)(b), references to the income, proceeds or assets transferred are to be read as including references to any assets derived from or representing the income, proceeds or assets.

"Tax"

12   (1)   References to "tax" are (unless in the context the reference is more specific) to income tax, capital gains tax or inheritance tax.

   (2)   References to "capital gains tax" do not include capital gains tax payable by companies in respect of chargeable gains accruing to them to the extent that those gains are NRCGT gains in respect of which the companies are chargeable to capital gains tax under section 14D or 188D of TCGA 1992 (see section 1(2A)(b) of that Act).

   (3)   In sub-paragraph (2) "company" has the same meaning as in TCGA 1992.

Correcting offshore tax non-compliance

13   (1)   This paragraph sets out how offshore tax non-compliance may be corrected.

   (2)   References to the correction of offshore tax non-compliance of any description are to the taking of any action specified in this paragraph as a means of correcting offshore tax non-compliance of that description.

   (3)   Offshore tax non-compliance consisting of a failure to notify chargeability may be corrected by—

    (a)   giving the requisite notice to HMRC (unless before doing so the person has received a notice requiring the person to make and deliver a tax return) and giving HMRC the relevant information by any means mentioned in paragraph (b),

    (b)   giving HMRC the relevant information—

        (i)   by making and delivering a tax return,

        (ii) using the digital disclosure service or any other service provided by HMRC as a means of correcting tax non-compliance,

652

*Finance (No. 2) Act 2017 (c. **32**)*
Schedule 18 — Requirement to correct certain offshore tax non-compliance
Part 1 — Liability for penalty for failure to correct

(iii) communicating it to an officer of Revenue and Customs in the course of an enquiry into the person's tax affairs, or

(iv) using a method agreed with an officer of Revenue and Customs.

(4) In sub-paragraph (3) "relevant information" means information relating to offshore tax that—

(a) had the requisite notice been given in time and the person given a notice to make and deliver a tax return, would have been required to be included in the tax return, and

(b) would have enabled or assisted HMRC to calculate the offshore tax due.

(5) Offshore tax non-compliance consisting of a failure to make or deliver a return or other document may be corrected by giving HMRC the relevant information by—

(a) making or delivering the requisite return or document,

(b) using the digital disclosure service or any other service provided by HMRC as a means of correcting tax non-compliance,

(c) communicating it to an officer of Revenue and Customs in the course of an enquiry into the person's tax affairs, or

(d) using a method agreed with an officer of Revenue and Customs.

(6) In subsection (5) "relevant information" means information relating to offshore tax that—

(a) should have been included in the return or other document, and

(b) would have enabled or assisted HMRC to calculate the offshore tax due.

(7) Offshore tax non-compliance consisting of making and delivering a return or other document containing an inaccuracy may be corrected by giving HMRC the relevant information by—

(a) in the case of an inaccurate tax document, amending the document or delivering a new document,

(b) using the digital disclosure service or any other service provided by HMRC as a means of correcting tax non-compliance,

(c) communicating it to an officer of Revenue and Customs in the course of an enquiry into the person's tax affairs, or

(d) using a method agreed with an officer of Revenue and Customs.

(8) In sub-paragraph (7) "relevant information" means information relating to offshore tax that—

(a) should have been included in the return but was not (whether due to an omission or the giving of inaccurate information), and

(b) would have enabled or assisted HMRC to calculate the offshore tax due.

(9) In this paragraph "offshore tax", in relation to any offshore tax non-compliance, means tax corresponding to the offshore PLR in respect of the non-compliance.

Finance (No. 2) Act 2017 (c. 32)
Schedule 18 — Requirement to correct certain offshore tax non-compliance
Part 2 — Amount of penalty

653

PART 2

AMOUNT OF PENALTY

Amount of penalty

14   (1) The penalty payable under paragraph 1 is 200% of the offshore PLR attributable to the uncorrected offshore tax non-compliance (subject to any reduction under a provision of this Part of this Schedule).

   (2) In this Part of this Schedule "the uncorrected offshore tax non-compliance" means —

    (a)   the relevant offshore tax non-compliance, in a case where none of it is corrected within the RTC period, or

    (b)   so much of the relevant offshore tax non-compliance as has not been corrected within the RTC period, in a case where part of it is corrected within that period.

Offshore PLR

15   (1) In this Schedule "offshore PLR", in relation to any offshore tax non-compliance means the potential loss of revenue attributable to that non-compliance, to be determined as follows.

   (2) The potential lost revenue attributable to any offshore tax non-compliance is (subject to sub-paragraphs (5) and (6)) —

    (a)   if the non-compliance is a failure to notify chargeability, the potential lost revenue under the applicable provisions of paragraph 7 of Schedule 41 to FA 2008 (or, where the original offshore tax non-compliance took place before 1 April 2010, the amount referred to in section 7(8) of TMA 1970),

    (b)   if the non-compliance is a failure to deliver a return or other document, the amount of the liability to tax under the applicable provisions of paragraph 24 of Schedule 55 to FA 2009 (or, where the original offshore tax non-compliance took place before 1 April 2011, the amount of liability to tax that would have been shown in the return as defined in section 93(9) of TMA 1970), and

    (c)   if the non-compliance is delivering a return or other document containing an inaccuracy, the potential lost revenue under the applicable provisions of paragraphs 5 to 8 of Schedule 24 to FA 2007 (or, where the original offshore tax non-compliance took place before 1 April 2008, the difference described in section 95(2) of TMA 1970).

   (3) In its application for the purposes of sub-paragraph (2)(c) above, paragraph 6 of Schedule 24 to FA 2007 has effect as if —

    (a)   for sub-paragraph (1) there were substituted —

         "(1) Where—

            (a)   P is liable to a penalty in respect of two or more inaccuracies (each being an inaccuracy in a return or other document listed in paragraph 8(3) or (4) of Schedule 18) to F(No 2)A 2017) in relation to a tax year or, in the case of inheritance tax, a single transfer of value,

654

Finance (No. 2) Act 2017 (c. 32)
Schedule 18 — Requirement to correct certain offshore tax non-compliance
Part 2 — Amount of penalty

     (b)   in relation to any one (or more than one) of those inaccuracies, the delivery of the return or other document containing it constitutes offshore tax non-compliance, and

     (c)   the calculation of potential lost revenue attributable to each of those inaccuracies depends on the order in which they are corrected,

the potential lost revenue attributable to any offshore tax non-compliance constituted by any one of those inaccuracies is to be taken to be such amount as is just and reasonable.

     (1A)   In sub-paragraph (1) "offshore tax non-compliance" has the same meaning as in Schedule 18 to F(No2)A 2017."; and

  (b)   in sub-paragraph (4), for paragraphs (b) to (d) there were substituted —

     "(b)   other understatements."

(4) In sub-paragraphs (5) and (6) "combined tax non-compliance" is tax non-compliance that—

     (a)   involves an offshore matter or an offshore transfer, but

     (b)   also involves an onshore matter.

(5) Any combined tax non-compliance is to be treated for the purposes of this Schedule as if it were two separate acts of tax non-compliance, namely—

     (a)   the combined tax non-compliance so far as it involves an offshore matter or an offshore transfer (which is then offshore tax non-compliance within the meaning of this Schedule), and

     (b)   the combined tax non-compliance so far as it involves an onshore matter.

(6) The potential lost revenue attributable to the offshore tax non-compliance referred to in sub-paragraph (5)(a) is to be taken to be such share of the potential lost revenue attributable to the combined tax non-compliance as is just and reasonable.

Reduction of penalty for disclosure etc by person liable to penalty

16 (1) This paragraph provides for a reduction in a penalty under paragraph 1 for any uncorrected relevant offshore tax non-compliance if the person ("P") who is liable to the penalty discloses any matter mentioned in sub-paragraph (2) that is relevant to the non-compliance or its correction or to the assessment or enforcement of the offshore tax attributable to it.

(2) The matters are—

     (a)   chargeability to income tax or capital gains tax (where the tax non-compliance is a failure to notify chargeability),

     (b)   a missing tax return,

     (c)   an inaccuracy in a document,

     (d)   a supply of false information or a withholding of information, or

     (e)   a failure to disclose an under-assessment.

(3) A person discloses a matter for the purposes of this paragraph only by—

     (a)   telling HMRC about it,

Finance (No. 2) Act 2017 (c. 32)
Schedule 18 — Requirement to correct certain offshore tax non-compliance
Part 2 — Amount of penalty

655

    (b)   giving HMRC reasonable help in relation to the matter (for example by quantifying an inaccuracy in a document),

    (c)   informing HMRC of any person who acted as an enabler of the relevant offshore tax non-compliance or the failure to correct it, and

    (d)   allowing HMRC access to records—

        (i)   for any reasonable purpose connected with resolving the matter (for example for the purpose of ensuring that an inaccuracy in a document is fully corrected), and

        (ii)   for the purpose of ensuring that HMRC can identify all persons who may have acted as an enabler of the relevant offshore tax non-compliance or the failure to correct it.

(4) Where a person liable to a penalty under paragraph 1 discloses a matter HMRC must reduce the penalty to one that reflects the quality of the disclosure.

(5) But the penalty may not be reduced below 100% of the offshore PLR.

(6) In relation to disclosure or assistance, "quality" includes timing, nature and extent.

(7) For the purposes of sub-paragraph (3) a person "acted as an enabler" of relevant offshore tax non-compliance by another if the person encouraged, assisted or otherwise facilitated the conduct by the other person that constituted the offshore tax non-compliance.

17 (1) If they think it right because of special circumstances, HMRC may reduce a penalty under paragraph 1.

    (2) In sub-paragraph (1) "special circumstances" does not include—

       (a)   ability to pay, or

       (b)   the fact that a potential loss of revenue from one taxpayer is balanced by a potential overpayment by another.

    (3) In sub-paragraph (1) the reference to reducing a penalty includes a reference to—

       (a)   staying a penalty, or

       (b)   agreeing a compromise in relation to proceedings for a penalty.

Procedure for assessing penalty, etc

18 (1) Where a person is found liable for a penalty under paragraph 1 HMRC must—

       (a)   assess the penalty,

       (b)   notify the person, and

       (c)   state in the notice—

          (i)   the uncorrected relevant offshore tax non-compliance to which the penalty relates, and

         (ii)   the tax period to which that offshore tax non-compliance relates.

    (2) A penalty must be paid before the end of the period of 30 days beginning with the day on which notification of the penalty is issued.

    (3) An assessment of a penalty—

656

Finance (No. 2) Act 2017 (c. 32)
Schedule 18 — Requirement to correct certain offshore tax non-compliance
Part 2 — Amount of penalty

     (a) is to be treated for procedural purposes in the same way as an assessment to tax (except in respect of a matter expressly provided for by this Schedule),

     (b) may be enforced as if it were an assessment to tax, and

     (c) may be combined with an assessment to tax.

(4) A supplementary assessment may be made in respect of a penalty if an earlier assessment operated by reference to an underestimate of the liability to tax that would have been shown in a return.

(5) Sub-paragraph (6) applies if —

     (a) an assessment in respect of a penalty is based on a liability to offshore tax that would have been shown on a return, and

     (b) that liability is found by HMRC to have been excessive.

(6) HMRC may amend the assessment so that it is based upon the correct amount.

(7) But an amendment under sub-paragraph (6) —

     (a) does not affect when the penalty must be paid, and

     (b) may be made after the last day on which the assessment in question could have been made under paragraph 19.

19 (1) An assessment of a penalty under paragraph 1 in respect of uncorrected relevant offshore tax non-compliance must be made before the end of the relevant period for that non-compliance.

(2) If the non-compliance consists of a failure to notify chargeability, the relevant period is the period of 12 months beginning with —

     (a) the end of the appeal period for the assessment of tax unpaid by reason of the failure, or

     (b) if there is no such assessment, the date on which the amount of tax unpaid by reason of the failure is ascertained.

(3) If the non-compliance consists of a failure to submit a return or other document, the relevant period is the period of 12 months beginning with —

     (a) the end of the appeal period for the assessment of the liability to tax which would have been shown in the return, or

     (b) if there is no such assessment, the date on which that liability is ascertained.

(4) If the non-compliance consists of making and delivering a tax document containing an inaccuracy, the relevant period is the period of 12 months beginning with —

     (a) the end of the appeal period for the decision correcting the inaccuracy, or

     (b) if there is no assessment to the tax concerned within paragraph (a), the date on which the inaccuracy is corrected.

(5) In this paragraph references to the appeal period are to the period during which —

     (a) an appeal could be brought, or

     (b) an appeal that has been brought has not been finally determined or withdrawn.

Finance (No. 2) Act 2017 (c. 32) 657
Schedule 18 — Requirement to correct certain offshore tax non-compliance
Part 2 — Amount of penalty

Appeals

20   A person may appeal against—

       (a)   a decision of HMRC that a penalty under paragraph 1 is payable by that person, or

       (b)   a decision of HMRC as to the amount of a penalty under paragraph 1 payable by the person.

21   (1) An appeal under paragraph 20 is to be treated in the same way as an appeal against an assessment to the tax at stake (including by the application of any provision about bringing the appeal by notice to HMRC, about HMRC review of the decision or about determination of the appeal by the First-tier Tribunal or Upper Tribunal).

    (2) Sub-paragraph (1) does not apply—

       (a)   so as to require the person bringing the appeal to pay a penalty before an appeal against the assessment of the penalty is determined,

       (b)   in respect of any other matter expressly provided for by this Schedule.

22   (1) On an appeal under paragraph 20(a) that is notified to the tribunal, the tribunal may affirm or cancel HMRC's decision.

    (2) On an appeal under paragraph 20(b) that is notified to the tribunal, the tribunal may—

       (a)   affirm HMRC's decision, or

       (b)   substitute for that decision another decision that HMRC had power to make.

    (3) If the tribunal substitutes its own decision for HMRC's, the tribunal may rely on paragraph 16 or 17 (or both)—

       (a)   to the same extent as HMRC (which may mean applying the same percentage reduction as HMRC to a different starting point),

       (b)   to a different extent, but only if the tribunal thinks that HMRC's decision in respect of the application of that paragraph was flawed.

    (4) In sub-paragraph (3)(b) "flawed" means flawed when considered in the light of the principles applicable in proceedings for judicial review.

    (5) In this paragraph "tribunal" means the First-tier Tribunal or Upper Tribunal (as appropriate by virtue of paragraph 21(1)).

Reasonable excuse

23   (1) Liability to a penalty under paragraph 1 does not arise in relation to a particular failure to correct any relevant offshore tax non-compliance within the RTC period if the person concerned (P) satisfies HMRC or the relevant tribunal (as the case may be) that there is a reasonable excuse for the failure.

    (2) For this purpose—

       (a)   an insufficiency of funds is not a reasonable excuse, unless attributable to events outside P's control,

       (b)   where P relied on any other person to do anything, that cannot be a reasonable excuse unless P took reasonable care to avoid the failure,

658

Finance (No. 2) Act 2017 (c. 32)
Schedule 18 — Requirement to correct certain offshore tax non-compliance
Part 2 — Amount of penalty

    (c)   where P had a reasonable excuse but the excuse has ceased, P is to be treated as continuing to have the excuse if the failure is remedied without unreasonable delay after the excuse ceased, and

    (d)   reliance on advice is to be taken automatically not to be a reasonable excuse if it is disqualified under sub-paragraph (3).

(3) Advice is disqualified (subject to sub-paragraph (4)) if —

    (a)   the advice was given to P by an interested person,

    (b)   the advice was given to P as a result of arrangements made between an interested person and the person who gave the advice,

    (c)   the person who gave the advice did not have appropriate expertise for giving the advice,

    (d)   the advice failed to take account of all P's individual circumstances (so far as relevant to the matters to which the advice relates), or

    (e)   the advice was addressed to, or was given to, a person other than P.

(4) Where advice would otherwise be disqualified under any of paragraphs (a) to (d) of sub-paragraph (3) the advice is not disqualified if at the end of the RTC period P—

    (a)   has taken reasonable steps to find out whether or not the advice falls within that paragraph, and

    (b)   reasonably believes that it does not.

(5) In sub-paragraph (3) "an interested person" means, in relation to any relevant offshore tax non-compliance—

    (a)   a person (other than P) who participated in relevant avoidance arrangements or any transaction forming part of them, or

    (b)   a person who for any consideration (whether or not in money) facilitated P's entering into relevant avoidance arrangements.

(6) In this paragraph "avoidance arrangements" means arrangements as respects which, in all the circumstances, it would be reasonable to conclude that their main purpose, or one of their main purposes, is the obtaining of a tax advantage.

(7) But arrangements are not avoidance arrangements for the purposes of this paragraph if (although they fall within sub-paragraph (6))—

    (a)   they are arrangements which accord with established practice, and

    (b)   HMRC had, at the time the arrangements were entered into, indicated its acceptance of that practice.

(8) Where any relevant offshore tax non-compliance arose originally because information was submitted to HMRC on the basis that particular avoidance arrangements had an effect which they did not have, those avoidance arrangements are "relevant avoidance arrangements" in relation to that tax non-compliance.

(9) In sub-paragraph (6)—

    (a)   "arrangements" includes any agreement, understanding, scheme, transaction or series of transactions (whether or not legally enforceable), and

    (b)   a "tax advantage" includes—

        (i)   relief or increased relief from tax,

        (ii)   repayment or increased repayment of tax,

Finance (No. 2) Act 2017 (c. 32)
Schedule 18 — Requirement to correct certain offshore tax non-compliance
Part 2 — Amount of penalty

659

     (iii)   avoidance or reduction of a charge to tax or an assessment to tax,

     (iv)   avoidance of a possible assessment to tax,

     (v)   deferral of a payment of tax or advancement of a repayment of tax.

Double jeopardy

24   (1) Where by reason of any conduct a person —

     (a)   has been convicted of an offence, or

     (b)   is liable to a penalty otherwise than under paragraph 1 for which the person has been assessed (and the assessment has not been successfully appealed against or withdrawn),

that conduct does not give rise to liability to a penalty under paragraph 1.

    (2) In sub-paragraph (1) the reference to a penalty otherwise than under paragraph 1 —

     (a)   includes a penalty under paragraph 6 of Schedule 55 to FA 2009, but does not include penalties under any other provision of that Schedule, and

     (b)   includes a penalty under subsection (5) of section 93 of TMA 1970 but, does not include penalties under any other provision of that section.

    (3) But the aggregate of —

     (a)   the amount of a penalty under paragraph 1, and

     (b)   the amount of a penalty under paragraph 5 of Schedule 55 which is determined by reference to a liability to tax,

must not exceed 200% of that liability to tax.

    (4) In sub-paragraph (1) "conduct" includes a failure to act.

Application of provisions of TMA 1970

25   Subject to the provisions of this Part of this Schedule, the following provisions of TMA 1970 apply for the purposes of this Part of this Schedule as they apply for the purposes of the Taxes Acts —

     (a)   section 108 (responsibility of company officers),

     (b)   section 114 (want of form), and

     (c)   section 115 (delivery and service of documents).

PART 3

FURTHER PROVISIONS RELATING TO THE REQUIREMENT TO CORRECT

Extension of period for assessment etc of offshore tax

26   (1) This paragraph applies where —

     (a)   at the end of the tax year 2016-17 a person has relevant offshore tax non-compliance to correct, and

     (b)   the last day on which it would (disregarding this paragraph) be lawful for HMRC to assess the person to any offshore tax falls within the period beginning with 6 April 2017 and ending with 4 April 2021.

660

Finance (No. 2) Act 2017 (c. 32)
Schedule 18 — Requirement to correct certain offshore tax non-compliance
Part 3 — Further provisions relating to the requirement to correct

(2) The period in which it is lawful for HMRC to assess the person to the offshore tax is extended by virtue of this paragraph to end with 5 April 2021.

(3) In this paragraph "offshore tax", in relation to any relevant offshore tax non-compliance, means tax corresponding to the offshore PLR in respect of the non-compliance.

Further penalty in connection with offshore asset moves

27 (1) Schedule 21 to FA 2015 (penalties in connection with offshore asset moves) is amended as follows.

(2) In paragraph 2 (original penalties triggering penalties under Schedule 21) omit "and" after paragraph (b) and after paragraph (c) insert ", and

   "(d)   a penalty under paragraph 1 of Schedule 18 to FA 2017 (requirement to correct relevant offshore tax non-compliance)."

(3) In paragraph 3 (meaning of deliberate failure) after paragraph (c) insert—

   "(d)   in the case of a penalty within paragraph 2(d), P was aware at any time during the RTC period that at the end of the 2016-17 tax year P had relevant offshore tax non-compliance to correct;

   and terms used in paragraph (d) have the same meaning as in Schedule 18 to FA 2017."

(4) In paragraph 5 (meaning of "relevant time") after sub-paragraph (4) insert—

   "(5)   Where the original penalty is under paragraph 1 of Schedule 18 to FA 2017, the relevant time is the time when that Schedule comes into force."

Asset-based penalty in addition to penalty under paragraph 1

28 (1) Schedule 22 to FA 2016 (asset-based penalty for offshore inaccuracies and failures) is amended as follows.

(2) In paragraph 2 (meaning of standard offshore penalty)—

   (a)   in sub-paragraph (1) for "or (4)" substitute "(4) or (4A)",

   (b)   after sub-paragraph (4) insert—

   "(4A)   A penalty falls within this paragraph if—
      (a)   it is imposed on a person under paragraph 1 of Schedule 18 to FA 2017 (requirement to correct relevant offshore tax non-compliance),
      (b)   the person was aware at any time during the RTC period that at the end of the 2016-17 tax year P had relevant offshore tax non-compliance to correct, and
      (c)   the tax at stake is (or includes) capital gains tax, inheritance tax or asset-based income tax.", and

   (c)   after sub-paragraph (5) insert—

   "(5A)   Sub-paragraph (5) does not apply to a penalty imposed under paragraph 1 of Schedule 18 to FA 2017."

(3) In paragraph 3 (tax year to which standard offshore penalty relates) after

Finance (No. 2) Act 2017 (c. 32)
Schedule 18 — Requirement to correct certain offshore tax non-compliance
Part 3 — Further provisions relating to the requirement to correct

661

sub-paragraph (3) insert —

"(4) Where a standard offshore penalty is imposed under paragraph 1 of Schedule 18 to FA 2017, the tax year to which that penalty relates is —

(a) if the tax at stake in relation to the uncorrected relevant offshore tax non-compliance is income tax or capital gains tax, the tax year or years to which the failure or inaccuracy constituting the relevant offshore tax non-compliance in question relates;

(b) if the tax at stake in relation to the uncorrected relevant offshore tax non-compliance is inheritance tax, the year, beginning on 6 April and ending on the following 5 April, in which the liability to tax first arose.

(5) In sub-paragraph (4) references to uncorrected relevant offshore tax non-compliance are to the relevant offshore tax non-compliance in respect of which the standard offshore penalty is imposed."

(4) In paragraph 5 (meaning of offshore PLR), in sub-paragraph (1)(a) after "FA 2008" insert "or Schedule 18 to FA 2017".

(5) In paragraph 6 (restriction on imposition of multiple asset-based penalties for same asset), in sub-paragraph (1)(a) after "penalty" insert "(other than one imposed under paragraph 1 of Schedule 18 to FA 2017)".

(6) After paragraph 6 insert —

"6A   Where —

(a) a penalty has been imposed on a person under paragraph 1 of Schedule 18 to FA 2017, and

(b) the potential loss of revenue threshold has been met,

only one asset-based penalty is payable by the person in relation to any given asset."

(7) In paragraph 13 (asset-based income tax) after sub-paragraph (2) insert —

"(2A) In relation to cases where the standard offshore penalty is a penalty falling within paragraph 2(4A), each reference to provisions of ITTOIA 2005 in column 1 of the Table in sub-paragraph (2) includes a reference —

(a) to the corresponding provisions of the legislation in force immediately before those provisions of ITTOIA 2005 came into force (and to any previous text of those corresponding provisions), and

(b) to any other provision that had the same purpose as, or a similar purpose to, any of those corresponding provisions (or any earlier text mentioned in paragraph (a)), if and so far as that other provision was in force —

(i) on or after 6 April 1997, but

(ii) before the corresponding provisions (or the earlier text mentioned in paragraph (a)) came into force.""

(8) In paragraph 19(2) (interpretation: incorporation of definitions from other legislation for "or Schedule 55 to FA 2009" substitute "Schedule 55 to FA 2009 or Part 1 of Schedule 18 to FA 2017".

662

Finance (No. 2) Act 2017 (c. 32)
Schedule 18 — Requirement to correct certain offshore tax non-compliance
Part 3 — Further provisions relating to the requirement to correct

29 (1) TMA 1970 is amended as follows.

(2) In section 103ZA (disapplication of sections 100 to 103 in the case of certain penalties) omit the "or" after paragraph (j) and after paragraph (k) insert ", or

(l)   Schedule 18 to the Finance Act 2017."

(3) In section 107A (relevant trustees) —

(a)   in subsection (2)(a) after "Finance Act 2009" insert or Schedule 18 to the Finance Act 2017", and

(b)   in subsection (3), after paragraph (c) insert—

"(d)   in relation to—

(i)   a penalty under Schedule 18 to the Finance Act 2017, or

(ii)   interest under section 101 of the Finance Act 2009 on a penalty within sub-paragraph (i),

the end of the RTC period (within the meaning of Schedule 18 to the Finance Act 2017);".

Publishing details of persons assessed to penalty or penalties under paragraph 1

30 (1) The Commissioners for Her Majesty's Revenue and Customs ("the Commissioners") may publish information about a person (P) if in consequence of an investigation they consider that sub-paragraph (2) or (3) applies in relation to P.

(2) This sub-paragraph applies if—

(a)   P has been found to have incurred one or more relevant penalties under paragraph 1 (and has been assessed or is the subject of a contract settlement), and

(b)   the offshore potential lost revenue in relation to the penalty, or the aggregate of the offshore potential lost revenue in relation to each of the penalties, exceeds £25,000.

(3) This sub-paragraph applies if P has been found to have incurred 5 or more relevant penalties under paragraph 1.

(4) A penalty incurred by P under paragraph 1 is "relevant" if —

(a)   P was aware at any time during the RTC period that at the end of the 2016-17 tax year the person had relevant offshore tax non-compliance to correct, and

(b)   the penalty relates to the failure to correct that non-compliance.

(5) The information that may be published is—

(a)   P's name (including any trading name, previous name or pseudonym),

(b)   P's address (or registered office),

(c)   the nature of any business carried on by P,

(d)   the amount of the penalty or penalties,

(e)   the offshore potential lost revenue in relation to the penalty or the aggregate of the offshore potential lost revenue in relation to each of the penalties,

(f)   the periods or times to which the uncorrected relevant offshore tax non-compliance relates,

Finance (No. 2) Act 2017 (c. 32)
Schedule 18 — Requirement to correct certain offshore tax non-compliance
Part 3 — Further provisions relating to the requirement to correct

663

(g)   any other information that the Commissioners consider it appropriate to publish in order to make clear the person's identity.

(6)   In sub-paragraph (5)(f) the reference to the uncorrected relevant offshore tax non-compliance is to so much of P's relevant offshore tax non-compliance at the end of the 2016-17 tax year as P failed to correct within the RTC period.

(7)   The information may be published in any manner that the Commissioners consider appropriate.

(8)   Before publishing any information the Commissioners must—
(a)   inform P that they are considering doing so, and
(b)   afford P the opportunity to make representations about whether it should be published.

(9)   No information may be published before the day on which the penalty becomes final or, where more than one penalty is involved, the latest day on which any of the penalties becomes final.

(10) No information may be published for the first time after the end of the period of one year beginning with that day.

(11) No information may be published (or continue to be published) after the end of the period of one year beginning with the day on which it is first published.

(12) No information may be published if the amount of the penalty—
(a)   is reduced under paragraph 16 to the minimum permitted amount (being 100% of the offshore PLR), or
(b)   is reduced under paragraph 17 to nil or stayed.

(13) For the purposes of this paragraph a penalty becomes final—
(a)   if it has been assessed, when the time for any appeal or further appeal relating to it expires or, if later, any appeal or final appeal relating to it is finally determined, and
(b)   if a contract settlement has been made, at the time when the contract is made.

(14) In this paragraph "contract settlement", in relation to a penalty, means a contract between the Commissioners and the person under which the Commissioners undertake not to assess the penalty or (if it has been assessed) not to take proceedings to recover it.

31   (1)   The Treasury may by regulations amend paragraph 30(2) to vary the amount for the time being specified in paragraph (b).

(2)   Regulations under this paragraph are to be made by statutory instrument.

(3)   A statutory instrument under this paragraph is subject to annulment in pursuance of a resolution of the House of Commons.

PART 4

SUPPLEMENTARY

Interpretation: minor

32   (1)   In this Schedule (apart from the amendments made by Part 3)—

664

Finance (No. 2) Act 2017 (c. 32)
Schedule 18 — Requirement to correct certain offshore tax non-compliance
Part 4 — Supplementary

"HMRC" means Her Majesty's Revenue and Customs;

"tax period" means a tax year or other period in respect of which tax is charged (or in the case of inheritance tax, the year beginning with 6 April and ending on the following 5 April in which the liability to tax first arose);

"tax year", in relation to inheritance tax, means a period of 12 months beginning on 6 April and ending on the following 5 April;

"UK" means the United Kingdom, including its territorial sea.

(2) A reference to making a return or doing anything in relation to a return includes a reference to amending a return or doing anything in relation to an amended return.

(3) References to delivery (of a document) include giving, sending and any other similar expressions.

(4) A reference to delivering a document to HMRC includes—

    (a) a reference to communicating information to HMRC in any form and by any method (whether by post, fax, email, telephone or otherwise, and

    (b) a reference to making a statement or declaration in a document.

(5) References to an assessment to tax, in relation to inheritance tax, are to a determination.

(6) An expression used in relation to income tax has the same meaning as in the Income Tax Acts.

(7) An expression used in relation to capital gains tax has the same meaning as in the enactments relating to that tax.

(8) An expression used in relation to inheritance tax has the same meaning as in IHTA 1984.

Terms defined or explained for purposes of more than one paragraph of this Schedule

Term	Paragraph
assets (in paragraphs 9 to 11)	paragraph 9(7)
capital gains tax	paragraph 12(2)
HMRC	paragraph 32(1)
involves an offshore matter (in relation to failure to notify chargeability)	paragraph 9(2)
involves an offshore matter (in relation to failure to deliver a return or other document)	paragraph 10(2) and (3)
involves an offshore matter (in relation to delivery of a return or other document containing an inaccuracy)	paragraph 11(2) and (3)
involves an offshore transfer (in relation to failure to notify chargeability)	paragraph 9(3) to (6)
involves an offshore transfer (in relation to failure to deliver a return or other document)	paragraph 10(4) to (8)

Finance (No. 2) Act 2017 (c. 32)
Schedule 18 — Requirement to correct certain offshore tax non-compliance
Part 4 — Supplementary

665

Term	Paragraph
involves an offshore transfer (in relation to delivery of a return or other document containing an inaccuracy)	paragraph 11(4) to (8)
involves an onshore matter (in relation to any tax non-compliance)	paragraph 7(2)
offshore tax non-compliance	paragraph 7(1)
offshore PLR	paragraph 15(1)
potential lost revenue	paragraph 15(2)
RTC period	paragraph 1(b)
relevant offshore tax non-compliance	paragraph 3
tax non-compliance	paragraph 8(1)
tax period	paragraph 32(1)
tax year (in relation to inheritance tax)	paragraph 32(1)
tax	paragraph 12(1)
UK	paragraph 32(1)
uncorrected offshore tax non-compliance (in Part 2)	paragraph 14(2)